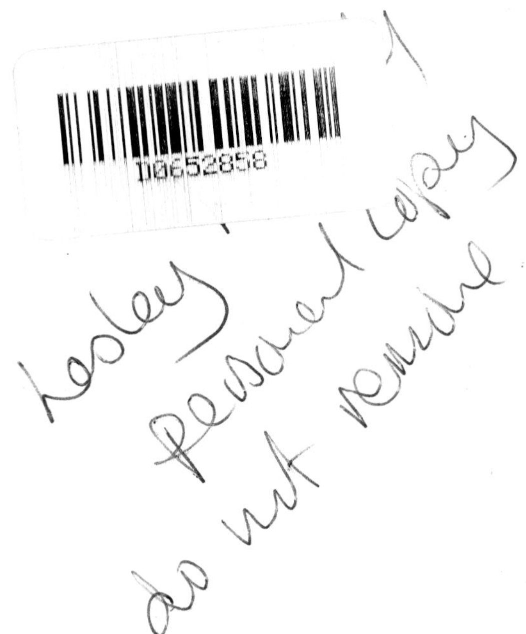

Business Accounts

David Cox FCCA FCIB Cert Ed

Osborne Books

First published 1991, reprinted 1992, 1993, 1994, 1995 (with revisions), 1996, 1997 (with revisions)

Published by Osborne Books Limited,
Unit 1B, Everoak Estate, Bromyard Road,
St Johns, Worcester, WR2 5HN
Tel 01905 748071

Printed by The Bath Press, Bath

A CIP catalogue record for this book is available from the British Library

ISBN 0-9510650-7-6

contents

about this book

aims

Business Accounts has been written to provide an up-to-date study of the principles of accounting for students commencing their studies. It covers first-level courses in accounting such as:

- BTEC National and Higher National
- first year of Business Studies and Accounting degree courses
- National Vocational Qualifications (NVQ) and Scottish Vocational Qualifications (SVQ)
- the examinations and assessments of
  - The Association of Accounting Technicians (AAT), Foundation and Intermediate Stages
  - RSA Examinations Board, stages I and II
  - Pitman Examinations Institute (PEI), levels 1, 2 and 3
  - London Chamber of Commerce and Industry (LCC), first level, second level
  - The Institute of Certified Book-keepers, levels 1 and 2
  - GCSE
  - GCE 'A' level
  - The Chartered Institute of Bankers (CIB), Banking Certificate and Pre-Associateship Route
  - The Institute of Chartered Secretaries and Administrators (ICSA), Pre-Professional
  - The Chartered Institute of Management Accountants (CIMA), Stage 1
  - The Association of Chartered Certified Accountants (ACCA), Technician and Foundation Stages
  - The Institute of Chartered Accountants in England and Wales (ICAEW), Foundation Stage

For whatever course you are studying, you must obtain:

- an up-to-date syllabus, or units of performance criteria
- copies of past examination papers, or assessments

These will give an indication of the depth of study required in each topic, the type of questions asked, and the style of recent examination papers or assessments. Many courses, and especially those which are competence-based, set out the performance criteria and thus indicate the exact level of study required.

contents

Business Accounts is a practical text which shows the *how* and *why* of accounting. It contains progressive sections covering:

- the basics of double-entry book-keeping, including the use of computers
- the trial balance, and preparation of final accounts
- accounting concepts and their application to final accounts
- the use of advanced accounting techniques, such as control accounts, suspense accounts, incomplete records
- final accounts for different types of organisations, such as clubs and societies, partnerships and limited companies
- the interpretation of accounts

Throughout the book, final accounts are presented in the modern vertical format, and Appendix A (page 484) gives a sample layout.

Each chapter is complete in itself and contains appropriate questions. The questions have been carefully graded within each chapter to ensure that the first ones test basic principles, and the later questions test more advanced techniques. Where a chapter covers more than one topic, the questions on each topic are grouped together in the same order as the topics appear in the chapter.

Dates used throughout the book in examples and questions, for the sake of simplicity, are expressed as 19-1, 19-2, 19-3, etc. In some instances you should note that 19-9 is followed by 19-0, ie the decade changes from, for example, 1989 to 1990.

Answers to selected questions – those marked with an asterisk (*) – are given in Appendix B (page 486). Answers are given in fully displayed form: this will assist in showing you the correct layouts – which is important in accounting.

There are also ten sets of multiple-choice questions placed throughout the book. Although not used on all courses, they are a popular method of testing progress. Answers to multiple-choice questions are given in Appendix B (page 486).

case studies

The book contains three Case Studies which consolidate major sections of work:

Case Study One is a fully-developed example of the use of computer accounting – an important aspect of business accounts today

Case Study Two is a fully worked example of a handwritten book-keeping system and follows a month's routine business transactions through to the production of final accounts

Case Study Three uses material from Case Study Two and incorporates the year-end adjustments to the final accounts

acknowledgements

In writing this book I have been helped by a number of people. In particular, I would like to thank:

Roger Petheram, Senior Lecturer in Accounting at Worcester College of Technology, for reading the text, commenting upon it, checking answers, and always being prepared to discuss any aspect of the book.

Sandra Smallwood, Lecturer in Computing at Worcester College of Technology, who helped with the computer accounting Case Study.

Michael Fardon, of Osborne Books, for his continued assistance and support.

Jean Cox, my wife, who keyed the text into the computer and prepared the page layouts.

Thanks are also due to the following for permission to reproduce material: The Sage Group plc, and The Controller of Her Majesty's Stationery Office.

Questions from past examination papers are reproduced by kind permission of:

—London East Anglian Group, *GCSE Accounting*

—Midland Examining Group, *GCSE Accounting*

—Northern Examining Association, *GCSE Accounting*

—Northern Ireland Schools Examinations and Assessment Council, *GCSE Accounting, 'A' level Accounting* (© 1991)

—Southern Examining Group, *GCSE Accounting*

—Welsh Joint Education Committee, *GCSE Accounting*

—Pitman Examinations Institute, *Book-keeping and Accounts levels 1 and 2*

—London Chamber of Commerce and Industry, *Book-keeping (first level), Book-keeping and Accounts (second level), and Accounting (third level)*

—RSA Examinations Board, *Book-keeping stage I, and Accounting stages II and III*

—The Chartered Institute of Bankers, *Introduction to Accounting (Banking Certificate)*

—Association of Accounting Technicians, *Basic Accounting (Certificate in Accounting), Basic Accounting, paper 1, and Accounting, paper 5*

—The Chartered Institute of Management Accountants, *Accounting, stage I*

—The Chartered Association of Certified Accountants, *Accounting, paper 1.1*

Where answers are given, they are the responsibility of the author, not the examining body.

the author

David Cox is a freelance lecturer and writer. Until recently he was a Senior Lecturer in the Management and Professional Studies Department at Worcester College of Technology. He is a fellow of The Chartered Association of Certified Accountants and has over twenty years' full-time teaching experience, during which time he has taught accounting students at all levels. He worked for Midland Bank plc for a number of years and is a fellow of The Chartered Institute of Bankers. He is particularly interested in the development of computer accounting material for teaching purposes. He is the author of a number of accounting and banking textbooks, and is co-author, with Michael Fardon, of *Finance, Accounting, Financial Recording, Financial Planning & Monitoring* and *Business Record Keeping* from Osborne Books.

1 What are Business Accounts?

1.1 What is meant by accounting?

Accounting – known as 'the language of business' – is essential to the recording and presentation of business activities in the form of *business accounts*. Accounting involves:

- recording business transactions in financial terms
- reporting financial information to the owner of the business and other interested parties
- advising the owner – and other parties – how to use the financial reports to assess the past performance of the business, and to make decisions for the future

We will see, in Section 1.10 of this chapter, that the three main elements of the definition – *recording, reporting* and *advising* - are often carried out by different types of accounting personnel. First, though, we will look at an outline of the *accounting system*.

1.2 The accounting system

Businesses need to record financial transactions in the form of business accounts for very practical reasons:

- they need to quantify items such as sales, expenses and profit
- they need to present these figures in a meaningful way to measure the success of the business

Business financial records can be very complex, and one of the problems that you face as a student of business accounts is having difficulty in relating what you are learning to the accounting system of the business as a whole. In this chapter we will summarise how a typical business records and presents financial information in the form of accounts. The process follows a number of distinct stages which are illustrated in full in fig. 1.1 on the next page.

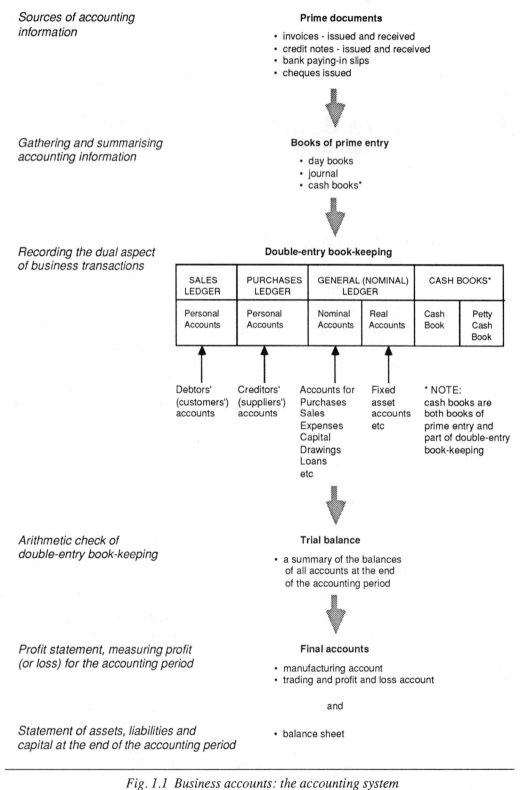

Sources of accounting information

Prime documents

- invoices - issued and received
- credit notes - issued and received
- bank paying-in slips
- cheques issued

Gathering and summarising accounting information

Books of prime entry

- day books
- journal
- cash books*

Recording the dual aspect of business transactions

Double-entry book-keeping

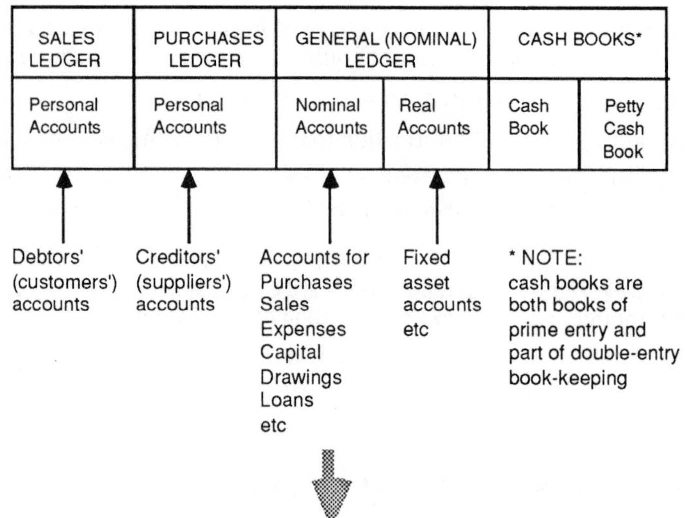

SALES LEDGER	PURCHASES LEDGER	GENERAL (NOMINAL) LEDGER		CASH BOOKS*	
Personal Accounts	Personal Accounts	Nominal Accounts	Real Accounts	Cash Book	Petty Cash Book
Debtors' (customers') accounts	Creditors' (suppliers') accounts	Accounts for Purchases Sales Expenses Capital Drawings Loans etc	Fixed asset accounts etc		

* NOTE: cash books are both books of prime entry and part of double-entry book-keeping

Arithmetic check of double-entry book-keeping

Trial balance

- a summary of the balances of all accounts at the end of the accounting period

Profit statement, measuring profit (or loss) for the accounting period

Final accounts

- manufacturing account
- trading and profit and loss account

and

Statement of assets, liabilities and capital at the end of the accounting period

- balance sheet

Fig. 1.1 Business accounts: the accounting system

The accounting system can be summarised as follows:

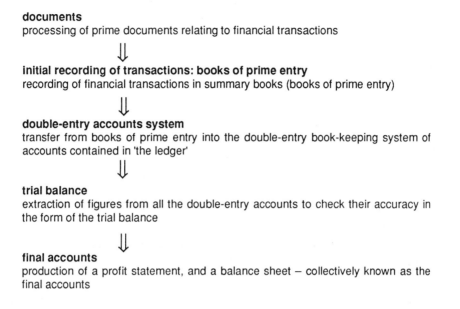

documents
processing of prime documents relating to financial transactions

initial recording of transactions: books of prime entry
recording of financial transactions in summary books (books of prime entry)

double-entry accounts system
transfer from books of prime entry into the double-entry book-keeping system of accounts contained in 'the ledger'

trial balance
extraction of figures from all the double-entry accounts to check their accuracy in the form of the trial balance

final accounts
production of a profit statement, and a balance sheet – collectively known as the final accounts

The rest of this book covers these stages – the accounting system – in detail. If you should at any time lose sight of where your studies are taking you, refer back to this chapter, and it should help to place your work in context.

Before summarising each stage in the accounting system we will first examine what form accounting records can take.

1.3 Accounting records

Accounting records are usually kept in one of two forms:

- handwritten records
- computer records

Written accounting records

This is the traditional form of keeping 'the books', particularly for the smaller business. The main record is *the ledger* which, at one time, would be a large leather-bound volume, neatly ruled, into which the book-keeper would enter each business transaction in immaculate copperplate handwriting into individual accounts. In modern times, the handwritten ledger is still used, and stationery shops sell ledgers and other accounting books, designed especially for the smaller business.

Computer accounting records

Nowadays, computers are relatively cheap so that they can be afforded by all but the smallest business. With computer accounting, business transactions are input into the computer and stored on disk. The major advantage of computer accounting is that it is a very accurate method of recording business transactions; the disadvantage is that it may be cumbersome and time-consuming to set up, particularly for the smaller business. Interestingly, the word 'ledger' has survived into the computer age but, instead of being a bound volume, it is represented by data files held on a computer disk.

Whether business transactions are recorded by hand, or by using a computer, the basic principles remain the same. The first few chapters of this book concentrate on these basic principles, and Chapter Ten and Case Study One see how computers can be used in accounting.

Practical points

When maintaining business accounts you should bear in mind that they should be kept

- accurately
- up-to-date
- confidentially, ie not revealed to people outside the business

Maintaining business accounts is a discipline, and you should develop disciplined accounting skills as you study with this book. Your study of business accounts will involve you in working through many questions and practical examples. These will require you to apply logical thought to the skills you have learned. In particular, when attempting questions you should:

- be neat in the layout of your work
- use ink (in accounting, the use of pencil shows indecision)
- not use correcting fluid (errors should be crossed through neatly with a single line and the correct version written on the line below)

The reason for not using correcting fluid in handwritten accounts is because, in practice, the accounts will be audited (checked by accountants): correcting fluid may hide errors, but it can also conceal fraudulent transactions.

1.4 Business documents

Business transactions generate documents. You will already be familiar with many of these. In this section we will relate them to the type of transaction involved and also introduce other accounting terminology which is essential to your studies.

Sale and purchase of goods and services – the invoice

When a business buys or sells goods or service the seller prepares an invoice stating

- the amount owing
- when it should be paid
- details of the goods sold or service provided

An invoice is illustrated on page 39.

Cash sales and credit sales – debtors and creditors

An invoice is prepared by the seller for

- *cash sales* – where payment is immediate, whether by cash or by cheque. (Note that not all cash sales will require an invoice to be prepared by the seller – shops, for instance, normally issue a *receipt* for the amount paid.)
- *credit sales* – where payment is to be made at a later date (often 30 days later)

A *debtor* is a person who owes you money when you sell on credit.

A *creditor* is a person to whom you owe money when you buy on credit.

Return of goods – the credit note

If the buyer returns goods which are bought on credit (they may be faulty or incorrect) the seller will prepare a credit note (see page 41 for an example) which is sent to the buyer, reducing the amount of money owed. The credit note, like the invoice, states the money amount and the goods and services to which it relates.

Banking transactions – paying-in slip and cheque

Businesses, like anyone else with a bank account, need to pay in money, and draw out cash and make payments. Paying-in slips and cheques are used frequently in business as source documents for bank account transactions.

Further reading

The subject of business documents is covered in detail in Chapter Four, which you should read if you are unfamiliar with the documents mentioned so far.

1.5 Initial recording of transactions – books of prime entry

Many businesses issue and receive large quantities of invoices, credit notes and banking documents, and it is useful for them to list these in summary form, during the course of the working day. These summaries are known as books of *prime (or original) entry*.

These books include

- *sales day book* – a list of sales made, compiled from invoices issued
- *purchases day book* – a list of purchases made, compiled from invoices received
- *sales returns day book* – a list of 'returns in', ie goods returned by customers, compiled from credit notes issued
- *purchases returns day book* – a list of 'returns out', ie goods returned by the business to suppliers, compiled from credit notes received
- *cash book* – the business' record of the bank account and the amount of cash held, compiled from receipts, paying-in slips and cheques
- *petty cash book* – a record of small cash (notes and coin) purchases made by the business, compiled from petty cash vouchers.
- *journal* – a record of non-regular transactions, which are not recorded in any other book of prime entry.

The books of prime entry are explained in detail in Chapter Six. The point you should bear in mind is that they provide the information for the double-entry book-keeping system.

1.6 Double-entry accounts: the ledger

The basis of the accounting system is the *double-entry book-keeping system* which is embodied in a series of records known as the *ledger*. This is divided into a number of separate *accounts*.

Double-entry book-keeping

Double-entry book-keeping involves making *two* entries in the accounts for each transaction: for instance, if you are paying wages by cheque you will make an entry in bank account and an entry in wages account. The reasoning behind this procedure and the rules involved are explained in detail in Chapters Two and Three. If you are operating a manual accounting system you will make the two entries by hand, if you are operating a computer accounting system you will make one entry on the keyboard, but indicate to the machine where the other entry is to be made by means of a numerical code.

Accounts

The sources for the entries you make are the books of prime entry. The ledger into which you make the entries is normally a bound book (in a non-computerised system) divided into separate *accounts,* eg a separate account for sales, purchases, each type of business expense, each debtor, each creditor, and so on. Each account will be given a specific name, and a number for reference purposes (or input code, if you use a computer system).

Division of the ledger

Because of the large number of accounts involved, the ledger has traditionally been divided into a number of sections. These same sections are used in computer accounting systems.

- *sales ledger* – personal accounts of debtors, ie customers to whom the business has sold on credit
- *purchases ledger* – personal accounts of creditors, ie suppliers to whom the business owes money
- *cash books* – a cash book comprising cash account and bank account, and a petty cash book for petty cash account (small purchases). Note: the cash books are *also* books of prime entry.
- *general (or nominal) ledger* – the remainder of the accounts: *nominal accounts*, eg sales, purchases, expenses, and *real accounts* for items owned by the business

1.7 Trial balance

Double-entry book-keeping, because it involves making two entries for each transaction, is open to error. What if the book-keeper writes in £45 in one account and £54 in another? The trial balance – explained in full in Chapter Five – effectively checks the entries made over a given period and will pick up most errors. It sets out the *balances* of all the double-entry accounts, ie the totals of the accounts for a certain period. It is, as well as being an arithmetic check, the source of valuable information which is used to help in the preparation of the *final accounts* of the business.

1.8 Final accounts

The final accounts of a business comprise the profit statement and the balance sheet.

Profit statement

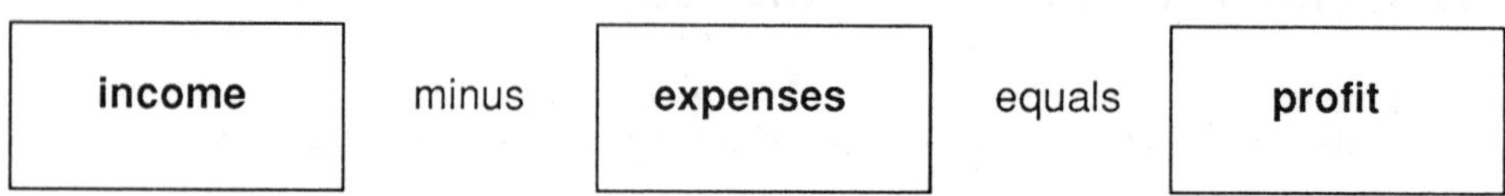

The profit statement of a business includes the *trading and profit and loss account,* and if the business manufactures goods, a *manufacturing account.* The object of these statements is to calculate the profit due to the owner(s) of the business after certain expenses have been deducted from income:

- *manufacturing account* shows the costs of producing a quantity of finished goods
- *trading and profit and loss account* shows the profit (or loss) after the deduction of cost of goods sold to give gross profit, and also after the deduction of *all* expenses to give net profit

The figures for these calculations – sales, purchases, expenses of various kinds – are taken from the double-entry system. The format for profit statements is explained in Chapter Eleven.

Balance sheet

The double-entry system also contains figures for

assets	items the business *owns,* which can be • fixed assets – items bought for use in the business, eg premises, vehicles, computers • current assets – items used in the everyday running of the business, eg stock, debtors (money owed by customers), and money in the bank
liabilities	items that the business *owes,* eg bank loans and overdrafts, and creditors (money owed to suppliers)
capital	money or assets introduced by the owner(s) of the business; capital is in effect owed by the business to the owner

The balance sheet is so called because it balances in numerical (money) terms:

Assets What a business owns	minus	**Liabilities** What a business owes	equals	**Capital** How the business has been financed

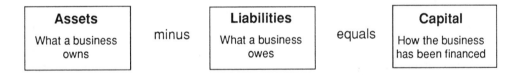

The layout of a balance sheet is explained in Chapter Twelve.

The accounting equation

The balance sheet illustrates a concept important to accounting theory, known as *the accounting equation.* This equation is illustrated in the diagram above, namely

Assets – Liabilities = Capital

Every business transaction will change the balance sheet and the equation, as each transaction has a *dual effect* on the accounts. However, the equation will always balance.

Consider the following transactions:

Transaction	*Effect on equation*
1. Business pays creditor	decrease in asset (bank) decrease in liability (money owed to creditor)
2. Business buys computer	increase in asset (computer) decrease in asset (bank)
3. The owner introduces new capital by paying a cheque into the bank	increase in asset (bank) increase in capital (money owed by business to owner)

How is the equation affected by these particular transactions?

1. Assets and liabilities both decrease by the amount of the payment; capital remains unchanged.
2. Assets remain the same because the two transactions cancel each other out in the assets section: value is transferred from the asset of bank to the asset of computer.
3. Both sides of the equation increase by the amount of the capital introduced.

In short, the equation always balances, as will the balance sheet of a business.

In conclusion, every business transaction has a *dual aspect*, as two entries are involved: this is the basis of the theory of double-entry book-keeping, and will be described in detail in Chapters Two and Three.

1.9 Accounting concepts

Accounting concepts are broad assumptions which underlie the preparation of all accounting reports. For the moment, we will consider two very important aspects:

- business entity
- money measurement

Business entity means that the accounts record and report on the financial transactions of a particular business: for example, the accounts of J Smith Ltd record and report on that business only. The problem is that, when a business is run by a sole trader, the owner's personal financial transactions can be sometimes mixed in with the business' financial transactions: the two should be kept entirely separate.

Money measurement means that the accounting system uses money as the common denominator in recording and reporting all business transactions. Thus, it is not possible to record, for example, the loyalty of a firm's workforce or the quality of a product, because these cannot be reported in money terms.

1.10 Who uses accounts?

Before answering the question of who uses the accounts, and why, it is important to draw a distinction between the two processes of book-keeping and accounting.

Book-keeping is the basic recording of business transactions in financial terms – literally 'keeping the books of account'. This task can be carried out by anyone – the owner, or by a full-time or part-time book-keeper. The book-keeper should be able to record transactions, and extract a trial balance (see Chapter Five).

Accounting involves taking the information recorded by the book-keeper and presenting it in the form of financial reports to the owners or managers of the business. Such reports are either *retrospective:*

- profit statement and balance sheet

or *forward looking:*

- forecast, or budgeted, accounts

In each case, these reports help the owners or managers to monitor the financial progress of the business, and to make decisions for the future.

Information for the owner(s)

The accounting system will be able to give information on:

- purchases of goods (for resale) to date
- sales/turnover to date
- expenses to date
- debtors – both the total amount owed to the business, and also the names of individual debtors and the amount owed by each
- creditors – both the total owed by the business, and the amount owed to each creditor
- assets owned by the business
- liabilities owed by the business
- profit made by the business during a particular time period

The owner will want to know how profitable the business is, and what it may be worth.

Information for outside bodies

Other people interested in the accounts of a business include:

- the bank manager, if the business wants to borrow from the bank
- the Inland Revenue – the business will have to pay tax on its profits
- HM Customs and Excise (the VAT authorities) if a business is registered for Value Added Tax
- financial analysts who may be advising investors in the business
- official bodies, eg Companies House, who need to see the final accounts of limited companies
- creditors, who wish to assess the likelihood of receiving payment
- employees and trade unions, who wish to check on the financial prospects of the business

1.11 Accounting personnel

If you are studying business accounts you will encounter references to different types of professional accountant. It is important to have a general idea of who does what in the accounting world – see fig. 1.2.

Financial accountant

The function of the financial accountant is to take further the information prepared by the book-keeper. This will involve the preparation of final accounts, ie trading and profit and loss account, and balance sheet. The financial accountant may be also required to negotiate with the Inland Revenue on taxation matters. Where the business is a limited company, the financial accountant will be also involved in preparing final accounts which comply with the requirements of the Companies Act 1985 (as amended by the Companies Act 1989). This Act requires the directors of a company to report annually to shareholders, with certain minimum financial accounting information being disclosed. The financial accountant of a limited company will usually report to the finance director.

Cost and management accountant

The *cost accountant* obtains information about the recent costs of the business, eg raw materials and labour, and estimates costs for the future. Often the cost accountant reports to the *management accountant* who prepares reports and makes recommendations to the owner(s) or managers of the business. The management accountant will usually report to the finance director.

Auditors

Auditors are accountants whose role is to check that accounting procedures have been followed correctly. There are two types of auditors:

- external auditors
- internal auditors

External auditors are independent of the firm whose accounts are being audited. The most common type of audit carried out by external auditors is the statutory audit of a limited company. In this, the auditors are reporting directly to the shareholders of the company, stating that the legal requirements laid down in the Companies Acts 1985 (as amended by the Companies Act 1989) have been complied with, and that the accounts represent a 'true and fair view' of the state of the business. External auditors are usually appointed by the shareholders at the Annual General Meeting of the company.

Internal auditors are employees of the business which they audit. They are concerned with the internal checking and control procedures of the business: for example, procedures for the control of cash, authorisation of purchases, and disposal of property. The nature of their work requires that they should have a degree of independence within the business and, in a limited company, they will usually report directly to the finance director.

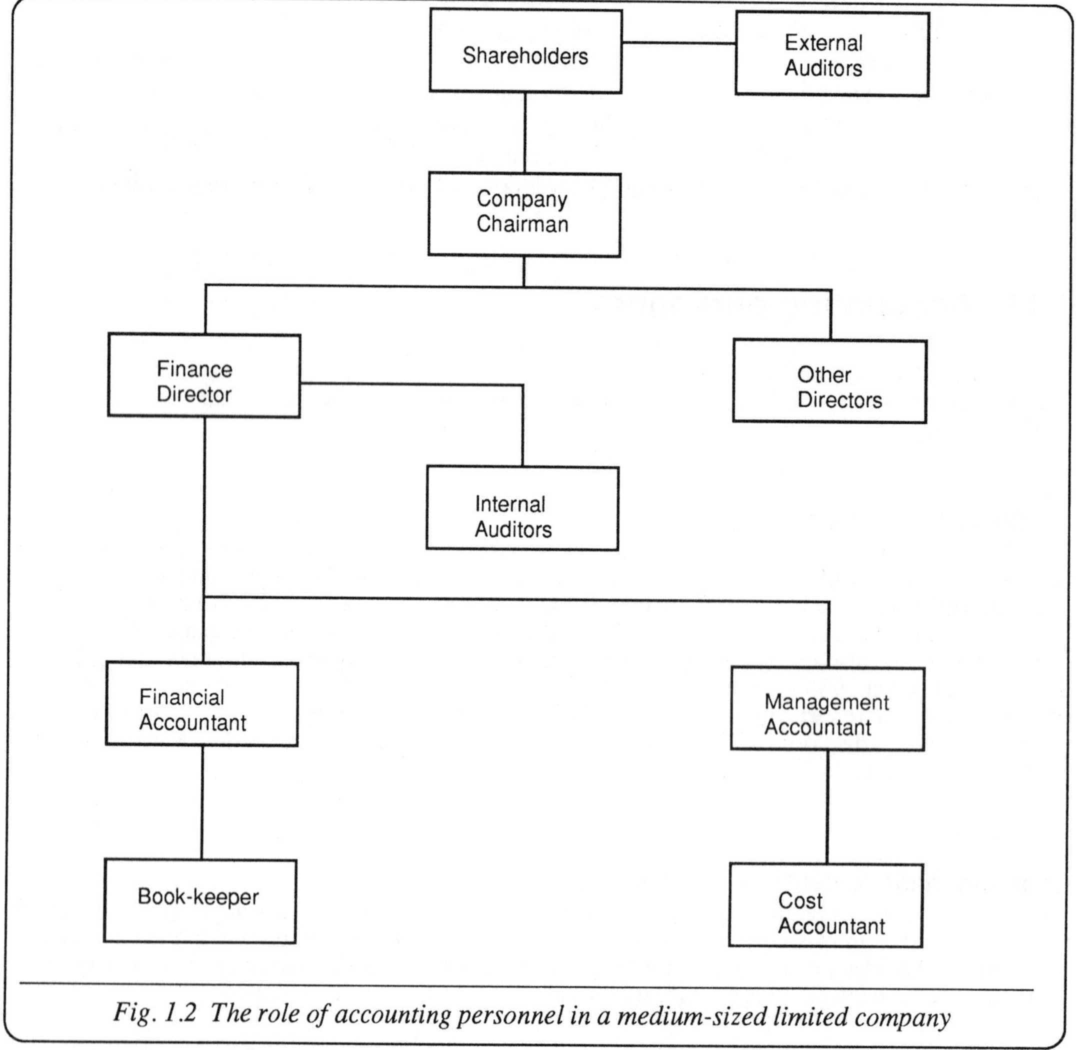

Fig. 1.2 The role of accounting personnel in a medium-sized limited company

1.12 Accounting terms

In the course of this chapter a number of specific accounting terms have been introduced. You should now study this section closely to ensure that you are clear about these definitions:

- **accounts** – financial records, where business transactions are entered
- **ledger** – the set of accounts of a business
- **assets** – items owned by a business
- **liabilities** – items owed by a business
- **capital** – the amount of the owner's (or owners') stake in the business
- **debtors** – individuals or businesses who owe money in respect of goods or services supplied by the business
- **creditors** – individuals or businesses to whom money is owed by the business
- **purchases** – goods bought, either on credit or for cash, which are intended to be resold later
- **credit purchases** – goods bought, with payment to be made at a later date
- **cash purchases** – goods bought and paid for immediately
- **sales** – the sale of goods, whether on credit or for cash, in which the business trades
- **credit sales** – goods sold, with payment to be received at an agreed date in the future
- **cash sales** – goods sold, with immediate payment received in cash, by cheque, by credit card, or by debit card
- **turnover** – the total of sales, both cash and credit, for a particular time period
- **profit** – the gain made by a business from selling goods during a particular time period
- **expenses** – the costs of running the business, eg wages, rent, rates, telephone, etc
- **trial balance** – list of the balances of all the double-entry accounts

1.13 Chapter summary

❑ Accounting is known as 'the language of business'

❑ The accounting system comprises a number of specific stages of recording and presenting business transactions
  - the originating document
  - the book of prime entry
  - the double-entry system of ledgers
  - the trial balance
  - final accounts

❑ Accounting records call for the development of skills of accuracy and neatness.

❑ The balance sheet uses the accounting equation:

Assets – Liabilities = Capital

- ❑ Two basic accounting concepts which apply to all business accounts are *business entity* and *money measurement.*

- ❑ Business accounts are used both by the managers of the business and also by outside bodies.

- ❑ There are several different types of accounting personnel, including:
  - book-keeper
  - financial accountant
  - cost and management accountant
  - auditors, external and internal

- ❑ Accounting involves the use of very specific terminology which should be learnt.

In the next chapter we will look at some financial transactions that are to be found in most business accounts. By studying these we will begin to understand the principles of double-entry book-keeping.

1.14 Questions

Note: An asterisk (*) after the question number means that an answer to the question is given in Appendix B (page 486).

1.1* Fill in the missing words from the following sentences:

(a) The set of double-entry accounts of a business is called the ....

(b) A .... is a person who owes you money when you sell on credit.

(c) A .... is a person to whom you owe money when you buy on credit.

(d) The .... is a list of sales made, compiled from invoices issued.

(e) The business' record of bank account and amount of cash held is kept in the ....

(f) Accounts such as sales, purchases, expenses are kept in the ....

(g) The accounting equation is:

.... minus .... equals ....

(h) Accounts record and report on the financial transactions of a particular business: this is the application of the .... concept.

(i) .... are accountants who check that accounting procedures have been followed correctly.

1.2 Describe the main stages in the accounting system. State five pieces of information that can be found from the accounting system that will be of interest to the owner of the business.

1.3 What types of accounting jobs are advertised in your local paper? Classify them in relation to accounting personnel described in this chapter. What tasks do the jobs involve?

1.4 Explain the accounting concepts of:

(a) business entity
(b) money measurement

1.5 Distinguish between:

- assets and liabilities
- debtors and creditors
- purchases and sales
- credit purchases and cash purchases

1.6 Show the dual aspect, as it affects the accounting equation (assets – liabilities = capital), of the following transactions for a particular business:

- owner starts in business with capital of £8,000 in the bank
- buys a computer for £4,000, paying by cheque
- obtains a loan of £3,000 by cheque from a friend
- buys a van for £6,000, paying by cheque

1.7* Fill in the missing figures:

Assets	*Liabilities*	*Capital*
£	£	£
20,000	0	....
15,000	5,000	....
16,400	....	8,850
....	3,850	10,250
25,380	....	6,950
....	7,910	13,250

1.8* Compare the columns below, ie (a) with (b), (b) with (c), etc, and identify the accounting transactions that have taken place.

	(a) £	(b) £	(c) £	(d) £	(e) £	(f) £
Assets						
Office equipment	–	2,000	2,000	2,000	2,000	2,000
Van	–	–	–	10,000	10,000	10,000
Bank	10,000	8,000	14,000	4,000	6,000	3,000
Liabilities						
Loan	–	–	6,000	6,000	6,000	3,000
Capital	10,000	10,000	10,000	10,000	12,000	12,000

2 Double-entry Book-keeping: First Principles

As we have seen in Chapter One, book-keeping is the basic recording of business transactions in financial terms. Before studying business accounts in detail it is important to study the principles of double-entry book-keeping, as these form the basis of all that we shall be doing in the rest of the book.

In the previous chapter we looked briefly at the dual aspect of accounting – each time there is a business transaction there are two effects on the accounting equation. This chapter shows how the dual aspect is used in the principles of book-keeping. In particular, we shall be looking at accounts for:

- bank
- cash
- capital
- fixed assets
- expenses
- income
- drawings
- loans

2.1 Ledger accounts

Double-entry book-keeping, as its name suggests, recognises that each transaction has a dual aspect. Once the dual aspect of each transaction has been identified, the two book-keeping entries can be made in the *ledger accounts* of the accounting system. An account is kept in the ledger to record each different type of transaction. In a handwritten book-keeping system, the ledger will consist either of a bound book, or a series of separate sheets of paper – each account in the ledger will occupy a separate page; in a computerised system, the ledger will consist of a computer file, divided into separate accounts. Whether a handwritten or computerised system is being used, the principles remain the same.

A commonly-used layout for an account is set out on the next page. Entries in ledger accounts always include dates. Please note that dates used throughout the book, for the sake of simplicity, are expressed as 19-1, 19-2, 19-3, etc, unlike in a real business where the actual year date is shown. Occasionally in this book 19-9 is followed by 19-0, ie when the decade changes.

Debit		Name of Account, eg Wages Account					Credit
Date	**Details**	**Folio**	**£ p**	**Date**	**Details**	**Folio**	**£ p**
↑ of trans-action	↑ name of other account	↑ page or reference number of other account	↑ amount of trans-action				

Note the following points about the layout of this account:

- the name of the account is written at the top
- the account is divided into two identical halves, separated by a central double vertical line
- the left-hand side is called the 'debit' side ('debit' is abbreviated to 'Dr.' – short for DebitoR)
- the right-hand side is called the 'credit' (or 'Cr.') side
- the date, details and amount of the transaction are entered in the account
- the 'folio' column is used as a cross-referencing system (see Case Study Two) to the other entry of the double-entry book-keeping transaction
- in the 'details' column is entered the name of the other account involved in the book-keeping transaction

In practice, each account would occupy a whole page in a handwritten book-keeping system but, to save space when doing exercises, it is usual to put several accounts on a page. In future, in this book, the account layout will be simplified to give more clarity as follows:

Dr.	Wages Account		Cr.
19-1	£	19-1	£

This layout is often known in accounting jargon as a 'T' account; it will be used extensively in this book because it separates in a simple way the two sides – debit and credit – of the account. An alternative style of account has three money columns: debit, credit and balance. This type of account is commonly used for bank statements, building society passbooks and computer accounting statements. Because the balance of the account is calculated after every transaction, it is known as a *running balance account* (see Section 2.11).

2.2 Debits and credits

The principle of double-entry book-keeping is that for every business transaction:

- one account is debited, and
- one account is credited

Debit entries are on the left-hand side of the appropriate account, while credit entries are on the right. The rules for debits and credits are:

- *debit entry* – the account which gains value, or records an asset, or an expense
- *credit entry* – the account which gives value, or records a liability, or an income item

This is illustrated as follows:

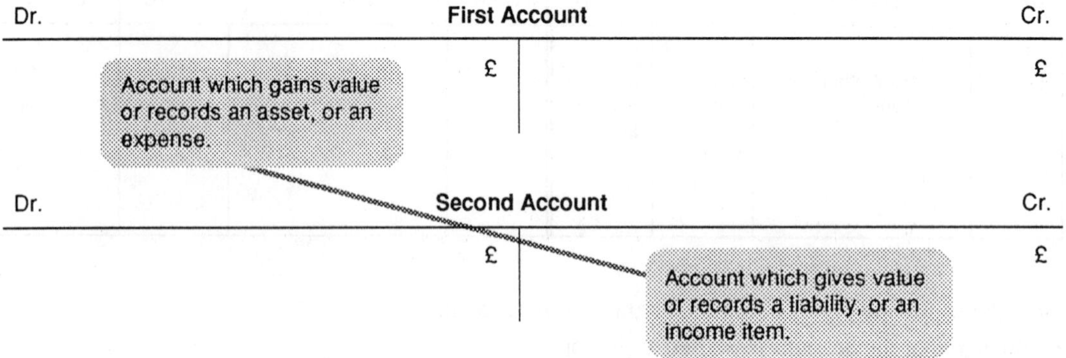

When one entry has been identified as a debit or credit, the other entry will be on the *opposite* side of the other account.

2.3 Example transactions

In order to put the theory of double-entry book-keeping into practice, we will look at some financial transactions undertaken by a new business which has just been set up by Jayne Hampson:

19-1	
1 Sep.	Started in business with capital of £5,000, a cheque paid into the bank
4 Sep.	Bought office equipment £2,500, paying by cheque
7 Sep.	Paid rent of office £500, by cheque
10 Sep.	Received commission of £100, by cheque
12 Sep.	Withdrew £250 from the bank for own use (drawings)
16 Sep.	Received a loan of £1,000 from James Henderson by cheque

All of these transactions involve the bank, and the business will enter them in its *bank account.* The bank account records money in the form of bank receipts and payments, ie cheques, standing orders, direct debits, bank giro credits, credit card transactions, and debit card transactions. (Most businesses also use a *cash account* to record transactions which involve money in the form of cash.)

With both bank account and cash account, the rules for debit and credit are:

- *money in* is recorded on the debit side
- *money out* is recorded on the credit side

Using these rules, the bank account of Jayne Hampson's business, after entering the transactions listed above, appears as:

Dr.		Bank Account			Cr.
19-1		£	19-1		£
1 Sep.	Capital	5,000	4 Sep.	Office equipment	2,500
10 Sep.	Commission	100	7 Sep.	Rent paid	500
16 Sep.	J Henderson: loan	1,000	12 Sep.	Drawings	250
	Money in			Money out	

Note: the bank account shows the firm's record of how much has been paid into, and drawn out of, the bank - it is not exactly the same as the record of receipts and payments kept by the bank (we will compare the two in Chapter Nine).

To complete the double-entry book-keeping transactions we need to:

- identify on which side of the bank account the transaction is recorded – debit (money in), or credit (money out)
- record the other double-entry transaction on the *opposite side* of the appropriate account
- note that business transactions involving cash will be entered in the *cash account*

The other accounts involved can now be recorded, and we shall now look at the principles involved for each transaction.

2.4 Capital

Capital is the amount of money invested in the business by the owner (or owners). The amount is *owed* by the business back to the owner, although it is unlikely to be repaid immediately as the business would cease to exist. A *capital account* is used to record the amount(s) paid into the business; the book-keeping entries are:

- **capital introduced**
  —*debit* bank account, as in the case of Jayne Hampson, or cash account (or a fixed asset account – see below – where these form part of the capital)
  —*credit* capital account

Example transaction

1 Sep. 19-1 Started in business with capital of £5,000, a cheque paid into the bank.

Dr.		Capital Account			Cr.
19-1		£	19-1		£
			1 Sep.	Bank	5,000

Note: The dual aspect is that bank account has gained value and has been debited already (see account at top of page); capital account records a liability (to the owner) and is credited. Remember that the business is a *separate entity* (see Chapter 1.9), and this book-keeping entry looks at the transaction from the point of view of the business. The introduction of capital into a business is often the very first business transaction entered into the books of account.

2.5 Fixed assets

Fixed assets are items purchased by a business for use on a semi-permanent basis. Examples are premises, motor vehicles, machinery and office equipment. All of these are bought by a business with the intention that they will be used for some time in the business. Without fixed assets, it would be difficult to continue in business, eg without machinery it would prove difficult to run a factory; without delivery vans and lorries it would be difficult to transport the firm's products to its customers.

When a business buys fixed assets, the expenditure is referred to as *capital expenditure*. This means that items have been bought for use in the business for some years to come. By contrast, *revenue expenditure* (see Section 2.6) is where the items bought will be used by the business quite quickly. For example, the purchase of a car is capital expenditure, while the cost of petrol for the car is revenue expenditure.

There is more on the difference between capital expenditure and revenue expenditure in Chapter Twelve.

Fixed assets and double-entry book-keeping

When fixed assets are bought, a separate account for each type of fixed asset is used, eg premises account, motor vehicles account, machinery account, etc. The book-keeping entries are:

- **purchase of a fixed asset**
  —*debit* fixed asset account (using the appropriate account)
  —*credit* bank account (or cash account)

Example transaction

4 Sep. 19-1 Bought office equipment £2,500, paying by cheque.

Dr.		Office Equipment Account			Cr.
19-1		£	19-1		£
4 Sep.	Bank	2,500			

The other part of the dual aspect of this transaction is a credit to bank account: this has been entered already (see account at the top of page 17).

2.6 Expenses

Businesses pay various running expenses, such as rent, wages, electricity, telephone, vehicle running expenses, etc. These day-to-day expenses of running the business are termed *revenue expenditure*. A separate account is used in the accounting system for each main class of revenue expenditure, eg rent account, wages account, etc.

The book-keeping entries are:

- **payment of an expense**
  —*debit* expense account (using the appropriate account)
  —*credit* bank account (or cash account)

Example transaction

7 Sep. 19-1 Paid rent of office £500, by cheque.

Dr.		Rent Account			Cr.
19-1		£	19-1		£
7 Sep.	Bank	500			

Note: The accounting rules followed are that we have debited the account which has gained value (rent – the business has had the use of the office for a certain time). The account which has given value (bank) has already been credited (see page 17).

2.7 Income

From time-to-time a business may receive amounts of income, eg rent received, commission received, or fees received. These are recorded in separate accounts for each category of income, eg rent received account, commission received account. The book-keeping entries are:

- **receipt of income**
  —*debit* bank account (or cash account)
  —*credit* income account (using the appropriate account)

Example transaction

10 Sep. 19-1 Received commission of £100, by cheque.

Dr.		Commission Received Account			Cr.
19-1		£	19-1		£
			10 Sep.	Bank	100

Note: We have already debited the account which has gained value (bank – see page 17) and credited the account which has given value (commission received).

2.8 Owner's drawings

Drawings is the term used when the owner takes money, in cash or by cheque (or sometimes goods), from the business for personal use. A *drawings account* is used to record such amounts; the book-keeping entries for withdrawal of money are:

- **owner's drawings**
  —*debit* drawings account
  —*credit* bank account (or cash account)

Example transaction

12 Sep. 19-1 Withdrew £250 from the bank for own use.

Dr. **Drawings Account** Cr.

19-1		£	19-1		£
12 Sep.	Bank	250			

The other part of the dual aspect of this transaction is a credit to bank account: this has been entered already (see page 17).

2.9 Loans

When a business receives a loan, eg from a relative or the bank, it is the cash account or bank account which gains value, while a loan account (in the name of the lender) records the liability.

- **loan received**
  —*debit* bank account (or cash account)
  —*credit* loan account (in name of the lender)

Example transaction

16 Sep. 19-1 Received a loan of £1,000 from James Henderson by cheque

Dr. **James Henderson: Loan Account** Cr.

19-1		£	19-1		£
			16 Sep.	Bank	1,000

The debit entry has already been made in bank account (see page 17).

2.10 Further transactions

Using the accounts which we have seen already, here are some further transactions:

- **loan repayment**
  —*debit* loan account
  —*credit* bank account (or cash account)
- **sale of a fixed asset, or return of an unsuitable fixed asset**
  —*debit* bank account (or cash account)
  —*credit* fixed asset account

  Note: sale of fixed assets is dealt with more fully in Chapter Thirteen.
- **withdrawal of cash from the bank for use in the business**
  —*debit* cash account
  —*credit* bank account
- **payment of cash into the bank**
  —*debit* bank account
  —*credit* cash account

2.11 Running balance accounts

The layout of accounts that we have used has a debit side and a credit side. Whilst this layout is very useful when learning the principles of book-keeping, it is not particularly appropriate for practical business use. Most 'real-life' accounts have three money columns: debit transactions, credit transactions, and balance. A familiar example of this type of account is a bank statement and a building society passbook. With a three-column account, the balance is calculated after each transaction has been entered – hence the name *running balance* accounts. For handwritten accounts, it would be rather tedious to calculate the balance after each transaction (and a potential source of errors) but, using computer accounting, the calculation is carried out automatically.

The following is the bank account used earlier in this chapter (page 17), set out in 'traditional' format:

Bank Account

Dr.					Cr.
19-1		£	19-1		£
1 Sep.	Capital	5,000	4 Sep.	Office equipment	2,500
10 Sep.	Commission	100	7 Sep.	Rent paid	500
16 Sep.	J Henderson: loan	1,000	12 Sep.	Drawings	250

The account does not show the balance, and would need to be balanced (see Chapter Five).

In 'running balance' layout, the account appears as:

Bank Account

19-1		*Debit* £	*Credit* £	*Balance* £
1 Sep.	Capital	5,000		5,000 Dr.
4 Sep.	Office equipment		2,500	2,500 Dr.
7 Sep.	Rent paid		500	2,000 Dr.
10 Sep.	Commission	100		2,100 Dr.
12 Sep.	Drawings		250	1,850 Dr.
16 Sep.	J Henderson: loan	1,000		2,850 Dr.

With a running balance account, it is necessary to state after each transaction whether the balance is debit (Dr.) or credit (Cr.). Note that the bank account in the books of this business has a *debit* balance, ie there is money in the bank – an asset.

2.12 Chapter summary

- Every business transaction has a dual aspect.
- Business transactions are recorded in ledger accounts using double-entry book-keeping principles.
- Each double-entry book-keeping transaction involves a debit entry and a credit entry.
- Entries in the bank account and cash account are:
  —*debit* money in
  —*credit* money out
- Capital is the amount of money invested in the business by the owner. Capital introduced is recorded as:
  —*debit* bank account or cash account (or an asset account if an asset is introduced)
  —*credit* capital account
- Fixed assets are items purchased by a business for use on a semi-permanent basis, eg premises, motor vehicles, machinery and office equipment. The purchase of such items is called *capital expenditure.*
- The purchase of fixed assets is recorded in the business accounts as:
  —*debit* fixed asset account
  —*credit* bank account (or cash account)
- Running expenses of a business, such as rent, wages, electricity, etc are called *revenue expenditure.*
- Expenses are recorded in the business accounts as:
  —*debit* expense account
  —*credit* bank account (or cash account)
- Receipt of income, eg rent received, commission received, fees received, is recorded as:
  —*debit* bank account (or cash account)
  —*credit* income account
- Drawings is where the owner takes money (or goods) from the business for personal use. The withdrawal of money is recorded as:
  —*debit* drawings account
  —*credit* bank account (or cash account)
- When a business receives a loan, it will be recorded as:
  —*debit* bank account (or cash account)
  —*credit* loan account in the name of the lender

In the next chapter we will continue with double-entry book-keeping and look at regular business transactions for purchases, sales and returns.

2.13 Questions

Note: An asterisk (*) after the question number means that an answer to the question is given in Appendix B (page 486).

2.1 James Anderson has kept his bank account up-to-date, but has not got around to the other double-entry book-keeping entries. Rule up the other accounts for him, and make the appropriate entries.

Dr.		**Bank Account**			Cr.
19-1		£	19-1		£
1 Feb.	Capital	7,500	6 Feb.	Computer	2,000
14 Feb.	Bank loan	2,500	8 Feb.	Rent paid	750
20 Feb.	Commission received	145	12 Feb.	Wages	425
			23 Feb.	Drawings	200
			25 Feb.	Wages	380
			28 Feb.	Van	6,000

2.2* The following are the business transactions of Tony Long for the month of May 19-2:

19-2
1 May Started a business with capital of £6,000 in the bank
4 May Bought a machine for £3,500, paying by cheque
6 May Bought office equipment for £2,000, paying by cheque
10 May Paid rent £350, by cheque
12 May Obtained a loan of £1,000 from a friend, Lucy Warner, and paid her cheque into the bank
15 May Paid wages £250, by cheque
17 May Commission received £150, by cheque
20 May Drawings £85, by cheque
25 May Paid wages £135, by cheque

You are to:

(a) Write up Tony Long's bank account

(b) Complete the double-entry book-keeping transactions

2.3 Enter the following transactions into the double-entry book-keeping accounts of Jean Lacey:

19-5
1 Aug. Started in business with capital of £5,000 in the bank
3 Aug. Bought a computer for £1,800, paying by cheque
7 Aug. Paid rent £100, by cheque
10 Aug. Received commission £200, *in cash*
12 Aug. Bought office fittings £2,000, paying by cheque
15 Aug. Received a loan, £1,000 by cheque, from a friend, Sally Orton
17 Aug. Drawings £100, *in cash*
20 Aug. Returned some of the office fittings (unsuitable) and received a refund cheque of £250
25 Aug. Received commission £150, by cheque
27 Aug. Made a loan repayment to Sally Orton of £150, by cheque

2.4* Tom Griffiths has recently set up in business. He has made some errors in writing up his bank account. You are to set out the bank account as it should appear, rule up the other accounts for him, and make the appropriate entries.

Dr.		**Bank Account**			Cr.
19-2		£	19-2		£
4 Mar.	Office equipment	1,000	1 Mar.	Capital	6,500
12 Mar.	Drawings	175	5 Mar.	Bank loan	2,500
			7 Mar.	Wages	250
			8 Mar.	Commission received	150
			10 Mar.	Rent paid	200
			15 Mar.	Van	6,000

2.5 Enter the following transactions into the double-entry book-keeping accounts of Caroline Yates:

19-7
1 Nov. Started in business with capital of £75,000 in the bank
3 Nov. Bought a photocopier for £2,500, paying by cheque
7 Nov. Received a bank loan of £70,000
10 Nov. Bought office premises £130,000, paying by cheque
12 Nov. Paid business rates of £3,000, by cheque
14 Nov. Bought office fittings £1,500, paying by cheque
15 Nov. Received commission of £300, in cash
18 Nov. Drawings in cash £125
20 Nov. Paid wages £250, by cheque
23 Nov. Paid £100 of cash into the bank
25 Nov. Returned some of the office fittings (unsuitable) and received a refund cheque for £200
28 Nov. Received commission £200, by cheque

2.6 Write up the bank account from question 2.5 in the form of a 'running balance' account.

2.7* The following account appears in the books of Peter Singh:

Dr.		**Bank Account**			Cr.
19-4		£	19-4		£
1 Jan.	Capital	10,000	2 Jan.	Office equipment	3,000
4 Jan.	Commission received	500	3 Jan.	Business rates	1,500
7 Jan.	Bank loan	2,500	5 Jan.	Cash	250
			6 Jan.	Drawings	500
			8 Jan.	Van	7,500

Taking each transaction in turn, describe to Peter Singh the transaction undertaken by his business, and explain the other account in which each appears in his double-entry accounts.

3 Double-entry Book-keeping: Further Transactions

This chapter continues with the principles of double-entry book-keeping and builds on the skills established in the previous chapter. We shall be looking at the dual aspect and the book-keeping required for the business transactions of:

- cash purchases
- cash sales
- credit purchases
- credit sales
- returns
- carriage

3.1 Purchases and sales

Common business transactions are to buy and sell goods. These transactions are recorded in *purchases account* and *sales account* respectively. These two accounts are used to record the purchase and sale of the *goods in which the business trades*. For example, a shoe shop will buy shoes from the manufacturer and will record this in purchases account; as shoes are sold, the transactions will be recorded in sales account. Note that the book-keeping system does *not* use a 'goods account': instead, when buying goods, a purchases account is used; when selling goods, a sales account is used.

The normal entry on a purchases account is on the debit side – the account has gained value, ie the business has bought goods for resale. The normal entry on a sales account is on the credit side – the account has given value, ie the business has sold goods.

When a business buys an item for use in the business, eg a computer, this is debited to a separate account, because a *fixed asset* – see Chapter 2.5 – has been purchased. Likewise, when a fixed asset is sold, it is not entered in the sales account.

3.2 Purchases and sales: an example

In order to put the theory of double-entry book-keeping for purchases and sales into practice, we will look at some financial transactions undertaken by Temeside Traders, a business which started trading on 1 October 19-1:

19-1
1 Oct. Started in business with capital of £7,000 paid into the bank
2 Oct. Bought goods for £5,000, paying by cheque
3 Oct. Sold some of the goods for £3,000, a cheque being received
5 Oct. Bought equipment £700, paying by cheque
10 Oct. Bought goods for £2,800, paying by cheque
12 Oct. Sold some of the goods for £5,000, a cheque being received
15 Oct. Paid rent £150, by cheque

These transactions are entered into the book-keeping system as follows:

Bank Account

Dr.			Cr.		
19-1		£	19-1		£
1 Oct.	Capital	7,000	2 Oct.	Purchases	5,000
3 Oct.	Sales	3,000	5 Oct.	Equipment	700
12 Oct.	Sales	5,000	10 Oct.	Purchases	2,800
			15 Oct.	Rent paid	150

Capital Account

Dr.			Cr.		
19-1		£	19-1		£
			1 Oct.	Bank	7,000

Purchases Account

Dr.			Cr.		
19-1		£	19-1		£
2 Oct.	Bank	5,000			
10 Oct.	Bank	2,800			

Sales Account

Dr.			Cr.		
19-1		£	19-1		£
			3 Oct.	Bank	3,000
			12 Oct.	Bank	5,000

Equipment Account

Dr.			Cr.		
19-1		£	19-1		£
5 Oct.	Bank	700			

Rent Account

Dr.			Cr.		
19-1		£	19-1		£
15 Oct.	Bank	150			

Notes:

- Only one purchases account and one sales account is used to record the two different movements of the goods in which a business trades (a 'goods account' is *not* used).
- The equipment is a fixed asset, so its purchase is entered to a separate equipment account.
- The purchases and sales made in the transactions above are called *cash purchases* and *cash sales,* because payment is immediate.

3.3 Credit transactions

In the previous section, we looked at the book-keeping for cash purchases and cash sales, ie where payment is made immediately. However, in business, many transactions for purchases and sales are made on credit, ie the goods are bought or sold now, with payment (in cash, or by cheque) to be made at a later date. It is an important aspect of double-entry book-keeping to record the credit transaction as a purchase or a sale, and then record the second entry in an account in the name of the creditor or debtor, ie to record the amount owing *by* the firm to a creditor, or *to* the firm by a debtor.

Note that the term *credit transactions* does not refer to the side of an account. Instead, it means the type of transaction where money is not paid at the time of making the sale: payment will be made at a later date.

3.4 Credit purchases

Credit purchases are goods obtained from a supplier, with payment to take place at a later date. From the buyer's viewpoint, the supplier is a *creditor.*

The book-keeping entries are:

- **credit purchase**
  — *debit* purchases account
  — *credit* creditor's (supplier's) account

When payment is made to the creditor the book-keeping entries are:

- **payment made to creditor**
  — *debit* creditor's account
  — *credit* bank account or cash account

3.5 Credit sales

With credit sales, goods are sold to a customer who is allowed to settle the account at a later date. From the seller's viewpoint, the customer is a *debtor.*

The book-keeping entries are:

- **credit sale**
  — *debit* debtor's (customer's) account
  — *credit* sales account

When payment is received from the debtor the book-keeping entries are:

- **payment received from debtor**
  — *debit* bank account or cash account
  — *credit* debtor's account

3.6 Credit transactions: an example

A local business, Wyvern Wholesalers, has the following transactions:

19-1	
18 Sep.	Bought goods, £250, on credit from Malvern Manufacturing Co, with payment to be made in 30 days' time
20 Sep.	Sold goods, £175, on credit to Strensham Stores, payment to be made in 30 days' time
18 Oct.	Paid £250 by cheque to Malvern Manufacturing Co
20 Oct.	Received a cheque for £175 from Strensham Stores

These transactions will be recorded in the book-keeping system (previous transactions on accounts, if any, not shown) as follows:

Dr. **Purchases Account** Cr.

19-1		£	19-1		£
18 Sep.	Malvern Manufacturing Co	250			

Dr. **Sales Account** Cr.

19-1		£	19-1		£
			20 Sep.	Strensham Stores	175

Dr. **Malvern Manufacturing Co** Cr.

19-1		£	19-1		£
18 Oct.	Bank	250	18 Sep.	Purchases	250

Dr.		Strensham Stores			Cr.
19-1		£	19-1		£
20 Sep.	Sales	175	20 Oct.	Bank	175

Dr.		Bank Account			Cr.
19-1		£	19-1		£
20 Oct.	Strensham Stores	175	18 Oct.	Malvern Manufacturing Co	250

Note: the name of the *other account* involved has been used in the details column as a description.

Balancing off accounts

In the example above, after the transactions have been recorded in the books of Wyvern Wholesalers, the accounts of Malvern Manufacturing Co and Strensham Stores have the same amount entered on both debit and credit side. This means that nothing is owing to Wyvern Wholesalers, or is owed by it, ie the accounts have a 'nil' balance. In practice, as a business trades, there will be a number of entries on both sides of such accounts, and we shall see in Chapter Five how accounts are 'balanced off' at regular intervals.

Fixed assets bought on credit

Fixed assets are often purchased on credit terms. As with the purchase of goods for resale, an account is opened in the name of the creditor, as follows:

- **purchase of a fixed asset on credit**
  — *debit* fixed asset account
  — *credit* creditor's (supplier's) account

When payment is made to the creditor the book-keeping entries are:

- **payment made to creditor**
  — *debit* creditor's account
  — *credit* bank account or cash account

3.7 Purchases returns and sales returns

From time-to-time goods bought or sold are returned, perhaps because the wrong items have been supplied (eg wrong type, size or colour), or because the goods are unsatisfactory. We will now see the book-keeping entries for returned goods.

Purchases returns (or *returns out*) is where a business returns goods to a creditor (supplier).

The book-keeping entries are:

— *debit* creditor's (supplier's) account

— *credit* purchases returns (or returns outwards) account

Purchases returns are kept separate from purchases, ie they are entered in a separate purchases returns account rather than being credited to purchases account.

Sales returns (or *returns in*) is where a debtor (customer) returns goods to the business.

The book-keeping entries are:

— *debit* sales returns (or returns in) account

— *credit* debtor's (customer's) account

Sales returns are kept separate from sales, ie they are entered in a separate sales returns account rather than being debited to sales account

Example transactions

Wyvern Wholesalers has the following transactions:

19-1	
7 Oct.	Bought goods, £280, on credit from B Lewis Ltd
10 Oct.	Returned unsatisfactory goods, £30, to B Lewis Ltd
11 Oct.	Sold goods, £125, on credit to A Holmes
17 Oct.	A Holmes returned goods, £25
26 Oct.	Paid the amount owing to B Lewis Ltd by cheque
29 Oct.	A Holmes paid the amount owing in cash

Note: 'Ltd' is the abbreviation for 'limited', and is used to indicate a *private limited company* – a common form of business entity.

The transactions will be recorded in the book-keeping system (previous transactions on accounts, if any, not shown) as follows:

Dr. **Purchases Account** Cr.

19-1		£	19-1		£
7 Oct.	B Lewis Ltd	280			

Dr. **B Lewis Ltd** Cr.

19-1		£	19-1		£
10 Oct.	Purchases Returns	30	7 Oct.	Purchases	280
26 Oct.	Bank	250			

Dr.		Purchases Returns Account			Cr.
19-1		£	19-1		£
			10 Oct.	B Lewis Ltd	30

Dr.		Sales Account			Cr.
19-1		£	19-1		£
			11 Oct.	A Holmes	125

Dr.		A Holmes			Cr.
19-1		£	19-1		£
11 Oct.	Sales	125	17 Oct.	Sales Returns	25
			29 Oct.	Cash	100

Dr.		Sales Returns Account			Cr.
19-1		£	19-1		£
17 Oct.	A Holmes	25			

Dr.		Bank Account			Cr.
19-1		£	19-1		£
			26 Oct.	B Lewis Ltd	250

Dr.		Cash Account			Cr.
19-1		£	19-1		£
29 Oct.	A Holmes	100			

3.8 Carriage inwards and carriage outwards

When goods are bought and sold, the cost of transporting the goods is referred to as 'carriage'.

Carriage inwards is where the buyer pays the carriage cost of purchases, eg an item is purchased by mail order, and the buyer has to pay the additional cost of post (and possibly packing also).

Carriage outwards is where the seller pays the carriage charge, eg an item is sold to the customer and described as 'post free'.

Both carriage inwards and carriage outwards are expenses and their cost should be debited to two separate accounts, *carriage inwards account* and *carriage outwards account* respectively.

3.9 General principles of debits and credits

By now you should have a good idea of the principles of debits and credits. From the transactions we have considered in this and the previous chapter, the 'rules' can be summarised as follows:

Debits include

- *purchases* of goods for resale
- *sales returns* (or *returns in*) when goods previously sold are returned to the business
- *purchase of fixed assets* for use in the business
- *expenses* incurred by the business
- *debtors* where money is owed to the business
- *money received* through cash account or bank account
- *drawings* made by the owner of the business
- *loan repayment,* where a loan liability is reduced/repaid

Credits include

- *sales* of goods by the business
- *purchases returns* (or *returns out*) of goods previously bought by the business
- *sale of fixed assets*
- *income* received by the business
- *creditors* where money is owed by the business
- *money paid out* through cash account or bank account
- *capital* introduced into the business by the owner(s)
- *loan* received by the business

It is important to ensure, at an early stage, that you are clear about the principles of debits and credits. They are important for an understanding of book-keeping, and are essential for your later studies in business accounts.

To summarise the double-entry book-keeping 'rules':

- *debit entry*—the account which gains value, or records an asset, or an expense
- *credit entry*—the account which gives value, or records a liability, or an income item

3.10 Types of accounts

Within a book-keeping system there are different types of accounts: a distinction is made between *personal* and *impersonal* accounts. Personal accounts are in the names of people or businesses, eg the accounts for debtors and creditors. Impersonal accounts are the other accounts; these are usually divided between *real accounts,* which represent things such as cash, bank, computers, motor vehicles, machinery, etc, and *nominal accounts,* which record income and expenses such as sales, purchases, wages, etc.

Fig. 3.1 distinguishes between the different types of accounts.

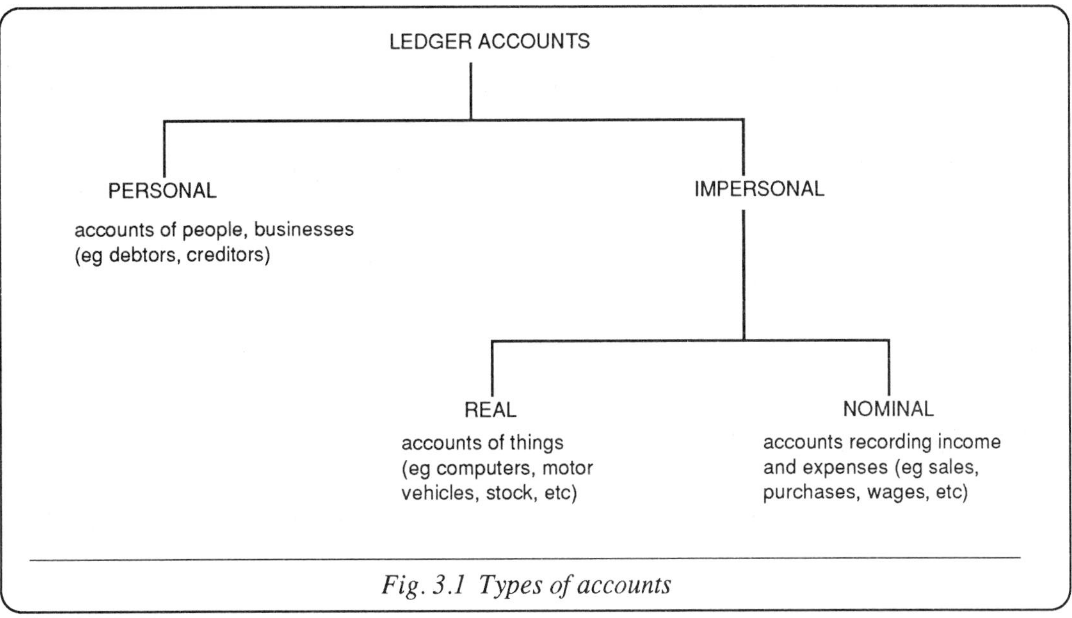

Fig. 3.1 Types of accounts

3.11 Chapter summary

- ❑ Purchases account is used to record the purchase of goods in which the business trades: the normal entry is on the debit side.
- ❑ Sales account is used to record the sale of goods in which the business trades: the normal entry is on the credit side.
- ❑ The purchase of goods is recorded as:
  — *debit* purchases account
  — *credit* bank/cash account or, if bought on credit, creditor's account
- ❑ The sale of goods is recorded as:
  — *debit* bank/cash account or, if sold on credit, debtor's account
  — *credit* sales account

- Purchases returns (or returns out) are recorded as:
  — *debit* creditor's account
  — *credit* purchases returns account

- Sales returns (or returns in) are recorded as:
  — *debit* sales returns account
  — *credit* debtor's account

- 'Carriage' is the expense of transporting goods:
  — *carriage inwards* is the cost of carriage paid on purchases
  — *carriage outwards* is the cost of carriage paid on sales

- Accounts are divided between personal (the accounts of people, firms, eg debtors and creditors; also capital account), and impersonal accounts; impersonal accounts are sub-divided between real (the accounts of things), and nominal (the accounts of income and expenses).

Case Study Two (page 164) gives a fully worked example showing business transactions entered into the double-entry accounts.

In the next chapter we will look at the business documents used when goods are sold on credit to another business.

3.12 Questions

Note: An asterisk (*) after the question number means that an answer to the question is given in Appendix B (page 486).

3.1 The following are the business transactions of Evesham Enterprises for the month of October 19-2:

19-2
1 Oct. Started in business with capital of £2500 in the bank
2 Oct. Bought goods, £200, paying by cheque
4 Oct. Sold goods, £150, a cheque being received
6 Oct. Bought goods, £90, paying by cheque
8 Oct. Sold goods, £125, a cheque being received
12 Oct. Received a loan of £2,000 from J Smithson by cheque
14 Oct. Bought goods, £250, paying by cheque
18 Oct. Sold goods, £155, a cheque being received
22 Oct. Bought a secondhand delivery van, £4,000, paying by cheque
25 Oct. Paid wages, £375, by bank giro credit
30 Oct. Sold goods, £110, a cheque being received

You are to:

(a) Write up the firm's bank account
(b) Complete the double-entry book-keeping transactions

3.2* The following are the business transactions of Oxford Trading Company for the month of February 19-1:

19-1
1 Feb. Started in business with capital of £3,000 in the bank
2 Feb. Sold goods, £250, a cheque being received
3 Feb. Bought goods, £100, paying by cheque
5 Feb. Paid wages, £150, by bank giro credit
7 Feb. Sold goods, £300, a cheque being received
12 Feb. Bought goods, £200, paying by cheque
15 Feb. Received a loan of £1,000 from James Walters by cheque
20 Feb. Bought a computer for £1,950, paying by cheque
25 Feb. Sold goods, £150, a cheque being received
27 Feb. Paid wages, £125, by bank giro credit

You are to:

(a) Write up the firm's bank account

(b) Complete the double-entry book-keeping transactions

3.3* Write up the bank account from question 3.2 in the form of a 'running balance' account.

3.4* The following are the business transactions of Pershore Packaging for the month of January 19-1:

19-1
4 Jan. Bought goods, £250, on credit from AB Supplies Ltd
5 Jan. Sold goods, £195, a cheque being received
7 Jan. Sold goods, £150, cash being received
10 Jan. Received a loan of £1,000 from J Johnson by cheque
15 Jan. Paid £250 to AB Supplies Ltd by cheque
17 Jan. Sold goods, £145, on credit to L Lewis
20 Jan. Bought goods, £225, paying by cheque
22 Jan. Paid wages, £125, in cash
26 Jan. Bought office equipment, £160, on credit from Mercia Office Supplies Ltd
29 Jan. Received a cheque for £145 from L Lewis
31 Jan. Paid the amount owing to Mercia Office Supplies Ltd by cheque

You are to record the transactions in the books of account.

3.5 The following are the business transactions for April 19-2 of William King, who runs a food wholesaling business:

19-2
2 Apr. Bought goods, £200, on credit from Wyvern Producers Ltd
4 Apr. Bought goods, £250, on credit from A Larsen
5 Apr. Sold goods, £150, on credit to Pershore Patisserie
7 Apr. Sold goods, £175, a cheque being received
9 Apr. Returned goods, £50, to Wyvern Producers Ltd
12 Apr. Sold goods, £110, a cheque being received
15 Apr. Pershore Patisserie returned goods, £25
17 Apr. Bought a weighing machine for use in the business £250, on credit from Amery Scales Ltd
20 Apr. Paid Wyvern Producers Ltd £150, by cheque
22 Apr. Pershore Patisserie paid the amount owing by cheque
26 Apr. Returned goods, £45, to A Larsen
28 Apr. Sold goods, £100, cash received
29 Apr. Paid wages in cash, £90
30 Apr. Paid the amount owing to Amery Scales Ltd by cheque

You are to record the transactions in the books of account.

3.6 The following are the business transactions for June 19-3 of Helen Smith who trades as 'Fashion Frocks':

19-3
2 Jun. Bought goods, £350, on credit from Designs Ltd
4 Jun. Sold goods, £220, a cheque being received
5 Jun. Sold goods, £115, cash received
6 Jun. Returned goods, £100, to Designs Ltd
7 Jun. Bought goods, £400, on credit from Mercia Knitwear Ltd
10 Jun. Sold goods, £350, on credit to Wyvern Trade Supplies
12 Jun. Sold goods, £175, a cheque being received
15 Jun. Wyvern Trade Supplies returned goods, £50
17 Jun. Returned goods, £80, to Mercia Knitwear Ltd
18 Jun. Paid the amount owing to Designs Ltd by cheque
20 Jun. Sold goods, £180, cash received
23 Jun. Bought goods, £285, on credit from Designs Ltd
26 Jun. Paid rent in cash, £125
28 Jun. Received a cheque from Wyvern Trade Supplies for the amount owing

You are to record the transactions in the books of account.

3.7 For each transaction below, complete the table to show the accounts which will be debited and credited:

(a) Bought goods, paying by cheque
(b) Cheque received for sales
(c) Bought goods on credit from Teme Traders
(d) Sold goods on credit to L Harris
(e) Returned unsatisfactory goods to Teme Traders
(f) L Harris returns unsatisfactory goods
(g) Received a loan from D Perkins, by cheque
(h) Withdrew cash from the bank for use in the business

Transaction	*Account debited*	*Account credited*
(a)		
(b)		
(c)		
(d)		
(e)		
(f)		
(g)		
(h)		

4 Business Documents

Business documents are important because they are the prime source for the recording of business transactions. In this chapter we will look at the following documents:

- purchase order
- delivery note
- invoice
- credit note
- statement of account

We will also look at how cash discount – an allowance off the invoice price for quick settlement – is recorded in the book-keeping system.

4.1 Documents for a credit transaction

You will see that the documents to be explained involve *credit transactions,* ie selling or buying with payment to be made at a later date. The normal stages in a credit transaction are:

- buyer prepares
  —*purchase order*
- seller prepares
  —*delivery note*
  —*invoice*
  —*statement of account*
- buyer prepares
  —*cheque* or *bank giro credit* in payment

If some or all of the goods are unsatisfactory and are returned, the seller prepares a *credit note*. The flow of these documents is shown in fig. 4.1.

4.2 Purchase order

A purchase order is prepared by the buyer, and is sent to the seller. Details found on a purchase order include:

- number of purchase order
- name and address of buyer
- name and address of seller
- full description of the goods, reference numbers, quantity required and unit price
- date of issue
- signature of person authorised to issue the order

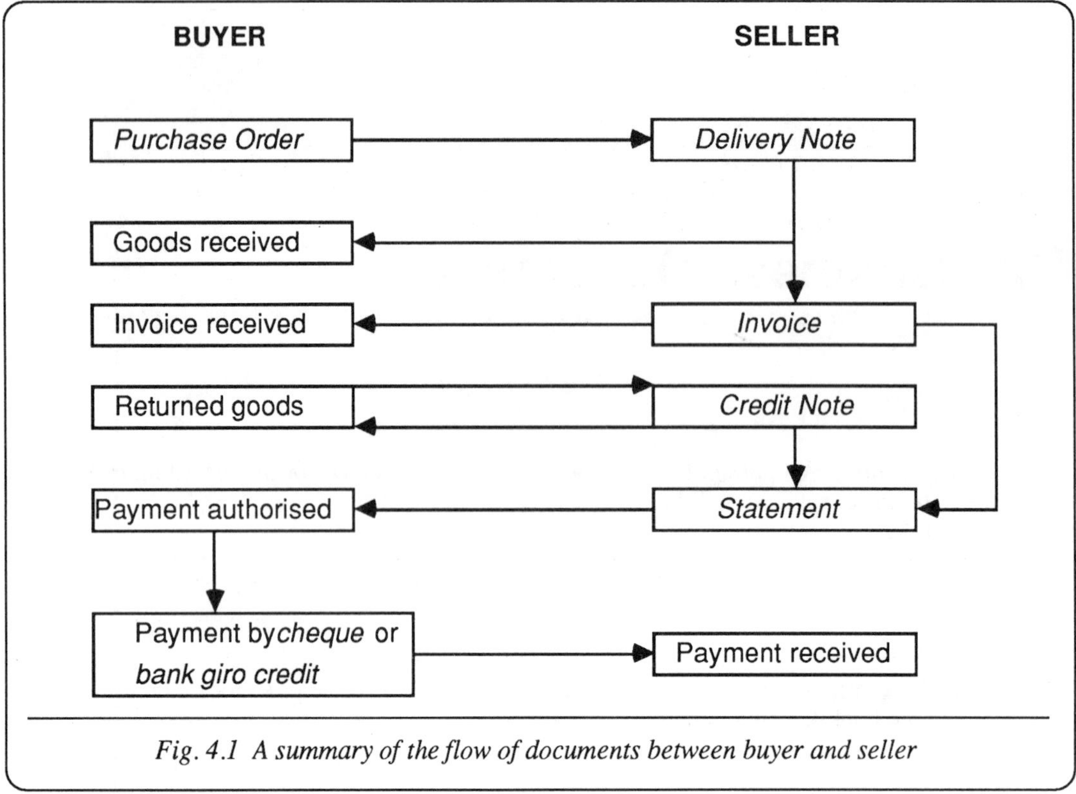

Fig. 4.1 A summary of the flow of documents between buyer and seller

In order to keep control over purchases many businesses authorise certain people as buyers. In this way, purchases are controlled so that duplicate or unauthorised goods are not ordered.

4.3 Delivery note

When the business that is selling the goods despatches them to the buyer, a delivery note is prepared. This accompanies the goods and gives details of what is being delivered. When the goods are received by the buyer, a check can be made to ensure that the correct goods have been delivered.

4.4 Invoice

The invoice (see fig. 4.2) is the most important document in a business transaction. It is prepared by the seller and is sent to the buyer. The invoice gives details of the goods supplied, and states the money amount to be paid by the buyer. The information to be found on an invoice includes:

- invoice number (serially numbered)
- name and address of seller
- name and address of buyer
- date of sale
- date of goods supplied, including reference numbers, quantity supplied and unit price
- details of trade discount allowed (if any)
- total amount of money due
- terms of trade

INVOICE **No. 1234**

W Chapel (Shoe Manufacturers) Ltd.
The Last Works
Welt Street
NORTHAMPTON NN5 2AB

Tel: (0604) 841271
Fax: (0604) 841461
VAT Reg No 928 1793 20

Date/Tax Point: 15 October 19-9

To:
The Shoe Shop
High Street
WYVERN
WY1 1XZ

Order No. 4321

Quantity	Description	Unit Price	Total Amount
5 pairs	Ladies shoes, L45, size 6	£40.00 per pair	£200.00
4 pairs	Gents shoes, G78, size 9	£50.00 per pair	£200.00
			£400.00
		less trade discount at 40%	£160.00
		Sub-total	£240.00
		Value Added Tax at 17½%	£42.00
		Invoice Total	£282.00

Terms: Net 30 days from invoice date

Fig. 4.2 An example of an invoice

Where the seller is registered for Value Added Tax (VAT), tax must be charged at the current rate (17½%) on all sales subject to VAT. The invoice, in addition to the items listed above must state:

- seller's VAT Registration Number
- date for tax purposes (the tax-point) on which the sale is made
- amount of VAT charged
- total amount of money due including VAT.

If the buyer of the goods is VAT-registered, then the amount of VAT on the invoice can be claimed back from the VAT authorities (HM Customs and Excise). The accounting implications of VAT are looked at in Chapter Seven.

Terms of trade are stated on an invoice to indicate the date by which the invoice amount is to be paid. The term 'net' on an invoice means that the invoice total is the amount to be paid; 'net 30 days' means that the amount is payable within 30 days of the invoice date.

Trade discount is the amount sometimes allowed as a reduction when goods are supplied to other businesses, but not when the sale is made to the general public. VAT is calculated on the net amount of the invoice, ie after deducting any trade discount allowed. (Note that trade discount is never shown in the accounts – only the amount after deduction of trade discount is recorded.)

Cash discount is an allowance off the invoice amount for quick settlement, eg 2% cash discount for settlement within seven days: the buyer can choose whether to take up the cash discount by paying promptly, or whether to take longer to pay, perhaps thirty days from the invoice date, without cash discount. When cash discount is taken, it needs to be recorded in the accounts – see Section 4.8.

Important note: Where a cash discount is offered, VAT is calculated on the net amount of the invoice (ie value of goods supplied, less any trade discount allowed), *less* the amount of the cash discount, whether or not this discount is subsequently taken by the buyer. For example:

	Net 30 days	*2% cash discount for settlement in 7 days, otherwise net 30 days*
Net invoice amount	£100.00	£100.00
VAT @ 17½%	£17.50	£17.15*
Invoice total	£117.50	£117.15

* VAT amount is: (£100.00 - £2.00 cash discount) x 17½% = £17.15. In the first example, the amount of £117.50 is due within 30 days of the invoice date. In the second example, £117.15 is due within 30 days of the invoice date (no cash discount taken); however, if the buyer settles within seven days (cash discount taken), the amount to be paid will be:

(£100.00 - £2.00 cash discount) + VAT £17.15 = £115.15.

Invoices (like other business documents) can be handwritten or typed on printed forms, or books of invoices can be bought in most stationers' shops. Invoicing is an ideal function for computerised accounting (see Chapter Ten) and, for this purpose, pre-printed invoices are available in the form of continuous stationery. Also, increasingly nowadays, invoices are in electronic form (EDI – electronic data interchange) and the information needs to be 'captured' and put into the accounting system.

4.5 Credit note

If a buyer returns goods for some reason, eg faulty goods supplied, the seller prepares a credit note (see fig. 4.3) to record the amount of the allowance made to the buyer. A credit note is often printed in red.

Another use of a credit note is when the seller has overcharged the buyer on an invoice, eg higher prices have been charged in error. A credit note is issued to show the amount allowed to the buyer. (By contrast, if the seller has undercharged on an invoice, a *debit note* is issued which shows the extra amount to be charged to the buyer.)

CREDIT NOTE

No. CN567

W Chapel (Shoe Manufacturers) Ltd.
The Last Works
Welt Street
NORTHAMPTON NN5 2AB

Tel: (0604) 841271
Fax: (0604) 841461
VAT Reg No 928 1793 20

Date/Tax Point: 26 October 19-9

To:
The Shoe Shop
High Street
WYVERN
WY1 1XZ

Order No. 4321

Quantity	Description	Unit Price	Total Amount
1 pair	Gents shoes, G78, size 9	£50.00 per pair	£50.00
		less trade discount at 40%	£20.00
		Sub-total	£30.00
		Value Added Tax at 17½%	£5.25
		Invoice Total	£35.25

Reason for credit: Faulty stitching

Fig. 4.3 An example of a credit note

4.6 Statement of account

At regular intervals, often at the end of each month, the seller sends a statement of account (see fig. 4.4) to each debtor. This gives a summary of the transactions that have taken place since the previous statement and shows how much is currently owed. The details on a statement are:

- name and address of seller
- name and address of the debtor (buyer)
- date of the statement
- details of transactions, eg invoices, debit notes, credit notes, payments
- balance currently due

STATEMENT OF ACCOUNT

W Chapel (Shoe Manufacturers) Ltd.
The Last Works
Welt Street
NORTHAMPTON NN5 2AB

Tel: (0604) 841271
Fax: (0604) 841461
VAT Reg No 928 1793 20

Statement date: 31 October 19-9

To:
The Shoe Shop
High Street
WYVERN
WY1 1XZ

Date	No.	Details	Debit £ p	Credit £ p	Balance £ p
19-9					
15 Oct	1234	Invoice	282. 00		282. 00 Dr
26 Oct	CN567	Credit Note		35. 25	246. 75 Dr
				Amount now due	246. 75

Fig. 4.4 An example of a statement of account

Most statements have three money columns: debit, credit and balance. The debit column is used to record the money amount of invoices and debit notes sent to the debtor; the credit column is for payments received and credit notes issued; the balance column shows the amount due, and is prepared on the 'running balance' (see Chapter 2.11) basis, ie a new balance is shown after each transaction. The balance is usually debit (shown on the statement as 'Dr.'), which indicates that the buyer is a debtor in the seller's accounting records. Some statements of account also incorporate a *remittance advice* as a tear-off slip; this is returned to the seller together with the payment.

4.7 Payment

Before payment is made to the seller, the buyer must check that the goods have been received and are as ordered. The payment can then be authorised by an appointed employee and made by means of either a cheque or a bank giro credit. The payment sent to the seller is usually accompanied by a *remittance advice*, which shows the amount of the payment, and the transactions to which it relates.

Sometimes a remittance advice for the use of the debtor is incorporated into a statement of account as a tear-off slip – the debtor ticks the items being paid. Large companies often use a computer to print the details on payment cheques, and attached to the cheque is a remittance advice showing the items being paid. Bank giro credits can also be prepared by computer, either in the form of a paper voucher, or a magnetic tape containing details of payments to be made. Paper vouchers are passed through the banking system to the seller's bank account, while magnetic tapes are passed through the BACS (Bankers Automated Clearing Services) system for the credit of the seller's bank account.

4.8 Recording cash discount in the book-keeping system

We saw earlier (in Section 4.4) that *cash discount* is an allowance off the invoice amount for quick settlement, eg 2% cash discount for settlement within seven days. A business can be involved with cash discount in two ways:

- discount allowed to debtors
- discount received from creditors

(Note that, although the terms *discount allowed* and *discount received* do not use the word 'cash', they do refer to cash discount.)

Discount allowed

When cash discount is taken by a debtor it is entered into the accounts as shown by the following transactions:

10 Oct. 19-2	Sold goods, £100, on credit to P Henry, allowing her a cash discount of 2% for settlement within seven days
15 Oct. 19-2	P Henry pays £98 by cheque

Sales Account

Dr.			Cr.		
19-2		£	19-2		£
			10 Oct.	P Henry	100

P Henry

Dr.			Cr.		
19-2		£	19-2		£
10 Oct.	Sales	100	15 Oct.	Bank	98
			15 Oct.	Discount allowed	2
		100			100

Bank Account

Dr.			Cr.		
19-2		£	19-2		£
15 Oct.	P Henry	98			

Discount Allowed Account

Dr.			Cr.		
19-2		£	19-2		£
15 Oct.	P Henry	2			

Note:

- The amount of the payment received from the debtor is entered in the bank account.
- The amount of discount allowed is entered in both the debtor's account and discount allowed account:
  —*debit* discount allowed account
  —*credit* debtor's account
- Discount allowed is an expense of the business, because it represents the cost of collecting payments more speedily from the debtors.
- The account of P Henry has been totalled to show that both the debit and credit money columns are the same – thus her account now has a nil balance (the method of balancing accounts is looked at in the next chapter).

Discount received

With cash discount received, a business is offered cash discount for quick settlement by its creditors. The following transactions give an example of this:

20 Oct. 19-2 Bought goods, £200, on credit from B Lewis Ltd; 2½% cash discount is offered for settlement by the end of October

30 Oct. 19-2 Paid B Lewis Ltd £195 by cheque

Purchases Account

Dr.			Cr.		
19-2		£	19-2		£
20 Oct.	B Lewis Ltd	200			

B Lewis Ltd

Dr.			Cr.		
19-2		£	19-2		£
30 Oct.	Bank	195	20 Oct.	Purchases	200
30 Oct.	Discount received	5			
		200			200

Bank Account

Dr.			Cr.		
19-2		£	19-2		£
			30 Oct.	B Lewis Ltd	195

Discount Received Account

Dr.			Cr.		
19-2		£	19-2		£
			30 Oct.	B Lewis Ltd	5

Note:

- The business is *receiving* cash discount from its creditor, and the amount is entered as:
  —*debit* creditor's account
  —*credit* discount received account
- Discount received account is an income account.
- The money columns of the account of B Lewis Ltd have been totalled to show that the account now has a nil balance.

Summary

- Cash discount – when taken – is recorded in the debtors' and creditors' accounts.
- Both discount allowed (an expenses account) and discount received (an income account) store up information until the end of the financial year, when it is used in the firm's profit and loss account – see Chapter Eleven.
- The cash book (see Chapter Eight) is usually used for listing the amounts of discount received and allowed – transfers are then made at the end of each month to the respective discount accounts.
- *Trade discount* is never recorded in the double-entry accounts; only the net amount of an invoice, after trade discount has been deducted, is recorded.

4.9 Chapter summary

- ❑ Correct documentation is important for businesses to be able to record accurately buying and selling transactions.
- ❑ There are a number of documents involved – the two most important are the purchase order and the invoice.
- ❑ A purchase order is a document which states the requirements of the buyer, and is sent to the seller.
- ❑ The invoice is prepared by the seller and states the value of goods sold and, hence, the amount to be paid by the buyer.
- ❑ Trade discount is often deducted when goods are sold to other businesses.
- ❑ Cash discount is an allowance off the invoice amount for quick settlement.
- ❑ Cash discount allowed is entered in the accounts as:
  —*debit* discount allowed account
  —*credit* debtor's account
- ❑ Cash discount received is entered as:
  —*debit* creditor's account
  —*credit* discount received account
- ❑ A credit note shows that the buyer is entitled to a reduction in the amount charged by the seller; it is used if:
  —some of the goods delivered were faulty, or incorrectly supplied
  —the price charged on the invoice was too high
- ❑ Statements of account are sent out regularly to each debtor of a business to show the amount currently due.

This chapter has looked at business documentation; the next chapter returns to double-entry book-keeping and looks at how accounts are balanced, and a trial balance is extracted.

4.10 Questions

4.1* Fill in the missing words from the following sentences:

(a) A .... is prepared by the buyer and sent to the seller and describes the goods to be supplied.

(b) The seller prepares the ...., which gives details of the goods supplied, and states the money amount to be paid by the buyer.

(c) .... is a deduction made in the price if the purchaser pays within a stated time.

(d) When the purchaser is in business, an amount of .... is sometimes allowed as a reduction in the price.

(e) The term .... on an invoice means that the invoice total is the amount to be paid.

(f) A government tax added to an invoice is called ....

(g) If a buyer returns goods, the seller prepares a ....

(h) If a seller has undercharged on an invoice, a .... is issued which shows the extra amount to be charged to the buyer.

(i) At regular intervals the seller sends a summary of transactions to the buyer in the form of a ....

4.2* Calculate the invoice price exclusive of VAT, the VAT chargeable (at 17½ per cent), and the total due for the order below, assuming the three following apply (three separate amounts due are to be calculated):

- Terms: net
- Terms: 2½% 30 days
- Terms: 5% 30 days

Order details:
One office desk, price £175.00

4.3 You work for Jane Smith, a wholesaler of fashionwear, who trades from Unit 21, Eastern Industrial Estate, Wyvern, Wyvernshire, WY1 3XJ. A customer, Excel Fashions of 49 Highland Street, Longtown, Mercia, LT3 2XL, orders the following:

5 dresses at £30 each
3 suits at £45.50 each
4 coats at £51.50 each

Value Added Tax is to be charged at 17½ per cent on all items and a 2½ per cent cash discount is offered for full settlement within 14 days.

You are to prepare invoice number 2451, under today's date, to be sent to the customer.

4.4 You work for Deansway Trading Company, a wholesaler of office stationery, which trades from The Model Office, Deansway, Rowcester, RW1 2EJ. A customer, The Card Shop of 126 The Cornbow, Teamington Spa, Wyvernshire, WY33 0EG, orders the following:

5 boxes of assorted rubbers at £5 per box
100 shorthand notebooks at £4 for 10
250 ring binders at 50p each

Value Added Tax is to be charged at 17½ per cent on all the items and a 2½ per cent cash discount is offered for full settlement within 14 days.

You are to prepare invoice number 8234, under today's date, to be sent to the customer.

4.5 You have the following financial details about J Wilson, a customer of your organisation:

1 Mar.	Balance due, £145
3 Mar.	Goods sold to J Wilson, £210, invoice number 8119
10 Mar.	Cheque received from J Wilson, £145
23 Mar.	Goods returned by J Wilson, £50, credit note number CN 345 issued
28 Mar.	Goods sold to J Wilson, £180, invoice number 8245

You are to prepare the statement of account to be sent to the customer on 31 March. This should show clearly the balance due at the month-end.

4.6* Study carefully the following document received by W Hoddle Ltd.

STATEMENT OF ACCOUNT

F. RAMSEY & SON
31 NORTH STREET
LIVERPOOL

W Hoddle Ltd
Blackpool Road
Manchester

31 July 19-7

Date	Reference	Dr.	Cr.	Balance
19-7				
July 1	B/F			Dr 522.80
July 8	62290	178.00		700.80
July 12	63492	132.80		833.60
July 14	Cash & Disc		522.80	310.80
July 17	89247	480.00		790.80
July 20	864		58.00	732.80
July 30	91082	347.20		1,080.00

Cash Discount 5% if paid within ONE month of the date of this Statement.

(a) In the above transactions, who is the supplier of the goods?

(b) Explain the transactions that gave rise to the entries dated
(i) 12 July
(ii) 14 July
(iii) 20 July

(c) If W Hoddle Ltd paid the above account on 18 August 19-7, how much cash discount did they receive?

(d) Assume W Hoddle Ltd prepared a balance sheet on 31 July 19-7, state where, in the balance sheet, F Ramsey & Son's balance should have appeared.

(e) In the ledger of F Ramsey & Son, show W Hoddle Ltd's account up to and including 14 July 19-7.
[Midland Examining Group]

4.7 Enter the following transactions into the double-entry book-keeping accounts of Sonya Smith:

19-4
2 Feb. Bought goods £200, on credit from G Lewis
4 Feb. Sold goods £150, on credit to L Jarvis
7 Feb. Sold goods £240, on credit to G Patel
10 Feb. Paid G Lewis the amount owing by cheque, after deducting a cash discount of 5%
12 Feb. L Jarvis pays the amount owing by cheque, after deducting a cash discount of 2%
16 Feb. Bought goods £160, on credit from G Lewis
20 Feb. G Patel pays the amount owing by cheque, after deducting a cash discount of 2½%
24 Feb. Paid G Lewis the amount owing by cheque, after deducting a cash discount of 5%

Multiple-choice questions: chapters 1-4

- Read each question carefully
- Choose the *one* answer you think is correct (calculators may be needed)
- Answers are on page 486

1. Which of the following accounting personnel concerned with the accounts of a business is *not* an employee of that business?

A external auditor
B financial accountant
C management accountant
D internal auditor

2. The purchase of goods for resale on credit is recorded in the accounts as:

	Debit	*Credit*
A	supplier's account	purchases account
B	purchases account	cash account
C	purchases account	supplier's account
D	supplier's account	sales account

3. The sale of goods to Williams for cash is recorded in the accounts as:

	Debit	*Credit*
A	Williams' account	sales account
B	sales account	Williams' account
C	sales account	cash account
D	cash account	sales account

4. Unsatisfactory goods are returned to the supplier. This is recorded in the accounts as:

	Debit	*Credit*
A	sales returns account	supplier's account
B	purchases returns account	supplier's account
C	supplier's account	purchases returns account
D	supplier's account	purchases account

5. Which one of the following is a nominal account?

A purchases
B motor vehicles
C J Smith, a debtor
D bank

6. A business buys a machine for use in the business on credit. This is recorded in the accounts as:

	Debit	*Credit*
A	machinery account	supplier's account
B	purchases account	supplier's account
C	machinery account	bank account
D	supplier's account	machinery account

7. The payment of wages in cash is recorded in the accounts as:

	Debit	*Credit*
A	wages account	drawings account
B	cash account	wages account
C	capital account	wages account
D	wages account	cash account

8. A loan is received from John Box. This is recorded in the accounts as:

	Debit	*Credit*
A	bank account	capital account
B	bank account	loan account: John Box
C	drawings account	loan account: John Box
D	loan account: John Box	bank account

9. The owner of the business transfers a computer to the business from personal assets. This is recorded in the accounts as:

	Debit	*Credit*
A	computer account	capital account
B	purchases account	computer account
C	capital account	computer account
D	computer account	sales account

10. Which of the following business documents is issued when goods are sold to another business?

A invoice
B credit note
C purchase order
D debit note

11. A business sells goods with a retail value of £500. The customer is allowed 20 per cent trade discount, and a cash discount of 2½ per cent for settlement within seven days. If the invoice is settled within the seven day period, and ignoring VAT, the business will receive a cheque for:

A £487.50
B £400.00
C £390.00
D £387.50

12. A business sells goods with a retail value of £1000, plus VAT at 17½ per cent. The customer is allowed 25 per cent trade discount, and a cash discount of 2½ per cent for settlement within seven days. How much VAT will be charged on the invoice?

A £175.00
B £170.62
C £131.25
D £127.96

5 Balancing Accounts; the Trial Balance

With the 'traditional' form of account (a 'T' account) that we have used in Chapters Two and Three, it is necessary to calculate the balance of each account from time-to-time, according to the needs of the business, and at the end of each financial year. The balance of an account is the total of that account to date, eg the amount of wages paid, the amount of sales made. In this chapter we shall see how this *balancing of accounts* is carried out.

We shall then use the balances from each account in order to check the double-entry book-keeping by extracting a *trial balance,* which is a list of the balances of ledger accounts.

5.1 Balancing the accounts

At regular intervals, often at the end of each month, accounts are balanced in order to show the amounts, for example:

- owing to each creditor
- owing by each debtor
- of sales
- of purchases
- of sales returns (returns in)
- of purchases returns (returns out)
- of expenses incurred by the business
- of fixed assets, eg premises, machinery, etc owned by the business
- of capital and drawings of the owner of the business
- of other liabilities, eg loans

We have already noted earlier that, where running balance accounts (see Chapter 2.11) are used, there is no need to balance each account, because the balance is already calculated – either manually or by computer – after each transaction.

5.2 Method of balancing accounts

On the next page is an example of an account which has been balanced at the month-end:

Dr.		Bank Account			Cr.
19-1		£	19-1		£
1 Sep.	Capital	5,000	2 Sep.	Computer	1,800
5 Sep.	J Jackson: loan	2,500	6 Sep.	Purchases	500
10 Sep.	Sales	750	12 Sep.	Drawings	100
			15 Sep.	Wages	200
			30 Sep.	Balance c/d	5,650
		8,250			8,250
1 Oct.	Balance b/d	5,650			

The steps involved in balancing accounts are:

Step 1
The entries in the debit and credit money columns are totalled; these totals are not recorded in ink on the account at this stage, but can be recorded either as sub-totals in pencil on the account, or noted on a separate piece of paper. In the example above, the debit side totals £8,250, while the credit side is £2,600.

Step 2
The difference between the two totals is the balance of the account and this is entered on the account:

- on the side of the smaller total
- on the next available line
- with the date of balancing (often the last day of the month)
- with the description 'balance c/d', or 'balance carried down'

In the bank account above, the balance carried down is £8,260 – £2,600 = £5,650, entered in the credit column.

Step 3
Both sides of the account are now totalled, including the balance which has just been entered, and the totals (the same on both sides) are entered *on the same line* in the appropriate column, and double underlined. The double underline indicates that the account has been balanced at this point using the figures above the total: the figures above the underline should not be added in to anything below the underline.

In the bank account above, the totals on each side of the account are £8,250.

Step 4
As we are using double-entry book-keeping, there must be an opposite entry to the 'balance c/d' calculated in Step 2. The same money amount is entered on the *other side of the account* below the double-underlined totals entered in Step 3. We have now completed both the debit and credit entry. The date is usually recorded as the next day after 'balance c/d', ie often the first day of the following month, and the description can be 'balance b/d' or 'balance brought down'.

In the example above, the balance brought down on the bank account on 1 October 19-1 is £5,650 debit; this means that, according to the firm's accounting records, there is £5,650 in the bank.

A practical point
When balancing accounts, use a pen and not a pencil. If any errors are made, cross them through neatly with a single line, and write the corrected version on the line below. Do *not* use correcting fluid: at best it conceals errors, at worst it conceals fraudulent transactions.

5.3 Further examples of balancing accounts

Wages Account

Dr.		£	Cr.		£
19-1		£	19-1		£
9 Apr.	Bank	750	30 Apr.	Balance c/d	2,250
16 Apr.	Bank	800			
23 Apr.	Bank	700			
		2,250			2,250
1 May	Balance b/d	2,250			

The above wages account has transactions on one side only, but is still balanced in the same way. This account shows that the total amount paid for wages is £2,250.

B Lewis Ltd

Dr.		£	Cr.		£
19-1		£	19-1		£
10 Apr.	Purchases Returns	30	7 Apr.	Purchases	280
26 Apr.	Bank	250			
		280			280

This account in the name of a creditor has a 'nil' balance after the transactions for April have taken place. The two sides of the account are totalled and, as both debit and credit side are the same amount, there is nothing further to do, apart from entering the double-underlined total.

A Holmes

Dr.		£	Cr.		£
19-1		£	19-1		£
1 Apr.	Balance b/d	105	10 Apr.	Bank	105
11 Apr.	Sales	125	11 Apr.	Sales Returns	25
			30 Apr.	Balance c/d	100
		230			230
1 May	Balance b/d	100			

This is the account of a debtor and, at the start of the month, there was a debit balance of £105 brought down from March. After the various transactions for April, there remains a debit balance of £100 owing at 1 May.

Office Equipment Account

Dr.		£	Cr.		£
19-1		£	19-1		£
12 Apr.	Bank	2,000			

This account has just the one transaction and, in practice, there is no need to balance it. It should be clear that the account has a debit balance of £2,000, which is represented by the asset of office equipment.

Dr.		Malvern Manufacturing Co			Cr.
19-1		£	19-1		£
29 Apr.	Bank	250	18 Apr.	Purchases	250

This creditor's account has a 'nil' balance, with just one transaction on each side. All that is needed here is to double underline the amount on both sides.

5.4 Extracting a trial balance

The book-keeper extracts a trial balance from the accounting records in order to check the arithmetical accuracy of the double-entry book-keeping, ie that the debit entries equal the credit entries.

A trial balance is a list of the balances of every account forming the ledger, distinguishing between those accounts which have debit balances and those which have credit balances.

A trial balance is extracted at regular intervals – often at the end of each month.

Example of a trial balance

Trial balance of A-Z Suppliers as at 31 January 19-1

	Dr. £	*Cr.* £
Name of account		
Purchases	750	
Sales		1,600
Sales returns	25	
Purchases returns		50
J Brown (debtor)	155	
T Sweet (creditor)		110
Rent paid	100	
Wages	150	
Heating and lighting	125	
Office equipment	500	
Machinery	1,000	
Cash	50	
Bank	455	
J Williams – loan		800
Capital		1,000
Drawings	250	
	3,560	3,560

Notes:

- The debit and credit columns have been totalled and are the same amount. Thus the trial balance proves that the accounting records are arithmetically correct. (A trial balance does *not* prove the *complete* accuracy of the accounting records – see Section 5.7.)
- The heading for a trial balance gives the name of the business whose accounts have been listed and the date it was extracted, ie the end of the accounting period.

- The balance for each account transferred to the trial balance is the figure brought down after the accounts have been balanced.
- As well as the name of each account, it is quite usual to show in the trial balance the account number. Most accounting systems give numbers to accounts – see Case Study Two (page 164) and the computer trial balances in Case Study One (page 133) – and these can be listed in a separate 'folio' or 'reference' column.

5.5 Debit and credit balances – guidelines

Certain accounts always have a debit balance, while others always have a credit balance. You should already know these, but the lists set out below will act as a revision guide, and will also help in your understanding of trial balances.

Debit balances include:

- cash account
- purchases account
- sales returns account (returns in)
- fixed asset accounts, eg premises, motor vehicles, machinery, office equipment, etc
- expenses accounts, eg wages, telephone, rent paid, carriage outwards, carriage inwards
- drawings account
- debtors' accounts (often, for the purposes of a trial balance, the balances of individual debtors' accounts are totalled, and the total is entered in the trial balance as 'debtors')

Credit balances include:

- sales account
- purchases returns account (returns out)
- income accounts, eg rent received, commission received, fees received
- capital account
- loan account
- creditors' accounts (often a total is entered in the trial balance, rather than the individual balances of each account)

Note: bank account can be either debit or credit – it will be debit when the business has money in the bank, and credit when it is overdrawn.

5.6 If the trial balance doesn't balance . . .

If the trial balance fails to balance, ie the two totals are different, there is an error (or errors):

- *either* in the addition of the trial balance
- *and/or* in the double-entry book-keeping

The procedure for finding the error(s) is as follows:

- check the addition of the trial balance
- check that the balance of each account has been correctly entered in the trial balance, and under the correct heading, ie debit or credit

- check that the balance of every account in the ledger has been included in the trial balance
- check the calculation of the balance on each account
- calculate the amount that the trial balance is wrong, and then look in the accounts for a transaction for this amount: if one is found, check that the double-entry book-keeping has been carried out correctly
- halve the amount by which the trial balance is wrong, and look for a transaction for this amount: if it is found, check the double-entry book-keeping
- if the amount by which the trial balance is wrong is divisible by nine, then the error may be a reversal of figures, eg £65 entered as £56, or £45 entered as £54
- if the trial balance is wrong by a round amount, eg £10, £100, £1,000, the error is likely to be in the calculation of the account balances
- if the error(s) is still not found, it is necessary to check the book-keeping transactions since the date of the last trial balance, by going back to the original documents and books of prime entry

5.7 Errors not shown by a trial balance

As mentioned earlier, a trial balance does not prove the complete accuracy of the accounting records. There are six types of errors that are not shown by a trial balance.

1. Error of omission

Here a business transaction has been completely omitted from the accounting records, ie both the debit and credit entries have not been made.

2. Reversal of entries

With this error, the debit and credit entries have been made in the accounts but *on the wrong side* of the two accounts concerned. For example, a cash sale has been entered wrongly as debit sales account, credit cash account. (This should have been entered as a debit to cash account, and a credit to sales account.)

3. Mispost/error of commission

Here, a transaction is entered to the wrong person's account. For example, a sale of goods on credit to A T Hughes has been entered as debit A *J* Hughes' account, credit sales account. Here, double-entry book-keeping has been completed but, when A J Hughes receives a statement of account, he or she will soon complain about being debited with goods not ordered or received.

4. Error of principle

This is when a transaction has been entered in the wrong type of account. For example, the cost of petrol for vehicles has been entered as debit motor vehicles account, credit bank account. The error is that motor vehicles account represents fixed assets, and the transaction should have been debited to the expense account for motor vehicle running expenses.

5. Error of original entry (or transcription)

Here, the correct accounts have been used, and the correct sides: what is wrong is that the amount has been entered incorrectly in *both* accounts. This could be caused by a 'bad figure' on an invoice or a cheque, or it could be caused by a 'reversal of figures', eg an amount of £45 being entered in both accounts as £54. Note that both debit and credit entries need to be made incorrectly for the trial balance still to balance; if one entry has been made incorrectly and the other is correct, then the error will be shown.

6. Compensating error

This is where two errors cancel each other out. For example, if the balance of purchases account is calculated wrongly at £10 too much, and a similar error has occurred in calculating the balance of sales account, then the two errors will compensate each other, and the trial balance will not show the errors.

Correction of errors is covered fully in Chapter Eighteen.

5.8 Importance of the trial balance

A business will extract a trial balance on a regular basis to check the arithmetic accuracy of the book-keeping. However, the trial balance is also used as the starting point in the production of the *final accounts* of a business. These final accounts, which are produced once a year (often more frequently) comprise:

- trading account
- profit and loss account
- balance sheet

The final accounts show the owner(s) how profitable the business has been, what the business owns, and how the business is financed. The preparation of final accounts is an important aspect of Business Accounts and one which we shall be coming to in later chapters. For the moment, we can say that extraction of a trial balance is an important exercise in the business accounts process: it proves the book-keeper's accuracy, and also lists the account balances which form the basis for the final accounts of a business.

5.9 Chapter summary

❑ The traditional 'T' account needs to be balanced at regular intervals – often at the month-end.

❑ When balancing accounts, the book-keeper must adhere strictly to the rules of double-entry book-keeping.

❑ When each account in the ledger has been balanced, a trial balance can be extracted.

❑ A trial balance is a list of the balances of every account forming the ledger, distinguishing between those accounts which have debit balances and those which have credit balances.

❑ A trial balance does not prove the complete accuracy of the accounting records; errors not shown by a trial balance are:
—error of omission
—reversal of entries
—mispost/error of commission
—error of principle
—error of original entry
—compensating error

❑ The trial balance is used as the starting point for the preparation of a business' final accounts.

Case Study Two (page 164) gives a fully worked example showing business transactions entered into the double-entry accounts, which are then balanced and a trial balance extracted.

In the next chapter we will look at the *division of the ledger* into manageable sections, and we will see how an expanding accounting system uses *books of original entry* to cope with large numbers of routine transactions.

5.10 Questions

5.1 The following are the business transactions of Robert Jefferson, a bookshop owner, for the months of January and February 19-1:

Transactions for January

19-1

1 Jan. Started in business with capital of £5,000 in the bank
2 Jan. Paid rent on premises £200, by cheque
4 Jan. Bought shop fittings £2,000, by cheque
5 Jan. Bought stock of books £2,500, on credit from Northam Publishers
8 Jan. Book sales £1,200, paid into bank
9 Jan. Book sales £1,000, paid into bank
12 Jan. Bought books £5,000, on credit from Broadheath Books
15 Jan. Book sales £1,500 to Teme School, a cheque being received
17 Jan. Book sales, £1,250, paid into bank
19 Jan. Bought books from Financial Publications £2,500, by cheque
23 Jan. Teme School returned unsuitable books £580, cheque refund sent
30 Jan. Sold books on credit to Wyvern College, £1,095

Transactions for February

19-1

3 Feb. Book sales £2,510, paid into bank
5 Feb. Paid rent on premises £200, by cheque
7 Feb. Bought shop fittings £1,385, by cheque
10 Feb. Book sales £3,875, paid into bank
11 Feb. Sent cheque, £2,500, to Northam Publishers
13 Feb. Bought books £1,290, on credit from Northam Publishers
14 Feb. Sent cheque, £5,000, to Broadheath Books
17 Feb. Book sales £1,745, paid into bank
18 Feb. Wyvern College returned books, £250
21 Feb. Book sales £1,435, paid into bank
24 Feb. Bought books £1,250, on credit from Associated Publishers
28 Feb. Book sales £3,900, paid into bank

You are to:

(a) Record the January transactions in the books of account, and balance each account at 31 January 19-1

(b) Draw up a trial balance at 31 January 19-1

(c) Record the February transactions in the books of account, and balance each account at 28 February 19-1

(d) Draw up a trial balance at 28 February 19-1

5.2* A Thompson commenced business on 1 February 19-0, paying £500 into a business bank account.

During the next two months the following transactions took place. All payments are made by cheque and all receipts are banked.

February		£
1	Bought goods for resale	150
5	Paid rent	50
10	Business takings to date	290
22	Paid for advertising	25
26	A Thompson's drawings	100
27	Business takings	240
March		
2	Bought goods for resale	100
5	Paid rent	50
14	Received a loan, L Lock	450
16	Business takings	330
23	A Thompson's drawings	75
26	Business takings	180
29	Paid for advertising leaflets	30

You are required to:

(a) write up the bank account, balancing at the end of each month

(b) write up all the other accounts and balance the accounts at the end of the two month period

(c) extract a trial balance as at 31 March 19-0

[RSA Examinations Board]

5.3 Produce the trial balance of Jane Greenwell as at 28 February 19-1. She has omitted to open a capital account.

	£
Bank overdraft	1,250
Purchases	850
Cash	48
Sales	730
Purchases returns	144
Creditors	1,442
Equipment	2,704
Van	3,200
Sales returns	90
Debtors	1,174
Wages	1,500
Capital	?

5.4 A trial balance is extracted to check the arithmetical accuracy of a set of books. If the trial balance fails to agree, errors must have been made. However, if the trial balance does agree, it does not prove the accuracy of the accounts. There are errors which a trial balance does not reveal.

Required:

Name and briefly describe *four* types of error which would **not** stop a trial balance from balancing. Give one example of each type of error.

[London Chamber of Commerce]

5.5* The following account appears in the ledger of Celia Donithorn.

Dr.		Georgina Harrison			Cr.
		£			£
1 Feb.	Balance b/d	200	3 Feb.	Bank	190
6 Feb.	Goods	80	3 Feb.	Discount	10
			10 Feb.	Returns	15

(a) What is the meaning of each item recorded in the above account? 1 February has been completed as an example.
1 Feb. Georgina Harrison owes Celia Donithorn £200

(b) What percentage cash discount was deducted on 3 February?

(c) Who owes whom how much at close of business on 10 February?

[Northern Examining Association]

5.6* Below are two ledger accounts in the books of Devenish Interiors. Study them carefully.

Dr.		M Johnston			Cr.
		£			£
1 Apr.	Balance b/d	150	10 Apr.	Bank	150
20 Apr.	Sales	200	22 Apr.	Returns	10
			28 Apr.	Bank	100
			30 Apr.	Balance c/d	90
		350			350
1 May	Balance b/d	90			

Dr.		J Kelly			Cr.
		£			£
7 Apr.	Returns	20	1 Apr.	Balance b/d	220
10 Apr.	Bank	200	6 Apr.	Purchases	110
15 Apr.	Bank	105	18 Apr.	Purchases	100
15 Apr.	Discount received	5			
20 Apr.	Returns	20			
30 Apr.	Balance c/d	80			
		430			430
			1 May	Balance c/d	80

Required:

(a) Explain the opening balance in the account of:
(i) M Johnston
(ii) J Kelly

(b) Which of the accounts is a debtor account on 30 April?

(c) Explain the 22 April entry in M Johnston/s account.

(d) Explain the 15 April *entries* in J Kelly's account.

(e) What documents should have been received from J Kelly for 7 April and 20 April transactions?

[© Northern Ireland Schools Examinations and Assessment Council]

6 Division of the Ledger; Books of Prime Entry

As we saw in Chapter One, the double-entry system involves the recording of transactions in accounts in the ledger. In this Chapter we will see how, in order to cope with an expanding book-keeping system, the ledger is divided into separate sections: this is called *division of the ledger.* We will also examine how a business makes use of *books of prime entry* to summarise business transactions before they are entered into the double-entry system.

6.1 Division of the ledger

Double-entry book-keeping involves, as we have seen, making two entries in the ledger accounts for each business transaction. The traditional meaning of a *ledger* is a weighty leather-bound volume into which each account was entered on a separate page. With such a hand-written book-keeping system, as more and more accounts were opened, the point was reached where another ledger book was needed. Finally, in order to sort the accounts into a logical order, the accounting system was divided into four main sections, and this practice continues today:

- *sales ledger,* containing the accounts of debtors
- *purchases ledger,* containing the accounts of creditors
- *cash books,* containing the main cash book and the petty cash book
- *general (or nominal) ledger,* containing the nominal accounts (expenses, etc) and the real accounts (fixed assets, etc)

These four divisions comprise *the ledger,* and are illustrated in full in fig. 6.1. Computer accounting programs (see Chapter Ten) are used for each of the four divisions of the ledger.

6.2 Use of the divisions of the ledger

To see how the divisions of the ledger are used, we will look at five business transactions and see which ledgers are used and in which accounts the transactions are recorded:

Purchase of goods on credit
- general ledger — *debit* purchases account
- purchases ledger — *credit* the account of the creditor (supplier)

Purchase of goods by cheque
- general ledger — *debit* purchases account
- cash book — *credit* bank account

SALES LEDGER

Sales ledger contains the accounts of debtors, and records:

- sales made on credit to customers of the business
- sales returns by customer
- payments received from debtors
- cash discount allowed for prompt settlement

Sales ledger does *not* record cash sales.

Sales ledger contains an account for each debtor and records the transactions with that debtor. The total of the sales ledger account balances is the debtors figure which appears in the trial balance.

PURCHASES LEDGER

Purchases ledger contains the accounts of creditors, and records:

- purchases made on credit from suppliers of the business
- purchases returns made by the business
- payments made to creditors
- cash discount received for prompt settlement

Purchases ledger does *not* record cash purchases.

Purchases ledger contains an account for each creditor and records the transactions with that creditor. The total of the purchases ledger account balances is the creditors figure which appears in the trial balance.

CASH BOOKS

The cash books (see also Chapter Eight) comprise:

- *Cash Book*
  — records all transacions for bank account and cash account
  — cash book is also often used for listing the amounts of cash discount received and allowed and Value Added Tax
- *Petty Cash Book*
  — records low value cash payments too small to be entered in the main cash book

GENERAL (NOMINAL) LEDGER

The general (or nominal) ledger contains the other accounts of the business:

- *Nominal Accounts*
  — sales account (cash *and* credit sales)
  — purchases account (cash *and* credit purchases)
  — sales returns, purchases returns
  — expenses and income
  — loan
  — capital, drawings
  — Value Added Tax (where the business is VAT-registered)
  — trading and profit and loss (see Chapter Eleven)
- *Real Accounts*
  — fixed assets
  — stock (see Chapter Eleven)

Fig. 6.1 Division of the ledger

Sale of goods on credit
- sales ledger — *debit* the account of the debtor (customer)
- general ledger — *credit* sales account

Sale of goods for cash
- cash book — *debit* cash account
- general ledger — *credit* sales account

Purchase of a computer for use in the business, paying by cheque
- general ledger — *debit* computer account (fixed asset)
- cash book — *credit* bank account

6.3 Books of prime entry

The place where a business transaction is recorded for the first time, prior to entry in the ledger, is known as a *book of prime entry* or a *book of original entry*. These comprise:
- sales day book (or sales journal)
- purchases day book (or purchases journal)
- sales returns day book (or sales returns journal)
- purchases returns day book (or purchases returns journal)
- cash book (see Chapter Eight)
- petty cash book (see Chapter Eight)
- general journal (see Chapter Seventeen)

In the rest of this chapter we will see how the first four of these – the day books – fit into the accounting system. The other books of prime entry will be looked at in more detail in later chapters. We have already used cash account and bank account which, together, make up a business' cash book. In Chapter Eight, we will see how the two accounts are brought together in one book. Cash book is the book of prime entry for receipts and payments in the forms of cash or cheque. Petty cash book is used mainly for small cash expenses and will also be looked at in Chapter Eight. General journal (often known more simply as *the* journal) is covered in Chapter Seventeen.

6.4 Sales day book

The sales day book (which can also be called a sales journal, or sales book) is used by businesses that have a lot of separate sales transactions. The day book is simply a list of transactions, the total of which, at the end of the day, week, or month, is transferred to sales account. (When used as a weekly or monthly record, it is still called a *day* book.) Note that the day book is *not* part of double-entry book-keeping, but is used as a book of prime entry to give a total which is then entered into the accounts. By using a day book for a large number of transactions in this way, there are fewer transactions passing through the double-entry accounts. Also, the work of the accounts department can be divided up – one person can be given the task of maintaining the day book, while another can concentrate on keeping the ledger up-to-date.

The most common use of a sales day book is to record credit sales from invoices issued. We will see how it is used and will also incorporate Value Added Tax, at a rate of 17½ per cent, into the transactions (VAT is looked at more fully in Chapter Seven).

Example transactions

19-1
3 Jan. Sold goods, £80 + VAT*, on credit to E Doyle, invoice no 901
8 Jan. Sold goods, £200 + VAT, on credit to A Sparkes, invoice no 902
12 Jan. Sold goods, £80 + VAT, on credit to T Young, invoice no 903
18 Jan. Sold goods, £120 + VAT, on credit to A Sparkes, invoice no 904

* VAT = 17½%

The sales day book is written up as follows:

Sales Day Book

Date	*Details*	*Invoice No*	*Folio*	*Net*	*VAT*	*Gross*
19-1				£	£	£
3 Jan.	E Doyle	901	SL 58	80	14	94
8 Jan.	A Sparkes	902	SL 127	200	35	235
12 Jan.	T Young	903	SL 179	80	14	94
18 Jan.	A Sparkes	904	SL 127	120	21	141
31 Jan.	Totals for month			480	84	564

Notes:

- Total net credit sales for the month are £480, and this amount is transferred to sales account in the general ledger.
- Total VAT charged on sales for the month has been totalled (£84), and is transferred to the credit side of VAT account in the general ledger. This is the amount of VAT charged by the business on sales made, and is due to the VAT authorities, HM Customs and Excise.
- The credit sales transactions are recorded in the personal accounts of the firm's debtors in the sales ledger, the amount debited to each account being the VAT-*inclusive* (gross) figure.
- The sales day book incorporates a folio column which cross-references each transaction to the personal account of each debtor. In this way, an *audit trail* is created so that a particular transaction can be traced from prime document (invoice), through the book of prime entry (sales day book), to the debtor's ledger account.
- The gross total (£564) is entered into the sales ledger control account (see Chapter Nineteen).

The accounts to record the above transactions are:

GENERAL LEDGER

Sales Account

Dr.			Cr.		
19-1		£	19-1		£
			31 Jan.	Sales Day Book	480

Value Added Tax Account

Dr.			Cr.		
19-1		£	19-1		£
			31 Jan.	Sales Day Book	84

SALES LEDGER

Dr.		**E Doyle** (account no 58)			Cr.
19-1		£	19-1		£
3 Jan.	Sales	94			

Dr.		**A Sparkes** (account no 127)			Cr.
19-1		£	19-1		£
8 Jan.	Sales	235			
18 Jan.	Sales	141			

Dr.		**T Young** (account no 179)			Cr.
19-1		£	19-1		£
12 Jan.	Sales	94			

Summary

Sales day book fits into the accounting system in the following way:

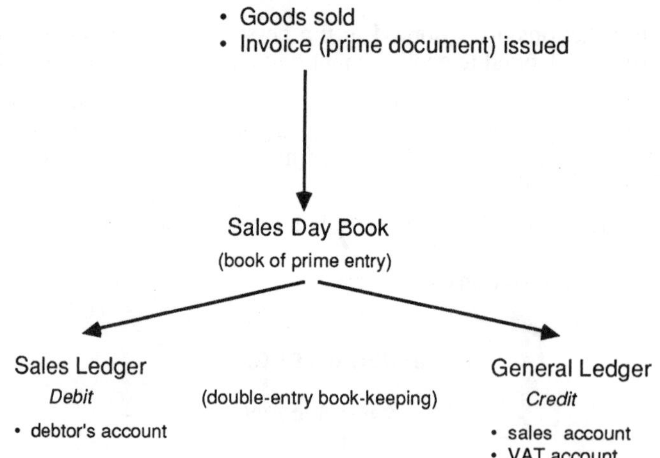

6.5 Purchases day book

This book of prime entry is used by businesses that have a lot of separate purchases transactions. The purchases day book lists the transactions for credit purchases from invoices received and, at the end of the day, week or month, the total is transferred to purchases account.

Example transactions

19-1
2 Jan. Bought goods, £80 + VAT*, on credit from P Bond, his invoice no 1234
11 Jan. Bought goods, £120 + VAT, on credit from D Webster, her invoice no A373
16 Jan. Bought goods, £160 + VAT, on credit from P Bond, his invoice no 1247
* VAT = 17½%

The purchases day book is written up as follows:

Purchases Day Book

Date	*Details*	*Invoice No*	*Folio*	*Net*	*VAT*	*Gross*
19-1				£	£	£
2 Jan.	P Bond	1234	PL 525	80	14	94
11 Jan.	D Webster	A373	PL 730	120	21	141
16 Jan.	P Bond	1247	PL 525	160	28	188
31 Jan.	Totals for month			360	63	423

Notes:

- Total net credit purchases for the month are £360, and this amount is transferred to purchases account in the general ledger.
- Total VAT payable on purchases for the month has been totalled (£63), and is transferred to the debit side of VAT account in the general ledger. This is the amount of VAT charged to the business by suppliers and can be claimed back by the business (provided it is registered for VAT), or offset against VAT due to the HM Customs and Excise (see also Chapter Seven).
- The credit purchases transactions are recorded in the personal accounts of the firm's debtors in the purchases ledger, the amount credited to each account being the VAT-*inclusive* (gross) figure.
- The folio column gives a cross-reference to the creditors' accounts and provides an audit trail.
- The gross total (£423) is entered into the purchases ledger control account (see Chapter Nineteen).

The accounts to record the above transactions (including a previous transaction on the VAT account) are:

GENERAL LEDGER

Purchases Account

Dr.			Cr.		
19-1		£	19-1		£
31 Jan.	Purchases Day Book	360			

Value Added Tax Account

Dr.			Cr.		
19-1		£	19-1		£
31 Jan.	Purchases Day Book	63	31 Jan.	Sales Day Book	84

PURCHASES LEDGER

Dr.		**P Bond** (account no 525)		Cr.
19-1	£	19-1		£
		2 Jan.	Purchases	94
		16 Jan.	Purchases	188

Dr.		**D Webster** (account no 730)		Cr.
19-1	£	19-1		£
		11 Jan.	Purchases	141

Summary

Purchases day book fits into the accounting system in the following way:

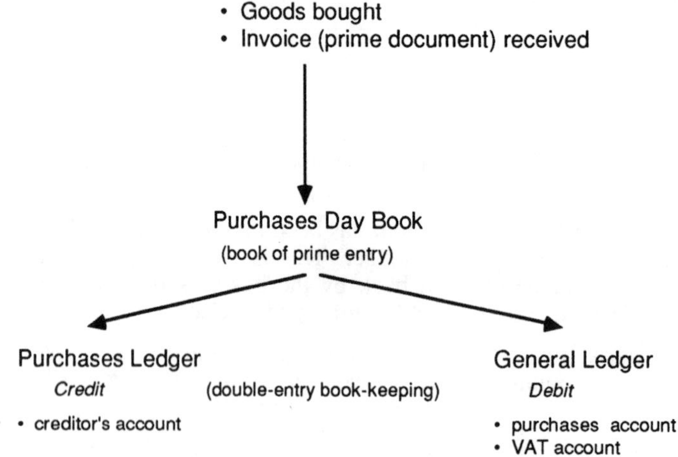

6.6 Returns day books

Where a business has a sufficient number of sales returns and purchases returns each day, week or month, it will make use of the two returns books:

- *Sales Returns Day Book* — for goods previously sold on credit and now being returned to the business by its customers
- *Purchases Returns Day Book* — for goods purchased on credit by the business, and now being returned to the suppliers

The two returns day books operate in a similar way to the other day books: they are used to store information about returns until such time as it is transferred to the appropriate returns account. Note that, like all day books, the transactions are recorded from prime documents (credit notes issued for sales returns, and credit notes received for purchases returns). The returns day books are books of prime entry and do not form part of the double-entry book-keeping system: the information from the day book must be transferred to the appropriate account in the ledger.

Example transactions

19-1
6 Jan. Returned goods, £40 + VAT* to P Bond, credit note no 406 received
15 Jan. T Young returns goods, £40 + VAT, credit note no CN702 issued
20 Jan. Returned goods, £40 + VAT to D Webster, credit note no 123 received
25 Jan. A Sparkes returns goods, £120 + VAT, credit note no CN703 issued

* VAT = 17½ per cent

The sales returns day book and purchases returns day book are written up as follows:

Sales Returns Day Book

Date	*Details*	*Credit Note No*	*Folio*	*Net*	*VAT*	*Gross*
19-1				£	£	£
15 Jan.	T Young	CN702	SL 179	40	7	47
25 Jan.	A Sparkes	CN703	SL 127	120	21	141
31 Jan.	Totals for month			160	28	188

Purchases Returns Day Book

Date	*Details*	*Credit Note No*	*Folio*	*Net*	*VAT*	*Gross*
19-1				£	£	£
6 Jan.	P Bond	406	PL 525	40	7	47
20 Jan.	D Webster	123	PL 730	40	7	47
31 Jan.	Totals for month			80	14	94

Notes:

- Total net sales returns and net purchases returns have been transferred to the sales returns account and purchases returns account respectively in the general ledger.
- Total VAT amounts are transferred to VAT account in the general ledger.
- The VAT-inclusive amounts of sales returns are credited to the debtors' personal accounts in the sales ledger; purchases returns are debited to the creditors' accounts in the purchases ledger.
- The gross totals will be entered into the sales ledger control account and purchases ledger control account (see Chapter Nineteen).

The accounts to record the above transactions (including any other transactions already recorded on these accounts) are:

GENERAL LEDGER

Sales Returns Account

Dr.			Cr.		
19-1		£	19-1		£
31 Jan.	Sales Returns Day Book	160			

Dr.	Purchases Returns Account				Cr.
19-1		£	19-1		£
			31 Jan.	Purchases Returns Day Book	80

Dr.	Value Added Tax Account*				Cr.
19-1		£	19-1		£
31 Jan.	Purchases Day Book	63	31 Jan.	Sales Day Book	84
31 Jan.	Sales Returns Day Book	28	31 Jan.	Purchases Returns Day Book	14

* We will see in the chapter on Value Added Tax (Chapter Seven) the significance of the balance on this account, and how it is dealt with.

SALES LEDGER

Dr.	**A Sparkes** (account no 127)				Cr.
19-1		£	19-1		£
8 Jan.	Sales	235	25 Jan.	Sales Returns	141
18 Jan.	Sales	141			

Dr.	**T Young** (account no 179)				Cr.
19-1		£	19-1		£
12 Jan.	Sales	94	15 Jan.	Sales Returns	47

PURCHASES LEDGER

Dr.	**P Bond** (account no 525)				Cr.
19-1		£	19-1		£
6 Jan.	Purchases Returns	47	2 Jan.	Purchases	94
			16 Jan.	Purchases	188

Dr.	**D Webster** (account no 730)				Cr.
19-1		£	19-1		£
20 Jan.	Purchases Returns	47	11 Jan.	Purchases	141

Summary

The two returns day books fit into the accounting system as follows:

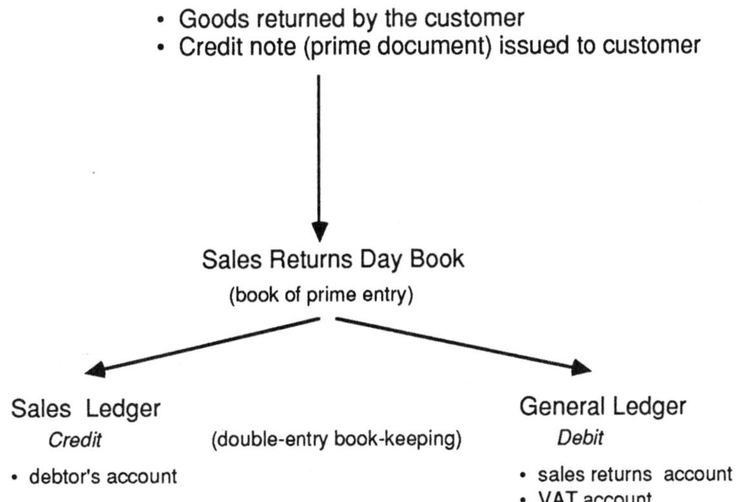

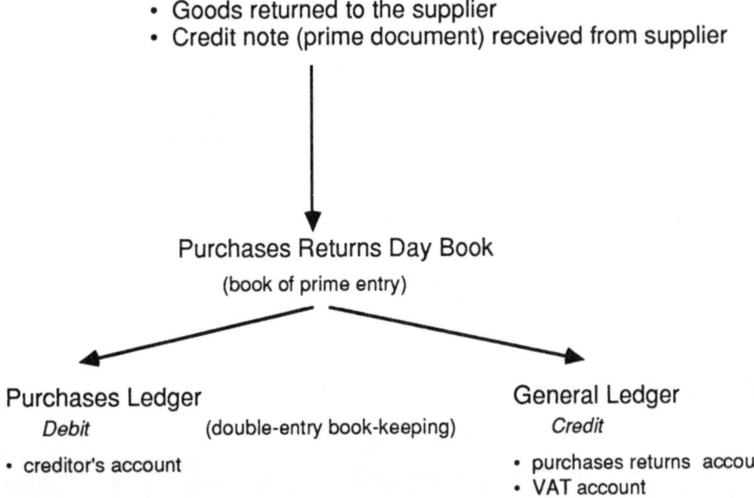

6.7 Analysed day books

An analysed day book is used whenever a business needs to split its purchases, sales or returns between different categories of products, or between different departments. For example, a paint and wallpaper shop may decide to write up its purchases day book (invoice and folio columns not shown) as follows:

Purchases Day Book

Date	*Details*	*Paint*	*Wallpaper*	*Net*	*VAT*	*Gross*
19-1		£	£	£	£	£
8 Aug.	DIY Wholesalers Ltd	75	125	200	35	235
12 Aug.	Luxor Paints Ltd	120	-	120	21	141
16 Jan.	P Bond	180	100	280	49	329
22 Aug.	Southern Manufacturing Co	60	100	160	28	188
31 Aug.	Totals for month	435	325	760	133	893

By using analysed day books, a business can keep track of the purchases, sales, etc of departments and assess the performance of each (see also Chapter Twenty-seven).

6.8 Chapter summary

❑ Division of the ledger means that the accounts are divided between four sections:
—sales ledger
—purchases ledger
—cash books
—general (or nominal) ledger

❑ Books of prime (original) entry include:
—sales day book
—purchases day book
—sales returns day book
—purchases returns day book
—cash book
—petty cash book
—general journal

❑ A day book is a listing device which is used to take pressure off the main double-entry book-keeping system, and also allows the work of the accounts department to be split up amongst staff.

❑ Most businesses use day books for credit transactions only.

❑ An analysed day book is used when a business needs to know the purchases, sales, etc made by different departments or divisions of the business.

Having included Value Added Tax in the day books used in this chapter, and seen VAT applied to business documents in Chapter Four, in the next chapter we will look in more detail at this tax and how it affects businesses.

6.9 Questions

6.1 The following invoices, in respect of purchases of goods for resale, have been received:

19-2		
2 January	T F Day	£850.45
10 January	B G Moon	£1,226.48
14 January	D S Cox	£912.14
18 January	T F Day	£1,009.63
25 January	B G Moon	£461.92
28 January	T F Day	£227.39
30 January	D S Cox	£1,013.27

***Note:* ignore VAT**

Required:

(a) rule up the purchases day book and enter the above invoices in it

(b) total the purchases day book for the month

(c) open the suppliers accounts and the purchases account

(d) post the necessary entries from the day book to these accounts

[London Chamber of Commerce]

6.2* Lucinda Lamille operates a clothes wholesaling business. All the goods she buys and sells are subject to Value Added Tax (at 17½ per cent). The following transactions are to be entered in the purchases day book or sales day book, as appropriate.

19-6	
1 Feb.	Bought goods from Flair Clothing Co for £520 + VAT
2 Feb.	Sold goods to Wyvern Fashions for £200 + VAT
4 Feb.	Bought goods from Modernwear for £240 + VAT
10 Feb.	Sold goods to Zandra Smith for £160 + VAT
15 Feb.	Sold goods to Just Jean for £120 + VAT
18 Feb.	Bought goods from Quality Clothing for £800 + VAT
23 Feb.	Sold goods to Peter Sanders Menswear for £320 + VAT
24 Feb.	Sold goods to H Wilson for £80 + VAT
26 Feb.	Sold goods to Mercian Models for £320 + VAT
28 Feb.	Bought goods from Flair Clothing Co for £200 + VAT

You are to:

(a) write up the sales day book and the purchases day book

(b) show how the VAT account will appear in her general ledger

6.3 James Scriven started in business as a furniture wholesaler on 1 February 19-2. He has registered for Value Added Tax. During the first month of business, the following credit transactions took place.

19-2	
1 Feb.	Bought furniture for resale and received invoice no 961 from Softseat Ltd, £320 + VAT*
2 Feb.	Bought furniture for resale and received invoice no 068 from PRK Ltd, £80 + VAT
8 Feb.	Sold furniture and issued invoice no 001 to High Street Stores, £440 + VAT
14 Feb.	Sold furniture and issued invoice no 002 to Peter Lounds Ltd, £120 + VAT
15 Feb.	Bought furniture for resale and received invoice no 529 from Quality Furnishings, £160 + VAT
18 Feb.	Sold furniture and issued invoice no 003 to Carpminster College, £320 + VAT
19 Feb.	Bought furniture for resale and received invoice no 984 from Softseat Ltd, £160 + VAT
25 Feb.	Sold furniture and issued invoice no 004 to High Street Stores, £200 + VAT

*** VAT = 17½%**

You are to:

(a) enter the above transactions in James Scriven's books of prime entry, and total the columns for the month

(b) record the accounting entries in James Scriven's purchases ledger, sales ledger and general ledger

6.4 Anne Green owns a shop selling paint and decorating materials; she is registered for Value Added Tax. She has two suppliers, Wyper Ltd (account no 301) and M Roper & Sons (account no 302). During the month of May 19-2 Anne received the following business documents from her suppliers:

19-2	
2 May	Invoice no 562 from M Roper & Sons for £190 + VAT*
4 May	Invoice no 82 from Wyper Ltd for £200 + VAT
10 May	Invoice no 86 from Wyper Ltd for £210 + VAT
18 May	Invoice no 580 from M Roper & Sons for £180 + VAT
18 May	Credit note no 82 from M Roper & Sons for £30 + VAT
21 May	Invoice no 91 from Wyper Ltd for £240 + VAT
23 May	Credit note no 6 from Wyper Ltd for £40 + VAT
25 May	Invoice no 589 from M Roper & Sons for £98 + VAT
28 May	Credit note no 84 from M Roper & Sons for £38 + VAT

*** VAT = 17½% (ignore fractions of a penny, ie round down to a whole penny)**

You are to:

(a) enter the above transactions in the appropriate day books which are to be totalled at the end of May

(b) enter the transactions in the appropriate accounts in Anne Green's ledgers. (The credit balances of Wyper Ltd and M Roper & Sons at the beginning of the month were £100 and £85 respectively.)

(c) balance each account and bring down a balance on 1 June 19-2

6.5* Lorna Pratt runs a computer software business, specialising in supplies to educational establishments. The business is registered for Value Added Tax. At the beginning of January 19-2 the balances in her ledgers were as follows:

Purchases ledger	Macstrad plc (account no 101)	£1,050.75 credit
	Amtosh plc (account no 102)	£2,750.83 credit
Sales ledger	Mereford College (account no 201)	£705.35 debit
	Carpminster College (account no 202)	£801.97 debit

During the course of the month the following business documents are issued (all plus VAT at 17½%):

19-2		
2 Jan.	Invoice from Macstrad plc, M1529	£2,900.00
3 Jan.	Invoice from Amtosh plc, A7095	£7,500.00
5 Jan.	Invoice to Mereford College, 1093	£3,900.00
7 Jan.	Invoice to Carpminster College, 1094	£8,500.00
10 Jan.	Credit note from Macstrad plc, MC105	£319.75
12 Jan.	Credit note from Amtosh plc, AC730	£750.18
13 Jan.	Credit note to Mereford College, CN109	£850.73
14 Jan.	Invoice to Carpminster College, 1095	£1,800.50
14 Jan.	Invoice to Mereford College, 1096	£2,950.75
18 Jan.	Invoice from Macstrad plc, M2070	£1,750.00
19 Jan.	Invoice from Amtosh plc, A7519	£5,500.00
20 Jan.	Invoice to Carpminster College, 1097	£3,900.75
22 Jan.	Invoice to Mereford College, 1098	£1,597.85
23 Jan.	Credit note from Macstrad plc, MC120	£953.07
27 Jan.	Credit note to Mereford College, CN110	£593.81

Note: when calculating VAT amounts, ignore fractions of a penny, ie round down to a whole penny.

You are to:

(a) enter the above transactions in the appropriate day books which are to be totalled at the end of January

(b) record the accounting entries in Lorna Pratt's purchases ledger, sales ledger and general ledger

6.6* For each transaction below, state
—the source document
—book of prime entry
—account to be debited
—account to be credited

(a) bought goods on credit from A Cotton
(b) sold goods on credit to D Law
(c) cheque received for sales
(d) returned damaged goods to A Cotton
(e) paid gas bill by cheque
(f) D Law returns damaged goods

6.7 C Emberson, a sole trader, buys and sells goods on credit. A bank account is kept through which all amounts received and paid are entered. On 30 November 19-9 the following balances remain in the books:

	£	£
C Hills		154
L Howe		275
K Harris	330	
Bank	740	
Capital		641
	1,070	1,070

You are required to:

(a) open appropriate ledger accounts for the above and enter balances as at 1 December 19-9

(b) post the transactions indicated in the subsidiary books direct to the ledger and open any other accounts which may be required

(c) balance the accounts where necessary and extract a trial balance on 31 December 19-9

Purchases Day Book		£	VAT	Total
Dec.				
13	C Hills	100	10	110
20	C Hills	150	15	165
21	L Howe	60	6	66
		310	31	341

Sales Day Book		£	VAT	Total
Dec.				
11	K Harris	240	24	264
15	K Harris	80	8	88
		320	32	352

Payments Received		£
Dec.		
16	K Harris	594

Payments Made		£
Dec.		
8	C Hills	154
15	Printing expenses	20

Author's note: in this question a rate of VAT of 10 per cent has been used.

[RSA Examinations Board]

Multiple-choice questions: chapters 5-6

- Read each question carefully
- Choose the *one* answer you think is correct (calculators may be needed)
- Answers are on page 486

1. A firm's cash account is as follows:

Dr.		Cash Account		Cr.
19-1	£	19-1		£
1 Jan. Capital	1,000	10 Jan.	Computer	500
19 Jan. Sales	650	12 Jan.	Purchases	400
		27 Jan.	Purchases	350
		29 Jan.	Electricity	75

At 31 January 19-1, the balance of the account is:

A credit £325
B debit £1,650
C debit £325
D credit £1,325

2. A debit balance of £125 on the bank account in a firm's book-keeping system means:

A the firm has money in the bank of £125
B the firm is overdrawn at the bank by £125
C the owner's capital is £125
D the balance of cash held by the firm is £125

3. A credit balance of £265 on T Smith's account in the books of J Wilson means:

A Smith owes Wilson £265
B Wilson has paid Smith £265
C Wilson owes Smith £265
D Smith has bought goods from Wilson for £265

4. Which one of the following *always* has a debit balance?

A capital account
B purchases account
C sales account
D purchases returns account

5. Which one of the following *always* has a credit balance?

A cash account
B premises account
C capital account
D drawings account

6. An amount has been entered into the book-keeping system as £65 instead of £56. The error is called:

   A compensating error
   B mispost
   C error of principle
   D error of original entry

7. The cost of petrol for motor vehicles has been debited in error to motor vehicles account. The error is called:

   A mispost
   B error of principle
   C error of original entry
   D error of omission

8. Which one of the following is *not* a division of the ledger?

   A general ledger
   B sales account
   C sales ledger
   D cash books

9. Sales ledger contains:

   A creditors' accounts
   B sales account
   C debtors' accounts
   D sales returns account

10. Which one of the following accounts is *not* contained in general ledger?

    A bank account
    B purchases returns account
    C motor vehicles account
    D loan account

11. Which one of the following is a book of original entry?

    A sales ledger
    B trial balance
    C general ledger
    D petty cash book

12. The book of prime entry for a credit note received from a supplier is:

    A purchases returns day book
    B sales day book
    C sales returns day book
    D general journal

7 Value Added Tax

We have already seen (in Chapter Four) how Value Added Tax (VAT) is added to invoices by businesses registered for VAT, and (in Chapter Six) how the tax is dealt with in day books and in the book-keeping system. In this chapter we shall look at:

- the nature of VAT
- the business account that needs to be kept for VAT
- how to complete a *Value Added Tax Return*

7.1 Registering for VAT

In Britain, most businesses with a turnover, ie sales, of more than £48,000 must be registered for VAT. The turnover figure is increased from time-to-time as a part of the Chancellor of the Exchequer's budget proposals. The figure quoted here was set in November 1996.

Once registered, a business is issued with a VAT registration number which must be quoted on all invoices and on other business documents. VAT is charged at the standard rate (quoted as 17½ per cent in this chapter) on all taxable supplies (except for domestic fuel, where the rate is currently 8 per cent), ie whenever the business sells goods, or supplies a service. From the supplier's viewpoint, the tax so charged is known as *output tax*. A number of items are *zero-rated* and no tax is charged when they are supplied: for example, food and children's clothing are zero rated.

Businesses registered for VAT must pay to the VAT authorities (HM Customs and Excise Department):

- the amount of VAT collected on sales (output tax)
- *less* the amount of VAT charged to them (input tax) on all taxable supplies bought in, eg purchases, expenses, fixed assets

If the amount of input tax is larger than the output tax, the business claims a refund of the difference from HM Customs and Excise.

A VAT return (see page 81) has to be completed every three months, although some businesses submit a return on an annual basis. Payment of VAT due (if the business is not claiming a refund) is made when the VAT return is submitted.

7.2 Exempt supplies

A few types of goods and services are neither standard-rated nor zero-rated for VAT: instead they are *exempt*. The effect of this is that the seller of such goods cannot charge VAT on outputs (as is the case with zero-rated goods). However, unlike the seller of zero-rated goods, the seller of exempt goods cannot claim back all the tax which has been paid on inputs. Examples of exempt supplies include postal services, loans of money, sale of land or property, and certain types of education and health care.

7.3 A tax on the final consumer

VAT is a tax which is paid by the final consumer or user of the goods (except where the final user is registered for VAT). For example, a member of the public buying a computer at a total cost of £705 is paying VAT of £105 (ie 17½ per cent of £600). This final consumer or user has to bear the cost of the VAT, but the tax is actually paid to HM Customs and Excise by all those involved in the manufacturing and selling process. This procedure is illustrated by the flow chart shown in fig. 7.1 on the next page: the right-hand column shows the amount of VAT paid to HM Customs and Excise at each stage of the process. Note that, if the final consumer had been a business registered for VAT, it would be able to claim the £105 of VAT as an input tax, and would record the purchase in its books as:

— *debit* computer account	£600
— *debit* Value Added Tax account	£105
— *credit* bank account (or creditor's account)	£705

7.4 VAT account

We have seen in the previous chapter how a VAT-registered business keeps a *Value Added Tax Account* as part of the book-keeping system in the general ledger. This records:

Debits (input tax)

- VAT on purchases
- VAT on fixed assets (except cars)
- VAT on expenses
- VAT on sales returns

Credits (output tax)

- VAT on sales and/or services
- VAT on purchases returns
- VAT on the sale of fixed assets

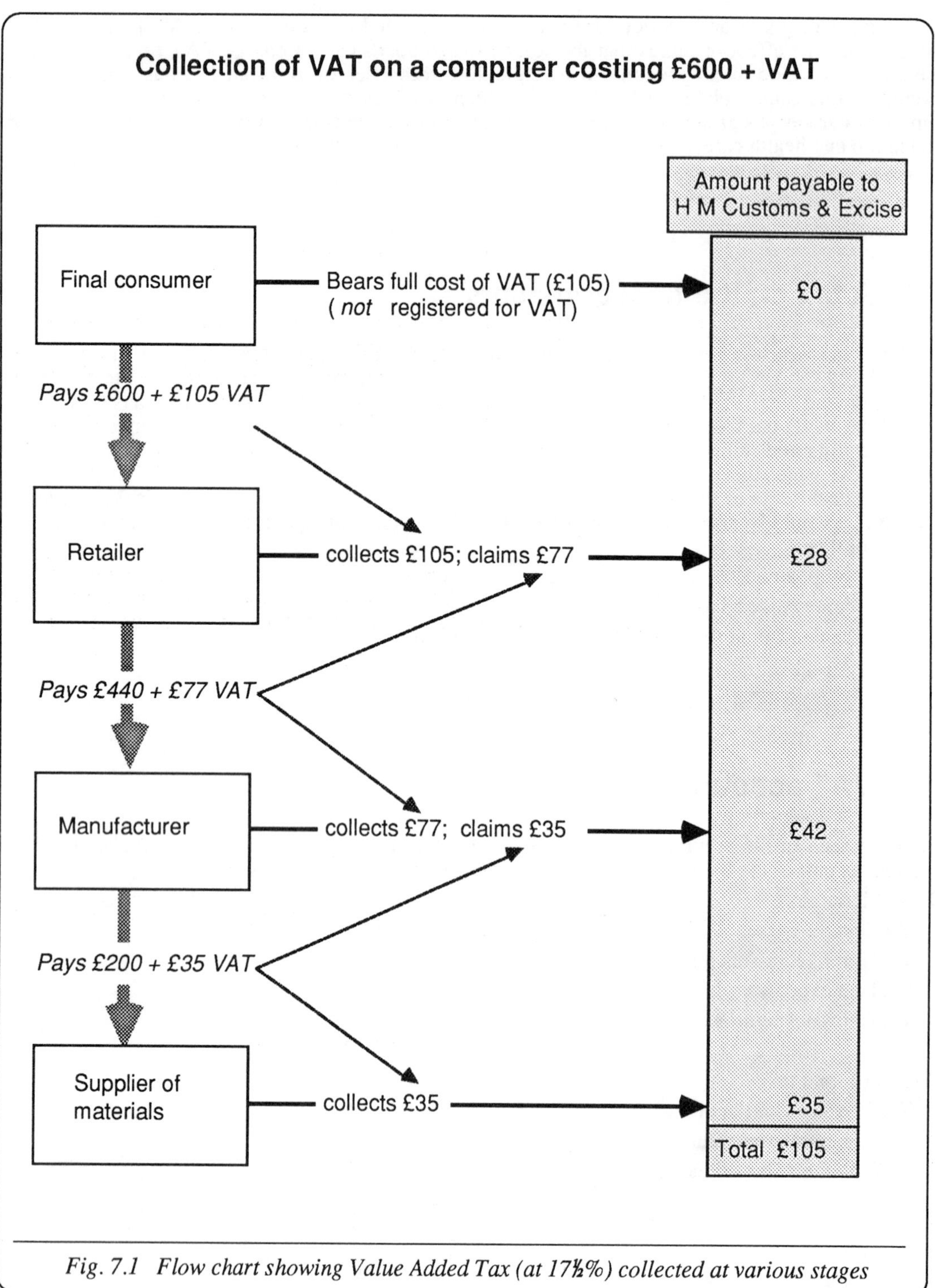

Fig. 7.1 Flow chart showing Value Added Tax (at 17½%) collected at various stages

The VAT account shown in the previous chapter (see page 68) for the month of January 19-1 is as follows:

Value Added Tax Account

Dr.			Cr.		
19-1		£	19-1		£
31 Jan.	Purchases Day Book	63	31 Jan.	Sales Day Book	84
31 Jan.	Sales Returns Day Book	28	31 Jan.	Purchases Returns Day Book	14
31 Jan.	Balance c/d	7			
		98			98
			1 Feb.	Balance b/d	7

At the end of January 19-1, the account has a credit balance of £7. This amount is owing to HM Customs and Excise and will be paid at the end of the three-month VAT period, along with the VAT due for the other two months of the VAT quarter. For example, if January is the first month of the VAT quarter, the account will be continued for a further two months until, at the end of March, the credit balance will be the amount owing to Customs and Excise. The amount will be paid in April (not later than the end of the month) by making the following book-keeping transaction:

— *debit* Value Added Tax account

— *credit* bank account (cheque made payable to 'HM Customs and Excise')

If, at the end of the VAT quarter, there is a debit balance on the VAT account, this represents the amount due from Customs and Excise. A VAT return is completed and a payment is received (usually by bank giro credit) from Customs and Excise. This is recorded in the accounting records as:

— *debit* bank account

— *credit* Value Added Tax account

7.5 Value Added Tax Return

For most businesses, a *Value Added Tax Return* (form VAT 100) must be completed every three months. The return is then sent to HM Customs and Excise, either with a payment for VAT due for the period, or a claim for repayment when input tax exceeds output tax.

Example

Wyvern (Office Products) Ltd has the following transactions, all of which are subject to VAT at 17½%, for the three months ended 31 March 19-1:

19-1	*Purchases*	*Expenses*	*Fixed assets*	*Sales*
	£	£	£	£
January	5 000	1 000	-	10 000
February	6 000	1 400	3 000	12 000
March	7 000	1 800	-	14 000
Total	18 000	4 200	3 000	36 000

The VAT account will be written up as follows:

Dr.		Value Added Tax Account			Cr.
19-1		£	19-1		£
31 Jan.	Purchases Day Book	875	31 Jan.	Sales Day Book	1,750
	Expenses	175	28 Feb.	Sales Day Book	2,100
28 Feb.	Purchases Day Book	1,050	31 Mar.	Sales Day Book	2,450
	Expenses	245			
	Fixed assets	525			
31 Mar.	Purchases Day Book	1,225			
	Expenses	315			
	*Sub-total**	4,410			
	Balance c/d	1,890			
		6,300			6,300
20 Apr.	Bank	1,890	1 Apr.	Balance b/d	1,890

* sub-totalled here for illustrative purposes (see below)

As can be seen from the account, the amount due to Customs and Excise on 1 April (£1,890) has been paid on 20 April. In this way the balance of the account is reduced to 'nil', and the account is ready to be used again in recording VAT transactions for the next VAT quarter.

The payment will be sent to Customs and Excise, along with the firm's Value Added Tax Return (see fig. 7.2). This has been completed as follows (the notes refer to the box numbers on the VAT return):

BOX 1 VAT due on sales and other outputs
This refers to the tax charged as output tax on sales invoices: here, it is £6,300.

BOX 2 deals with VAT due to HM Customs and Excise in respect of goods bought from VAT-registered businesses in the other member states of the European Union: there is nothing to complete on this occasion.

BOX 3 is the total of boxes 1 and 2.

BOX 4 VAT reclaimed on purchases and other inputs
This is the input tax on purchases, expenses and fixed assets: the total for the quarter is £4,410.

BOX 5 Net VAT to be paid to Customs or reclaimed
This is the difference between boxes 1 and 2, ie £6,300 – £4,410 = £1,890. As tax on outputs is greater than on inputs, this is the amount to be paid to Customs and Excise. If box 2 is greater than box 1, this indicates that a repayment is due from Customs and Excise.

BOX 6 Total value of sales and all other outputs
Here is shown the value of sales made during the period covered by the VAT return. In this example, the amount is £36,000. Note that this figure excludes any VAT.

BOX 7 Total value of purchases and all other inputs
This is the value of purchases, and other inputs such as expenses and fixed assets, for the period; here the amount is £18,000 + £4,200 + £3,000 = £25,200. Note that this figure excludes any VAT.

BOXES 8 and 9 are completed with the total of any sales to, and any purchases from, other European Union member states.

The box on the left-hand lower section of the form is ticked to indicate that payment is enclosed. Finally, the *declaration* has to be signed and dated by an authorised person of the business.

Value Added Tax Return

HM Customs and Excise

For the period
01 01 -1 **to** 31 03 -1

For Official Use

Registration Number: 841 1160 11

Period: 03 -1

You could be liable to a financial penalty if your completed return and all the VAT payable are not received by the due date.

Due date: 30 04 -1

WYVERN (OFFICE PRODUCTS) LTD
12 LOWER HYDE STREET
MEREFORD
MR1 2JF

For Official Use

Before you fill in this form please read the notes on the back and the VAT leaflet *"Filling in your VAT return"*. Fill in all boxes clearly in ink, and write 'none' where necessary. Don't put a dash or leave any box blank. If there are no pence write **"00"** in the pence column. **Do not** enter more than one amount in any box.

For official use

		£	p
VAT due in this period on **sales** and other outputs	1	6,300	00
VAT due in this period on **acquisitions** from other **EC Member States**	2	NONE	
Total VAT due **(the sum of boxes 1 and 2)**	3	6,300	00
VAT reclaimed in this period on **purchases** and other inputs (including acquisitions from the EC)	4	4,410	00
Net VAT to be paid to Customs or reclaimed by you (Difference between boxes 3 and 4)	5	1,890	00
Total value of **sales** and all other outputs excluding any VAT. **Include your box 8 figure**	6	36,000	00
Total value of **purchases** and all other inputs excluding any VAT. **Include your box 9 figure**	7	25,200	00
Total value of all **supplies** of goods and related services, excluding any VAT, to other **EC Member States**	8	NONE	00
Total value of all **acquisitions** of goods and related services, excluding any VAT, from other **EC Member States**	9	NONE	00

Retail schemes. If you have used any of the schemes in the period covered by this return, enter the relevant letter(s) in this box.

If you are enclosing a payment please tick this box. ✓

DECLARATION: You, or someone on your behalf, must sign below.

I, MATTHEW LLOYD declare that the
(Full name of signatory in BLOCK LETTERS)
information given above is true and complete.

Signature Matthew Lloyd Date 20 April 19-1

A false declaration can result in prosecution.

Y

CD 2859/N3(08/93)

F 3790 (February 1994)

VAT 100

Fig. 7.2 Value Added Tax Return – Crown copyright

7.6 VAT calculations

It is easy to calculate the VAT amount when the price of goods before the addition of VAT is known; eg using a rate of VAT of 17½ per cent, goods costing £100 plus VAT of £17.50 gives a total cost of £117.50.

When the total cost *including* VAT is known, the amount of VAT is found by multiplying the amount by 17.5 and dividing by 117.5. For example:

Total cost	=	£117.50
Amount of VAT is $^{17.5}/_{117.5}$ of £117.50	=	£ 17.50
VAT-exclusive cost	=	£100.00

The VAT-exclusive price can be found by dividing the amount by 1.175. For example:

$$\frac{£117.50}{1.175} = \text{VAT-exclusive cost of £100}$$

Note that the divisor of 1.175 applies only with a rate of VAT of 17½%. With a rate of 10%, for example, the divisor is 1.1.

When calculating VAT amounts, fractions of a penny are ignored, ie the tax is rounded down to a whole penny.

7.7 Chapter summary

- ❑ VAT-registered businesses charge VAT on all taxable supplies (sales).
- ❑ Most types of goods and services are taxable, but some are zero-rated, while others are exempt.
- ❑ A VAT account is used to record the amount of VAT charged on sales (output tax), and paid on purchases and expenses (input tax).
- ❑ A VAT-registered business must complete a Value Added Tax Return at certain intervals, commonly every three months, and either pay over to HM Customs and Excise the net amount of tax collected, or seek a refund where tax on inputs exceeds that on outputs.

In the next chapter we will return to books of prime entry by looking at cash book and petty cash book – these are the books of prime entry for cash and bank transactions.

7.8 Questions

7.1* The following is a summary of purchases and sales, excluding VAT, made by Wyvern Computers for the three months ended 30 June 19-4:

Purchases	April £5,400, May £4,800, June £6,800
Sales	April £8,200, May £9,400, June £10,800

All purchases and sales are subject to Value Added Tax at a rate of 17½ per cent.

You are to:

(a) calculate the VAT amounts for each month

(b) show the VAT account for the quarter as it will appear in the general ledger, and balance the account at 30 June 19-4

(c) explain the significance of the balance of the VAT account at 30 June 19-4 and how it will be dealt with

7.2 The following amounts *include* VAT at a rate of 17½%:

• £11.75	• £10.34	• £0.94
• £14.10	• £6.50	• £2.21

You are to calculate for each amount:

(a) the amount of VAT

(b) the VAT-exclusive amount

7.3 Sarah Matthews owns a specialist plant and floristry business. She employs an accounts clerk, Derek Miller, who maintains a full accounting system.

At the end of April 19-0, Derek Miller had not completed the VAT account for the month. However, the following VAT totals have been taken from the four day books:

	£
purchases	360
sales	690
returns out	25
returns in	42

Note: there was no balance brought forward on the VAT account on 1 April 19-0.

Required:

(a) In the books of Sarah Matthews, the VAT account for April 19-0. (The account should be balanced at the month end.)

(b) An explanation of the meaning of the balance on the VAT account on 30 April 19-0.

(c) Advice for Derek Miller on how he should treat this VAT account balance when preparing the business balance sheet on 30 April 19-0.

[Southern Examining Group, 1990]

7.4* Computer Supplies Ltd issued the following sales invoices (SI) and credit notes (CN) to customers during the week commencing 19 August 19-1. All sales are subject to Value Added Tax at 17½% and the amounts shown are the *gross* values.

Date	*Number*	*Customer*	*Gross Amount*
19-1			£
19 Aug.	SI 1547	E Newman	183.30
20 Aug.	SI 1548	Wyvern Traders Ltd	267.90
21 Aug.	SI 1549	Teme Supplies	411.25
22 Aug.	SI 1550	Lugg Brothers & Co	1,410.00
22 Aug.	CN 121	Wyvern Traders Ltd	267.90
23 Aug.	SI 1551	E Newman	470.00
23 Aug.	CN 122	E Newman	91.65

Required:

(a) Prepare Computer Supplies Ltd's sales day book and sales returns day book for the week commencing 19 August 19-1, totalling the columns on 23 August 19-1.

(b) The balance brought down on E Newman's account as at 1 August 19-1 was £440.00. Computer Supplies Ltd received a cheque on 7 August 19-1 for this amount less 5% cash discount. There were no other transactions with E Newman during the month of August other than those detailed above.

Show E Newman's personal account for August 19-1 as it would appear in Computer Supplies Ltd's ledger. Balance the account at the end of the month.

8 Control of Cash: Cash Book and Petty Cash Book

Cash and money in the bank is the lifeblood of any business. A firm can have an excellent product or service and be making good sales, but a shortage of cash may mean that wages and other day-to-day running expenses cannot be paid as they fall due: this could lead to the rapid failure of the business.

For most businesses, control of cash – including bank and cash transactions – takes place in the cash books, these comprise:

- cash book
- petty cash book

As already seen in Chapter Six, these are the books of original entry for cash transactions.

8.1 Cash Book

We have already used a separate cash account and bank account for double-entry book-keeping transactions. These two accounts are, in practice, brought together into one book under the title of *cash book.* This cash book is, therefore, used to record the money side of book-keeping transactions and is part of the double-entry system. The cash book is used for:

- cash transactions
  — all receipts in cash
  — most payments for cash, except for low-value expense payments (which are paid through *petty cash book:* see later in this chapter)
- bank transactions
  — all receipts by cheque (or payment of cash into the bank)
  — all payments by cheque (or withdrawal of cash from the bank)

The cash book is usually controlled by a cashier who:

- records receipts and payments by cheque and in cash
- makes cash payments, and prepares cheques for signature by those authorised to sign
- pays cash and cheques received into the bank
- has control over the firm's cash, either in a cash till or cash box
- issues cash to the petty cashier, as and when required

It is important to note that transactions passing through the cash book must be supported by documentary evidence in order to establish the audit trail (a link which can be checked and followed through the accounting system from prime document, through books of prime entry, to the double-entry accounts), and also for taxation purposes – both for Value Added Tax, and for the Inland Revenue. This applies to both receipts and payments: for example, the cashier will be responsible for issuing a formal receipt for cash (and sometimes cheques) received; payments in cash and by cheque can only be made against documents (eg an invoice received) showing the amount due. In this way, the cash book becomes part of the audit trail, and provides evidence of receipts and payments for tax purposes.

8.2 Layout of the cash book

Although a cash book can be set out in many forms to suit the requirements of a particular business, a common format is the *columnar cash book*. This is set out like other double-entry accounts, with debit and credit sides, but there may be several money columns on each side. An example of a *three column cash book* (with three money columns on each side) is shown below:

Dr. **Cash Book** Cr.

Date	Details	Folio	Discount allowed	Cash	Bank	Date	Details	Folio	Discount received	Cash	Bank
			£	£	£				£	£	£

The debit side is used for receipts, with one money column for cash and one for bank receipts. The credit side is used for payments with a money column for cash payments, and one for bank (cheque) payments. The third money column on each side is used to record cash *discount allowed* on the debit side, and cash *discount received* on the credit side. (To remind you, cash discount is an allowance offered for quick settlement of the amount due, eg 2% cash discount for settlement within seven days.) Note that the discount columns are *not* part of the double-entry book-keeping system — they are used in the cash book as a listing device or memorandum column and, as we will see below, are totalled at the end of the week or month, and the totals are then transferred into the double-entry system.

A *two column cash book* has money columns on each side for cash and bank only, but no other money columns.

8.3 Cash Book: example transactions and balancing

We will now look at some example transactions and then see how the three-column cash book is balanced at the month-end. The transactions are:

19-1
1 Apr. Balances at start of month: cash £300, bank £550
4 Apr. Received a cheque from S Wright for £98 - we have allowed her £2 cash discount
7 Apr. Paid a cheque to S Crane for £145 - he has allowed £5 cash discount
12 Apr. Paid wages in cash £275
14 Apr. Paid by cheque the account of T Lewis £120, deducting 2½% cash discount
17 Apr. J Jones settles in cash her account of £80, deducting 5% cash discount
20 Apr. Withdrew £100 in cash from the bank for use in the business
23 Apr. Received a cheque for £45 from D Whiteman in full settlement of her account of £48
28 Apr. Paid cash of £70 to S Ford in full settlement of our account of £75

All cheques are banked on the day of receipt.

The cash book records these transactions (as shown below) and, after they have been entered, is balanced on 30 April. (The other part of the double-entry book-keeping transaction is not shown here, but has to be done in order to record the transactions correctly.)

Dr. **Cash Book** Cr.

Date	Details	Folio	Discount allowed	Cash	Bank	Date	Details	Folio	Discount received	Cash	Bank
19-1			£	£	£	19-1			£	£	£
1 Apr.	Balances b/d			300	550	7 Apr.	J Crane		5		145
4 Apr.	S Wright		2		98	12 Apr.	Wages			275	
17 Apr.	J Jones		4	76		14 Apr.	T Lewis		3		117
20 Apr.	Bank	C		100		20 Apr.	Cash	C			100
23 Apr.	D Whiteman		3		45	28 Apr.	S Ford		5	70	
						30 Apr.	Balances c/d			131	331
			9	476	693				13	476	693
1 May	Balances b/d			131	331						

Note: The transaction on 20 April – £100 withdrawn from the bank for use in the business – involves a transfer of money between cash and bank. As each transaction is both a receipt and a payment within the cash book, it is usual to indicate both of them in the folio column with a 'c' – this stands for *contra* and shows that both parts of the transaction are in the *same* book.

A cash book is balanced as follows:

- add the two cash columns and subtotal in pencil (ie £476 in the debit column, and £345 in the credit column); remember to erase the subtotals afterwards
- deduct the lower total from the higher (payments from receipts) to give the balance of cash remaining (£476 – £345 = £131)
- the higher total is recorded at the bottom of both cash columns in a totals 'box' (£476)
- the balance of cash remaining (£131) is entered as a balancing item above the totals box (on the credit side), and is brought down underneath the total on the debit side as the opening balance for next month (£131)
- the two bank columns are dealt with in the same way (£693 – £362 = £331)

Notice that, in the cash book shown above, the cash and bank balances have been brought down on the debit side. It may happen that the balance at bank is brought down on the credit side: this occurs when payments exceed receipts, and indicates a bank overdraft.

It is very important to appreciate that the bank columns of the cash book represent the firm's own records of bank transactions and the balance at bank – the bank statement may well show different figures (see Chapter Nine).

At the end of the month each discount column is totalled separately – no attempt should be made to balance them. At this point, amounts recorded in the columns and the totals are not part of the double-entry system. However, the two totals are transferred to the double-entry system as follows:

- the total on the debit side (£9 in the example above) is debited to *discount allowed account* in the general (or nominal) ledger
- the total on the credit side (£13 in the example) is credited to *discount received account,* also in the general (or nominal) ledger

The opposite book-keeping entries will have already been entered in the debtors and creditors accounts respectively (see Chapter 4.8).

The accounts appear as follows:

Discount Allowed Account

Dr.			Cr.		
19-1		£	19-1		£
30 Apr.	Cash Book	9			

Discount Received Account

Dr.			Cr.		
19-1		£	19-1		£
			30 Apr.	Cash Book	13

The two discount accounts represent an expense and an income respectively and, at the end of the firm's financial year, the totals of the two accounts will be used in the calculation of profit.

Where control accounts (see Chapter Nineteen) are in use, the total of discount allowed will be credited to the sales ledger control account, while the total of discount received will be debited to the purchases ledger control account.

8.4 Checking the cash book

In business there is little point in keeping records of cash and bank transactions if we cannot, from time-to-time, prove that the records are accurate. How can we check the cash book?

Cash columns

To check the cash columns is easy. It is simply a matter of counting the cash in the cash till or box, and agreeing it with the balance shown by the cash book. In the example in Section 8.3, there should be £131 in the firm's cash till at 30 April 19-1. If the cash cannot be agreed in this way, the discrepancy needs to be investigated urgently.

Bank columns

How are these to be checked? We could, perhaps, enquire at the bank and ask for the balance at the month-end, or we could arrange for a bank statement to be sent to us at the end of each month. However, the balance of the account at the bank may well not agree with that shown by the bank columns of the cash book. There are several reasons why there may be a difference: for example, a cheque that has been written out recently to pay a bill may not yet have been recorded on the bank statement, ie it has been entered in the cash book, but is not yet on the bank statement. To agree the bank columns of the cash book and the bank statement, it is usually necessary to prepare a *bank reconciliation statement,* and this topic is dealt with fully in the next chapter.

8.5 Cash book incorporating VAT

A cash book can be adapted to suit the needs of a business – already we have seen how a three-column cash book uses a memorandum column for discounts allowed and received. Another common layout uses a fourth money column, for VAT, as shown in the example which follows. The VAT columns act as memorandum columns and, at the end of the week or month, are transferred to VAT account.

Worked example

Question

On Monday, 2 June 19-8, the cash book of Eveshore Growers showed balances of £86 in cash and £248 in the bank. Transactions for the week were:

19-8	
2 June	Paid insurance premium of £130 by cheque
3 June	Cash sales of £282, including Value Added Tax
3 June	Paid travel expenses in cash £17
3 June	Paid an invoice for £100 from A–Z Supplies by cheque after deducting 5% cash discount
4 June	Received a cheque for £117 from a debtor, P Lovall, who was settling his account balance of £120 after deducting 2½% cash discount
5 June	Cash sales of £423, including Value Added Tax
6 June	Cash purchase of £188, including Value Added Tax
6 June	Paid wages of £205, partly by cheque for £105 and partly in cash £100
6 June	Transferred £250 of cash into the bank

The rate of Value Added Tax is 17½%

Required:

- Write up the cash book of Eveshore Growers for the week commencing 2 June 19-8, using separate columns for discount, VAT, cash and bank.
- Balance the cash book at 6 June 19-8.
- Explain how the totals for the discount and VAT columns will be entered in the ledger of Eveshore Growers.

Answer

Dr.					Cash Book								Cr.
Date	Details	Folio	Disc allwd	VAT	Cash	Bank	Date	Details	Folio	Disc recd	VAT	Cash	Bank
19-8			£	£	£	£	19-8			£	£	£	£
2 Jun	Balances b/d				86	248	2 Jun	Insurance	GL				130
3 Jun	Sales	GL		42	282		3 Jun	Travel exp	GL			17	
4 Jun	P Lovall	SL	3			117	3 Jun	A–Z Supplies	PL	5			95
5 Jun	Sales	GL		63	423		6 Jun	Purchases	GL		28	188	
6 Jun	Cash	C				250	6 Jun	Wages	GL			100	105
							6 Jun	Bank	C			250	
							7 Jun	Balances c/d				236	285
			3	105	791	615				5	28	791	615
8 Jun	Balances b/d				236	285							

Notes:

- The folio columns have been completed as follows:
  —GL = general ledger (or NL for nominal ledger)
  —SL = sales ledger
  —PL = purchases ledger
  —C = contra (both parts of the transaction in the same book)
- With transactions involving sales ledger (ie P Lovall) and purchases ledger (ie A–Z Supplies), no amount for VAT is shown in the VAT columns. This is because VAT has been charged on invoices issued and received and was recorded in the VAT account when the sale or purchase was made.
- VAT on cash sales and purchases, and other transactions, is recorded in the two VAT analysis columns.

The discount and VAT columns:

- *discount allowed column* – the total of £3 will be debited to discount allowed account in the general (or nominal) ledger
- *discount received column* – the total of £5 will be credited to discount received account in the general (or nominal) ledger
- *VAT columns* — the total of £105 will be credited to VAT account in the general (or nominal) ledger, while the total of £28 will be debited to VAT account

8.6 Petty cash book

A petty cash book is used to record low-value cash payments for various small purchases by a business, eg small items of stationery, postages, etc. It would not be appropriate for such expenses to be entered in the main cash book, as a large number of payments would clutter it up. Instead, an amount of cash is handed by the main cashier to a member of staff, the *petty cashier,* who will be responsible for security of the money, and will make payments as appropriate.

In order to operate a petty cash system, the petty cashier needs the following:

- a *petty cash book* in which to record transactions
- a lockable *petty cash box* in which to keep the money
- a stock of blank *petty cash vouchers* (see page 91) for claims on petty cash to be made
- a *lockable desk drawer* in which to keep these items

8.7 What items can be passed through petty cash book?

Petty cash is used to make small cash payments for expenses incurred by the business. Examples of the type of payments made from petty cash include:

- stationery items
- casual wages
- window cleaning
- bus, rail and taxi fares (incurred on behalf of the business)
- meals (incurred on behalf of the business)
- postages
- tips and donations

For example, an employee might be asked to buy an item of stationery for the business: he or she will be reimbursed from petty cash. However, petty cash should not be used to pay for private expenses of employees, eg tea, coffee, and milk, unless the business has agreed these in advance. Usually the petty cashier will have a list of approved expenses which can be reimbursed.

A business will also decide on the maximum value of each transaction that can be paid out of petty cash; for example, £20 is a common maximum.

8.8 The imprest system

Most petty cash books operate on the *imprest system*. With this method the petty cashier starts each week (or month) with a certain amount of money – the imprest amount. As payments are made during the week (or month) the amount of money will reduce and, at the end of the period, the cash will be made up by the main cashier to the imprest amount. For example:

	Started week with imprest amount	£100.00
Less	Total of petty cash amounts paid out during week	£80.50
	Cash held at end of week	£19.50
Add	Amount drawn from cashier to restore imprest amount	£80.50
	Cash at start of next week, ie imprest amount	£100.00

If, at any time, the imprest amount proves to be insufficient, further amounts of cash can be drawn from the cashier. Also, from time-to-time, it may be necessary to increase the imprest amount so that regular shortfalls are avoided.

8.9 Petty cash voucher

The petty cashier, who is likely also to have other tasks within the firm, is responsible for control of the petty cash, making cash payments when appropriate, keeping records of payments made, and balancing the petty cash book at regular intervals.

Payments out of petty cash are made only against correct documentation – usually a petty cash voucher (see fig. 8.1). Petty cash vouchers are completed as follows:

- details and amount of expenditure
- signature of the person making the claim and receiving the money
- signature of the person authorising the payment to be made

- additionally, most petty cash vouchers are numbered, so that they can be controlled, the number being entered in the petty cash book
- any relevant documentation, eg receipt, should be attached to the petty cash voucher

Petty Cash Voucher

No 807

Date *11 May 19-1*

For what required	AMOUNT £	p
Envelopes	1	55
10 Floppy disks	6	10
	7	65

Signature *T. Harris*

Passed by *D. Adams*

Fig. 8.1 An example of a petty cash voucher

8.10 Layout of a petty cash book

Receipts	Date	Details	Voucher No.	Total Payment	Analysis columns				
					VAT	Postages	Stationery	Travel	Ledger
£				£	£	£	£	£	£

The layout shows that:

- receipts from the main cashier are entered in the column on the extreme left
- there are columns for the date and details of all receipts and payments
- there is a column for the petty cash voucher number
- the total payment (ie the amount paid out on each petty cash voucher) is in the next column
- then follow the analysis columns which analyse each transaction entered in the 'total payment' column (note that VAT may need to be calculated – see Section 8.11 below)

A business or organisation will use whatever analysis columns are most suitable for it and, indeed, there may be more than the columns shown.

8.11 Petty cash and VAT

As we have already seen in Chapter Seven, Value Added Tax is charged by VAT-registered businesses on their taxable supplies. Therefore, there will often be VAT included as part of the expense paid out of petty cash. However, not all expenses will have been subject to VAT. There are four possible circumstances:

- VAT has been charged at the standard rate
- VAT has not been charged because the supplier is not VAT-registered
- the zero rate of VAT applies, eg food and drink (but not meals which are standard-rated), books, newspapers, transport (but not taxis and hire cars)
- the supplies are exempt (eg financial services, postal services)

Often the indication of the supplier's VAT registration number on a receipt or invoice will tell you that VAT has been charged at the standard rate.

Where VAT has been charged, the amount of tax might be indicated separately on the receipt or invoice. However, for small money amounts it is quite usual for a total to be shown without indicating the amount of VAT. To calculate the VAT amount, with VAT at a rate of 17½%, the full amount of the receipt or invoice is multiplied by 17.5 and divided by 117.5. For example:

Amount of receipt		£4.70
Therefore VAT is 17.5/117.5 of £4.70	=	£0.70
Amount, net of VAT	=	£4.00

Here £0.70 will be entered in the VAT column in the petty cash book, £4.00 in the appropriate expense column, and the full £4.70 in the total payment column.

Remember that, when calculating VAT amounts, fractions of a penny are ignored, ie the tax is rounded down to a whole penny.

8.12 Petty cash book: example transactions

A business keeps a petty cash book, which is operated on the imprest system. There are a number of transactions (all of which, unless otherwise indicated, include VAT at 17½%) to be entered for the week in the petty cash book:

19-1
10 Apr. Started the week with an imprest amount of £50.00
10 Apr. Paid stationery £3.76 on voucher no. 47
10 Apr. Paid taxi fare £2.82 on voucher no. 48
11 Apr. Paid postages £0.75 (no VAT) on voucher no. 49
12 Apr. Paid taxi fare £4.70 on voucher no. 50
12 Apr. Paid J Jones, a creditor, £6.00 (no VAT shown in petty cash book – amount will be on VAT account already) on voucher no. 51
13 Apr. Paid stationery £3.76 on voucher no. 52
13 Apr. Paid postages £2.85 (no VAT) on voucher no. 53
14 Apr. Paid taxi fare £6.11 on voucher no. 54
14 Apr. Cash received to restore imprest amount, and petty cash book balanced at the end of the week

The petty cash book is written up as follows:

Receipts	Date	Details	Voucher No.	Total Payment	Analysis columns				
					VAT	Postages	Stationery	Travel	Ledger
£	19-1			£	£	£	£	£	£
50.00	10 Apr.	Balance b/d							
	10 Apr.	Stationery	47	3.76	0.56		3.20		
	10 Apr.	Taxi fare	48	2.82	0.42			2.40	
	11 Apr.	Postages	49	0.75		0.75			
	12 Apr.	Taxi fare	50	4.70	0.70			4.00	
	12 Apr.	J Jones	51	6.00					6.00
	13 Apr.	Stationery	52	3.76	0.56		3.20		
	13 Apr.	Postages	53	2.85		2.85			
	14 Apr.	Taxi fare	54	6.11	0.91			5.20	
				30.75	3.15	3.60	6.40	11.60	6.00
30.75	14 Apr.	Cash received							
	14 Apr.	Balance c/d		50.00					
80.75				80.75					
50.00	14 Apr.	Balance b/d							

Note the following points:

- The totals of the analysis columns add up to the total payment
- the amount of cash received from the main cashier to restore the imprest amount is the same as the total paid out during the week
- The petty cashier will give the firm's book-keeper details of the total of each analysis column – see Section 8.13 below – so that the amounts can be recorded in the double-entry book-keeping system

8.13 Petty cash and double-entry book-keeping

In the petty cash book looked at in Section 8.12 above, each analysis column has been totalled. In order to record the amounts in the double-entry system, the total of each column is debited to the relevant account in the general ledger. For example:

Dr.		Postages Account			Cr.
19-1		£	19-1		£
14 Apr.	Petty cash book	3.60			

Thus, from the petty cash book, debits are passed to:

- VAT account, £3.15
- postages account, £3.60
- stationery account, £6.40
- travel expenses account, £11.60

The amount in the ledger analysis column is debited to the appropriate creditor's account – in this case, the account of J Jones in the purchases ledger must be debited with £6.00

Total debits in the example are £30.75 and this is the amount drawn from the main cashier on 14 April. This amount is credited in the cash book, so completing double-entry book-keeping. If a trial balance is extracted on 14 April (after the analysis columns have been debited to the respective accounts, and a credit entered in cash book to restore the imprest amount) the balance of petty cash, £50.00, must be included as a debit balance.

8.14 Chapter summary

- ❑ The cash book records receipts (debits) and payments (credits) both in cash (except for low-value expense payments) and by cheque.
- ❑ A basic layout for a cash book has money columns for cash transactions and bank transactions on both the debit and credit sides, together with a further column on each side for discounts.
- ❑ In the discount columns are recorded cash discounts: discounts allowed (to customers) on the debit side, and discounts received (from suppliers) on the payments side.
- ❑ Another common cash book layout incorporates columns for VAT.
- ❑ The petty cash book records payments for a variety of low-value business expenses.
- ❑ The person responsible for maintaining the petty cash book is the petty cashier.
- ❑ Most petty cash books operate on the imprest system.
- ❑ Payment can only be made from the petty cash book against correct documentation – usually a petty cash voucher, which must be signed by the person authorising payment.
- ❑ Where a business is registered for Value Added Tax, it must record VAT amounts paid on petty cash purchases in a separate column in the petty cash book.
- ❑ At regular intervals – weekly or monthly – the petty cash book will be balanced – the main cashier will restore the imprest amount of cash and the total of each analysis column will be debited to the relevant account.

The bank columns of the cash book and the balance calculated are unlikely to agree exactly with the bank statement: in order to agree them it is necessary to prepare a *bank reconciliation statement* which we will look at in the next chapter.

8.15 Questions

8.1 (a) List *three* ways in which a trader can pay debts other than by cash or cheque.

(b) On 1 July year 7, the debit balances in the cash book of E Rich were:

Cash £419
Bank £3,685

His transactions for the month of July were:

2 July	Received cheque from A Wood £296
6 July	Paid wages in cash £102
9 July	Paid C Hill £211 by cheque in full settlement of his account of £224
12 July	Received £146 cash for sale of damaged stock
12 July	Paid T Jarvis £1,023 by cheque in full settlement of his account of £1,051
13 July	Paid wages in cash £104
17 July	Received cheque for £500 from Atlas & Company
19 July	Paid £21 in cash for postage stamps
20 July	Paid wages in cash £102
23 July	Withdrew £200 from bank for office cash
25 July	Paid W Moore £429 by cheque
26 July	Paid wages in cash £105
28 July	Received £317 cash from T Phillips in full settlement of his account of £325, paid into bank the same day
31 July	Paid £260 cash into bank

Required:
Prepare the three-column cash book for the month of July year 7 and balance it at 31 July, bringing the balances down at 1 August.

[London Chamber of Commerce]

8.2* Walter Harrison is a sole trader who records his cash and bank transactions in a *three-column* cash book. The following are the transactions for June:

19-2	
1 June	Balances: cash £280; bank overdraft £2,240
3 June	Received a cheque from G Wheaton for £195, in full settlement of a debt of £200
5 June	Received cash of £53 from T Francis, in full settlement of a debt of £55
8 June	Paid the amount owing to F Lloyd by cheque: the total amount due is £400 and you take advantage of a 2½ per cent cash discount for prompt settlement
10 June	Paid wages in cash £165
12 June	Paid A Morris in cash, £100 less 3 per cent cash discount
16 June	Withdrew £200 in cash from the bank for use in the business
18 June	Received a cheque for £640 from H Watson in full settlement of a debt of £670
20 June	Paid R Marks £78 by cheque
24 June	Paid D Farr £65 by cheque, in full settlement of a debt of £67
26 June	Paid telephone account £105 in cash
28 June	Received a cheque from M Perry in settlement of his account of £240 – he has deducted 2½ per cent cash discount
30 June	Received cash £45 from K Willis

You are to:

(a) enter the above transactions in Harrison's three-column cash book, balance the cash and bank columns, and carry the balances down to 1 July

(b) total the two discount columns and transfer them to the appropriate accounts

8.3* Choose from the statements **A-L** given below the **one** which you think best explains the meaning of each entry shown in the cash book. Enter the letter **A-L** of your choice in the space provided in the brackets at the side of each entry.

CASH BOOK (credit side only)

		Discount £	*Cash* £	*Bank* £
2 Jan.	Balance b/d			380 (........)
4 Jan.	M Hughes	30 (........)		570 (........)
9 Jan.	Bank		240 (........)	
16 Jan.	Motor van			5,850 (........)
20 Jan.	Purchases		735 (........)	
31 Jan.	Balances c/d		25 (........)	260 (........)
		30	1,000	7,060

A Cash paid for the purchase of goods
B The amount of the bank overdraft
C Discount allowed by a creditor for prompt payment
D Cheque received for the sale of a motor van
E Cash withdrawn from bank
F The balance in the firm's bank account
G Value of a cheque received from a debtor
H Cash paid into bank
I Purchase of a motor van, paid for by cheque
J Discount allowed to a debtor for prompt payment
K Value of a cheque sent to a creditor
L Cash in hand at the end of the month

[Northern Examining Association]

8.4 A business commenced trading for the week commencing 28 May 19-0 with £79 in cash and a bank overdraft of £515.

The following receipts and payments occurred during the week ending 3 June 19-0.

28 May Paid travelling expenses of £37 in cash
29 May Paid a telephone bill of £115 (including £15 Value Added Tax) by cheque
29 May Grant Degan, a credit customer, settled an invoice for £90 paying £81 in cash and receiving £9 discount for prompt settlement
30 May Made cash sales totalling £460 including £60 Value Added Tax. The amount was received by cheque and was immediately banked
31 May Paid an invoice for £100 from Gaga Ltd by cheque for £92. £8 discount was received for prompt settlement.
1 June Made cash purchases totalling £115 including Value Added Tax of £15 paying by cheque
1 June Made cash sales of £230 inclusive of Value Added Tax of £30
2 June Paid staff wages of £300. This was partly paid by cheques totalling £230, the balance being paid in cash
2 June Paid £200 from the till into the business bank account

Required:

(a) Draw up a cash book with separate columns for dates, narrations, folios, discount, VAT, bank and cash. Enter the opening balances and record the transactions for the week commencing 28 May 19-0. Balance the cash book as at 3 June 19-0.

(b) Describe how the totals for the discount and VAT columns will be entered into the ledger.

[Association of Accounting Technicians]

Author's note: this question was set in June 1990 when the rate of Value Added Tax was 15%.

8.5* On 1 October 19-0 the Cash Book of Hawksworth Ltd showed a cash balance of £142 and an overdraft at the bank of £177. The business has been registered for VAT (Value Added Tax) and during the first week of October the following transactions took place:

1 Oct. Settlement made by cheque between Hawksworth Ltd and HM Customs and Excise relating to the last VAT return. This showed £2,890 as being the total VAT paid on purchases and £3,425 as the total VAT collected on sales.
1 Oct. Withdrew £250 cash from the bank for use within the business.
2 Oct. Paid telephone bill for £207, inclusive of VAT, by cheque.
3 Oct. During September credit sales had been made to P Donavon for £200 plus VAT and to G Stevens for £600 plus VAT.
The two customers have now paid by cheque.
3 Oct. Sold goods for £736 inclusive of VAT, the customer paying by cheque.
4 Oct. Received a cheque for £90 from S Turnbull.
4 Oct. Paid a cheque for £297 to M Palmer in repayment of a debt.
4 Oct. A cheque drawn by N Collins for £110 and originally paid into the bank in September has now been dishonoured and returned by the bank "Refer to Drawer".
5 Oct. Sold goods to M Peters for £380 plus VAT. M Peters paid in cash.
5 Oct. £450 cash was paid into the bank.

The rate of Value Added Tax is 15%.

Required:

(a) Write up Hawksworth Ltd's cash book for the week and then balance off at the end of the week. The cash book should have separate columns for VAT, cash and bank. Folio numbers are not required.
(b) Show how the totals of the VAT columns would appear in the VAT account.
(c) Show how the payment made on 2 October would appear in the telephones account.

[Association of Accounting Technicians]

Author's note: this question was set in December 1990 when the rate of Value Added Tax was 15%.

8.6 You operate a petty cash book with an imprest of £150. The following expenses, supported by vouchers, were paid out of the petty cash:

Voucher Nos			
1	3 February	Postage	£10.00
2	5 February	Travelling expenses	£6.50
3	9 February	Cleaner's wages	£25.00
4	12 February	Stationery	£7.20
5	15 February	Postage	£10.00
6	18 February	Travelling expenses	£7.30
7	20 February	Cleaner's wages	£25.00
8	24 February	Stationery	£4.75
9	26 February	T B Collins, a creditor	£3.90
10	27 February	Miscellaneous	£4.15
11	27 February	Postage	£10.00
12	28 February	Cleaner's wages	£25.00

At 1 February you had a balance of £18.26 and received cash on that date to make up the figure to the imprest amount.

Required:

Draw up the petty cash book for the month of February, including the balancing and the amount paid on 1 March year 7 to make up the imprest figure. The analysis column headings are postage, travelling expenses, stationery, wages, miscellaneous and ledger.

[London Chamber of Commerce]

8.7 F Salmon keeps her petty cash book on the imprest system. The imprest figure was set at £350. On 1 November year 8 the balance of petty cash brought forward was £155. The following transactions took place during November year 8:

Year 8
1 Nov. Drew cash from the bank to restore the imprest
4 Nov. Postage stamps £20
6 Nov. Train fare reimbursed £25
9 Nov. Petrol £15
10 Nov. Stationery £38
12 Nov. Bus fares £2
15 Nov. Paid £16 to P Gates – this was to refund an overpayment on his account in the sales ledger
16 Nov. Stamps £30
18 Nov. Motor van repairs £35
20 Nov. Stationery £47
23 Nov. Petrol £28
25 Nov. Miscellaneous expenses £17
28 Nov. Parcel post charges £19
30 Nov. Travelling expenses £38

Required:

Draw up F Salmon's petty cash book, using the following analysis columns: postage; travelling expenses; motor van expenses; stationery; miscellaneous expenses; ledger accounts. Balance the account at 30 November, bring down the balance of cash in hand at that date, and show the amount of cash drawn from the bank to restore the imprest on 1 December year 8.

[London Chamber of Commerce]

8.8* The Oakhill Printing Co Ltd operates its petty cash account on the imprest system. It is maintained at a figure of £80 on the first day of each month.

At 30 April 19-7 the petty cash box held £19.37 in cash.

During May 19-7, the following petty cash transactions arose:

Date		*Amount*
19-7		£
1 May	Cash received to restore imprest	to be derived
1 May	Bus fares	0.41
2 May	Stationery	2.35
4 May	Bus fares	0.30
7 May	Postage stamps	1.70
7 May	Trade journal	0.95
8 May	Bus fares	0.64
11 May	Correcting fluid	1.29
12 May	Typewriter ribbons	5.42
14 May	Parcel postage	3.45
15 May	Paper clips	0.42
15 May	Newspapers	2.00
16 May	Photocopier repair	16.80
19 May	Postage stamps	1.50
20 May	Drawings pins	0.38
21 May	Train fare	5.40
22 May	Photocopier paper	5.63
23 May	Display decorations	3.07
23 May	Correcting fluid	1.14
25 May	Wrapping paper	0.78

27 May	String	0.61
27 May	Sellotape	0.75
27 May	Biro pens	0.46
28 May	Typewriter repair	13.66
30 May	Bus fares	2.09
1 June	Cash received to restore imprest	to be derived

Required:

Open and post the company's petty cash account for the period 1 May to 1 June 19-7 inclusive and balance the account at 30 May 19-7.

In order to facilitate the subsequent double-entry postings, all items of expense appearing in the 'payments' column should then be analysed individually into suitably labelled expense columns.

[The Chartered Association of Certified Accountants]

8.9* Draw up a petty cash book with appropriate analysis columns and a VAT column, and enter the following transactions for the month. The voucher amounts include VAT at 17½% unless indicated:

19-1

1 May	Balance of cash £150.00
1 May	Postages £7.00, voucher no 455, travel £2.85, voucher no 456 (no VAT on postages and travel)
2 May	Meal allowance £6.11, voucher no 457 (no VAT)
3 May	Taxi £4.70, voucher no 458
4 May	Stationery £3.76, voucher no 459
7 May	Postages £5.25, voucher no 460 (no VAT)
8 May	Travel £6.50, voucher no 461 (no VAT)
9 May	Meal allowance £6.11, voucher no 462 (no VAT)
10 May	Stationery £8.46, voucher no 463
14 May	Taxi £5.17, voucher no 464
17 May	Stationery £4.70, voucher no 465
21 May	Travel £3.50, voucher no 466, postages £4.50, voucher no 467 (no VAT on travel and postages)
23 May	Bus fares £3.80, voucher no 468 (no VAT)
26 May	Catering expenses £10.81, voucher no 469
27 May	Postages £3.50, voucher no 470 (no VAT), stationery £7.52, voucher no 471
28 May	Travel expenses £6.45, voucher no 472 (no VAT)
31 May	Cash received from cashier to restore imprest amount to £150.00

9 Bank Reconciliation Statements

In the last chapter we saw that the bank columns of the cash book record the organisation's own internal record of the bank transactions, and the balance at the end of the week or month. However, the bank statement received from the bank may show a rather different balance. There are two main reasons for this:

- *timing differences* caused by unpresented cheques, ie the time delay between, for example, writing out (drawing) a cheque and recording it in the cash book, and the cheque being entered on the bank statement
- *the cash book has not been updated* with items which appear on the bank statement and should also appear in the cash book, eg bank charges

Assuming that there are no errors, both cash book and bank statement are correct, but need to be reconciled with each other, ie the closing balances need to be agreed.

While the majority of this chapter is concerned with bank reconciliation statements, in Section 9.7 we look at the reconciliation of statements of account received from suppliers with the balance on the creditor's (supplier's) account in the purchases ledger of the business.

9.1 Timing differences

The two main timing differences between the bank columns of the cash book and the bank statement are:

- cheques drawn, not yet recorded on the bank statement
- amounts paid into the bank, not yet recorded on the bank statement

The first of these – unpresented cheques – is caused because, when a cheque is written out, it is immediately entered on the payments side of the cash book, even though it may be some days before the cheque passes through the bank clearing system and is recorded on the bank statement. Therefore, for a few days at least, the cash book shows a lower balance than the bank statement in respect of this cheque. When the cheque is recorded on the bank statement, the difference will disappear. We have looked at only one cheque here, but a business will often be issuing many cheques each day, and the difference between the cash book balance and the bank statement balance may be considerable.

With the second timing difference – amounts paid in, not yet recorded on the bank statement – the firm's cashier will record a receipt in the cash book as he or she prepares the bank paying-in slip. However, the receipt may not be recorded by the bank on the bank statement for a day or so, particularly if it is paid in late in the day (when the bank will put it into the next day's work), or if it is paid in at a bank branch other than the one at which the account is maintained. Until the receipt is recorded by the bank the cash book will show a higher bank account balance than the bank statement. Once the receipt is entered on the bank statement, the difference will disappear.

These two timing differences are involved in the calculation known as the *bank reconciliation statement*. The business cash book *must not be altered* for these because, as we have seen, they will correct themselves on the bank statement as time goes by.

9.2 Updating the cash book

Besides the timing differences described above, there may be other differences between the bank columns of the cash book and the bank statement, and these *do* need to be entered in the cash book to bring it up-to-date. For example, the bank might make an automatic standing order payment on behalf of a business – such an item is correctly debited by the bank, and it might be that the bank statement acts as a reminder to the business cashier of the payment: it should then be entered in the cash book.

Examples of items that show in the bank statement and need to be entered in the cash book include:

Receipts

- standing order and BACS (Bankers' Automated Clearing Services) receipts credited by the bank, eg payments from debtors (customers)
- bank giro credit (credit transfer) amounts received by the bank, eg payments from debtors (customers)
- dividend amounts received by the bank
- interest credited by the bank

Payments

- standing order and direct debit payments
- bank charges and interest
- unpaid cheques debited by the bank (ie cheques from creditors paid in by the business which have 'bounced' and are returned by the bank marked 'refer to drawer')

For each of these items, the cashier needs to check to see if they have been entered in the cash book; if not, they need to be recorded (provided that the bank has not made an error). If the bank has made an error, it must be notified as soon as possible and the incorrect transactions reversed by the bank in its own accounting records.

9.3 The bank reconciliation statement

This forms the link between the balances shown in the cash book and the bank statement:

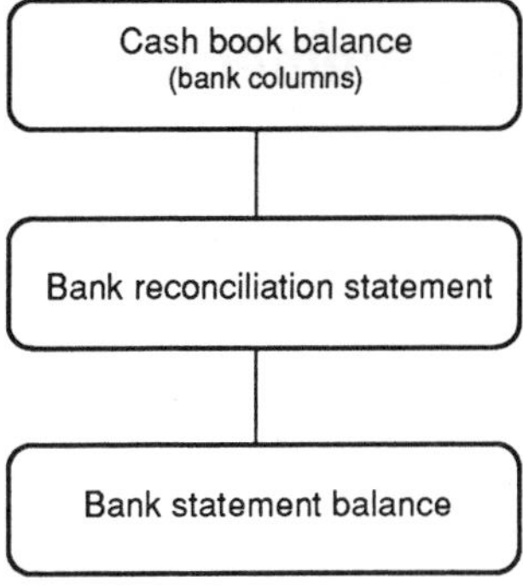

Upon receipt of a bank statement, reconciliation of the two balances is carried out in the following way:

- tick off the items that appear in *both* cash book and bank statement
- the unticked items on the bank statement are entered into the bank columns of the cash book to bring it up-to-date (provided none are errors made by the bank)
- the bank columns of the cash book are now balanced to find the revised figure
- the remaining unticked items from the cash book will be the timing differences
- the timing differences are used to prepare the bank reconciliation statement, which takes the following format (with example figures):

XYZ TRADING LTD
Bank Reconciliation Statement as at 31 October 19-1

		£	£
Balance at bank as per cash book			525
Add: cheques drawn, not yet recorded on the bank statement			
J Lewis	cheque no. 0012378	60	
ABC Ltd	cheque no. 0012392	100	
Eastern Oil Co	cheque no. 0012407	80	
			240
			765
Less: amounts paid in, not yet recorded on the bank statement		220	
		300	
			520
Balance at bank as per bank statement			245

Notes:

- The layout shown above starts from the cash book balance, and works towards the bank statement balance. A common variation of this layout is to start with the bank statement balance and to work towards the cash book balance (see page 105).
- If a bank overdraft is involved, brackets should be used around the numbers to indicate this for the cash book or bank statement balance. The timing differences are still added or deducted, as appropriate.
- Once the bank reconciliation statement agrees, it should be filed because it proves that the cash book (bank columns) and bank statement were reconciled at a particular date. If, next time it is prepared, it fails to agree, the previous statement is proof that reconciliation was reached at that time.

9.4 Bank reconciliation statement: example

The cashier of Severn Trading Co has written up the firm's cash book for the month of February 19-2, as follows (the cheque number is shown against payments):

Cash Book

Dr. Cr.

Date	Details	Cash	Bank	Date	Details	Cash	Bank
19-2		£	£	19-2		£	£
1 Feb.	Balances b/d	250.75	1,340.50	3 Feb.	Appleton Ltd 123456		675.25
7 Feb.	A. Abbott		208.50	5 Feb.	Wages	58.60	
9 Feb.	Sales	145.25		12 Feb.	Rent 123457		125.00
13 Feb.	Sales	278.30		14 Feb.	Transfer to bank c	500.00	
14 Feb.	Transfer from cash c		500.00	17 Feb.	D. Smith & Co 123458		421.80
20 Feb.	Sales	204.35		23 Feb.	Stationery	75.50	
21 Feb.	D. Richards Ltd.		162.30	24 Feb.	G. Christie 123459		797.55
26 Feb.	Sales	353.95		27 Feb.	Transfer to bank c	500.00	
27 Feb.	Transfer from cash c		500.00	28 Feb.	Balances c/d	98.50	954.00
28 Feb.	P. Paul Ltd.		262.30				
		1,232.60	2,973.60			1,232.60	2,973.60
1 Mar.	Balances b/d	98.50	954.00				

The cash balance of £98.50 shown by the cash columns on 1 March has been agreed with the cash held in the firm's cash box. The bank statement for February 19-2 has just been received:

National Bank plc

Branch Bartown

TITLE OF ACCOUNT Severn Trading Co.

ACCOUNT NUMBER 67812318

STATEMENT NUMBER 45

DATE	PARTICULARS	PAYMENTS	RECEIPTS	BALANCE
19-2		£	£	£
1 Feb.	Balance brought forward			1,340.50 CR
9 Feb.	Credit		208.50	1,549.00 CR
10 Feb.	Cheque no. 123456	675.25		873.75 CR
16 Feb.	Credit		500.00	1,373.75 CR
17 Feb.	Cheque no. 123457	125.00		1,248.75 CR
23 Reb.	Credit		162.30	1,411.05 CR
24 Feb.	Bank Giro Credit: J Jarvis Ltd.		100.00	1,511.05 CR
26 Feb.	Cheque no. 123458	421.80		1,089.25 CR
26 Feb.	Direct Debit: A-Z Finance Co.	150.00		939.25 CR
28 Feb.	Credit		500.00	1,439.25 CR
28 Feb.	Bank Charges	10.00		1,429.25 CR

Note that the bank statement is prepared from the bank's viewpoint: thus a credit balance shows that the customer is a creditor of the bank, ie the bank owes the balance to the customer. In the customer's own cash book, the bank is shown as a debit balance, ie an asset.

As the month-end balance at bank shown by the cash book, £954.00, is not the same as that shown by the bank statement, £1,429.25, it is necessary to prepare a bank reconciliation statement. The steps are:

1. Tick off the items that appear in *both* cash book and bank statement.
2. The unticked items on the bank statement are entered into the bank columns of the cash book to bring it up-to-date. These are:
   - *receipt* 24 Feb. Bank Giro Credit; J Jarvis Ltd £100.00
   - *payments* 26 Feb. Direct Debit, A-Z Finance Co £150.00
     28 Feb. Bank Charges, £10.00

   In double-entry book-keeping, the other part of the transaction will need to be recorded in the accounts, eg in J Jarvis Ltd's account in the sales ledger, etc.
3. The cash book is now balanced to find the revised balance:

Dr. **Cash Book** (bank columns) Cr.

19-2		£	19-2		£
	Balance b/d	954.00	26 Feb.	A-Z Finance Co.	150.00
24 Feb.	J. Jarvis Ltd.	100.00	28 Feb.	Bank Charges	10.00
			28 Feb.	Balance c/d	894.00
		1,054.00			1,054.00
1 Mar.	Balance b/d	894.00			

4. The remaining unticked items from the cash book are used in the bank reconciliation statement:
   - *receipt* 28 Feb. P Paul Ltd £262.30
   - *payment* 24 Feb. G Christie (cheque no. 123459) £797.55

   These items are timing differences, which should appear on next month's bank statement.
5. The bank reconciliation statement is now prepared, starting with the re-calculated balance of £894.00.

SEVERN TRADING CO.
Bank Reconciliation Statement as at 28 February 19-2

	£
Balance at bank as per cash book	894.00
Add: cheque drawn, not yet recorded on the bank statement	797.55
	1,691.55
Less: amount paid in, not yet recorded on the bank statement	262.30
Balance at bank as per bank statement	1,429.25

With the above, a statement has been produced which starts with the amended balance from the cash book, and finishes with the bank statement balance, ie the two figures are reconciled.

Notes:

- *Cheque drawn, not yet recorded on the bank statement* is added back to the cash book balance because, until it is recorded by the bank, the cash book shows a lower balance than the bank statement.
- *Amounts paid in, not yet recorded on the bank statement* are deducted from the cash book balance because, until they are recorded by the bank, the cash book shows a higher balance than the bank statement.

The layout used above starts with the cash book balance and finishes with the bank statement balance. However, there is no reason why it should not commence with the bank statement balance and finish with the cash book balance: with this layout it is necessary to *deduct* cheques drawn, not yet recorded on the bank statement, and to *add* amounts paid in, not yet recorded. The bank reconciliation statement of Severn Trading Co. would then appear as:

	£
Balance at bank as per bank statement	1,429.25
Less: cheque drawn, not yet recorded on the bank statement	797.55
	631.70
Add: amount paid in, not yet recorded on the bank statement	262.30
Balance at bank as per cash book	894.00

9.5 Importance of bank reconciliation statements

1. A bank reconciliation statement is important because, in its preparation, the transactions in the bank columns of the cash book are compared with those recorded on the bank statement. In this way, any errors in the cash book or bank statement will be found and can be corrected (or advised to the bank, if the bank statement is wrong).

2. The bank statement is an independent accounting record, therefore it will assist in deterring fraud by providing a means of verifying the cash book balance.

3. By writing the cash book up-to-date, the organisation has an amended figure for the bank balance to be shown in the trial balance and balance sheet.

4. Unpresented cheques over six months old – 'stale' cheques – can be identified and written back in the cash book (any cheque dated more than six months' ago will not be paid by the bank).

9.6 Worked example

We will now look at a more difficult example of a bank reconciliation statement, taken from a past examination paper. Try attempting the question before looking at the answer.

Question

Jane Banks, who is in business as a car dealer, prepares a bank reconciliation statement weekly. The bank reconciliation statement as at 5 November 19-8, in addition to bank charges of £25.60 not then recorded in the cash book, included only the following unpresented cheques:

Cheque number	£
162358	95.10
162361	147.64
162362	16.00
162364	38.90

The cash book, bank columns only, of Jane Banks for the week ended 12 November 19-8 is as follows:

19-8		£	19-8		Cheque no	£
7 Nov.	Balance b/d	2,823.28	7 Nov.	K Supplies	162365	16.41
8 Nov.	Sun Blinds Ltd	110.00	7 Nov.	J Bay	162366	273.69
8 Nov.	John Bell	210.80	8 Nov.	L Simms	162367	116.20
9 Nov.	Thomas Jones Ltd	169.00	8 Nov.	M Dint	162368	1,399.38
9 Nov.	Jean Hill	1,921.00	8 Nov.	D Feint	162369	200.00
10 Nov.	Andrew Wall - Cheque	710.00	9 Nov.	W Young	162370	70.00
	- Discount	6.00	9 Nov.	S M Hotels	162371	47.00
11 Nov.	Direct Dealers Ltd	29.00	10 Nov.	Bank charges		25.60
12 Nov.	Balance c/d	312.20	10 Nov.	H Meng	162372	139.10
			10 Nov.	F Grundy	162373	17.20
			11 Nov.	P Waters	162374	101.00
			11 Nov.	V Neall	162375	385.70
			12 Nov.	H Dent	162376	3,500.00
		6,291.28				6,291.28
			14 Nov.	Balance b/d		312.20

The following bank statement has been received by Jane Banks:

Central Bank Plc, Northtown Branch — Statement of account

Jane Banks — Account number 547892

19-8			*Payments* £	*Receipts* £	*Balance* £
8 Nov.	Opening balance				3,095.32
8 Nov.		162366	273.69		2,821.63
8 Nov.		162362	16.00		2,805.63
8 Nov.	Bank Giro Credit			110.00	2,915.63
9 Nov.		162368	1,399.38		1,516.25
9 Nov.		162361	147.64		1,368.61
9 Nov.		162365	16.41		1,352.20
10 Nov.	Bank Giro Credit			379.80	1,732.00
10 Nov.		162369	200.00		1,532.00
10 Nov.		162367	116.20		1,415.80
11 Nov.		162373	17.20		1,398.60
11 Nov.	Car Dealers' Association - Standing Order		25.00		1,373.60
11 Nov.		162372	139.10		1,234.50
11 Nov.	Bank Giro Credit			2,631.00	3,865.50

The cheque prepared in favour of S M Hotels on 9 November was not despatched and has now been cancelled; a proposed visit of Jane Banks to the Central Hotel owned by S M Hotels is not now to take place.

Required:

- Prepare a bank reconciliation statement as at 12 November 19-8.
- Explain why it is necessary to prepare bank reconciliation statements.

[Association of Accounting Technicians]

Answer

1. In preparing the bank reconciliation statement, the first point to note is that the opening balances of cash book and bank statement are not the same: this is usually the 'real life' situation for most organisations. The two can be reconciled as follows:

	£	£
Balance at bank as per cash book (7 November)		2,823.28
Add: cheques drawn, not yet recorded on the bank statement		
cheque no 162358	95.10	
cheque no 162361	147.64	
cheque no 162362	16.00	
cheque no 162364	38.90	
		297.64
		3,120.92
Less: bank charges, not yet recorded in the cash book		25.60
Balance at bank as per bank statement		3,095.32

2. The items that appear in *both* cash book and bank statement can now be ticked off (including the items listed above). Note that cheques listed individually in the cash book are combined on the bank paying-in slip:

- cheque received from John Bull £210.80
  cheque received from Thomas Jones Ltd £169.00
  bank giro credit on 10 November £379.80

- cheque received from Jean Hill £1,921.00
  cheque received from Andrew Wall* £ 710.00
  bank giro credit on 11 November £2,631.00

* Note that the discount allowed to Andrew Wall (£6) has been debited in error in the cash book: it should have been entered in the memorandum column for discount allowed. The cash book will need crediting in order to correct this error.

3. The following items need to be entered into the cash book to bring it up-to-date:
   - standing order for £25 to the Car Dealers' Association
   - cancelled cheque for £47 in favour of S M Hotels
   - correction of discount allowed of £6 (see 2, above)

   The cash book is then balanced to find the revised balance:

Dr. **Cash Book** (bank columns) Cr.

19-8		£	19-8		£
	Cancelled cheque (162371)	47.00	14 Nov.	Balance b/d	312.20
14 Nov.	Balance c/d	296.20		Car Dealers' Association	25.00
				Discount allowed (debited in error)	6.00
		343.20			343.20
			14 Nov.	Balance b/d	296.20

Note that the question, as set, does not ask for the cash book to be written up-to-date. Instead, these amounts can form the first three items of the bank reconciliation statement:

	£	£
Balance at bank as per cash book		(312.20)
Add: cancelled cheque no 162371		47.00
		(265.20)
Less: Car Dealers' Association standing order	25.00	
discount allowed (debited in error)	6.00	
		(31.00)
Adjusted cash book balance		(296.20)

These amounts will need to be entered into the cash book.

4. The unticked items from the cash book are now used in the bank reconciliation statement, as follows:

JANE BANKS, CAR DEALER
Bank Reconciliation Statement as at 12 November 19-8

	£	£
Balance at bank as per cash book (see 3, above)		(296.20)
Add: cheques drawn, not yet recorded on the bank statement		
cheque no 162358	95.10	
cheque no 162364	38.90	
cheque no 162370	70.00	
cheque no 162374	101.00	
cheque no 162375	385.70	
cheque no 162376	3,500.00	
		4,190.70
		3,894.50
Less: amount paid in, not yet recorded on the bank statement		29.00
Balance at bank as per bank statement		3,865.50

Reasons why it is necessary to prepare bank reconciliation statements:

- to verify the cash book balance
- to identify unpresented cheques, and amounts paid into the bank, not yet recorded on the bank statement
- to identify errors – either in the cash book or on the bank statement
- to identify 'stale' unpresented cheques, ie those over six months old

9.7 Other types of reconciliation statements

Besides bank reconciliation statements, it is often necessary to reconcile the balance shown on a statement of account (see Chapter 4.6) received from a supplier with the supplier's (creditor's) account in the buyer's books:

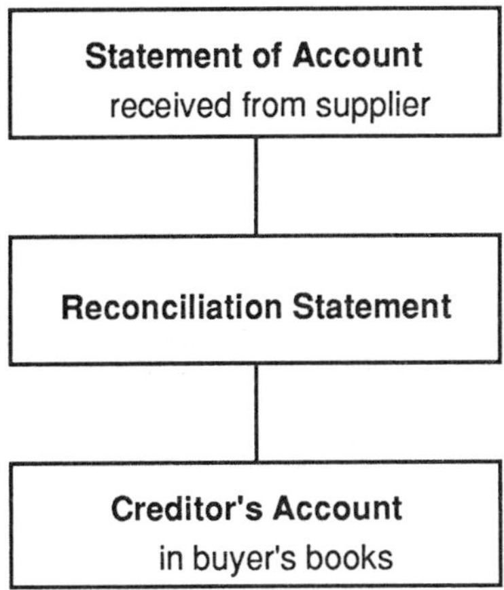

Assuming that there are no errors either on the statement of account or in the creditor's account, the discrepancies are caused by:

- *items in transit,* which have been invoiced by the supplier, but the invoice is not yet recorded by the buyer
- *payments in the post or banking system,* recorded by the buyer, but not yet received and recorded on the supplier's statement
- *purchases returns,* made by buyer but not yet recorded by the supplier

These three discrepancies are all caused by *timing differences,* ie the business document – invoice, payment, credit note – has not yet been recorded in the accounts of both buyer and seller. The reconciliation statement must take note of these.

Worked example

Question

The following creditor's account appears in the purchases ledger of A Jarvis:

T Smith

Dr.			Cr.		
19-1		£	19-1		£
10 Jan.	Bank	200	1 Jan.	Balance b/d	200
30 Jan.	Bank	150	12 Jan.	Purchases	150
31 Jan.	Purchases returns	25	25 Jan.	Purchases	125
31 Jan.	Balance c/d	100			
		475			475
			1 Feb.	Balance b/d	100

The following statement of account is received from T Smith on 2 February:

Statement of Account: A Jarvis

19-1		Dr. £	Cr. £	Balance £	
1 Jan.	Balance b/d	200		200	*Dr.*
9 Jan.	Invoice no 374	150		350	*Dr.*
14 Jan.	Payment received: thank you		200	150	*Dr.*
20 Jan.	Invoice no 382	125		275	*Dr.*
29 Jan.	Invoice no 413	100		375	*Dr.*

Reconcile the creditor's account balance with that of the statement received by A Jarvis.

Answer

Reconciliation of T Smith's statement of account as at 31 January 19-1

	£	
Balance of account at 31 January 19-1	100	*Cr.*
Add: payment sent on 30 January, not yet appearing on statement	150	
	250	*Cr.*
Add: invoice no 413 sent by T Smith on 29 January, not yet received	100	
	350	
Add: purchases returns to T Smith on 31 January, not yet appearing on statement	25	
Balance of statement at 31 January 19-1	375	

As each of these items are timing differences, they will correct themselves within a few days as they are entered into the accounts of buyer and seller.

9.8 Chapter summary

❏ A bank reconciliation statement is used to agree the balance shown by the bank columns of the cash book with that shown by the bank statement.

❏ Certain differences between the two are timing differences. The two main timing differences are:
- cheques drawn, not yet recorded on the bank statement
- amounts paid into the bank, not yet recorded on the bank statement

These differences will be corrected by time and, most probably, will be recorded on the next bank statement.

❏ Certain differences appearing on the bank statement need to be entered in the cash book to bring it up-to-date. These include:

Receipts
- standing order and BACS receipts credited by the bank
- bank giro credit amounts received by the bank
- dividend amounts received by the bank
- interest credited by the bank

Payments
- standing order and direct debit payments
- bank charges and interest
- unpaid cheques debited by the bank

- The bank reconciliation statement makes use of the timing differences.
- Once prepared, a bank reconciliation statement is proof that the cash book (bank columns) and the bank statement were agreed at a particular date.
- Statements of account received from creditors may need to be reconciled with the creditor's account; discrepancies are caused by:
  - items in transit
  - payments in the post or banking system
  - purchases returns

The next chapter looks at how computers are used to handle accounting records.

9.9 Questions

9.1 Below is the cash book (bank columns only) of Andrew Clark for the month of May 19-0 together with his bank statement for the same period.

Andrew Clark
CASH BOOK

Dr.					Cr.
19-0		Bank	19-0		Bank
		£			£
1 May	Balance b/d	4,200	2 May	Cheque no 422	136
14 May	Sales	1,414	7 May	Cheque no 423	204
21 May	Sales	1,240	27 May	Cheque no 424	214
28 May	Sales	1,160			

BANK STATEMENT

Southern Bank plc
Northbrook Branch

In account with:
Mr Andrew Clark

Date	*Detail*	*Debit*	*Credit*	*Balance*
		£	£	£
19-0				
1 May				4,200
5 May	Cheque no 422	136		4,064
10 May	Cheque no 423	204		3,860
15 May	Counter credit		1,414	
15 May	National Insurance Company	284		4,990
22 May	Counter credit		1,240	6,230
31 May	Service charges	100		6,130

You are to:

(a) rewrite the cash book making any adjustments you consider necessary

(b) balance the cash book and bring the balance down

(c) prepare a bank reconciliation statement as at 31 May 19-0

[Pitman Examinations Institute]

9.2* Given below are the bank account and bank statement of C Cod for the month of May 19-9.

C Cod's Bank Account

		£			£
1 May	Balance	144.00	9 May	M Roe	108.00
10 May	Sales	134.00	7 May	Drawings	80.00
19 May	F Haddock	300.00	18 May	Cash	30.00
31 May	V Perch	90.00	19 May	E Skate	84.00
31 May	B Tench	48.00	24 May	British Gas	36.00
			29 May	N Fish	108.00

THE IZAAK WALTON BANK PLC

STATEMENT OF ACCOUNT

C Cod
14 Pond Street
Banktown

123578

31 May 19-9

Date	*Detail*	*Debit*	*Credit*	*Balance*
1 May	Balance			144.00 (cr)
9 May	00820	108.00		36.00
10 May	Sundries		134.00	170.00
11 May	00821	80.00		90.00
18 May	00822	30.00		60.00
24 May	Cheque		300.00	360.00
24 May	00823	84.00		276.00
29 May	Mortgage SO	90.00		186.00
31 May	00824	36.00		150.00
31 May	Charges	14.00		136.00

You are to:

(a) Starting with the final balance on the bank account, which you have to calculate, bring the bank account up-to-date by referring to the bank statement of account.

(b) Prepare a bank reconciliation statement for C Cod as on 31 May 19-9.

[Midland Examining Group]

9.3* On 5 June 19-0 J Kearns received his monthly bank statement for the month of May. The statement contained the following details:

Date	*Particulars*	*Payments* £	*Receipts* £	*Balance* £
1 May	Balance			830
3 May	LGT		440	1,270
6 May	Fee	22		1,248
9 May	236129	42		1,206
12 May	236128	337		869
17 May	DD	32		837
23 May	236130	78		759
23 May	236132	131		628
25 May	CT		22	650
27 May	LGT		305	955

LGT = Lodgment
DD = Direct Debit
CT = Credit Transfer

For the corresponding period J Kearns' own cash book (bank columns) contained the following:

Dr.						Cr.
Date	Details	£	Date	Details	Cheque No	£
1 May	Balance b/d	830	5 May	Purchases	128	337
2 May	Sales	440	6 May	Electricity	129	42
27 May	Sales	305	16 May	Purchases	130	78
31 May	Sales	375	18 May	Rent	131	30
			20 May	Purchases	132	131
			30 May	Wages	133	250
			31 May	Cleaning Ltd	134	27
			31 May	Balance c/d		1,055
		1,950				1,950
1 June	Balance b/d	1,055				

Required:

(a) Show the additional entries to be made in the cash book on 31 May and bring down the new balance.

(b) Prepare a statement reconciling the balance on 31 May, as given by the bank statement, with the revised cash book balance.

[© Northern Ireland Schools Examinations and Assessment Council]

9.4 Kirsty McDonald has recently received the following bank statement:

National Bank plc

Kirsty McDonald Statement of Account

Date	*Details*	*Debits* £	*Credits* £	*Balance* £
19-0				
30 Oct.	Balance			841
31 Oct.	606218	23		818
5 Nov.	Sundry Credit		46	864
7 Nov.	606219	161		703
9 Nov.	Direct Debit	18		685
12 Nov.	606222	93		592
15 Nov.	Sundry Credit		207	799
19 Nov.	606223	246		553
19 Nov.	Bank Giro Credit		146	699
20 Nov.	Bank Giro Credit		246	945
21 Nov.	606221	43		902
21 Nov.	Sundry Credit		63	965
22 Nov.	Bank Giro Credit		79	1,044
23 Nov.	Loan Interest	391		653
26 Nov.	606220	87		566
26 Nov.	Deposit A/C Interest		84	650
27 Nov.	606226	74		576
28 Nov.	Sundry Credit		88	664
30 Nov.	606225	185		479

Her cash book showed the following details:

19-0		£	*19-0*		*Cheque No*	£
1 Nov.	Balance b/d	818	2 Nov.	Rent	219	161
5 Nov.	B Mason	46	5 Nov.	H Gibson	220	87
8 Nov.	K Dean	146	7 Nov.	G Wise	221	43
14 Nov.	G Hunt	207	8 Nov.	T Allen	222	93
16 Nov.	C Charlton	79	12 Nov.	Gas	223	246
19 Nov.	D Banks	63	15 Nov.	F Causer	224	692
26 Nov.	P Perry	88	19 Nov.	M Lewis	225	185
28 Nov.	A Palmer	29	23 Nov.	G Bridges	226	74
30 Nov.	J Dixon	17	29 Nov.	L Wilson	227	27
30 Nov.	Balance c/d	206	29 Nov.	P Brown	228	91
		1,699				1,699

Required:

(a) Bring the cash book balance of £206 up-to-date as at 30 November 19-0.

(b) Draw up a bank reconciliation statement as at 30 November 19-0.

[Association of Accounting Technicians]

9.5 The cashier of Wrecker Ltd balanced the company's cash book at the end of July 19-0 and found that it showed an overdraft of £27,392. The balance on the company's bank statement of the same date was an overdraft of £23,570.

Investigation showed the difference between these two balances to be caused by the following:

1. A standing order for rates of £1,700 was charged in the bank statement on 2 July 19-0.
2. An entry on the bank statement dated 31 July showed that Buyit Ltd, a debtor of Wrecker Ltd, had settled its outstanding balance of £3,400 by a direct credit of £3,200; the difference was due to a prompt payment discount.
3. A cheque for £532 had been wrongly charged to Wrecker Ltd's bank account; it should have been charged to the account of Wretched Ltd, a company which banks at the same branch.
4. Bank charges of £1,853 for the three months to 30 June 19-0 were charged to the account on 2 July 19-0.
5. At 31 July 19-0 cheques drawn by Wrecker Ltd but not yet presented amounted to £15,326.
6. The cashier had entered the firm's receipts of £10,619 for 31 July 19-0 in the cash book on that date and taken them to the bank, but they did not appear on the statement until 1 August.

Required:

(a) Complete the cash book of Wrecker Ltd for the period to 31 July 19-0, starting with the overdrawn balance of £27,392.

(b) Reconcile the balance on Wrecker Ltd's bank statement with the corrected cash book balance computed for part (a).

(c) State what action should be taken in respect of the items which appear in the bank reconciliation at 31 July 19-0.

(d) State *two* general benefits to be derived from the regular preparation of bank reconciliation statements.

[The Chartered Institute of Bankers, Autumn 1990]

9.6* JC Limited uses a computerised accounting system to record its transactions and produce a trial balance. The trial balance which was produced by the system at 31 March 19-0 showed that the bank balance was £12,879 overdrawn, but the bank statement which is reproduced below showed a balance on the same date of £5,467 credit. A bank account control report was printed by the accountant of JC Limited so that the transactions could be compared.

JC LIMITED
COMPUTERISED ACCOUNTING SYSTEM
CONTROL REPORT
BANK ACCOUNT CODE 99 TRANSACTIONS FROM 01.03/-0 TO 31/03/-0

DATE		*DR* £	*CR* £	*BAL* £
01/03/-0	Balance			4,201
02/03/-0	J Smith & Sons	1,405		
	White Brothers	697		6,303
04/03/-0	Brown & Co	234		6,537
07/03/-0	543987		279	
	543988		1,895	
	543989		11,987	(7,624)
10/03/-0	J Lake	1,386		(6,238)
12/03/-0	543990		1,497	
	543991		547	
	543992		296	(8,578)
17/03/-0	Grey Enterprises	2,569		
	Hunt Lodges	34		
	B Black	643		(5,332)
24/03/-0	543993		2,305	(7,637)
31/03/-0	543994		5,242	(12,879)

The bank statement for the same month was as follows:

NATTOWN BANK STATEMENT OF ACCOUNT 31/03/-0

DATE		*DR* £	*CR* £	*BAL* £
MARCH				
1	Balance			3,529
3	Counter credit		2,489	6,018
4	543986	237		5,781
6	Counter credit		2,102	7,883
7	Bank charges	195		
	543988	1,895		5,793
9	Counter credit		234	6,027
11	543985	68		5,959
13	Brown & Co cheque dishonoured	234		
	543989	1,197		4,528
14	Counter credit		1,486	6,014
17	543990	1,497		
	543992	296		4,221
23	Counter credit		5,332	9,553
25	Standing order: rates	4,029		5,524
27	543991	57		5,467
31	Balance			5,467

The balances on 1 March 19-0 were reconciled, the difference being partly due to the following cheques which were unpresented on that date:

Cheque	543984	£1,512
	543985	£68
	543986	£237

You are required to:

(a) prepare a bank reconciliation statement at 31 March 19-0

(b) list *three* reasons why bank reconciliation statements should be prepared regularly

[The Chartered Institute of Management Accountants]

9.7 A young and inexperienced book-keeper is having great difficulty in producing a bank reconciliation statement at 31 December. He gives you his attempt to produce a summarised cash book, and also the bank statement received for the month of December. These are shown below. You may assume that the bank statement is correct. You may also assume that the trial balance at 1 January did indeed show a bank overdraft of £7,000.12.

Cash Book Summary - draft

	£	£	£		
Jan 1					
Opening overdraft		7,000.12	35,000.34	payments Jan-Nov	
Jan-Nov receipts	39,500.54				
Add: discounts	500.02				
		40,000.56	12,000.34	balance Nov 30	
		47,000.68	47,000.68		
Dec 1		12,000.34		payments Dec	Cheque No
Dec receipts	178.19		37.14		7654
	121.27		192.79		7655
	14.92		5,000.00		7656
	16.88		123.45		7657
		329.26	678.90		7658
			1.47		7659
Dec receipts	3,100.00		19.84		7660
	171.23		10.66		7661
	1,198.17				
		4,469.40	10,734.75	Balance c/d	
		16,799.00	16,799.00		
Dec 31 balance		10,734.75			

Bank Statement - December 31

	Withdrawals £	*Deposits* £		*Balance* £
			1 December	800.00
7650	300.00	178.19		
7653	191.91	121.27		
7654	37.14	14.92		
7651	1,111.11	16.88		
7656	5,000.00	3,100.00		
7655	129.79	171.23		
7658	678.90	1,198.17		
Standing order	50.00	117.98		
7659	1.47			
7661	10.66			
Bank charges	80.00		31 December	3,472.34

Required:

(a) A corrected cash book summary and a reconciliation of the balance on this revised summary with the bank statement balance as at 31 December, as far as you are able.

(b) A brief note as to the likely cause of any remaining difference.

[The Chartered Association of Certified Accountants]

9.8* The following account appears in your purchases ledger:

Convex Co Ltd

19-9		£	19-9		£
7 Oct.	Bank	711	1 Oct.	Balance b/d	776
7 Oct.	Discount	37	4 Oct.	Purchases	498
30 Oct.	Bank	1,235	25 Oct.	Purchases	1,022
	Discount	65			
31 Oct.	Balance c/d	248			
		2,296			2,296
			1 Nov.	Balance b/d	248

During the first week in November a statement of account was received from Convex Co Ltd as follows:

19-9		£	£	£
1 Oct.	Balance			1,000
4 Oct.	Sales	498		1,498
5 Oct.	Bank		220	
	Discount		4	1,274
10 Oct.	Bank		711	
	Discount		37	526
25 Oct.	Sales	1,022		1,548

You are required to:

(a) reconcile the opening balance of £1,000 on the statement with that of £776 in your books

(b) reconcile the closing balance of £248 on your ledger account with that of £1,548 shown on the statement

[RSA Examinations Board]

Multiple-choice questions: chapters 7-9

- Read each question carefully
- Choose the *one* answer you think is correct (calculators may be needed)
- Answers are on page 486

1. For a VAT-registered business, which of the following is output tax?

   A VAT on purchases
   B VAT on sales
   C VAT on expenses
   D VAT on fixed assets

2. A VAT-registered business buys a machine for £2000 excluding VAT, and pays by cheque. If VAT is at 17½%, this transaction is recorded as:

	Debit	*Credit*
A	machinery account £2,350	bank account £2,350
B	machinery account £2,000	bank account £1,650 VAT account £350
C	machinery account £2,000 VAT account £350	bank account £2,350
D	machinery account £2,000	bank account £2,000

3. A credit balance on a firm's VAT account means:

   A there is a book-keeping error - VAT account always has a debit balance
   B the firm owes VAT to HM Customs and Excise
   C the firm sells only zero-rated goods
   D the VAT authorities owe VAT to the firm

4. A pack of envelopes costs £5.17 including VAT at 17½%. How much is the price *excluding* VAT?

   A £6.07
   B £4.80
   C £3.63
   D £4.40

5. The cash book records:

   A receipts and payments in cash only
   B receipts and payments by cheque only
   C all receipts and payments both in cash and by cheque
   D receipts and payments both in cash (except for low-value expense payments) and by cheque

6. The discount received column of the cash book is totalled at regular intervals and transferred to:

   A the credit side of discount received account
   B the debit side of discount received account
   C the debit side of general expenses account
   D the credit side of the trial balance

7. Most petty cash books operate on the *imprest system*. This means that:

A the petty cashier draws money from the main cashier as and when required
B the main cashier has to authorise each petty cash payment
C a carbon copy has to be kept of each petty cash voucher
D the petty cashier starts each week or month with a certain amount of money

8. Which one of the following expenses is not normally allowed to be paid from petty cash?

A casual wages
B staff tea and coffee
C window cleaning
D small items of stationery

9. A petty cash book is balanced at the end of each week and the cash float returned by the main cashier. At the start of a particular week the cash float is £50. Petty cash vouchers for the week total £34.56. How much will be received from the main cashier at the end of the week?

A £50.00
B £15.44
C £34.56
D £84.56

10. When preparing a bank reconciliation statement, which one of the following is a timing difference?

A cheques issued, but not yet recorded on the bank statement
B bank charges and interest
C bank giro credits received by the bank
D standing order payments made by the bank

11. A firm's cash book shows a balance at bank of £250; cheques drawn not yet presented for payment total £350; cheques paid in to the bank but not yet credited total £200. What is the balance at bank as per the bank statement?

A £100
B £200
C £250
D £400

12. Which one of the following will be entered in the cash book, but will not appear on the bank statement?

A a dishonoured cheque
B payment of cash to the petty cashier
C wages cheque
D bank charges and interest

10 Computer Accounting: Theory

Many small businesses and almost all large businesses use computers to handle their accounting records.

Computers are ideal where there are large quantities of routine data; common uses in accounting are:

- preparing invoices to be sent out to customers
- keeping the sales ledger (debtors' accounts) up-to-date
- keeping the purchases ledger (creditors' accounts) up-to-date
- stock control
- recording receipts and payments
- payroll, ie handling the information on wages and salaries of employees

In addition to handling routine data, computers are able to print out management reports, including the production of a trial balance and final accounts (see Chapter Eleven). These give information on various aspects of the business, and should enable the business to be run more efficiently.

This chapter looks at the theory of computer accounting; Case Study One (page 133) which follows, deals with a practical example of computerised book-keeping.

10.1 Computer hardware

For smaller businesses the hardware, ie the computer itself, consists of a microcomputer, a *micro*. These are quite compact machines which can be placed on a desktop. Some micros are designed to be portable and can be used when travelling. Large businesses usually use a *mainframe* computer, which is a very large machine with enormous capacity (or memory): such a machine will be used by organisations such as local authorities, banks, building societies, large companies, etc. Often the computers of a business are linked together in a *network,* so that the computers can communicate with each other and share resources, eg a printer. A network can be a local area network (LAN), eg in the same building, or a wide area network (WAN), where computers can be linked by means of telephone lines over the whole country.

The hardware of a computer system consists of:

Microprocessor

This is the heart of the computer where a network of electrical circuits store and manipulate data.

Keyboard
This enables the input of data and instructions to the computer.

Screen
The screen, or monitor, is similar to that on a television set, but is designed to give a clear picture. Information contained in the computer is presented in a readable form on the screen.

Disk drive
This is a mechanism which reads information contained on magnetic disks and transfers it at high speed to the microprocessor. Microcomputers store information on small 'floppy' disks of 3½ inch or 5¼ inch diameter; some use hard disks which have a much larger capacity. Mainframe computer systems use hard disks and high speed tapes.

Printer
Computer systems use a printer to enable information from the computer to be presented in a permanent form that can be read by the human eye. Printers vary in price and quality with, at the lower end of the scale, dot-matrix printers, extending through daisy-wheel printers, to ink-jet and laser printers.

Fig. 10.1 shows the arrangement of the hardware in a typical small business computer application.

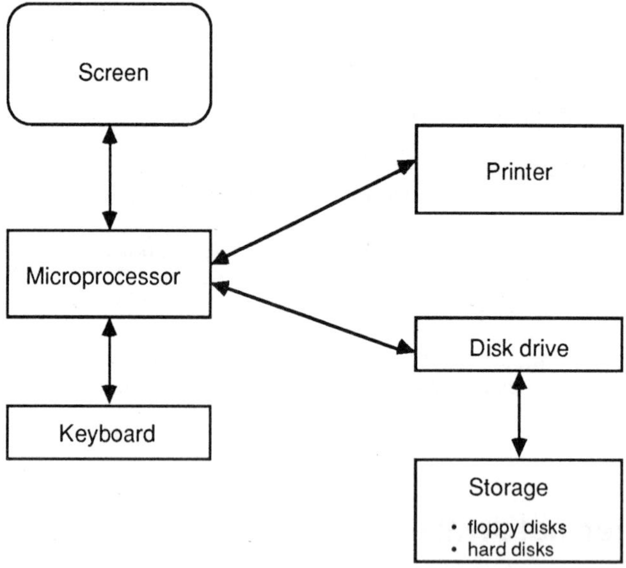

Fig. 10.1 Computer hardware for a small business application

10.2 Computer software

Software consists of the programs, or packages, that give the operating instructions to the computer. Programs are contained in magnetic form on a disk, which is inserted into the disk drive in order that the instructions can be read and passed to the computer. Programs can also be stored on the hard disk, where they are ready for use at any time.

For accounting purposes there are basically two types of programs: the simple *cash trader* program, and the *complete ledger* system.

Cash trader programs

These simple systems assume that the business keeps only a cash book, and needs to keep track of money received and money spent, and to analyse the expenditure. Such programs are inexpensive and are suitable for small businesses which deal on a cash-only basis.

Complete ledger systems

These are more suitable for the larger business, and common applications include:

- invoicing
- sales ledger (ie the debtors' accounts)
- purchases ledger (ie the creditors' accounts)
- nominal ledger
- stock control
- payroll

Often, such programs for business record keeping are fully integrated so that a business transaction can be recorded in a number of different records at the same time. For example, when an invoice is prepared for the sale of goods, an integrated program will reduce the stock of goods held and will record, in the sales ledger, that an increased amount is now owed by the debtor concerned. Integrated programs include a *nominal ledger* (also known as general ledger) which brings together the totals from the other records, and can also be used to record fixed assets and expenses, and produce a trial balance and final accounts. The nominal ledger also usually includes the cash book. Fig. 10.2 shows the various programs that can be brought together in an integrated system.

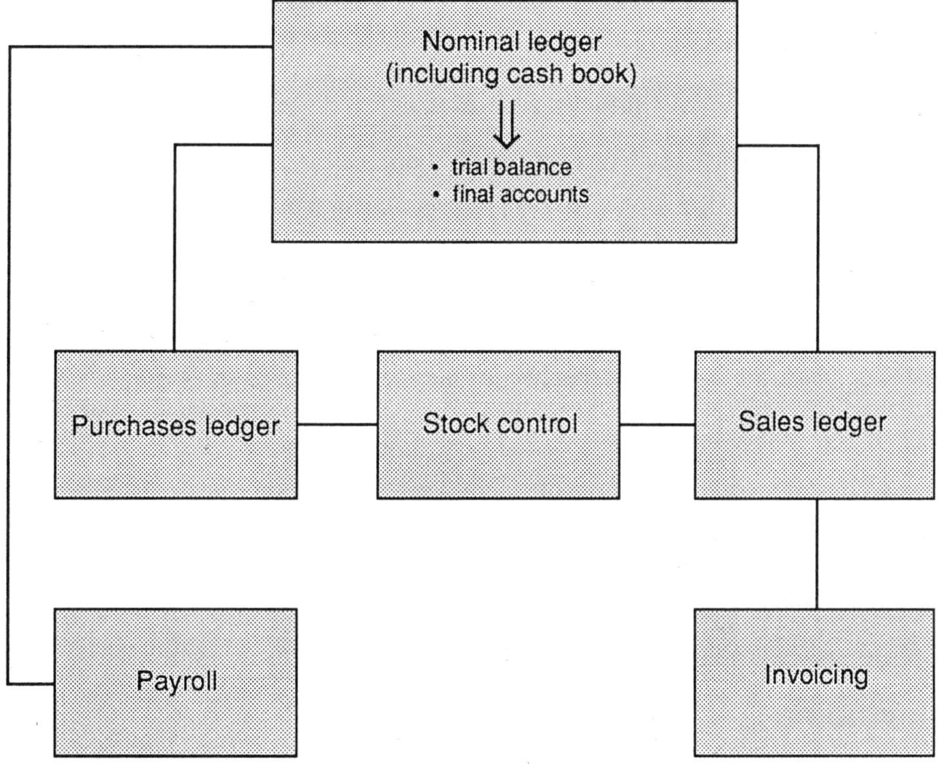

Fig. 10.2 An integrated computer accounting system

10.3 Using computer programs

When using computer programs, it is usual to *batch* a series of transactions, eg to deal with a number of sales ledger transactions, or purchases ledger transactions. By batching, there is less need to keep changing from one area of the program to another. Before entering a batch of transactions, it is usual to *pre-list* them on a separate form such as that shown below for a batch of sales invoices:

Sales Invoice Batch

Customer		*Invoice*		*Net*	*VAT*	*Gross*
Account No	*Name*	*Date*	*No*	£	£	£
			Check list totals			

The sales invoice batch form will be completed from invoices which have been prepared separately. The transactions will then be entered from the invoices into the computer. The computer screen will show the total money amount of invoices and this is compared with the check list total from the sales invoice batch form; if there is a discrepancy, the error must be located and corrected.

At first, entering transactions using a computer is relatively slow because it is necessary to set up a number of *data files*. For example, in sales ledger it is necessary to set up a data file for each customer to whom the business sells: the file will contain an account reference or number, the name and address of the customer, credit limit, perhaps a contact name and telephone number, etc. The data file is usually held in magnetic form on a separate disk from that of the program. This is because the computer will need to be able to read information from both at various times when transactions are being processed. Therefore computer accounting is best done on a computer with either a hard disk or with twin disk drives.

In computer accounting, much use is made of numbers and letters to code items. For example, each debtor's account in the sales ledger will be given a number or an abbreviated name; likewise, each item of stock that a business sells will have a number or a letter. This makes for faster processing of transactions: by entering a number, a short name or a letter, the particular account or stock item can be displayed on screen.

10.4 Invoicing

In order to produce invoices with an invoicing program, two data files are needed:

- *customer file,* which contains the name, address and account number of the customer
- *product file,* which contains details, selling prices and unit quantities of each product the firm sells

The computer operator builds up an invoice on the screen. First is entered the customer's account reference or number (this puts name, address, etc. on screen). Next the product code and the quantity of goods being sold is entered (these items then appear on screen). Trade discounts and Value Added Tax are calculated by the invoicing program.

The on-screen invoice can then either be printed immediately, or it can be stored on disk for later printing of a batch of invoices. Specially printed stationery is often used for computer-printed invoices; an example is shown in fig. 10.3. If an integrated program is used, each invoice produced will automatically update the customer's account in the sales ledger, and adjust the stock records.

10.5 Sales ledger

A computerised sales ledger handles all the debtors' accounts. A *customer file* is maintained for each customer which contains details of:

- name
- address
- account number or short name
- credit limit (ie balance beyond which the debtor's account should not go)

Sales ledger programs, like most accounting programs, are *menu driven*: this means that the program asks the operator to choose what is to be done. The main menu that will appear on computer screen at the start of a sales ledger program will be similar to that shown below:

<u>SALES LEDGER</u>
Customer details
Batched data entry
Reports

The operator chooses one of these. For example, selecting 'customer details' enables accounts to be opened for new customers or amendment of existing customer details, eg change of address, increase in credit limit, etc. Selection of 'batched data entry' will lead to a sub-menu appearing on screen similar to the following:

<u>BATCHED DATA ENTRY</u>
Sales invoices
Sales credit notes

By selecting one of these, the operator can input a batch of sales invoices (if not already entered automatically from an invoicing program) or sales credit notes.

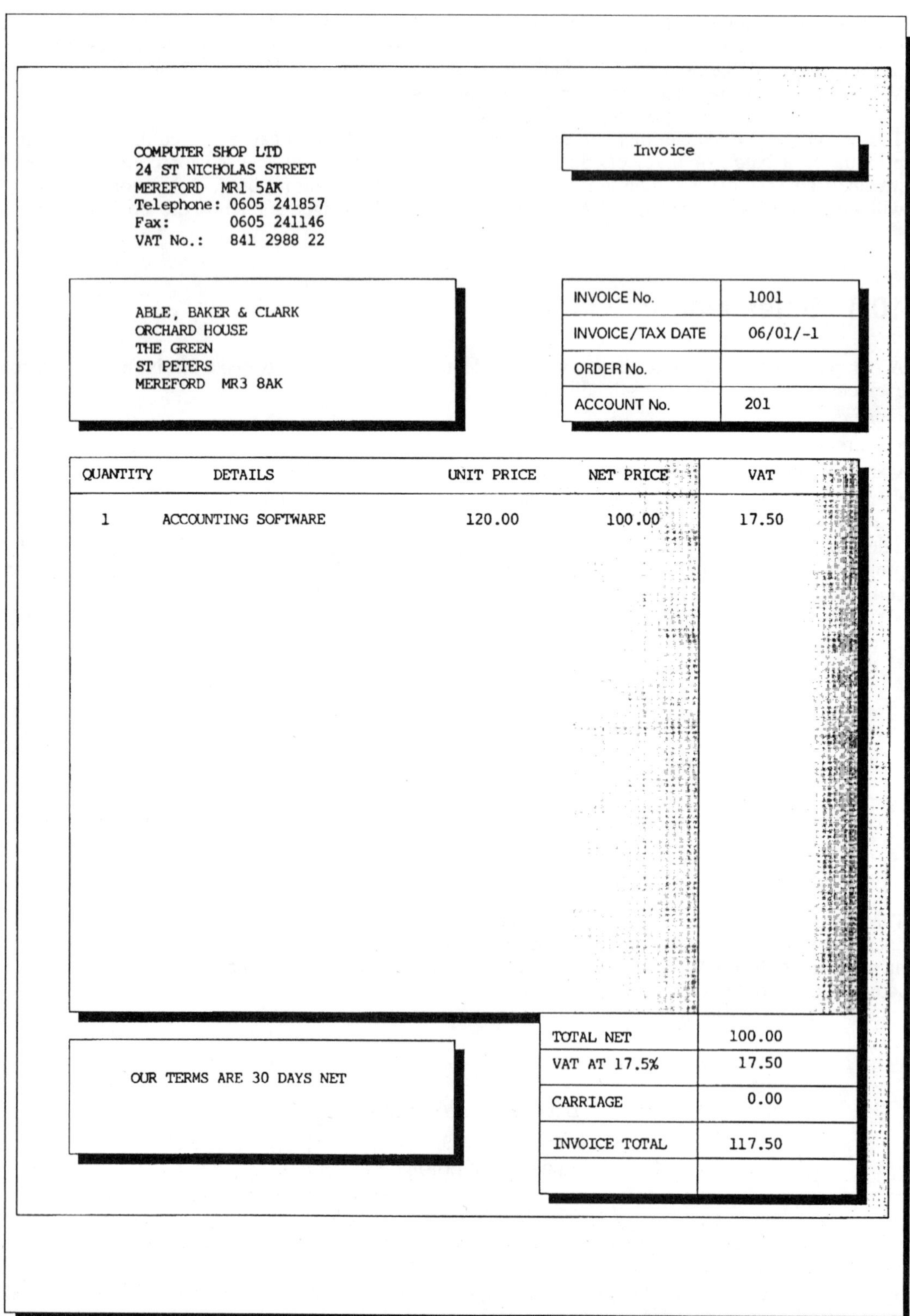

COMPUTER SHOP LTD
24 ST NICHOLAS STREET
MEREFORD MR1 5AK
Telephone: 0605 241857
Fax: 0605 241146
VAT No.: 841 2988 22

Invoice

ABLE, BAKER & CLARK
ORCHARD HOUSE
THE GREEN
ST PETERS
MEREFORD MR3 8AK

INVOICE No.	1001
INVOICE/TAX DATE	06/01/-1
ORDER No.	
ACCOUNT No.	201

QUANTITY	DETAILS	UNIT PRICE	NET PRICE	VAT
1	ACCOUNTING SOFTWARE	120.00	100.00	17.50

OUR TERMS ARE 30 DAYS NET

TOTAL NET	100.00
VAT AT 17.5%	17.50
CARRIAGE	0.00
INVOICE TOTAL	117.50

Fig. 10.3 Computer-printed invoice

'Reports' from the main menu enables information to be printed from the sales ledger program. This information may be sent out to customers in the form of statements of account, or may be for the use of management in the business. Most sales ledger programs can produce the following reports:

- day book listing, showing transactions posted during the day
- statements of account, to be sent to each customer at regular intervals
- aged debtors' schedule, showing each debtor balance analysed over the current month and each of the previous two or three months – useful for 'chasing' slow payers; an example of such a schedule is shown in fig. 10.4.
- debtors' letters, printing reminder letters to those customers whose accounts are overdue
- customer lists, giving names and addresses of customers in alphabetical or account number order

COMPUTER SHOP LTD   Sales Ledger - Account Balances (Aged)   Date : 0103-2
Page : 1

A/C	Account Name		Turnover	Credit Limit	Balance	Current	30 Days	60 Days	Older
201	Able, Baker & Clark		370.00	1000.00	164.50	164.50	0.00	0.00	0.00
202	Hitech Trading Co		320.00	750.00	376.00	376.00	0.00	0.00	0.00
204	Sixth Form College	*	1730.00	1000.00	1632.75	799.00	833.75	0.00	0.00
205	Teleservice	*	2025.00	500.00	1926.88	1880.00	46.88	0.00	0.00
208	Stone, Wall Ltd		425.00	750.00	499.38	499.38	0.00	0.00	0.00
		Totals :	4870.00	4000.00	4599.51	3718.88	880.63	0.00	0.00

Fig. 10.4 Aged debtors' schedule
(an asterisk indicates debtors whose balances are above the credit limit)

10.6 Purchases ledger

A purchases ledger deals with the creditors or suppliers of a business. A purchases ledger program operates in much the same way as that for sales ledger.

A *supplier file* maintains for each account details of the name, address, and credit terms allowed by the supplier. Accounts are updated from batches of invoices and credit notes received, and payments made. Purchases ledger programs can, using special stationery, print remittance advices (sent to the creditor with the payment) and, for larger businesses, can also print payment cheques and bank giro credits, or prepare computer data where payment is to be made electronically through BACS (Bankers' Automated Clearing Services).

Reports include:

- day book listing, showing transactions posted
- aged creditors' schedule, showing amounts owing to creditors analysed between the current month, and each of the previous two or three months
- supplier lists, giving names and addresses of creditors in alphabetical order

10.7 Stock control

The stock of a business consists of the quantity of goods held for resale. Control of stock (see also Chapter Sixteen) is an important aspect for any business and the use of a computer program enables the stock records to be kept up-to-date as:

- stocks are received from suppliers
- stocks are dispatched to customers

At any time, the stock control program will be able to show the current stock held for each type of stock. Most stock control programs will give the minimum levels for each type of stock that should be held, together with the quantities in which the stock item is re-ordered, eg 100 units, etc.

The *stock file* has information on the:

- stock number allocated to a particular stock item
- description of the stock item
- name and address of supplier
- level at which stock should be re-ordered
- re-order quantities
- quantity of stock currently held
- stock allocated to known future needs, eg delivery to a customer at a future date
- valuation of stock currently held

The main menu for a stock control program will appear on the computer screen and will be similar to the following:

STOCK CONTROL
Update stock details
Stock received
Stock issued
Reports

Selecting one of the choices will take the user to a sub-menu which leads to each section of the stock control program. For example, by selecting 'Stock received' the user can record the delivery of stock.

The most common report to be produced from a stock control program is that showing the *stock valuation,* ie details of how many units of each stock item are held, the unit cost, and the total value of stock held. A stock valuation report is shown in fig. 10.5. Other reports available include:

- a list of items stocked by the business
- details of items out-of-stock, or below minimum stock level
- stock that needs to be re-ordered (some programs can print the purchase order)
- slow moving stock items
- names and addresses of suppliers

STOCK VALUATION REPORT

Date 2802-1 Page 1

Stock number	Description	Quantity	Unit cost (£)	Total value (£)
75001	Floppy disks 3½" double density (packs of 10)	100	8.00	800.00
75002	Floppy disks 3½" high density (packs of 10)	40	15.00	600.00
75003	Floppy disks 5¼" double density (packs of 10)	150	5.00	750.00
75004	Floppy disks 5¼" high density (packs of 10)	30	12.50	375.00

Fig. 10.5 Stock valuation report

10.8 Nominal ledger

Nominal ledger contains all the accounts of the business, except for debtors (sales ledger) and creditors (purchases ledger). Thus it contains accounts for:

- sales
- purchases
- cash and bank
- expenses
- sundry income
- VAT
- fixed assets
- liabilities
- capital and owner's drawings

Most computer accounting programs include a 'default' layout for nominal ledger, ie the accounts have been set up already and it is for the user of the software either to accept these accounts, or to set up a different structure. For a small business, the default layout is perfectly acceptable and, indeed, amendments can be made easily to change the names of accunts to suit the needs of the business, and to insert new accounts.

There are links between nominal ledger and sales and purchases ledgers. When transactions are posted to sales and purchases ledgers – eg credit sales, credit purchases, credit notes, receipts and payments – it is necessary to specify at the appropriate point the nominal account involved in the other half of the book-keeping transaction. For example, when posting invoices to the sales ledger, the program will ask for the account number of sales account in the nominal ledger.

Besides the management reports associated with the other areas of computer accounting, nominal ledger can be used to help in the production of:

- VAT returns (see Chapter Seven)
- trial balance (see Chapter Five)
- final accounts – trading and profit and loss account and balance sheet (see Chapter Eleven)

10.9 Payroll

Payroll programs enable the speedy processing of employees' wages and salaries (see also Chapter Twenty-eight), and sick pay. The *employee file* held for each employee contains:

- employee's name
- work's number
- National Insurance number
- tax code
- wage or salary rate
- overtime rate

The main menu for a payroll program will be similar to the following:

PAYROLL
Employee details
Parameters
Payroll processing
Reports

By selecting 'employee details', a new employee can be added to the employee file, or a person who has left can be deleted; also, wage and salary rates, tax code, etc. can be changed. The 'parameters' option allows details of tax codes, National Insurance Contributions, etc. to be altered: normally this information changes annually and will apply to all employees – the program must, therefore, be revised. 'Payroll processing' allows information for the current pay week or month to be entered, eg hours worked, overtime, etc. 'Reports' enables printouts and other information to be obtained from the program.

To process the payroll, it is necessary to input information of hours worked for hourly-paid employees; for those earning a fixed wage or salary this information does not need to be entered, but overtime hours will need to be input. The program automatically calculates each employee's gross pay, tax deductions, National Insurance Contributions, and pension contributions.

For each pay period, eg a week or a month, the program can be used to print out pay slips, together with either a cheque or a bank giro credit. Where employees are paid in cash, a notes and coin analysis is printed which shows the quantities of each bank note and coin required to make up employees' pay packets. Where employees are paid by BACS (Bankers' Automated Clearing Services), the payroll program will give the details necessary to prepare the computer data enabling the electronic transfer of money from the employer's bank account into the bank account of the employee.

Printouts and reports include:

- payslips
- cheques, bank giro credits
- notes and coin analysis
- end-of-year summaries of income tax, National Insurance Contributions, and pension deductions
- list of employees

10.10 Other uses for the business computer

So far we have looked solely at the use of a computer to keep the accounting records. However, the purchase of a computer system will also enable a business to improve its performance by allowing the introduction of other programs such as word processing, databases, and spreadsheets.

Word processing programs are now used widely in any efficient office.

Databases are computer filing systems which enable a large amount of information, such as customer names and addresses to be held on file and accessed immediately.

Spreadsheets enable a large amount of numeric data to be tabulated, manipulated and processed.

10.11 Passwords and 'backing up' data

Passwords

Most computer accounting programs require the user to key in the correct password before data can be accessed and transactions posted. The password should be known only by those staff authorised to use the program: in this way confidentiality of the accounting information held by the program is maintained, in the same way that handwritten accounting records are confidential. The computer accounting program allows the password to be changed from time-to-time, and it is advisable to do this at regular intervals, although how often will vary depending on the size of the business and the number of accounting staff.

Backing up data

It is a standard computer procedure to take back up copies of files that have been worked on, eg files on the working disk – hard disk or floppy disk – saved from time-to-time on another disk. In computer accounting it is particularly important to back up files regularly – after each thirty minutes of work would be advisable. (Some computer programs are designed to back up at regular intervals automatically to either a floppy disk or a separate hard disk.) Accounting files cannot be considered to be properly entered until they are backed up.

At the end of each day files should be backed up and the back up copy should be placed in a fire-proof safe for overnight storage. The disk should be labelled with the date.

Many businesses operate a ten disk set of back-ups so that, at any one time, they have a record of all the changes made to files in the last two working weeks. At the end of each day, the oldest back up is taken out and the latest files saved to it (and the date changed on the label). Disks wear out in time and, at regular intervals, it would be prudent to use a new set of disks.

At the end of each financial year, it is practice to keep the year-end disks, as they will be needed for audit purposes.

10.12 Chapter summary

- Computer accounting enables a business to handle a large volume of routine business transactions in the most efficient way.
- Computer accounting systems can be either a simple cash trader program or a full ledger system.
- Common applications for computer accounting include:
  - invoicing
  - sales ledger
  - purchases ledger
  - nominal ledger
  - stock control
  - payroll

'Hands-on' experience is essential to seeing how the programs work, and Case Study One, which follows, is a practice session on the use of computer book-keeping.

10.13 Questions

10.1 You have been asked to recommend to a small business a suitable computer, together with software for accounting, word-processing and spreadsheet functions. Obtain from your library or local newsagent copies of professional computing magazines. Investigate hardware and software from reviews and advertisements; send away for details if necessary. Draw up a shortlist of three suitable machines together with compatible software, bearing in mind the considerations of value for money and reliability.

10.2 Microcomputers are being used by many organisations of varying sizes either to prepare their accounts or to assist the managers of an organisation to control its activities.

(a) Describe how a microcomputer accounting package may be used to deal with accounting transactions.

(b) What are the advantages of using such accounting packages instead of a manual system?

[The Chartered Institute of Management Accountants]

10.3 Answer the following letter from Mrs Rose Turner, Arco Engineering, Unit 7, Westbury Trading Estate, Greenham GR6 9TY:

7 July 19-8

Mr J Rudd
White Peterhouse, Chartered Accountants
Castle View
GREENHAM

Dear Mr Rudd
I have been considering the possibility of computerising our accounts. As you know, we run a double-entry system here at Arco Engineering, and I want to convince the higher management that computerisation will bring great benefits. They are an old-fashioned lot, and are bound to bring up any number of objections. I shall be very grateful if you could set out for me the advantages of computerisation, particularly for management, and also the disadvantages, so that I can answer their criticisms. I know that you are expert in the field, so I hope you will be able to help me.

Yours sincerely
Rose Turner
Rose Turner, Accounts Manager

Case Study 1
Computer Accounting: Practice

This Case Study looks at the application of computers to:

- sales ledger
- purchases ledger
- nominal ledger

While the Case Study follows the use of Sage™ Book-keeping and Accounting programs, most other accounting programs designed for use with personal computers operate in a similar way.

To work through this Case Study you will need:

- a personal computer, preferably with a hard disk drive
- a printer
- a computer accounting program, such as Sage 'Book-keeper', 'Accountant', 'Accountant Plus', 'Financial Controller'

In order to demonstrate the use of computer accounting, we will follow the book-keeping transactions of a new business called Computer Shop Limited.

After each set of transactions, the trial balance is given so that you can check the accuracy of your work as you make progress.

1 Getting started

Firstly it is necessary for the accounting program to be configured to suit the type of computer being used, by following the instructions in the manual. This may well have been done for you already, in which case you should proceed as follows (hard disk computer):

- switch on the computer and printer
- at the C prompt (C>) key in SAGE (in upper or lower case) and press ↵ (enter)

If you are at a school or college it is likely that you will have your own data disk (which will have been configured with the program data files):

- switch on the computer and printer
- insert your data disk in the 'A' drive
- select the Sage program ('Book-keeper', 'Accountant', 'Accountant Plus', 'Financial Controller') from the menu, or key in SAGE and press ↵ (enter)

The date will appear on screen: as you will be making entries for the month of January, enter the date as 31 January, together with the year, eg '310195'.

Press ↵ (enter) and key in the password: this is set initially as LETMEIN. Press enter to take you to the main menu – other choices may appear, depending on the program you are running.

```
SALES LEDGER
PURCHASE LEDGER
NOMINAL LEDGER
UTILITIES
QUIT
```

Important note: To quit the program, always return to this menu and select [Quit]: by doing this the data files will be correctly updated. Never quit by just switching off or resetting the computer.

2 Situation

Computer Shop Limited is a new business which has just been set up by its owner, Richard Brown. The business operates from premises in St Nicholas Street, Mereford, where Richard sells computer hardware and software. He buys his stocks of hardware and software on credit terms from a number of suppliers. The business is registered for Value Added Tax.

Richard Brown intends that his main customers are to be the business community in Mereford. To these he must offer credit terms. In order to seek business, he has recently visited a number of firms and schools in the area offering the services of his company on credit terms of a 30 day payment period. A number of these have asked him to open an account for them.

You have just been appointed as an assistant in the shop and Richard Brown has asked you to set up an accounting system using the computer hardware and accounting software available to you.

3 Purchases ledger

Details of suppliers

Richard Brown has arranged to purchase hardware and software on credit from the following:

Supplier's name and address	*For your use - account number or short name**
Axis Supplies Ltd Unit 21 Ringway Trading Estate Barchester BR2 9JT	101 or AXIS
Bell Computers Ltd The Old Foundry Clapton-on-Sea CL9 8AJ	102 or BELL

* Note: With the Sage programs, any combination of up to six numbers and/or letters – selected by the user – identify each purchases ledger (and sales ledger) account.

Computer Supplies Ltd 35-40 Granbury Road Leeton LT1 8RZ	103 or COMP
Granta Trading Co Ltd Unit 6 Camside Industrial Estate Cambury CB5 2AQ	104 or GRANTA
Kingsway Technical Ltd 126 The Parade Kingsway Denham DM3 9PQ	105 or KINGS
Pratt and Co Ltd 28 Avon Lane Eveshore MR10 9HP	106 or PRATT

Opening accounts in the purchases ledger

- From the main menu, select [Purchase Ledger]; press enter.
- From the purchase ledger menu, select [Supplier Details]; press enter.
- The program will ask you for an account reference – for the first account, key in either the account number, 101, or the short name, AXIS, and press enter. (If the account reference has already been used, details of the account will show on the screen.) Press enter.
- The program will ask "Is this a new account: No Yes". The cursor will be positioned over the word No; move the cursor to the word Yes by pressing the [→] key, and then press enter.
- Now enter the name and address of the supplier. If you make any errors use the arrow keys to move up or down the screen, and make the corrections.
- Ignore other details that could be completed.
- When all the details of the first account have been entered on screen, press [ESC]. The program now asks "Do you want to: Post Edit Abandon" – notice that the cursor is already positioned over Post, which is the default, ie the answer the computer expects. If the details are correct, simply press enter and the data files will be updated.
- Repeat the process for the other supplier accounts.
- Return to the main menu by pressing [ESC] twice.

Purchases account in the nominal ledger

As Richard Brown's business buys computer hardware and software, it is appropriate to open separate purchases accounts in the nominal ledger for each of these aspects of his business.

Your data disk will already include a standard layout for nominal ledger, with accounts already numbered. The purchases accounts are 5000, 5001, 5002, 5003: we will use the first two numbers for hardware purchases and software purchases respectively. However, we need to name them as such.

- From the main menu, select [Nominal Ledger].
- From the nominal ledger menu, select [Nominal Account Structure], press enter; then, select [Account Names] from the sub-menu.
- You are now asked for an account reference: key in 5000.
- Change the account name by keying in Hardware Purchases and press enter.

- Press [ESC] and, at the prompt, select Post and press enter.
- Repeat the process for account reference 5001, which is to be called Software Purchases.
- To return to the main menu, press [ESC] three times.

Using the purchases ledger

Richard Brown's business, Computer Shop Ltd, has the following credit purchases transactions for his first month in business:

Note: *All purchases are subject to Value Added Tax. The amounts shown below need the addition of VAT: the program will calculate the amounts and will post them to the purchases VAT account. (The Case Study has been worked using the VAT rate of 17½ per cent.)*

January	
2	Bought software £500 from Axis Supplies Ltd, their invoice no 1341
3	Bought hardware £600 from Bell Computers Ltd, invoice no 1005
5	Bought software £350 from Granta Trading Co Ltd, invoice no T7648
7	Bought software £200 from Pratt and Co Ltd, invoice no A81721
8	Bought hardware £425 from Kingsway Technical Ltd, invoice no 900817
12	Bought software £200 from Axis Supplies Ltd, invoice no 1397
18	Bought hardware £365 from Granta Trading Co Ltd, invoice no T7721
22	Bought software £85 from Computer Supplies Ltd, invoice no 9987
27	Bought software £125 from Pratt & Co Ltd, invoice no A81795

Starting from the main menu, the purchases ledger transactions are entered as follows:

- Select [Purchase Ledger]; press enter.
- Select [Batched Data Entry]; press enter.
- Select [Purchase Invoices]; press enter, and the data entry screen now appears.

Data entry screen

- The cursor is in the 'A/C' column; enter the account number or short name of the first account you need. As this is Axis Supplies Ltd, key in 101 or AXIS (depending on how you opened the accounts earlier); press enter. Note that the supplier's account name appears at the top of the screen. (Pressing function key F4 – the Search Key – will show on screen a list of the suppliers' accounts.)
- The cursor will have moved automatically to the 'Date' column. Key in the required date, eg 020195 (2 January 1995), or press function key F5 to display the system date.
- The cursor will have moved to the 'Inv' column; key in the supplier's invoice number 1341 (up to six numbers/letters can be entered); press enter.
- The cursor will now be under the column 'N/C' – this stands for nominal code and here we must enter the nominal account number involved in the other half of the book-keeping transaction. As it is software that has been bought from Axis Supplies Ltd, the nominal code is 5001; enter this and press enter. (Pressing function key F4 will show on screen a list of nominal account codes. The up and down arrow keys – or 'Pg Up' and 'Pg Dn' keys – can be used to move the highlight to the correct account. Enter is pressed to accept the selected account.) Note that the name of the nominal account used shows at the top of the screen below the name of the supplier.
- The next column is 'Dep' (department); press enter to miss this out.
- In the 'Details' column can be entered Software (in this first transaction), or Hardware. Alternatively, the items on the invoice can be described (in up to 19 characters). Press enter.
- In the 'Nett Amt' column enter the amount before VAT: for this first transaction it is £500. Press enter.

- In the 'Tc' (tax code) column, key in T1 and press enter. VAT will be calculated and displayed at the standard rate of 17½ per cent. (Other tax codes available are T0 for zero-rated and T2 for exempt goods.) Function key F9 can also be used to input the T1 tax code. Press enter.
- Note that the batch total (top right-hand side of the screen) shows the total (value of goods, plus VAT) of the screen transactions.
- The cursor will now be at the start of the next line and you should enter the other credit purchases of Richard Brown's business.
- When all the other transactions have been entered, ensure that the cursor is on a blank line, and press [ESC]. The prompt "Do you want to: Post Edit Abandon" appears. If all the details are correct, select Post and press enter. The data files will now be updated. (If any items need to be edited, move the cursor by using the arrow keys, amend the details, press enter, and then move the cursor back to a clear line before pressing [ESC].)
- Press [ESC] twice to return to the purchase ledger sub-menu

Reports

The following reports can be displayed on screen, printed or filed on disk:

- Day book, showing purchases invoices
- Transaction history (for each account) – an asterisk against a money amount indicates that it has not yet been paid
- Account balances (aged) – after the first screen use the [→] key to display the aged balances

Select each in turn and follow the screen prompts. Press C if you wish to alter the specifications for the listing from those displayed on the screen. Press enter to move the cursor over the options. (If the data files were larger than those created so far, we would need to be more selective in order to avoid being inundated with information.) To produce a printout, key in P when the cursor reaches the "Display, Print or File" box. Continue to press enter to reach the bottom of the screen and print.

Do ensure that you print out the day book. When you have finished with reports, press [ESC] twice to return to the main menu.

Trial balance

Choose [Nominal Ledger] from the main menu, and then [Trial Balance] which can be displayed on screen, or printed (key in P) as follows:

Ref	*Account Name*	*Debit*	*Credit*
2100	CREDITORS CONTROL ACCOUNT		3348.77
2201	PURCHASES VAT CONTROL ACCOUNT	498.77	
5000	HARDWARE PURCHASES	1390.00	
5001	SOFTWARE PURCHASES	1460.00	
		3348.77	3348.77

Note that, instead of showing the balance of the account of each creditor, a total of all suppliers' accounts is shown under the heading *Creditors Control Account*. Control accounts (see Chapter Nineteen) are quite common in business accounts, and are used where there is a need to show a total for a ledger section. *Purchases VAT Control Account* shows the amount of Value Added Tax on purchases – the amount of VAT is recorded automatically as each transaction is entered. (A separate *Sales VAT Control Account* is used to record the VAT on sales, as shown in the next section.)

4 Sales ledger

Details of credit customers

The following customers have asked Richard Brown, the owner of Computer Shop Limited, to open credit accounts for them:

Customer's name and address and credit limit (decided by Richard Brown)	*For your use - account number or short name**
Able, Baker & Clark Orchard House The Green St Peters Mereford MR3 8AK Credit limit £1000	201 or ABLE
Hitech Trading Co Unit 16 Factory Estate Eveshore MR10 8PW Credit limit £750	202 or HITECH
Jones & Co Ltd 123 High Street Mereford MR1 2DB Credit limit £500	203 or JONES
Sixth Form College Whittington Avenue Mereford MR2 7QH Credit limit £1000	204 or SIXTH
Teleservice 78 Bruton Road Mereford MR2 4PT Credit limit £500	205 or TELE
Wyvern County Council County Hall Eveshore Road Mereford MR4 8AP Credit limit £2500	206 or WCC

* Note: With the Sage programs, any combination of up to six numbers and/or letters – selected by the user – identify each sales ledger (and purchases ledger) account.

Opening accounts in the sales ledger

- From the main menu, select [Sales Ledger]; press enter.
- From the sales ledger menu, select [Customer Details]; press enter.
- Key in the first account number, 201, or the short name, ABLE. Follow the same procedure as with purchase ledger. Remember to key in the credit limit for each customer.
- After the customer details have been entered, return to the main menu by pressing [ESC] twice.

Sales account in the nominal ledger

Two separate sales accounts are to be opened in the nominal ledger, one for hardware sales, the other for software sales. Follow the same procedure as for opening purchases accounts. The sales accounts to be opened are numbered:

4000 Hardware sales

4001 Software sales

Return to the main menu by pressing [ESC] three times.

Using the sales ledger

Richard Brown's business, Computer Shop Ltd, has the following credit sales transactions for his first month in business (all sales are subject to VAT):

January	
6	Sold software £100 to Able, Baker & Clark, invoice no 1001
10	Sold software £300 to Teleservice, invoice no 1002
13	Sold hardware £600 to Sixth Form College, invoice no 1003
15	Sold software £125 to Jones & Co Ltd, invoice no 1004
17	Sold hardware £700 to Wyvern County Council, invoice no 1005
20	Sold software £50 to Hitech Trading Co, invoice no 1006
23	Sold software £125 to Teleservice, invoice no 1007
24	Sold hardware £450 to Sixth Form College, invoice no 1008
27	Sold software £130 to Able, Baker & Clark, invoice no 1009

These transactions are entered to the sales ledger in a similar way as purchases are entered in the purchases ledger:

- Select [Sales Ledger] from the main menu; press enter.
- Select [Batched Data Entry]; press enter.
- Select [Sales Invoices]; press enter, and the data entry screen now appears.
- Enter the transactions in a similar way as purchases are recorded in the purchases ledger.
- When all transactions have been entered, press [ESC] and, at the prompt, select Post and press enter: the data files will now be updated.
- Press [ESC] to return to the sales ledger sub-menu.

Note: When the second entry for Sixth Form College is made (24 January), a red warning box appears on screen as follows:

Account credit limit will be exceeded Credit limit is 1000.00

Press enter to over-ride the warning and remove the box from the screen, you are now able to continue with data entry.

Reports

The following reports can be displayed on screen, printed or filed on disk:

- Day book, showing sales invoices
- Transaction history (for each account) – an asterisk indicates items that have not yet been paid
- Account balances (aged) – after the first screen use the [→] key to display the aged balances
- Statements

Ensure that you print out the day book.

For sales ledger, an aged analysis of debtor balances is particularly useful as a management report in order to see the amounts owing analysed in terms of 'current, 30 days, 60 days, 90 days, older'. Overdue debts can be identified and action taken to chase for payment.

Statements can be printed on commercially available forms: they can then be dispatched to the customers.

Press [ESC] twice to return to the main menu.

Trial balance

Choose [Nominal Ledger] from the main menu, and display or print the trial balance which now appears as:

Ref	*Account Name*	*Debit*	*Credit*
1100	DEBTORS CONTROL ACCOUNT	3031.51	
2100	CREDITORS CONTROL ACCOUNT		3348.77
2200	SALES VAT CONTROL ACCOUNT		451.51
2201	PURCHASES VAT CONTROL ACCOUNT	498.77	
4000	HARDWARE SALES		1750.00
4001	SOFTWARE SALES		830.00
5000	HARDWARE PURCHASES	1390.00	
5001	SOFTWARE PURCHASES	1460.00	
		6380.28	6380.28

Note that the *Debtors Control Account* totals the individual debtor balances; the *Sales VAT* and *Purchases VAT Control Accounts* show the Value Added Tax on sales and purchases respectively.

5 Recording receipts and payments

All receipts and payments pass through nominal account no 1200 'Bank Account': this is already open in the nominal ledger.

Receipts

Richard Brown's business has the following receipts from customers in the first month:

January

15	Received a cheque for £117.50 from Able, Baker & Clark
20	Received a cheque for £352.50 from Teleservice
24	Received a cheque for £400.00 from Sixth Form College
30	Received a cheque for £146.88 from Jones & Co Ltd

These receipts are entered as follows:

- Choose [Sales Ledger] from the main menu, and then [Receipts].
- Press enter to accept the nominal code of Bank (account no 1200).
- The data entry screen requires the account reference of the debtor, date of payment, cheque number (press enter if not giving a number), and the amount of the cheque.
- The screen now displays the outstanding transactions on the debtors account (or the first ten transactions, if there are more). At the bottom of the screen is asked "Method of Payment: Automatic Manual" with the cursor positioned over the default of Automatic.

Automatic allocation

This goes through the transactions in numerical order and pays off outstanding invoices until either the amount of the receipt reaches zero or there are no more invoices to pay off. If there is insufficient money to pay off an invoice in full, the remaining money will be used to partially pay the invoice. Press [ESC] if you are satisfied with the allocations made, and then press enter at the prompt "Do you want to: Post Edit Abandon" to post the receipts.

Manual allocation

This is selected in order to allocate payment to a particular invoice, either in full or partially. Simply move the cursor up or down by using the arrow keys. Now select one of the four payment options: 'Full, Part, Discount, or Cancel'. If part payment is selected, the amount needs to be keyed in. Once the allocations have been made, press [ESC], and then press enter at the prompt "Do you want to: Post Edit Abandon" to post the receipts.

- Use Automatic allocation (on this occasion) to post the receipts.
- After posting receipts, return to the main menu by pressing [ESC] twice.

Payments

Richard Brown makes the following payments to suppliers in the first month:

January	
22	Paid Pratt & Co Ltd a cheque for £235.00, cheque no 860005
27	Paid Axis Supplies Ltd a cheque for £587.50, cheque no 860006
31	Paid Bell Computers Ltd a cheque for £705.00, cheque no 860009

These payments are entered as follows:

- Select [Purchase Ledger] from the main menu, and then [Payments].
- Press enter to accept the nominal code of 'Bank'.
- At the data entry screen, follow the same procedure as for receipts (enter the cheque number).
- Choose between either automatic or manual allocation, and post the payments.
- Return to the main menu by pressing [ESC] twice.

Trial balance

Choose [Nominal Ledger] from the main menu, and display or print the trial balance which now appears as:

Ref	*Account Name*	*Debit*	*Credit*
1100	DEBTORS CONTROL ACCOUNT	2014.63	
1200	BANK CURRENT ACCOUNT		510.62
2100	CREDITORS CONTROL ACCOUNT		1821.27
2200	SALES VAT CONTROL ACCOUNT		451.51
2201	PURCHASES VAT CONTROL ACCOUNT	498.77	
4000	HARDWARE SALES		1750.00
4001	SOFTWARE SALES		830.00
5000	HARDWARE PURCHASES	1390.00	
5001	SOFTWARE PURCHASES	1460.00	
		5363.40	5363.40

Note that the bank is overdrawn.

6 Recording returned goods

Most computer accounting systems do not use separate purchases returns and sales returns accounts to record returned goods. Instead, they credit purchases account with purchases returns, and debit sales with sales returns.

Purchases returns

Richard Brown's business has the following purchases returns in the first month:

January

20 Returned software to Axis Supplies Ltd for £50, plus VAT, and received a credit note reference CN251

31 Returned hardware to Granta Trading Co Ltd for £120, plus VAT, and received a credit note reference 8524

These are entered as follows:

- Choose [Purchases Ledger] from the main menu, then [Batched Data Entry].
- From the sub-menu, select [Purchase Credit Notes].
- The data entry screen is similar to that for purchases invoices.
- When the entries have been recorded, press [ESC] and post the transactions.
- Press [ESC] three times to return to the main menu.

Sales returns

Richard Brown's business has the following sales returns in the first month:

January

24 Wyvern County Council returns hardware £300, plus VAT; credit note no. CN101

27 Hitech Trading Co returns software £50, plus VAT; credit note no. CN102

These are entered as follows:

- Choose [Sales Ledger] from the main menu, then [Batched Data Entry].
- From the sub-menu, select [Sales Credit Notes].
- The data entry screen is similar to that for sales invoices.
- When the entries have been recorded, press [ESC] and post the transactions.
- Press [ESC] twice to return to the main menu.

Trial balance

Choose [Nominal Ledger] from the main menu, and display or print the trial balance which now appears as:

Ref	*Account Name*	*Debit*	*Credit*
1100	DEBTORS CONTROL ACCOUNT	1603.38	
1200	BANK CURRENT ACCOUNT		510.62
2100	CREDITORS CONTROL ACCOUNT		1621.52
2200	SALES VAT CONTROL ACCOUNT		390.26
2201	PURCHASES VAT CONTROL ACCOUNT	469.02	
4000	HARDWARE SALES		1450.00
4001	SOFTWARE SALES		780.00
5000	HARDWARE PURCHASES	1270.00	
5001	SOFTWARE PURCHASES	1410.00	
		4752.40	4752.40

7 Other nominal account transactions

The standard default layout for nominal ledger comprises many accounts which are already numbered. In this section we will enter transactions to expenses accounts, capital and loans, and fixed assets.

Expenses

Richard Brown pays the following business expenses by cheque in his first month:

January

10	Paid travelling expenses (nominal account no 7400) £25.00, cheque no 860003
19	Paid staff salaries (account no 7003) £645.00, cheque no 860004
20	Paid stationery (account no 7504) £70.50 *including* VAT (see below), cheque no 860007
31	Paid shop rent (account no 7100) £176.25 *including* VAT (see below), cheque no 860008

The various expenses of the business, eg salaries, rent, electricity, etc do not usually pass through the purchase ledger. They are paid direct by cheque, and so the double-entry book-keeping is:
— *debit* appropriate expense account (with amount excluding VAT, if any)
— *debit* VAT account (with amount of VAT, if any)
— *credit* bank account

To see the nominal ledger accounts which are already open on your data disk:

- From the main menu select [Nominal Ledger], then [Nominal Account Structure], then [Account Names].
- Press function key F4 to see the existing accounts: use the arrow keys – or 'Pg Up' and 'Pg Dn' keys – to move up or down the list.
- Press [ESC] to remove the display.
- Press [ESC] twice to return to the main menu.

Where expenses are paid by cheque, transactions are entered by using the bank payments routine, as follows:

- From the main menu choose [Nominal Ledger], then [Bank Transactions], then [Bank Payments].
- At the data entry screen, press enter to accept the nominal account no 1200 for Bank. Enter the nominal account number for the expense and check that the correct account name shows towards the top of the screen.
- Enter the other details: note that the VAT tax code for travelling expenses will be T0 (zero-rated), while that for salaries will be T9 (outside the scope of VAT). With stationery and rent, which are subject to VAT at 17½ per cent, the amount paid *includes* VAT. The program can calculate the VAT amount:
  — enter the amount of the cheque (eg £70.50 for stationery) in the 'Nett Amnt' column
  — enter the tax code in the 'Tc' column, as T1 (or use function key F9)
  — in the 'Tax Amnt' column, press function key F10
  — the program will deduct tax from the figure in the net column and show the changed net value and amount of VAT
- When the entries have been recorded, press [ESC] and post the transactions.
- Press [ESC] three times to return to the main menu.

Note: Some business expenses may be made through purchase ledger if a creditor's account is opened. For example, a business may have an account open in the name of the local garage to which petrol, servicing and repair costs are credited, with settlement being made at the end of each month.

Capital and loans

Richard Brown's business, Computer Shop Ltd, has the following capital and loans transactions:

January

1 Started in business with ordinary share capital (nominal account no 3000) of £10,000, received by cheque

10 Received a loan (account no 2300) of £5,000, by cheque

These are entered through the bank receipts routine, as follows:

- From the main menu choose [Nominal Ledger], then [Bank Transactions], then [Bank Receipts]; press enter.
- At the data entry screen, enter the transactions: use the tax code T9 for both ordinary share capital and the loan (both transactions are outside the scope of VAT).
- When the entries have been recorded, press [ESC] and post the transactions.
- Press [ESC] three times to return to the main menu.

Fixed assets

Richard Brown's business buys the following fixed assets:

January

4 Bought office equipment (nominal account no 0030) for £2,350 *including* VAT, paying by cheque no 860001

8 Bought a delivery van (nominal account no 0050) for £9,400 *including* VAT, paying by cheque no 860002

These are entered in a similar way to expenses (see previous page) using the bank payments routine. Note that both of these purchases *include* VAT at the standard rate (tax code T1), so use function key F10 (as described in the expenses section above) to calculate the amount net of tax.

Trial balance

Choose [Nominal Ledger] from the main menu, and display or print the trial balance which now appears as:

Ref	*Account Name*	*Debit*	*Credit*
0030	OFFICE EQUIPMENT	2000.00	
0050	MOTOR VEHICLES	8000.00	
1100	DEBTORS CONTROL ACCOUNT	1603.38	
1200	BANK CURRENT ACCOUNT	1822.63	
2100	CREDITORS CONTROL ACCOUNT		1621.52
2200	SALES VAT CONTROL ACCOUNT		390.26
2201	PURCHASES VAT CONTROL ACCOUNT	2255.77	
2300	LOANS		5000.00
3000	ORDINARY SHARES		10000.00
4000	HARDWARE SALES		1450.00
4001	SOFTWARE SALES		780.00
5000	HARDWARE PURCHASES	1270.00	
5001	SOFTWARE PURCHASES	1410.00	
7003	STAFF SALARIES	645.00	
7100	RENT	150.00	
7400	TRAVELLING	25.00	
7504	OFFICE STATIONERY	60.00	
		19241.78	19241.78

If your trial balance fails to agree with that shown on the previous page, choose [Utilities] from the main menu, and then [Audit Trail]. Print out all the transactions for January and 'tick' them off against the transactions in this Case Study.

8 Saving data files to disk

As you worked through the chapter, each time you posted transactions the data files were updated, either on your data disk or on the hard disk. There is no requirement to save data at regular intervals during the processing. However, in a business, it makes good sense to save data at regular intervals throughout the day to a back-up disk. The techniques of backing-up have already been discussed in Chapter 10.11. With accounting data, we cannot consider to be correctly posted until it is backed-up on a separate disk.

9 Case Study summary

- ❑ We have used a computer accounting program to:
  - open debtors' accounts in the sales ledger
  - open creditors' accounts in the purchases ledger
  - enter business transactions in the sales ledger, purchases ledger and nominal ledger

- ❑ We have seen some of the reports that can be produced:
  - day books
  - transaction history for each account
  - statements of account for debtors
  - aged account balances
  - trial balance
  - audit trail

- ❑ It has only been possible to look at the main features of computer accounting. It may be that you will wish to investigate other aspects of the program. In addition you may have the opportunity to use other computer accounting programs, eg
  - invoicing
  - stock control
  - payroll

In the next chapter we will use the trial balance – whether produced by hand or computer – to produce the year-end accounts – or final accounts, as they are often called – for a business. Some computer accounting programs allow the production of final accounts from a trial balance.

10 Exercises

These exercises cover the transactions of Richard Brown's business, Computer Shop Ltd for the month of February. Before commencing, you must ensure that you have worked through the Case Study, recording the transactions for January, and ensure that your trial balance agrees with that shown on page 144.

Restart the program and use the data from January's transactions; enter the date at the end of February, eg 280295; now attempt the exercises which follow.

1. Open new accounts in the purchases ledger for:

- Software Supplies
  Unit 10
  Newtown Trading Estate
  Newtown NT1 7AJ
  Account no 107 or SOFT

- Trade Tech Ltd
  45-50 The High Road
  Dunton DT4 7AL
  Account no 108 or TRADE

2. • Enter the following credit purchases transactions for the month (all subject to VAT at $17^{1/2}$ per cent):

February	
4	Bought software £150 from Software Supplies, invoice no. AB452
5	Bought hardware £220 from Trade Tech Ltd, invoice no. H3974
7	Bought hardware £550 from Granta Trading Co Ltd, invoice no. T7849
10	Bought software £200 from Axis Supplies Ltd, invoice no. 1529
15	Bought hardware £320 from Kingsway Technical Ltd, invoice no. 901072
18	Bought hardware £525 from Bell Computers Ltd, invoice no. 1149
20	Bought software £110 from Computer Supplies Ltd, invoice no. 10105
23	Bought hardware £610 from Granta Trading Co Ltd, invoice no. T7927
25	Bought software £500 from Software Supplies, invoice no. AB641

- Print the day book for February, showing purchases invoices (transaction numbers 38 to 46)
- Print the trial balance

3. Open new accounts in the sales ledger for:

- Adams & Co
  The Old Rectory
  Church Street
  Eveshore MR8 7PP
  Account no 207 or ADAMS; credit limit £500

- Stone, Wall Ltd
  Builders Merchants
  Station Yard
  Mereford MR2 1BT
  Account no 208 or STONE; credit limit £750

4. • Enter the following credit sales transactions for the month (all subject to VAT at $17^{1/2}$ per cent):

February	
2	Sold software £350 to Adams & Co, invoice no. 1010
4	Sold hardware £1,100 to Wyvern County Council, invoice no. 1011
5	Sold software £425 to Stone, Wall Ltd, invoice no. 1012
8	Sold hardware £750 to Teleservice, invoice no. 1013
10	Sold hardware £630 to Sixth Form College, invoice no. 1014
12	Sold software £320 to Hitech Trading Co, invoice no. 1015
16	Sold hardware £450 to Sixth Form College, invoice no. 1016
20	Sold software £250 to Able, Baker & Clark, invoice no. 1017
24	Sold hardware £850 to Teleservice, invoice no. 1018

- Print the day book for February, showing sales invoices (transaction numbers 47 to 55)
- Print the trial balance

5. • Enter the following returns for the month (all subject to VAT at $17^1/_2$ per cent):

February	
	Purchases returns
18	Returned software to Software Supplies for £50, and received a credit note reference 3219
27	Returned hardware to Kingsway Technical Ltd for £220, and received a credit note reference CN681
	Sales returns
20	Sixth Form College returns hardware £400; credit note no. CN103 issued
26	Able, Baker & Clark return software £110; credit note no. CN104 issued

• Print the trial balance

6. • Enter the following receipts and payments for the month:

February	
	Receipts
4	Received a cheque for £152.75 from Able, Baker & Clark
19	Received a cheque for £411.25 from Adams & Co
20	Received a cheque for £100.00 from Teleservice
28	Received a cheque for £1,762.50 from Wyvern County Council
	Payments
5	Paid Axis Supplies Ltd a cheque for £176.25, cheque no 860010
10	Paid Kingsway Technical Ltd a cheque for £499.38, cheque no 860013
18	Paid Pratt & Co Ltd a cheque for £146.88, cheque no 860015
28	Paid Computer Supplies Ltd a cheque for £229.13, cheque no 860016

• Print the trial balance

7. • Enter the following nominal account transactions for the month:

February	
	Payments
6	Paid stationery £152.75 *including* VAT, cheque no 860011
10	Paid advertising £293.75 *including* VAT, cheque no 860012
15	Paid travelling expenses £30.00 (zero-rated – use tax code T0), cheque no 860014
28	Paid staff salaries £650.00 (outside the scope of VAT – use tax code T9), cheque no 860017
28	Bought office equipment £587.50 *including* VAT, cheque no 860018
	Receipts
15	Received a loan £1,500 (outside the scope of VAT – use tax code T9)

• Print the trial balance

8. Print out the aged account balances from the sales ledger at 1 March. Which account should be brought to the attention of Richard Brown, the owner of Computer Shop Ltd? What action would you advise him to take?

11 Final Accounts

So far we have looked at the format of business accounts and the recording of different types of transactions. All that we have covered is usually carried out by the book-keeper. We will now see how the financial accountant takes to a further stage the information prepared by the book-keeper. The financial accountant will use the information from the accounting system, which is summarised in the trial balance (see Chapter Five), in order to produce the *final accounts* of a business. For most businesses, the final accounts, which are produced at the end of each financial year, comprise:

- trading account
- profit and loss account
- balance sheet

The final accounts can be produced more often than once a year in order to give information to the owner(s) on how the business is progressing. However, it is customary to produce annual or final accounts for the benefit of the Inland Revenue, bank manager and other interested parties. Limited companies (see Chapter Twenty-four) have a legal responsibility to report to their shareholders each year, while non-trading organisations (such as clubs and societies – see Chapter Twenty-one) report financial results to the members annually.

Final accounts can be presented in a *vertical format,* or a *horizontal format.* In the chapter we shall look at both; however, the vertical format is more common nowadays and is used as the standard format in this book.

When preparing final accounts it is important to distinguish between *capital expenditure* and *revenue expenditure* – this topic is dealt with in Section 11.9.

11.1 Final accounts and the trial balance

The starting point for preparing final accounts is the trial balance prepared by the book-keeper. All the figures recorded on the trial balance are used in the final accounts. The trading account and the profit and loss account are both 'accounts' in terms of double-entry book-keeping. This means that amounts recorded in these accounts must also be recorded elsewhere in the book-keeping system. By contrast, the balance sheet is not an account, but is simply a statement of account balances remaining after the trading and profit and loss accounts have been prepared.

To help us with the preparation of final accounts we will use the trial balance, shown on the next page, which has been produced by a book-keeper at the end of a firm's financial year.

Trial Balance of Wyvern Wholesalers as at 31 December 19-1

	Dr.	Cr.
	£	£
Sales		250,000
Purchases	156,000	
Sales returns	5,400	
Purchases returns		7,200
Discount received		2,500
Discount allowed	3,700	
Stock 1 January 19-1	12,350	
Salaries	46,000	
Electricity and gas	3,000	
Rent and rates	2,000	
Sundry expenses	4,700	
Premises	100,000	
Equipment	30,000	
Vehicles	21,500	
Debtors	23,850	
Bank overdraft		851
Cash	125	
Creditors		15,516
Capital		110,000
Drawings	10,442	
Long-term loan		33,000
	419,067	419,067

Note: stock at 31 December 19-1 was valued at £16,300

You will see that the trial balance includes the stock value at the start of the year, while the end-of-year valuation is noted after the trial balance. For the purposes of financial accounting, the stock of goods for resale is valued by the business (and often verified by the auditor) at the end of each financial year, and the valuation is entered into the book-keeping system (see Section 11.6).

We will present the final accounts

- *before adjustments* for items such as accruals, prepayments, depreciation of fixed assets, bad debts written off, and provision for bad debts (each of which will be dealt with in Chapters Twelve to Fourteen)
- in *vertical format,* ie in columnar form (the alternative layout – *horizontal format* – is looked at in Section 11.7)

In Section 11.6 we will look at the double-entry book-keeping for amounts entered in the trading and profit and loss accounts.

11.2 Trading account

The main activity of a trading business is to buy goods at one price and then to sell the same goods at a higher price. The difference between the two prices represents a profit known as *gross profit.* Instead of calculating the gross profit on each item bought and sold, we have seen how the book-keeping system stores up the totals of all transactions for the year in purchases account and sales account. Further, any goods returned are recorded in purchases returns account and sales returns account.

At the end of the financial year (which can end at any date – it doesn't have to be the calendar year) the total of purchases and sales accounts, together with purchases returns and sales returns, are used to form the trading account. It is also necessary to take note of the value of stock of goods for resale held at the beginning and end of the financial year.

The trading account is set out as:

TRADING ACCOUNT OF WYVERN WHOLESALERS
FOR THE YEAR ENDED 31 DECEMBER 19-1

	£	£	£
Sales			250,000
Less Sales returns			5,400
Net sales (or *turnover*)			244,600
Opening stock (1 January 19-1)		12,350	
Purchases	156,000		
Carriage in	-		
Less Purchases returns	7,200		
Net purchases		148,800	
		161,150	
Less Closing stock (31 December 19-1)		16,300	
Cost of Goods Sold			144,850
Gross profit			99,750

Notes:

- Sales and purchases only include items in which the business trades – items to be kept for use in the business, such as machinery, are not included in sales and purchases but are classified as fixed assets.

- Adjustments are made for the value of stock in the store or warehouse at the beginning and end of the financial year. The opening stock is added to the purchases because it has been sold during the year. The closing stock is deducted from purchases because it has not been sold; it will form the opening stock for the next financial year, when it will be added to next year's figure for purchases.

- The figure for *cost of goods sold* (often written as *cost of sales*) represents the cost to the business of the goods which have been sold in this financial year. Cost of goods sold is:

  opening stock
  + purchases
  + carriage in (see below)
  – purchases returns
  – closing stock
  = cost of goods sold

- Gross profit is calculated as:

  sales
  – sales returns
  = net sales
  – cost of goods sold
  = gross profit

  If cost of goods sold is greater than net sales, the business has made a *gross loss*.

- 'Carriage in' is the expense to the business of having purchases delivered (eg if you buy from a mail order company, you often have to pay the post and packing – this is the 'carriage in' cost). The cost of carriage in is added to purchases.

- *Net sales* (often described as *turnover*) is:

  sales
  – sales returns
  = net sales

- *Net purchases* is:

  purchases
  + carriage in
  – purchases returns
  = net purchases

11.3 Profit and loss account

In the profit and loss account are listed the various running expenses (or *revenue expenditure*) of the business. The total of running expenses is deducted from gross profit to give *net profit* for the year. Net profit is an important figure: it shows the profitability of the business after all expenses, and how much has been earned by the business for the owner(s). It is on this profit, after certain adjustments, that the tax liability will be based.

The profit and loss account follows on from the trading account and is set out as follows:

PROFIT AND LOSS ACCOUNT OF WYVERN WHOLESALERS
FOR THE YEAR ENDED 31 DECEMBER 19-1

	£	£	£
Gross profit			99,750
Add Discount received			2,500
			102,250
Less:			
Discount allowed		3,700	
Salaries		46,000	
Electricity and gas		3,000	
Rent and rates		2,000	
Sundry expenses		4,700	
			59,400
Net profit			42,850

Notes:

- The various running expenses shown in the profit and loss account can be listed to suit the needs of a particular business: the headings used here are for illustrative purposes only.
- Amounts of income are also included in profit and loss account, eg discount received in the example; these are added to gross profit.
- The net profit is the amount the business earned for the owner(s) during the year; it is important to note that this is *not* the amount by which the cash/bank balance has increased during the year.
- If the total of expenses exceeds gross profit (and other income), the business has made a *net loss*.
- Drawings by the owner(s) are *not* listed as an expense in profit and loss account – instead, they are deducted from capital (see balance sheet below).
- If the owner of the business has taken goods for his or her own use, the amount should be deducted from purchases and added to drawings (see also Chapter 12.6).

The trading account and the profit and loss account are usually combined together, rather than being shown as separate accounts, in the following form:

TRADING AND PROFIT AND LOSS ACCOUNT OF WYVERN WHOLESALERS
FOR THE YEAR ENDED 31 DECEMBER 19-1

	£	£	£
Sales			250,000
Less Sales returns			5,400
Net sales			244,600
Opening stock (1 January 19-1)		12,350	
Purchases	156,000		
Carriage in	–		
Less Purchases returns	7,200		
Net purchases		148,800	
		161,150	
Less Closing stock (31 December 19-1)		16,300	
Cost of Goods Sold			144,850
Gross profit			99,750
Add Discount received			2,500
			102,250
Less:			
Discount allowed		3,700	
Salaries		46,000	
Electricity and gas		3,000	
Rent and rates		2,000	
Sundry expenses		4,700	
			59,400
Net profit			42,850

The trading and profit and loss account forms part of the double-entry book-keeping system, and we will look at the transactions to be recorded in the accounts later in this chapter – see Section 11.6.

The above presentation is in vertical format, ie in columnar form, but the trading and profit and loss account can also be set out in a horizontal presentation – see Section 11.7.

Service sector businesses

You should note that when preparing the final accounts of a service sector business – such as a secretarial agency, solicitors, estate agents, doctor – a trading account will not be prepared because, instead of trading in goods, the business supplies services. Thus the final accounts will consist of a profit and loss account and balance sheet. The profit and loss account, instead of starting with gross profit, will commence with the income from the business activity, such as 'fees', 'income from clients', 'charges', 'work done'. Other items of income, such as discount received, are added, and the expenses are then listed and deducted to give the net profit, or net loss, for the accounting period. An outline example is as follows:

PROFIT AND LOSS ACCOUNT OF WYVERN SECRETARIAL AGENCY
FOR THE YEAR ENDED 31 DECEMBER 19-1

	£
Income from clients	100,000
Less expenses	75,000
Net profit	25,000

11.4 Balance sheet

The trading and profit and loss account shows two types of profit – gross profit and net profit, respectively – *for the financial year* (or such other time period as may be chosen by the business). A balance sheet, by contrast, shows the state of the business *at one moment in time*. It lists the *assets* and the *liabilities* at a particular date, but is *not* part of the double-entry book-keeping system.

The balance sheet of Wyvern Wholesalers, using the figures from the trial balance on page 149, is as follows:

BALANCE SHEET OF WYVERN WHOLESALERS
AS AT 31 DECEMBER 19-1

	£	£	£
Fixed Assets			
Premises			100,000
Equipment			30,000
Vehicles			21,500
			151,500
Current Assets			
Stock		16,300	
Debtors		23,850	
Cash		125	
		40,275	
Less Current Liabilities			
Creditors	15,516		
Bank overdraft	851		
		16,367	
Working Capital			23,908
			175,408
Less Long-term Liabilities			
Loan			33,000
NET ASSETS			142,408
FINANCED BY:			
Capital			
Opening capital			110,000
Add net profit			42,850
			152,850
Less drawings			10,442
			142,408

Notes:

- **Assets** are items or amounts owned or owed to the business, and are normally listed in increasing order of liquidity, ie the most permanent assets are listed first.

  Fixed assets are long-term assets, and are divided between *tangible fixed assets,* which have material substance such as premises, equipment, vehicles, and *intangible fixed assets,* such as goodwill (see below).

  Current assets are short-term assets which continually change from day-to-day (eg stock, debtors, bank – if not overdrawn, cash).

- **Intangible fixed assets** (not shown in the balance sheet above) will appear on some balance sheets, and are listed before the tangible fixed assets. An *intangible asset* does not have material substance, but belongs to the business and has value. A common example of an intangible fixed asset is *goodwill,* which is where a business has bought another business and paid an agreed amount for the existing reputation and customer connections (the *goodwill*). Other examples are the value of brand names (eg Coca-Cola) and patents and trade marks.

- **Liabilities** are items or amounts owed by the business.

  Current liabilities are amounts owing at the balance sheet date and due for repayment within 12 months or less (eg creditors, bank overdraft).

  Long-term liabilities are borrowings where repayment is due in more than 12 months (eg loans, bank loans).

- **Capital** is money owed by the business to the owner. It is usual practice to show on the balance sheet the owner's investment at the start of the year *plus* net profit for the year *less* drawings for the year; this equals the owner's investment at the end of the year, ie at the balance sheet date.

- **Working capital** is the excess of current assets over current liabilities. Without working capital, a business cannot continue to operate.

Significance of the balance sheet

The balance sheet shows the assets used by the business and how they have been financed. The concept may be expressed as a formula:

Fixed assets
\+ Working capital
\- Long-term liabilities
= Net assets
= Capital

Thus it can be seen that the vertical presentation balance sheet agrees the figure for net assets (£142,408, in the example), with capital. An alternative style of balance sheet – the horizontal presentation – is shown in Section 11.7.

11.5 Preparation of final accounts from a trial balance

The trial balance contains the basic figures necessary to prepare the final accounts but, as we shall see in the next section, the figures are transferred from the double-entry accounts of the business. Nevertheless, the trial balance is a suitable summary from which to prepare the final accounts. The information needed for the preparation of each of the final accounts needs to be picked out from the trial balance; you will find the following guidelines helpful:

- go through the trial balance and write against the items the final account in which each appears
- 'tick' each figure as it is used – each item from the trial balance appears in the final accounts *once only*
- the year-end (closing) stock figure is not listed in the trial balance, but is shown as a note; the closing stock appears *twice* in the final accounts – firstly in the trading account, and secondly in the balance sheet (as a current asset).

If this routine is followed with the trial balance of Wyvern Wholesalers, it will then appear as shown on the next page:

Trial balance of Wyvern Wholesalers as at 31 December 19-1

	Dr.	Cr.		
	£	£		
Sales		250,000	*T*	✔
Purchases	156,000		*T*	✔
Sales returns	5,400		*T*	✔
Purchases returns		7,200	*T*	✔
Discount received		2,500	*P & L (income)*	✔
Discount allowed	3,700		*P & L (expense)*	✔
Stock 1 January 19-1	12,350		*T*	✔
Salaries	46,000		*P & L (expense)*	✔
Electricity and gas	3,000		*P & L (expense)*	✔
Rent and rates	2,000		*P & L (expense)*	✔
Sundry expenses	4,700		*P & L (expense)*	✔
Premises	100,000		*BS (fixed asset)*	✔
Equipment	30,000		*BS (fixed asset)*	✔
Vehicles	21,500		*BS (fixed asset)*	✔
Debtors	23,850		*BS (current asset)*	✔
Bank overdraft		851	*BS (current liability)*	✔
Cash	125		*BS (current asset)*	✔
Creditors		15,516	*BS (current liability)*	✔
Capital		110,000	*BS (capital)*	✔
Drawings	10,442		*BS (capital)*	✔
Long-term loan		33,000	*BS (long-term liability)*	✔
	419,067	419,067		
Stock at 31 December 19-1 was valued at £16,300			*T*	✔
			BS (current asset)	✔

Note: T = trading account; P & L = profit and loss account; BS = balance sheet

11.6 Double-entry book-keeping and the final accounts

We have already noted earlier in this chapter that the trading and profit and loss account forms part of the double-entry book-keeping system. Therefore, each amount recorded in this account must have an opposite entry elsewhere in the accounting system. In preparing the trading and profit and loss account we are, in effect, emptying each account that has been storing up a record of the transactions of the business during the course of the financial year and transferring it to the trading and profit and loss account.

Trading account

In the trading account of Wyvern Wholesalers the balance of purchases account will be transferred as follows (*debit* trading account; *credit* purchases account):

Purchases Account

Dr.			Cr.		
19-1		£	19-1		£
31 Dec.	Balance b/d (ie total for year)	156,000	31 Dec.	Trading account	156,000

The account now has a nil balance and is ready to receive the transactions for next year.

The balances of sales, sales returns, and purchases returns accounts will be cleared to nil in a similar way and the amounts transferred to trading account, as debits or credits as appropriate.

Stock account, however, is dealt with differently. Stock is valued for financial accounting purposes at the end of each year (it is also likely to be valued more regularly in order to provide management information). Only the annual stock valuation is recorded on stock account, and the account is not used at any other time. After the book-keeper has extracted the trial balance, but *before* preparation of the trading account, the stock account appears as follows:

Stock Account

Dr.			Cr.		
19-1		£	19-1		£
31 Dec.	Balance b/d	12,350			

This balance, which is the opening stock valuation for the year, is transferred to the trading account to leave a nil balance, as follows (*debit* trading account; *credit* stock account):

Stock Account

Dr.			Cr.		
19-1		£	19-1		£
31 Dec.	Balance b/d	12,350	31 Dec.	Trading account	12,350

The *closing* stock valuation for the year is now recorded on the account as an asset (*debit* stock account; *credit* trading account):

Stock Account

Dr.			Cr.		
19-1		£	19-1		£
31 Dec.	Balance b/d	12,350	31 Dec.	Trading account	12,350
31 Dec.	Trading account	16,300	31 Dec.	Balance c/d	16,300
19-2					
1 Jan.	Balance b/d	16,300			

The closing stock figure is shown on the balance sheet as a current asset, and will be the opening stock in next year's trading account.

Profit and loss account

Expenses and income items are transferred from the double-entry accounts to the profit and loss account. For example, the salaries account of Wyvern Wholesalers has been storing up information during the year and, at the end of the year, the total is transferred to profit and loss account, as shown on the next page (*debit* profit and loss account; *credit* salaries account):

Salaries Account

Dr.		£			Cr. £
19-1			19-1		
31 Dec.	Balance b/d (ie total for year)	46,000	31 Dec.	Profit and loss account	46,000

The salaries account now has a nil balance and is ready to receive transactions for 19-2, the next financial year.

Net profit

After the profit and loss account has been completed, the amount of net profit (or net loss) is transferred to the owner's capital account. The book-keeping entries are:

- net profit
  —*debit* profit and loss account
  —*credit* capital account
- net loss
  —*debit* capital account
  —*credit* profit and loss account

A net profit increases the owner's stake in the business by adding to capital account, while a net loss decreases the owner's stake.

At the same time the account for drawings, which has been storing up the amount of drawings during the year is also transferred to capital account:

—*debit* capital account
—*credit* drawings account

Thus the total of drawings for the year is debited to capital account.

When these transactions are completed, the capital account for Wyvern Wholesalers appears as:

Capital Account

Dr.		£			Cr. £
19-1			19-1		
31 Dec.	Drawings for year	10,442	31 Dec.	Balance b/d	110,000
31 Dec.	Balance c/d	142,408	31 Dec.	Profit and loss account (net profit for year)	42,850
		152,850			152,850
19-2			19-2		
			1 Jan.	Balance b/d	142,408

Note: It is the balance of capital account at the end of the year, ie £142,408, which forms the total for the capital section of the balance sheet. Whilst this figure could be shown on the balance sheet by itself, it is usual to show capital at the start of the year, with net profit for the year added, and drawings for the year deducted. In this way, the capital account is summarised on the balance sheet.

Balance sheet

Unlike the trading and profit and loss account, the balance sheet is not part of the double-entry accounts. The balance sheet is made up of those accounts which remain with balances after the trading and profit and loss account transfers have been made. Thus it consists of asset and liability accounts, not forgetting the asset of closing stock.

11.7 Horizontal presentation of final accounts

So far in this chapter we have used the *vertical presentation* for setting out the final accounts of a business, ie we have started at the top of the page and worked downwards in columnar or narrative style. An alternative method is the *horizontal presentation,* where each of the financial statements is presented in the format of a two-sided account. The set of final accounts presented earlier would appear, in horizontal style, as follows:

TRADING ACCOUNT OF WYVERN WHOLESALERS
FOR THE YEAR ENDED 31 DECEMBER 19-1

	£	£		£
Opening stock		12,350	Sales	250,000
Purchases	156,000		Less Sales returns	5,400
Carriage in	-		*Net sales*	244,600
Less Purchases returns	7,200			
Net purchases		148,800		
		161,150		
Less Closing stock		16,300		
Cost of Goods Sold		144,850		
Gross profit c/d		99,750		
		244,600		244,600

PROFIT AND LOSS ACCOUNT OF WYVERN WHOLESALERS
FOR THE YEAR ENDED 31 DECEMBER 19-1

	£		£
Discount allowed	3,700	Gross profit b/d	99,750
Salaries	46,000	Discount received	2,500
Electricity and gas	3,000		
Rent and rates	2,000		
Sundry expenses	4,700		
Net profit	42,850		
	102,250		102,250

BALANCE SHEET OF WYVERN WHOLESALERS
AS AT 31 DECEMBER 19-1

	£	£		£	£
Fixed Assets			**Capital**		
Premises		100,000	Opening capital		110,000
Equipment		30,000	Add net profit		42,850
Vehicles		21,500			152,850
		151,500	Less drawings		10,442
Current Assets					142,408
Stock	16,300		**Long-term liabilities**		
Debtors	23,850		Loan		33,000
Cash	125				175,408
		40,275	**Current Liabilities**		
			Creditors	15,516	
			Bank overdraft	851	
					16,367
		191,775			191,775

In your study of Business Accounts you will see both forms of presentation from time-to-time in the accounts of different businesses and organisations. The vertical format is more common nowadays and is used as the standard format in this book. As you will appreciate, both forms of presentation use the same information and, after a while, you will soon be able to 'read' either version.

11.8 Vertical presentation of final accounts – a 'pro-forma'

Many students studying final accounts for the first time find it helpful to be able to follow a set layout, or pro-forma – certainly in the early stages. A sample pro-forma for final accounts is included in Appendix A (page 484). There are some items included that will be covered in later chapters, and the layout will need to be amended to fit the needs of partnership (Chapter Twenty-two) and limited company (Chapter Twenty-four) final accounts.

11.9 Capital expenditure and revenue expenditure

When preparing final accounts it is important to distinguish between *capital expenditure* and *revenue expenditure.*

Capital expenditure can be defined as *expenditure incurred on the purchase, alteration or improvement of fixed assets.* For example, the purchase of a car for use in the business is capital expenditure. Capital expenditure includes the costs of delivering and installing fixed assets, also the legal costs of buying property.

Revenue expenditure is *expenditure incurred on running expenses.* For example, the cost of petrol for the car (above) is revenue expenditure. Included in revenue expenditure are the costs of

- maintaining fixed assets
- administration of the business
- selling and distributing the goods in which the business trades

Capital expenditure is shown on the balance sheet, while revenue expenditure is charged as an expense to the profit and loss account. It is important to classify these types of expenditure correctly in the accounting system. For example, if the cost of the car was shown as an expense in profit and loss account, then net profit would be reduced considerably, or a net loss recorded; meanwhile, the balance sheet would not show the car as a fixed asset – clearly this is incorrect as the business owns the asset.

In some circumstances we must take care to distinguish between capital and revenue expenditure. For example:

- *cost of building an extension to the factory £30,000, which includes £1,000 for repairs to the existing factory*
  —capital expenditure, £29,000
  —revenue expenditure, £1,000 (because it is for repairs to an existing fixed asset)
- *a piece of land has been bought for £20,000, the legal costs are £750*
  —capital expenditure £20,750 (the legal costs are included in the capital expenditure, because they are the cost of acquiring the fixed asset, ie the legal costs are *capitalised*)
- *own employees used to install a new air conditioning system: wages £1,000, materials £1,500*
  —capital expenditure £2,500 (an addition to the property). Note that, in cases such as this, revenue expenditure, ie wages and materials purchases, will need to be reduced to allow for the transfer to capital expenditure.

- *own employees used to repair and redecorate the premises: wages £500, materials £750* —revenue expenditure £1,250 (repairs and redecoration are running expenses)
- *purchase of a new machine £10,000, payment for installation and setting up £250* —capital expenditure £10,250 (costs of installation of a fixed asset are capitalised)

Only by allocating capital and revenue expenditure correctly between the balance sheet and the profit and loss account can the final accounts reflect accurately the state of the business.

11.10 Chapter summary

- ❑ The final accounts of a business comprise:
  - *trading account,* which shows gross profit
  - *profit and loss account,* which shows net profit
  - *balance sheet,* which shows the assets and liabilities of the business at the year-end

  Appendix A (page 484) gives a specimen layout for final accounts.
- ❑ The starting point for the preparation of final accounts is the summary of the information from the accounting records contained in the book-keeper's trial balance.
- ❑ Each item from the trial balance is entered into the final accounts once only.
- ❑ Any notes to the trial balance, such as the closing stock, affect the final accounts in two places.
- ❑ The trading account and profit and loss account form part of the double-entry book-keeping system – amounts entered must be recorded elsewhere in the accounts.
- ❑ The balance sheet is not part of the double-entry system; it lists the assets and liabilities at a particular date.
- ❑ Final accounts can be presented in either a vertical or a horizontal format.
- ❑ *Capital expenditure* is expenditure incurred on the purchase, alteration or improvement of fixed assets.
- ❑ *Revenue expenditure* is expenditure incurred on running expenses.

There is more material to cover in connection with final accounts, and the next few chapters (Twelve to Sixteen) deal with accruals and prepayments, depreciation of fixed assets, bad debts and provision for bad debts, and accounting concepts and stock valuation. In addition the more specialist final accounts of manufacturing businesses (Chapter Twenty-six), partnerships (Chapter Twenty-two), and limited companies (Chapter Twenty-four) will be studied. Final accounts can also be analysed and interpreted (Chapter Twenty-nine) to give the user of the accounts information about the financial state of the business.

Case Study Two follows after the questions at the end of this chapter; it looks at a fully worked example of a handwritten book-keeping system.

11.11 Questions

11.1* The following information has been extracted from the business accounts of Matthew Lloyd for his first year of trading which ended on 31 December 19-8:

	£
Purchases	94,350
Sales	125,890
Stock at 31 December 19-8	5,950
Business rates	4,850
Heating and lighting	2,120
Wages and salaries	10,350
Office equipment	8,500
Motor vehicles	10,750
Debtors	3,950
Bank balance	4,225
Cash	95
Creditors	2,200
Capital at start of year	20,000
Drawings for year	8,900

You are to prepare the trading and profit and loss account of Matthew Lloyd for the year ended 31 December 19-8, together with his balance sheet at that date.

11.2 (a) Complete the table below for each item (1) to (7) indicating with a tick:

(i) whether the item would normally appear in the debit or credit column of the trial balance, and

(ii) in which 'final account' the item would appear at the end of the accounting period.

	(i) TRIAL BALANCE		(ii) FINAL ACCOUNTS		
	Debit	Credit	Trading	Profit/Loss	Balance Sheet
1. Rent paid					
2. Motor van					
3. Sales					
4. Creditors					
5. Purchases					
6. Capital					
7. Salaries					

(b) Name one item not necessarily included in part (a), which could appear more than once in the final accounts at the year-end.

[London East Anglian Group, 1990]

11.3* You are to fill in the missing figures for the following businesses:

	Sales	Opening Stock	Purchases	Closing Stock	Gross Profit	Expenses	Net Profit/ (Loss)*
	£	£	£	£	£	£	£
Business A	20 000	5 000	10 000	3 000	....	4 000	....
Business B	35 000	8 000	15 000	5 000	....	....	10 000
Business C	....	6 500	18 750	7 250	18 500	11 750	....
Business D	45 250	9 500	....	10 500	20 750	....	10 950
Business E	71 250	....	49 250	9 100	22 750	24 450	....
Business F	25 650	4 950	13 750	....	11 550	....	(3 450)

* Note: net loss is indicated in brackets

11.4 The following trial balance was extracted from the books of Jane Walsh (who is the proprietor of a fabric shop) at the end of her financial year 30 April 19-0:

Trial balance as at 30 April 19-0

	Dr	*Cr*
	£	£
Sales		30,000
Purchases	15,700	
Shop fittings	13,000	
Capital		15,000
Opening stock (1 May 19-9)	4,700	
Bank	610	
Cash	100	
Shop wages	4,420	
Debtors	120	
Drawings	3,500	
Creditors		2,030
Light and heat	260	
Rent	4,500	
Insurance	120	
	47,030	47,030

In preparing the year-end accounts, the following should be accounted for:

- the stock at the end of the year was valued at £4,400

You are required to:

(a) prepare Jane's trading account for the year ended 30 April 19-0

(b) prepare Jane's profit and loss account for the year ended 30 April 19-0

(c) draft Jane's balance sheet as at 30 April 19-0

[Pitman Examinations Institute]

11.5* The following trial balance has been extracted by the book-keeper of John Adams at 31 December 19-7:

	£	£
Stock at 1 January 19-7	14,350	
Purchases	114,472	
Sales		259,688
Business rates	13,718	
Heating and lighting	12,540	
Wages and salaries	42,614	
Motor vehicle expenses	5,817	
Advertising	6,341	
Premises	75,000	
Office equipment	33,000	
Motor vehicles	21,500	
Debtors	23,854	
Bank	1,235	
Cash	125	
Capital at 1 January 19-7		62,500
Drawings	12,358	
Loan from bank		35,000
Creditors		19,736
	376,924	376,924

Stock at 31 December 19-7 was valued at £16,280.

You are to prepare the trading and profit and loss account of John Adams for the year ended 31 December 19-7, together with his balance sheet at that date.

11.6 The following trial balance has been extracted by the book-keeper of Clare Lewis at 31 December 19-4:

	£	£
Debtors	18,600	
Creditors		13,350
Bank overdraft		4,610
Capital at 1 January 19-4		25,250
Sales		144,810
Purchases	96,318	
Stock at 1 January 19-4	16,010	
Salaries	18,465	
Heating and lighting	1,820	
Rent and business rates	5,647	
Motor vehicles	9,820	
Office equipment	5,500	
Sundry expenses	845	
Motor vehicle expenses	1,684	
Drawings	13,311	
	188,020	188,020

Stock at 31 December 19-4 was valued at £13,735.

You are to prepare the trading and profit and loss account of Clare Lewis for the year ended 31 December 19-4, together with her balance sheet at that date.

Case Study 2
Handwritten Book-keeping System

This Case Study is a fully worked example of a handwritten book-keeping system. It looks at the routine transactions of a sole trader business, Wyvern Metal Supplies, which is a supplier of specialist steel and other metals to local businesses. Wyvern Metal Supplies is registered for Value Added Tax, and all its purchases and sales are subject to VAT.

1 The book-keeping system

The business operates a handwritten book-keeping system which is divided into:

- sales ledger
- purchases ledger
- general ledger
- cash book

Day books are used for sales, purchases, and returns. A journal (see Chapter Seventeen) is used for the year-end transfers to the trading and profit and loss account.

The business transactions are for the month of December 19-1; they include:

- credit sales
- credit purchases
- receipts and payments, including cash discount allowed and received
- expenses
- drawings

All transactions are cross-referenced in the accounts to show the use of the folio column. The abbreviations used are:

SL	= sales ledger	SDB	= sales day book
PL	= purchases ledger	PDB	= purchases day book
GL	= general ledger	SRDB	= sales returns day book
CB	= cash book	PRDB	= purchases returns day book
		C	= contra, ie both transactions within the same book

The firm's financial year ends on 31 December 19-1, at which date the final accounts are prepared. As this Case Study is intended to show routine transactions, no adjustments are shown in the final accounts for:

- accruals and prepayments (see Chapter Twelve)
- provision for depreciation of fixed assets (see Chapter Thirteen)
- bad debts written off, and provision for bad debts (see Chapter Fourteen)

These adjustments, covered in the next few chapters, as indicated above, and are brought together in Case Study Three on page 260.

2 Trial balance

The trial balance of the business at 30 November 19-1, after eleven months' trading in the financial year, is as follows:

TRIAL BALANCE OF WYVERN METAL SUPPLIES AS AT 30 NOVEMBER 19-1

		Folio	*Dr.*	*Cr.*
			£	£
Sales		GL101		180,500
Purchases		GL102	81,300	
Sales returns		GL103	850	
Purchases returns		GL104		430
Wages and salaries		GL105	45,800	
Vehicle running expenses		GL106	2,700	
Office expenses		GL107	7,810	
Business rates		GL108	4,030	
Rent		GL109	13,200	
Discount allowed		GL110	2,100	
Discount received		GL111		980
Delivery van		GL112	12,000	
Office equipment		GL113	5,000	
Stock (at 1 January 19-1)		GL114	16,170	
Value Added Tax		GL115		2,750
Capital		GL116		30,000
Drawings		GL117	18,700	
Cash		CB	255	
Bank		CB	5,785	
Debtors:	Eveshore Engineering Ltd	SL201	4,000	
	Wyvern Wiring Co Ltd	SL202	4,400	
	Speciality Forgings	SL203	6,720	
Creditors:	Axis Supplies Ltd	PL301		7,830
	Quality Alloys Ltd	PL302		5,330
	Midlands Steel Co Ltd	PL303		3,000
			230,820	230,820

3 Transactions for December 19-1

Note: VAT = 17½ per cent

1 Dec.	Bought goods, £2,000 + VAT, on credit from Quality Alloys Ltd; received invoice no 7651
2 Dec.	Sold goods, £1,000 + VAT, on credit to Wyvern Wiring Co Ltd; issued invoice no 5310
3 Dec.	Received a cheque from Eveshore Engineering Ltd in full settlement of the amount owing, less 2½ per cent cash discount
4 Dec.	Paid office expenses, £200 + VAT, by cheque
4 Dec.	Paid the amount owing to Midlands Steel Co Ltd by cheque, after deducting 2½ per cent cash discount
5 Dec.	Bought goods, £1,000 + VAT, on credit from Axis Supplies Ltd; received invoice no AS791
5 Dec.	Owner's drawings, £250, in cash
8 Dec.	Returned goods, £40 + VAT, to Quality Alloys Ltd; received credit note no 0278
8 Dec.	Withdrew £500 of cash from the bank for business use
9 Dec.	Sold goods, £1,440 + VAT, on credit to Speciality Forgings; issued invoice no 5311
10 Dec.	Bought office equipment, £320 + VAT, paying by cheque no 365129
10 Dec.	Wyvern Wiring Co Ltd returns goods, £80 + VAT; credit note no 159 issued
11 Dec.	Paid the amount owing to Quality Alloys Ltd by cheque
12 Dec.	Paid vehicle running expenses, £120 + VAT, in cash
12 Dec.	Sold goods, £800 + VAT, on credit to Eveshore Engineering Ltd; issued invoice no 5312
15 Dec.	Received a cheque from Wyvern Wiring Co Ltd for the amount owing on 1 December, less 2½ per cent cash discount
16 Dec.	Sold goods £2,200 + VAT, on credit to Speciality Forgings; issued invoice no 5313
16 Dec.	Paid wages and salaries £5,500 by cheque
17 Dec.	Bought goods, £1,520 + VAT, on credit from Midlands Steel Co Ltd; received invoice no 9432
17 Dec.	Eveshore Engineering Ltd returns goods, £200 + VAT, credit note no 160 issued
18 Dec.	Paid office expenses, £94 *including* VAT, by cheque
18 Dec.	Received a cheque from Speciality Forgings for £6720
19 Dec.	Returned goods, £120 + VAT, to Midlands Steel Co Ltd; received credit note no CN732
19 Dec.	Paid rent, £1,200 + VAT, by cheque
22 Dec.	Sold goods, £1,600 + VAT, on credit to Wyvern Wiring Ltd; issued invoice no 5314
22 Dec.	Bought goods, £1,800 + VAT, on credit from Quality Alloys Ltd; received invoice no 7943
23 Dec.	Sold goods, £1,320 + VAT, on credit to Eveshore Engineering Ltd; issued invoice no 5315
24 Dec.	Owner's drawings, £450, by cheque
29 Dec.	Received a cheque from Speciality Forgings for £4,000

At 31 December 19-1, the closing stock is valued at £20,200.

4 Day books

Sales Day Book

Date	*Details*	*Invoice No*	*Folio*	*Net*	*VAT*	*Gross*
19-1				£	£	£
2 Dec.	Wyvern Wiring Co Ltd	5310	SL202	1,000	175	1,175
9 Dec.	Speciality Forgings	5311	SL203	1,440	252	1,692
12 Dec.	Eveshore Engineering Ltd	5312	SL201	800	140	940
16 Dec.	Speciality Forgings	5313	SL203	2,200	385	2,585
22 Dec.	Wyvern Wiring Co Ltd	5314	SL202	1,600	280	1,880
23 Dec.	Eveshore Engineering Ltd	5315	SL201	1,320	231	1,551
31 Dec.	Totals for month			8,360	1,463	9,823
				GL101	GL115	

Purchases Day Book

Date	*Details*	*Invoice No*	*Folio*	*Net*	*VAT*	*Gross*
19-1				£	£	£
1 Dec.	Quality Alloys Ltd	7651	PL302	2,000	350	2,350
5 Dec.	Axis Supplies Ltd	AS791	PL301	1,000	175	1,175
17 Dec.	Midlands Steel Co Ltd	9432	PL303	1,520	266	1,786
22 Dec.	Quality Alloys Ltd	7943	PL302	1,800	315	2,115
31 Dec.	Totals for month			6,320	1,106	7,426
				GL102	GL115	

Sales Returns Day Book

Date	*Details*	*Credit Note No*	*Folio*	*Net*	*VAT*	*Gross*
19-1				£	£	£
10 Dec.	Wyvern Wiring Co Ltd	159	SL202	80	14	94
17 Dec.	Eveshore Engineering Ltd	160	SL201	200	35	235
31 Dec.	Totals for month			280	49	329
				GL103	GL115	

Purchases Returns Day Book

Date	*Details*	*Credit Note No*	*Folio*	*Net*	*VAT*	*Gross*
19-1				£	£	£
8 Dec.	Quality Alloys Ltd	0278	PL302	40	7	47
19 Dec.	Midlands Steel Co Ltd	CN732	PL303	120	21	141
31 Dec.	Totals for month			160	28	188
				GL104	GL115	

5 The ledger accounts

The ledger accounts include year-end transfers, where appropriate, to the trading and profit and loss account; these transfers are detailed in Section 7 (page 175).

GENERAL LEDGER

Sales (account no 101)

Dr.			£	Cr.				£
19-1			£	19-1				£
31 Dec.	Trading account		188,860	1 Dec.	Balance b/d			180,500
				31 Dec.	Sales Day Book*	SDB		8,360
			188,860					188,860

Purchases (account no 102)

Dr.				Cr.		
19-1			£	19-1		£
1 Dec.	Balance b/d		81,300	31 Dec.	Trading account	87,620
31 Dec.	Purchases Day Book*	PDB	6,320			
			87,620			87,620

Sales returns (account no 103)

Dr.				Cr.		
19-1			£	19-1		£
31 Dec.	Balance b/d		850	31 Dec.	Trading account	1,130
31 Dec.	Sales Returns Day Book*	SRDB	280			
			1,130			1,130

Purchases returns (account no 104)

Dr.			Cr.			
19-1		£	19-1			£
31 Dec.	Trading account	590	1 Dec.	Balance b/d		430
			31 Dec.	Purchases Returns Day Book*	PRDB	160
		590				590

* *Totals for the month taken from the appropriate day book*

Dr.			**Wages and salaries** (account no 105)		Cr.
19-1		£	19-1		£
1 Dec.	Balance b/d	45,800	31 Dec.	Profit and loss account	51,300
16 Dec.	Bank CB	5,500			
		51,300			51,300

Dr.			**Vehicle running expenses** (account no 106)		Cr.
19-1		£	19-1		£
1 Dec.	Balance b/d	2,700	31 Dec.	Profit and loss account	2,820
12 Dec.	Cash CB	120			
		2,820			2,820

Dr.			**Office expenses** (account no 107)		Cr.
19-1		£	19-1		£
1 Dec.	Balance b/d	7,810	31 Dec.	Profit and loss account	8,090
4 Dec.	Bank CB	200			
18 Dec.	Bank CB	80			
		8,090			8,090

Dr.			**Business rates** (account no 108)		Cr.
19-1		£	19-1		£
1 Dec.	Balance b/d	4,030	31 Dec.	Profit and loss account	4,030

Dr.			**Rent** (account no 109)		Cr.
19-1		£	19-1		£
1 Dec.	Balance b/d	13,200	31 Dec.	Profit and loss account	14,400
19 Dec.	Bank CB	1,200			
		14,400			14,400

Dr. **Discount allowed** (account no 110) Cr.

Date	Details	Folio	£	Date	Details	Folio	£
19-1			£	19-1			£
1 Dec.	Balance b/d		2,100	31 Dec.	Profit and loss account		2,310
31 Dec.	Cash Book*	CB	210				
			2,310				2,310

Dr. **Discount received** (account no 111) Cr.

Date	Details	Folio	£	Date	Details	Folio	£
19-1			£	19-1			£
31 Dec.	Profit and loss account		1,055	1 Dec.	Balance b/d		980
				31 Dec.	Cash Book*	CB	75
			1,055				1,055

Dr. **Delivery van** (account no 112) Cr.

Date	Details	Folio	£	Date	Details	Folio	£
19-1			£	19-1			£
1 Dec.	Balance b/d		12,000	31 Dec.	Balance c/d		12,000
19-2				19-2			
1 Jan.	Balance b/d		12,000				

Dr. **Office equipment** (account no 113) Cr.

Date	Details	Folio	£	Date	Details	Folio	£
19-1			£	19-1			£
1 Dec.	Balance b/d		5,000	31 Dec.	Balance c/d		5,320
10 Dec.	Bank	CB	320				
			5,320				5,320
19-2				19-2			
1 Jan.	Balance b/d		5,320				

Dr. **Stock** (account no 114) Cr.

Date	Details	Folio	£	Date	Details	Folio	£
19-1			£	19-1			£
1 Dec.	Balance b/d		16,170	31 Dec.	Trading account		16,170
31 Dec.	Trading account		20,200	31 Dec.	Balance c/d		20,200
19-2				19-2			
1 Jan.	Balance b/d		20,200				

** Totals for the month taken from the appropriate column in the cash book (see page 172)*

Value Added Tax (account no 115)

Dr.				Cr.			
19-1			£	19-1			£
31 Dec.	Purchases Day Book*	PDB	1,106	1 Dec.	Balance b/d		2,750
31 Dec.	Sales Returns Day Book*	SRDB	49	31 Dec.	Sales Day Book*	SDB	1,463
31 Dec.	Cash Book**	CB	336	31 Dec.	Purchases Returns Day Book*	PRDB	28
31 Dec.	Balance c/d		2,750				
			4,241				4,241
				19-2			
				1 Jan.	Balance b/d		2,750

Capital (account no 116)

Dr.				Cr.			
19-1			£	19-1			£
31 Dec.	Drawings	GL117	19,400	1 Dec.	Balance b/d		30,000
31 Dec.	Balance c/d		33,435	31 Dec.	Profit and loss account§		22,835
			52,835				52,835
19-2				19-2			
				1 Jan.	Balance b/d		33,435

Drawings (account no 117)

Dr.				Cr.			
19-1			£	19-1			£
1 Dec.	Balance b/d		18,700	31 Dec.	Capital	GL116	19,400
5 Dec.	Cash	CB	250				
24 Dec.	Bank	CB	450				
			19,400				19,400

* *Totals for the month taken from the appropriate day book*

** *Total for the month taken from the VAT column in the cash book (see page 172)*

§ *Net profit for the year, calculated in the profit and loss account on page 177*

Dr. **CASH BOOK** Cr.

Date	Details		VAT	Discount allowed	Cash	Bank	Date	Details		VAT	Discount received	Cash	Bank
19-1			£	£	£	£	19-1			£	£	£	£
1 Dec.	Balances b/d				255	5,785	4 Dec.	Office expenses	GL107	35			235
3 Dec.	Eveshore Engineering Ltd	SL201		100		3,900	4 Dec.	Midlands Steel Co Ltd	PL303		75		2,925
8 Dec.	Bank	C			500		5 Dec.	Drawings	GL117			250	
15 Dec.	Wyvern Wiring Co Ltd	SL202		110		4,290	8 Dec.	Cash	C				500
18 Dec.	Speciality Forgings	SL203				6,720	10 Dec.	Office equipment	GL113	56			376
29 Dec.	Speciality Forgings	SL203				4,000	11 Dec.	Quality Alloys Ltd	PL302				7,633
							12 Dec.	Vehicle running expenses	GL106	21		141	
							16 Dec.	Wages and salaries	GL105				5,500
							18 Dec.	Office expenses	GL107	14			94
							19 Dec.	Rent	GL109	210			1,410
							24 Dec.	Drawings	GL117				450
							31 Dec.	Balances c/d				364	5,572
				210	755	24,695				336	75	755	24,695
			GL 115	GL 110						GL 115	GL 111		
19-2							19-2						
1 Jan.	Balances b/d				364	5,572							

Note: In the VAT columns of the cash book, no VAT is shown for transactions involving the sales ledger (eg Eveshore Engineering Ltd) and purchases ledger (eg Midlands Steel Co Ltd). This is because VAT has been charged on invoices issued and received and was recorded in the VAT account (via the appropriate day book) when the sale or purchase was made. However, VAT on cash sales and purchases, and other transactions, is recorded in the VAT columns of the cash book.

SALES LEDGER

Eveshore Engineering Ltd (account no 201)

Dr.				Cr.			
19-1			£	19-1			£
1 Dec.	Balance b/d		4,000	3 Dec.	Bank	CB	3,900
12 Dec.	Sales	SDB	940	3 Dec.	Discount allowed	CB	100
23 Dec.	Sales	SDB	1,551	17 Dec.	Sales returns	SRDB	235
				31 Dec.	Balance c/d		2,256
			6,491				6,491
19-2				19-2			
1 Jan.	Balance b/d		2,256				

Wyvern Wiring Co Ltd (account no 202)

Dr.				Cr.			
19-1			£	19-1			£
1 Dec.	Balance b/d		4,400	8 Dec.	Sales returns	SRDB	94
2 Dec.	Sales	SDB	1,175	15 Dec.	Bank	CB	4,290
22 Dec.	Sales	SDB	1,880	15 Dec.	Discount allowed	CB	110
				31 Dec.	Balance c/d		2,961
			7,455				7,455
19-2				19-2			
1 Jan.	Balance b/d		2,961				

Speciality Forgings (account no 203)

Dr.				Cr.			
19-1			£	19-1			£
1 Dec.	Balance b/d		6,720	18 Dec.	Bank	CB	6,720
9 Dec.	Sales	SDB	1,692	29 Dec.	Bank	CB	4,000
16 Dec.	Sales	SDB	2,585	31 Dec.	Balance c/d		277
			10,997				10,997
19-2				19-2			
1 Jan.	Balance b/d		277				

PURCHASES LEDGER

Axis Supplies Ltd (account no 301)

Dr.				Cr.			
19-1			£	19-1			£
31 Dec.	Balance c/d		9,005	1 Dec.	Balance b/d		7,830
				5 Dec.	Purchases	PDB	1,175
			9,005				9,005
19-2				19-2			
				1 Jan.	Balance b/d		9,005

Quality Alloys Ltd (account no 302)

Dr.				Cr.			
19-1			£	19-1			£
8 Dec.	Purchases returns	PRDB	47	1 Dec.	Balance b/d		5,330
11 Dec.	Bank	CB	7,633	1 Dec.	Purchases	PDB	2,350
31 Dec.	Balance c/d		2,115	22 Dec.	Purchases	PDB	2,115
			9,795				9,795
19-2				19-2			
				1 Jan.	Balance b/d		2,115

Midlands Steel Co Ltd (account no 302)

Dr.				Cr.			
19-1			£	19-1			£
4 Dec.	Bank	CB	2,925	1 Dec.	Balance b/d		3,000
4 Dec.	Discount received	CB	75	17 Dec.	Purchases	PDB	1,786
19 Dec.	Purchases returns	PRDB	141				
31 Dec.	Balance c/d		1,645				
			4,786				4,786
19-2				19-2			
				1 Jan.	Balance b/d		1,645

6 Trial balance at the month-end

TRIAL BALANCE OF WYVERN METAL SUPPLIES AS AT 31 DECEMBER 19-1
(before preparation of the final accounts)

		Folio	*Dr.* £	*Cr.* £
Sales		GL101		188,860
Purchases		GL102	87,620	
Sales returns		GL103	1,130	
Purchases returns		GL104		590
Wages and salaries		GL105	51,300	
Vehicle running expenses		GL106	2,820	
Office expenses		GL107	8,090	
Business rates		GL108	4,030	
Rent		GL109	14,400	
Discount allowed		GL110	2,310	
Discount received		GL111		1,055
Delivery van		GL112	12,000	
Office equipment		GL113	5,320	
Stock (at 1 January 19-1)		GL114	16,170	
Value Added Tax		GL115		2,750
Capital		GL116		30,000
Drawings		GL117	19,400	
Cash		CB	364	
Bank		CB	5,572	
Debtors*:	Eveshore Engineering Ltd	SL201	2,256	
	Wyvern Wiring Co Ltd	SL202	2,961	
	Speciality Forgings	SL203	277	
Creditors*:	Axis Supplies Ltd	PL301		9,005
	Quality Alloys Ltd	PL302		2,115
	Midlands Steel Co Ltd	PL303		1,645
			236,020	236,020

* *Instead of showing the balance of individual debtors and creditors accounts, the total of each ledger section could be recorded: see also control accounts (Chapter Nineteen).*

In the trial balance above:

- the stock account balance of £16,170 is before the year-end transfers in respect of the closing stock – valued at £20,200 – are entered into the accounts (see Section 7, below)
- the capital account balance of £30,000, and drawings account balance of £19,400, are before the year-end transfers are made to capital account in respect of net profit from the profit and loss account – see page 177 – and drawings (see Section 7, below)

7 Year-end journal entries

At the end of the financial year a number of transfers are made to transfer the balances of certain accounts to the trading and profit and loss account, and also in connection with capital account and drawings account. We have already seen in Chapter 11.6 the double-entry book-keeping for these transfers. In order to keep an accurate record, an entry is made in the journal for each of these non-regular transactions. We shall look at journal entries in more detail in Chapter Seventeen.

The journal entries to be made in respect of the year-end transfers of Wyvern Metal Supplies are shown on the next page.

JOURNAL

Date	Details	Folio	Dr	Cr
19-1			£	£
31 Dec.	Trading account	*	87,620	
	Purchases	GL102		87,620
	Sales	GL101	188,860	
	Trading account			188,860
	Purchases returns	GL104	590	
	Trading account			590
	Trading account		1,130	
	Sales returns	GL103		1,130
	Trading account } opening stock		16,170	
	Stock } opening stock	GL114		16,170
	Stock } closing stock	GL114	20,200	
	Trading account } closing stock			20,200
	Transfer of purchases, sales, purchases returns, sales returns, and stock balance to the trading account in order to calculate gross profit for the year-ended 31 December 19-1			
31 Dec.	Discount received	GL111	1,055	
	Profit and loss account	*		1,055
	Profit and loss account		51,300	
	Wages and salaries	GL105		51,300
	Profit and loss account		2,820	
	Vehicle running expenses	GL106		2,820
	Profit and loss account		8,090	
	Office expenses	GL107		8,090
	Profit and loss account		4,030	
	Business rates	GL108		4,030
	Profit and loss account		14,400	
	Rent	GL109		14,400
	Profit and loss account		2,310	
	Discount allowed	GL110		2,310
	Transfer of income and expenditure to the profit and loss account in order to calculate net profit for the year-ended 31 December 19-1			
31 Dec.	Profit and loss account		22,835	
	Capital	GL116		22,835
	Capital	GL116	19,400	
	Drawings	GL117		19,400
	Transfer of net profit and drawings to capital account at the end of the financial year			

* *The trading and profit and loss account is located in the general ledger; however, because of its importance within the general ledger, it is not usual for it to be allocated an account number.*

8 Final accounts

WYVERN METAL SUPPLIES
TRADING AND PROFIT AND LOSS ACCOUNT FOR THE YEAR ENDED 31 DECEMBER 19-1

	£	£	£
Sales			188,860
Less Sales returns			1,130
Net sales			187,730
Opening stock		16,170	
Purchases	87,620		
Less Purchases returns	590		
Net purchases		87,030	
		103,200	
Less Closing stock		20,200	
Cost of Goods Sold			83,000
Gross Profit			104,730
Add: Discount received			1,055
			105,785
Less:			
Wages and salaries		51,300	
Vehicle running expenses		2,820	
Office expenses		8,090	
Business rates		4,030	
Rent		14,400	
Discount allowed		2,310	
			82,950
Net Profit			22,835

WYVERN METAL SUPPLIES
BALANCE SHEET AS AT 31 DECEMBER 19-1

	£	£	£
Fixed Assets			
Delivery van			12,000
Office equipment			5,320
			17,320
Current Assets			
Stock		20,200	
Debtors (total of sales ledger balances)		5,494	
Bank		5,572	
Cash		364	
		31,630	
Less Current Liabilities			
Creditors (total of purchases ledger balances)	12,765		
Value Added Tax (see note on next page)	2,750		
		15,515	
Working Capital			16,115
NET ASSETS			33,435

(Balance sheet continues on next page)

	£
FINANCED BY:	
Capital	
Opening capital	30,000
Add Net profit	22,835
	52,835
Less Drawings	19,400
	33,435

Note: In this balance sheet VAT is a liability and, assuming 31 December 19-1 is the end of the VAT quarter, the amount due to HM Customs and Excise will be paid by 31 January 19-2.

9 Case study summary

- In this Case Study we have looked at the routine business transactions passing through the handwritten book-keeping system of a sole trader.
- The books of prime entry used were:
  - sales day book
  - purchases day book
  - sales returns day book
  - purchases returns day book
  - journal (see Chapter Seventeen)
- The business transactions were then entered into the ledger. This was split into:
  - sales ledger
  - purchases ledger
  - general ledger
  - cash book
- A trial balance was extracted at the end of the month.
- Final accounts were prepared comprising:
  - trading and profit and loss account
  - balance sheet

  Transfers were recorded in the journal and made from the ledger to the trading and profit and loss account.

Case Study Three (on page 260) uses the information from the trial balance at 31 December 19-1 in this Case Study, and makes adjustments in the final accounts for:

- accruals and prepayments (see Chapter Twelve)
- provision for depreciation (see Chapter Thirteen)
- bad debts written off, and provision for bad debts (see Chapter Fourteen)

12 Accruals and Prepayments

In the last chapter we prepared the final accounts – trading and profit and loss account, and balance sheet. There are, however, a number of adjustments which may be made to the final accounts at the year-end in order to show a more realistic view of the state of the business. This chapter is concerned with the adjustments to be made for *accruals* and *prepayments* of expenses and income.

To illustrate the effect of adjustments for accruals and prepayments on final accounts we shall in this, and the next three chapters, be referring to the set of accounts of Wyvern Wholesalers – see Chapter Eleven, pages 152 and 153.

12.1 Accrual of expenses

An accrual is an amount due in an accounting period which is unpaid at the end of that period.

In the final accounts, accrued expenses are:

- added to the expense from the trial balance before listing it in the profit and loss account
- shown as a current liability in the year-end balance sheet

The reason for dealing with accruals in this way is to ensure that the profit and loss account records the cost that has been *incurred* for the year, instead of simply the amount that has been *paid.* In other words, the expense is adjusted to relate to the time period covered by the profit and loss account. The year-end balance sheet shows a liability for the amount that is due, but unpaid.

In this book, and generally in accounting exercises, details of accruals (and prepayments – see below) will usually appear as a note to the trial balance.

Example of an accrual expense

The trial balance of Wyvern Wholesalers (see page 149) shows a debit balance for electricity and gas of £3,000. Before preparing the final accounts, an electricity bill for £250 is received on 1 January 19-2, ie on the first day of the new financial year. As this bill is clearly for electricity used in 19-1, an adjustment needs to be made in the final accounts for 19-1 to record this *accrued expense.*

In the profit and loss account, the total cost of £3,250 (ie £3,000 from the trial balance, *plus* £250 accrued) will be recorded as an expense. In the balance sheet, £250 will be shown as a separate current liability of 'accruals'.

Accruals – the book-keeping records

In the double-entry records, accruals must be shown as an amount owing at the end of the financial year. Thus the account for electricity and gas in the records of Wyvern Wholesalers will appear as follows:

Dr.		Electricity and Gas Account			Cr.
19-1		£	19-1		£
31 Dec.	Balance b/d (trial balance total)	3,000	31 Dec.	Profit and loss account	3,250
31 Dec.	Balance c/d	250			
		3,250			3,250
19-2			19-2		
			1 Jan.	Balance b/d	250

Notes:

- The book-keeper's trial balance showed the debit side balance brought down of £3,000
- As £250 is owing for electricity at the end of the year, the transfer to profit and loss account is the cost that has been incurred for the year of £3,250
- The balance remaining on the account – a credit balance of £250 – is the amount of the accrual, which is listed on the balance sheet at 31 December 19-1 as a current liability
- Later on, for example on 5 January, the electricity bill is paid by cheque and the account for 19-2 now appears as:

Dr.		Electricity and Gas Account			Cr.
19-2		£	19-2		£
5 Jan.	Bank	250	1 Jan.	Balance b/d	250

The effect of the payment on 5 January is that the account now has a 'nil' balance and the bill received on 1 January will not be recorded as an expense in the profit and loss account drawn up at the end of 19-2.

Effect on profit

Taking note of the accrual of an expense has the effect of *reducing* a previously reported net profit. As the expenses have been increased, net profit is less (but there is no effect on gross profit). Thus, the net profit of Wyvern Wholesalers reduces by £250 from £42,850 to £42,600.

12.2 Prepayment of expenses

A prepayment is a payment made in advance of the accounting period to which it relates.

A prepayment is, therefore, the opposite of an accrual: with a prepayment of expenses, some part of the expense has been paid in advance.

In the final accounts, prepaid expenses are:

- deducted from the expense amount of the trial balance before listing it in the profit and loss account
- shown as a current asset in the year-end balance sheet

As with accruals, the reason for dealing with prepaid expenses in this way is to ensure that the profit and loss account records the cost incurred for the year, and not the amount that has been paid – the profit and loss account expense relates to the time period covered by the profit and loss account. The year-end balance sheet shows an asset for the amount that has been prepaid.

Example of a prepaid expense

The owner of Wyvern Wholesalers tells you that the trial balance (see page 149) figure for rent and rates of £2,000, includes £100 of rent paid in advance for January 19-2. An adjustment needs to be made in the final accounts for 19-1 to record this *prepaid expense.*

In the profit and loss account, the cost of £1,900 (ie £2,000 from the trial balance, *less* £100 prepaid) will be recorded as an expense. In the balance sheet, £100 will be shown as a separate current asset of 'prepayments'.

Prepayments – the book-keeping records

In the double-entry records, prepayments must be shown as an asset at the end of the financial year. Thus the account for rent and rates in the records of Wyvern Wholesalers will appear as follows:

Dr.				Rent and Rates Account	Cr.
19-1		£	19-1		£
31 Dec.	Balance b/d (trial balance total)	2,000	31 Dec.	Profit and loss account	1,900
			31 Dec.	Balance c/d	100
		2,000			2,000
19-2					
1 Jan.	Balance b/d	100			

Notes:

- The trial balance total for rent and rates is £2,000
- As £100 is prepaid at the end of the year, the transfer to profit and loss account is the cost that has been incurred for the year of £1,900
- The balance remaining on the account – a debit balance of £100 – is the amount of the prepayment, which is listed on the balance sheet at 31 December 19-1 as a current asset
- The debit balance of £100 on 1 January 19-2 will be included in the expenses for rent and rates for the year and will be transferred to profit and loss account on 31 December 19-2

Effect on profit

Taking note of the prepayment of an expense has the effect of *increasing* a previously reported net profit – expenses have been reduced, so net profit is greater.

Stocks of office supplies

At the end of a financial year most businesses have stocks of office supplies which have been recorded as expenses during the year, such as stationery, postage stamps (or a balance held in a franking machine). Technically, at the end of each year, these items should be valued and treated as a prepayment for next year, so reducing the expense in the current year's profit and loss account. However, in practice, this is done only when the stock of such items is substantial enough to affect the accounts in a material way. The firm's accountant will decide at what level the prepayment will apply.

To give an example of office stocks, the trial balance total for postages of a business at the year-end is £1,050; stocks of postage stamps at the same date are £150. The business will record an expense of £900 (£1,050, less £150) in the profit and loss account, while £150 is listed on the balance sheet as a current asset 'stocks of postage stamps'.

12.3 Accruals and prepayments in final accounts

We have looked at the separate effect of dealing with accruals and prepayments. Let us now see how they are presented in the final accounts of Wyvern Wholesalers (see pages 152 and 153). Remember that we are taking note of the following items at 31 December 19-1:

- electricity accrued £250
- rent prepaid £100

Trading and profit and loss account

As there is no effect on gross profit, the details of the trading account are not shown. The profit and loss section appears as follows (note that the calculations for accruals and prepayments do not appear in the final accounts; they are presented here for illustrative purposes only):

PROFIT AND LOSS ACCOUNT OF WYVERN WHOLESALERS
FOR THE YEAR ENDED 31 DECEMBER 19-1

		£	£	£
Gross profit				99,750
Add Discount received				2,500
				102,250
Less:				
Discount allowed			3,700	
Salaries			46,000	
Electricity and gas	3,000 + 250		3,250	
Rent and rates	2,000 – 100		1,900	
Sundry expenses			4,700	
				59,550
Net profit				42,700

The effect of taking note of accruals and prepayments is to alter net profit:

	£
Net profit (before adjustments)	42,850
Add rent prepaid	100
	42,950
Less electricity accrued	250
Net profit (after adjustments)	42,700

Balance sheet

The balance sheet is shown below with the accruals and prepayments shaded:

BALANCE SHEET OF WYVERN WHOLESALERS
AS AT 31 DECEMBER 19-1

	£	£	£
Fixed Assets			
Premises			100,000
Equipment			30,000
Vehicles			21,500
			151,500
Current Assets			
Stock		16,300	
Debtors		23,850	
Prepayments		100	
Cash		125	
		40,375	
Less Current Liabilities			
Creditors	15,516		
Accruals	250		
Bank	851		
		16,617	
Working Capital			23,758
			175,258
Less Long-term Liabilities			
Loan			33,000
NET ASSETS			142,258
FINANCED BY			
Capital			
Opening capital			110,000
Add net profit			42,700
			152,700
Less drawings			10,442
			142,258

12.4 Accruals and prepayments of income

Just as expenses can be accrued or prepaid at the end of a financial year, income amounts can be accrued or prepaid also.

Accrual of income

Here, income of a business is due but unpaid at the end of the financial year. For example, commission receivable might have been earned, but the payment is received after the end of the financial year to which it relates.

In the final accounts, accrual of income is:

- added to the income amount from the trial balance before listing it in the profit and loss account
- shown as a current asset (eg commission receivable) in the year-end balance sheet

Prepayment of income

Here, the income of a business has been paid in advance by the payer. For example, the rent receivable account for this financial year could include an advance payment received from a tenant in respect of the next financial year.

In the final accounts, prepayment of income is:

- deducted from the income amount from the trial balance before listing it in the profit and loss account
- shown as a current liability (eg rent receivable prepaid) in the year-end balance sheet

As with expenses, the objective of taking note of accruals and prepayments of income is to ensure that the money amount listed in the profit and loss account relates to the period covered by that account.

12.5 Opening balances on expense or income accounts

So far in this chapter, we have looked at adjustments which take place at the end of a financial year. We have seen, though, that these cause the account to have an opening balance at the beginning of the next financial year. With such an account there are likely to be four separate figures making up the expense or income account:

- amount owing or prepaid at the beginning of the year (opening balance)
- amount paid (or received, if an income account) during the course of the year
- amount to be transferred to profit and loss account at the end of the financial year
- amount owing or prepaid at the end of the year (closing balance)

For the purposes of examination questions, if any three of these are known, the fourth – or 'missing' figure – can be calculated. For example, we are given the following information about the car expenses account for 19-1:

- owing at beginning of year £35
- amount paid in year £350
- owing at end of year £55

The 'missing' figure here, is the amount to be transferred to profit and loss account at the year-end. It is calculated (in account form) as follows:

Dr.		Car Expenses Account			Cr.
19-1		£	19-1		£
	Bank	350	1 Jan.	Balance b/d	35
31 Dec.	Balance c/d	55	31 Dec.	Profit and loss account (missing figure)	370
		405			405
19-2			19-2		
			1 Jan.	Balance b/d	55

Applying the above principles will help you to solve quite complex expenses and income problems set as part of an examination question. For example, where an expense account deals with two expenses, such as electricity and gas account, and one expense is prepaid at the start of the year while the other is accrued!

12.6 Private expenses and goods for own use

Adjustments also have to be made in the final accounts for the amount of any business facilities that are used by the owner for private purposes. These adjustments are for private expenses and goods for own use.

Private expenses

Sometimes the owner of a business uses business facilities for private purposes, eg telephone, or car. The owner will agree that part of the expense shall be charged to him or her as drawings, while the other part represents a business expense.

For example, the balance of the telephone account is £600 at the year-end, and the owner agrees that this should be split as one-quarter private use, and three-quarters to the business. The book-keeping entries to record such adjustments are:

—*debit* drawings account
—*credit* telephone account
} with the amount of private use

—*debit* profit and loss account
—*credit* telephone account
} with the amount of business use

The telephone account will be completed at the end of the year as follows:

Dr.		**Telephone Account**			Cr.
19-1		£	19-1		£
31 Dec.	Balance b/d	600	31 Dec.	Drawings	150
			31 Dec.	Profit and loss account	450
		600			600

Goods for own use

When the owner of a business takes some of the goods in which the business trades for his or her own use, the double-entry book-keeping is:

—*debit* drawings account

—*credit* purchases account

When working from a trial balance to produce the final accounts, goods for own use should be deducted from purchases and added to drawings.

12.7 Income and expenditure accounting

In this chapter we have made adjustments for accruals and prepayments to ensure that the profit and loss account shows the correct amount of income and expenses for the financial year, ie what should have been paid, instead of what has actually been paid. In doing this we are adopting the principle of *income and expenditure accounting*. If we simply used the trial balance figures, we would be following the principle of *receipts and payments accounting*, ie comparing money coming in, with money going out: this would usually give a false view of the net profit for the year.

The principle of income and expenditure accounting is applied in the same way to purchases and sales, although no adjustments are needed because of the way in which these two are handled in the accounting records. For purchases, the amount is entered into the accounts when the supplier's invoice is received, although the agreement to buy will be contained in the legal contract which exists between buyer and seller. From the accounting viewpoint, it is receipt of the supplier's invoice that causes an accounting entry to be made; the subsequent payment is handled as a different accounting transaction. A business could have bought goods, not paid for them yet, but will have a purchases figure to enter into the trading account. Doubtless the creditors will soon be wanting payment!

Sales are recorded in a similar way – when the invoice for the goods is sent, rather than when payment is made. This applies the principle of income and expenditure accounting. In this way, a business could have made a large amount of sales, which will be entered in the trading account, but may not yet have received any payments.

The way in which accounts are adjusted to take note of accruals and prepayments is formally recognised in the accruals (or matching) concept, which is discussed in more detail in Chapter 16.2.

12.8 Chapter summary

❑ Final accounts are prepared on the income and expenditure basis, rather than the receipts and payments basis.

❑ An adjustment should be made at the end of the financial year in respect of accruals and prepayments.

❑ In the final accounts, accrued expenses are:
- added to the expense from the trial balance
- shown as a current liability in the balance sheet

❑ Prepaid expenses are:
- deducted from the expense from the trial balance
- shown as a current asset in the balance sheet

❑ An accrual of income is:
- added to the income amount from the trial balance
- shown as a current asset in the balance sheet

❑ A prepayment of income is:
- deducted from the income amount from the trial balance
- shown as a current liability in the balance sheet

❑ Adjustments also need to be made in the business accounts for:
- private expenses
- goods for own use

Accruals and prepayments are just one type of adjustment made at the end of a financial year in order to present the financial statements more accurately. The next chapter continues the theme by considering depreciation of fixed assets.

12.9 Questions

Note: When preparing final accounts you may wish to refer to the specimen layout given in Appendix A (page 484).

12.1 Explain how the following would be dealt with in the profit and loss account, and balance sheet of a business with a financial year end of 31 December 19-2:

(a) Wages and salaries paid to 31 December 19-2 amount to £55,640. However, at that date, £1,120 is owing: this amount is paid on 4 January 19-3.

(b) Business rates totalling £3,565 have been paid to cover the period 1 January 19-2 to 31 March 19-3.

(c) A computer is rented at a cost of £150 per month. The rental for January 19-3 was paid in December 19-2 and is included in the total payments during 19-2 which amount to £1,950.

12.2 John Smith runs a wholesale stationery business. The following information has been extracted from his business accounts for the year ended 31 December 19-4:

	£
Sales	257,258
Purchases	138,960
Stock at 1 January 19-4	18,471
Stock at 31 December 19-4	14,075
Rent and business rates	10,862
Electricity	2,054
Telephone	1,695
Salaries	55,891
Motor vehicle expenses	10,855

At 31 December 19-4 he tells you that:

- business rates prepaid are £250
- salaries owing are £365

You are to prepare the trading and profit and loss account of John Smith for the year ended 31 December 19-4.

12.3* The following balances remained in the books of G Williams, a sole trader, at 31 October 19-2:

	£
Trade creditors	2,065
Stock, 31 October 19-2	3,073
Wages owing	225
Premises	27,400
Cash	500
Trade debtors	5,127
Furniture and fittings	3,075
Vehicles	6,100
Plant and machinery	13,840
Bank overdraft	1,875
Insurance paid in advance	50
5 year loan from Loamshire Finance Co	7,500
Drawings	10,800
Net profit for year ended 31 October 19-2	12,970
Capital	?

You are required to:

(a) answer the following

(i) What is the meaning of the words 'as at' on a balance sheet heading?

(ii) Why is the stock shown above as being at 31 October 19-2 rather than at 1 November 19-1?

(b) prepare the balance sheet for G Williams, using the balances listed above, and thus calculate his capital at the balance sheet date; pay particular attention to layout and presentation

(c) prepare Williams' capital account, as it would appear in his ledger for his financial year to 31 October 19-2

[RSA Examinations Board]

12.4 The following trial balance was extracted from the books of Jane Osman who is the proprietor of a computer store, at the end of her financial year 31 March 19-2:

TRIAL BALANCE
as at 31 March 19-2

	Dr	*Cr*
	£	£
Sales		60,800
Purchases	31,400	
Shop fittings	26,000	
Capital		29,000
Opening Stock (1 April 19-1)	9,400	
Bank	1,220	
Cash	190	
Shop wages	8,850	
Debtors	230	
Drawings	7,000	
Creditors		4,550
Light and heat	520	
Rent	8,500	
Insurance	240	
Sales returns	800	
	94,350	94,350

In preparing the year-end accounts, the following should be accounted for:

1. the stock at the end of the year was valued at £8,800
2. there is an accrual on shop wages amounting to £350
3. the insurance is paid in advance by £60

You are required to:

(a) prepare Jane's trading account for the year ended 31 March 19-2

(b) prepare Jane's profit and loss account for the year ended 31 March 19-2

(c) draft Jane's balance sheet as at 31 March 19-2

[Welsh Joint Education Committee]

12.5* Sandra Black operates a secretarial service to farmers and the following trial balance was extracted from her books on 31 May 19-0.

	£	£
Income from clients		32,500
Commissions from other sources		800
Discounts received		150
Stationery	2,100	
Wages	7,600	
Equipment	4,500	
Vehicles	6,500	
Rent and rates	2,350	
Vehicle expenses	2,000	
Light and heat	800	
Insurance	850	
Telephone	280	
Sundry expenses	175	
Drawings	11,200	
Debtors	760	
Creditors		670
Bank overdraft		250
Cash in hand	175	
Capital		4,920
	39,290	39,290

Notes:

(a) At 31 May 19-0 there is an unpaid telephone bill of £52 and an unpaid electricity bill of £45.

(b) Business rates prepaid at 31 May 19-0 are £120.

(c) On 31 May 19-0 there is an unused stock of stationery valued at £150.

You are required to:

Prepare a profit and loss account for Sandra Black for the year ended 31 May 19-0 and a balance sheet as at that date, showing clearly therein the value of her capital, fixed assets, current assets and current liabilities.

[RSA Examinations Board]

12.6* The trial balance of Bilton Potteries prepared after calculation of the gross profit is shown below:

BILTON POTTERIES
Trial balance as at 31 January 19-2

	Debit £	*Credit* £
Capital		7,000
Premises	5,000	
Bank	3,218	
Debtors	434	
Stock (31 January 19-2)	1,000	
Creditors		870
Drawings	3,800	
Insurance	450	
Rent receivable		225
Rates	500	
Wages	5,200	
Gross profit for year-ended 31 January 19-2		11,507
	19,602	19,602

A detailed review by the accountant revealed that the following adjustments were outstanding:

(i) Rates amounting to £100 had been paid in advance.

(ii) Rent receivable of £75 was still outstanding at 31 January 19-2.

(iii) The insurance total included the payment of £50 for private house contents insurance.

(iv) Wages owing amounted to £300.

Requirements:

(a) Open up the appropriate ledger accounts and post the above adjustments. Balance off these ledger accounts.

(b) Prepare a profit and loss account for the year ended 31 January 19-2 and a balance sheet as at that date, after the above adjustments have been posted.

[RSA Examinations Board]

12.7 A Bush is a sole trader who occupies rented premises. The annual rental is £2,400 which he pays quarterly. His lease and financial year commenced on 1 August year 1.

During his first financial year, A Bush made the following payments in respect of rent:

		£
Year 1	1 August	600
	4 November	600
Year 2	31 March	600
	8 August	600

He paid rates on the premises as follows:

Year 1	31 August	£75 for period 1 August to 30 September year 1
	22 October	£220 for period 1 October to 31 March year 2
Year 2	17 April	£270 for period 1 April to 30 September year 2

He paid electricity bills as follows:

Year 1	17 October	£310
Year 2	21 January	£390
Year 2	10 April	£360

An electricity bill of £420 accrued due had not been paid.

Required:

(i) Open the following accounts and, for the year ended 31 July year 2, enter the payments and make the necessary year-end adjustments for prepayments or accruals. Enter the transfers to profit and loss account and bring down balances at 1 August year 2.

   (a) Rent payable

   (b) Rates

   (c) Electricity

(ii) Show the relevant extracts covering the above items from the balance sheet of A Bush as at 31 July year 2.

[London Chamber of Commerce]

12.8* Norman Rickets is the proprietor of a small retailing business in Bradthorpe. Although Norman would very much like to own the premises which he uses, unfortunately he does not have the necessary resources to make the purchase and therefore, since first setting up the business, he has had to use rented accommodation. Rent is paid to the landlord quarterly in arrears with a review of the amount payable taking place yearly on 30 June. Norman is also responsible for the rates on the property, which are paid 6 monthly in advance, and for the property insurance. His financial year runs from 1 April to 31 March and each year he makes the necessary arrangements for his accountant to produce a set of final accounts. This year, however, he thought he would prepare a first draft himself, his only concern in doing so being the charge to profit for the rent, rates and insurance. He appreciates that the figures should be calculated on an accruals basis but he is not quite sure how to approach this. As a starting point, he has extracted the following figures from his Cash Book as he feels that some or all of them might be relevant.

Cash Book Payment Extracts

		£
1 Oct.19-0	Insurance (premium for period to 31 March 19-2)	900
1 Jan. 19-1	Rates	560
31 Mar. 19-1	Rent	450
1 Jul. 19-1	Rent	480
1 Jul. 19-1	Rates	600
30 Sep. 19-1	Rent	480
1 Jan. 19-2	Rates	600
2 Jan. 19-2	Rent	480
12 Apr. 19-2	Rent	480
1 Jul. 19-2	Rates	630

You are to assist Norman by preparing certain ledger accounts which will show the various amounts to be used in the calculation of profit.

Required:

Construct the following accounts for the year ended 31 March 19-2, showing clearly the opening and closing balances for the period and any transfers to or from the profit and loss account:

(a) the rent account

(b) the rates account

(c) the insurance account

[Association of Accounting Technicians]

Multiple-choice questions: chapters 11-12

- Read each question carefully
- Choose the *one* answer you think is correct (calculators may be needed)
- Answers are on page 486

1. Gross profit is:

   A sales less sales returns, minus cost of goods sold
   B sales less sales returns, minus purchases, less purchases returns
   C sales, minus expenses
   D sales, less sales returns, minus closing stock

2. At the end of a financial year the cost of *carriage in* is:

   A debited to the profit and loss account
   B debited to carriage out account
   C debited to the trading account
   D debited to purchases account

3. Net profit is:

   A gross profit, plus other income, minus expenses
   B increase in the bank balance
   C sales minus expenses
   D capital account minus expenses

4. Which one of the following does not appear in profit and loss account?

   A salaries
   B machinery
   C rent received
   D salespersons' commission

Questions 5 to 9 relate to the following account:

Rent and Business Rates Account

Dr.			Cr.		
19-1		£	19-1		£
1 Jan.	Balance (rates) b/d	450	31 Dec.	Profit and loss account	4,350
31 Mar.	Bank (rent)	500	31 Dec.	Balance (rates) c/d	600
15 May	Bank (rates)	1,200			
1 Jul.	Bank (rent)	500			
3 Oct.	Bank (rent)	550			
20 Nov.	Bank (rates)	1,200			
31 Dec.	Balance (rent) c/d	550			
		4,950			4,950
19-2			19-2		
1 Jan.	Balance (rates) b/d	600	1 Jan.	Balance (rent) b/d	550

5. The balance on 1 January 19-1 is:

   A business rates prepaid
   B business rates for the year ended 31 December 19-0
   C business rates accrued
   D a refund due

6. The transfer to profit and loss account for business rates in respect of the year ended 31 December 19-1 is:

   A £600
   B £2,100
   C £2,250
   D £4,350

7. The transfer to profit and loss account for rent in respect of the year ended 31 December 19-1 is:

   A £550
   B £2,100
   C £2,250
   D £4,950

8. The amount *paid* in respect of business rates in the year ended 31 December 19-1 is:

   A £1,550
   B £2,400
   C £4,350
   D £4,950

9. The amount of rent accrued at 31 December 19-1 is:

   A Nil
   B £550
   C £600
   D £4,950

10. Wages accrued are shown as a:

    A current asset in the balance sheet
    B debit balance in wages account
    C fixed asset in the balance sheet
    D credit balance in wages account

11. Net assets are:

    A fixed assets + working capital – long-term liabilities
    B capital + working capital – long-term liabilities
    C fixed assets – working capital + long-term liabilities
    D fixed assets + capital + long-term liabilities

12. An example of an intangible fixed asset is:

    A premises
    B debtors
    C goodwill
    D bank loan

13 Depreciation of Fixed Assets

Fixed assets, for example machinery and vehicles, lose value as time goes by, largely as a result of wear and tear. This loss in value is known as depreciation. In business accounts it is necessary to record an estimate of depreciation in the accounting records.

In this chapter we will:

- define depreciation
- consider the methods of calculating depreciation
- look at the book-keeping entries for depreciation
- apply depreciation to the final accounts
- investigate the book-keeping entries when a fixed asset is sold
- see how a revaluation of assets is recorded in the accounting system

13.1 What is depreciation?

Depreciation is the estimate of the amount of the loss in value of fixed assets over an estimated time period.

Most fixed assets lose value over time and, in business accounts, it is necessary, in order to present a realistic view of the business, to record the amount of the loss in value. This is done by showing an expense – called 'provision for depreciation of fixed assets' – in the profit and loss account, and recording the asset at a lower value than cost price in the balance sheet. The profit and loss expense is called a *provision* for depreciation because it is an estimate of both the loss in value and the time period; the estimate is linked to the cost price of the asset. Depreciation is a further application of the accruals concept, because we are recognising the timing difference between payment for the fixed asset and the asset's loss in value.

The main factors which cause fixed assets to depreciate are:

- *wear and tear* through use, eg motor vehicles, machinery, etc
- *passage of time,* eg the lease on a building
- *depletion,* eg extraction of stone from a quarry
- *economic reasons*
  - —obsolescence, eg a new design of machine which does the job better and faster makes the old machine obsolete
  - —inadequacy, eg a machine no longer has the volume capacity to meet the needs of the business

Fixed assets – even buildings – are depreciated over their useful economic life. The only exception is land, which does not normally depreciate (unless it is a quarry or a mine, when it will have a limited useful economic life). Land and buildings are sometimes increased in value from time-to-time, ie a revaluation takes place, and this is recorded in the accounts (see Section 13.7).

13.2 Methods of calculating depreciation

There are several different ways in which we can allow for the loss in value of fixed assets. All of these are *estimates,* and it is only when the asset is sold or scrapped that we will know the accuracy of the estimate (see Section 13.6).

The two most common methods of calculating depreciation are:

- straight-line method
- reducing balance method (also called the diminishing balance method)

Other methods used include:

- units of output (or service)
- sum of the digits

For the calculations of depreciation amounts we will use the following data:

MACHINE

Cost price on 1 January 19-1		£2,000
Estimated life		4 years
Estimated production:		
	year 1	60,000 units
	year 2	50,000 units
	year 3	25,000 units
	year 4	25,000 units
	total	160,000 units
Estimated scrap value at end of four years		£400

Straight-line method

With this method, a fixed percentage is written off the *original cost* of the asset each year. For this example, twenty-five per cent will be written off each year by the straight-line method. The depreciation amount (ignoring for the moment any residual or scrap value) for *each year* is:

£2,000 x 25% = £500 per year

The depreciation percentage will be decided by a business on the basis of what it considers to be the useful economic life of the asset. Thus, twenty-five per cent each year gives a useful economic life of four years (assuming a nil residual value at the end of its life).

Different classes of fixed assets are often depreciated at different rates, eg motor vehicles may be depreciated at a different rate to office equipment. It is important that, once a particular method and rate of depreciation has been selected, depreciation should be applied consistently, ie methods and rates are not changed from year-to-year without good reason.

The method of calculating straight-line depreciation, taking into account the asset's estimated sale proceeds at the end of its useful economic life, is:

$$\frac{\text{cost of asset} - \text{estimated residual (scrap or salvage) sale proceeds}}{\text{number of years' expected use of asset}}$$

For example, the machine is expected to have a residual (scrap or salvage) value of £400, so the depreciation amount will be:

$$\frac{£2{,}000 - £400}{4 \text{ years}} = £400 \text{ per year (ie 20\% per annum on cost)}$$

Reducing balance method (diminishing balance method)

With this method, a fixed percentage is written off the *reduced balance* each year. The reduced balance is cost of the asset less depreciation to date. For example, the machine is to be depreciated by 33.3% (one-third) each year, using the reducing balance method. The depreciation amounts for the four years of ownership are:

Original cost	£2,000
Year 1 depreciation: 33.3% of £2,000	£667
Value at end of year 1	£1,333
Year 2 depreciation: 33.3% of £1,333	£444
Value at end of year 2	£889
Year 3 depreciation: 33.3% of £889	£296
Value at end of year 3	£593
Year 4 depreciation: 33.3% of £593	£193
Value at end of year 4	£400

Note: the figures have been rounded to the nearest £, and year 4 depreciation has been adjusted by £5 to leave a residual value of £400.

The formula to calculate the percentage of reducing balance depreciation is:

$$r = 1 - \sqrt[n]{\frac{s}{c}}$$

where:

r = percentage rate of depreciation
n = number of years
s = salvage (residual) value
c = cost of asset

In the example above the 33.3% is calculated as:

$$r - 1 - \sqrt[4]{\frac{400}{2{,}000}}$$

$4 = 1 - \sqrt[4]{0.2}$ (to find the fourth root press the square root key on your calculator twice)

$r = 1 - 0.669$

$r = 0.331$ or 33.1% (which is close to the 33.3% used above)

Straight-line and reducing balance methods compared

The following tables use the depreciation amounts calculated above.

Straight-line

Year	1 Original cost	2 Depreciation for year	3 Depreciation to date	4 Net book value (ie 1-3)
	£	£	£	£
1	2,000	400	400	1,600
2	2,000	400	800	1,200
3	2,000	400	1,200	800
4	2,000	400	1,600	400

Note: Net book value is cost, less depreciation to date, ie column 1, less column 3.

These calculations will be used in the final accounts (see Section 13.4) as follows: taking year 2 as an example, the profit and loss account will be charged with £400 (column 2) as an expense, while the balance sheet will record £1,200 (column 4) as the net book value.

Reducing balance

Year	1 Original cost	2 Depreciation for year	3 Depreciation to date	4 Net book value (ie 1-3)
	£	£	£	£
1	2,000	667	667	1,333
2	2,000	444	1,111	889
3	2,000	296	1,407	593
4	2,000	193	1,600	400

In the final accounts, using year 3 as an example, £296 (column 2) will be charged as an expense to profit and loss account, while £593 (column 4) is the net book value that will be shown in the balance sheet. We shall look in more detail at depreciation in the final accounts in Section 13.4.

Using the tables above, let us see how the two methods compare:

Straight-line

- Same money amount each year
- Lower depreciation percentage required to achieve same residual value
- Best used for fixed assets likely to be kept for the whole of their expected lives, eg machinery, office equipment, fixtures and fittings

Reducing balance

- Different money amounts each year: more than straight-line in early years, less in later years
- Higher depreciation percentage required to achieve same residual value – but can never reach a nil value
- Best used for fixed assets which depreciate more in early years and which are not kept for the whole of expected lives, eg vehicles

Other methods of calculating depreciation

- *Units of output (or service) method*
  This method estimates
  — the number of units to be produced by a machine, *or*
  — the number of hours of operation of a machine, *or*
  — the number of miles expected from a vehicle
  over its expected life. Depreciation for a given year is calculated by reference to the number of units/hours/miles for that year.

  For example, the machine referred to earlier is to be depreciated by £1,600 (ie £2,000 – £400 residual value). As the total number of units to be produced by the machine is expected to be 160,000, then each year's depreciation will be calculated at £100 for every 10,000 units produced (£1,600 ÷ 160,000 units).

  Depreciation amounts will be:

Year 1	£600	depreciation for year
Year 2	£500	depreciation for year
Year 3	£250	depreciation for year
Year 4	£250	depreciation for year
	£1,600	total depreciation

  This method has the benefit of linking usage (ie units/hours/miles) to the depreciation amount. In years of high usage, depreciation is higher than in years of low usage. As the asset gets older, so the usage may be lower, but repair costs may be increasing: in this way the total expense (depreciation + repair costs) will probably be a similar amount from year-to-year.

- *Sum of the digits method*
  With this method, the depreciation amount each year is calculated on the sum of the number of years of useful life. For example, the machine is expected to last for four years: the sum of the digits is 1 + 2 + 3 + 4 = 10. Depreciation is now applied to the amount to be written off, £1,600 (ie £2,000 – £400 residual value) as follows:

Year 1	$^{4}/_{10}$ x £1,600	= £640	depreciation for year
Year 2	$^{3}/_{10}$ x £1,600	= £480	depreciation for year
Year 3	$^{2}/_{10}$ x £1,600	= £320	depreciation for year
Year 4	$^{1}/_{10}$ x £1,600	= £160	depreciation for year
		£1,600	total depreciation

  In using this method, note that the digits count down from the number of years of estimated life, ie the depreciation for year 1 is higher than that for year 2, etc. In this way, sum of the digits depreciation is similar to the reducing balance method.

Note that whichever depreciation method is used, the total net profits of the business over the life of the asset are the same. The various depreciation methods will cause the net profit for individual years to be different but, overall, the same total depreciation is charged to the profit and loss account.

13.3 Book-keeping entries for depreciation

Once the amounts of depreciation have been calculated using the methods described in the previous section, they can be recorded in the book-keeping system. The procedure is to use two accounts for each class of fixed assets:

- *fixed asset account,* which records the cost price of the asset (remember that the value of the asset can include certain other capital costs, eg installation costs – see Chapter 11.9)
- *provision for depreciation account,* which records the amount of depreciation for the asset

Example book-keeping entries

A machine is purchased for £2,000 on 1 January 19-1. It is decided to depreciate it at twenty per cent each year, using the straight-line method. The firm's financial year runs from 1 January to 31 December. The accounting records for the first four years will be:

Machinery Account

Dr.			Cr.		
19-1		£	19-1		£
1 Jan.	Bank	2,000			

This account remains with the balance of £2,000, which is the cost price of the machine. (The other transaction on 1 January 19-1 is in the bank account – this has not been shown.)

Provision for Depreciation Account – Machinery

Dr.			Cr.		
19-1		£	19-1		£
31 Dec.	Balance c/d	400	31 Dec.	Profit and loss account	400
19-2			19-2		
31 Dec.	Balance c/d	800	1 Jan.	Balance b/d	400
			31 Dec.	Profit and loss account	400
		800			800
19-3			19-3		
31 Dec.	Balance c/d	1,200	1 Jan.	Balance b/d	800
			31 Dec.	Profit and loss account	400
		1,200			1,200
19-4			19-4		
31 Dec.	Balance c/d	1,600	1 Jan.	Balance b/d	1,200
			31 Dec.	Profit and loss account	400
		1,600			1,600
19-5			19-5		
			1 Jan.	Balance b/d	1,600

The provision for depreciation account stores up the amounts of depreciation year by year. Notice that, while the asset account of machinery has a debit balance, provision for depreciation has a credit balance. The difference between the two balances at any time will tell us the book value of the asset, ie what it is worth according to our accounting records. For example, at 31 December 19-3, the book value of the machine is £800 (£2,000 cost, less £1,200 depreciation to date).

When a business owns several fixed assets of the same class, eg several machines, it is usual practice to maintain only one asset account and one provision for depreciation account for that class. This does mean that the calculation of amounts of depreciation can become quite complex – particularly when assets are bought and sold during the year. It may be helpful, in an examination question, to calculate the separate depreciation amount for each machine, or asset, before amalgamating the figures as the year's depreciation charge.

We will look at how to deal with the sale of an asset in Section 13.6.

13.4 Depreciation and final accounts

Profit and loss account

The depreciation amount calculated for each class of asset is listed amongst the other expenses as a *provision for depreciation* for that particular class of asset. For example, to consider the machine depreciated in Section 13.3, the profit and loss account will show 'provision for depreciation: machinery £400' amongst the other expenses. You will, by now, appreciate that the double-entry book-keeping for depreciation is:

—*debit* profit and loss account
—*credit* provision for depreciation account } with the annual amount of depreciation

Balance sheet

Each class of fixed asset should be shown at cost price (or revaluation – see Section 13.7), less total *depreciation to date* (ie this year's depreciation, plus depreciation from previous years if any). The resulting figure is the net book value of the fixed asset.

The usual way of setting these out in a balance sheet (using figures for the machine in Section 13.3) is:

Balance sheet (extract) .... as at 31 December 19-1

	£ Cost	£ Dep'n to date	£ Net
Fixed Assets			
Machinery	2,000	400	1,600
Vehicles, etc	x	x	x
	x	x	x

Balance sheet (extract) .... as at 31 December 19-2

	£ Cost	£ Dep'n to date	£ Net
Fixed Assets			
Machinery	2,000	800	1,200
Vehicles, etc	x	x	x
	x	x	x

Notice, from the above, how depreciation to date increases with the addition of each further year's depreciation. At the same time, the net figure reduces – it is this net figure which is added to the other fixed assets to give a sub-total for this section of the balance sheet.

Trial balance figures

When preparing final accounts from a trial balance, the trial balance often gives separate figures for the cost of an asset and its depreciation to date *at the start of the year*. For example:

Trial Balance of .... as at 31 December 19-3

	Dr	Cr
	£	£
Machinery at cost	2,000	
Provision for depreciation: machinery		800
etc		

If a note to the trial balance then says, for example, to "provide for depreciation on machinery for the year at twenty per cent on cost", this indicates that the trial balance figure is at the start of the year. Accordingly, depreciation of £400 for 19-3 must be calculated and shown as an expense in profit and loss account.

The balance sheet will then show:

Balance sheet (extract) .... as at 31 December 19-3

	£	£	£
	Cost	Dep'n to date	Net
Fixed Assets			
Machinery	2,000	1,200	800
Vehicles, etc	x	x	x
	x	x	x

Depreciation policies of a business

In examination questions, information will be given – where it is needed – on the depreciation policies of the business whose accounts you are preparing. In particular, the information will be given on what to do when a fixed asset is bought part of the way through a firm's financial year. The choices here will be to allocate depreciation for the part of the year that it is owned; alternatively the firm may choose to provide for depreciation for the whole year on assets held at the end of the year. All the information will be given in the question (a worked example from a past examination question is given in Section 13.8).

13.5 Depreciation: a non-cash expense

It is very important to realise that depreciation is a non-cash expense: unlike the other expenses in the profit and loss account, no cheque is written out, or cash paid, for depreciation. In cash terms, depreciation causes no outflow of money. Nevertheless, it is correct, in the final accounts of a business, to show an allowance for depreciation in the profit and loss account, and to reduce the value of the fixed asset in the balance sheet. This is because the business has had the use of the asset, and needs to record the fall in value as an expense to present a true picture of its financial state. Thus we are led back to the definition of depreciation as "the estimate of the amount of the loss in value of fixed assets over an estimated time period", ie it is an accounting adjustment.

As depreciation is a non-cash expense, it should be noted that depreciation is *not* a method of providing a fund of cash which can be used to replace the asset at the end of its life. In order to do this, it is necessary to create a separate fund into which cash is transferred at regular intervals. This technique is often known as a *sinking fund,* and it needs to be represented by a separate bank account, eg a deposit account, which can be drawn against when the new fixed asset is to be purchased. This, however, is not a common practice.

13.6 Sale of fixed assets

When a fixed asset is sold or disposed, it is necessary to bring together:

- the original cost of the asset
- depreciation provided over the life of the asset
- sale proceeds

These figures are transferred from the appropriate accounts in the double-entry book-keeping system to a *disposals account* (also known as a *sale of assets account*). The disposals account will enable us to calculate the 'profit' or 'loss' on sale of the asset (more correctly the terms are 'over-provision' and 'under-provision' of depreciation, respectively).

The book-keeping transactions are:

- original cost of the asset

  — *debit* disposals account
— *credit* fixed asset account } with the cost price of the fixed asset now sold

- depreciation provided to date

  — *debit* provision for depreciation account
— *credit* disposals account } with depreciation provided over the life of the asset

  Note: The amount of depreciation provided to date may need to be calculated for the correct period, eg if disposal takes place part of the way through a financial year and the firm's policy is to charge part-years.

- sale proceeds

  — *debit* bank/cash account
— *credit* disposals account } with the sale proceeds of the asset

- loss on sale

  — *debit* profit and loss account
— *credit* disposals account } with the amount of under-provision of depreciation

- profit on sale

  — *debit* disposals account
— *credit* profit and loss account } with the amount of over-provision of depreciation

Small adjustments for under- or over-provision of depreciation will usually be needed because it is impossible, at the start of an asset's life, to predict exactly what it will sell for in a number of years' time.

Example of book-keeping entries

To illustrate the transactions described above, we will use the machine purchased for £2,000 on 1 January 19-1, which is depreciated at twenty per cent each year, using the straight-line depreciation method. On 31 December 19-3, the machine is sold for £700.

The calculations are:	£
cost price of machine	2,000
less provision for depreciation to date	1,200
net book value at date of sale	800
selling price	700
loss on sale	100

The book-keeping entries (excluding bank account) are:

Machinery Account

Dr.		£	Cr.		£
19-1			19-3		
1 Jan.	Bank	2,000	31 Dec.	Disposals account	2,000

Provision for Depreciation Account – Machinery

Dr.		£	Cr.		£
19-1			19-1		
31 Dec.	Balance c/d	400	31 Dec.	Profit and loss account	400
19-2			19-2		
31 Dec.	Balance c/d	800	1 Jan.	Balance b/d	400
			31 Dec.	Profit and loss account	400
		800			800
19-3			19-3		
31 Dec.	Disposals account	1,200	1 Jan.	Balance b/d	800
			31 Dec.	Profit and loss account	400
		1,200			1,200

Disposals Account

Dr.		£	Cr.		£
19-3			19-3		
31 Dec.	Machinery account	2,000	31 Dec.	Provision for dep'n account	1,200
			31 Dec.	Bank	700
			31 Dec.	Profit and loss account (loss on sale)	100
		2,000			2,000

Profit and loss account (extract) .... for the year ended 31 December 19-3

	£	£
Gross profit		x
Less:		
Provision for depreciation: machinery	400	
Loss on sale of machinery	100	

Notes:

- In the machinery account, which is always kept 'at cost', the original price of the asset is transferred at the date of sale to disposals account. In this example, a nil balance remains on machinery account; however it is quite likely that the machinery account includes several machines, only one of which is being sold – in this case, there would be a balance on machinery account comprising the cost prices of the remaining machines.
- In provision for depreciation account, the amount of depreciation relating to the machine sold is transferred to disposals account. In this example, as only one machine is owned, the whole balance is transferred. However, if there were machines remaining, only part of the balance would be transferred – the amount remaining on the account relates to the remaining machines.
- Disposals account would balance without the need for a profit and loss account transfer if the depreciation rate used reflected exactly the fall in value of the machine. In practice, this is unlikely to happen, so a transfer to profit and loss account must be made. In this example, it is an under-provision of depreciation (loss on sale), and the profit and loss account lists an extra expense. If there had been an over-provision of depreciation (profit on sale), an item of additional income would be shown in profit and loss account.

Part-exchange of an asset

Instead of selling an old fixed asset for cash, it is quite common to part-exchange it for a new asset. This is exactly the same as if a person trades in their old car for a new (or newer) one.

Once the part-exchange allowance has been agreed, the book-keeping entries for disposal are as detailed earlier except that, instead of sale proceeds, there will be:

— *debit* fixed asset account
— *credit* disposals account } with amount of part-exchange allowance

The remainder of the purchase cost of the new fixed asset paid by cheque is debited to fixed asset account and credited to bank account in the usual way.

For example, the machine referred to earlier in this section is part-exchanged on 31 December 19-3 at an agreed value of £700 for a new machine costing £2,500. The balance is paid by cheque.

Machinery account will now be shown as:

Machinery Account

Dr.		£			£ Cr.
19-1		£	19-3		£
1 Jan.	Bank	2,000	31 Dec.	Disposals account	2,000
19-3					
31 Dec.	Disposals account (part-exchange allowance)	700	31 Dec.	Balance c/d	2,500
31 Dec.	Bank (balance paid by cheque)	1,800			
		2,500			2,500
19-4					
1 Jan.	Balance b/d	2,500			

Notes:

- This gives two debits (£700 and £1,800) in machinery account for a single machine.
- Disposals account will be unchanged, except that the description for the credit transaction of £700 will be machinery account, instead of bank.

13.7 Revaluation of a fixed asset

From time-to-time fixed assets are revalued at a higher value. In practice, the most likely asset to be revalued is property. After an asset has been revalued, depreciation is calculated on the revalued amount.

When a fixed asset is revalued, a *reserve* is created which adds to the value of the owner's capital. The book-keeping procedure is:

- *debit* fixed asset account
- *credit* capital account

} with the amount of the increase in value

Example of revaluation

A business owns premises which is shown in the accounts on 1 January 19-1 at the original cost of £100,000. The premises have been revalued on 31 December 19-1 at £150,000 and it has been decided to record this value in the accounting system. The balance on the owner's capital account on 31 December 19-1 is £200,000 before the revaluation is recorded.

Premises Account

Dr.					Cr.
19-1		£	19-1		£
1 Jan.	Balance b/d	100,000			
31 Dec.	Capital account	50,000			

Capital Account

Dr.					Cr.
19-1		£	19-1		£
			1 Jan.	Balance b/d	200,000
			31 Dec.	Premises account (revaluation)	50,000

Notes:

- Both premises account and the owner's capital account have been increased by the amount of the revaluation. The owner's stake in the business is now £250,000.
- There is *no new cash* in the business – a non-cash book-keeping entry has recorded the increase in value. Clearly if the premises were sold for the revalued amount, cash would be received.
- The revaluation transaction has *not* been recorded in profit and loss account because it is a capital transaction rather than a revenue transaction. (When we come to dealing with company final accounts in Chapter Twenty-four – we shall see that a revaluation amount would be placed in a separate account which is grouped under the general heading of 'capital reserves'.)

13.8 Worked example

We will now look at a past examination question involving the purchase and sale of several assets of the same class. In particular, note how a schedule of depreciation has been prepared. Such a schedule is particularly useful when:

- there are several purchases and sales taking place in a year
- there has been a change of accounting policy, eg a switch from straight-line method to reducing balance, and it is decided to recalculate depreciation for previous years

Question

You are provided with the following information relating to Speed, a firm of delivery merchants, for the year to 31 October 19-5:

1. Balance sheet (extract) at 31 October 19-4:

	£
Vans, at cost	14,000
Less: Depreciation to date	6,000
Net book value	8,000

2. Purchases of vans:

Date	*Registration number*	*Cost* £
1.1.-1	AAT 10	2,000
1.5.-2	BAT 20	3,000
1.12.-2	CAT 30	4,000
1.8.-4	DAT 40	5,000
1.12.-4	EAT 50	6,000
1.8.-5	FAT 60	9,000

3. Sales of vans:

Date	*Registration number*	*Sale proceeds* £
30.11.-4	AAT 10	500
31.7.-5	CAT 30	2,000
30.9.-5	DAT 40	4,000

4. Vans are depreciated at a rate of 20% per annum on cost. A full year's depreciation is charged in the year of purchase, but no depreciation is charged in the year of disposal.

Required:

- enter the above transactions in the following accounts for the year to 31 October 19-5, being careful to bring down the balances as at 1 November 19-5: i) Vans Account; ii) Vans Depreciation Provision Account; and iii) Vans Disposal Account; and
- state briefly whether you think that the reducing balance method of depreciation would be a more appropriate method of depreciating delivery vans.

[Association of Accounting Technicians]

Answer

We will, firstly, agree the balances at 31 October 19-4:

- *Vans at cost* consists of

AAT 10 (purchased 1.1.-1)	£2,000
BAT 20 (purchased 1.5.-2)	£3,000
CAT 30 (purchased 1.12.-2)	£4,000
DAT 40 (purchased 1.8.-4)	£5,000
	£14,000

- *Depreciation to date* consists of

		Depreciation* for year ended:				
		31.10.-1	31.10.-2	31.10.-3	31.10.-4	TOTAL
		£	£	£	£	£
1.1.-1	AAT 10	400	400	400	400	1,600
1.5.-2	BAT 20	-	600	600	600	1,800
1.12.-2	CAT 30	-	-	800	800	1,600
1.8.-4	DAT 40	-	-	-	1,000	1,000
		400	1,000	1,800	2,800	6,000

* Depreciation is at the rate of 20% per annum on cost; a full year's depreciation is charged in the year of purchase.

A schedule for the year ended 31 October 19-5 is prepared:

		Depreciation brought forward (see above)	Depreciation for year ended 31.10.-5	Depreciation transferred to disposals account	Depreciation at year-end
		£	£	£	£
1.1.-1	AAT 10 (sold 30.11.-2)	1,600	- *	(1,600)	-
1.5.-2	BAT 20	1,800	600	-	2,400
1.12.-2	CAT 30 (sold 31.7.-3)	1,600	- *	(1,600)	-
1.8.-4	DAT 40 (sold 30.9.-3)	1,000	- *	(1,000)	-
1.12.-4	EAT 50	-	1,200	-	1,200
1.8.-5	FAT 60	-	1,800	-	1,800
		6,000	3,600	(4,200)	5,400
			charged to profit and loss account		balance of provision for depreciation account

* No depreciation charged in year of disposal

The accounts appear as:

Vans Account

Dr.		£	Cr.		£
19-4			19-4		
1 Nov.	Balance b/d	14,000	30 Nov.	Disposals account (AAT 10)	2,000
1 Dec.	Bank (EAT 50)	6,000	19-5		
19-5			31 Jul.	Disposals account (CAT 30)	4,000
1 Aug.	Bank (FAT 60)	9,000	30 Sep.	Disposals account (DAT 40)	5,000
			31 Oct.	Balance c/d	18,000
		29,000			29,000
19-5			19-5		
1 Nov.	Balance b/d	18,000			

Provision for Depreciation Account – Vans

Dr.		£	Cr.		£
19-4			19-4		
30 Nov.	Disposals account (AAT 10)	1,600	1 Nov.	Balance b/d	6,000
19-5			19-5		
31 Jul.	Disposals account (CAT 30)	1,600	31 Oct.	Profit and loss account	3,600
30 Sep.	Disposals account (DAT 40)	1,000			
31 Oct.	Balance c/d	5,400			
		9,600			9,600
19-5			19-5		
			1 Nov.	Balance b/d	5,400

Van Disposal Account

Dr.		£	Cr.		£
19-4			19-4		
30 Nov.	Vans account (AAT 10)	2,000	30 Nov.	Bank (AAT 10)	500
			30 Nov.	Provision for depreciation (AAT 10)	1,600
19-5			19-5		
31 Jul.	Vans account (CAT 30)	4,000	31 Jul.	Bank (CAT 30)	2,000
			31 Jul.	Provision for depreciation (CAT 30)	1,600
30 Sep.	Vans account (DAT 40)	5,000	30 Sep.	Bank (DAT 40)	4,000
			30 Sep.	Provision for depreciation (DAT 40)	1,000
			31 Oct.	Profit and loss account (loss on sale of vans)	300
		11,000			11,000

Notes:

- The vans disposal account shows an overall loss on sale of £300 for the three vans. The separate amounts are:

	£	
AAT 10	100	profit on sale
CAT 30	400	loss on sale
DAT 40	–	
Net	300	loss on sale

- The balance sheet extract at 31 October 19-5 is:

	£
Vans at cost	18,000
Less depreciation to date	5,400
Net book value	12,600

- In the second part of the question, the firm should consider the reducing balance method: see Section 13.2.

13.9 Chapter summary

- ❑ Depreciation is the estimate of the amount of the loss in value of fixed assets over an estimated time period.
- ❑ Two common methods of calculating depreciation are the straight-line method and the reducing balance method. Other methods include units of output (or service), and sum of the digits methods.
- ❑ In terms of book-keeping, two accounts are used for each class of fixed asset:
  - fixed asset account
  - provision for depreciation account
- ❑ The depreciation amount for each class of fixed asset is included amongst the expenses in profit and loss account, while the value of the asset, as shown in the balance sheet, is reduced by the same amount.
- ❑ Depreciation is a non-cash expense.
- ❑ When a fixed asset is sold, it is necessary to make an adjustment in respect of any under-provision (loss on sale) or over-provision (profit on sale) of depreciation during the life of the asset. The amount is calculated by means of a disposals account, and is then transferred to profit and loss account.
- ❑ When assets are revalued at a higher value, the owner's stake in the business is increased. This is a capital transaction (rather than revenue) and does not pass through profit and loss account.

In the next chapter we look at another expense to be shown in profit and loss account: bad debts, and provision for bad debts.

13.10 Questions

Note: When preparing final accounts you may wish to refer to the specimen layout given in Appendix A (page 484).

13.1 Bert Greenwood bought a new vending machine for his business on 1 January 19-8 at a cost of £8,000. He intends to write off depreciation of the machine at the end of each business year which is 31 December. Greenwood however cannot decide whether to write off the depreciation by the straight line method or the reducing balance method.

Required:

(a) Prepare the provision for depreciation of machinery account as it should appear for the years 19-8 and 19-9 under:

(i) straight line method at 12½% per annum;

(ii) reducing balance method at 15% per annum.

(b) The balance sheet extracts for the years 19-8 and 19-9 showing the book value of the machinery after depreciation by the reducing balance method.

[RSA Examinations Board]

13.2 From the following trial balance extracted from the books of Paulo Gavinci, restaurateur, you are required to prepare the trading and profit and loss account for the year ended 30 April 19-0 and the balance sheet as at that date.

Trial balance as at 30 April 19-0

	Dr	*Cr*
	£	£
Capital		75,000
Fixtures and fittings	95,000	
Delivery vehicle	8,000	
Opening stock	2,000	
Cash	450	
Bank		4,300
Bank loan (long-term)		30,000
Purchases	190,250	
Sales		300,000
Creditors		5,000
Wages	45,000	
Drawings	25,000	
Purchases returns		400
Rent	31,800	
General expenses	17,200	
	414,700	414,700

You should also take the following additional information into account:

(a) Closing stock at 30 April 19-0 was £1,600

(b) Depreciation is to be provided as follows on a straight line basis:

Fixtures and fittings – 20% on cost
Delivery vehcile – 25% on cost

(c) Paulo took goods for personal use amounting to £250 at cost and an adjustment needs to be made for this

(d) Provide for:

Rent prepaid £2,000
Wages accrued £1,000

[Pitman Examinations Institute]

13.3* The following trial balance has been extracted by the book-keeper of Hazel Harris at 31 December 19-4:

	£	£
Bank loan		75,000
Capital		125,000
Purchases and sales	465,000	614,000
Building repairs	8,480	
Motor vehicles at cost	12,000	
Provision for depreciation on motor vehicles		2,400
Motor expenses	2,680	
Land and buildings at cost	100,000	
Bank overdraft		2,000
Furniture and fittings at cost	25,000	
Provision for depreciation on furniture and fittings		2,500
Wages and salaries	86,060	
Discounts	10,610	8,140
Drawings	24,000	
Business rates and insurance	6,070	
Debtors and creditors	52,130	41,850
General expenses	15,860	
Stock at 1 January 19-4	63,000	
	870,890	870,890

Notes at 31 December 19-4:

- Stock was valued at £88,000
- Wages and salaries outstanding: £3,180
- Rates and insurance paid in advance: £450
- Depreciate motor vehicles at 20 per cent using the straight-line method
- Depreciate furniture and fittings at 10 per cent using the straight-line method

You are to prepare her trading and profit and loss accounts for the year ended 31 December 19-4, together with her balance sheet at that date.

13.4* On 1 January 19-1, Martin Jackson bought a car for £6,000. In his final accounts, which have a year-end of 31 December, he has been depreciating it at 25 per cent per annum using the reducing balance method. On 31 December 19-3 he sells the car for £2,750 (cheque received).

You are to show:

(a) The provision for depreciation account for 19-1, 19-2 and 19-3

(b) The balance sheet extract at 31 December 19-1 and 19-2

(c) The asset disposal account

13.5 P. Iglet's financial year runs from 1 April—31 March. On 1 April 19-0 he has one vehicle on his books valued at its original cost of £8,400. £3,360 had been written off to a separate provision for depreciation on motor vehicles account.

On 30 April 19-0 the vehicle was sold for £4,900 cash and replaced by a new vehicle bought on credit from Robin Motors Limited for £9,000.

P. Iglet depreciates vehicles at 24% per annum on cost. Depreciation is charged up to the date of disposal.

(a) Prepare P. Iglet's accounts for motor vehicles, provision for depreciation on motor vehicles, and disposal of motor vehicles.

Close the accounts on 30 April 19-0, bringing down any balance to 1 May 19-0.

(b) Prepare a profit and loss account extract for the month ended 30 April 19-0 showing relevant entries.

[London East Anglian Group, 1990]

13.6 Colin and Reena Tan have run a small road haulage firm since 19-6, when they started the business with three transit vans which cost £30,000 each in 19-6.

The accounts relating to the transit vans have been lost and you are required to prepare and update the accounts from the following details and information available:

A charge of 20% depreciation has been charged on the vans using the reducing balance method. On 1 January 19-9, a further transit van was purchased at a cost of £48,000 and on 30 June one of the original vans was sold for £10,000.

Depreciation is charged in the year of purchase but none in the year of sale.

You are required to prepare:

(a) vehicles account starting from 1 January 19-9;

(b) provision for depreciation of vehicles/transit vans;

(c) asset disposal account.

[RSA Examinations Board]

13.7 (a) "When a fixed asset is purchased, a business will use depreciation as a means to set aside cash each year so that it eventually has the funds to purchase a replacement when this becomes necessary."

Required
Comment briefly on the above statement.

(b) Jim Barlow is the owner of a taxi business and his financial year runs from 1 July to 30 June. On 1 July 19-9 he had two vehicles used by his drivers, one a Ford purchased on 10 January 19-7 for £10,000 and the other a Toyota purchased on 12 August 19-7 for £8,000.

During November 19-9 Jim decided to replace the Ford and trade it in for a new Mercedes costing £15,500. Jim took delivery of the new car on 14 November. The garage accepted the Ford together with a cheque for £9,500 in payment.

Vehicles are depreciated at 10% per annum reducing balance method. With a full year's depreciation charged in the year of purchase and no depreciation charged in the year of disposal.

Required:

(i) Calculate the value on 1 July 19-9 of both the Ford and the Toyota.

(ii) Draw up the motor vehicles account, the provision for depreciation—motor vehicles account and the motor vehicles disposal account as they would appear in the ledger for the year ended 30 June 19-0. Show clearly any transfers to or from the profit and loss account and any closing balances.

[Association of Accounting Technicians]

13.8* On 1 January 19-1 a business purchased a Minilab to process and print films. The Minilab cost £28,000 and has an estimated economic life of 4 years after which it will have no residual value. The financial year of the business ends on 31 December each year.

It is estimated that the output from the Minilab will be:

	Films processed
Year 1	40,000
Year 2	50,000
Year 3	55,000
Year 4	55,000
	200,000

(a) **Required**
Calculate the annual depreciation charges on the Minilab for each of the four years on each of the following bases:
(i) the straight line basis,
(ii) the diminishing balance method at 55% per annum, and
(iii) the units of output method.
Note: Your workings should be to the nearest £.

(b) Suppose that the business sold the Minilab half way through the third year for £10,000 and that depreciation had been provided for using the straight line method applied on a month for month basis.

Required:
Reconstruct the following accounts *for the third year ONLY:*
(i) the Minilab account,
(ii) the provision for depreciation—Minilab account, and
(iii) the assets disposals account.

[Association of Accounting Technicians]

13.9* The following table shows the cumulative effects of a succession of separate transactions on the assets and liabilities of a business:

Transactions:		*A*	*B*	*C*	*D*	*E*	*F*	*G*	*H*	*I*	*J*
	£000	£000	£000	£000	£000	£000	£000	£000	£000	£000	£000
Assets:											
Property	300	300	300	350	350	350	350	350	350	350	350
Motor vans	50	50	50	50	50	50	50	47	47	47	47
Stock	56	56	60	60	55	55	55	55	55	55	55
Debtors	65	65	65	65	72	72	72	72	72	72	65
Prepayments	10	10	10	10	10	10	10	10	10	10	10
Bank	17	47	47	47	47	44	34	38	33	32	39
Cash	2	2	2	2	2	5	5	5	5	5	5
	500	530	534	584	586	586	576	577	572	571	571
Liabilities:											
Capital	320	350	350	350	352	352	352	353	354	354	354
Loan	125	125	125	175	175	175	175	175	175	174	174
Creditors	42	42	46	46	46	46	46	46	40	40	40
Accruals	13	13	13	13	13	13	3	3	3	3	3
	500	530	534	584	586	586	576	577	572	571	571

Required:

Identify clearly and as fully as you can what transaction has taken place in each case. Do not copy out the table but use the reference letter for each transaction.

[Association of Accounting Technicians]

14 Bad Debts; Provision for Bad Debts; Discount on Debtors

Most businesses selling their goods and services to other businesses do not receive payment immediately. Instead, they often have to allow a period of credit and, until the payment is received, they have a current asset of *debtors*. Unfortunately, it is likely that not all debtors will eventually settle the amount they owe, ie the amounts are *bad debts* which have to be written off. At the same time a business needs to make a *provision for bad debts,* which allows for debtors who *may* not pay.

In this chapter we will:

- distinguish between *bad debts* and *provision for bad debts*
- prepare the accounting entries for bad debts, and consider the effect on the final accounts
- prepare the accounting entries to make a provision for bad debts, and consider the effect on the final accounts
- look at the procedures a business may use in order to minimise the risk of bad debts

Towards the end of the chapter we will see how a provision for discount on debtors is created.

14.1 Bad debts and provision for bad debts

A bad debt is a debt owing to a business which it considers will never be paid.

Let us consider a business with debtors of £10,000. This total will, most probably, be made up of a number of debtors' accounts. At any one time, a few of these accounts will be bad, and therefore the amount is uncollectable: these are *bad debts,* and they need to be written off, ie the business will give up trying to collect the debt and will accept the loss.

Provision for bad debts is the estimate by a business of the likely percentage of its debtors which may go bad during any one accounting period.

There are likely to be some debtors' accounts which, although they are not yet bad, may be giving some concern as to their ability to pay: a *provision for bad debts* (or *doubtful debts*) needs to be made in respect of these. The one thing the business with debtors of £10,000 cannot do is to show this debtors' amount as a current asset in the balance sheet: to do so would be to imply to the user of the balance sheet that the full £10,000 is collectable. Instead, this *gross* debtors' figure might be reduced in two stages, for example:

- debtors' accounts with balances totalling £200 are to be written off as bad
- a general provision for bad debts is to be made amounting, in this case, to two per cent of remaining debtors

Thus the debtors' figure becomes:

	£
Gross debtors	10,000
Less: bad debts written off	200
	9,800
Less: provision for bad debts at two* per cent	196
Net debtors (recorded in balance sheet)	9,604

* The amount of the provision for bad debts will vary from business to business, depending on the past experience of receiving payment, the nature of the business and the current economic climate.

14.2 Bad debts

Bad debts are written off when they become uncollectable. This means that all reasonable efforts to recover the amount owing have been exhausted, ie statements and letters have been sent to the debtor requesting payment and legal action, where appropriate, or the threat of legal action has failed to obtain payment.

In writing off a debtor's account as bad, the business is bearing the cost of the amount due. The debtor's account is closed and the amount (or amounts, where a number of accounts are dealt with in this way) is debited to *bad debts written off account*. This account stores up the amounts of account balances written off during the year (in much the same way as an expense account). At the end of the financial year, the balance of the account is transferred to profit and loss account, where it is described as *bad debts written off*.

In terms of book-keeping, the transactions are:

—*debit* bad debts written off account
—*credit* debtor's account
} with amount of the bad debt

At the end of the financial year, bad debts written off account is transferred to profit and loss account:

—*debit* profit and loss account
—*credit* bad debts written off account
} with the total of bad debts written off for the year

For example, the following debtor's account is in the sales ledger:

T Hughes

Dr.		£			Cr. £
19-1			19-1		
5 Jan.	Sales	55	8 May	Bank	25
			6 Jul.	Cash	5

It is now 15 December 19-1 and you are reviewing the debtors' accounts before the end of the financial year on 31 December. Your business has sent statements and 'chaser' letters to T Hughes – the last letter was dated 30 September, and was returned marked 'gone away, not known at this address'. Nothing further has been heard from T Hughes. You take the decision to write off this account as a bad debt; the account will be closed off as shown on the next page:

Dr.		T Hughes			Cr.
19-1		£	19-1		£
5 Jan.	Sales	55	8 May	Bank	25
			6 Jul.	Cash	5
			15 Dec.	Bad debts written off	25
		55			55

The balance is transferred to the 'holding' account, *bad debts written off,* together with other accounts written off. At the end of the financial year, the total of this account is transferred to profit and loss account:

Dr.		Bad Debts Written Off Account			Cr.
19-1		£	19-1		£
15 Dec.	T Hughes	25	31 Dec.	Profit and loss account	200
15 Dec.	A Lane	85			
15 Dec.	A Harvey	90			
		200			200

In final accounts, the effect of writing off debts as bad is to reduce the previously reported profit – in the example above, by £200.

Note: If you are preparing final accounts from a trial balance, and the figure for bad debts is shown in the trial balance (debit side), simply record the amount as an expense in profit and loss account – the debtors' figure will have been reduced already. If the bad debts figure is not already shown in the trial balance, and a note tells you to write off a certain debt as bad, you need to list the amount as an expense in profit and loss account *and* reduce the debtors' figure for the balance sheet.

Bad debts recovered

If, by chance, a former debtor whose account has been written off as bad, should make a payment, the book-keeping procedure is:

—*debit* cash/bank account
—*credit* either, bad debts written off account
or, bad debts recovered account
} with the amount of the payment

The latter account, *bad debts recovered,* would only be used where a business has substantial debtors and was successful in chasing its bad debts. If a recovery is a rare event – perhaps once a year – the practical accounting solution is to credit bad debts written off account. The one account you would *not* credit is the closed debtor's account – if the customer now wishes to buy goods, cash terms would be advisable for some time to come!

14.3 Provision for bad debts

This is different from writing off a bad debt because there is the possibility – not the certainty – of future bad debts. The debtors' figure (after writing off bad debts) is reduced either by totalling the balances of the accounts that may not pay or, more likely, by applying a percentage to the total figure for debtors. The percentage chosen will be based on past experience and will vary from business to business – for example, a hire purchase company may well use a higher percentage than a bank.

14.4 Initial creation of a provision for bad debts

The procedure for the provision for bad debts – also known as a *provision for doubtful debts* – comes *after* writing off bad debts (if any). The steps are:

1. A business, at the end of the financial year, estimates the percentage of its debtors which may go bad, say two per cent
2. The provision is calculated (eg £9,800 x 2% = £196)
3. The provision is recorded in the book-keeping system:
   —*debit* profit and loss account
   —*credit* provision for bad debts account
4. In the final accounts, the amount of the provision is:
   - listed in the profit and loss account as an expense *provision for bad debts*
   - deducted from the debtors' figure in the current assets section of the balance sheet, eg:

	£	£	£
Current Assets			
Stock		x	
Debtors	9,800		
Less provision for bad debts	196		
		9,604	
Prepayments		x	
Bank		x	
Cash		x	
		x	

Note that the business, in creating a *provision* for bad debts, is presenting a realistic and prudent estimate of its debtor position.

14.5 Adjustments to provision for bad debts

Once a provision for bad debts has been created, the only adjustments that need to be made to the provision for bad debts are as a result of:

- a *policy change* in the provision, eg an increase in the fixed percentage from 2% to 5%
- an *arithmetic adjustment* in the provision as a result of a change in the total of debtors, eg increase in debtors of £5,000 will require a higher provision

If, or when, either of these two situations arises, the adjustment to the existing position will be:

- either *upwards* (increase in provision percentage, or increase in debtor figure)
- or *downwards* (decrease in provision percentage, or decrease in debtor figure)

An ***increase in the provision*** is recorded in the book-keeping system as follows:

—*debit* profit and loss account*
—*credit* provision for bad debts account
} with the amount of the increase

* described as 'increase in provision for bad debts', and listed in the expenses section

For the purposes of the balance sheet, the amount of the increase is added to the existing provision to give the new figure for provision for bad debts (which is deducted from the debtors' figure), ie the balance at the end of the year is used.

A ***decrease in the provision*** is recorded as:

—*debit* provision for bad debts account
—*credit* profit and loss account* } with the amount of the decrease

* described as 'reduction in provision for bad debts', and listed in the income section

For the balance sheet, the amount of the new provision is shown, ie the lower amount (existing provision less amount of decrease).

Note that provision for bad debts and bad debts written off are completely separate adjustments: the two should not be confused. It is quite usual to see in a profit and loss account entries for both *bad debts* (written off) and *provision for bad debts* (the creation or adjustment of provision for bad debts).

14.6 Example of book-keeping entries for provision for bad debts

A business decides to create a provision for bad debts of five per cent of its debtors. After writing off bad debts, the debtors figures at the end of each of three years are:

19-1	£10,000
19-2	£15,000
19-3	£12,000

Book-keeping entries

Creating the provision (19-1)

—*debit* profit and loss account
—*credit* provision for bad debts account } with £10,000 x 5% = £500

Increasing the provision (19-2)

—*debit* profit and loss account
—*credit* provision for bad debts account } with £5,000 (*increase* in debtors) x 5% = £250

Decreasing the provision (19-3)

—*debit* provision for bad debts account
—*credit* profit and loss account } with £3,000 (*decrease* in debtors) x 5% = £150

The provision for bad debts account is as follows:

Dr.	**Provision for Bad Debts Account**				Cr.
19-1		£	19-1		£
31 Dec.	Balance c/d	500	31 Dec.	Profit and loss account	500
19-2			19-2		
31 Dec.	Balance c/d	750	1 Jan.	Balance b/d	500
			31 Dec.	Profit and loss account *(increase in provision)*	250
		750			750
19-3			19-3		
31 Dec.	Profit and loss account *(decrease in provision)*	150	1 Jan.	Balance b/d	750
31 Dec.	Balance c/d	600			
		750			750
19-4			19-4		
			1 Jan.	Balance b/d	600

The final accounts

The effect of the above transactions on the final accounts is shown in the following table:

Year	Profit and loss account		Balance sheet		
	Expense	Income	Debtors	Less provision for bad debts	Net debtors
	£	£	£	£	£
19-1	500	-	10,000	500	9,500
19-2	250	-	15,000	750	14,250
19-3	-	150	12,000	600	11,400

The profit and loss account and balance sheet extracts for each year are as follows:

Profit and loss account (extract) for the year ended 31 December 19-1

	£	£
Gross Profit		x
Less:		
Provision for bad debts	500	

Balance sheet (extract) as at 31 December 19-1

	£	£	£
Current Assets			
Stock		x	
Debtors	10,000		
Less provision for bad debts	500		
		9,500	

Profit and loss account (extract) for the year ended 31 December 19-2

	£	£
Gross Profit		x
Less:		
Increase in provision for bad debts	250	

Balance sheet (extract) as at 31 December 19-2

	£	£	£
Current Assets			
Stock		x	
Debtors	15,000		
Less provision for bad debts	750		
		14,250	

Profit and loss account (extract) for the year ended 31 December 19-3

	£	£
Gross Profit		x
Add:		
Reduction in provision for bad debts		150
		x

Balance sheet (extract) as at 31 December 19-3

	£	£	£
Current Assets			
Stock		x	
Debtors	12,000		
Less provision for bad debts	600		
		11,400	

Note: If you are preparing final accounts from a trial balance in an examination, there will be a note to the trial balance telling you to make an adjustment to the provision for bad debts. Sometimes you will be told a percentage figure, eg 'provision for bad debts is to be maintained at five per cent of debtors'; alternatively, you may be told the new provision figure (be careful of the wording – distinguish between 'increase the provision *to* £750' and 'increase the provision *by* £750').

14.7 Minimising the risk of bad debts

Having studied the technicalities of accounting for bad debts, and creating a provision for bad debts, it is appropriate to look at ways in which businesses selling on credit can minimise the risks. The following are some of the procedures that can be followed:

- When first approached by an unknown business wishing to buy goods on credit, the seller should ask for two references. One of these should be the buyer's bank, and the other a trader with whom the buyer has previously done business.

- The seller, before supplying goods on credit, should take up both references and obtain satisfactory replies. (Note that it is not possible to approach a bank direct for a reference on one of their customers – this can only be done bank-to-bank, and so the seller must ask his or her own bank to obtain a reference from the buyer's bank.)

- Once satisfactory replies have been received, a credit limit for the customer should be established, and an account opened in the sales ledger. The amount of the credit limit will depend very much on the expected amount of future business – for example, £1,000 might be appropriate. The credit limit should not normally be exceeded – the firm's credit controller or financial accountant will approve any transactions above the limit.

- Invoices and month-end statements of account should be sent out promptly; invoices should state the terms of trade (see Chapter 4.4), and statements should analyse the balance to show how long it has been outstanding, eg 'over 30 days, over 60 days, over 90 days' – computer-produced statements can show this automatically.

- If a customer does not pay within a reasonable time, the firm should follow established procedures in order to chase up the debt promptly. These procedures are likely to include 'chaser' letters, the first of which prints out that the account is overdue, with a later letter threatening legal action. Whether or not legal action is taken will depend on the size of the debt – for a small amount the costs and time involved in taking legal action may outweigh the benefits of recovering the money.

The use of an aged schedule of debtors

To help with credit control, many firms produce an *aged schedule of debtors* at the end of each month. This analyses individual debtor balances into the time that the amount has been owing. Thus it shows the long outstanding debts that are, potentially, bad debtors, against whom early action is necessary. An aged schedule is easily produced using a computer accounting system (see Chapter 10.5).

An aged schedule of debtors can also be used to calculate the provision for bad debts. For example, a business has the following schedule of debtors at the end of its financial year:

Days outstanding	*Debtors*
	£
Current (up to 30 days)	50,000
31 to 60	26,000
61 to 90	10,000
91 and over	4,000
	90,000

Provision for bad debts is to be calculated by providing for 25% on debts which have been outstanding for 91 days and over, 10% on debts outstanding for 61-90 days, and 2% on debts outstanding for 31-60 days. No provision is to be made on current debts.

Provision for bad debts is calculated as:

			£
Current	£50,000 (no provision)	=	nil
31-60 days	£26,000 x 2%	=	520
61-90 days	£10,000 x 10%	=	1,000
91 days and over	£4,000 x 25%	=	1,000
Provision for bad debts to be created (or adjusted) to			2,520

14.8 Provision for discount on debtors

As well as making a provision for bad debts, some businesses make a *provision for discount on debtors*. This allows for the fact that a cash discount for quick settlement will be taken by some debtors. Therefore an estimate of the amount of discount to be allowed to the debtors needs to be recorded as an expense in the profit and loss account in the year that the sale was made. At the same time, the balance sheet records the net debtors figure after both provision for bad debts and provision for discount on debtors have been deducted: the resultant figure represents the best estimate of the amount that is owing to the business by its debtors.

In calculating the amount of provision for discount on debtors a fixed percentage is usually used, eg two per cent. The calculations and book-keeping entries for provision for discount on debtors are very similar to those for provision for bad debts. Note, however, that the provision for discount on debtors is calculated *after* deduction from debtors of the provision for bad debts.

Example of book-keeping entries

Refer back to the example debtors figures shown in Section 14.6 (page 218). Here the debtors figures (after writing off bad debts) at the end of each of three years are:

19-1	£10,000
19-2	£15,000
19-3	£12,000

The business has already created a provision for bad debts of five per cent of its debtors. In addition it now decides to create a provision for discount on debtors of two per cent. The calculations are:

	Debtors (after writing off bad debts)	Provision for bad debts (five per cent of debtors)	Provision for discount on debtors (two per cent of *debtors less provision for bad debts)*	Net debtors (balance sheet figure)
19-1	£10,000	£500	£190	£9,310
19-2	£15,000	£750	£285	£13,965
19-3	£12,000	£600	£228	£11,172

Provision for Discount on Debtors Account

Dr.		£	Cr.		£
19-1			19-1		
31 Dec.	Balance c/d	190	31 Dec.	Profit and loss account *(creating the provision)*	190
19-2			19-2		
31 Dec.	Balance c/d	285	1 Jan.	Balance b/d	190
			31 Dec.	Profit and loss account *(increasing the provision, ie £285 - £190)*	95
		285			285
19-3			19-3		
31 Dec.	Profit and loss account *(decreasing the provision, ie £285 - £228)*	57	1 Jan.	Balance b/d	285
31 Dec.	Balance c/d	228			
		285			285
			19-4		
			1 Jan.	Balance b/d	228

Profit and loss account (extract) for the year ended 31 December 19-1

	£	£
Gross Profit		x
Less:		
Provision for discount on debtors	190	

Balance sheet (extract) as at 31 December 19-1

	£	£	£
Current Assets			
Stock		x	
Debtors	10,000		
Less provision for bad debts	500		
	9,500		
Less provision for discount on debtors	190		
		9,310	

Profit and loss account (extract) for the year ended 31 December 19-2

	£	£
Gross Profit		x
Less:		
Increase in provision for discount on debtors	95	

Balance sheet (extract) as at 31 December 19-2

	£	£	£
Current Assets			
Stock		x	
Debtors	15,000		
Less provision for bad debts	750		
	14,250		
Less provision for discount on debtors	285		
		13,965	

Profit and loss account (extract) for the year ended 31 December 19-3

	£	£
Gross Profit		x
Add:		
Reduction in provision for discount on debtors		57
		x

Balance sheet (extract) as at 31 December 19-3

	£	£	£
Current Assets			
Stock		x	
Debtors	12,000		
Less provision for bad debts	600		
	11,400		
Less provision for discount on debtors	228		
		11,172	

14.9 Chapter summary

- ❑ A bad debt is a debt owing to a business which it considers will never be paid.
- ❑ A provision for bad debts is the estimate by a business of the likely percentage of its debtors which may go bad during any one accounting period.
- ❑ The specific order should be followed:
  - write off bad debts (if any)
  - create (or adjust) provision for bad debts
- ❑ To write off a bad debt:
  - *debit* bad debts written off account
  - *credit* debtor's account

  At the end of the financial year the bad debts written off account is transferred as an expense, to profit and loss account.
- ❑ A provision for bad debts is often based on a fixed percentage of debtors at the year-end.

- ❑ To create a provision for bad debts:
  - *debit* profit and loss account
  - *credit* provision for bad debts account
- ❑ In the balance sheet, provision for bad debts is deducted from debtors.
- ❑ Having created a provision for bad debts, it will usually be adjusted either upwards or downwards in later years in line with the change in the level of debtors.
- ❑ A business should follow set procedures when opening new accounts in order to minimise the risk of bad debts.
- ❑ Some businesses make a provision for discount on debtors, being an estimate of the amount of cash discount to be allowed to debtors. The amount is usually calculated as a fixed percentage of debtors, after deducting provision for bad debts.
- ❑ To create a provision for discount on debtors:
  - *debit* profit and loss account
  - *credit* provision for discount on debtors
- ❑ In the balance sheet, provision for discount on debtors is deducted from debtors, after first deducting provision for bad debts.
- ❑ Having created a provision for discount on debtors, it will usually be adjusted either upwards or downwards in later years in line with the change in the level of debtors.

The next chapter looks at how the various adjustments considered in the last four chapters can be shown formally on the trial balance. This technique is known as the *extended trial balance.*

14.10 Questions

Note: When preparing final accounts you may wish to refer to the specimen layout given in Appendix A (page 484).

14.1* On 31 December year 7, at the end of his first year's trading, J Richards balanced his accounts and found that his debtors amounted to £32,350.

Included in this total were three debts that Richards decided were irrecoverable and wrote off as bad, namely:

D Rice £420 T Higgs £310 C Clay £120

He *then* decided to make a provision for bad and doubtful debts of 5% of his total debtors.

During year 8, Richards wrote off two debts as irrecoverable, namely:

H Carr – £640 on 1 July

A Moore – £290 on 1 October

On 31 December year 8, Richards balanced his books and found that his debtors amounted to £36,500 and he decided to adjust his provision for bad and doubtful debts to 5% of his total debtors.

Required:

(i) Balancing the accounts at the end of *each* year, prepare:

(a) the provision for bad and doubtful debts account

(b) the bad debts account

(ii) Show the balance sheet entries for debtors as at 31 December year 7 and 31 December year 8.

[London Chamber of Commerce]

14.2 The following data is available in relation to Thermogen Suppliers:

		£
• Balance of debtors at 31 December year 6 —*before* writing off bad debts	–	81,600
• Bad debts written off in year 6	–	1,200
• A provision of 2% of debtors for doubtful debts was set up at 31 December year 6		
• Bad debts written off in year 7	–	1,800
• Balance of debtors at 31 December year 7 —*before* writing off bad debts	–	122,700
• The provision for doubtful debts is increased to 4% at 31 December year 7		
• Bad debts written off in year 8	–	2,100
• Balance of debtors at 31 December year 8 —*after* writing off bad debts	–	103,500
• The provision for doubtful debts is reduced to 3% at 31 December year 8		

Required:

(a) Prepare the following accounts for years 6, 7 and 8, showing the transfer to profit and loss account at the end of each year:
(i) bad debts account
(ii) provision for doubtful debts account

(b) Show balance sheet extracts in respect of debtors at the following dates:
31 December year 6
31 December year 7
31 December year 8

(c) If one of the debts, written off early in year 8, was to be recovered later in year 8, what accounting entries would you expect to be made?

[London Chamber of Commerce]

14.3 The following trial balance was extracted from the books of Paula Jones, a retail grocer, at the end of her financial year 31 March 19-0.

Trial balance as at 31 March 19-0

	Dr £	*Cr* £
Capital		200,000
Debtors	6,000	
Creditors		4,000
Drawings	38,000	
Cash in hand	100	
Cash at bank		4,630
Sales		168,000
Purchases	96,000	
Opening stock	6,400	
Sales returns	1,000	
Carriage inwards	400	
Discount received		250
Discount allowed	380	
Premises	187,000	
Fixtures and fittings (at cost)	20,000	
Provision for depreciation on fixtures		6,000
Rates	4,400	
Insurance	1,200	
Wages and salaries	22,000	
	382,880	382,880

In preparing the year-end accounts, the following should be accounted for:

1. The closing stock was valued at £6,800
2. Wages and salaries due but not paid amount to £1,000
3. There is a prepayment on rates amounting to £600
4. A debt amounting to £120 is considered irrecoverable
5. Depreciation on fixtures is to be provided at the rate of 10% per annum on cost

You are required to:

(a) prepare Paula's trading account for the year ended 31 March 19-0

(b) prepare Paula's profit and loss account for the year

(c) draft Paula's balance sheet as at 31 March 19-0

[Welsh Joint Education Committee]

14.4 The following trial balance was extracted from the books of Sandra Shenstone, a sole trader, as at the close of business on 30 June year 5:

	Dr £	*Cr* £
Capital account		6,400
Wages and salaries	6,800	
Discounts allowed and received	260	340
Purchases and sales	12,830	26,700
Rent	2,600	
Bad debts written off	420	
Drawings	2,450	
Delivery van	1,800	
Bank overdraft		2,200
Returns inwards	340	
Office furniture and equipment, at cost	1,600	
Van running expenses	780	
Rates and insurance	760	
Debtors and creditors	4,650	2,950
General office expenses	320	
Stock, 1 July year 4	2,930	
Cash in hand	50	
	38,590	38,590

The following adjustments are to be made:

- Provide for depreciation as follows:
  Delivery van – £600
  Office furniture and equipment – 25% per annum on cost
- A provision of 2% of Debtors is to be created for doubtful debts
- Stock, 30 June year 5 – £3,160

Required:

Prepare a trading and profit and loss account for the year ended 30 June year 5, together with a balance sheet at that date.

[London Chamber of Commerce]

14.5* The following is the trial balance extracted from the ledger of Stamper, a sole trader who runs a shop, at 31 December 19-9:

	£	£
Capital 1 January 19-9		52,500
Drawings	20,000	
Sales		150,750
Purchases	112,800	
Stock at 1 January 19-9	25,600	
Wages	12,610	
Rent	2,500	
Motor expenses	1,240	
Motor vehicle:		
at cost	17,000	
accumulated depreciation at 1 January 19-9		3,000
Equipment:		
at cost	15,000	
accumulated depreciation at 1 January 19-9		4,500
Bank	900	
Debtors	9,950	
Creditors		8,100
Cash float	250	
Insurance	1,000	
	218,850	218,850

You are given the following additional information:

1. Stock at 31 December 19-9 was valued at £27,350.
2. Rent of £500 (included in the figure of £2,500 above) was prepaid at 31 December 19-9.
3. Motor expenses of £140 are to be accrued at 31 December 19-9.
4. A bad debt of £200 is to be written off.
5. An invoice for insurance of £450 was wrongly recorded as purchases, and is included under purchases in the trial balance.
6. The motor vehicle is depreciated on the straight line basis assuming a life of four years and a residual value of £5,000; the equipment is depreciated on the reducing balance basis using an annual rate of 30%.

Required:

Prepare the trading and profit and loss account of Stamper for the year to 31 December 19-9 and the balance sheet at that date.

[The Chartered Institute of Bankers, Spring 1990]

14.6 The following trial balance was extracted from the books of Percival Porteous at 31 May 19-0.

Trial balance as at 31 May 19-0

	£	£
Capital		54,960
Drawings	8,280	
Premises at cost	54,000	
Sundry debtors and creditors	7,500	6,228
Stock at 1 June 19-9	11,100	
Salaries	5,280	
Carriage inwards	2,190	
Carriage outwards	2,340	
Rates and insurance	2,790	
Purchases and sales	102,000	145,185
Returns inwards and outwards	780	1,440
Advertising	1,041	
Bad debts	240	
Rent receivable		960
Office equipment at cost	6,000	
Shop fittings at cost	18,000	
Provision for depreciation:		
Office equipment		1,200
Shop fittings		4,800
Cash in hand	1,020	
Bank overdraft		7,488
Provision for bad debts at 1 June 19-9		300
	222,561	222,561

You are given the following additional information:

(i) Stock valued at 31 May 19-0 £12,600

(ii) Salaries due but unpaid £1,800

(iii) Rates and insurance prepaid £310

(iv) The provision for bad debts is to be adjusted to 5% of debtors outstanding on 31 May 19-0

(v) Depreciation is written off fixed assets as follows:
Office equipment 10% per annum using the straight line basis
Shop fittings 5% per annum using the reducing balance

You are required to:

Prepare Porteous's trading and profit and loss account for the year ended 31 May 19-0 showing clearly

(a) the cost of goods sold

(b) gross profit and net profit

and the balance sheet as at 31 May 19-0, highlighting the net working capital.

(Note: Your accounts should be in vertical form)

[RSA Examinations Board]

14.7* The following table shows the cumulative effects of a succession of separate transactions on the assets and liabilities of a business. Each letter identifies the assets and liabilities *after each single transaction.*

Transactions:		*A*	*B*	*C*	*D*	*E*	*F*	*G*	*H*	*I*	*J*
Assets:	£000	£000	£000	£000	£000	£000	£000	£000	£000	£000	£000
Buildings, at cost/valuation	200	200	200	200	200	200	200	250	250	250	250
Equipment, at cost	100	100	100	100	125	125	125	125	125	125	125
Stock, at cost	35	35	46	32	32	22	22	22	22	22	22
Trade debtors	48	43	43	43	43	43	43	43	40	40	40
Prepaid expenses	5	5	5	5	5	5	5	5	5	5	3
Bank	0	0	0	15	15	15	15	15	15	10	10
Cash	3	3	3	3	3	3	1	1	1	1	3
	391	386	397	398	423	413	411	461	458	453	453
Liabilities:											
Capital	235	235	235	241	241	231	230	280	277	278	278
Loan	80	80	80	80	105	105	105	105	105	105	105
Trade creditors	55	55	66	66	66	66	66	66	66	60	60
Accrued expenses	11	11	11	11	11	11	10	10	10	10	10
Bank overdraft	10	5	5	0	0	0	0	0	0	0	0
	391	386	397	398	423	413	411	461	458	453	453

Required:

Identify clearly as fully as you can what transaction has taken place in each case. Use the reference letters from the table to identify each transaction. There is no need to copy out the table.

[Association of Accounting Technicians]

Multiple-choice questions: chapters 13-14

- Read each question carefully
- Choose the *one* answer you think is correct (calculators may be needed)
- Answers are on page 486

1. A machine costs £5,000 and is expected to last for five years. At the end of this time, it is estimated it will have a residual (scrap) value of £500. The annual amount of depreciation, using the straight-line method will be:

   A £900
   B £1,000
   C £1,100
   D £1,250

2. A car costs £12,000 and is expected to be kept for four years. At the end of this time, it is estimated that it will be sold for £4,000. Using the reducing balance method of depreciation, what percentage (to the nearest whole number) will be used each year?

   A 20%
   B 24%
   C 25%
   D 26%

3. A car is being depreciated using the reducing balance method. The original cost of the car was £15,000. At the end of year three it has a net book value of £5,145. What percentage of reducing balance is being used?

   A 20%
   B 25%
   C 30%
   D 35%

4. A computer is being depreciated over five years using the sum of the digits method. The original cost was £8,000 and the estimated residual (scrap) value is £500. How much will be the depreciation amount for year 4?

   A £2,000
   B £1,600
   C £1,500
   D £1,000

5. A bus costs £85,000 and is expected to last for five years during which time it will cover 250,000 miles. It is then expected to be sold for £10,000. Depreciation is on the units of output method. How much will be the depreciation amount for this year, during which it has covered 60,000 miles?

   A £17,000
   B £15,000
   C £18,000
   D £20,000

6. The depreciation charge in profit and loss account will reduce:

A gross profit
B net profit
C bank balance
D current assets

7. The book-keeping entries to record a profit on sale of fixed assets are:

	Debit	*Credit*
A	fixed asset account	profit and loss account
B	disposals account	profit and loss account
C	profit and loss account	disposals account
D	bank account	profit and loss account

8. A machine, which originally cost £1,000, is sold for £350. The provision for depreciation account relevant to this machine shows a balance of £620. This means that there is:

A a loss on sale of £380
B a profit on sale of £350
C a loss on sale of £30
D a profit on sale of £30

9. The book-keeping entries to record a decrease in provision for bad debts are:

	Debit	*Credit*
A	profit and loss account	provision for bad debts account
B	bad debts written off account	profit and loss account
C	provision for bad debts account	profit and loss account
D	bank account	provision for bad debts account

10. An increase in provision for bad debts will:

A decrease net profit for the year
B increase gross profit for the year
C decrease the cash/bank balance
D increase net profit for the year

11. A trial balance shows debtors of £48,000 and a provision for bad debts of £2,200. It is decided to make the provision for bad debts equal to five per cent of debtors. What book-keeping entry will be made on the provision for bad debts account?

A debit £200
B debit £2,400
C credit £200
D credit £2,200

12. The profit and loss account of a business has been prepared showing a net loss of £2,350. A reduction of £150 in the provision of bad debts should have been made, and bad debts of £70 should have been written off. Net loss will now be:

A £2,130
B £2,270
C £2,430
D £2,570

15 The Extended Trial Balance

In the previous four chapters we have looked at the preparation of year-end accounts from a trial balance, including adjustments for accruals and prepayments, depreciation of fixed assets, bad debts written off, and provision for bad debts. In this chapter we shall see how these adjustments can be shown formally on the trial balance, and then the various figures from the trial balance can be shown in columns and allocated to the trading account, profit and loss account and balance sheet. This technique is known as the *extended trial balance* and is often used by accountancy firms preparing year-end accounts for their clients.

15.1 The dual aspect of adjustments

When preparing final accounts in the previous chapters, we have seen how each adjustment needs to be reflected in two aspects of the year-end accounts. The following are examples of how we have dealt with the main adjustments:

- Closing stock
  — deduct in trading account, so reducing cost of goods sold
  — current asset in balance sheet

- Accruals of expenses
  — increase expenses in profit and loss account
  — current liability in balance sheet

- Prepayment of expenses
  — decrease expense in profit and loss account
  — current asset in balance sheet

- Provision for depreciation
  — expense in profit and loss account
  — fixed asset value reduced

- Increase in provision for bad debts
  — expense in profit and loss account
  — debtors' figure reduced

15.2 Layout of the extended trial balance

Like a number of accounting statements, the extended trial balance can be set out in a way that best suits the user. A comprehensive layout is shown in fig. 15.1 and a completed extended trial balance in fig. 15.2.

Starting with the trial balance extracted from the book-keeping records, accruals and prepayments are made, together with other adjustments, and the final totals are recorded under the appropriate headings of trading, profit and loss account, and balance sheet. For example, if £150 was owing for electricity at the end of the year, this amount is entered as a debit to electricity in the adjustments column and the total for electricity of £2,900 (£2,750 + £150) is shown as a debit in the profit and loss account column; to complete double-entry, the amount owing is credited to accrued expenses in the adjustments column, and is then shown as a creditor in the balance sheet column.

15.3 Worked example

Using the trial balance shown in fig. 15.2, the following adjustments are to be made as at 31 December 19-1:

- closing stock is valued at £20,000
- electricity is accrued by £150
- rent is prepaid by £250
- the provision for bad debts is to be increased to five per cent of debtors
- the shop equipment is to be depreciated at twenty per cent per annum using the straight-line method

These adjustments are recorded in the appropriate columns (as shown in fig. 15.2). Notice that:

- the trading account columns show gross profit for the year (on the debit side), and this is transferred to the credit side of the profit and loss account columns
- likewise, net profit is transferred to the balance sheet (and will be added to the owner's capital account)
- closing stock is credited in the trading account, and shown as an asset in the balance sheet
- accruals and prepayments are shown in the adjustments column in order to alter the amount of the relevant expense for profit and loss account; the amounts for accruals and prepayments are shown in the balance sheet
- increase in provision for bad debts is shown in the adjustments column (credit side), and is then debited to profit and loss account, and the new total (existing provision plus increase) is shown as a liability in the balance sheet
- increase in provision for depreciation is dealt with in the same way

The extended trial balance does not present final accounts in the conventional format used by accountants, but it does ensure that the dual aspect of each adjustment is dealt with correctly, and that no item from the trial balance is overlooked. Using the 'conventional' format, the year-end accounts of H Jarvis will be presented as shown on page 237.

The use of an extended trial balance is one way in which adjustments to the accounts can be picked up and incorporated into the final accounts. Its use is particularly helpful when dealing with complex adjustments.

H JARVIS

	Trial balance as at 31 December 19-1		Adjustments		Trading account		Profit and loss account		Balance Sheet *Assets* *Liabilities*	
	Dr £	Cr £	Dr £	Cr £	Dr £	Cr £	Dr £	Cr £	Dr £	Cr £
Sales		122,000								
Purchases	78,500									
Debtors	5,000									
Creditors		10,500								
Stock at 1 Jan. 19-1	17,500									
Bad debts	850									
Rent	10,500									
Electricity	2,750									
Wages	20,500									
Provision for bad debts		200								
Shop equipment (cost)	25,000									
Provision for depreciation		5,000								
Bank	14,600									
Capital		50,000								
Drawings	12,500									
	187,700	187,700								
Stock at 31 Dec. 19-1:										
• trading account										
• balance sheet										
Accrued expenses										
Prepaid expenses										
Provision for bad debts										
Provision for depreciation										
Gross profit (balancing figure)										
Net profit (balancing figure)										

Fig. 15.1 Layout of an extended trial balance

H JARVIS

	Trial balance as at 31 December 19-1		Adjustments		Trading account		Profit and loss account		Balance Sheet *Assets Liabilities*	
	Dr £	Cr £	Dr £	Cr £	Dr £	Cr £	Dr £	Cr £	Dr £	Cr £
Sales		122,000				122,000				
Purchases	78,500				78,500					
Debtors	5,000								5,000	
Creditors		10,500								10,500
Stock at 1 Jan. 19-1	17,500				17,500					
Bad debts	850						850			
Rent	10,500			250			10,250			
Electricity	2,750		150				2,900			
Wages	20,500						20,500			
Provision for bad debts		200		50						250
Shop equipment (cost)	25,000								25,000	
Provision for depreciation		5,000		5,000						10,000
Bank	14,600								14,600	
Capital		`50,000								50,000
Drawings	12,500								12,500	
	187,700	187,700								
Stock at 31 Dec. 19-1:										
• trading account				20,000		20,000				
• balance sheet			20,000						20,000	
Accrued expenses				150						150
Prepaid expenses			250						250	
Provision for bad debts			50				50			
Provision for depreciation			5,000				5,000			
Gross profit (balancing figure)					46,000			46,000		
Net profit (balancing figure)							6,450			6,450
			25,450	25,450	142,000	142,000	46,000	46,000	77,350	77,350

Fig. 15.2 Use of an extended trial balance

**TRADING AND PROFIT AND LOSS ACCOUNT OF H JARVIS
FOR THE YEAR ENDED 31 DECEMBER 19-1**

	£	£
Sales		122,000
Opening stock	17,500	
Purchases	78,500	
	96,000	
Less Closing Stock	20,000	
Cost of Goods Sold		76,000
Gross Profit		46,000
Less:		
Bad debts written off	850	
Rent	10,250	
Electricity	2,900	
Wages	20,500	
Increase in provision for bad debts	50	
Provision for depreciation	5,000	
		39,550
Net Profit		6,450

BALANCE SHEET OF H JARVIS AS AT 31 DECEMBER 19-1

	£	£	£
Fixed Assets	*Cost*	*Dep'n to date*	*Net*
Shop equipment	25,000	10,000	15,000
Current Assets			
Stock		20,000	
Debtors	5,000		
Less provision for bad debts	250		
		4,750	
Prepayment		250	
Bank		14,600	
		39,600	
Less Current Liabilities			
Creditors	10,500		
Accrual	150		
		10,650	
Working Capital			28,950
NET ASSETS			43,950
FINANCED BY			
Capital			
Opening capital			50,000
Add net profit			6,450
			56,450
Less drawings			12,500
			43,950

15.4 Chapter summary

- The extended trial balance formally records adjustments for accruals and prepayments, depreciation of fixed assets, bad debts written off, and provision for bad debts.

- Once adjusted, the various figures from the trial balance are allocated to the trading account, profit and loss account, and balance sheet.
- The extended trial balance is often used by accountancy firms in preparing year-end accounts on behalf of their clients.

Having looked, in the last few chapters, at some specific methods of adjusting accounts to take note of accruals and prepayments, depreciation, and bad debts, the next chapter considers the basic framework – or concepts – within which financial statements are prepared, and looks at stock valuation.

15.5 Questions

15.1* The following figures have been extracted from the books of Henry as at 31 December 19-9:

	Trial balance as at 31.12.-9		Adjustments		Trading account		Profit & loss account		Balance Sheet	
	Dr	Cr	Dr	Cr	Dr	Cr	Dr	Cr	Dr	Cr
	£	£	£	£	£	£	£	£	£	£
Sales		185,500								
Purchases	97,250									
Debtors	10,500									
Creditors		9,000								
Stock at 1 Jan.19-9	15,250									
Bad debts	500									
Rent	12,750									
Wages	33,250									
Provision for bad debts		1,000								
Fixed assets (cost)	120,000									
Provision for depreciation		36,000								
Bank	11,500									
Capital		95,000								
Drawings	25,500									
	326,500	326,500								

The following adjustments are to be made at 31 December 19-9:

- the stock at 31 December 19-9 is valued at £18,500
- the provision for doubtful debts is to be increased to 10% of debtors
- rent is accrued by £1,000
- wages have been prepaid by £500
- fixed assets are to be depreciated at ten per cent per annum using the straight-line method

Required:

Prepare an extended trial balance for Henry as at 31 December 19-9.

Other questions for which an extended trial balance can be prepared are 12.4, 12.5, 13.2, 13.3, 14.3 and 14.4.

16 Accounting Concepts; Stock Valuation

In this chapter we will look at the basic rules which are always followed in the preparation of final accounts. These rules, or *accounting concepts* (sometimes known as *accounting conventions*) form a theoretical framework within which the final accounts of all businesses are constructed. By following the same concepts, broad comparisons can then be made between the financial results of different businesses.

Later in this chapter we will see how one of the accounting concepts is applied in the valuation of stock. We will also look, in more detail, at stock valuation.

16.1 Basic accounting concepts

We have already looked (in Chapter 1.9) at the two concepts of:

- business entity
- money measurement

Both of these are so basic that they are followed in all circumstances. Another basic accounting concept is that of *materiality* (see below).

Business entity concept

This refers to the fact that final accounts record and report on the activities of one particular business. They do not include the assets and liabilities of those who play a part in owning or running the business.

Money measurement concept

This means that, in the final accounts, all items are expressed in the common denominator of money. Only by using money can items be added together to give, for example, net profit, or a balance sheet total. The disadvantage of money measurement is that it is unable to record items which cannot be expressed in money terms. For example, a business with an efficient management, and good labour relations, will appear to have the same value as one that is overstaffed and has poor labour relations: only in the longer term, with different levels of profit and balance sheet structure, will the differences between the two become apparent.

A further disadvantage of money measurement is that it cannot take note of inflation. For example, a business achieved sales of £100,000 in 19-1 and £105,000 in 19-2. Is this an improvement? It depends on the general level of inflation – if inflation was greater than five per cent per year, there sales have increased in real terms. The problem of how to handle the effects of inflation in final accounts is one that has, so far, defeated accountants – despite the spending of much time, effort and money.

Materiality concept

Some items in accounts are of such a low value that it is not worthwhile recording them separately, ie they are not 'material'.

Examples:

- Small expense items, such as donations to charities, the purchase of plants for the office, window cleaning, etc, do not justify their own separate expense account; instead they are grouped together in a sundry expenses account.
- End-of-year stocks of office stationery, eg paper clips, staples, photocopying paper, etc, are often not valued for the purpose of final accounts, because the amount is not material and does not justify the time and effort involved. This does mean, however, that the cost of all stationery purchased during the year is charged as an expense to profit and loss account – technically wrong, but not material enough to affect the final accounts (see also Chapter 12.2).
- Low-cost fixed assets are often charged as an expense in profit and loss account, instead of being classed as capital expenditure, eg a stapler, waste-paper basket, etc. Strictly, these should be treated as fixed assets and depreciated each year over their estimated life; in practice, because the amounts involved are not material, they are treated as profit and loss account expenses.

Materiality depends very much on the size of the business. A large company may consider that items of less than £1,000 are not material; a small company will usually use a much lower figure. What is material, and what is not becomes a matter of judgement for the accountant.

16.2 Further accounting concepts

The concepts we have considered so far are fundamental to all final accounts. Four further accounting concepts should also be applied:

- going concern
- accruals
- consistency
- prudence

Going concern concept

This presumes that the business to which the final accounts relate will continue to trade in the foreseeable future. The trading and profit and loss account and balance sheet are prepared on the basis that there is no intention to reduce significantly the size of the business or to liquidate the business. If the business was not a going concern, assets would have very different values, and the balance sheet would be affected considerably. For example, a large, purpose-built factory has considerable value to a going concern business but, if the factory had to be sold, it is likely to have a limited use for other industries, and therefore will have a lower market value. The latter case is the opposite of the going concern concept and would be described as a *gone concern*. Also, in a gone concern situation, extra depreciation would need to be charged as an expense to profit and loss account to allow for the reduced value of fixed assets.

Accruals (or matching) concept

This means that expenses and revenues must be matched so that they concern the same goods and the same time period. We have already put this concept into practice in Chapter Twelve, where expenses and revenues were adjusted to take note of prepayments and accruals. The trading and profit and loss account should always show the amounts of the expense that should have been incurred, ie the expenditure for the year, whether or not it has been paid. This is the principle of income and expenditure accounting, rather than using receipts and payments as and when they fall due. Further examples of the accruals concept are debtors, creditors, provision for depreciation, and the opening and closing stock adjustments in the trading account.

Consistency concept

This requires that, when a business adopts particular accounting methods, it should continue to use such methods consistently. For example, a business that decides to make a provision for depreciation on machinery at ten per cent per annum, using the straight-line method, should continue to use that percentage and method for future final accounts for this asset. Of course, having once chosen a particular method, a business is entitled to make changes provided there are good reasons for so doing, and a note to the final accounts would explain what has happened. By applying the consistency concept, direct comparison between the final accounts of different years can be made. Further examples of the use of the consistency concept are stock valuation (see later in this chapter), and the application of the materiality concept.

Prudence concept

This concept, also known as conservatism in accounting, requires that final accounts should always, where there is any doubt, report a conservative figure for profit or the valuation of assets. To this end, profits are not to be anticipated and should only be recognised when it is reasonably certain that they will be realised; at the same time all known liabilities should be provided for. A good example of the prudence concept is where a provision is made for bad debts (see Chapter Fourteen) – the debtors have not yet gone bad, but it is expected, from experience, that a certain percentage will eventually need to be written off as bad debts. The valuation of stock (see later in this chapter) also follows the prudence concept. 'Anticipate no profit, but anticipate all losses' is a summary of the concept which, in its application, prevents an over-optimistic presentation of a business through the final accounts.

Note: These concepts apply equally to the final accounts of sole traders, partnerships and limited companies. In the case of limited companies the concepts are given legal force in the Companies Act 1985 (as amended by the Companies Act 1989), and a company which does not apply them will receive a qualified audit report from its external auditors.

16.3 Accounting standards

Over the last twenty-five years, a number of accounting standards have been produced to provide the rules, or framework, of accounting. The intention has been to reduce the variety of alternative accounting treatments. At present the rules of accounting are represented by:

- Statements of Standard Accounting Practice
- Statements of Recommended Practice
- Financial Reporting Standards

Statements of Standard Accounting Practice – or SSAPs, as they are more usually known – were issued by the Accounting Standards Committee, now superseded by the Accounting Standards Board. This Board requires accountants to observe the applicable accounting standards, and to disclose and explain significant departures from the standards. A number of SSAPs have been replaced by Financial Reporting Standards (see below) as part of an attempt to reduce the number of permissible accounting treatments.

We have just looked at the four accounting concepts (in Section 16.2). These are detailed in SSAP 2, which is entitled 'Disclosure of accounting policies'. These concepts apply to all final accounts and, in the case of limited companies, are given legal force by the Companies Act.

In Chapter Thirteen, when dealing with depreciation, we have already covered the main requirements of SSAP 12 'Accounting for depreciation'. Later in this chapter, we shall look at aspects of SSAP 9 'Stocks and long-term contracts'.

Statements of Recommended Practice (SORPs) are a means of setting out the current best accounting practice to deal with problems of accounting treatments that apply to a particular sector of industry, or the public sector. SORPs are developed by bodies recognised by the Accounting Standards Board. SORPs are not mandatory but are designed to narrow the areas of difference and variety in accounting treatment, and to make accounting information more useful to the users.

Financial Reporting Standards (FRSs) are issued by the Accounting Standards Board which wishes to ensure that standards are consistent, and that there are few options allowed in the preparation of final accounts. An example of an FRS is FRS1 'Cash Flow Statements' (see Chapter Thirty). In your continuing studies in accounting it is certain that you will make use of other Financial Reporting Standards.

Statutory support for accounting standards

The Companies Act 1989 introduced a requirement that limited company accounts must state that they have been prepared in accordance with applicable accounting standards and, if there have been any material departures, must give details and the reasons for such departures.

To enforce this part of the Act, the Secretary of State for Trade and Industry, and other authorised bodies (principally the Financial Reporting Review Panel) are able to apply to the courts for an order requiring the directors of the company to make revisions to defective accounts.

16.4 Valuation of stock

The control and valuation of stock is an important aspect in the efficient management of a business. Manual or computer records (see Chapter 10.7) are used to show the amount of stock held and its value at any time during the year. However, at the end of the financial year it is essential for a business to make a physical *stock-take* for use in the final accounts. This involves stock control personnel going into the stores, the shop, or the warehouse and counting each item. The counted stock for each type of stock held is then valued as follows:

number of items held x stock valuation per item = stock value

The auditors of a business – probably both the internal and external auditors – will make random checks to ensure that the stock value is correct.

The value of stock at the beginning and end of the financial year is used in the trading account, as we have seen (Chapter Eleven), to calculate the figure for cost of goods sold. Therefore, the stock value has an effect on the gross and net profit for the year.

Stock is valued at either:

- what it cost the business to buy the stock, or
- if the goods are old, deteriorated or have gone out of fashion, and their selling price is *less* than the original purchase price, then they will be valued at this selling price (less any costs of selling and distribution).

This stock valuation is often described as being *at the lower of cost and net realisable value*. This valuation is taken from SSAP 9 and applies the prudence concept (see Section 16.2 above). It is illustrated as follows:

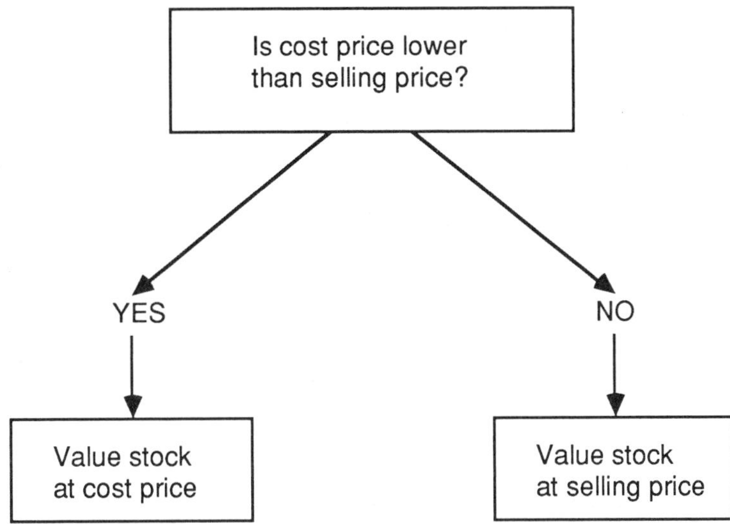

The difficulty in stock valuation is in finding out the cost price of stock – this is not easy when quantities of a particular stock item are continually being bought in – often at different prices – and then sold. Some businesses will have stock in a number of different forms, eg a manufacturing business (see Chapter Twenty-six) will have stocks of raw materials, work-in-progress and finished goods.

16.5 Different methods used in stock valuation

Firms use different methods to calculate the cost price of stock. Three commonly used methods are:

- *FIFO (first in, first out)* This method assumes that the first stocks acquired are the first to be sold or used, so that the valuation of stock on hand at any time consists of the most recently acquired stock.
- *LIFO (last in, first out)* Here it is assumed that the last stocks acquired are the first to be sold or used, so that the stock on hand is made up of earlier purchases.
- *AVCO (average cost)* Here the average cost of items held at the beginning of the year is calculated; as new stocks are bought a new average cost is calculated (based on a weighted average, using the number of units bought as the weighting).

The use of a particular method does not necessarily correspond with the method of physical distribution adopted in a firm's stores. For example, in a car factory one starter motor of type X is the same as another, and no-one will be concerned if the storekeeper issues one from the last batch received, even if the FIFO system has been adopted. However, perishable goods are always physically handled on the basis of first in, first out, even if the accounting stock records use another method.

Having chosen a suitable stock valuation method, a business will continue to use that method unless there are good reasons for making the change. This is in line with the *consistency concept* of accounting.

16.6 Stock valuation records

In order to be able to calculate accurately the price at which stocks of materials are issued to production, and to ascertain quickly a valuation of closing stock, the following method of recording stock data is suggested:

DATE	RECEIPTS		ISSUES		BALANCE		
19..	Quantity	Price	Quantity	Price*	Quantity	Price	Total

* Note that this price is the cost price to the business, *not* the selling price – virtually all stock records are kept at cost price.

16.7 Stock records: an example

In order to show how the stock records would appear under FIFO, LIFO and AVCO, the following data has been used for each:

19-1

January	Opening stock of 40 units at a cost of £3.00 each
February	Bought 20 units at a cost of £3.60 each
March	Sold 36 units for £6 each
April	Bought 20 units at a cost of £3.75 each
May	Sold 25 units for £6 each

FIFO

Date	Receipts			Issues			Balance					
19-1	Quantity		Price	Quantity		Price	Quantity		Price		Total
January	Balance b/d						40	x	£3.00	=	£120.00
February	20	@	£3.60				40 20 60	x x	£3.00 £3.60	= =	£120.00 £72.00 £192.00
March				36	@	£3.00	4 20 24	x x	£3.00 £3.60	= =	£12.00 £72.00 £84.00
April	20	@	£3.75				4 20 20 44	x x x	£3.00 £3.60 £3.75	= = =	£12.00 £72.00 £75.00 £159.00
May				4 20 1	@ @ @	£3.00 £3.60 £3.75	19	x	£3.75	=	£71.25

LIFO

Date	Receipts			Issues			Balance				
19-1	Quantity		Price	Quantity		Price	Quantity		Price		Total
January	Balance b/d						40	x	£3.00	=	£120.00
February	20	@	£3.60				40 20 60	x x	£3.00 £3.60	= =	£120.00 £72.00 £192.00
March				20 16	@ @	£3.60 £3.00	24	x	£3.00	=	£72.00
April	20	@	£3.75				24 20 44	x x	£3.00 £3.75	= =	£72.00 £75.00 £147.00
May				20 5	@ @	£3.75 £3.00	19	x	£3.00	=	£57.00

AVCO

Date	Receipts			Issues			Balance				
19-1	Quantity		Price	Quantity		Price	Quantity		Price		Total
January	Balance b/d						40	x	£3.00	=	£120.00
February	20	@	£3.60				40 20 60	x x x	£3.00 £3.60 £3.20	= = =	£120.00 £72.00 £192.00
March				36	@	£3.20	24	x	£3.20	=	£76.80
April	20	@	£3.75				24 20 44	x x x	£3.20 £3.75 £3.45	= = =	£76.80 £75.00 £151.80
May				25	@	£3.45	19	x	£3.45	=	£65.55

The closing stock valuations at the end of May under each method show cost prices of:
FIFO £71.25
LIFO £57.00
AVCO £65.55

There is quite a difference, and this has come about because different stock methods have been used.

Effect on profit

In the example above, the selling price was £6 per unit. The effect on gross profit of using different stock valuations is shown in the following trading accounts:

	FIFO £	LIFO £	AVCO £
Sales: 61 units at £6	366.00	366.00	366.00
Opening stock: 40 units at £3	120.00	120.00	120.00
Purchases: 20 units at £3.60, 20 Units at £3.75	147.00	147.00	147.00
	267.00	267.00	267.00
Less Closing stock: 19 units	71.25	57.00	65.55
Cost of Goods Sold	195.75	210.00	201.45
Gross profit	170.25	156.00	164.55
	366.00	366.00	366.00

In times of rising prices, FIFO produces the highest profit, LIFO the lowest, and AVCO between the other two. However, over the life of a business, total profit is the same in total, whichever method is chosen: the profit is allocated to different years depending on which method is used.

16.8 Advantages and disadvantages to a business of FIFO, LIFO and AVCO

FIFO (first in, first out)

Advantages:

- realistic, ie it assumes that goods are issued in order of receipt
- it is easy to calculate
- stock valuation comprises actual prices at which items have been bought
- the closing stock valuation is close to the most recent prices

Disadvantages:

- prices at which goods are issued are not necessarily the latest prices
- in times of rising prices, profits will be higher than with other methods (resulting in more tax to pay)

LIFO (last in, first out)

Advantages:

- goods are issued at the latest prices
- it is easy to calculate

Disadvantages:

- illogical, ie it assumes goods are issued in reverse order from that in which they are received
- the closing stock valuation is not usually at most recent prices
- when stocks are being run down, issues will 'dip into' old stock at out-of-date prices

AVCO (average cost)

Advantages:

- over a number of accounting periods reported profits are smoothed, ie both high and low profits are avoided
- fluctuations in purchase price are evened out so that issues do not vary greatly
- logical, ie it assumes that identical units, even when purchased at different times, have the same value
- closing stock valuation is close to current market values (in times of rising prices, it will be below current market values)

Disadvantages:

- difficult to calculate, and calculations may be to several decimal places
- issues and stock valuation are usually at prices which never existed
- issues may not be at current prices and, in times of rising prices, will be below current prices

The important point to remember is that a business must adopt a *consistent* stock valuation policy, ie it should choose one method of finding the cost price, and not change it without good reason. FIFO and AVCO are more commonly used than LIFO; in particular, LIFO usually results in a stock valuation for the final accounts which bears little relationship to recent costs.

16.9 Categories of stock

Statement of Standard Accounting Practice No 9 requires that, in calculating the lower of cost and net realisable value, note should be taken of

— separate items of stock, or

— groups of similar items

This means that the stock valuation 'rule' must be applied to each separate item of stock, or each group or category of similar stocks. The *total* cost cannot be compared with the *total* net realisable value. For example, a decorator's shop has two main categories of stock, paints and wallpapers; they are valued as follows:

	Cost	*Net realisable value*
	£	£
Paints	2,500	2,300
Wallpapers	5,000	7,500
	7,500	9,800

The correct stock valuation is £7,300, which takes the lower of cost and net realisable value for each *group* of stock, ie

	£
Paints (at net realisable value)	2,300
Wallpapers (at cost)	5,000
	7,300

Note that this valuation is the lowest possible choice, so indicating that stock valuation follows the prudence concept of accounting.

16.10 Stock losses

From time-to-time an event such as a fire, a flood, or a theft may cause stock losses. After such an event it is necessary to calculate the amount of stock losses for insurance purposes; this topic is looked at in Chapter 20.8.

16.11 Chapter summary

❑ The basic accounting concepts of business entity, money measurement and materiality always apply to the preparation of final accounts.

❑ In order to improve the usefulness of final accounts the four concepts of going concern, accruals, consistency and prudence should also be applied.

❑ The usual valuation for stock is *at the lower of cost and net realisable value* (SSAP 9).

❑ Common methods of accounting for stock include:
- FIFO (first in, first out)
- LIFO (last in, first out)
- AVCO (average cost, based on a weighted average)

❑ Having chosen one stock valuation method, a business should apply it consistently.

In the last five chapters we have looked at the preparation of final accounts, and a number of adjustments, in some detail. Case Study Three (page 260) puts these adjustments into context by bringing them all together in a set of final accounts.

So far in our studies of *Business Accounts*, we have concerned ourselves with the accounts of a sole trader business – later in the book we will consider the more specialist final accounts of manufacturing businesses (Chapter Twenty-six), partnerships (Chapter Twenty-two), and limited companies (Chapter Twenty-four).

For the next chapter we will see how the journal is used to record adjustments to final accounts, and other transactions.

16.12 Questions

16.1 The use of certain concepts is fundamental to the preparation of accounts.

The fundamental concepts are referred to as

(i) the going concern concept;

(ii) the accruals concept;

(iii) the consistency concept; and

(iv) the prudence concept.

You are required to explain any *three* of these concepts, using an example to identify the importance of the concept.

[The Chartered Institute of Management Accountants]

16.2 One of the well known accounting concepts is that of materiality.

Required:

(a) Explain what is meant by this concept.

(b) State and explain three types of situation to which this concept might be applicable.

(c) State and explain two specific difficulties in applying this concept.

[The Chartered Association of Certified Accountants]

16.3* A discussion is taking place between Wendy Adams, a sole trader, who owns a furniture shop, and her husband, John, who solely owns an engineering business. The following points are made:

(a) John says that, having depreciated his firm's machinery last year on the reducing balance method, for this year he intends to use the straight-line method. By doing this he says that he will deduct less depreciation from profit and loss account, so his net profit will be higher and his bank manager will be impressed. He says he might revert back to reducing balance method next year.

(b) At the end of her financial year, Wendy comments that the stock of her shop had cost £10,000. She says that, as she normally adds 50 per cent to cost price to give the selling price, she intends to put a value of £15,000 for stock in the trading account and balance sheet.

(c) John's car is owned by his business but he keeps referring to it as *my car.* Wendy reminds him that it does not belong to him, but to the firm. He replies that of course it belongs to him and, furthermore, if the firm went bankrupt, he would be able to keep the car.

(d) On the last day of her financial year, Wendy sold a large order of furniture, totalling £3,000, to a local hotel. The furniture was invoiced and delivered from stock that day, before year-end stocktaking commenced. The payment was received early in the new financial year and Wendy now asks John if she will be able to put this sale through the accounts for the new year, instead of the old, but without altering the figures for purchases and closing stock for the old year.

(e) John says that his accountant talks of preparing his accounts on a going concern basis. John asks Wendy if she knows of any other basis that can be used, and which it is usual to follow.

You are to take each of the points and state the correct accounting treatment, referring to appropriate accounting concepts.

16.4 The following information relates to Maynard Autos Limited:

	Purchases	*Sales*
June 19-1	800 units @ £6.00	
July 19-1		700 units
September 19-1	1,200 units @ £7.00	
December 19-1		600 units
February 19-2	1,000 units @ £8.00	
April 19-2		400 units
May 19-2	700 units @ £10.00	

You have been asked to value the stock:
(i) using the FIFO method
(ii) using the LIFO method

[RSA Examinations Board]

16.5* A and B are in business, buying and selling goods for resale. Neither of them are accountants but A has read a book on stock control whereas B has purchased a software package for daily stock records. During September 19-9 the following transactions occurred:

1 September	Balance brought forward: NIL
3 September	Bought 200 units @ £1.00 each
7 September	Sold 180 units
8 September	Bought 240 units @ £1.50 each
14 September	Sold 170 units
15 September	Bought 230 units @ £2.00 each
21 September	Sold 150 units

A prepares the stores ledger card using the LIFO method and B uses the same data to test the software package which uses the weighted average method of pricing.

You are required to:

(a) show the ledger cards as they would appear for *each* method (calculations should be made to two decimal places of £1.00);

(b) comment on the effect on profits of using *each* method of valuing stock.

[The Chartered Institute of Management Accountants]

16.6* D Swift maintains manually prepared stock record cards for the recording of the receipts and issues of various items of stock held in the stores.

You are required to:

(i) draw up a stock record card showing the following rulings and headings:

Item *STOCK CARD*

Date	*Details*	*Receipts*		*Issues*		*Balance*	
		Units	*£*	*Units*	*£*	*Units*	*£*
1 Sep.	Balance					12	144

(ii) record the following movements of the item of stock reference number DW/04 for the month of September 19-9. The cost price of each item is £12 and there were 12 items in stock at 1 September 19-9.

Receipts

8 September	Invoice no 784	20 units
15 September	Invoice no 847	48 units
22 September	Invoice no 984	20 units

Issues

6 September	Issue Note no A237	8 units
17 September	Issue Note no D534	18 units
24 September	Issue Note no B631	64 units

On making a physical stockcheck on 30 September 19-9, Swift discovered that there were 8 units in stock. Adjust the stock record card for this difference and give some explanation.

[RSA Examinations Board]

16.7 The following stores ledger card records the cost of receipts and issues of stock item EJ 89 for the month of May. Issues have been priced on a FIFO basis.

Receipts				*Issues*					*Balance*	
Date	Qty.	Cost	Amount	Date	Qty.		Cost	Amount	Qty.	Amount
1 May	Opening balance b/f								100	£114.00
5 May	150	£1.25	£187.50						250	£301.50
				May 17	60 @		£1.10	£66.00	190	£235.50
				May 18	40 @		£1.20	£48.00	150	£187.50
20 May	200	£1.00	£200.00						350	£387.50
				May 21	30 @		£1.25	£37.50	320	£350.00
				May 25	200	120 @	£1.25	£150.00	200	£200.00
						80 @	£1.00	£80.00	120	£120.00
28 May	100	£1.30	£130.00						220	£250.00
				May 30	210	120 @	£1.00	£120.00	100	£130.00
						90 @	£1.30	£117.00	10	£13.00

Required:

(a) Explain by reference to the above stores ledger card the FIFO method of issuing items from stock.

(b) Redraft the stores ledger card using the LIFO method of pricing issues.

(c) Identify and describe any one basis other than FIFO and LIFO for pricing issues from stock.

[Association of Accounting Technicians]

16.8* Mary Smith commenced trading on 1 September 19-0 as a distributor of the Straight Cut garden lawn mower, a relatively new product which is now becoming increasingly popular.

Upon commencing trading, Mary Smith transferred £7,000 from her personal savings to open a business bank account.

Mary Smith's purchases and sales of the Straight Cut garden lawn mower during the three months ended 30 November 19-0 are as follows:

19-0	*Bought*	*Sold*
September	12 machines at £384 each	-
October	8 machines at £450 each	4 machines at £560 each
November	16 machines at £489 each	20 machines at £680 each

Assume all purchases are made in the first half of the month and all sales are in the second half of the month.

At the end of October 19-0, Mary Smith decided to take one Straight Cut garden lawn mower out of stock for cutting the lawn outside her showroom. It is estimated that this lawn mower will be used in Mary Smith's business for 8 years and have a nil estimated residual value. Mary Smith wishes to use the straight line basis of depreciation.

Additional information:

1. Overhead expenses paid during the three months ended 30 November 19-0 amounted to £1,520.
2. There were no amounts prepaid on 30 November 19-0, but sales commissions payable of 2½% of the gross profit on sales were accrued due on 30 November 19-0.
3. Upon commencing trading, Mary Smith resigned a business appointment with a salary of £15,000 per annum.
4. Mary Smith is able to obtain interest of 10% per annum on her personal savings.
5. One of the lawn mowers not sold on 30 November 19-0 has been damaged in the showroom and is to be repaired in December 19-0 at a cost of £50 before being sold for an expected £400.

Note: Ignore taxation.

Required:

(a) Prepare, in as much detail as possible, Mary Smith's trading and profit and loss account for the quarter ended 30 November 19-0 using:

(i) the first in first out basis of stock valuation, and

(ii) the last in first out basis of stock valuation.

(b) Using the results in (a)(i) above, prepare a statement comparing Mary Smith's income for the quarter ended 30 November 19-0 with that for the quarter ended 31 August 19-0.

(c) Give one advantage and one disadvantage of each of the bases of stock valuations used in (a) above.

[Association of Accounting Technicians]

17 The Journal

We have already seen in Chapter Six how a business uses day books (or journals) as books of prime entry for sales, purchases and returns transactions. Besides these books for routine transactions, a further book of prime entry – called the journal – is used as a book of prime entry for non-regular transactions. The journal is *not* part of double-entry book-keeping; instead it is used to list transactions before they are entered into the accounts.

17.1 Uses of the general journal

The journal is used for listing transactions which are not recorded in any other book of prime entry. The categories of such transactions are:

- opening entries
- purchase and sale of fixed assets on credit
- correction of errors
- other transfers

We shall look at each of these uses in this chapter, except for correction of errors, which is covered in Chapter Eighteen.

The journal is a book of prime entry and is, therefore, not part of the double-entry book-keeping system. The journal is used to list the transactions that are then to be put through the accounts.

The reasons for using a journal are:

- to eliminate the need for remembering why non-regular transactions were put through the accounts – the journal acts as a notebook
- to reduce the risk of fraud, by making it difficult for unauthorised transactions to be entered in the accounting system
- to reduce the risk of errors, by listing the transactions that are to be put into the double-entry accounts
- to ensure that entries can be traced back to a prime document, thus providing an audit trail for non-regular transactions

17.2 Opening entries

These are the transactions which open the accounts of a business. For example, a first business transaction is:

1 Jan. 19-1 Started in business with £10,000 in the bank

This non-regular transaction is entered in the journal as follows:

Date	Details	Folio	Dr	Cr
19-1			£	£
1 Jan.	Bank account	CB	10,000	
	Capital account	GL		10,000
	Opening capital introduced			

Notes:

- The names of the accounts to be debited and credited in the book-keeping system are written in the details column. It is customary to show the debit transaction first.
- The money amounts of each debit and credit are stated in the columns (which are used for debit and credit purposes – like a trial balance).
- A journal entry always balances.
- It is usual to include a brief narrative explaining why the transaction is being carried out, and making reference to the prime document whenever possible. (In examinations you should always include a narrative unless specifically told otherwise.)
- Each journal entry is complete in itself and is ruled off to separate it from the next entry.

Here is another opening entries transaction to be recorded in the journal:

1 Feb. 19-2 Started in business with cash £100, bank £5,000, stock £1,000, machinery £2,500, creditors £850.

The journal entry is:

Date	Details	Folio	Dr	Cr
19-2			£	£
1 Feb.	Cash account	CB	100	
	Bank account	CB	5,000	
	Stock account	GL	1,000	
	Machinery account	GL	2,500	
	Creditors accounts	PL		850
	Capital account*	GL		7,750
			8,600	8,600
	Assets and liabilities at the start of business			

* Note that capital is the balancing figure, ie assets minus liabilities. The amounts will now need to be recorded in the double-entry book-keeping system.

17.3 Purchase and sale of fixed assets on credit

The purchase and sale of fixed assets are non-regular business transactions which are recorded in the journal as the book of prime entry. Strictly, only *credit* transactions are entered in the journal (because cash/bank transactions are recorded in the cash book as the book of prime entry). However, a business (or an examination question) may choose to journalise cash entries: strictly, though, this is incorrect as two books of prime entry are being used.

15 Apr. 19-1 *Bought a machine for £1,000 plus VAT at 17½ per cent (the buyer is registered for VAT), on credit from Machinery Supplies Ltd.*

Date	Details	Folio	Dr	Cr
19-1			£	£
15 Apr.	Machinery account	GL	1,000	
	VAT account	GL	175	
	Machinery Supplies Ltd*	GL		1,175
			1,175	1,175
	Purchase of machine: purchase order no. 28/19-1			

20 May 19-1 *Car sold for £2,500 on credit to Wyvern Motors Ltd (no VAT chargeable).*

Date	Details	Folio	Dr	Cr
19-1			£	£
20 May	Wyvern Motors Ltd*	GL	2,500	
	Car account	GL		2,500
	Sale of car, registration no Q201 HAB			

Note that disposal of the car will require calculation of any profit or loss. The journal entries for a disposal are shown in Section 17.5 below.

* A general ledger account has been opened for the creditor (Machinery Supplies Ltd) and the debtor (Wyvern Motors Ltd). This has been done to avoid confusion with trade creditors (in the purchases ledger) and trade debtors (in the sales ledger).

17.4 Correction of errors

This topic, including the use of appropriate journal entries, is covered in the next chapter.

17.5 Other transfers

All other non-regular transactions need to be recorded in the journal. Many of these take place at the end of a firm's financial year and are concerned with:

- transfers to the trading and profit and loss account
- accruals and prepayments
- expenses charged to owner's drawings
- provision for depreciation
- disposal of fixed assets
- bad debts written off
- provision for bad debts

Examples of these are as follows:

31 Dec. 19-3 Balance of wages and salaries account, £35,500, transferred to profit and loss account

Date	Details	Folio	Dr	Cr
19-3			£	£
31 Dec.	Profit and loss account		35,500	
	Wages and salaries account	GL		35,500
	Transfer to profit and loss account of expenditure for the year			

31 Dec. 19-3 Closing stock has been valued at £10,400 and is to be entered into the accounts

Date	Details	Folio	Dr	Cr
19-3			£	£
31 Dec.	Stock account	GL	10,400	
	Trading account			10,400
	Stock valuation at 31 December 19-3 transferred to trading account			

Do not be confused by this entry. Remember that closing stock is an asset at the year-end and, therefore, must be debited to stock account. This means that the trading account must be credited – although the usual way in which this is shown is as a deduction from purchases.

31 Dec. 19-3 The balance of electricity account is £550. Of this £500 relates to 19-3, while £50 is a prepayment for 19-4

Date	Details	Folio	Dr	Cr
19-3			£	£
31 Dec.	Profit and loss account		500	
	Electricity account	GL		500
	Transfer to profit and loss account of expenditure for the year			

31 Dec. 19-3 The balance of telephone account is £600. Of this, one-quarter is the estimated cost of the owner's private usage

Date	Details	Folio	Dr	Cr
19-3			£	£
31 Dec.	Profit and loss account		450	
	Drawings account	GL	150	
	Telephone account	GL		600
			600	600
	Transfer to profit and loss account of expenditure for the year; transfer of private use to drawings account			

31 Dec. 19-3 Depreciation on a machine is calculated at £400 for the year

Date	Details	Folio	Dr	Cr
19-3			£	£
31 Dec.	Profit and loss account		400	
	Provision for depreciation account – machinery	GL		400
	Annual depreciation charge			

31 Dec. 19-3 A machine was bought on 1 January 19-1 (ie three years' ago) for £2000. Depreciation to date (including the current year) totals £1200. On 31 December 19-3 the machine is sold for £700, a cheque being received (ignore VAT)

Date	Details	Folio	Dr	Cr
19-3			£	£
31 Dec.	Disposals account	GL	2,000	
	Machinery	GL		2,000
	Provision for depreciation account – machinery	GL	1,200	
	Disposals account	GL		1,200
	Bank account	CB	700	
	Disposals account	GL		700
	Profit and loss account		100	
	Disposals account	GL		100
			4,000	4,000
	Sale of machine no. 123456; loss on sale £100 transferred to profit and loss account			

(If you wish to check the book-keeping entries for this transaction, they are set out in full on page 203.)

31 Dec. 19-3 Bad debts written off for the year are £125

Date	Details	Folio	Dr	Cr
19-3			£	£
31 Dec.	Profit and loss account		125	
	Bad debts written off account	GL		125
	Total of bad debts written off for the year transferred to profit and loss account			

31 Dec. 19-3 A provision for bad debts of £500 is to be created

Date	Details	Folio	Dr	Cr
19-3			£	£
31 Dec.	Profit and loss account		500	
	Provision for bad debts account	GL		500
	Creation of a provision for bad debts			

31 Dec. 19-4 The existing provision for bad debts is to be reduced by £100

Date	Details	Folio	Dr	Cr
19-4			£	£
31 Dec.	Provision for bad debts account		100	
	Profit and loss account	GL		100
	Reduction in provision for bad debts			

17.6 Chapter summary

- ❑ The journal is used to list non-regular transactions.
- ❑ The journal is a book of prime entry – it is *not* a double-entry account.
- ❑ The journal is used for:
  - opening entries
  - purchase and sale of fixed assets on credit
  - correction of errors
  - other transfers (particularly year-end transfers)

Case Study Three follows the questions at the end of this chapter: this shows how the adjustments for accruals and prepayments, depreciation, bad debts, and provision for bad debts are made in a set of accounts, together with the journal entries.

In the next chapter we will look at correction of errors, and the use of the journal for listing such non-regular transactions.

17.7 Questions

17.1 On 1 May 19-0 the financial position of Carol Green was as follows:

	£
Freehold premises	45,000
Fixtures and fittings	12,500
Motor vehicles	9,500
Bank overdraft	2,800
Cash in hand	650
Stock in hand	1,320
F Hardy (a trade debtor)	160
A Darby (a trade creditor)	270

You are required to:
make a journal entry for the above showing clearly the capital of Carol Green on 1 May 19-0.

[RSA Examinations Board]

17.2 Melanie Manson has been organising the accounting section of her business. She has decided that the following books of prime (original) entry should be used:

Journal
Sales Journal
Purchases Journal
Returns Inwards Journal
Returns Outwards Journal
Cash Book

Subsequently, the following take place:

1. An invoice is issued to K Lowe for £120 of goods.
2. An electricity bill for £200 is paid by cheque.
3. An invoice is received from Ideal Machinery Ltd relating to £5,000 of machinery purchased on credit.
4. Cash sales are made for £63.
5. An invoice for £800 is received from Champion Supplies Ltd relating to the supply of goods on credit.
6. A credit note for £24 is issued to K Lowe.
7. J Wardle, a credit customer, clears his account with a cheque for £146.
8. A debit note for £36 is sent to Champion Supplies Ltd.
9. J Jones, who owes £42, is written off as an irrecoverable debt.
10. Melanie Manson withdraws £50 cash for her own use.

Required:
For each of the events listed above, identify which book of prime entry would be used, the name of the account which would be debited and the name of the account which would be credited. Present your answer in the form of a table as follows:

	Book of Prime Entry	*Account to be Debited*	*Account to be Credited*
1.			
2.			
etc			

[Association of Accounting Technicians]

17.3* W E Carryit set up in business as a haulage contractor on 1 November 19-7. He decides to maintain his vehicle account at cost and to keep a separate provision for depreciation account. Vehicles are to be depreciated by 25% per annum using the reducing balance method. Depreciation is to be calculated on assets in existence at the end of each year, a full year's depreciation being charged in the year of purchase and none being charged in the year of disposal.

1 November 19-7	Bought lorry costing £12,000, paying by cheque.
6 December 19-8	Bought lorry costing £18,000, paying by cheque.
1 January 19-9	The lorry bought on 1 November 19-7 was written off in an accident; the insurance company paying £8,450 in full settlement of the claim.
7 March 19-0	A new lorry costing £28,000 was bought on credit from Supatruks Ltd; they allowing £13,500 (ie its book value) in part exchange for the lorry bought on 6 December 19-8. The balance is to be paid in one year's time.

You are required to:

(a) prepare the vehicle accounts and provision for depreciation accounts for the years ended 31 October 19-8, 19-9 and 19-0, and to show how vehicles would have appeared in the balance sheet as at those dates.

(b) give journal entries for the transactions which took place on 1 January 19-9 and 7 March 19-0.

Note: Disposal accounts are not required.

[RSA Examinations Board]

Case Study 3
Year-end Adjustments to Final Accounts

This Case Study uses the trial balance, from Case Study Two, of Wyvern Metal Supplies at 31 December 19-1 and makes adjustments to the final accounts. The adjustments are for:

- accruals
- prepayments
- provision for depreciation
- bad debts written off
- provision for bad debts

Appropriate journal entries (see Chapter Seventeen) are made in order to keep a record of these non-regular transactions.

1 The trial balance

This Case Study starts with the trial balance extracted by the book-keeper of Wyvern Metal Supplies at 31 December 19-1 (see page 164) in Case Study Two.

2 Adjustments to be made

The owner of Wyvern Metal Supplies, in conjunction with the firm's accountant, has decided to make the following year-end adjustments at 31 December 19-1:

- Wages and salaries of £1,100 are owing
- Business rates are prepaid by £600
- Depreciation for the year, using the straight-line method, is to be provided for on the delivery van at twenty per cent per annum and on the office equipment at ten per cent per annum. The provision for depreciation is to apply to assets held at the end of the financial year.
- A debtor, Speciality Forgings, has gone out of business and it is decided to write this account off as a bad debt (ignore any possibility of VAT relief on the bad debt)
- A five per cent provision for bad debts (to nearest £) is to be made against the remaining debtors

3 Journal entries

Each adjustment requires a journal entry, and these are as follows:

JOURNAL

Date	Details	Folio	Dr	Cr
19-1			£	£
31 Dec.	Profit and loss account		52,400	
	Wages and salaries	GL105		52,400
	Transfer to profit and loss account of expenditure for the year: amount paid in year £51,300 add amount owing £1,100 transfer to profit and loss £52,400			
31 Dec.	Profit and loss account		3,430	
	Business rates	GL108		3,430
	Transfer to profit and loss account of expenditure for the year: amount paid in year £4,030 less prepayment £600 transfer to profit and loss £3,430			
31 Dec.	Profit and loss account		2,400	
	Provision for depreciation: delivery van	GL118		2,400
	Annual depreciation, using the straight-line method, at twenty per cent per annum on delivery van			
31 Dec.	Profit and loss account		532	
	Provision for depreciation: office equipment	GL119		532
	Annual depreciation, using the straight-line method, at ten per cent per annum on office equipment			
31 Dec.	Bad debts written off	GL120	277	
	Speciality Forgings	SL203		277
	Bad debt written off on written instruction of credit controller: see correspondence file reference			
31 Dec.	Profit and loss account		277	
	Bad debts written off	GL120		277
	Transfer to profit and loss account at the year-end			
31 Dec.	Profit and loss account		261	
	Provision for bad debts	GL121		261
	Creation of provision for bad debts at five per cent of debtors (5% x £5,217)			

4 The ledger accounts

Shown below are the ledger accounts which are:

- *either* existing accounts affected by the adjustments to the final accounts
- *or* new accounts

The accounts, as originally prepared by the book-keeper, ie before adjustment, are shown in Case Study Two (pages 164-178). Accounts which are not affected by the adjustments to the final accounts have not been reprinted here – see Case Study Two.

GENERAL LEDGER

Dr. **Wages and salaries** (account no 105) Cr.

			£			£
19-1				19-1		
1 Dec.	Balance b/d		45,800	31 Dec.	Profit and loss account	52,400
16 Dec.	Bank	CB	5,500			
31 Dec.	Balance c/d		1,100			
			52,400			52,400
19-2				19-2		
				1 Jan.	Balance b/d	1,100

Note: The credit balance of £1,100 on the account at the end of the year is recorded on the balance sheet as an accrual.

Dr. **Business rates** (account no 108) Cr.

		£			£
19-1			19-1		
1 Dec.	Balance b/d	4,030	31 Dec.	Profit and loss account	3,430
			31 Dec.	Balance c/d	600
		4,030			4,030
19-2			19-2		
1 Jan.	Balance b/d	600			

Note: The debit balance of £600 on the account at the end of the year is recorded on the balance sheet as a prepayment.

Dr. **Provision for depreciation: delivery van** (account no 118) Cr.

		£			£
19-1			19-1		
31 Dec.	Balance c/d	2,400	31 Dec.	Profit and loss account	2,400
19-2			19-2		
			1 Jan.	Balance b/d	2,400

Dr.	**Provision for depreciation: office equipment** (account no 119)				Cr.
19-1		£	19-1		£
31 Dec.	Balance c/d	532	31 Dec.	Profit and loss account	532
19-2			19-2		
			1 Jan.	Balance b/d	532

Note: The credit balances on the two provision for depreciation accounts are shown on the balance sheet as deductions from their respective fixed asset accounts: this gives the net book value figure for each asset. In subsequent years further provisions for depreciation will be made to these accounts.

Dr.	**Bad debts written off** (account no 120)					Cr.
19-1			£	19-1		£
31 Dec.	Speciality Forgings	SL203	277	31 Dec.	Profit and loss account	277

Note: See also the account of the debtor, Speciality Forgings, below. Bad debts written off account stores up amounts written off during the year. At the year-end, the total of the account is transferred to profit and loss account as an expense.

Dr.	**Provision for bad debts** (account no 121)				Cr.
19-1		£	19-1		£
31 Dec.	Balance c/d	261	31 Dec.	Profit and loss account	261
19-2			19-2		
			1 Jan.	Balance b/d	261

Note: The credit balance on this account is shown on the balance sheet as a deduction from debtors to give the net debtors figures which represents the estimate of debtors which are collectable. In subsequent years the balance of this account will need to be adjusted for changes in the level of debtors, or changes in the percentage of the provision.

SALES LEDGER

Dr.	**Speciality Forgings** (account no 203)						Cr.
19-1			£	19-1			£
1 Dec.	Balance b/d		6,720	18 Dec.	Bank	SRDB	6,720
9 Dec.	Sales	SDB	1,692	29 Dec.	Bank	CB	4,000
16 Dec.	Sales	SDB	2,585	31 Dec.	Bad debts written off	GL120	277
			10,997				10,997

5 Adjusted final accounts

After incorporating the year-end adjustments the final accounts appear as follows (there is no change to gross profit):

WYVERN METAL SUPPLIES
TRADING AND PROFIT AND LOSS ACCOUNT FOR THE YEAR ENDED 31 DECEMBER 19-1

	£	£	£
Sales			188,860
Less Sales returns			1,130
Net sales			187,730
Opening stock		16,170	
Purchases	87,620		
Less Purchases returns	590		
Net purchases		87,030	
		103,200	
Less Closing stock		20,200	
Cost of Goods Sold			83,000
Gross Profit			104,730
Add: Discount received			1,055
			105,785
Less:			
Wages and salaries		52,400	
Vehicle running expenses		2,820	
Office expenses		8,090	
Business rates		3,430	
Rent		14,400	
Discount allowed		2,310	
Bad debt written off		277	
Provision for bad debts		261	
Provision for depreciation:			
delivery van		2,400	
office equipment		532	
			86,920
Net Profit			18,865

Note: As the net profit is different from that calculated in Case Study Two, the transfer from profit and loss account to capital account will be £18,865.

WYVERN METAL SUPPLIES
BALANCE SHEET AS AT 31 DECEMBER 19-1

	£	£	£
Fixed Assets	*Cost*	*Dep'n to date*	*Net*
Delivery van	12,000	2,400	9,600
Office equipment	5,320	532	4,788
	17,320	2,932	14,388
Current Assets			
Stock		20,200	
Debtors	5,217		
Less provision for bad debts	261		
		4,956	
Prepayment		600	
Bank		5,572	
Cash		364	
		31,692	
Less Current Liabilities			
Creditors	12,765		
Value Added Tax	2,750		
Accrual	1,100		
		16,615	
Working Capital			15,077
NET ASSETS			29,465
FINANCED BY:			
Capital			
Opening capital			30,000
Add Net profit			18,865
			48,865
Less Drawings			19,400
			29,465

6 Case study summary

- This Case Study has looked at adjustments to the final accounts for:
  - accruals
  - prepayments
  - provision for depreciation
  - bad debts written off
  - provision for bad debts

- These adjustments are made to enable the final accounts to show a more realistic view of the state of the business. The adjustments are examples of the application of the accounting concepts set out in Statement of Standard Accounting Practice No. 2, 'Disclosure of accounting policies' (see pages 240-242):
  - *accruals concept* – accruals and prepayments, provision for depreciation, stock valuation
  - *consistency concept* – provision for depreciation, provision for bad debts, stock valuation
  - *prudence concept* – provision for depreciation, provision for bad debts, stock valuation
  - *going concern* – stock valuation, asset values

18 Correction of Errors

In any book-keeping system there is always the possibility of an error. Ways to avoid errors, or ways to reveal them sooner, include:

- division of the accounting function between a number of people, so that no one person is responsible for both the debit and credit entries of a business transaction
- regular circulation of statements to debtors, who will check the transactions on their accounts and advise any discrepancies
- checking of statements received from creditors
- extraction of a trial balance at regular intervals
- the preparation of bank reconciliation statements
- checking cash and petty cash balances against cash held
- the use of control accounts (see Chapter Nineteen)

Despite all of these, errors will still occur from time-to-time and, in this chapter, we shall look at:

- correction of errors not shown by a trial balance
- correction of errors shown by a trial balance, using a suspense account
- the effect of correcting errors on profit and the balance sheet

18.1 Errors not shown by a trial balance

In Chapter 5.7 we have already seen that some types of errors in a book-keeping system are not revealed by a trial balance. These are:

- error of omission
- reversal of entries
- mispost/error of commission
- error of principle
- error of original entry (or transcription)
- compensating error

Although these errors are not shown by a trial balance, they are likely to come to light if the procedures suggested in the introduction, above, are followed. For example, a debtor will soon let you know if her account has been debited with goods she did not buy. When an error is found, it needs to be corrected by means of a journal entry which shows the book-keeping entries that have been passed.

We will now look at an example of each of the errors not shown by a trial balance, and will see how it is corrected by means of a journal entry. (A practical hint which may help in correcting errors is to write out the 'T' accounts as they appear with the error. Then write in the correcting entries and see if the result has achieved what was intended.)

Error of omission

Credit sale of goods, £100, to H Jarvis completely omitted from the accounting system; the error is corrected on 10 May 19-2

Date	Details	Folio	Dr	Cr
19-2			£	£
10 May	H Jarvis	SL	100	
	Sales account	GL		100
	Invoice no. xxx omitted from the accounts			

This type of error can happen in a very small business – often where the book-keeping is done by one person. For example, an invoice, when typed out, is 'lost' down the back of a filing cabinet. In a large business, particularly one using a computer accounting system, it *should* be impossible for this error to occur. Also, if documents are numbered serially, then none should be mislaid.

Reversal of entries

A payment, on 3 May 19-2 by cheque of £50 to a creditor, S Wright, has been debited in the cash book and credited to Wright's account; the error is corrected on 12 May 19-2

Date	Details	Folio	Dr	Cr
19-2			£	£
12 May	S Wright	PL	50	
	Bank account	CB		50
	S Wright	PL	50	
	Bank account	CB		50
	Correction of £50 reversal of entries: receipt no. xxx			

To correct this type of error it is best to reverse the entries that have been made incorrectly (the first two journal entries), and then to put through the correct entries. Although it will correct the error, it is wrong to debit Wright £100 and credit bank £100. This is because there was never a transaction for this amount – the original transaction was for £50.

As noted earlier, it is often an idea to write out the 'T' accounts, complete with the error, and then to write in the correcting entries. As an example, the two accounts involved in this last error are shown with the error made on 3 May, and the corrections made on 12 May indicated by the shading (the opening credit balance of S Wright's account is shown as £50):

S Wright

Dr.		£		Cr.	£
19-2		£	19-2		£
12 May	Bank	50	1 May	Balance b/d	50
12 May	Bank	50	3 May	Bank	50
		100			100

Cash Book (bank columns)

Dr.		£		Cr.	£
19-2		£	19-2		£
3 May	S. Wright	50	12 May	S Wright	50
			12 May	S Wright	50

The accounts now show a net debit transaction of £50 on S Wright's account, and a net credit transaction of £50 on bank account, which is how this payment to a creditor should have been recorded in order to clear the balance on the account.

Mispost/error of commission

Credit sales of £40 have been debited to the account of J Adams, instead of the account of J Adams Ltd; the error is corrected on 15 May 19-2

Date	Details	Folio	Dr	Cr
19-2			£	£
15 May	J Adams Ltd	SL	40	
	J Adams	SL		40
	Correction of mispost of invoice no. xxx			

This type of error can be avoided, to some extent, by the use of account numbers, and by persuading the customer to quote the account number or reference on each transaction. All computer accounting systems use numbers/references to identify accounts, but it is still possible to post a transaction to the wrong account.

Error of principle

The cost of petrol, £15, has been debited to vehicles account; the error is corrected on 20 May 19-2

Date	Details	Folio	Dr	Cr
19-2			£	£
20 May	Vehicle running expenses account	GL	15	
	Vehicles account	GL		15
	Correction of error: voucher no. xxx			

This type of error is similar to a mispost except that, instead of the wrong *person's* account being used, it is the wrong *class* of account. In the above example, the vehicle running costs must be kept separate from the cost of the asset – vehicles. Correcting this error will have an effect on both profit and loss account and balance sheet (if already prepared) – see Section 18.3.

Error of original entry

Credit sale of goods, £45, to J Lamb entered in the accounts as £54; the error is corrected on 27 May 19-2

Date	Details	Folio	Dr	Cr
19-2			£	£
27 May	Sales account	GL	54	
	J Lamb	SL		54
	J Lamb	SL	45	
	Sales account	GL		45
	Correction of error: invoice no. xxx entered into the accounts wrongly			

This error could have been corrected by debiting sales, crediting J Lamb with £9, being the difference between the two amounts. However, there was no original transaction for this amount, and it is better to reverse the wrong transaction and put through the correct one.

A reversal of figures, as above, either has a difference of nine, or an amount divisible by nine. An error of original entry can also be a 'bad' figure on a cheque or an invoice, which is entered wrongly into both accounts.

Compensating error

Business rates account is over-cast (over-added) by £100; sales account is also over-cast by the same amount; the error is corrected on 31 May 19-2

Date	Details	Folio	Dr	Cr
19-2			£	£
31 May	Sales account	GL	100	
	Business rates account	GL		100
	Correction of over-cast on rates account and sales account			

Here, an account with a debit balance – business rates – has been over-cast; this is compensated by an over-cast on an account with a credit balance – sales. There are several permutations on this theme, eg two debit balances, one over-cast, one under-cast; a debit balance under-cast, a credit balance under-cast.

Important note

We have just looked at several journal entries in connection with the correction of errors. Remember that the journal entry lists the transactions that must then be recorded in the book-keeping system.

18.2 Errors shown by a trial balance: use of suspense account

There are many types of errors revealed by a trial balance. Included amongst these are:

- omission of one part of the double-entry transaction
- recording two debits or two credits for a transaction
- recording a different amount for a transaction on the debit side from the credit side
- errors in the calculation of balances (not compensated by other errors)
- error in transferring the balance of an account to the trial balance

When errors are shown, the trial balance is 'balanced' by recording the difference in a *suspense account*. For example, on 31 December 19-1 the trial balance totals are:

	Dr	Cr
	£	£
Trial balance totals	100,000	99,850
Suspense account		150
	100,000	100,000

A suspense account is opened in the general ledger with, in this case, a credit balance of £150:

Suspense Account

Dr.		£	Cr.		£
19-1			19-1		
			31 Dec.	Trial balance difference	150

A detailed examination of the book-keeping system is now made in order to find the errors. As errors are found, they are corrected by means of a journal entry. The journal entries will balance, with one part of the entry being either a debit or credit to suspense account. In this way, the balance on suspense account is eliminated by book-keeping transactions. Taking the above suspense account, the following errors are found and corrected on 15 January 19-2:

- sales account is under-cast by £100
- a payment to a creditor, A Wilson, for £65, has been recorded in the bank as £56
- telephone expenses of £55 have not been entered in the expenses account
- stationery expenses £48 have been debited to both the stationery account and the bank account

These errors are corrected by journal entries:

Date	Details	Folio	Dr	Cr
19-2			£	£
15 Jan.	Suspense account	GL	100	
	Sales account	GL		100
	Under-cast on . . . . . . now corrected			
15 Jan.	Bank account	CB	56	
	Suspense account	GL		56
	Suspense account	GL	65	
	Bank account	CB		65
	Payment to A Wilson for £65 (cheque no. xxx) on . . . entered in bank as £56 in error			
15 Jan.	Telephone expenses account	GL	55	
	Suspense account	GL		55
	Omission of entry in expenses account: paid by cheque no xxx			
15 Jan.	Suspense account	GL	48	
	Bank account	CB		48
	Suspense account	GL	48	
	Bank account	CB		48
	Correction of error: payment by cheque no xxx debited in error to bank account			

After these journal entries have been recorded in the accounts, suspense account appears as:

Suspense Account

Dr.			Cr.		
19-2		£	19-1		£
15 Jan.	Sales	100	31 Dec.	Trial balance difference	150
15 Jan.	Bank	65	19-2		
15 Jan.	Bank	48	15 Jan.	Bank	56
15 Jan.	Bank	48	15 Jan.	Telephone expenses	55
		261			261

Thus all the errors have now been found, and suspense account has a nil balance.

Note:
If final accounts have to be prepared after creating a suspense account but before the errors are found, the balance of suspense account is shown, depending on the balance, as either a current asset (debit balance) or a current liability (credit balance). Nevertheless, the error must be found at a later date and suspense account eliminated.

18.3 Effect on profit and balance sheet

The correction of errors, whether shown by a trial balance or not, often has an effect on the profit figure calculated before the errors were found. For example, an undercast of sales account, when corrected, will increase gross and net profits and, of course, the profit figure shown in the balance sheet. Some errors, however, only affect the balance sheet, eg an error involving a creditor's account. Fig. 18.1 shows the effect of errors when corrected on gross profit, net profit and the balance sheet.

Correction of error	Gross profit	Net profit	Balance sheet
Trading account			
• sales undercast/understated	increase	increase	net profit increase
• sales overcast/overstated	decrease	decrease	net profit decrease
• purchases undercast/understated	decrease	decrease	net profit decrease
• purchases overcast/overstated	increase	increase	net profit increase
• opening stock undervalued	decrease	decrease	net profit decrease
• opening stock overvalued	increase	increase	net profit increase
• closing stock undervalued	increase	increase	net profit increase stock increase
• closing stock overvalued	decrease	decrease	net profit decrease stock decrease
Profit and loss account			
• expense undercast/understated	-	decrease	decrease in net profit
• expense overcast/overstated	-	increase	increase in net profit
• income undercast/understated	-	increase	increase in net profit
• income overcast/overstated	-	decrease	decrease in net profit
Balance sheet			
• asset undercast/understated	-	-	increase asset
• asset overcast/overstated	-	-	decrease asset
• liability undercast/understated	-	-	increase liability
• liability overcast/overstated	-	-	decrease liability

Fig. 18.1 Effect of correction of errors on profit and balance sheet

Some examination questions on correction of errors require the preparation of a statement showing the amended profit after errors have been corrected. We will look at the errors shown on page 270 and see how their correction affects the net profit (assume the net profit before adjustments is £10,000).

Statement of corrected net profit for the year ended 31 December 19-1

	£
Net profit (unadjusted)	10,000
Add sales undercast	100
	10,100
Less additional telephone expenses	55
Adjusted net profit	10,045

Note: the other two errors do not affect net profit

The effect on the balance sheet of correcting the errors is:

- net profit increases £45
- bank balance reduces £105 (+£56, –£65, –£48, –£48)
- the credit balance of £150 in suspense account (shown as a current liability) is eliminated

The balance sheet will now balance without the need for a suspense account – the errors have been found and corrected.

18.4 Chapter summary

❑ Correction of errors is always a difficult topic to put into practice: it tests your knowledge of book-keeping procedures and it is all too easy to make the error worse than it was in the first place! The secret of dealing with this topic well is to write down – in account format – what has gone wrong. It should then be relatively easy to see what has to be done to put the error right.

❑ Errors not shown by a trial balance: error of omission, reversal of entries, mispost/error of commission, error of principle, error of original entry (or transcription), compensating error.

❑ Errors shown by a trial balance include: omission of one part of the book-keeping transaction, recording two debits/credits for a transaction, recording different amounts in the two accounts, calculating balances, transferring balances to the trial balance.

❑ All errors are non-regular transactions and need to be corrected by means of a journal entry: the book-keeper then needs to record the correcting transactions in the accounts.

❑ When error(s) are shown by a trial balance, the amount is placed into a suspense account. As the errors are found, journal entries are made which 'clear out' the suspense account.

❑ Correction of errors may have an effect on gross profit and net profit, and on the figures in the balance sheet. It may be necessary to restate net profit and to adjust the balance sheet.

In the next chapter we shall look at the use of control accounts which are used as a checking device for a section of the ledgers.

18.5 Questions

18.1 For each of the errors listed below, name the type of error and show how each error would be corrected by writing down the accounts which would be debited and credited.

(a) Cash sales £56 had not been entered in the books of account.
(b) £128 paid to Amanda Crisp had been debited to Amanda Cripp's account.
(c) The purchase of fixtures £200 had been debited to the purchases account.
(d) The totals of the returns inwards day book and the sales day book had both been undercast by £20.

	Type of error	*Account debited*	*Account credited*
(a)	....	....	....
(b)	....	....	....
(c)	....	....	....
(d)	....	....	....

[Northern Examining Association]

18.2* The Cashier extracts a trial balance which fails to agree; he then places the difference in a suspense account and tries to find the errors which have caused his trial balance to disagree.

The following errors are found:

(a) Discount allowed to Forest and Company entered as £35 debited to their account.
(b) Purchases of goods for £910 from Drystone Brothers posted to their account in error as £700.
(c) Sales day book had been overcast by £70.
(d) Balance on Clair and Sons' account of £245 in the sales ledger extracted in error as £385.

Show the suspense account after the above errors have been adjusted and the amount of the original error has been placed in the account.

[Pitman Examinations Institute]

18.3 Sally Jones was not able to balance her trial balance at 30 April 19-0 so she opened a suspense account to balance the trial balance.

Subsequently she discovered the following errors:

1. the sale proceeds of an old delivery van amounting to £700 were placed to the sales account
2. discount allowed amounting to £400 were entered as a credit balance in the trial balance
3. debtors amounting to £500 had not been included in the trial balance total

You are required to:

(a) make appropriate journal entries to rectify the errors

(b) draft the suspense account after the errors have been corrected showing the original balance

(c) Sally also wishes to create a provision for bad debts for £500 and write off a bad debt for Simon Joseph for £250

Draft the journal entry for these items

[Pitman Examinations Institute]

18.4* On 31 December 19-2 a firm's net profit, as shown by the profit and loss account, was £3,700.

Subsequently it was discovered that:

(a) the total of the sales day book had been overcast by £420

(b) although rates prepaid were £68, the figure of £86 had been used in the drafting of the profit and loss account

(c) discounts received during the period amounting to £100 had been omitted from the profit and loss account

(d) wages during the period had been recorded as £3,860, whereas the correct amount was £3,720

(e) during stocktaking, an item had been recorded twice, the amount of the item being £30

You are required to make up a statement only (journal entries not necessary) of the adjusted profit, to give the corrected net profit figure as at 31 December 19-2.

[Pitman Examinations Institute]

18.5 William Trent, in business as a dealer in hardware goods, found that his trial balance at 30 September year 12 did not agree and accordingly opened a suspense account. A subsequent search revealed the following errors or omissions:

1. Goods returned by F Mortimer £124 had been credited to his account and entered in the returns outwards book.
2. A cheque for £47 received from L Johnson had been dishonoured and posted in error from the cash book to the general expenses account. Trent had no intention as yet of treating the debt as irrecoverable.
3. Trent had taken goods, value £225 at cost, for his personal use: no entry had been made in the books.
4. A credit note for £850 in respect of a trade-in allowance obtained on one of the business motor vans had been incorrectly credited to both sales account and motor vans disposal account.
5. A payment by cheque of £45 for having the computer installation serviced had been posted to the computer asset account.

Required:

(i) Journal entries correcting these errors/omissions, including narrations.

(ii) The suspense account

Note: If no entry is required in respect of any item, state this as a note beneath the account.

(iii) A statement, in the following form, showing the effect of each of these errors/omissions on the profit of the business:

	Profit under-stated	*Profit over-stated*
	£	£
1.		
2.		
3.		
4.		
5.		

[London Chamber of Commerce]

18.6 The following balances were extracted from the books of Headly Bishop on 31 December 19-9 in order to prepare a trial balance:

	£
Sundry expenses	24,741
Purchases	90,191
Sales	160,327
Returns inwards	874
Returns outwards	627

Premises	120,135
Drawings	12,161
Stock at 1 January 19-9	8,324
Discounts allowed	535
Discounts received	346
Debtors	14,295
Creditors	10,392
Cash	1,650
Capital	100,794

Unfortunately, the two sides of the trial balance did not agree and the difference was posted to a suspense account until such time as the errors could be found. An investigation into the books subsequently revealed the following:

1. A £40 discount given by one of the suppliers, although correctly dealt with in that suppliers account, had been entered in the discounts allowed column of the cash book.
2. The sales journal had been overcast by £100.
3. A credit note for £225 issued to a customer, Paul Blackburn, had been posted to the wrong side of his account.
4. An invoice for £98 received from DDC Ltd had been entered in the purchases journal as £89.
5. In attempting to balance off the cash account, the entries on the credit side have been over-added by £10.

Required:

(a) The journal entries to show how the above errors would be corrected. Dates, folio numbers and narratives are not required.

(b) A corrected trial balance as at 31 December 19-9.

[Association of Accounting Technicians]

18.7* The financial year of Naveen Traders ended on 31 May 19-0. The following end of year adjustments have still to be entered into the ledger.

1. Closing stock as at the close of business on 31 May 19-0 was valued at £33,600.
2. Depreciation for the year ended 31 May 19-0 has still to be provided for as follows:

on property	£22,000
on equipment	£24,000
on motor vehicles	£40,000

3. The provision for bad debts is to be reduced by £3,660.
4. An invoice for £1,440 received from XJ Supplies has been entered erroneously in the purchases book as £1,044 and has been posted into the double-entry system as such.
5. An invoice for £770 made out to P Next has been correctly entered into the sales book but has been posted in error to B Necht's account.
6. The discount allowed column of the cash book has been overcast by £99.
7. A page of the returns outwards book was correctly totalled at £1,220 but has been erroneously carried forward to the next page as £1,770.

Naveen Traders does not maintain control accounts for debtors and creditors as part of the double-entry system. You may assume that any difference in the trial balance as at 31 May 19-0 has been posted temporarily to a suspense account.

Required:

(a) Draw up journal entries to show how the above adjustments would be incorporated into Naveen Traders' ledger. Dates and narrations are not required.

(b) Suppose that a draft calculation of net profit for the year ended 31 May 19-0 before taking into account the above adjustments was £677,220. Compute the revised figure for net profit after taking the above information into account.

[Association of Accounting Technicians]

Multiple-choice questions: chapters 15-18

- Read each question carefully
- Choose the *one* answer you think is correct (calculators may be needed)
- Answers are on page 486

1. A business should not, without good reason, change its method of depreciation. This follows the concept of:

   A money measurement
   B going concern
   C prudence
   D consistency

2. 'Anticipate no profit, but anticipate all losses' is a summary of the concept of:

   A accruals
   B prudence
   C consistency
   D business entity

3. Stock is valued at:

   A cost price
   B net realisable value
   C lower of cost and net realisable value
   D replacement price

4. One of the main advantages of FIFO as a stock valuation method is that:

   A it is realistic and assumes that goods are issued in order of receipt
   B goods are issued at the latest prices
   C fluctuations in purchase price are evened out
   D in times of rising prices, profits will be higher

5. Which one of the following transactions will *not* be recorded in the general journal?

   A credit purchase of a fixed asset
   B credit sale of goods to a customer
   C write off of a bad debt
   D transfer of expenses at the year-end to profit and loss account

6. The payment for business rates has been debited to the premises account. This is:

   A an error of original entry
   B an error of principle
   C an error of commission
   D a reversal of entries

7. A credit purchase of £63 from T Billington has been entered in the accounts as £36. This is:

A a reversal of entries
B an error of original entry
C a compensating error
D an error of omission

8. A receipt of £20 by cheque from L Jarvis, a customer, has been debited to Jarvis' account and credited to bank account in error. Which entry will correct the error?

	Debit	*Credit*
A	Bank account £20	L Jarvis £20
	Bank account £20	L Jarvis £20
B	Bank account £20	L Jarvis £20
C	L Jarvis £40	Bank account £20
D	L Jarvis £20	Bank account £20
	L Jarvis £20	Bank account £20

9. A trial balance fails to agree by £75 and the difference is placed to a suspense account. Later it is found that a credit sale for this amount has not been entered in the sales account. Which entry will correct the error?

	Debit	*Credit*
A	Suspense account £75	Sales account £75
B	Suspense account £150	Sales account £150
C	Sales account £75	Suspense account £75
D	–	Sales account £75

10. The book-keeper has entered a receipt of £100 from a customer on the wrong side of the debtor's account. Assuming that there are no other errors, the trial balance will show:

A debit side £100 more than credit side
B debit side £200 more than credit side
C credit side £100 more than debit side
D credit side £200 more than debit side

11. Sales account has been undercast by £100. When this is corrected:

A gross and net profits will decrease by £100
B gross and net profits will not change
C the balance sheet will not be affected
D gross and net profits will increase £100

12. Closing stock is found to be overvalued by £250. When this is corrected:

A gross and net profits will decrease by £250
B gross and net profits will increase by £250
C the balance sheet will not be affected
D gross and net profits will not change

19 Control Accounts

Control accounts, as their name suggests, are used as 'master' accounts to control a number of subsidiary ledger accounts in the following way:

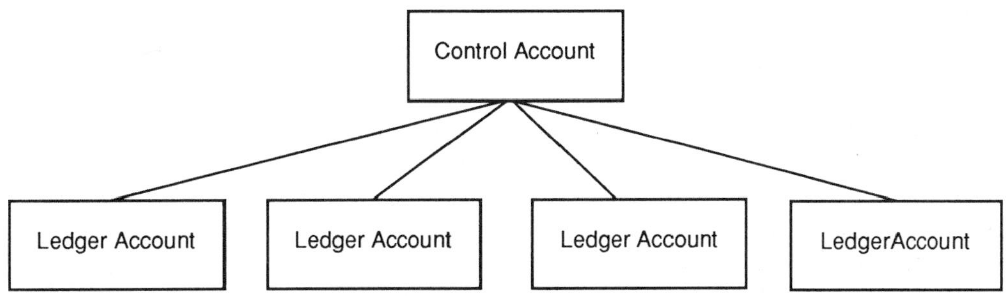

The control account (also known as a *totals account*) is used to record the totals of transactions passing through the subsidiary accounts. In this way, the balance of the control account will always be equal (unless an error has occurred) to the total balances of the subsidiary accounts. Two commonly-used control accounts are:

- sales ledger control account – the total of the debtors
- purchases ledger control account – the total of the creditors

In this chapter we shall look at:

- the concept of control accounts
- the layout of sales ledger and purchases ledger control accounts
- the use of control accounts as an aid to the management of a business

19.1 The concept of control accounts

In the illustration above we have seen how a control account acts as a master account for a number of subsidiary accounts. The principle is that, if the *total* of the opening balances for subsidiary accounts is known, together with the *total* of amounts increasing these balances, and the *total* of amounts decreasing these balances, then the *total* of the closing balances for the subsidiary accounts can be calculated.

Sales Ledger Control Account

Dr.					Cr.
19-1		£	19-1		£
1 Jan.	Balances b/d	500	31 Jan.	Bank	443
31 Jan.	Sales	700	31 Jan.	Discount allowed	7
			31 Jan.	Sales returns	70
			31 Jan.	Balances c/d	680
		1,200			1,200
1 Feb.	Balances b/d	680			

A Ackroyd

Dr.					Cr.
19-1		£	19-1		£
1 Jan.	Balance b/d	100	10 Jan.	Bank	98
5 Jan.	Sales	150	10 Jan.	Discount allowed	2
			31 Jan.	Balance c/d	150
		250			250
1 Feb.	Balance b/d	150			

C Cox

Dr.					Cr.
19-1		£	19-1		£
1 Jan.	Balance b/d	50	18 Jan.	Bank	50
15 Jan.	Sales	200	29 Jan.	Sales returns	20
			31 Jan.	Balance c/d	180
		250			250
1 Feb.	Balance b/d	180			

B Barnes

Dr.					Cr.
19-1		£	19-1		£
1 Jan.	Balance b/d	200	12 Jan.	Bank	195
10 Jan.	Sales	250	12 Jan.	Discount allowed	5
			25 Jan.	Sales returns	50
			31 Jan.	Balance c/d	200
		450			450
1 Feb.	Balance b/d	200			

D Douglas

Dr.					Cr.
19-1		£	19-1		£
1 Jan.	Balance b/d	150	30 Jan.	Bank	100
20 Jan.	Sales	100	31 Jan.	Balance c/d	150
		250			250
1 Feb.	Balance b/d	150			

Fig. 19.1 An example of the use of sales ledger control account

For example:

	£
Total of opening balances	50,000
Add increases	10,000
	60,000
Less decreases	12,000
Total of closing balances	48,000

The total of the closing balances can now be checked against a separate listing of the subsidiary accounts to ensure that the two figures agree. If so, it proves that the ledgers within the section are correct (subject to any errors such as misposts and compensating errors). Let us now apply this concept to one of the divisions of the ledger – sales ledger.

Fig. 19.1 shows the personal accounts which form the entire sales ledger of a particular business (in practice there would, of course, be more than four accounts involved). The sales ledger control account acts as a totals account, which records totals of the transactions passing through the individual accounts which it controls. Notice that transactions appear in the control account *on the same side* as they appear in the individual accounts. It follows that the control account acts as a checking device for the individual accounts which it controls. Thus, control accounts act as an aid to locating errors: if the control account and subsidiary accounts agree, then the error is *likely* to lie elsewhere. In this way the control account acts as an intermediate checking device – proving the arithmetical accuracy of the ledger section.

Normally the whole of a ledger section is controlled by one control account, eg sales ledger control account and purchases ledger control account. However, it is also possible to have a number of separate control accounts for subdivisions of the sales ledger and purchases ledger, eg sales ledger control account A-K, purchases ledger control account S-Z, etc. It is for a business – the user of the accounting system – to decide what is most suitable, taking into account the number of accounts in the sales and purchases ledger, together with the type of book-keeping system – manual or computerised.

In the example in fig. 19.1, the control account and subsidiary accounts were agreed at the end of the month. However, the time period is for the business to decide – weekly, monthly, quarterly or annually.

19.2 Sales ledger control account

We have already seen in fig. 19.1 the set-out of a sales ledger control account (or debtors' control account). The following includes some additional items (explained below) and can be used as a 'pro-forma' layout:

Sales Ledger Control Account

Dr.	£	Cr.	£
Balances b/d (large amount)		Balances b/d (small amount)	
Credit sales		Cash/cheques received from debtors	
Returned cheques		Cash discount allowed	
Interest charged to debtors		Sales returns	
Balances c/d (small amount)		Bad debts written off	
		Set-off/contra entries	
		Balances c/d (large amount)	
Balances b/d (large amount)		Balances b/d (small amount)	

Notes:

- **Balances b/d**

In the layout above there is a figure for balances b/d on both the debit side *and* the credit side of the control account. The usual balance on a debtor's account is debit and so this will form the large balance on the debit side. However, from time-to-time, it is possible for some debtors to have a credit balance on their accounts. This may come about, for example, because they have paid for goods, and then returned them, or because they have overpaid in error: the business owes them the amount due, ie they have a credit balance for the time being. Such credit balances are always going to be in the minority and so they will be for the smaller amount. Clearly, if there are small credit balances at the beginning of the month, there are likely to be credit balances at the month-end, and these need to be recorded *separately* as balances carried down – do not 'net off' the two types of balances. In a balance sheet, the small credit balances should be included with creditors.

- **Credit sales**

Only credit sales – and not cash sales – are entered in the control account because it is this transaction that is recorded in the debtors' accounts. The total sales of the business will comprise both credit and cash sales.

- **Returned cheques**

If a debtor's cheque is returned unpaid by the bank, ie the cheque has 'bounced', then entries have to be made in the book-keeping system to record this. These entries are:

— *debit* debtor's account

— *credit* cash book (bank columns)

As a transaction has been made in a debtor's account, then the amount must also be recorded in the sales ledger control account – on the debit side.

- **Interest charged to debtors**

Sometimes a business will charge a debtor for slow payment of an account. The accounting entries are:

— *debit* debtor's account

— *credit* interest received account

As a debit transaction has been made in the debtor's account, so a debit entry must be recorded in the control account.

- **Bad debts written off**

The book-keeping entries for writing off a bad debt (see Chapter Fourteen) are:

— *debit* bad debts written off account

— *credit* debtor's account

As you can see, a credit transaction is entered in a debtor's account. The control account 'masters' the sales ledger and so the transaction must also be recorded as a credit transaction in the control account.

Note, however, that *provision for bad debts* (see Chapter Fourteen) is not entered in the control account. The book-keeping entries to create a provision are:

— *debit* profit and loss account

— *credit* provision for bad debts account

As neither of these transactions involves a debtor's personal account, there is no entry in the control account. (Watch out for this 'trap' in examination questions!)

- **Set-off/contra entries**

See Section 19.4 below.

19.3 Purchases ledger control account

The 'pro-forma' layout for the purchases ledger control account (or creditors' control account) is:

Purchases Ledger Control Account

Dr.	£		Cr. £
Balances b/d (small amount)		Balances b/d (large amount)	
Cash/cheques paid to creditors		Credit purchases	
Cash discount received		Interest charged by creditors	
Purchases returns		Balances c/d (small amount)	
Set-off/contra entries			
Balances c/d (large amount)			
Balances b/d (small amount)		Balances b/d (large amount)	

Notes:

- **Balances b/d**

As with sales ledger control account, it is possible to have balances on both sides of the account. For purchases ledger, containing the accounts of creditors, the large balance b/d is always on the credit side. However, if a creditor has been overpaid, the result may be a small debit balance b/d. It may also be that there are closing balances on both sides of the account at the end of the period. In the balance sheet, any small debit balances should be included with debtors.

- **Credit purchases**

Only credit purchases – and not cash purchases – are entered in the control account. However, the total purchases of the business will comprise both credit and cash purchases.

- **Interest charged by creditors**

If creditors charge interest because of slow payment, this must be recorded on both the creditor's account and the control account.

- **Set-off/contra entries**

See below.

19.4 Set-off/contra entries

These entries occur when the same person or business has an account in both sales ledger and purchases ledger, ie they are both buying from, and selling to, the business whose accounts we are preparing. For example, M Patel Ltd has the following accounts in the sales and purchases ledgers:

SALES LEDGER

A Smith

Dr.	£		Cr. £
Balance b/d	200		

PURCHASES LEDGER

Dr.	A Smith		Cr.
	£		£
		Balance b/d	300

From these accounts we can see that:

- A Smith owes M Patel Ltd £200 (sales ledger)
- M Patel Ltd owes A Smith £300 (purchases ledger)

To save each having to write out a cheque to send to the other, it is possible (with A Smith's agreement) to set-off one account against the other, so that they can settle their net indebtedness with one cheque. The book-keeping entries in M Patel's books will be:

— *debit* A Smith (purchases ledger) £200

— *credit* A Smith (sales ledger) £200

The accounts will now appear as:

SALES LEDGER

Dr.	A Smith		Cr.
	£		£
Balance b/d	200	Set-off: purchases ledger	200

PURCHASES LEDGER

Dr.	A Smith		Cr.
	£		£
Set-off: sales ledger	200	Balance b/d	300

The net result is that M Patel Ltd owes A Smith £100. The important point to note is that, because transactions have been recorded in the personal accounts, an entry needs to be made in the two control accounts:

— *debit* purchases ledger control account
— *credit* sales ledger control account } with the amount set-off

19.5 Sources of information for control accounts

Control accounts use totals (remember that their other name is *totals accounts*) for the week, month, quarter or year – depending on what time period is decided upon by the business. The totals come from a number of sources in the accounting system:

Sales ledger control account

- total credit sales (including VAT) – from the sales day book
- total sales returns (including VAT) – from the sales returns day book
- total cash/cheques received from debtors – from the cash book
- total discount allowed – from the discount allowed column (cash book), or discount allowed account
- bad debts – from the journal

Purchases ledger control account

- total credit purchases (including VAT) – from the purchases day book
- total purchases returns (including VAT) – from the purchases returns day book
- total cash/cheques paid to creditors – from the cash book
- total discount received – from the discount received column (cash book), or discount received account

19.6 Control accounts as an aid to management

- When the manager of a business needs to know the figure for debtors or creditors – important information for the manager – the balance of the appropriate control account will give the information immediately. There is no need to add up the balances of all the debtors' or creditors' accounts. With a computer accounting system, the control accounts can be printed at any time.

- The use of a control account makes fraud more difficult – particularly in a manual accounting system. If a fraudulent transaction is to be recorded on a personal account, the transaction must also be entered in the control account. As the control account will be either maintained by a supervisor, and/or checked regularly by the manager, the control account adds another level of security within the accounting system.

- We have already seen in this chapter how control accounts can help in locating errors. Remember, though, that a control account only proves the arithmetical accuracy of the accounts which it controls – there could still be errors, such as misposts and compensating errors, within the ledger section.

19.7 Control accounts and book-keeping

A business can choose how far to include control accounts into the double-entry system. In this chapter we have used them as a 'checking device' for a ledger section, with the ledgers that they control being part of double-entry book-keeping.

Another approach is to use the control accounts as the double-entry system, ie the balances of the sales and purchases ledger control accounts are recorded in the trial balance as debtors and creditors respectively. Using this system, the personal accounts are not part of double-entry, but are *memorandum accounts* which record how much each debtor owes, and how much is owed to each creditor. From time-to-time, the balances of the memorandum accounts will be agreed with the balance of the appropriate control account.

19.8 Chapter summary

- Control accounts (or *totals accounts*) are 'master' accounts, which control a number of subsidiary accounts.

- Two commonly used control accounts are:
  - sales ledger control account
  - purchases ledger control account

- Transactions are recorded on the same side of the control account as on the subsidiary accounts.

- Set-off/contra entries occur when one person has an account in both sales and purchases ledger, and it is agreed to set-off one balance against the other to leave a net balance. This usually results in the following control account entries:
  —*debit* purchases ledger control account
  —*credit* sales ledger control account

- Control accounts are an aid to management:
  - in giving immediate, up-to-date information on the total of debtors or creditors
  - by making fraud more difficult
  - in helping to locate errors

- Control accounts can form part of the double-entry system, with the subsidiary accounts forming memorandum accounts.

In the next chapter we shall use control accounts in a somewhat different way. There we shall be preparing accounts from *incomplete records* – where the owner of the business has not followed double-entry book-keeping principles. Control accounts will be used to help us find missing figures.

19.9 Questions

19.1 The following balances are included in the purchase ledger of Ambrose Artichoke as at 1 January 19-0:

J Carrot	£86.14
F Parsnip	£20.28
B Sprout	£14.10
C Beetroot	£3.90

During January the following transactions took place:

3 January	Purchased stock on credit from F Parsnip £19.72 and from M Mushroom £55.90
10 January	Purchases on credit from C Beetroot £11.91, B Sprout £25.90 and M Mushroom £28.32
15 January	Returned goods to J Carrot £6.00 and B Sprout £7.40
25 January	Paid by cash J Carrot £20.00 on account
30 January	Paid F Parsnip by cheque the balance owing on her account after deducting a 5% cash discount

You are required to:

(a) write up and balance off the personal accounts in the purchase ledger

(b) prepare a purchase ledger control account as at 31 January 19-0

(c) make up a simple reconciliation of the control account balance with the actual creditors as at 31 January 19-0

[RSA Examinations Board]

19.2* The sales ledgers of John Hine Limited were split into two sections and each section was balanced separately. Section 1 covered all dealings with food. Section 2 covered all dealings with clothing.

On 1 January the sales ledger balances were:

Section 1	£84,200	debit	Section 2	£136,200	debit
Section 1	£190	credit	Section 2	£1,260	credit

During the twelve months to 31 December the books of original entry showed the following:

	Section 1	*Section 2*
Sales	678,672	497,285
Cash received from debtors	697,384	526,294
Returns inwards	3,475	1,226
Discount allowed	2,760	887
Bad debts written off	3,660	1,284

At 31 December the credit balances in the sales ledger were:

Section 1 £281 Section 2 £1,328

You are required to prepare control accounts for the two sections for the year ended 31 December and to carry down the balances as at that date.

[Pitman Examinations Institute]

19.3 On 1 January 19-7, the balances in the bought ledger (*purchases ledger*) of John Matthews & Co, were £13,140.

During the half-year ending 30 June 19-7, transactions had taken place which resulted as follows:

	£
Purchases	69,010
Cash paid to creditors	59,328
Discount receivable	2,472
Purchases returns	930
Interest charged by creditors	150
Transfers to credit accounts in sales ledger	220
Cash overpaid returned	20

(a) Prepare the bought ledger control account for the half-year.

(b) Give *two* reasons for keeping such an account.

[Midland Examining Group]

19.4* Rocker Ltd keeps control accounts for its sales and purchases ledgers which it balances at the end of each month. The balances on these accounts at 31 March 19-0 were:

	Debit	*Credit*
	£	£
Purchases ledger	782	78,298
Sales ledger	95,617	613

The following transactions and adjustments took place during April 19-0:

	£
Sales on credit	759,348
Purchases on credit	621,591
Cash sales	202,651
Cash purchases	7,985
Returns from credit customers	3,549
Returns to credit suppliers	4,581
Cash received from credit customers	703,195
Cash paid to credit suppliers	612,116
Discounts received	8,570
Discounts allowed	25,355
Bad debts written off	5,123
Provision for doubtful debts increased by	458

At 30 April 19-0, there were credit balances on the sales ledger totalling £161 and debit balances on the purchases ledger totalling £329.

Required:
Prepare the sales ledger control account and purchases ledger control account of Rocker Ltd for April 19-0, carrying down the balances as at 30 April 19-0.

[The Chartered Institute of Bankers, Spring 1990]

19.5 Mr James Ip keeps both sales and purchases ledgers. From the following details relating to his debtors and creditors, write up the sales ledger control account and the purchases ledger control account for the month of May 19-0. Explain why Mr Ip would prepare such control accounts and give two reasons for a credit balance on a customer's account.

19-0		£
1 May	Sales ledger – debit balances	9,134
	Sales ledger – credit balances	44
	Purchases ledger – credit balances	13,086
	Purchases ledger – debit balances	53
31 May	Transactions for the month:	
	Sales (including cash sales of £2,794)	14,318
	Purchases (including cash purchases of £3,122)	24,677
	Cash received from debtors	970
	Cheques received from debtors	9,564
	Cheques paid out to creditors	10,532
	Discount allowed	382
	Discount received	532
	Bad debts	250
	Sales returns	200
	Purchases returns	908
	Dishonoured cheques	58
	Transfer of a credit balance from the purchases ledger to the sales ledger	160
	Sales ledger – debit balances	9,226
	Sales ledger – credit balances	80
	Purchases ledger – credit balances	22,572
	Purchases ledger – debit balances	116

[RSA Examinations Board]

19.6* The financial year of Michael Brown Ltd ended on 31 May 19-0. A trial balance extracted as at that date shows up a difference of £90 in the books. It is decided to draw up a sales ledger control account and a purchases ledger control account to help locate any errors.

The figures for trade debtors and trade creditors as per the trial balance as at 31 May 19-0 were £38,120 and £21,560 respectively. These were calculated by aggregating the balances on the individual accounts in the sales and purchases ledgers respectively. All purchases and sales were made on credit.

The following totals are available from the books of original entry:

	£
Cash Book:	
Discounts allowed	5,410
Cash and cheques from customers	133,880
Discounts received	3,710
Cash and cheques paid to suppliers	150,960
Refunds given to customers	440
Customers' cheques dishonoured	110
Journal:	
Bad debts written off	750
Decrease in the provision for bad debts	130
Set offs	690
Sales Journal	157,220
Purchases Journal	161,090
Returns In Journal	4,220
Returns Out Journal	4,040

The audited balance sheet as at 1 June 19-9 showed trade debtors and trade creditors of £25,300 and £19,960 respectively.

Required:

(a) Draw up the relevant control accounts.

(b) Use the control accounts to suggest where an error might have been made.

[Association of Accounting Technicians]

19.7* Aries Ltd maintains a creditors ledger control account in its general ledger as part of its double-entry system. Individual accounts for suppliers are maintained on a memorandum basis in a separate creditors ledger.

The following totals are available for the financial year ended 30 November 19-0:

	£
Discounts received	3,608
Cash and cheques paid to suppliers (per Cash Book)	231,570
Set offs to sales ledger control account	818
Credit purchases	249,560
Returns outwards	4,564

The audited total for creditors as at 1 December 19-9 was £45,870.

Required:

(a) Reconstruct the creditors ledger control account for the year ended 30 November 19-0.

(b) The total of the balances on the individual creditors' accounts as at 30 November 19-0 was £51,120. Following a checking of the records the following errors were discovered:

1. An invoice for £1,125 which was correctly entered into the purchases book has not been posted to the individual supplier's account.
2. Another invoice for £1,850 has been omitted from the purchases book.

3. A credit note from a supplier for £870 has been completely omitted from the records.
4. During the year ended 30 November 19-0 petty cash payments to suppliers totalled £625. These have been correctly recorded in the petty cash book and posted to the individual suppliers' accounts but no other entry has been made.
5. The total of the individual creditors' balances as at 30 November 19-0 has been undercast by £2,000.

Required:

Prepare a clear calculation of:

(i) the corrected balance on the creditors ledger control account, and

(ii) the corrected total of the balances on the individual creditors' accounts as at 30 November 19-0.

[Association of Accounting Technicians]

19.8 The sales ledger control account of C Limited is shown below.

Sales Ledger Control

	DR £		*CR* £
Balance b/d	70,814.16	Balances b/d	1,198.73
Sales	54,738.36	Sales returns	2,344.39
Dishonoured cheque	607.15	Payments received	68,708.27
Debt collection fees	108.81	Contra	378.82
Balance c/d	1,194.26	Bad debts written off	474.16
		Balance c/d	54,358.37
	127,462.74		127,462.74

A listing of the individual customer balances in the sales ledger gives the following totals:
Debits £55,136.65 Credits £1,194.26 (used above)

The following facts have been discovered:

1. No entries have been made in the sales ledger for the debt collection charges or bad debts written off.
2. A credit balance of £673.46 has been taken as a debit balance in the listing of the customer balances.
3. The sales day book has been over-added by £500.00
4. The account of the customer who settled by contra was debited with £378.82.
5. A balance on a customer's account of debit £347.58 has been entered on the listing of balances as debit £374.85.
6. The sales returns day book had been under-added by £10.00.
7. The dishonoured cheque has been entered in the sales ledger as credit £601.75.

You are required to:

(a) correct the sales ledger control account (commencing with the closing balances given) and reconcile the listing of the individual balances to the new sales ledger control account balances

(b) explain the purposes of control accounts

[The Chartered Institute of Management Accountants]

20 Incomplete Records

So far in our studies of business accounts we have concentrated on the double-entry system and, from this, have extracted a trial balance and prepared final accounts. However, many smaller businesses do not use the double-entry system, and no trial balance can be extracted. The business keeps some records – *incomplete records* – and, at the end of the year, it is the task of the accountant to construct the final accounts from these.

In this chapter we will

- look at the information available to the accountant in constructing final accounts from incomplete records
- see what information may not be available and how 'missing' figures can be calculated

Many students of business accounts find incomplete records a difficult topic. This problem is caused because each incomplete records question is different from the others in terms of information given. The problem is solved by working out what information has been given and what needs to be calculated. In Section 20.6 we will look at a past examination question to see how questions can be tackled.

In Section 20.8 we shall see how *stock losses* – goods 'lost' as a result of fire, flood or theft – are calculated for insurance purposes.

20.1 Information available to the accountant

The basic financial record kept by most businesses is a cash book, often operated as a *single-entry* system. In practice, even if a cash book has not been kept, it is usually possible to reconstruct it from banking records, although this task can be time-consuming for the accountant and therefore costly for the owner in terms of accountant's fees. Other financial information will be available so that, in all, the accountant has the following to work from:

- cash book – the basic record for any single entry system
- banking details – statements, paying-in books, cheque counterfoils
- invoices – both received (for purchases) and sent (for sales) during the year
- expenses – during the year
- assets and liabilities – fixed and current assets, long-term and current liabilities, both at the beginning and the end of the year
- fixed assets – bought or sold during the year

Information which may not be available, and will need to be calculated includes:

- capital at the beginning of the financial year
- purchases and sales for the year
- cash book summary
- gross and net profits for the year

In the sections which follow, we will see how each of these can be calculated. To give us some figures from which to work, we will use the following information taken from the incomplete records of the business of William Penny, who runs a small stationery wholesaling business:

STATEMENT OF ASSETS AND LIABILITIES

	1 Jan 19-5	31 Dec 19-5
	£	£
Shop fittings	8,000	8,000
Stock	25,600	29,800
Debtors	29,200	20,400
Bank	15,000	not known
Creditors	20,800	16,000
Expenses owing	200	300

BANK SUMMARY FOR 19-5

	£
Receipts from debtors	127,800
Payments to creditors	82,600
Drawings	10,000
Business expenses	30,600

20.2 Opening capital

In order to calculate the capital at the beginning of the financial year, we use the following formula:

- assets *less* liabilities = capital

This is usually presented as a *statement of assets and liabilities,* or *statement of affairs*, in the following form:

STATEMENT OF ASSETS AND LIABILITIES OF WILLIAM PENNY AS AT 1 JANUARY 19-5

	£	£
Assets		
Shop fittings		8,000
Stock		25,600
Debtors		29,200
Bank		15,000
		77,800
Less Liabilities		
Creditors	20,800	
Expenses owing	200	
		21,000
Capital at 1 January 19-5		56,800

20.3 Cash book summary

It is often necessary to prepare a summary cash book to find out the cash and bank balances at the year-end. (Sometimes this is not necessary in examination questions, as the cash book will have been prepared already.) In practice, the entries on the firm's bank statement can be used to produce a summary of receipts and payments for the year. In the case of William Penny's business, the cash book (bank columns) will appear as:

Dr.		Cash Book (bank columns)			Cr.
19-5		£	19-5		£
1 Jan.	Balance b/d	15,000		Payments to creditors	82,600
	Receipts from debtors	127,800		Drawings	10,000
				Expenses	30,600
			31 Dec.	Balance c/d	19,600
		142,800			142,800
19-6			19-6		
1 Jan.	Balance b/d	19,600			

Note that the balance at bank on 31 December 19-5 is calculated by filling in the missing figure.

20.4 Purchases and sales

In calculating purchases and sales, we need to take note of the creditors and debtors at both the beginning and the end of the year. The important point to note is that payments to creditors are *not* the same as purchases for the year (because of the change in the level of creditors). Likewise, receipts from debtors are not the same as sales (because of the change in debtors). Only in a business which trades solely on cash terms and has no debtors/creditors would the receipts and payments be the figures for sales and purchases – such businesses are unheard of in examinations!

Calculating purchases and sales

The method of calculating the purchases and sales figures is:

- **purchases for year** = payments to creditors in year, *less* creditors at the beginning of the year, *plus* creditors at the end of the year
- **sales for year** = receipts from debtors in year, *less* debtors at the beginning of the year, *plus* debtors at the end of the year

(When calculating purchases and sales, also take note of any discounts allowed and received, and bad debts written off.)

The figures from William Penny's business are:

- purchases = £82,600 - £20,800 + £16,000 = £77,800
- sales = £127,800 - £29,200 + £20,400 = £119,000

Use of control accounts

Having learned how to use control accounts in the last chapter, their use is recommended for calculating purchases and sales in incomplete records questions. We can use the information for purchases given in the question as follows:

Purchases Ledger Control Account

Dr.		£			Cr. £
19-5		£	19-5		£
	Payments to creditors	82,600	1 Jan.	Balances b/d	20,800
31 Dec.	Balances c/d	16,000		Purchases *(missing figure)*	?
		98,600			98,600
19-6			19-6		
			1 Jan.	Balances b/d	16,000

The missing figure of purchases for the year can be calculated as £98,600 - £20,800 = £77,800.

In a similar way, the sales figure can be calculated:

Sales Ledger Control Account

Dr.		£			Cr. £
19-5		£	19-5		£
1 Jan.	Balances b/d	29,200		Receipts from debtors	127,800
	Sales *(missing figure)*	?	31 Dec.	Balances c/d	20,400
		148,200			148,200
19-6			19-6		
1 Jan.	Balances b/d	20,400			

The missing figure of sales for the year is £148,200 - £29,200 = £119,000.

The control account method, although its use is not essential in incomplete records questions, does bring a discipline to calculating the two important figures of purchases and sales. Do not forget that the control accounts give the figures for *credit* purchases and sales: cash purchases and sales need to be added, where applicable, to obtain total purchases and sales for the year.

Purchases and sales – summary

Whichever method of calculating purchases or sales is preferred – calculation, or a control account – four pieces of information are usually being used:

- opening balance
- closing balance
- payments or receipts for the year
- purchases or sales for the year

Provided that any three are known, the fourth can be calculated – the figure for purchases and sales was the missing figure in the examples above. However, if an examiner gives us, for example, the opening and closing debtors totals, together with sales for the year, it is a simple matter to calculate the missing figure for receipts from debtors.

Remember that if an examination question includes discounts allowed and received, and bad debts written off, these should also be incorporated into the calculations or control accounts.

20.5 Preparation of the final accounts

Trading account

Having calculated the figures for purchases and sales (in Section 20.4), we can now prepare the trading account.

TRADING ACCOUNT OF WILLIAM PENNY FOR THE YEAR ENDED 31 DECEMBER 19-5

	£	£
Sales		119,000
Opening stock	25,600	
Purchases	77,800	
	103,400	
Less Closing stock	29,800	
		73,600
Gross profit		45,400

Profit and loss account

The profit and loss account follows on from the trading account but, before we are able to complete this, we need to know the figure for expenses for the year. The relevant information from page 292 is:

- bank payments during year, £30,600
- expenses owing at 1 January 19-5, £200
- expenses owing at 31 December 19-5, £300

Like the calculation of purchases and sales, we cannot simply use the bank payments figure for expenses; we must take note of cash payments, together with accruals (and prepayments). The calculation is:

- **expenses for year** = bank payments *less* accruals at the beginning of the year (or *plus* prepayments), *plus* accruals at the end of the year (or *less* prepayments)

Thus the figure for William Penny's business expenses is: £30,600 - £200 + £300 = £30,700.

Alternatively, expenses can be calculated by means of a control account:

Expenses Control Account

Dr.			Cr.		
19-5		£	19-5		£
	Cash/bank	30,600	1 Jan.	Balance b/d	200
31 Dec.	Balance c/d	300	31 Dec.	Profit and loss account *(missing figure)*	?
		30,900			30,900
19-6			19-6		
			1 Jan.	Balance b/d	300

The missing figure is £30,900 - £200 = £30,700.

PROFIT AND LOSS ACCOUNT OF WILLIAM PENNY FOR THE YEAR ENDED 31 DECEMBER 19-5

	£	£
Gross profit		45,400
Less		
Expenses		30,700
Net profit		14,700

Balance sheet

The balance sheet can now be prepared using mainly the assets and liabilities listed on page 292.

BALANCE SHEET OF WILLIAM PENNY AS AT 31 DECEMBER 19-5

	£	£	£
Fixed Assets			
Shop fittings			8,000
Current Assets			
Stock		29,800	
Debtors		20,400	
Bank		19,600	
		69,800	
Less Current Liabilities			
Creditors	16,000		
Accruals	300		
		16,300	
Working Capital			53,500
NET ASSETS			61,500
FINANCED BY			
Capital			
Opening capital			56,800
Add net profit			14,700
			71,500
Less drawings			10,000
			61,500

20.6 Worked example

We will now look at a past examination question on incomplete records. This incorporates points on depreciation and the sale of a fixed asset. You might like to work through the question yourself before comparing your answer with the one shown.

Question

Mary Grimes, retail fruit and vegetable merchant, does not keep a full set of accounting records. However, the following information has been produced from the business records:

- Summary of the bank account for the year ended 31 August 19-8.

	£		£
1 Sep. 19-7 Balance brought forward	1,970	Payments to suppliers	72,000
Receipts from trade debtors	96,000	Purchase of motor van (E471 KBR)	13,000
Sale of private yacht	20,000	Rent and rates	2,600
Sale of motor van (A123 BWA)	2,100	Wages	15,100
		Motor vehicle expenses	3,350
		Postages and stationery	1,360
		Drawings	9,200
		Repairs and renewals	650
		Insurances	800
		31 Aug.19-8 Balance carried forward	2,010
	120,070		120,070
1 Sep. 19-8 Balance brought forward	2,010		

- Assets and liabilities, other than balance at bank:

As at			*1 Sep. 19-7*	*31 Aug. 19-8*
			£	£
Trade creditors			4,700	2,590
Trade debtors			7,320	9,500
Rent and rates accruals			200	260
Motor vans:	A123 BWA -	At cost	10,000	-
		Provision for depreciation	8,000	-
	E471 KBR -	At cost	-	13,000
		Provision for depreciation	-	To be determined
Stock in trade			4,900	5,900
Insurances prepaid			160	200

- All receipts are banked and all payments are made from the business bank account.
- A trade debt of £300 owing by John Blunt and included in the trade debtors at 31 August 19-8 (see above) is to be written off as a bad debt.
- It is Mary Grimes' policy to provide depreciation at the rate of 20% on the cost of motor vans held at the end of each financial year; no depreciation is provided in the year of sale or disposal of a motor van.
- Discounts received during the year ended 31 August 19-8 from trade creditors amounted to £1,100.

Required:

- Prepare Mary Grimes' trading and profit and loss account for the year ended 31 August 19-8.
- Prepare Mary Grimes' balance sheet as at 31 August 19-8.

[Association of Accounting Technicians]

Answer

- **Opening capital**

STATEMENT OF ASSETS AND LIABILITIES OF MARY GRIMES AS AT 1 SEPTEMBER 19-7

	£	£
Assets		
Motor van (A123 BWA) at cost	10,000	
Less provision for depreciation	8,000	
		2,000
Stock		4,900
Debtors		7,320
Insurance prepaid		160
Bank		1,970
		16,350
Less Liabilities		
Creditors	4,700	
Rent and rates accruals	200	
		4,900
Capital at 1 September 19-7		11,450

- **Purchases and sales**

Purchases Ledger Control Account

Dr.		£	Cr.		£
19-7/8		£	19-7/8		£
	Payments to creditors	72,000	1 Sep.	Balances b/d	4,700
	Discounts received	1,100		Purchases *(missing figure)*	70,990
31 Aug.	Balances c/d	2,590			
		75,690			75,690

Sales Ledger Control Account

Dr.		£	Cr.		£
19-7/8		£	19-7/8		£
1 Sep.	Balances b/d	7,320		Receipts from debtors	96,000
	Sales *(missing figure)*	98,180	31 Aug.	Bad debt written off	300
			31 Aug.	Balances c/d	9,200
		105,500			105,500

Note: the balance carried down is the debtors figure at 31 August 19-8, *less* bad debt written off, ie £9500 - £300 = £9200.

- **Cash book summary**

This has already been done and is included in the question. The balance at bank on 31 August 19-8 is £2010.

- **Expenses**

There are accruals for rent and rates, and prepayments for insurances. There is also a profit or loss on the sale of van, registration number A123 BWA.

Rent and Rates Control Account

Dr.		£	Cr.		£
19-7/8		£	19-7/8		£
	Cash/bank	2,600	1 Sep.	Balances b/d	200
31 Aug.	Balance c/d	260	31 Aug.	Profit and loss account*	2,660
		2,860			2,860

* missing figure

Insurances Control Account

Dr.		£	Cr.		£
19-7/8		£	19-7/8		£
1 Sep.	Balance b/d	860	31 Aug.	Profit and loss account*	760
	Cash/bank	100	31 Aug.	Balance c/d	200
		960			960

* missing figure

Disposals Account: Motor Van (A123 BWA)

Dr.	£	Cr.	£
19-7/8	£	19-7/8	£
Motor van at cost	10,000	Provision for depreciation	8,000
Profit and loss account*	100	Bank - sale proceeds	2,100
	10,100		10,100

* missing figure - 'profit' on sale

- **The year-end accounts**

TRADING AND PROFIT AND LOSS ACCOUNT OF MARY GRIMES
FOR THE YEAR ENDED 31 AUGUST 19-8

	£	£
Sales		98,180
Opening stock	4,900	
Purchases	70,990	
	75,890	
Less Closing stock	5,900	
Cost of Goods Sold		69,990
Gross profit		28,190
Add: Discount received		1,100
Profit on sale of motor van		100
		29,390
Less:		
Rent and rates	2,660	
Wages	15,100	
Motor vehicle expenses	3,350	
Postages and stationery	1,360	
Repairs and renewals	650	
Insurances	760	
Depreciation on motor van	2,600	
Bad debt written off	300	
		26,780
Net profit		2,610

BALANCE SHEET OF MARY GRIMES AS AT 31 AUGUST 19-8

	£	£	£
Fixed Assets	Cost	Dep'n to date	Net
Motor van	13,000	2,600	10,400
Current Assets			
Stock		5,900	
Debtors		9,200	
Prepayment (insurance)		200	
Bank		2,010	
		17,310	
Less Current Liabilities			
Creditors	2,590		
Accrual (rent and rates)	260		
		2,850	
Working Capital			14,460
NET ASSETS			24,860
FINANCED BY			
Capital			
Opening capital			11,450
Add addition to capital (sale of private yacht)			20,000
			31,450
Add net profit			2,610
			34,060
Less drawings			9,200
			24,860

20.7 The use of accounting ratios and percentages

Sometimes it is necessary to use accounting ratios and percentages in the preparation of final accounts from incomplete records. (The topic of ratios and percentages is covered fully in Chapter Twenty-nine.) Two common percentages are:

- gross profit mark-up
- gross profit margin

It is quite common for a business to establish its selling price by reference to either a mark-up or a margin. The difference between the two is that:

- mark-up is a profit percentage added to *buying* or *cost* price
- margin is a percentage profit based on the *selling* price

For example, a product is bought by a retailer at a cost of £100; the retailer sells it for £125, ie

cost price + gross profit = selling price

£100 + £25 = £125

The *mark-up* is:

$$\frac{\text{gross profit}}{\text{cost price}} \times \frac{100}{1} = \frac{£25}{£100} \times \frac{100}{1} = 25\%$$

The *margin* is:

$$\frac{\text{gross profit}}{\text{selling price}} \times \frac{100}{1} = \frac{£25}{£125} \times \frac{100}{1} = 20\%$$

In incomplete records accounting, knowing the mark-up or the margin percentages can enable us to calculate either cost of goods sold (which, if we know opening stock and closing stock will enable us to calculate purchases) or sales.

Example:

- Cost of goods sold is £150,000
- Mark-up is 40%
- What is sales?

- Gross profit = £150,000 x $\frac{40}{100}$ = £60,000
- Sales is cost of goods sold + gross profit, ie £150,000 + £60,000 = £210,000

Example:

- Sales is £450,000
- Margin is 20%
- Opening stock is £40,000; closing stock is £50,000
- What is purchases?

- Gross profit = £450,000 x $\frac{20}{100}$ = £90,000
- Cost of sales is sales - gross profit, ie £450,000 – £90,000 = £360,000
- Purchases is:

Opening stock	£40,000
+ Purchases (missing figure)	?
- Closing stock	£50,000
Cost of goods sold	£360,000

Therefore purchases is £370,000.

20.8 Stock losses

A loss of stock may occur as a result of an event such as a fire, a flood or a theft. When such a loss occurs, an estimate of the value of the stock lost needs to be made in order for the business to make an insurance claim (always assuming that the stock was adequately insured). The value is calculated by preparing an account similar to a trading account to the date of the event, and often making use of margins and mark-ups (see Section 20.7 above). The calculations are best carried out in three steps:

1. Opening stock
   + Purchases
   = Cost of stock available for sale

2. Sales
   – Gross profit (using normal gross profit percentage)
   = Cost of goods sold

3. Cost of stock available for sale (from 1, above)
   – Cost of goods sold (2, above)
   = Estimated closing stock
   – Value of stock remaining or salvaged
   = Value of stock lost, ie amount of insurance claim

Worked example

Question

On 20 April 19-4, a fire destroyed part of the stock of Teme Traders, and damaged the remainder. The accounting records were saved and showed the following information for the period from 1 January 19-4 (the start of the financial year) to 20 April:

	£
Stock at 1 January	55,000
Purchases for period	245,000
Sales for period	320,000

The firm's gross profit margin on sales last year was twenty per cent and the same percentage was expected for this year. After the fire, the remaining damaged stock was sold for £4,000.

Calculate the amount of the insurance claim for stock.

Answer

Calculation of stock loss on 20 April 19-4

	£	£
Opening stock		55,000
Purchases		245,000
Cost of stock available for sale		300,000
Sales	320,000	
Less Normal gross profit percentage (20%)	64,000	
Cost of Goods Sold		256,000
Estimated closing stock		44,000
Less Value of stock salvaged and sold		4,000
Value of stock lost (ie insurance claim)		40,000

Note: Some questions may give the percentage mark-up on the buying price, rather than the margin on the selling price. Under these circumstances, cost of goods sold must be calculated. For example, if the mark-up is twenty-five per cent in the question above, then:

$$\text{Sales} \times \frac{100}{125^*} = \text{cost of goods sold}$$

* 100 + percentage mark-up

$$\text{ie } £320{,}000 \times \frac{100}{125} = £256{,}000 \text{ cost of goods sold}$$

The value of stock lost is then calculated by filling in the missing figure, as follows:

	£	£
Opening stock		55,000
Purchases		245,000
		300,000
Less:		
Value of stock salvaged and sold	4,000	
Value of stock lost *(missing figure)*	40,000	
		44,000
Cost of Goods Sold (see calculation above)		256,000
Gross profit (25% of cost of goods sold)		64,000
Sales		320,000

20.9 Chapter summary

- Incomplete records is the term used to describe a book-keeping system where double-entry principles are not used.
- In order to prepare final accounts, the accountant may well have to calculate:
  - capital at the beginning of the financial year
  - purchases and sales for the year
  - cash book summary
  - gross and net profits for the year
- On the basis of these calculations, the accountant can then construct the final accounts without recourse to a trial balance.
- Mark-up is the gross profit percentage added to buying price.
- Margin is the percentage profit based on the selling price.
- The value of stock losses caused by fire, flood or theft is calculated using margins and mark-ups.

In the next chapter we will look at a specialised type of account for clubs and societies - income and expenditure accounts. Normally such accounts are *not* prepared on the double-entry system and you will need to apply your incomplete records skills!

20.10 Questions

20.1 Bill Brown took out a statement of his financial position on 1 April 19-9 which showed the following:

	£
Sundry creditors	8,505
Sundry debtors	7,200
Stock in trade	1,350
Cash and bank	450
Furniture and fittings	2,655

After one year, during which Bill Brown introduced additional capital of £500 and withdrew £2,250 for his own requirements, his position was:

	£
Sundry creditors	6,831
Sundry debtors	5,400
Stock in trade	840
Cash and bank	1,350
Furniture and fittings	2,390

Required:

(a) statements of affairs to show Bill Brown's capital position as at 1 April 19-9 and his new capital position one year later.

(b) a statement showing the profit or loss made by Bill Brown for the year.

[RSA Examinations Board]

20.2* Brian Withers runs a medium-sized family business as a general trader. He knows a great deal about selling but, sadly, very little about accounting. Brian is being very hard pressed to produce some trading results, and has asked your help in calculating his new profit or loss for the year to 30 April 19-0.

The only information available to you is a statement of his assets and liabilities at 1 May 19-9 and 30 April 19-0; details of these are given below:

	1 May 19-9	*30 April 19-0*
	£	£
Cash at bank	720	790
Stock in trade	6,400	6,700
Trade debtors	6,240	6,430
Trade creditors	1,330	1,450
Fixed assets	45,000	46,500
Insurance paid in advance	140	180
Wages paid in arrears	70	50
Loan from father	5,000	4,000

During the year Brian had taken monies from the business for his own private use to the value of £700 per month. During the financial year Brian had a small win on the football pools amounting to £2,000 which he paid into the business.

You are required to:

(a) prepare a statement of affairs at 1 May 19-9

(b) prepare a statement of affairs at 30 April 19-0

(c) calculate Brian's net profit or loss for the year

(d) give *three* advantages which a formal double-entry book-keeping system would have for Brian and his business

(e) explain why Brian should take account of payments in advance and payments in arrears

[Welsh Joint Education Committee]

20.3 D Bradley, a retailer, does not keep any books of account, but does operate a business bank account. A summary of the bank statements for the year ending 30 June 19-5 is given below.

	£		£
Receipts from customers	22,820	Opening balance	2,025
Additional capital paid in	5,500	Payments to creditors	18,682
		Electricity	1,825
		Rent and rates	2,350
		Motor van	2,400
		Closing balance	1,038
	28,320		28,320

During the year he paid expenses direct from cash received and these were estimated as £5,280 for wages and £1,250 for general expenses and D Bradley took drawings of £100 each week for himself.

D Bradley supplied the following details of his assets and liabilities at the year-end for the years 30 June 19-4 and 19-5:

	19-4	*19-5*
	£	£
Fixtures at cost	1,800	1,800
Motor van at cost		2,400
Stock	13,680	12,790
Debtors	4,250	4,925
Creditors	2,575	3,520
Accrued electricity	485	520
Prepaid rates	280	340
Cash in till	120	210

Depreciation is to be provided at Fixtures 10%
Motor van 25%

You are required to prepare a trading and profit and loss account for the year ending 30 June 19-5 and a balance sheet as at 30 June 19-5.

[Pitman Examinations Institute]

20.4* Gerald Ash started up in business on his own account as a painter and decorator on 1 December 19-9 with capital of £20,000 paid into a business bank account. He also borrowed £10,000 as a loan repayable over five years. During the financial year ended 30 November 19-0 Mr Ash made loan payments totalling £3,500 which can be analysed as follows:

	£
Interest due to 30 November 19-0	1,500
Repayment of amount borrowed	2,000
	3,500

On 1 December 19-9 a motor vehicle costing £14,000 and equipment costing £11,000 were purchased for use in the business. These were paid for in cash and are to be written off equally over their expected economic life of 5 years.

During the year ended 30 November 19-0 Mr Ash received cash and cheques totalling £52,080 for work done for customers. As at 30 November 19-0 there were unpaid invoices totalling £2,400 for work done but Mr Ash expects £180 of this to be uncollectable and provision is to be made accordingly.

Payments to suppliers during the year for painting and decorating materials totalled £15,000 and Mr Ash still had outstanding suppliers' invoices totalling £3,400 as at 30 November 19-0. The cost of unused materials as at 30 November 19-0 was £560.

Mr Ash's business premises were rented as from 1 December 19-9. The annual rental is £1,200 but the rent for November 19-0 was still outstanding as at 30 November 19-0. On 1 June 19-0 Mr Ash found it necessary to engage an assistant at an annual salary of £9,800. This is payable monthly in arrears and all payments due had been made by 30 November 19-0. Mr Ash also withdrew £1,000 each month from the business bank account for personal use during the year ended 30 November 19-0.

Other expenses of operating the business for its first financial year totalled £8,640. Operating expenses accrued and prepaid as at 30 November 19-0 were £65 and £120 respectively.

Required
Prepare in so far as the above information permits, Mr Ash's profit and loss account for the year ended 30 November 19-0 and his balance sheet as at 30 November 19-0.

Note: You may insert the bank balance as at 30 November 19-0 as a balancing figure in the financial statements—there is no need to reconstruct the bank account for the year.

[Association of Accounting Technicians]

20.5 At 1 July year 6, the financial position of John Marcus, a dealer in fancy goods, was as follows:

	£	£		£
Fixtures and fittings:			Capital account – J Marcus	28,000
At cost	16,000		Trade creditors	3,050
Less aggregate depreciation	6,400	9,600	Electricity charges accrued	290
Stock-in-trade		12,400		
Trade debtors		2,900		
Prepayments (rates)		340		
Balance at bank		6,100		
		31,340		31,340

Marcus does not keep a full set of account records but he was able to arrive at the following summarised data for the year which ended on 30 June year 7:

1. Sales for the year amounted to £117,460. Gross profit is 25% of sales.
2. Stock-in-trade, at cost, at 30 June year 7, has increased by 25% over the previous year.
3. Trade debtors at 30 June year 7 amounted to £5,200.
4. Trade creditors at 30 June year 7 amounted to £4,650.
5. Cash discounts for the year were as follows: allowed £720; received £560.
6. During the year he had acquired a motor van for £4,200 in cash.
7. Payments were made during the year as follows:

Wages	£12,680
Rent, rates, electricity	£8,950

8. At 30 June year 7, electricity charges accrued were £260 and rent prepaid amounted to £520.
9. Marcus had written off bad debts amounting to £180 during the year.

Additional information:

- Depreciation was to be provided as follows:

Fixtures and fittings	10% on cost
Motor van	25% on cost

- Marcus wished to make a provision of 5% of debtors for bad debts at 30 June year 7. No such provision had been made at 30 June year 6.

Required:

Prepare for John Marcus:

(a) a trading and profit and loss account for the year ended 30 June year 7

(b) a balance sheet at 30 June year 7

[London Chamber of Commerce]

20.6 The assets and liabilities as at the close of business on 30 October 19-9 of J Patel, retailer, are summarised as follows:

	£	£
Motor vehicles:		
At cost	9,000	
Provision for depreciation	1,800	
		7,200
Fixtures and fittings:		
At cost	10,000	
Provision for depreciation	6,000	
		4,000
Stock		16,100
Trade debtors		19,630
Cash		160
		47,090
Capital—J Patel		30,910
Bank overdraft		6,740
Trade creditors		9,440
		47,090

All receipts from credit customers are paid intact into the business bank account whilst cash sales receipts are banked after deduction of cash drawings and providing for the shop till cash float. The cash float was increased from £160 to £200 in September 19-0.

The following is a summary of the transactions in the business bank account for the year ended 31 October 19-0.

Receipts	£	*Payments*	£
Credit sales	181,370	Drawings	8,500
Cash sales	61,190	Motor van (bought 1 May 19-0)	11,200
Proceeds of sale of land owned privately by J Patel	16,000	Purchases	163,100
		Establishment and administrative expenses	33,300
		Sales and distribution expenses	29,100

Additional information for the year ended 31 October 19-0:

1. A gross profit of $33\frac{1}{3}$% has been achieved on all sales.
2. Bad debts of £530 have been written off during the year.
3. Trade debtors at 31 October 19-0 were reduced by £8,130 as compared with a year earlier.
4. Trade creditors at 31 October 19-0 amounted to £12,700.
5. Depreciation is to be provided at the following annual rates on cost:

Motor vehicles	20%
Fixtures and fittings	10%

6. Stock at 31 October 19-0 has been valued at £23,700.

Required:

A trading and profit and loss account for the year ended 31 October 19-0 and a balance sheet as at that date for J Patel.

[Association of Accounting Technicians]

20.7* JB, a sole trader, does not maintain a set of ledgers to record his accounting transactions. Instead, he relies on details of cash receipts/payments, bank statements and files of invoices. He started business on 1 June 19-7 with private capital of £5,000 which comprised a second-hand van valued at £1,500 and £3,500 cash which he deposited in a business bank account on that date. He has not prepared any accounts since he commenced trading and you have agreed to prepare his first set of accounts for him in respect of the 18 months ended 31 December 19-8.

You have discovered:

1. A summary of his cash transactions from his cash book for the period was:

		£	£
Receipts:	Capital introduced	3,500	
	Cash sale receipts	21,250	
	Sale of motor van	850	
			25,600
Payments:	Cash paid to bank	21,350	
	Cash purchases	2,160	
	Postage and stationery	474	
	Motor expenses	919	
			24,903
Cash in hand at 31 December 19-8			697

2. A summary of his bank statements shows:

		£	£
Receipts:	Cash paid into bank	21,190	
	Bank loan	4,500	
	Credit sale receipts	1,955	
			27,645
Payments:	Purchase of goods	7,315	
	Office equipment	1,280	
	Motor van	4,000	
	Drawings	5,400	
	Rent and rates	1,850	
	Light and heat	923	
			20,768
Balance at 31 December 19-8			6,877

3. The office equipment was purchased on 1 October 19-7.
4. The new motor van was purchased on 1 April 19-8 to replace the original second-hand van which was sold on the same date.
5. JB expects the office equipment to last five years but to have no value at the end of its life. The motor van bought on 1 April 19-8 is expected to be used for three years and to be sold for £700 at the end of that time.
6. The cost of goods unsold on 31 December 19-8 was £1,425. JB thought he would sell these for £2,560, with no item being sold for less than its original cost.
7. On 31 December 19-8 JB owed £749 for goods bought on credit and was owed £431 for goods sold on credit. Of these amounts £189 was due from/to XEN Limited which is both a customer and supplier of JB. A contra settlement arrangement has been agreed by both JB and XEN Limited.
8. Rent and rates paid includes an invoice for £1,200 for the rates due for the year to 31 March 19-9.
9. No invoice was received for light and heat in respect of November and December 19-8 until 25 February 19-9. This showed that the amount due for the three months ended 31 January 19-9 was £114.
10. The bank loan was received on 1 January 19-8. Interest is charged at 10% per annum on the amount outstanding.

You are required to prepare JB's trading and profit and loss account for the period ended 31 December 19-8 and his balance sheet at that date in vertical format.

[The Chartered Institute of Management Accountants]

20.8 What is the estimated closing stock at cost given the following information?

Opening stock	£3,000
Purchases	£15,000
Sales	£19,375

Normal rate of gross profit on cost price is 25 per cent.

Explain when you might want to make such a calculation.

[Pitman Examinations Institute]

20.9* John Amos Limited (Wholesalers) had a fire at their warehouse on 30 November, the greater part of the stock being destroyed. Some stock was able to be salvaged and this was valued at £6,800.

The accounting records were kept in an office away from the fire and the accountant of John Amos was able to establish that in the last four months, sales were £251,200 and purchases £187,600.

The stock records showed that on 1 August stock had amounted to £94,300. The average gross profit on turnover during the last two years had been 22%. The business was fully insured against fire.

You are required to prepare the claim to be submitted to the insurance company in respect of stock destroyed by fire.

[Pitman Examinations Institute]

20.10 The premises of Scott Welch Limited suffered a fire on the night of 1 November 19-9, which destroyed a quantity of stock together with the stock records.

The stock was insured against fire and the company wishes to submit a claim, the following information is available:

Year end accounts were completed on 30 June 19-9 and the balance sheet at that date showed stock in trade £84,800, debtors £49,000 and creditors for purchases £53,000.

During the period 1 July – 1 November 19-9, the following transactions took place:

	£
Cash collected from debtors	116,000
Cash sales	43,500
Drawings from stock	2,200
Discount received	1,900
Discount allowed	1,800
Cash paid to creditors	76,600

The following balances remained in the ledgers:

Debtors owed £63,000 and creditors were owed £48,500; a stock take carried out immediately after the fire, showed the value of undamaged stock to be £21,150; the company makes a gross profit of 25% on the selling price of its goods.

You are required to prepare a statement showing the value of the stock lost in the fire.

[RSA Examinations Board]

21 Club and Society Accounts

The title of this book is 'Business Accounts' and, up until now, we have been concerned with the accounting records of business organisations. The primary objective of a business is to make a profit, and we have become used to calculating this in the trading and profit and loss account. We now turn to the accounts of clubs and societies and non-profit making organisations; here the primary objective is to provide facilities and services to members.

In this chapter we will look at:

- differences in accounting terminology between business and non-profit making organisations
- the preparation of club/society year-end accounts
- the different accounting treatments for certain aspects of club/society accounts

It is for the treasurer of the club/society to maintain proper accounting records, and these will be audited either by another member, or by an outside accountant. The important point is that the highest standards of financial recording should still be maintained, and many accountants find themselves elected to the job of treasurer.

21.1 Accounting terminology

As mentioned above, there are differences in aims and accounting terminology between businesses and non-profit making organisations.

Business	**Non-profit making organisations**
• Primary objective: to make a profit for the owners	• Primary objective: to provide facilities and and services to members
• Profit and loss account	• Income and expenditure account
• Profit	• Surplus (of income over expenditure)
• Loss	• Deficit (of expenditure over income)
• Capital	• Accumulated fund

21.2 Accounting records of a club/society

Few clubs and societies keep accounting records in double-entry form. For most clubs, the treasurer keeps a cash book, which is a simple version of the cash book used by businesses. It records receipts paid into the bank and payments made from the bank, together with cash receipts and payments. The cash book is ruled off and balanced at the end of the financial year.

Often a summary of the cash book is presented to members in the form of a *receipts and payments account* (see example on page 313); for a very small club, this information forms the 'year-end accounts'. However, there are two accounting problems in using a receipts and payments account:

- accruals and prepayments cannot be made
- the distinction between capital and revenue expenditure cannot be made

Thus, whilst a receipt and payments account may be suitable for a small club which meets infrequently or deals in small amounts of money, a larger club needs to produce final accounts in the form of:

- income and expenditure account
- balance sheet

21.3 Income and expenditure account

The income and expenditure account of a club or society lists the income first and then deducts the expenditure using a similar layout to a profit and loss account. The account will then show:

- *either* a surplus of income over expenditure
- *or* a deficit of expenditure over income

An example of an income and expenditure account is shown below:

CROWN HEATH CRICKET CLUB
INCOME AND EXPENDITURE ACCOUNT FOR THE YEAR ENDED 31 DECEMBER 19-8

	£	£
Income		
Subscriptions		905
Gross profit on bar		1,450
Sale of programmes		235
		2,590
Less Expenditure		
Rent	250	
Heating oil	900	
Electricity	127	
Groundsman's wages	1,050	
Sundry expenses	35	
Provision for depreciation: lawnmower	75	
		2,437
Surplus of income over expenditure		153

The income and expenditure account is prepared from the receipts and payments account, taking note of:

- accruals
- prepayments
- provision for depreciation on fixed assets

Capital expenditure, eg the purchase of a new lawnmower, is not recorded in the income and expenditure account, although depreciation of the lawnmower will be shown.

A major source of income for a club is members' subscriptions. Some members will prepay subscriptions for the next financial year, while others will be late in paying, or may never pay at all, ceasing to be members. In examination questions you should, unless told otherwise, calculate the subscriptions that *should have been received,* ie

subscriptions received in year
less subscriptions paid in advance at the end of the year
plus subscriptions due but unpaid at the end of the year
equals subscription income for year to be shown in the income and expenditure account

(*Note:* it will also be necessary to adjust for any subscriptions prepaid and accrued at the start of the year.)

In the balance sheet of the club, subscriptions in advance are recorded as a current liability, while subscriptions due but unpaid are a current asset – debtors for subscriptions. This method of handling subscriptions takes note of prepayments and accruals and is the way in which we would deal with such items in the accounts of a business. However, in practice, the treasurer of a club is unlikely to record subscriptions due but unpaid as debtors because, unlike a business, the club will not sue for unpaid amounts. The most realistic approach is to ignore such subscriptions – if they are subsequently paid, they can be brought into that year's income. For examination purposes though, and unless the question tells you differently, treat subscriptions due as debtors.

Other sources of income for clubs/societies include:

- trading activities (see Section 21.5)
- donations received
- room lettings to other organisations
- special activities, eg jumble sale, dinner dance

21.4 Balance sheet

The balance sheet of a club/society is presented in a very similar way to that of a business. The major difference is that, instead of capital, a club has an *accumulated fund.* If the accumulated fund is not known at the start of the financial year, it is calculated as:

- assets *less* liabilities = accumulated fund

In the balance sheet a surplus from the income and expenditure account is added, while a deficit is deducted.

An example club balance sheet is shown at the end of Section 21.7.

21.5 Trading activities

Although the primary objective of clubs and societies and other non-profit making organisations is to provide facilities and services to members, many organisations carry out an activity on a regular basis with the intention of making a profit. Examples of such trading activities include:

- a bar for the use of members
- provision of catering facilities for members
- the purchase of goods to sell to members on favourable terms, eg seeds and fertilisers by a gardening society

In the year-end accounts, the treasurer should prepare a separate *trading account* for such activities so as to show the profit or loss. The layout of this account is exactly the same as that for a business, with opening stock, closing stock, purchases and sales. Any direct costs associated with the trading activity – such as a barperson's wages – will be included in the trading account. The profit or loss on trading activities is then taken to the income and expenditure account. An example of a trading account is shown in Section 21.7.

21.6 Fund-raising events

Most clubs and societies organise fund-raising events from time-to-time, eg jumble sales, raffles, coffee mornings, etc. It is usual to show the separate profit or loss on such events within the income and expenditure account. This is done by linking the income and the expenses together, for example:

	£	£
Income		
Christmas Fayre		
takings	550	
less expenses	210	
profit		340

21.7 Worked example

Question

The following account has been prepared by the treasurer of the Phoenix Model Engineering Society:

Receipts and payments statement for the year ended 31 March 19-9

	£		£
1 Apr. 19-8 Opening balance b/fwd	894	Purchase of building land	8,000
Subscriptions received	12,000	Purchase of machinery and tools	17,500
Sales of machinery and tools	21,000	Rent of temporary office and meeting room	600
Sale of wooden hut	1,100	Printing, stationery and postages	860
Sales of tickets for annual national exhibition	300	Deposit in building society investment account	7,500
		Secretary's honorarium	150
		Coach to annual national exhibition	110
		Admission charges to annual national exhibition	220
		31 Mar. 19-9 Closing balance c/fwd	354
	35,294		35,294

The following additional information has been obtained from the Society's records:

1. In addition to the balances at bank shown in the above receipts and payments statement, the Society's assets and liabilities were:

As at	*1 April 19-8*	*31 March 19-9*
	£	£
Stocks of machinery and tools at cost	1,200	600
Subscriptions due to the Society	150	250
Wooden hut at valuation	1,300	-
Subscriptions prepaid by members	300	To be determined
Outing to annual national exhibition	-	See note 4 below

2. The annual subscription for the year ended 31 March has been £50 per member since 1 April 19-7.
All subscriptions due at 1 April 19-8 have now been paid.
The Society's membership was 238 during the year ended 31 March 19-9.

3. All sales of machinery and tools are to members on a strictly cash basis.

4. *Annual National Exhibition.* £40 for tickets was owing by a member to the Society on 31 March 19-9 and at that date the Society owed £45 for the purchase of exhibition programmes distributed to members without charge.

5. Since preparing the above receipts and payments statement, the treasurer has received a bank statement showing bank charges of £14 debited in the Society's bank account on 30 March 19-9; no adjustment was made for these charges in the above statement.

6. Since the sale of the wooden hut on 1 July 19-8, the Society has rented a temporary office and meeting room at an annual rent of £600 payable in advance.

Required:

Prepare an income and expenditure account for the year ended 31 March 19-9 and a balance sheet as at that date for the Society.

Note: **The income and expenditure account should show clearly the overall result of the trade in machinery and tools and the profit or loss of the visit to the annual national exhibition.**

[Association of Accounting Technicians]

Answer

In preparing the answer, notice that the question gives a receipts and payments account for the year; also, assets and liabilities at the beginning and end of the year are listed.

- **Accumulated fund at start of year**

Statement of Assets and Liabilities as at 1 April 19-8

	£	£
Assets		
Stocks of machinery and tools at cost		1,200
Subscriptions due to the society (note that the Society's policy appears to treat these as debtors)		150
Wooden hut at valuation		1,300
Bank*		894
		3,544
Less Liabilities		
Subscriptions prepaid		300
Accumulated fund as at 1 April 19-8		3,244

* opening balance of receipts and payments account – always check to see if it is money in the bank (asset), or an overdraft (liability).

- **Subscriptions**

This is best prepared by means of a control account:

Dr.		Subscriptions Control Account			Cr.
		£			£
19-8/9			19-8/9		
1 Apr.	Balance b/d (subscriptions owing)	150	1 Apr.	Balance b/d (subscriptions prepaid)	300
31 Mar.	Income and expenditure account (238 @ £50)	11,900		Subscriptions received	12,000
31 Mar.	Balance c/d *(missing figure)*	500	31 Mar.	Balance c/d	250
		12,550			12,550

- **Rent**

Note that £150 of rent is prepaid, ie to 30 June 19-9.

- **Income and expenditure account and balance sheet**

As the society sells machinery and tools to members, and the question requires the accounts to show the overall result of the trade in machinery and tools, the income and expenditure account is preceded by a trading account for this aspect of the society's activities.

THE PHOENIX MODEL ENGINEERING SOCIETY
TRADING ACCOUNT FOR MACHINERY AND TOOLS FOR THE YEAR ENDED 31 MARCH 19-9

	£	£
Sales		21,000
Opening stock	1,200	
Purchases	17,500	
	18,700	
Less Closing stock	600	
Cost of Goods Sold		18,100
Gross profit		2,900

INCOME AND EXPENDITURE ACCOUNT FOR THE YEAR ENDED 31 MARCH 19-9

	£	£	£
Income			
Members' subscriptions			11,900
Gross profit on machinery and tools			2,900
			14,800
Less Expenditure			
Rent of temporary office and meeting room		450	
Printing, stationery and postages		860	
Secretary's honorarium		150	
Sale of wooden hut:			
valuation 1 April 19-8	1,300		
less sale proceeds	1,100		
loss on sale		200	
Annual national exhibition:			
coach	110		
admission charges	220		
exhibition programmes	45		
	375		
less sale of tickets	340		
loss		35	
Bank charges		14	
			1,709
Surplus of income over expenditure			13,091

BALANCE SHEET AS AT 31 MARCH 19-9

	£	£	£
Fixed Assets			
Building land			8,000
Current Assets			
Stock of machinery and tools		600	
Subscriptions due		250	
Prepayment of rent		150	
Due for annual exhibition tickets		40	
Building society investment account		7,500	
Bank	354		
Less bank charges	14		
		340	
		8,880	
Less Current Liabilities			
Prepayment of subscriptions	500		
Accrual – annual national exhibition programmes	45		
Working Capital		545	
			8,335
			16,335
REPRESENTED BY			
Accumulated fund			3,244
Add surplus of income over expenditure for year			13,091
			16,335

21.8 Club accounts: problem areas

There are a number of possible areas that need to be clarified by a newly appointed treasurer of a club or society. These are the club's policy on:

- overdue subscriptions
- life membership
- entrance/joining fees
- donations received
- depreciation

The club's rules should state how these are to be handled in the accounts; if not, a new treasurer will have to see how they were dealt with in previous years, or ask the committee for a decision.

Overdue subscriptions

We have already seen in Section 21.3 that the practical policy adopted by most treasurers is to ignore overdue subscriptions (but an adjustment *is* made for prepaid subscriptions). However, an examination question may instruct you to treat overdue subscriptions as debtors.

Life membership

Some clubs and societies offer life membership in exchange for a one-off payment. The problem for the treasurer is whether to record this payment as income for the year in which it is received, or to credit it to a reserve account (eg Life Subscriptions Account), the balance of which is then transferred bit-by-bit over a number of years to the income and expenditure account. The time period for this will depend on the nature of the club: for example, the 'Over-eighties Gentleman's Dining Club' is likely to transfer its life subscriptions account to income rather more quickly than will a stamp collecting club.

Two clubs of which I am a member have these different policies:

"Three per cent of the life subscriptions account is released to income each year."

"Life subscription income is credited to life membership reserve and taken to income and expenditure account in equal annual instalments over the number of years represented by the ratio of the life membership subscription to the annual adult subscription."

An examination question will always give you guidance on this point.

Entrance or joining fees

Often a one-off charge is made in the year of joining a club as an entrance fee. It is possible to justify making such a charge by arguing that it covers the cost of processing new members' applications; on the other hand it gives extra income to the club and, once a person is a member, it acts as an incentive for them to remain a member (because, if their membership lapsed, the joining fee would be payable again upon rejoining).

The treasurer needs to know how to account for the joining fee:

- *either,* it is treated as income for the year of joining (but this could distort income if a membership 'drive' was held in one particular year)
- *or,* it is credited to an entrance fees account which is transferred to income over a number of years

Again, an examination question will give guidance.

Donations received

There are two alternative accounting treatments which can be used for donations received:

- record the amount as income in the income and expenditure account, *or*
- record the amount as an addition to the accumulated fund in the balance sheet

The first method treats the donation as income for the year, while the second capitalises the amount (ie records it on the balance sheet). As to which is to be used depends very much on the amount of the donation in relation to the size of the club's activities. For example, a £10 donation would normally be recorded as income; however, a legacy of several thousands of pounds from a deceased club member ought to be capitalised and added to the accumulated fund. If the club rules do not state how donations received are to be dealt with in the accounts, the treasurer must use his or her own judgement and will probably apply the materiality concept.

Remember that, in practice, donations will not always be cash amounts, other assets could be donated, eg a piece of land, a work of art. Here the asset will need to be valued and recorded in the accounts. In the case of assets other than cash, it is likely that they will need to be capitalised and recorded on the balance sheet.

Depreciation

As in business accounts, fixed assets should be depreciated in club accounts; the same principles will apply (see Chapter Thirteen). Provision for depreciation for the year is charged as an expense in the income and expenditure account, while the asset is shown in the balance sheet at cost less depreciation to date, to give the net book value.

In examination questions, details will usually be given of the club's policy on depreciation. Some questions will simply state the value of fixed assets at the beginning and the end of the financial year: if there have been no acquisitions or sales, the fall in value is the provision for depreciation for the year which is to be charged as an expense in the income and expenditure account. The asset will then be shown at the reduced value in the year-end balance sheet.

21.9 Practical points

As noted in the introduction to this chapter, the treasurer of a club/society is responsible for maintaining proper accounting records. The same high standards of financial recording as would be applied to business accounts should be used by the club treasurer. Two areas are of particular importance:

- *Authority to spend*
  Before making payments, the treasurer must ensure that he or she has the authority to spend the club's money. For 'one-off' transactions, eg the purchase of a new lawnmower by a cricket club, the minutes of the relevant committee meeting will show that the purchase was agreed. For regular activities eg small expenses such as printing, electricity, the club's rules will authorise the treasurer to make payment against invoices received.

- *Documentary evidence*
  The treasurer should ensure that there is documentary evidence for every transaction passing through the accounts of the club. For example, payments should only be made against invoices received in the name of the club, while a receipt should be given for all money received. In this way, an audit trail is created. All documents should be retained for the use of the club's auditor, who will check the accounting records after the end of each financial year. The documents should then be stored for at least six years in case there are subsequent queries.

21.10 Chapter summary

❑ Unlike a business, a club, society or other non-profit making organisation does not base its activities on profit, but operates for the benefit of its members.

❑ Many clubs and societies have large sums of money passing through their hands and, like businesses, need tight accounting controls.

❑ The year-end accounts of a club consist of
- income and expenditure account
- balance sheet

❑ Where a club carries out an activity on a regular basis with the intention of making a profit, a trading account is prepared for the activity.

❑ Accounting policies on which the treasurer needs guidance from the club's committee are:
- overdue subscriptions
- life membership
- entrance/joining fees
- donations received
- depreciation

In the next chapter we return to business accounts and look at the year-end accounts of a partnership.

21.11 Questions

21.1* On 1 January 19-9, the Carlton Sports Club had £1,000 in the bank.

At the end of the first year their receipts and payments account was as follows:

Receipts and Payments Account

	£		£
Balance b/d	1,000	Equipment	840
Subscriptions	481	Postage and stationery	176
Entry fees for competitions	143	Tuck shop purchases	690
Tuck shop receipts	832	Competition expenses	98
		Rent	120
		Balance c/d	532
	2,456		2,456
Balance b/d	532		

(a) Prepare an income and expenditure account for the year ending 31 December 19-9, taking note of the following information:
(i) subscriptions in arrears £23
(ii) equipment to be depreciated by 5%
(iii) rent owing £30

(b) Prepare a balance sheet as at 31 December 19-9

[© Northern Ireland Schools Examinations and Assessment Council]

21.2 A group of young musicians intend to form a music society, meeting once a week commencing 1 September 19-0. They present the following financial estimates for your consideration:

1. The club would expect 300 members, but only 50% of this target would be achieved in the first year. The membership fee would be £20 per annum.
2. They can hire a hall for £20 per meeting, plus £5 weekly for light and heat.
3. At the outset, they would need to buy stereo equipment costing £1,200.
4. The equipment would be depreciated on a straight line basis over 4 years.
5. The annual premium for all risks insurance will be £90 payable on commencement.
6. Records costing £1,000 would be bought during the year. They would be treated as an expense of the society.
7. It is estimated that each member would spend an average of £40 per annum on light refreshments. It is hoped to sell the refreshments at twice the purchase price.

You are required to:

(a) Prepare an estimated receipts and payments account for the society's first year which would end on 31 August 19-1

(b) Draw up an estimated income and expenditure account for the year ending 31 August 19-1

(c) Draft the society's estimated balance sheet as at 31 August 19-1

[Welsh Joint Education Committee]

21.3 The Secretary of the Greenroom Social Club issued the following receipts and payments account to members:

Receipts and Payments Account for the year to 30 June

	£		£
Cash balance	1,620	Wages	15,300
Subscriptions	22,410	Secretary's salary	2,700
Bank loan	4,500	Rent of hall	900
Games' fees	270	Printing and postage	2,115
Drink machine receipts	936	Purchase of new chairs	3,240
		Loss on dance	198
		Cash balance	5,283
	29,736		29,736

The Secretary gave the following information:

Subscriptions included £180 from previous year, £72 received in respect of advance payment for next year, and that £225 was due but unpaid.

Games' fees included £27 paid in advance for the following year's matches.

The cleaner had not been paid £108 for the month of June and was to be paid this amount in July.

Stationery purchased during the year and held in stock on 30 June was valued at £180. The furniture at 30 June was valued at £3,105 and this included what was purchased during the year. The accumulated fund at the previous 1 July was £1,800.

You are required to prepare an income and expenditure account for the club for the year ended 30 June and a balance sheet at that date.

[Pitman Examinations Institute]

21.4* The assets and liabilities of the East Sutton Social Club as at 1 November 19-8 were:

Cash held at bank £380; furniture and equipment £420; bar stock £120; rent owing on premises £30.

The following is a summary of receipts and payments for the club for the year ended 31 October 19-9:

Receipts	£	*Payments*	£
Balance 1 November 19-8	380	Bar purchases	1,485
Subscriptions	1,420	Annual dance expenses	580
Annual dance	750	Rent of premises	840
Bar sales	2,040	Secretary's expenses	225
		Purchase of furniture	200
		Wages of caretaker	580
		Balance 31 October 19-9	680
	4,590		4,590

The following information was also available:

(i) Bar stock at 31 October 19-9 was £150;

(ii) Rent for premises of £110 was owing at 31 October 19-9.

You are required to:

(a) calculate the accumulated fund at 1 November 19-8

(b) prepare an income and expenditure account for the year ended 31 October 19-9, showing clearly the profit/loss on the bar and the dance

(c) prepare a balance sheet for the club as at 31 October 19-9

[RSA Examinations Board]

21.5 The treasurer of the local amateur dramatic society, of which you are a member, has reported that the society has made a healthy surplus for the year to 30 June 19-0. He supports this statement by pointing to the fact that the cash in the society's current account at the bank has risen by £1,100, from £320 to £1,420, as shown in the following summary of receipts and payments which he has prepared:

Receipts	£	*Payments*	£
Balance brought down	320	Hire of halls	300
Subscriptions	1,000	Purchase of refreshments for resale	1,500
Box office takings	4,500	Royalty payments for performance rights	2,500
Transfer from deposit account	2,000		
Interest on deposit account	200	Purchase of lighting, scenery and costumes	3,000
Sales of refreshments	2,300		
		Incidental expenses	1,600
		Balance carried down	1,420
	10,320		10,320

You wonder whether the treasurer's optimism is justified, and ascertain that the following balances existed at the start and end of the year:

	At 30 June 19-9	*At 30 June 19-0*
	£	£
Creditors for purchases of refreshments	50	350
Deposit account	2,000	0
Lighting, scenery and costumes at written down value	10,000	To be calculated
Royalties prepaid	500	300

The annual charge for depreciation of scenery, lighting and costumes should be calculated as 20% of the written down balance brought forward plus any additions during the year.

There were no stocks and no subscriptions in advance or arrears at the start or end of the year.

Required:

(a) Calculate the value of the society's accumulated fund at 30 June 19-9.

(b) Prepare the income and expenditure account of the society for the year to 30 June 19-0 and its balance sheet at that date.

(c) To what extent do you agree with the treasurer that the society's financial progress during the year has been satisfactory?

[The Chartered Institute of Bankers, Autumn 1990]

21.6 The following trial balance was extracted from the books of New Town Cricket Club at 30 September year 7:

Trial balance

	Dr	*Cr*
	£	£
Sports ground at cost	10,000	
Pavilion at cost	4,000	
Provision for depreciation of pavilion 1 October year 6		800
Cricket equipment at written down value 1 October year 6	2,300	
Subscriptions		9,560
Salary of secretary	2,500	
Wages of groundsman	3,600	
Electricity and telephone	420	
Fixtures and fittings at written down value 1 October year 6	1,800	
Rates and insurance	480	
Sundry expenses	350	
Balance at bank	3,120	
Cash in hand	40	
Accumulated fund		18,250
	28,610	28,610

Additional information as at 30 September year 7:

1. Subscriptions accrued due, not yet paid, amounted to £70. Subscriptions paid in advance for year to 30 September year 8 amounted to £30.
2. Rates prepaid £40.
3. Electricity accrued due £25.
4. The club has agreed to provide for depreciation as follows:

pavilion	– 10% on cost per annum
cricket equipment	– 30% on written down value
fixtures and fittings	– 20% on written down value

Required:

(a) the income and expenditure account for the year ended 30 September year 7.

(b) a balance sheet at 30 September year 7.

[London Chamber of Commerce]

21.7* The honorary treasurer of the Capella Choir, a club for choral music enthusiasts, has prepared the following receipts and payments account for the year ended 31 May 19-0:

Capella Choir

Receipts and Payments Account for the year ended 31 May 19-0

	£		£
Cash and bank balances b/f	410	Secretarial expenses	550
Members' subscriptions	1,480	Rent of rehearsal room	850
Donations	220	Other rehearsal expenses	350
Sales of concert tickets	2,680	Fees and expenses	2,870
Grants and subsidies	2,500	Purchase of music	1,300
		Travelling expenses	490
		Stationery and printing	670
		Cash and bank balances c/f	210
	7,290		7,290

The following valuations are also available:

	1 June 19-9	*31 May 19-0*
	£	£
Subscriptions in arrears	200	120
Subscriptions in advance	50	140
Owing to suppliers of music	510	660
Stocks of music, at valuation	6,160	7,100
Grants and subsidies receivable	950	1,400
Travelling expenses accrued	0	210

Required:

(a) Prepare a calculation of the accumulated fund of the Capella Choir as at 1 June 19-9.

(b) Draw up a summary subscriptions account for the year ended 31 May 19-0.

(c) Prepare calculations of the following:

1. the depreciation charge on music for the year ended 31 May 19-0, and
2. grants and subsidies for the year ended 31 May 19-0.

(d) Prepare the income and expenditure account for the Capella Choir for the year ended May 19-0 showing clearly the surplus or deficit for the year.

[Association of Accounting Technicians]

21.8* The HB tennis club was formed on 1 April 19-0 and has the following receipts and payments account for the six months ended 30 September 19-0:

Receipts	£	*Payments*	£
Subscriptions	12,600	Purchase of equipment	4,080
Tournament fees	465	Groundsman's wages	4,520
Bank interest	43	Rent and business rates	636
Sale of club ties	373	Heating and lighting	674
Life membership fees	4,200	Postage and stationery	41
		Court maintenance	1,000
		Tournament prizes	132
		Purchase of club ties	450
		Balance c/d	6,148
	17,681		17,681

Notes:

1. The annual subscription fee is £300. On 30 September there were five members who had not paid their subscription, but this money was received on 4 October 19-0.
2. The equipment is expected to be used by the club for five years, after which time it will need to be replaced. Its estimated scrap value at that time is £50.
3. During the six months, the club purchased 100 ties printed with its own design. Forty of these ties remained unsold at 30 September 19-0.
4. The club has paid business rates in advance on 30 September 19-0 of £68.
5. The club treasurer estimates that the following amounts should be accrued for expenses:

	£
Groundsman's wages	40
Postage and stationery	12
Heating and lighting	53

6. The life membership fees received relate to payments made by four families. The scheme allows families to pay £1,050 which entitles them to membership for life without further payment. It has been agreed that such receipts would be credited to income and expenditure in equal instalments over 10 years.

You are required to:

(a) prepare the club's income and expenditure account for the six months ended 30 September 19-0

(b) prepare the club's balance sheet at 30 September 19-0

[The Chartered Institute of Management Accountants]

Multiple-choice questions: chapters 19-21

- Read each question carefully
- Choose the *one* answer you think is correct (calculators may be needed)
- Answers are on page 486

1. Which one of the following does *not* appear in purchases ledger control account?

   A cash discount allowed
   B set off/contra entry
   C cash/cheques paid to creditors
   D purchases returns

2. Which one of the following does *not* appear in sales ledger control account?

   A cash discount allowed
   B returned cheques
   C bad debts written off
   D provision for bad debts

3. You have the following information:

• opening creditor balances at the start of the month	£18,600
• cash/cheques paid to creditors during month	£9,400
• purchases returns	£800
• creditor balances at the month-end	£17,500

   What is the amount of credit purchases for the month?

   A £9,100
   B £9,700
   C £10,000
   D £11,300

4. You have the following information:

• opening debtor balances at the start of the month	£12,500
• cash/cheques received from debtors during month	£7,300
• credit sales during month	£6,600
• sales returns during month	£500

   What is the amount of the debtor balances at the month-end?

   A £11,300
   B £12,300
   C £12,700
   D £13,200

5. You are to set off a sales ledger debit balance of £100 against a purchases ledger credit balance of £150. The entries in the control accounts will be:

	Debit	*Credit*
A	purchases ledger control account £150	sales ledger control account £150
B	sales ledger control account £100	purchases ledger control account £100
C	purchases ledger control account £100	sales ledger control account £100
D	sales ledger control account £150	purchases ledger control account £150

6. You are preparing a trading account from incomplete records. Debtors at the start of the year were £2,500, and at the end were £3,250. Cheques received from debtors total £17,850; cash sales total £2,500. What is the sales figure for the year?

   A £17,850
   B £19,600
   C £20,350
   D £21,100

7. • Cost of goods sold for the year is £200,000.
   • Mark-up is 30%.
   • What are sales for the year?

   A £60,000
   B £140,000
   C £200,000
   D £260,000

8. • Sales for the year are £100,000.
   • Gross profit margin is 25%.
   • Opening stock is £10,000; closing stock is £12,000.
   • What are purchases for the year?

   A £25,000
   B £73,000
   C £77,000
   D £125,000

9. A club's receipts and payments account is:

   A similar to a balance sheet
   B a summarised cash and bank account
   C similar to a profit and loss account
   D a deposit account at the bank

10. The loss made by a club is recorded in its accounts as:

    A drawings
    B deficit
    C surplus
    D depreciation

11. In a club balance sheet, subscriptions paid in advance are recorded as:

    A a current asset
    B a current liability
    C an addition to the accumulated fund
    D a fixed asset

12. Members' subscriptions of £30 were overdue at the beginning of the year. £2,020 was received during the year, including the overdue amount, and £18 for subscriptions in advance for the following year. What amount will be shown for subscriptions in the income and expenditure account for the year?

    A £1,972
    B £2,008
    C £2,038
    D £2,068

22 Partnership Accounts

So far, when discussing business accounts, we have considered the accounts of sole traders, ie one person in business. In this chapter we will see how the accounts are presented where two or more people own a business in the form of a partnership. Normally, partnerships consist of between two and twenty partners (exceptions being large professional firms, eg solicitors and accountants).

In this chapter we will look at:

- the definition of a partnership
- the accounting requirements of the Partnership Act 1890
- the use of capital accounts and current accounts
- the appropriation of profits
- the layout of the capital section of the balance sheet

In Section 22.8, a past examination is shown as a worked example.

22.1 Definition of a partnership

The Partnership Act of 1890 defines a partnership as
the relation which subsists between persons carrying on a business in common with a view of profit.

The partnership is a common form of business; examples include:

- sole traders who have joined forces with others in order to raise finance and expand operations
- established family firms such as manufacturers, traders and builders
- professional firms such as solicitors, accountants, estate agents, doctors and dentists

On a practical note, it is important for potential partners to know each other well before going into business together: the rigours of business and the financial aspects will test to the limits the best of relationships.

The main disadvantage of partnerships is that each partner is fully liable for the business debts of the *whole* firm. This can be overcome by the comparatively rare *limited partnerships* created under the Limited Partnerships Act 1907. A limited partner contributes a stated amount of capital and is not liable for the debts of the partnership beyond that amount. In any limited partnership there must always be at least one general partner who is responsible for partnership debts.

A partnership is a very different form of business from a limited company, which we will look at in Chapter Twenty-four. The two should never be confused, despite the 'and company' designation of some partnerships.

22.2 Accounting requirements of the Partnership Act 1890

Unless the partners agree otherwise, the Partnership Act states the following accounting rules:

- profits and losses are to be shared equally between the partners
- no partner is entitled to a salary
- partners are not entitled to receive interest on their capital
- interest is not to be charged on partners' drawings
- when a partner contributes more capital than agreed, he or she is entitled to receive interest at five per cent per annum on the excess

These rules *must* be followed unless the partners agree amongst themselves, by means of a *partnership agreement* (see Section 22.4), to follow different accounting rules.

22.3 Year-end accounts of a partnership

A partnership prepares the same type of year-end accounts as a sole trader business:

- trading and profit and loss account
- balance sheet

The main difference is that, immediately after the profit and loss account, follows an *appropriation section* (often described as an appropriation account). This shows how the net profit from profit and loss account is shared amongst the partners.

For example, Able, Baker and Crow are partners sharing profits and losses equally; their profit and loss account for the current year shows a net profit of £30,000. The appropriation of profits appears as:

ABLE, BAKER AND CROW
PROFIT AND LOSS APPROPRIATION ACCOUNT FOR THE YEAR ENDED . . .

	£
Net profit	30,000
Share of profits	
Able	10,000
Baker	10,000
Crow	10,000
	30,000

The above is a simple appropriation of profits. A more complex appropriation account (see Section 22.6) deals with other accounting points from the partnership agreement (see next section).

22.4 Partnership agreement

The accounting rules from the Partnership Act are often varied with the agreement of all partners, by means of a partnership agreement. In particular, a partnership agreement will usually cover the following:

- division of profits and losses between partners
- partners' salaries/commission
- whether interest is to be allowed on capital and at what rate
- whether interest is to be charged on partners' drawings, and at what rate

The money amounts involved for each of these points (where allowed by the partnership agreement) are shown in the partnership appropriation account (see Section 22.6).

Division of profits and losses between partners

The Partnership Act states that, in the absence of an agreement to the contrary, profits and losses are to be shared equally. A partner's share of the profits is normally taken out of the business in the form of drawings. Clearly, if one partner has contributed much more capital than the other partner(s), it would be unfair to apply this clause from the Act. Consequently, many partnerships agree to share profits and losses on a different basis – often in the same proportions as they have contributed capital. The important point, though, is that if the partnership agreement (or an examination question) is silent on this matter, then the Partnership Act applies and profits and losses are shared equally.

Partners' salaries/commission

Although the Act says that no partner is entitled to a salary, it is quite usual in the partnership agreement for one or more partners to be paid a salary. The reason for doing this is that often in a partnership, one of the partners spends more time working in the partnership than the other(s). The agreement to pay a salary is in recognition of the work done. Note that partners' salaries are not shown as an expense in profit and loss account; instead, they appear in the partnership appropriation account (see Section 22.6).

Many professional partnerships, such as solicitors and accountants, have *junior partners* who receive a partnership salary because they work full-time in the business. Most junior partners have not contributed any capital, but they are liable for business debts. (In a partnership, there may not be a requirement to contribute capital – unless the partnership agreement states otherwise – however, most partners will do so.)

As an alternative to a salary, a partner might be paid a *commission on sales*. As with a salary, this is not shown as an expense in the profit and loss account, but appears in the partnership appropriation account.

Interest allowed on capital

Many partnerships include a clause in their partnership agreement which allows interest to be paid on capital; the rate of interest will be stated also. This clause is used to compensate partners for the loss of use of their capital, ie it is not available to invest elsewhere. Often, interest is allowed on capital in partnerships where profits and losses are shared equally – it is one way of partly adjusting for different capital balances. As noted earlier, the Partnership Act does not permit interest to be paid on capital, so reference to it must be made in the partnership agreement.

When calculating interest on capital, it may be necessary to allow for part years. For example:

- 1 January 19-1 – capital balance £10,000
- 1 July 19-1 – additional capital contributed £2,000
- the rate of interest allowed on capital is 10 per cent per annum
- the partnership's financial year-end is 31 December

Interest allowed on capital is calculated as:

1 January - 30 June £10,000 x 10%	=	£500
1 July - 31 December £12,000 x 10%	=	£600
Interest allowed on capital for year		£1,100

Interest charged on partners' drawings

In order to discourage partners from drawing out too much money from the business early in the financial year, the partnership agreement may stipulate that interest is to be charged on partners' drawings, and at what rate. This acts as a penalty against early withdrawal when the business may be short of cash. For example:

- a partner's drawings for the year total £12,000
- £3,000 was withdrawn at the end of each quarter, ie 31 March, 30 June, 30 September and 31 December
- the rate of interest charged on partners' drawings is 10 per cent per annum
- the partnership's financial year-end is 31 December

Interest charged is calculated as:

31 March	£3,000 x 10% x 9 months	=	£225
30 June	£3,000 x 10% x 6 months	=	£150
30 September	£3,000 x 10% x 3 months	=	£75
Interest charged on partner's drawings for year			£450

(No interest charged on the withdrawal on 31 December, because it is at the end of the financial year.)

The amount of interest charged on drawings for the year is shown in the partnership appropriation account (see Section 22.6), where it increases the profit to be shared amongst the partners.

Other points

- *Interest on loans*
  If a partner makes a loan to the partnership, the rate of interest to be paid needs to be agreed, otherwise the rate specified in the Partnership Act 1890 applies – five per cent per annum.

  Interest on loans is charged as an expense in the profit and loss account, and is *not* shown in the appropriation account.

- *Interest on current accounts*
  The partnership agreement may state that interest is to be allowed at a specified rate on the credit balance of partners' current accounts (see Section 22.5 below), and is to be charged on debit balances.

22.5 Capital accounts and current accounts

The important book-keeping difference between a sole trader and a partnership is that each partner usually has a capital account and a current account. The capital account is normally *fixed,* and only alters if a permanent increase or decrease in capital contributed by the partner takes place. The current account is *fluctuating* and it is to this account that:

- share of profits is credited
- share of loss is debited
- salary (if any), or commissions, are credited
- interest allowed on partners' capital is credited
- drawings are debited
- interest charged on partners' drawings is debited

Thus, the current account is treated as a *working* account, while capital account remains fixed, except for capital introduced or withdrawn.

A partner's current account will have the following layout:

Dr.		Partner A: Current Account			Cr.
		£			£
19-1			19-1		
	Drawings			Balance b/d	
	Interest charged on drawings*			Share of net profit	
	Balance c/d			Salary (or commissions)*	
				Interest allowed on capital*	

* if these items are allowed by the partnership agreement

Note that whilst the normal balance on a partner's current account is credit, when the partner has drawn out more than his or her share of the profits, then the balance will be debit.

22.6 Appropriation of profits

As we have seen earlier in this chapter, the appropriation section (often described as the appropriation account) follows the profit and loss account and shows how net profit has been divided amongst the partners. The example which follows shows a partnership salary (*not* to be shown in profit and loss account), interest allowed on partners' capital, and interest charged on partners' drawings.

Example

Fox and Gun are in partnership sharing profits and losses 60 per cent and 40 per cent respectively. Net profit for the year ended 31 March 19-5 is £21,000.

At 1 April 19-4 (the start of the year), the partners have the following balances:

	Capital account	*Current account*
	£	*£*
Fox	20,000	1,000 Cr.
Gun	15,000	200 Cr.

There have been no changes to the capital accounts during the year; interest is allowed on partners' capitals at the rate of eight per cent per year.

Gun is entitled to a salary of £8,000 per year.

On 30 September 19-4 (half-way through the financial year), partners' drawings were made: Fox £9,000, Gun £12,000; there were no other drawings. Interest is charged on partners' drawings at the rate of ten per cent per year.

The appropriation of profits will be made as follows:

FOX AND GUN
PROFIT AND LOSS APPROPRIATION ACCOUNT FOR THE YEAR ENDED 31 MARCH 19-5

	£	£
Net profit		21,000
Add interest charged on partners' drawings:		
Fox (£9,000 ÷ 2 x 10%)	450	
Gun (£12,000 ÷ 2 x 10%)	600	
		1,050
		22,050
Less appropriation of profits:		
Salary: Gun		8,000
Interest allowed on partners' capitals:		
Fox	1,600	
Gun	1,200	
		2,800
		11,250
Share of remaining profits:		
Fox (60%)	6,750	
Gun (40%)	4,500	
		11,250

Note that *all* of the available profit, after allowing for any salary, and interest charged and allowed, is shared amongst the partners, in the ratio in which they share profits and losses.

The partners' current accounts for the year appear as:

Partners' Current Accounts

Dr.	Fox	Gun		Cr.	Fox	Gun
	£	£			£	£
19-4/-5			19-4/-5			
31 Mar. Drawings for year	9,000	12,000	1 Apr.	Balances b/d	1,000	200
31 Mar. Interest on drawings	450	600		Salary	–	8,000
31 Mar. Balance c/d	–	1,300	31 Mar.	Interest on capital	1,600	1,200
			31 Mar.	Share of profits	6,750	4,500
			31 Mar.	Balance c/d	100	-
	9,450	13,900			9,450	13,900
19-5/-6			19-5/-6			
1 Apr. Balance b/d	100	–	1 Apr.	Balance b/d	–	1,300

Note that Fox has drawn more out of the current account than the balance of the account; accordingly, at the end of the year, Fox has a debit balance on the account with the partnership. By contrast, Gun has a credit balance of £1,300 on current account.

22.7 Balance sheet

Within the balance sheet of a partnership must be shown the year-end balances on each partner's capital and current account. However, it is usual to show the transactions that have taken place on each account in summary form, in the same way that, in a sole trader's balance sheet, net profit for the year is added and drawings for the year are deducted.

The other sections of the balance sheet – fixed assets, current assets and current liabilities – are presented in the same way as for a sole trader.

The following is an example balance sheet layout for the 'Financed by' section (the other sections of the balance sheet are not shown). It details the capital and current accounts of the partnership of Fox and Gun (see Section 22.6).

BALANCE SHEET (EXTRACT) OF FOX AND GUN AS AT 31 MARCH 19-5

FINANCED BY	£	£	£
Capital Accounts			
Fox		20,000	
Gun		15,000	
			35,000
Current Accounts	FOX	GUN	
Opening balance	1,000	200	
Add: salary	-	8,000	
interest on capital	1,600	1,200	
share of profit	6,750	4,500	
	9,350	13,900	
Less: drawings	9,000	12,000	
interest on drawings	450	600	
	(100)	1,300	
			1,200
			36,200

Note that an examination question will call either for the preparation of the partners' current accounts, as shown in Section 22.6 (above), or for the detailed balance sheet extract, as shown here.

22.8 Worked example

We will now look at a past examination question. This includes a partner's salary, interest paid on capital and charged on drawings. The trading account has already been completed and the trial balance gives a figure for gross profit for the year. We are asked to prepare the profit and loss account and appropriation account. The question does not require production of a balance sheet, but this is shown in the answer for illustrative purposes.

Question

Blackwell and Rosewall are in partnership. They have agreed to share profits and losses in the ratio Blackwell 60%: Rosewall 40%. The following trial balance was extracted on 31 December 19-9:

		Dr	*Cr*
		£	£
Drawings:	Blackwell	15,000	
	Rosewall	10,000	
Capital accounts:	Blackwell		80,000
	Rosewall		45,000
Current accounts at 1 January 19-9:	Blackwell		1,250
	Rosewall		350
Gross profit for the year			40,000
Machinery at cost		84,000	
Motor vehicles at cost		20,000	
Provision for depreciation at 1 January 19-9:	Machinery		8,400
	Motor Vehicles		4,000
Bad debts		1,300	
Provision for doubtful debts			770
Stock at 31 December 19-9		12,600	
Debtors		9,850	
Creditors			7,230
Bank		29,760	
Sundry expenses		4,490	
		187,000	187,000

Other information relating to the business is as follows:

1. An additional debt of £250 owed by Frank Parsons is now considered to be bad and should be written off.
2. On 31 December 19-8 the debtors totalled £7,700. The provision for doubtful debts is to be maintained at the same percentage of the new debtors' figure, having first dealt with the account of Frank Parsons.
3. Machinery is being depreciated over 20 years to a zero scrap value using the straight line method.
4. Motor vehicles are being depreciated at 20% per annum reducing balance method.
5. Blackwell is entitled to a salary of £5,000.
6. Interest is allowed on capital account balances at 10% per annum.
7. Interest on drawings have been calculated as Blackwell £720 and Rosewall £410.

Required:

Prepare the partners' Profit and Loss Account and Profit and Loss Appropriation Account for the year ended 31 December 19-9.

[Association of Accounting Technicians]

Answer

BLACKWELL AND ROSEWALL, IN PARTNERSHIP
PROFIT AND LOSS ACCOUNT FOR THE YEAR ENDED 31 DECEMBER 19-9

	£	£
Gross profit		40,000
Less		
Provision for depreciation:		
machinery (£84,000 x 5%)	4,200	
motor vehicles (£16,000 x 20%)	3,200	
Bad debts written off (£1,300 + £250)	1,550	
Increase in provision for bad debts (10% provision £960 - £770)	190	
Sundry expenses	4,490	
		13,630
Net profit		26,370
Add interest charged on partners' drawings:		
Blackwell	720	
Rosewall	410	
		1,130
		27,500
Less appropriation of profits:		
Salary: Blackwell		5,000
Interest allowed on partners' capitals:		
Blackwell	8,000	
Rosewall	4,500	
		12,500
		10,000
Share of remaining profits:		
Blackwell (60%)	6,000	
Rosewall (40%)	4,000	
		10,000

Note how the appropriation section follows on as part of the profit and loss account.

The question, as set, did not require preparation of a balance sheet. However, in order to show the layout of the partners' capital and current accounts, the balance sheet now follows on the next page:

BLACKWELL AND ROSEWALL, IN PARTNERSHIP
BALANCE SHEET AS AT 31 DECEMBER 19-9

	£	£	£
Fixed Assets	*Cost*	*Dep'n to date*	*Net*
Machinery	84,000	12,600	71,400
Motor vehicles	20,000	7,200	12,800
	104,000	19,800	84,200
Current Assets			
Stock		12,600	
Debtors (£9,850 - £250)	9,600		
Less provision for bad debts	960		
		8,640	
Bank		29,760	
		51,000	
Less Current Liabilities			
Creditors		7,230	
Working Capital			43,770
NET ASSETS			127,970
FINANCED BY			
Capital Accounts			
Blackwell		80,000	
Rosewall		45,000	
			125,000
Current Accounts	BLACKWELL	ROSEWALL	
Opening balance	1,250	350	
Add: salary	5,000	-	
interest on capital	8,000	4,500	
share of profit	6,000	4,000	
	20,250	8,850	
Less: drawings	15,000	10,000	
interest on drawings	720	410	
	4,530	(1,560)	2,970
			127,970

22.9 Chapter summary

- A partnership is formed when two or more (usually up to a maximum of twenty) people set up in business.
- The Partnership Act 1890 states certain accounting rules, principally that profits and losses must be shared equally.
- Many partnerships over-ride the accounting rules of the Act by creating a partnership agreement which covers
  - division of profits and losses between partners
  - partners' salaries/commissions
  - whether interest is to be allowed on capital, and at what rate
  - whether interest is to be charged on partners' drawings, and at what rate
- The usual way to account for partners' capital is to maintain a fixed capital account for each partner. This is complemented by a fluctuating current account which is used as a working account for share of profits, drawings, etc.

- The final accounts of partnerships are similar to those of sole traders, but incorporate
  - an appropriation account as a continuation of the profit and loss account
  - individual capital and current accounts for each partner shown in the balance sheet

In the next chapter we continue the theme of partnerships and look at changes in partnerships, such as the admission of a new partner, retirement of a partner.

22.10 Questions

22.1 (a) Thomas and Finney own a sports shop. Their first financial year ended on 31 December 19-7. From the following particulars prepare the firm's appropriation account and the partners' current accounts.

Capital: Thomas—£30,000; Finney—£24,000

Interest on capital is to be allowed at 10% pa

Partnership salaries: Thomas—£4,500; Finney—£3,000

Profits and losses are to be shared equally.

Drawings: Thomas—£6,430; Finney—£6,700

The firm's net profit for the year was £16,420.

(b) (i) Name the Act of Parliament which regulates partnerships.

(ii) Name the document which sets out the rules governing individual partnerships.

(iii) Give an example of one of the rules mentioned in (ii) above.

[Midland Examining Group]

22.2* J Eel is a partner in a business and is entitled to one-third of the profits and a partnership salary of £1,800 per annum. On 1 January 19-8 his capital account showed a credit balance of £6,000, but there was a debit balance of £136 on his current account.

You are given the following information:

16 January Eel paid £136 into the partnership bank account to settle the balance in his current account.

30 June £800 of the partnership salary was entered in Eel's account. He also paid in £2,000 additional capital into the firm.

Repairs to Eel's private car, £30, previously charged to the firm, were transferred to his account.

31 December Eel was allowed interest on his capital at the rate of 5% per annum. The balance of his partnership salary was entered in his account.

His drawings during the year were:

31 March £700
30 June £900
1 September £800

At the end of the year the partnership profit, after deducting all interest and partnership salaries, was £3,600.

Using the above information, prepare

(a) Eel's capital account
(b) Eel's current account
(c) a balance sheet extract showing the balances of these two accounts

[Midland Examining Group]

22.3 Rexton, Sareeta and Sonia are in partnership, the capital invested in the partnership is £60,000, £35,000 and £20,000 respectively.

During the financial year ended 30 June 19-9 the partnership earned a net profit of £38,000.

The partners have agreed the following:
(i) interest is to be allowed on capital at 12% per annum
(ii) Sareeta and Sonia are to receive salaries of £10,000 and £8,600 respectively
(iii) profits and losses are to be shared in the ratio of 4:3:1

The partners had the following balances in their current accounts as at 30 June 19-9:

	£
Rexton	1,400 Cr
Sareeta	2,900 Dr
Sonia	1,165 Dr

During the year to 30 June 19-9, the partners withdrew the following amounts from the partnership:

	£
Rexton	6,300
Sareeta	4,700
Sonia	9,800

You are required to prepare the appropriation account for the partnership and show each of the partner's current accounts as at 30 June 19-9.

[RSA Examinations Board]

22.4 D Brook and T Stream went into partnership on 1 January 19-2, each contributing £16,000 and £12,000 respectively as capital.

They agreed to share profits and losses equally and for T Stream to transfer £2,000 annually from 31 December 19-2 from his current account at each year end and until such time as his capital is the same as D Brook, the first payment being due on 31 December 19-2. Interest is to be allowed on capital at 10 per cent.

The following trial balance was prepared on 31 December 19-2:

		£	£
Capital accounts	D Brook		16,000
	T Stream		12,000
Drawings	D Brook	3,500	
	T Stream	3,000	
Purchases and sales		48,200	72,620
Debtors and creditors		2,000	2,200
Premises		25,000	
Equipment and fixtures		7,000	
Bank		1,260	
Salaries		8,420	
Rates		2,100	
Advertising		320	
Carriage inwards		180	
Motor van rental		1,260	
Discount allowed and received		320	480
Bad debts		210	
Heating and lighting		530	
		103,300	103,300

The following information is available to complete the final accounts:

	£
• stock as at 31 December 19-2	6,280
• a payment for advertising is due	60
• rates were paid in advance to 30 June 19-3	700

- equipment and fixtures are to be depreciated by 20 per cent per annum
- T Stream is to be given a commission of 2 per cent of the sales figure for the year but this is not in the accounts

You are required to prepare:

(a) the partnership trading account for the year
(b) the profit and loss account for the year
(c) the appropriation account for the year
(d) the current accounts for the year
(e) a balance sheet of the partnership as at 31 December 19-2

[Pitman Examinations Institute]

22.5* Wave and Trough run a shop together as partners. The following is the trial balance extracted from the firm's ledger at 30 June 19-0:

	£	£
Capital 30 June 19-9:		
Wave		90,000
Trough		75,000
Drawings:		
Wave	16,000	
Trough	15,800	
Current account balances at 30 June 19-9:		
Wave	1,000	
Trough		10,600
Sales		611,300
Purchases	426,100	
Stock at 30 June 19-9	35,500	
Rates on premises	15,000	
Wages	36,900	
Motor expenses	6,300	
Land and buildings at cost	134,000	
Motor vehicle:		
at cost	20,000	
accumulated depreciation at 30 June 19-9		3,000
Fixtures and fittings:		
at cost	55,200	
accumulated depreciation at 30 June 19-9		10,000
Bank		15,100
Debtors and creditors	101,800	35,500
Bank charges and interest	3,600	
Advertising	21,200	
Discounts allowed and received	9,800	2,700
Long-term loan at 10%		50,000
Interest on long-term loan	5,000	
	903,200	903,200

You are given the following additional information:

1. Stock at 30 June 19-0 was valued at £42,700.
2. The rates account contains a payment of £8,000 made in April 19-0 for the six months to 30 September 19-0.
3. Some advertising was undertaken in April 19-0, and the invoice for £4,300 was received in July. This is not included in the trial balance.
4. During the year to 30 June 19-0, Wave took goods for his own use which cost £1,500. No record of this was made in the firm's books.

5. The motor vehicle is depreciated on the straight line basis assuming a life of six years and a residual value of £2,000; the fixtures and fittings are also depreciated on the straight line basis assuming a life of 10 years and a residual value of £5,200.
6. The partners agree that profits and losses should be shared equally, after giving each partner interest on his capital account balance of 12% a year and an annual salary of £20,000 to Wave and £30,000 to Trough.
7. Capital account balances are to remain unchanged.

Required:

Prepare the trading and profit and loss account of Wave and Trough for the year to 30 June 19-0 and the balance sheet at that date.

[The Chartered Institute of Bankers, Autumn 1990]

22.6 Gore and Pryor are in partnership with a partnership agreement which provides for the following:

(i) Commission of 2% of sales to Gore
(ii) Salary of £2,000 per annum payable to Pryor
(iii) Interest on partners' drawings: Gore £60; Pryor £50
(iv) Interest on capital at 10% per annum for each partner
(v) Interest on Gore's loan at 12% per annum
(vi) Profit or loss sharing ratio: Gore 60%; Pryor 40%

The trial balance extracted from the partnership books at 31 December 19-9 was as follows:

	DR	*CR*
	£	£
Premises	29,600	
Equipment	5,000	
Staff salaries	4,200	
Administration expenses	7,200	
Selling expenses	5,400	
Bad debts written off	300	
Provision for bad debts (1 January 19-9)		100
Debtors	3,800	
Creditors		4,900
Stock (1 January 19-9)	8,500	
Cash	820	
Sales		92,000
Purchases	53,000	
Carriage inwards	500	
Gore—Capital at 1 January 19-9		12,000
Gore—Current account at 1 January 19-9		900
Gore—Drawings	3,000	
Pryor—Capital at 1 January 19-9		8,000
Pryor—Current account at 1 January 19-9	1,080	
Pryor—Drawings	2,500	
Gore—Loan account		7,000
	124,900	124,900

Notes:

(i) Stock at 31 December 19-9 was valued at £7,000
(ii) Administration expenses paid in advance £400 and selling expenses outstanding at the year end £600
(iii) Provision for doubtful debts at the year end to be adjusted to 5% of debtors
(iv) Depreciation is charged on the book value of the equipment at 1 January 19-9 at the rate of 20% per annum

You are required to prepare from the information provided above, the

(a) partnership trading and profit and loss account and appropriation account for the year ended 31 December 19-9
(b) partnership balance sheet in vertical format as at 31 December 19-9

[RSA Examinations Board]

22.7* The following list of balances as at 30 September 19-0 has been extracted from the books of Brick and Stone, trading in partnership, sharing the balance of profits and losses in the proportions 3:2 respectively:

	£	
Printing, stationery and postages	3,500	
Sales	322,100	
Stock in hand at 1 October 19-9	23,000	
Purchases	208,200	
Rent and rates	10,300	
Heat and light	8,700	
Staff salaries	36,100	
Telephone charges	2,900	
Motor vehicle running costs	5,620	
Discounts allowable	950	
Discounts receivable	370	
Sales returns	2,100	
Purchases returns	6,100	
Carriage inwards	1,700	
Carriage outwards	2,400	
Fixtures and fittings: at cost	26,000	
provision for depreciation	11,200	
Motor vehicles: at cost	46,000	
provision for depreciation	25,000	
Provision for doubtful debts	300	
Drawings: Brick	24,000	
Stone	11,000	
Current account balances at 1 October 19-9		
Brick	3,600	credit
Stone	2,400	credit
Capital account balances at 1 October 19-9		
Brick	33,000	
Stone	17,000	
Debtors	9,300	
Creditors	8,400	
Balance at bank	7,700	

Additional information:

1. £10,000 is to be transferred from Brick's capital account to a newly opened Brick loan account on 1 July 19-0.

   Interest at 10 per cent per annum on the loan is to be credited to Brick.
2. Stone is to be credited with a salary at the rate of £12,000 per annum from 1 April 19-0.
3. Stock in hand at 30 September 19-0 has been valued at cost at £32,000.
4. Telephone charges accrued due at 30 September 19-0 amounted to £400 and rent of £600 prepaid at that date.
5. During the year ended 30 September 19-0, Stone has taken goods costing £1,000 for his own use.
6. Depreciation is to be provided at the following annual rates on the straight line basis:

Fixtures and fittings	10%
Motor vehicles	20%

Required:

(a) Prepare a trading and profit and loss account for the year ended 30 September 19-0

(b) Prepare a balance sheet as at 30 September 19-0 which should include summaries of the partners' capital and current accounts for the year ended on that date.

Note: In both (a) and (b) vertical forms of presentation should be used.

[Association of Accounting Technicians]

23 Changes in Partnerships

In this chapter we will continue our study of partnerships by looking at the principles involved, and the accounting entries, for:

- admission of a new partner
- retirement of a partner
- death of a partner
- changes in profit-sharing ratios
- revaluation of assets
- dissolution of a partnership

Before we look at each of these, we need to consider the *goodwill* of the business, which will feature in each of the changes listed above.

23.1 Goodwill

The balance sheet of a partnership, like that of many businesses, rarely indicates the true 'going concern' value of the business: usually the recorded figures under-estimate the worth of a business. There are two main reasons for this:

- *Prudence concept.* If there is any doubt about the value of assets, they are stated at the lowest possible figure.
- *Goodwill.* A going concern business will often have a value of goodwill, because of various factors, eg the trade that has been built up, the reputation of the business, the location of the business – leading to increased trade, the skill of the workforce, and the success at developing new products.

Definition of goodwill

Goodwill can formally be defined in accounting terms as:

the excess of the going-concern realisable value of a business as a whole, over the sum of the replacement or realisable values of its separable assets, less liabilities.

Thus goodwill has a value as an intangible asset to the owner or owners of a going concern business, whether or not it is recorded on the balance sheet. As you will see in the sections which follow, a valuation has to be placed on goodwill whenever a change takes place in a partnership.

Valuation of goodwill

The valuation of goodwill is always subject to negotiation between the people concerned if, for instance, a partnership business is to be sold. Two commonly-used methods of valuing goodwill are:

- average profits
- super profits

With the *average profits method,* goodwill is valued at the average net profit over the last, say, three years multiplied by an agreed figure, perhaps five times. For example:

- net profit 19-1 £10,000, 19-2 £14,000, 19-3 £12,000
- goodwill is to be valued at five times the average profit of the last three years

Goodwill, therefore, is valued at £12,000 x 5 = £60,000

For the *super profits method,* goodwill is based on the extra profit generated by the business above the amount that would be earned if the capital of the business was invested elsewhere with similar risks. For example:

- the capital of a partnership is £100,000
- profits after payment of a salary to each partner are £15,000 per year
- the general level of interest for savers is ten per cent per year, gross of tax
- goodwill is to be valued at five times the super profits

The profits of this partnership are £5,000 per year higher than would be earned if the capital was invested in a bank or building society account: this is the amount of the super profits. Goodwill, therefore, is valued at £5,000 x 5 = £25,000.

In a balance sheet, goodwill is shown as an intangible asset. It is *only* recorded on the balance sheet when it has been purchased, eg a sole trader or a partnership purchasing goodwill when taking over another business. It should then:

- *either,* be written off in profit and loss account as an expense (in a similar way to depreciation) over a period not exceeding its 'useful economic life' (taken to mean not exceeding twenty years, and usually much less)
- *or,* written off in full, in the appropriation account, to capital (or, in the case of limited companies, to reserves - see page 363)

We will now see how goodwill is used whenever changes are made to partnerships, eg the admission of a new partner, retirement of a partner, etc. For each of these changes, a value for goodwill is agreed and this amount is *temporarily* debited to goodwill account, and credited to the partners' capital accounts in their profit-sharing ratio; after the change in the partnership, as you will see, the partners' capital accounts are debited and goodwill account is credited. Thus a 'nil' balance remains on goodwill account and, therefore, it is not recorded on the partnership balance sheet. This follows the prudence concept, and is the method commonly followed when changes are made to partnerships.

23.2 Admission of a new partner

A new partner – who can only be admitted with the consent of all existing partners – is normally charged a premium for goodwill. This is because the new partner will start to share in the profits of the business immediately and will benefit from the goodwill established by the existing partners. If the business was to be sold shortly after the admission of a new partner, a price will be agreed for goodwill and this will be shared amongst all the partners (including the new partner). To make allowance for this benefit it is necessary to make book-keeping adjustments in the partners' capital accounts. The most common way of doing this is to use a goodwill account which is opened by the old partners with the agreed valuation of goodwill and, immediately after the admission of the new partner, is closed by transfer to the partners' capital accounts, including that of the new partner.

The procedures on admission of a new parter are:

- agree a valuation for goodwill
- old partners
  — *debit* goodwill
  — *credit* partners' capital accounts (in their old profit-sharing ratio) } with the amount of goodwill
- old partners + new partner
  — *debit* partners' capital accounts (in their new profit-sharing ratio) } with the amount of goodwill
  — *credit* goodwill

The effect of this is to charge the new partner with a premium for goodwill.

Worked example

Question

X and Y are in partnership sharing profits and losses equally. Their balance sheet as at 31 December 19-1 is as follows:

BALANCE SHEET OF X AND Y AS AT 31 DECEMBER 19-1

	£
Net assets	80,000
Capital accounts:	
X	45,000
Y	35,000
	80,000

On 1 January 19-2 the partners agree to admit Z into the partnership, with a new profit-sharing ratio of 2:2:1. Goodwill has been agreed at a valuation of £25,000. Z will bring in £20,000 of cash into the business as his capital and premium for goodwill.

Show the procedures on the admission of Z into the partnership.

Answer

- goodwill has been valued at £25,000
- old partners:
  — *debit* goodwill £25,000
  — *credit* capital accounts (in their old profit-sharing ratio)
  X £12,500
  Y £12,500
- old partners + new partner
  — *debit* capital accounts (in their new profit-sharing ratio)
  X £10,000
  Y £10,000
  Z £5,000
  — *credit* goodwill £25,000

The capital accounts of the partners, after the above transactions have been recorded, appear as:

Partners' Capital Accounts

Dr.	X	Y	Z		X	Y	Z Cr.
	£	£	£		£	£	£
Goodwill written off	10,000	10,000	5,000	Balances b/d	45,000	35,000	-
Balances c/d	47,500	37,500	15,000	Goodwill created	12,500	12,500	-
				Bank	-	-	20,000
	57,500	47,500	20,000		57,500	47,500	20,000
				Balances b/d	47,500	37,500	15,000

The balance sheet, following the admission of Z, appears as:

BALANCE SHEET OF X, Y AND Z AS AT 1 JANUARY 19-2

	£
Net assets	100,000
Capital accounts:	
X (£45,000 + £12,500 - £10,000)	47,500
Y (£35,000 + £12,500 - £10,000)	37,500
Z (£20,000 - £5,000)	15,000
	100,000

In this way, the new partner has paid to the existing partners a premium of £5,000 for a one-fifth share of the profits of a business with a goodwill value of £25,000. Note that, although a goodwill account has been used, it has been fully utilised and, therefore, does not appear on the balance sheet.

23.3 Retirement of a partner

When a partner retires it is necessary to calculate how much is due to the partner in respect of capital and profits. The partnership deed normally includes provision for retirement. The most common procedure requires goodwill to be valued and operates in a similar way to the admission of a new partner, as follows:

- agree a valuation for goodwill
- old partners
  — *debit* goodwill
  — *credit* partners' capital accounts (in their old profit-sharing ratio) } with the amount of goodwill
- remaining partners
  — *debit* partners' capital accounts (in their new profit-sharing ratio)
  — *credit* goodwill } with the amount of goodwill

The effect of this is to credit the retiring partner with the amount of the goodwill built up whilst he or she was a partner. This amount, plus the retiring partner's capital and current account balances can then be paid out of the partnership bank account. (If there is insufficient money for this, it is quite usual for a retiring partner to leave some of the capital in the business as a loan, which is repaid over a period.)

Worked example

Question

M, N and O are in partnership sharing profit and losses in the ratio of 2:2:1 respectively. Partner M decides to retire, at the date of which the partnership balance sheet is as follows:

BALANCE SHEET OF M, N AND O AS AT . . . .

	£
Net assets	100,000
Capital accounts:	
M	35,000
N	45,000
O	20,000
	100,000

Goodwill is agreed at a valuation of £30,000. N and O are to continue in partnership and will share profits and losses in the ratio of 2:1 respectively. M agrees to leave £20,000 of the amount due to her as a loan to the new partnership.

Show the procedures on the retirement of M from the partnership.

Answer

- goodwill has been valued at £30,000
- old partners:
  — *debit* goodwill £30,000
  — *credit* capital accounts (in their old profit-sharing ratio of 2:2:1)
  M £12,000
  N £12,000
  O £6,000
- remaining partners
  — *debit* capital accounts (in their new profit-sharing ratio of 2:1)
  N £20,000
  O £10,000
  — *credit* goodwill £30,000

The balance of M's capital account is now £47,000 (ie £35,000 + goodwill of £12,000). Of this, £20,000 will be retained in the business as a loan, and £27,000 will be paid from the partnership bank account.

The balance sheet, after the retirement of M, appears as:

BALANCE SHEET OF N AND O AS AT . . . .

	£
Net assets (£100,000 - £27,000 paid to M)	73,000
Less loan account of M	20,000
	53,000
Capital accounts:	
N (£45,000 + £12,000 - £20,000)	37,000
O (£20,000 + £6,000 - £10,000)	16,000
	53,000

The effect of this is that the remaining partners have bought out M's £12,000 share of the goodwill of the business, ie it has cost N £8,000, and O £4,000. If the business was to be sold later, N and O would share the goodwill obtained from the sale in their new profit-sharing ratio.

23.4 Death of a partner

The accounting procedures on the death of a partner are very similar to those for a partner's retirement. The only difference is that the amount due to the deceased partner is placed in an account called 'Executors (or Administrators) of X deceased' pending payment.

23.5 Changes in profit-sharing ratios

It may be necessary, from time-to-time, to change the profit-sharing ratios of partners. A partner's share of profits might be increased because of an increase in capital in relation to the other partners, or because of a more active role in running the business. Equally, a share of profits may be decreased if a partner withdraws capital or spends less time in the business. Clearly the agreement of all partners is needed to make changes, and the guidance of the partnership deed should be followed.

Generally, a change in profit-sharing ratios involves establishing a figure for goodwill, even if the partnership is to continue with the same partners; this is to establish how much goodwill was built up while they shared profits in their old ratios. Each partner will, therefore, receive a value for the goodwill based on the old profit-sharing ratio.

Worked example

Question

C and D are in partnership sharing profits and losses equally. The balance sheet at 31 December 19-1 is as follows:

BALANCE SHEET OF C AND D AS AT 31 DECEMBER 19-1

	£
Net assets	60,000
Capital accounts:	
C	35,000
D	25,000
	60,000

The partners agree that, as from 1 January 19-2, C will take a two-thirds share of the profits and losses, with D taking one-third. It is agreed that goodwill shall be valued at £30,000.

Show the procedures on the change in the profit-sharing ratio.

Answer

- goodwill has been valued at £30,000
- old profit-sharing ratio:
  — *debit* goodwill £30,000
  — *credit* capital accounts (in their old profit-sharing ratio of 1:1)
  C £15,000
  D £15,000
- new profit-sharing ratio:
  — *debit* capital accounts (in their new profit-sharing ratio of 2:1)
  C £20,000
  D £10,000
  — *credit* goodwill £30,000

The balance sheet at 1 January 19-2 appears as:

BALANCE SHEET OF C AND D AS AT 1 JANUARY 19-2

	£
Net assets	60,000
Capital accounts:	
C (£35,000 + £15,000 – £20,000)	30,000
D (£25,000 + £15,000 – £10,000)	30,000
	60,000

The effect is that C has 'paid' D £5,000 to increase his/her share of the profits from half to two-thirds. This may seem inequitable but neither partner is worse off in the event of the business being sold, assuming that the business is sold for £90,000 (£60,000 assets + £30,000 goodwill). *Before* the change in the profit-sharing ratio they would have received:

C £35,000 capital + £15,000 half-share of goodwill = £50,000
D £25,000 capital + £15,000 half-share of goodwill = £40,000

After the change, they will receive:

C £30,000 capital + £20,000 two-thirds share of goodwill = £50,000
D £30,000 capital + £10,000 one-third share of goodwill = £40,000

Thus, as far as the capital positions are concerned, the partners remain unchanged: it is only the profit-sharing ratios that will be different as from 1 January 19-2. Also, any *increase* in goodwill above the £30,000 figure will be shared in the new ratio.

23.6 Revaluation of assets

So far in this chapter we have looked at the adjustments made for goodwill in various changes made to partnerships. Goodwill, however, reflects only one aspect of a partner's interest in the business. For example, some of the assets may have appreciated in value, but adjustments may not have been made in the accounts; other assets may have fallen in value, while provisions for depreciation and/or bad debts may have been too much or too little. With a change in the personnel of a partnership, a *revaluation account* may be needed to correct any discrepancies in values. The accounting procedure is:

- increase in the value of an asset
  — *debit* asset account
  — *credit* revaluation account
  } with the amount of the increase
- reduction in the value of an asset
  — *debit* revaluation account
  — *credit* asset account
  } with the amount of the reduction
- increase in provision for depreciation/bad debts
  — *debit* revaluation account
  — *credit* provision account
  } with the amount of the increase
- reduction in provision for depreciation/bad debts
  — *debit* provision account
  — *credit* revaluation account
  } with the amount of the reduction

After these adjustments have been recorded in the books of account, the balance of the revaluation account is divided among the partners in their profit-sharing ratios.

Worked example

Question

Question E, F and G are in partnership sharing profits and losses equally. On 31 December 19-1 their balance sheet is as follows:

BALANCE SHEET OF E, F AND G AS AT 31 DECEMBER 19-1

	£	£	£
Fixed Assets	*Cost*	*Dep'n to date*	*Net*
Premises	100,000	-	100,000
Machinery	50,000	10,000	40,000
	150,000	10,000	140,000
Current Assets			
Stock		30,000	
Debtors		20,000	
Bank		5,000	
		55,000	
Less Current Liabilities			
Creditors		25,000	
Working Capital			30,000
NET ASSETS			170,000
FINANCED BY:			
Capital accounts			
E			60,000
F			60,000
G			50,000
			170,000

G decides to retire at 31 December 19-1; E and F are to continue the partnership and will share profits and losses equally. The following valuations are agreed:

Goodwill	£30,000
Premises	£150,000
Machinery	£30,000
Stock	£21,000

A provision for bad debts equal to five per cent of debtors is to be made.

G agrees that the moneys owing on retirement are to be retained in the business as a long-term loan.

Show the revaluation account, and adjusted balance sheet at 1 January 19-2 to record the above transactions.

Answer

Revaluation Account

Dr.		£			Cr. £
19-1			19-1		
31 Dec.	Provision for depreciation:		31 Dec.	Goodwill	30,000
	machinery	10,000		Premises	50,000
	Stock	9,000			
	Provision for bad debts	1,000			
	Capital accounts:				
	E (one-third)	20,000			
	F (one-third)	20,000			
	G (one-third)	20,000			
		80,000			80,000

Note that the amount of goodwill has been credited to revaluation account (and thus to the capital accounts); it will, later, be debited to the capital accounts of the two remaining partners - in this way it will not feature on the balance sheet.

BALANCE SHEET OF E AND F AS AT 1 JANUARY 19-2

	£	£	£
Fixed Assets	*Cost*	*Dep'n to date*	*Net*
Premises	150,000	-	150,000
Machinery	50,000	20,000	30,000
	200,000	20,000	180,000
Current Assets			
Stock		21,000	
Debtors	20,000		
Less provision for bad debts	1,000		
		19,000	
Bank		5,000	
		45,000	
Less Current Liabilities			
Creditors		25,000	
Working Capital			20,000
			200,000
Less Long-term Liabilities			
Loan account of G (£50,000 + £20,000)			70,000
NET ASSETS			130,000
FINANCED BY			
Capital accounts			
E (£60,000 + £20,000 – £15,000 goodwill debited)			65,000
F (£60,000 + £20,000 – £15,000 goodwill debited)			65,000
			130,000

23.7 Partnership changes: split years

Any of the changes in partnerships that we have looked at so far in this chapter may occur during the course of an accounting year, rather than at the end of it. For example, part-way through the year:

- the partners may decide to admit a new partner
- a partner might retire, or die
- the partners may decide to change their profit-sharing ratios

To avoid having to prepare final accounts at the date of the change, it is usual to continue the accounts until the normal year-end. Then, when profit for the year has been calculated, it is necessary to apportion the profit between the two parts of the financial year, ie to split the year into the period *before* the change, and the period *after* the change. This is often done by assuming that the profit for the year has been earned at an equal rate throughout the year. The apportionment is done by dividing the appropriation account between the two time periods.

Worked example

Question

J and K are in partnership; their partnership agreement states:

- interest is allowed on partners' capital accounts at the rate of ten per cent per annum
- K receives a partnership salary of £18,000 per annum
- the balance of partnership profits and losses are shared between J and K in the ratio 2:1 respectively

At the beginning of the financial year, on 1 January 19-1, the balances of the partners' capital accounts were:

J £70,000
K £50,000

During the year ended 31 December 19-1, the net profit of the partnership was £50,500 before appropriations. The profit arose uniformly throughout the year.

On 1 October 19-1, J and K admitted L as a partner. L introduced £40,000 in capital on this date.

The partnership agreement was amended on 1 October 19-1 as follows:

- interest is allowed on partners' capital accounts at the rate of ten per cent per annum
- K and L are each to receive a partnership salary of £12,000 per annum
- the balance of partnership profits and losses are to be shared between J, K and L in the ratio of 2:2:1 respectively

Prepare the appropriation account of the partnership for the year.

Answer

PROFIT AND LOSS APPROPRIATION ACCOUNT OF J, K AND L
FOR THE YEAR ENDED 31 DECEMBER 19-1

		9 months to 30 September	*3 months to 31 December*	*Total for year*
		£	£	£
Net profit		37,875	12,625	50,500
Less appropriation of profits:				
Salaries:				
K	£18,000 pa x 9 months	13,500	–	16,500
	£12,000 pa x 3 months		3,000	
L	£12,000 pa x 3 months		3,000	3,000
Interest on partners' capitals:				
J	£70,000 @ 10% pa x 9 months	5,250	–	7,000
	£70,000 @ 10% pa x 3 months	–	1,750	
K	£50,000 @ 10% pa x 9 months	3,750	–	5,000
	£50,000 @ 10% pa x 3 months	–	1,250	
L	£40,000 @ 10% pa x 3 months	–	1,000	1,000
		15,375 *	2,625 **	18,000
Share of remaining profits:				
	J	(2/3) 10,250	(2/5) 1,050	11,300
	K	(1/3) 5,125	(2/5) 1,050	6,175
	L	–	(1/5) 525	525
		15,375	2,625	18,000

* J and K shared profits 2:1 respectively
** J, K and L shared profits 2:2:1 respectively

23.8 Dissolution of a partnership

There are various reasons why a partnership may come to an end:

- a partnership may be formed for a fixed term or for a specific purpose and, at the end of that term or when that purpose has been achieved, it is dissolved
- a partnership might be dissolved as a result of bankruptcy, or because a partner retires or dies and no new partners can be found to keep the firm going
- sales may fall due to changes in technology and product obsolescence, with the partners not feeling it is worthwhile to seek out and develop new products
- at the other end of the scale, the business might expand to such an extent that, in order to acquire extra capital needed for growth, the partnership may be dissolved and a limited company formed to take over its assets and liabilities (see Chapter 25.6)

Whatever the reason for dissolving the partnership, the accounts have to be closed. A *realisation account* is used to record the closing transactions, and this account shows the net gain or loss that is available for distribution among the partners. The Partnership Act 1890 requires that moneys realised from the sale of assets are to be applied in the following order:

- in settlement of the firm's debts, other than those to partners
- in repayment of partners' *loans*
- in settlement of partners' capital and current accounts

Steps to close the books of a partnership

- Asset accounts (except for cash and bank) are closed by transfer to realisation account:
  — *debit* realisation account
  — *credit* asset accounts
- Provisions accounts, eg depreciation, bad debts, are transferred to realisation account:
  — *debit* provision account
  — *credit* realisation account
- As assets are sold, the proceeds are placed to cash/bank account, and the sum recorded in realisation account:
  — *debit* cash/bank account
  — *credit* realisation account
- If a partner takes over any assets, the value is agreed and the amount is deducted from the partner's capital account and transferred to realisation account:
  — *debit* partner's capital account
  — *credit* realisation account
- As expenses of realisation are incurred, they are paid from cash/bank account and entered in realisation account:
  — *debit* realisation account
  — *credit* cash/bank account
- Creditors are paid off:
  — *debit* creditors' accounts
  — *credit* cash/bank account
- The balance of realisation account, after all assets have been sold and all creditors have been paid, represents the profit or loss on realisation, and is transferred to the partners' capital accounts in the proportion in which profits and losses are shared. If a profit has been made, the transactions are:
  — *debit* realisation account
  — *credit* partners' capital accounts
  Where a loss has been made, the entries are reversed
- Partners' loans (if any) are repaid:
  — *debit* partners' loan accounts
  — *credit* cash/bank account
- Partners' current accounts are transferred to capital accounts:
  — *debit* partners' current accounts
  — *credit* partners' capital accounts
  If a partner has a debit balance on current account, the entries will be reversed
- If any partner now has a debit balance on capital account, he or she must introduce cash to clear the balance:
  — *debit* cash/bank account
  — *credit* partner's capital account
- The remaining cash and bank balances are used to repay the credit balances on partners' capital accounts:
  — *debit* partners' capital accounts
  — *credit* cash/bank account

Worked example

Question

P, Q and R are in partnership, sharing profits and losses equally. As a result of falling sales they decide to dissolve the partnership as from 31 December 19-2. The balance sheet at that date was as shown on the next page:

BALANCE SHEET OF P, Q AND R AS AT 31 DECEMBER 19-2

	£ *Cost*	£ *Dep'n to date*	£ *Net*
Fixed Assets			
Machinery	25,000	10,000	15,000
Delivery van	10,000	5,000	5,000
	35,000	15,000	20,000
Current Assets			
Stock		12,000	
Debtors		10,000	
Bank		3,000	
		25,000	
Less Current Liabilities			
Creditors		8,000	
Working Capital			17,000
NET ASSETS			37,000
FINANCED BY			
Capital accounts			
P			13,000
Q			12,000
R			12,000
			37,000

The sale proceeds of the assets are machinery £12,000, stock £8,000, debtors £9,000. P is to take over the delivery van at an agreed valuation of £3,000. The expenses of realisation amount to £2,000.

Show the realisation account, partners' capital accounts and bank account to record the dissolution of the partnership.

Answer

Dr.		**Realisation Account**	Cr.
	£		£
Machinery	25,000	Provisions for depreciation:	
Delivery van	10,000	machinery	10,000
Stock	12,000	delivery van	5,000
Debtors	10,000	Bank: machinery	12,000
Bank: realisation expenses	2,000	Bank: stock	8,000
		Bank: debtors	9,000
		P's capital account: van	3,000
		Loss on realisation:	
		P (one-third)	4,000
		Q (one-third)	4,000
		R (one-third)	4,000
	59,000		59,000

Partners' Capital Accounts

Dr.	P	Q	R		P	Q	R Cr.
	£	£	£		£	£	£
Realisation account: delivery van	3,000	-	-	Balances b/d	13,000	12,000	12,000
Realisation account: loss	4,000	4,000	4,000				
Bank	6,000	8,000	8,000				
	13,000	12,000	12,000		13,000	12,000	12,000

Bank Account

Dr.	£		£ Cr.
Balance b/d	3,000	Realisation account: expenses	2,000
Machinery	12,000	Creditors	8,000
Stock	8,000	Capital accounts:	
Debtors	9,000	P	6,000
		Q	8,000
		R	8,000
	32,000		32,000

As can be seen from the above accounts, the assets have been realised, the liabilities paid, and the balances due to the partners have been settled; the partnership has been dissolved.

23.9 Chapter summary

❑ Goodwill is an intangible fixed asset.

❑ There are several methods of valuing goodwill; two commonly-used methods are
- average profits
- super profits

❑ Goodwill should only be shown in the balance sheet when it has been purchased; it should then be:
- *either,* written off to profit and loss account as an expense over a period not exceeding its 'useful economic life'
- *or,* written off in full, in the appropriation account, to capital (or, in the case of a limited company, to reserves)

❑ With partnerships, goodwill is normally calculated for transactions involving changes in the structure of the business to cover:
- admission of a new partner
- retirement of a partner
- death of partner
- changes in profit-sharing ratios

In accordance with the prudence concept, a goodwill account is normally created just before the change, and then deleted immediately after the change, ie it does not appear on the partnership balance sheet.

When changes take place part-way through the financial year, it is necessary to apportion the profit between the two parts of the financial year, usually by assuming that the profit has been earned at a uniform rate throughout the year.

- A *revaluation account* is used whenever assets are revalued prior to making changes to the personnel of the partnership.

- When a partnership is dissolved, a *realisation account* is used to record the sale proceeds of assets, and to calculate any profit or loss on realisation due to the partners.

In the next chapter we shall look at another form of business entity: the limited liability company. This is different from sole traders and partnerships in that it has its own corporate identity in law, and more stringent accounting requirements.

23.10 Questions

23.1 Al and Bert are in partnership, sharing profits equally. At 30 June they have balances on their capital accounts of £12,000 (Al) and £15,000 (Bert). On that day they agree to bring in their friend Hall as a third partner. All three partners are to share profits equally from now on. Hall is to introduce £20,000 as capital into the business. Goodwill on 30 June is agreed at £18,000.

Required:

(a) Show the partners' capital accounts for 30 June and 1 July on the assumption that the goodwill, previously unrecorded, is to be included in the accounts.

(b) Show the additional entries necessary to eliminate goodwill again from the accounts.

(c) Explain briefly what goodwill is. Why are adjustments necessary when a new partner joins a partnership?

[The Chartered Association of Certified Accountants]

23.2* Rose, Tulip and Crocus are in partnership sharing profits and losses $^1/_7$, $^2/_7$ and $^4/_7$ respectively.

They are to dissolve the partnership and at the date of dissolution, the balances in the partnership books are:

		£
Sundry creditors		3,815
Stock		7,945
Sundry debtors		4,417
Premises		23,177
Loan from Crocus		2,450
Capital accounts	Rose (credit)	9,170
	Tulip (credit)	10,290
	Crocus (credit)	12,432
Cash		2,618

On sale of the assets the amount realised was:

Stock	£7,812
Premises	£21,000
Debtors	£4,305

and the loan and all the creditors were paid off.

You are required to close all the above accounts and give the amounts each partner received.

[Pitman Examinations Institute]

23.3 Alpha and Beta are in partnership. They share profits equally after Alpha has been allowed a salary of £4,000 pa. No interest is charged on drawings or allowed on current accounts or capital accounts. The trial balance of the partnership at 31 December 19-9 before adjusting for any of the items below, is as follows:

	Dr *£000*	*Cr* *£000*
Capital —Alpha		30
—Beta		25
Current —Alpha		3
—Beta		4
Drawings —Alpha	4	
—Beta	5	
Sales		200
Stock 1 January 19-9	30	
Purchases	103	
Operating expenses	64	
Loan —Beta (10%)		10
—Gamma (10%)		20
Land and buildings	60	
Plant and machinery:		
—cost	70	
—depreciation to 31 January 19-9		40
Debtors and creditors	40	33
Bank	—	11
	376	376

(i) Closing stock on hand at 31 December was £24,000.

(ii) On 31 December Alpha and Beta agree to take their manager, Gamma, into partnership. Gamma's loan account balance is to be transferred to a capital account as at 31 December. It is agreed that in future Alpha, Beta and Gamma will all share profits equally. Alpha will be allowed a salary of £4,000 as before, and Gamma will be allowed a salary of £5,000 pa (half of what he received in 19-9 as manager, included in operating expenses).

The three partners agree that the goodwill of the business at 31 December should be valued at £12,000, but is not to be recorded in the books. It is also agreed that land and buildings are to be revalued to a figure of £84,000 and that this revalued figure is to be retained and recorded in the accounts.

(iii) Interest on the loan has not been paid.

(iv) Included in sales are two items sold on 'sale or return' for £3,000 each. Each item had cost the business £1,000. One of these items was in fact returned on 4 January 19-0 and the other one was formally accepted by the customer on 6 January 19-0.

Required:

(a) Submit with appropriately labelled headings and subheadings:
   (i) partners' capital accounts in columnar form;
   (ii) partners' current accounts in columnar form;
   (iii) trading, profit and loss and appropriation account for 19-9;
   (iv) balance sheet as at 31 December 19-9

(b) Write a brief note to Gamma, who cannot understand why his capital account balance seems so much less than those of Alpha and Beta. Explain to him the adjustments you have made.

[The Chartered Association of Certified Accountants]

23.4* Owing to staff illnesses, the draft final accounts for the year ended 31 March 19-0 of Messrs Stone, Pebble and Brick, trading in partnership as the Bigtime Building Supply Company, have been prepared by an inexperienced, but keen, clerk. The draft summarised balance sheet as at 31 March 19-0 is as follows:

	£	£
Tangible fixed assets: at cost less depreciation to date		45,400
Current assets	32,290	
Less: Trade creditors	6,390	25,900
		71,300

Represented by:	*Stone*	*Pebble*	*Brick*	*Total*
	£	£	£	£
Capital accounts: at 1 April 19-9	26,000	18,000	16,000	60,000
Current accounts:				
Share of net profit for the year ended 31 March 19-0	12,100	12,100	12,100	
Drawings year ended 31 March 19-0	(8,200)	(9,600)	(7,200)	
At 31 March 19-0	3,900	2,500	4,900	11,300
				71,300

The partnership commenced on 1 April 19-9 when each of the partners introduced, as their partnership capital, the net tangible fixed and current assets of their previously separate businesses. However, it has now been discovered that contrary to what was agreed, no adjustments were made in the partnership books for the goodwill of the partners' former businesses now incorporated in the partnership. The agreed valuations of goodwill at 1 April 19-9 are as follows:

	£
Stone's business	30,000
Pebble's business	20,000
Brick's business	16,000

It is agreed that a goodwill account should not be opened in the partnership's books.

It has now been discovered that effect has not been given in the accounts to the following provisions in the partnership agreement effective from 1 January 19-0:

1. Stone's capital to be reduced to £20,000, the balance being transferred to a loan account upon which interest at the rate of 11% per annum will be paid on 31 December each year.
2. Partners to be credited with interest on their capital account balances at the rate of 5% per annum.
3. Brick to be credited with a partner's salary at the rate of £8,500 per annum.
4. The balance of the net profit or loss to be shared between Stone, Pebble and Brick in the ratio 5:3:2 respectively.

Notes:

1. It can be assumed that the net profit indicated in the draft accounts accrued uniformly throughout the year.
2. It has been agreed between the partners that no adjustments should be made for any partnership goodwill as at 1 January 19-0.

Required:

(a) Prepare the profit and loss appropriation account for the year ended 31 March 19-0.

(b) Prepare a corrected statement of the partners' capital and current accounts for inclusion in the partnership balance sheet as at 31 March 19-0.

[Association of Accounting Technicians]

23.5 Peter Pale, who has been in business for several years as a sole trader, was joined in partnership on 1 April 19-7 by Roger Rains.

Roger Rains brought into the partnership, as his initial capital, his existing business whose summarised balance sheet as at 31 March 19-7 was as follows:

	£
Tangible fixed assets	40,000
Net current assets	11,000
	51,000
Capital—R Rains	51,000

For purposes of the partnership, the business of Roger Rains was valued at £60,000 at 1 April 19-7.

It has been agreed that the accounting records of Peter Pale will become those of the partnership from 1 April 19-7; however, it has now been discovered Roger Rains initial capital at 1 April 19-7 has not been brought into the partnership accounts nor has effect been given to the goodwill at 1 April 19-7 of Roger Rains.

The following summarised trial balance at 31 March 19-8 has been extracted from the partnership accounts:

	£	£
Tangible fixed assets	100,000	
Net current assets	123,000	
Capital account: Peter Pale		170,000
Current accounts: Peter Pale		18,000
Roger Rains	3,000	
Net profit for the year ended 31 March 19-8		38,000
	226,000	226,000

The net profit for the year ended 31 March 19-8 as stated above arose uniformly throughout the year.

The partnership agreement includes the following:

1. A goodwill account is not to be maintained.
2. Roger Rains is to be credited with a partner's salary of £8,000 per annum.
3. Partners are to be credited with interest on their capital account balances at the rate of 5% per annum.
4. As from 1 October 19-7, £40,000 is to be transferred from Peter Pale's capital account to the credit of a loan account in that partner's name; interest is to be credited at the rate of 10% per annum.
5. The balance of profits and losses are to be shared between Peter Pale and Roger Rains as follows:
   - up to 30 September 19-7 – Peter Pale 3/5ths, Roger Rains 2/5ths
   - from 1 October 19-7 – equally

Required:

(a) Prepare the partnership's profit and loss appropriation account for the year ended 31 March 19-8.

(b) Prepare the partners' capital accounts for the year ended 31 March 19-8.

(c) Prepare the partners' current accounts for the year ended 31 March 19-8.

[Association of Accounting Technicians]

24 Limited Company Accounts

In the last two chapters we have looked at the accounting requirements of partnerships, a business entity which is a collection of individuals with *unlimited* liability who own and *are* the firm. In this chapter we will turn to the limited liability company, which has its own *corporate* identity in law, and more stringent accounting requirements.

A limited liability company is a legal entity which has a separate identity from its shareholder owners, whose liability for the company's debts is limited.

The shareholder owners (members of the company) receive shares in return for their capital contribution. The directors, who manage the company, are strictly speaking employees of the company, although they will also be shareholders, and in the case of smaller companies will probably own the majority of the shares.

24.1 Advantages of forming a limited company

Individuals setting up in business, or partners considering changing the constitution of their partnership may *incorporate* (form a limited liability company), for a number of reasons:

Limited liability

The shareholders (members) of a company are liable for company debts to the extent of any money unpaid on their shares (unpaid instalments on new share issues, for example). Thus, if the company concerned became insolvent, shareholders would have to pay any unpaid instalments to pay off the creditors. As this is an extremely unlikely occurance, shareholders are in a very safe position: their personal assets, unless pledged as security to a lender, *are not available to the company's creditors.* (By contrast, in a partnership, excluding limited partnerships, *every partner is personally liable for the whole debt of the partnership.*)

Separate legal entity

A limited company is a separate legal entity from its owners. Anyone taking legal action proceeds against the company. This is in contrast to sole traders and partnerships, where legal action is taken against the individual or the partners.

Ability to raise finance

A limited company can raise substantial funds from outside sources by the issue of shares, either from the public on the Stock Exchange and Unlisted Securities Market, for the larger company, or privately, for the smaller company.

Membership

A member of a limited company is a person who owns at least one share in that company. The minimum number of members is two, but there is no upper limit. By contrast, most partnerships are normally restricted to twenty partners.

24.2 The Companies Acts

Limited companies are regulated by the Companies Act 1985, as amended by the Companies Act 1989. Under the terms of the 1985 Act there are two main types of limited company: the larger *public limited company* (abbreviated to "Plc"), which is defined in the Act, and the smaller company, traditionally known as a *private limited company* (abbreviated to "Ltd"), which is any other limited company. A further type of company is *limited by guarantee.*

Public limited company (Plc)

A company may become a public limited company if it has

- issued share capital of over £50 000
- at least two members (shareholders) and at least two directors

A public limited company may raise capital from the public on the Stock Exchange or related markets, and the various new issues and privatisations are examples of this. A public limited company does *not have to* raise funds on the Stock Markets, and not all do so.

Private limited company (Ltd)

The private limited company is the most common form of limited company. The term *private* is not set out in the Companies Act 1985, but it is traditional description, and well describes the smaller company, often in family ownership. A private limited company has

- no minimum requirement for issued share capital
- at least two members (shareholders) and at least one director

The shares are not traded publicly, but are transferable between individuals, although valuation will be more difficult for shares not quoted on the Stock Market.

Company limited by guarantee

A company limited by guarantee is not formed with share capital, but relies on the guarantee of its members to contribute a stated amount in the event of the company's insolvency. Examples of such companies include charities, artistic and educational organisations, and some football clubs.

24.3 Governing documents of companies

There are a number of documents required by the Companies Act in the setting-up of a company. Two essential governing documents are:

- *Memorandum of Association,* the constitution of the company, which contains five main clauses:
    1. name of the company
    2. capital of the company (the amount that can be issued in shares)

3. 'objects' of the company, ie what activities the company can engage in; under the Companies Act 1989, the objects can be stated as being those of "a general commercial company", ie the company can engage in any commercial activity
4. registered office of the company (not the address, but whether it is registered in England and Wales, or in Scotland)
5. a statement that the liability of the members is limited

- *Articles of Association,* regulate the administration of the company, including the powers of directors and the holding of company meetings

24.4 Statutory books

All limited companies are required to keep certain registers, books and records — collectively known as the *statutory books*. These are:

- **Accounting records,** *containing*
  — the day-to-day entries of all receipts and expenditure of the company
  — a record of the assets and liabilities of the company
  — statements of stock held and sales and purchases of goods

- **Register of directors and secretaries,** *containing*
  — name, address, nationality, and business occupation (if any) of the persons concerned
  — particulars of other directorships held within the past five years

- **Register of directors' interests,** *containing*
  — details of directors' holdings of the shares and debentures (secured loans – see Section 24.7) in the company
  — details of holdings of shares and debentures in the names of each director's spouse and children

- **Register of members,** *containing*
  — details of shareholders, to include name, address, number of shares held and their members (if any)

- **Register of substantial shareholdings (public companies only),** *containing*
  — details of holders of five per cent or more of a company's shares
  — personal details of the shareholder, and the amount of the shareholding

- **Register of charges,** *containing*
  — details of charges (eg mortgages) given by the company over assets
  — description of property charged, amount of the charge, persons in whose favour the charge is made

- **Minute books of directors' meetings,** *containing*
  — details of matters discussed
  — record of decisions made

- **Minute book of general meetings,** *containing*
  — details of matters discussed
  — record of decisions made

- **Register of directors' service contracts,** *containing*
  — written copy of every directors' service agreement or, where not in writing, a written memorandum

24.5 Accounting requirements of the Companies Act

The Companies Act 1985 (as amended by the Companies Act 1989) not only requires the production of accounts, but also states the detailed information that must be disclosed. The accounts are audited by external auditors – this is a costly and time-consuming exercise, and may be a deterrent to someone wishing to form a limited company. The accounts must be filed within nine months of the financial year-end on a central register at Companies House in Cardiff, where they are available for public inspection. A copy of the accounts is sent to all shareholders.

In this chapter we will look at the 'internal use' accounts, rather than being concerned with the detailed accounting requirements of the Companies Act. It might be that, as part of your future accountancy studies you will be required to prepare such 'published accounts', as they are often known.

Before we examine the year-end accounts in detail we will first look at the principal ways in which a company raises finance: shares. There are different types of shares which appear in a company's balance sheet as a capital item.

24.6 Types of shares issued by limited companies

One clause contained in the Memorandum of Association (the document setting out the powers and objects of a company) states the share capital of that company and its division into shares of a fixed amount. This is known as the *authorised share capital,* ie the share capital that the company is allowed to issue. The authorised share capital may not be the same as the amount that the company has actually issued – this is known as the *issued share capital.* The latter can never exceed the former; if a company which has issued the full extent of its authorised share capital wishes to make an increase, it must first pass the appropriate resolution at a general meeting of the shareholders.

The authorised and issued share capital is divided into a number of classes or types of share, the principal of which are *ordinary shares* and *preference shares*. Each share has a *nominal value* – or face value – which is entered in the accounts. Shares may be issued with nominal values of 5p, 10p, 25p, 50p or £1, or indeed for any amount. Thus a company with an authorised share capital of £100,000 might state in its Memorandum of Association that this is divided up into:

100,000 ordinary shares of 50p each	£50,000
50,000 ten per cent preference shares of £1 each	£50,000
	£100,000

The nominal value of a share often bears little relationship to its *market value*. It is easy to find out the value of shares in a public limited company – if they are quoted on the Stock Exchange, the price may well be listed in the *Financial Times*. Shareholders receive *dividends* on their shares, being a distribution of a part of the company's earnings for a year or half-year. The dividend paid half-way through a financial year is known as an *interim dividend,* while that paid at the end of a year is a *final dividend.*

Ordinary (equity) shares

These are the most commonly issued class of share. They take a share of the profits available for distribution after allowance has been made for all expenses of the business, including loan interest, taxation, and after preference dividends (if any). When a company makes large profits, it will have the ability to pay higher dividends to the ordinary shareholders; when losses are made, the ordinary shareholders may receive no dividend. Companies rarely pay out all of their profits in the form of dividends; most retain some profits as reserves. These can always be used to enable a dividend to be paid in a year when the company makes little or no profit, always assuming that the company has sufficient cash in the bank to make the payment. Ordinary shareholders, in the event of the company ceasing to trade or 'winding up', will be the last to receive any repayment of their investment: other creditors will have to be paid off first.

Preference shares

Such shares usually carry a fixed rate of dividend – eg ten per cent of nominal value – which, as their name suggests, is paid in preference to the ordinary shareholders; but it is only paid if the company makes profits. In the event of winding up the company, the 'preference' will also extend to repayment of capital before the ordinary shareholders.

Preference shares may be non-cumulative or cumulative:

- *non-cumulative* — if insufficient profits are made during a certain year to pay the preference dividend and the shares are designated as non-cumulative, then there is no provision for 'catching up' with missed dividends in future years
- *cumulative* — if the dividend on these is not paid in one year, it accumulates and will be paid in the future. In this way missing dividends will always be paid provided that the company makes sufficient profits in the future.

All preference shares are cumulative unless otherwise stated.

24.7 Loans and debentures

In addition to money provided by shareholders, who are the owners of the company, further funds can be obtained by borrowing in the form of loans or debentures, for example, from a bank. The term 'debenture' usually refers to a formal certificate issued by a company acknowledging that a sum of money is owing to a specified person. Both loans and debentures usually carry a fixed rate of interest that must be paid, just like other business expenses, whether a company makes profits or not. As loan and debenture interest is a business expense, this is shown in the profit and loss account along with all other expenses. In the event of the winding-up of the company, loan and debenture-holders would be repaid before any shareholders. Often debentures are secured, being backed by assets of the company pledged as security. In the event of winding up, the assets would be sold and used to repay the debenture holders first. Unsecured debentures – sometimes known as *naked* debentures – do not have this backing, but they will be repaid before any shareholders receive their funds.

24.8 Reserves

Unlike a sole trader or partnership, where all profits are added to the owner's capital, a company will rarely distribute all its profits. Instead, it will often keep part of the profits earned each year in the form of reserves. As we shall see later – in Section 24.10 – there are two types of reserves:

- *capital reserves,* which are created as a result of a non-trading profit
- *revenue reserves,* which are retained profits from profit and loss account

Revenue reserves are often left as the balance of the appropriation section (see Section 24.9 below) of the profit and loss account: this balance is commonly described as 'profit and loss account balance' or 'balance of retained profits'. Alternatively, they may be transferred from the appropriation section to a named revenue reserve account, such as *general reserve,* or a revenue reserve for a specific purpose, such as *reserve for the replacement of machinery*. Transfers to or from these named revenue reserve accounts are made in the appropriation section of the profit and loss account.

It should be noted that reserves – both capital and revenue – are *not* a cash fund to be used whenever the company needs money, but are in fact represented by assets shown on the balance sheet. The reserves record the fact that the assets belong to the shareholders via the company.

24.9 Limited companies: trading and profit and loss accounts

A limited company uses the same type of final accounts as a sole trader or partnership. However there are two items commonly found in the profit and loss account of a limited company that are not found in those of other business units:

- **Directors' remuneration** ie amounts paid to directors. As directors are employed by the company, their *pay* appears amongst the expenses of the company.
- **Debenture interest** as already noted, when debentures are issued by companies, the interest is shown as an expense in the profit and loss account.

In a similar way to a partnership, a limited company follows the profit and loss account with an *appropriation section* (often described as an appropriation account) to show how the net profit has been distributed. The following is an example of a simple appropriation account:

	£
Net profit for year	100,000
Less corporation tax	20,000
Profit after taxation	80,000
Less proposed ordinary dividend	50,000
Retained profit for year	30,000
Add balance of retained profits at beginning of year	35,000
Balance of retained profits at end of year	65,000

Notes:

- The company has recorded a net profit of £100,000 in its profit and loss account – this is brought into the appropriation section.
- Corporation tax, the tax that a company has to pay, based on its profits, is shown in the appropriation account. (At this level of your studies of Business Accounts you will not be concerned with corporation tax computations – examination questions will state the amount of corporation tax payable.)
- The company proposes to distribute £50,000 to the ordinary shareholders as a dividend. This will be paid in the early part of the next financial year. Note that a dividend is often expressed as an amount per share, based on the nominal value, eg 5p per 50p nominal value share (which is the same as a ten per cent dividend).
- Added to net profit is a balance of £35,000. This represents profits of the company from previous years that have not been distributed as dividends. You will note that the appropriation section shows a balance of retained profits at the year-end of £65,000. Such retained profits form a *revenue reserve* of the company.

A more comprehensive appropriation account follows:

APPROPRIATION ACCOUNT OF ORION LTD
FOR THE YEAR ENDED 31 DECEMBER 19-4

	£	£
Net profit for year before taxation		43,000
Less corporation tax		15,000
Profit for year after taxation		28,000
Less: interim dividends paid		
ordinary shares	5,000	
preference shares	2,000	
final dividends proposed		
ordinary shares	10,000	
preference shares	2,000	
		19,000
		9,000
Less transfer to general reserve		5,000
Retained profit for year		4,000
Add balance of retained profits at beginning of year		16,000
Balance of retained profits at end of year		20,000

24.10 Limited companies: balance sheet

Balance sheets of limited companies follow the same layout as those of sole traders and partnerships but the capital section is more complex because of the different classes of shares that may be issued, and the various reserves. Fig. 24.1 (on next page) shows the balance sheet of Orion Ltd. as an example.

A word of explanation about some of the items appearing in company balance sheets is appropriate at this point.

Fixed assets

Like the fixed asset section in other balance sheets, this comprises those items that do not change daily and are likely to be retained for use in the business for some time to come. It is usual for fixed assets, with the possible exception of freehold land, to be depreciated over a period of time or with use. The headings used for fixed assets in a balance sheet read: *cost, depreciation to date* and *net* (see fig. 24.1). When a company has both intangible and tangible fixed assets, it would be appropriate to show the subdivision within the fixed assets section of the balance sheet. Goodwill (see Chapter 23.1) is an example of an intangible fixed asset.

Current assets

The usual current assets will be included, ie stocks, debtors, balance at bank, and cash in hand.

Current liabilities

As with the balance sheets of sole traders and partnerships, this section contains those liabilities that are normally due to be paid within twelve months from the date of the balance sheet, eg creditors, bank overdraft. For limited companies, this section also contains the amount of proposed dividends (but not dividends that have been *paid* in the year) and the amount of corporation tax to be paid within the next twelve months. Both of these amounts are also included in the appropriation account.

BALANCE SHEET OF ORION LTD AS AT 31 DECEMBER 19-4

Fixed Assets	*Cost*	*Dep'n to date*	*Net*
	£	£	£
Freehold land and buildings	180,000	20,000	160,000
Machinery	280,000	110,000	170,000
Fixtures and fittings	100,000	25,000	75,000
	560,000	155,000	405,000
Current Assets			
Stock		50,000	
Debtors		38,000	
Bank		22,000	
Cash		2,000	
		112,000	
Less Current Liabilities			
Creditors	30,000		
Proposed dividends	12,000		
Corporation tax	15,000		
		57,000	
Working Capital			55,000
			460,000
Less long-term Liabilities			
12% debentures			60,000
NET ASSETS			400,000
FINANCED BY			
Authorised Share Capital			
100,000 10% preference shares of £1 each			100,000
600,000 ordinary shares of £1 each			600,000
			700,000
Issued Share Capital			
40,000 10% preference shares of £1 each, fully paid			40,000
300,000 ordinary shares of £1 each, fully paid			300,000
			340,000
Capital Reserve			
Share premium account			10,000
Revenue Reserves			
General reserve*		30,000	
Profit and loss account		20,000	
			50,000
SHAREHOLDERS' FUNDS			400,000

* including transfer of £5,000 (see appropriation account on page 365)

Fig. 24.1 An example of a limited company balance sheet

Long-term liabilities

These are generally considered to be liabilities that are due to be repaid more than twelve months from the date of the balance sheet, eg loans and debentures.

Authorised share capital

As already explained, this is the share capital of the company and its division into shares of a fixed amount as authorised by the company's Memorandum of Association. It is included on the balance sheet 'for information', but is not added into the balance sheet total, as it may not be the same amount as the issued share capital.

Issued share capital

Here are detailed the classes and number of shares that have been isued. As stated earlier the issued share capital cannot exceed the amount authorised. In the balance sheet of Orion Ltd, the shares are described as being *fully paid,* meaning that the company has received the full amount of the value of each share from the shareholders. Sometimes shares will be *partly paid*, eg ordinary shares of £1, but 75p paid. This means that the company can make a *call* on the shareholders to pay the additional 25p to make the shares fully paid. Companies often issue partly paid shares and then make calls at certain times: for example, a company that is issuing shares to raise the finance for a new factory may wish to receive the proceeds of issue at different stages of the building and equipment of the factory. For the purpose of entering the amount of issued share capital in the balance sheet, always multiply the number of shares by the amount paid on them, eg 100,000 ordinary shares of £1 each, 75p paid = £75,000 (the other £25,000 will be called by the company at a later date).

Capital reserves

A capital reserve is created as a result of a non-trading profit. Examples are:

- *Revaluation reserve.* This occurs when a fixed asset, most probably property, is revalued in the balance sheet. The amount of the revaluation is placed in a revaluation reserve where it increases the value of the shareholders' investment in the company. Note, however, that this is purely a 'book' adjustment, no cash has changed hands and the reserve cannot be used to fund the payment of dividends.

  For example:

BALANCE SHEET OF STAR LTD

	£
Before revaluation	
Property at cost	500,000
Ordinary shares of £1 each	500,000
After revaluation	
Property at revaluation	750,000
Ordinary shares of £1 each	500,000
Capital reserve: Revaluation reserve	250,000
	750,000

- *Share premium account.* An established company may well issue additional shares to the public at a higher amount than the nominal value. For example, Orion Ltd (fig. 24.1) seeks finance for further expansion by issuing additional ordinary shares. Although the shares have a nominal value of £1 each, because Orion is a well-established company, the shares are issued at £1.50 each. Of this amount, £1 is recorded in the issued share capital section, and the extra 50p is the share premium.

A capital reserve cannot be used for the payment of dividends: one of its few uses is the issue of bonus shares (see Section 24.11 below).

Revenue reserves

The reserves from profits are the amounts which the directors of the company have retained in the business. Examples of revenue reserves include *general reserve, profit and loss account,* and more specific reserves such as *debenture redemption reserve.*

Revenue reserves can be used when goodwill (see Chapter 23.1) is written off. The accounting entries for this are:

- *debit* profit and loss appropriation account (or other revenue reserve) } with the amount of goodwill being written off
- *credit* goodwill*

(* Remember that goodwill is an asset, ie it has a debit balance, so the write-off will be a *credit* to goodwill account.)

Shareholders' funds

This total represents the stake of the shareholders in the company. It comprises issued share capital (ordinary and preference shares), plus reserves (capital and revenue reserves).

24.11 Bonus shares

A company that has built up substantial capital or revenue reserves may decide to capitalise them (ie turn them into permanent share capital) by issuing free or *bonus* shares to existing shareholders. For example, Orion Ltd (fig. 24.1) might decide to use the £10,000 of capital reserve held on share premium account, and £20,000 of its general reserve to provide bonus shares to the existing ordinary shareholders. These would be issued on the basis of one bonus share for every ten ordinary shares held. The 'financed by' section of the balance sheet now appears as:

	£	£
Issued Share Capital		
40,000 10% preference shares of £1 each, fully paid		40,000
330,000 ordinary shares of £1 each, fully paid		330,000
		370,000
Capital Reserve		
Share premium account		-
Revenue Reserves		
General reserve	10,000	
Profit and loss account	20,000	
		30,000
SHAREHOLDERS' FUNDS		400,000

Notice that no cash has flowed into or out of the company, and that the shareholders are no better off: the only change that has taken place is that the company's net assets are spread among a greater number of shares.

If a choice can be made between using capital or revenue reserves for a bonus issue, then the capital reserve is normally used first – this is because it is one of the few uses of a capital reserve, which cannot be used to fund the payment of dividends.

24.12 Provisions and reserves

We have seen in Section 24.8 how companies use reserve accounts for retained profits (either trading or non-trading). In earlier chapters (Thirteen and Fourteen), we have seen how businesses make provisions, for example, provision for depreciation and provision for bad debts. The difference between provisions and reserves is:

- **Provisions.** These are methods of providing for known liabilities of the business, the amounts of which cannot be determined with complete accuracy. Provisions are costs of running the business and, as such, are charged in profit and loss account before calculating the profit available to the shareholders. Examples are:
  - — provision for depreciation
  - — provision for bad debts
  - — provision for corporation tax (where an estimate of the amount is allowed for in the appropriation account – the exact amount of the tax will be agreed with the Inland Revenue later)

- **Reserves.** These provide for possible future, but – at the present time – unknown, liabilities of the business. They are not a cost of running the business and transfers to reserves are made out of the profit available to shareholders. By not distributing all of the available profit as dividends, the directors retain funds for use within the business to meet possible future liabilities such as:
  - — to enable dividends to continue to be paid in the future if profits should fall
  - — to fund expansion of the business
  - — to fund possible redemption of shares or debentures
  - — to meet any other contingency which may occur but which is unknown at present

24.13 Chapter summary

- ❑ A limited company, unlike a sole trader or a partnership, has a separate legal entity from its owners.
- ❑ A company is regulated by the Companies Act 1985 (as amended by the Companies Act 1989), and is owned by shareholders and managed by directors.
- ❑ A limited company may be either a public limited company or a private limited company.
- ❑ The liability of shareholders is strictly limited to any money unpaid on their shares.
- ❑ The main types of shares issued by companies are ordinary shares and preference shares.
- ❑ Borrowings in the form of loans and debentures are a further source of finance.
- ❑ The final accounts of a company include an appropriation section, which follows the profit and loss account.
- ❑ The balance sheet of a limited company is similar to that of sole traders and partnerships but the capital and reserves section reflects the ownership of the company by its shareholders:
  - — a statement of the authorised and issued share capital
  - — details of capital reserves and revenue reserves

In the next chapter we will look at business conversions and purchases.

24.14 Questions

24.1 Mason Motors Limited is a second-hand car business. The following information is available for the year ended 31 December 19-1:

- balance of retained profits from previous years stands at £100,000
- net profit for the year was £75,000
- it has been agreed that a transfer to a general reserve of £20,000 is to be made
- corporation tax of £20,050 is to be paid on the year's profit
- it has been agreed that a dividend of 10% is to be paid on the issued share capital of £100,000

You are to:

(a) Set out the appropriation account for Mason Motors Limited for the year ended 31 December 19-1.

(b) One of the directors of the company asks if the £20,000 being transferred to general reserve could be used to rebuild the garage forecourt. How would you reply?

24.2* Swift Traders plc has an authorised share capital of £300,000 divided into 100,000 8% preference shares of £1 each and 200,000 ordinary shares of £1 each. All the preference shares have been issued at par and are fully paid: 150,000 of the ordinary shares have been issued at a premium of 25p per share and are fully paid.

The company also had loan capital consisting of £200,000 of 12% debentures.

On 1 November 19-9 the company's balance sheet showed retained profits of £12,890 and a general reserve of £22,760.

During the year ended 31 October 19-0 the company made a profit of £52,000 out of which the directors decided to:

(i) transfer £5,000 to general reserve

(ii) pay the preference dividend for the year

(iii) declare an ordinary dividend of 12 pence per share

You are required to:

prepare the company's profit and loss appropriation account for the year ended 31 October 19-0 and the capital section of the balance sheet as at that date.

[RSA Examinations Board]

24.3 Under United Kingdom law, all limited companies are required to maintain certain registers, books and records which are collectively referred to as statutory books.

Required:

(a) List the names of any four such statutory books.

(b) State the contents of each book you have listed in (a) above and explain the purpose for which each is maintained.

[The Chartered Association of Certified Accountants]

24.4 The authorised share capital of Highwood Co Ltd is 500,000 ordinary shares of £1 each. The following trial balance was extracted from the books of the company at the close of business on 31 December year 4.

	£	£
Issued and paid-up capital		200,000
Premises	180,000	
Fixtures and fittings at cost	70,000	
Purchases and sales	327,000	509,000
Debtors and creditors	79,000	32,000
Provision for depreciation on fixtures and fittings		15,000
Wages and salaries	72,000	
Returns inwards	7,000	
General expenses	39,000	
Interest on debentures, half-year to 30 June year 4	3,000	
Insurance	5,000	
Bad debts	2,000	
Provision for bad and doubtful debts		2,000
Stock at 1 January year 4	28,000	
Bank balance	23,000	
Profit and loss account at 1 January year 4		17,000
10% debentures		60,000
	835,000	835,000

Additional information:

1. Stock at 31 December year 4 was valued at £29,000
2. Wages due amounted to £2,000
3. Insurance paid in advance amounted to £1,000
4. The provision for doubtful debts is to be increased to £3,000
5. The provision for depreciation on fixtures and fittings is to be increased by 10% of the cost price
6. A dividend of £0.15 per ordinary share is proposed for year 4

Required:

(i) A trading and profit and loss account for the year ended 31 December year 4

(ii) A balance sheet in vertical form as at 31 December year 4

[London Chamber of Commerce]

24.5 (a) Distinguish between *provisions* and *reserves*

(b) Indicate which of the following are provisions and which are reserves:

(i) depreciation of motor vehicles

(ii) share premium account

(iii) amount retained for the replacement of machinery

(iv) amount set aside for bad debts

24.6* The following trial balance was extracted from the books of Sidbury Trading Co. Ltd., a local stationery supplies firm, as at 31 December 19-2:

	£	£
Share capital		240,000
Freehold land and buildings at cost	142,000	
Motor vans at cost	55,000	
Provision for depreciation on motor vans at 1 January 19-2		21,800
Purchases and sales	189,273	297,462
Rent and rates	4,000	
General expenses	9,741	
Wages and salaries	34,689	
Bad debts written off	948	
Provision for doubtful debts at 1 January 19-2		1,076
Directors' salaries	25,000	
Debtors and creditors	26,482	16,974
Retained profit at 1 January 19-2		18,397
Stock at 1 January 19-2	42,618	
Bank	65,958	
	595,709	595,709

You are given the following additional information:

- The authorised share capital is 300,000 ordinary shares of £1 each; all the shares which have been issued are fully paid
- Wages and salaries outstanding at 31 December 19-2 amounted to £354
- The provision for doubtful debts is to be increased by £124
- Stock at 31 December 19-2 is valued at £47,288
- Rent and rates amounting to £400 were paid in advance at 31 December 19-2
- It is proposed to pay a dividend of £8,000 for 19-2
- Depreciation on motor vans is to be charged at the rate of 20 per cent per annum on cost
- Corporation tax of £12,000 is to be provided for

You are to prepare appropriate final accounts for the year 19-2, together with a balance sheet at 31 December 19-2.

24.7 Playfair Ltd has an authorised share capital of 50,000 ordinary shares of £1 each and 10 000 8% preference shares of £1 each. At 31 December 19-3, the following trial balance was extracted:

	£	£
Ordinary share capital		50,000
8% preference share capital		8,000
Plant and machinery at cost	34,000	
Motor vehicles at cost	16,000	
Debtors and creditors	34,980	17,870
Bank	14,505	
10% debentures		9,000
Stock (1 January 19-3)	25,200	
General expenses	11,020	
Purchases and sales	164,764	233,384
Bad debts written off	2,400	
Debenture interest	900	
Discounts	325	640
Salaries	24,210	
Insurance	300	
Provision for depreciation:		
plant and machinery		16,000
motor vehicles		7,200
Directors' fees	17,000	
Interim preference dividend paid	320	
Profit and loss account (1 January 19-3)		3,300
Provision for bad debts (1 January 19-3)		530
	345,924	345,924

Additional information:

- Stock at 31 December 19-3 is valued at £28,247
- Depreciation on plant and machinery is to be provided for at the rate of 10 per cent per annum calculated on cost
- Depreciation on motor vehicles is to be provided for at the rate of 20 per cent per annum using the reducing balance method
- Insurance prepaid at 31 December 19-3 amounted to £60
- General expenses owing at 31 December 19-3 amounted to £110
- The provision for bad debts is to be increased to £750
- The directors propose to pay an ordinary dividend of 6 per cent to the ordinary shareholders and to pay the remaining dividend due to the preference shareholders
- £2,000 is to be transferred to General Reserve
- Corporation tax of £4,000 is to be provided for

You are to prepare appropriate final accounts for the year ended 31 December 19-3, together with a balance sheet at that date.

24.8* The following balances remain in the books after the completion of the profit and loss account of Maginn Company Ltd for the year ended 31 December 19-9.

	£
Profit and loss account balance (1 January 19-9)	17,400
Net profit before tax and dividends (31 December 19-9)	36,720
Authorised Share Capital:	
175,000 £1 ordinary shares	175,000
50,000 8% preference shares of £1 each	50,000
Issued Share Capital:	
150,000 £1 ordinary shares	150,000
37,500 8% preference shares of £1 each	37,500
Premises at cost	112,500
Fixtures and fittings at cost	60,000
Office equipment at cost	6,750
Motor vans at cost	30,000
Provisions for depreciation (31 December 19-9):	
Fixtures and fittings	28,500
Office equipment	2,550
Motor vans	18,750
Share premium account	15,000
12½% £1 mortgage debentures	13,975
Interim dividends:	
Preference shareholders	1,500
Ordinary shareholders	7,500
Reserves	15,000
Debtors	60,375
Creditors	38,400
Stock at 31 December 19-9	59,730
Expenses outstanding	1,365
Expenses prepaid	1,800
Bank balance	35,005

The directors decide to recommend to:

(i) transfer £7,500 to the reserves

(ii) provide for the final preference dividend and for a recommended final ordinary dividend of 7.5 pence in the £

From the information provided, you are required to prepare:

(a) Maginn Company Ltd's profit and loss appropriation account for the year ended 31 December 19-9

(b) the company's balance sheet in vertical format as at 31 December 19-9

(Note: Ignore taxation)

[RSA Examinations Board]

Multiple-choice questions: chapters 22-24

- Read each question carefully
- Choose the *one* answer you think is correct (calculators may be needed)
- Answers are on page 486

1. In the absence of a partnership agreement, which one of the following contravenes the provisions of the Partnership Act 1890?

   A no partner is entitled to a salary
   B profits and losses are to be shared in proportion to capital
   C partners are not entitled to receive interest on their capital
   D interest is not to be charged on partners' drawings

2. A partnership may choose to over-ride some or all of the accounting rules in the Partnership Act 1890 by the partners entering into a separate:

   A appropriation account
   B memorandum of association
   C partnership agreement
   D articles of association

3. Profits of a two-person partnership are £32,800 before the following are taken into account:
   - interest on partners' capital accounts, £1,800
   - interest on partners' drawings, £200
   - salary of one partner, £10,000

   If the remaining profits are shared equally, how much will each partner receive?

   A £10,600
   B £11,400
   C £12,200
   D £16,400

4. Where changes in partnerships take place, a goodwill account is opened, usually temporarily. After the change has taken place, goodwill account is usually written off. This follows the accounting concept of:

   A prudence
   B accruals
   C going concern
   D consistency

5. A final debit balance on a partnership realisation account means that there is:

   A an error in the book-keeping records
   B a profit on realisation
   C goodwill
   D a loss on realisation

6. On dissolution of a partnership, the Partnership Act 1890 requires that moneys realised from the sale of assets are to be applied first to:

A settlement of partners' current accounts
B repayments of partners' loans
C settlement of partners' capital accounts
D settlement of the firm's debts

7. Which one of the following does *not* appear in the appropriation account of a limited company?

A corporation tax
B proposed dividends
C directors' remuneration
D transfer to general reserve

8. In the final accounts of a limited company debenture interest is:

A debited in the trading account
B debited in the profit and loss account
C debited in the appropriation account
D shown as a long-term liability in the balance sheet

9. Reserves in a company belong to the:

A ordinary shareholders
B directors
C debenture holders
D creditors

10. Revenue reserves in a limited company balance sheet are:

A the difference between the cost and book value of fixed assets
B amount of proposed dividends
C the total of provisions for depreciation and bad debts
D profit retained in the business

11. Which one of the following is *not* a revenue reserve?

A general reserve
B revaluation reserve
C debenture redemption reserve
D profit and loss account

12. Which one of the following is not included in shareholders' funds?

A ordinary share capital
B debentures
C preference share capital
D capital reserves

25 Business Conversions and Purchases

In the last three chapters we have looked at the final accounts of partnerships and limited companies; much earlier in the book we looked at sole trader final accounts. In this chapter, we will see the accounting transactions involved for business conversions from one type of business formation to another. While there are several combinations of business conversions, we shall look at:

- conversion of two sole trader businesses into a partnership
- conversion of a partnership into a limited company

By learning the principles used here you will be able to apply them to other business conversions, eg conversion of two (or more) partnerships into a limited company, conversion of a sole trader into a limited company.

In the second half of the chapter we will look at the purchase of one business by another:

- a sole trader buys another sole trader
- a partnership buys a sole trader
- a limited company buys a partnership

Again, by learning these principles you will be able to apply them in other circumstances, eg a limited company buys a sole trader, a partnership buys another partnership.

25.1 Conversion of two sole traders into a partnership

Put simply, conversion of two sole trader businesses into a partnership, in accounting terms, merely requires the two separate balance sheets to be merged to form the opening balance sheet of the new partnership. In this way the capital from the sole trader accounts becomes the balance of the partner's capital account at commencement. Sometimes it is agreed that certain assets should be kept by the sole trader and not introduced into the partnership; the opening capital would then be adjusted accordingly to the value of net assets (ie assets minus liabilities) taken over by the partnership. A journal entry (see below) is needed showing the assets and liabilities at the commencement of the partnership, and stating the amount of the respective capital accounts.

Revaluation of assets

On the formation of a partnership from two sole trader businesses, revaluations are often agreed in respect of the assets taken over by the partnership. Some assets may be increased in value, others may be reduced; a valuation may also be placed on the goodwill of each separate business. Such revaluations affect the opening capital of each partner: increases are credited, while decreases are debited.

Worked example

Question

A and B are two sole traders who have decided to form a partnership, AB, from 1 January 19-2. A summary of their separate balance sheets at 31 December 19-1 is as follows:

BALANCE SHEETS OF A AND B, AS SOLE TRADERS, AS AT 31 DECEMBER 19-1

	A	B
	£	£
Fixed assets (net book values)	55,000	80,000
Net current assets	25,000	15,000
	80,000	95,000
Capital	80,000	95,000

The new partners agree that:

- Profits and losses are to be shared equally
- The fixed assets of A are to be valued at £60,000; those of B are to be valued at £75,000
- Goodwill is agreed at A £12,000, B £18,000

Prepare the balance sheet of A and B, in partnership, as at 1 January 19-2.

Answer

BALANCE SHEET OF A AND B, IN PARTNERSHIP, AS AT 1 JANUARY 19-2

	£
Fixed assets (£60,000 + £75,000)	135,000
Net current assets (£25,000 + £15,000)	40,000
	175,000
Capital accounts	
A (£80,000 + £5,000 revaluation – £3,000 goodwill*)	82,000
B (£95,000 – £5,000 revaluation + £3,000 goodwill*)	93,000
	175,000

** Goodwill calculations based on total goodwill of £30,000:*

Capital Accounts		*Debit*	*Credit*	*Net*
A	goodwill creation		£12,000	£3,000 debit
	goodwill deletion	£15,000		
B	goodwill creation		£18,000	£3,000 credit
	goodwill deletion	£15,000		

Following the concept of prudence the goodwill account has been created and then deleted, ie it does not show on the balance sheet.

The journal entry to record the opening transactions (after adjustment for goodwill) in the books of the partnership appears as:

Date	Details	Dr	Cr
19-2		£	£
1 Jan.	Fixed assets	135,000	
	Net current assets	40,000	
	Capital accounts		
	A		82,000
	B		93,000
		175,000	175,000
	Assets and liabilities at the commencement of the partnership of A and B.		

25.2 Conversion of a partnership into a limited company

The logical step for a partnership growing in size and needing access to more capital is the formation of a limited company. The assets and liabilities of the partnership are taken over by the company, and the partners are issued with shares in the new company. The shares will be issued in proportion to their capital account balances in the partnership, or in the proportion in which they share profits and losses, or by some other method agreed between themselves.

The book-keeping entries in the partnership accounts are similar to those on dissolution (see Chapter 23.8).

Worked example

Question

C and D have been trading in partnership for several years, sharing profits and losses in the ratio of 2:1 respectively. They have decided to convert the partnership into a limited company, CD Ltd, as from 1 January 19-2. They agree that £1 ordinary shares should be allocated on the basis of their former profit and loss sharing ratio. A summary of their balance sheet is as follows:

BALANCE SHEET OF C AND D, IN PARTNERSHIP, AS AT 31 DECEMBER 19-1

	£
Fixed assets (net book values)	60,000
Current assets	30,000
	90,000
Less current liabilities	15,000
	75,000
Capital accounts	
C	45,000
D	30,000
	75,000

All the assets are to be transferred to the company and, by agreement with the creditors, the company will become liable to settle their accounts. The purchase consideration is calculated as follows:

	£
Fixed assets revalued at	90,000
Current assets revalued at	40,000
Goodwill agreed at	20,000
	150,000
Less current liabilities	15,000
Purchase consideration	135,000

What are the entries required to close the accounts of the partnership, including the number of £1 ordinary shares to be allocated to each partner?

Answer

The steps are:

- The asset and liability accounts that are being taken over by the new limited company are closed off by transfer to a realisation account
- Any profit or loss on realisation is transferred to the partners' capital accounts in the ratio in which they share profits and losses
- The shares are allocated between the partners – in this case in their profit and loss sharing ratio
- It may be necessary for one partner to make a cash contribution to the other partner in order to bring the capital account balances into line with the number of shares issued to each partner

The accounts of the partnership are dealt with as follows:

Realisation Account

Dr.		Cr.	
	£		£
Fixed assets	60,000	Current liabilities	15,000
Current assets	30,000	CD Ltd	135,000
Profit on realisation:			
C (two-thirds)	40,000		
D (one-third)	20,000		
	150,000		150,000

Fixed Assets

Dr.		Cr.	
	£		£
Balance b/d	60,000	Realisation account	60,000

Current Assets

Dr.		Cr.	
	£		£
Balance b/d	30,000	Realisation account	30,000
Capital account: C	5,000	Capital account: D	5,000
	35,000		35,000

Current Liabilities

Dr.		Cr.	
	£		£
Realisation account	15,000	Balance b/d	15,000

CD Ltd

Dr.		Cr.	
	£		£
Realisation account	135,000	Ordinary shares in CD Ltd	135,000

Capital Accounts

Dr.	C	D		C	D Cr.
	£	£		£	£
Ordinary shares in CD Ltd	90,000	45,000	Balances b/d	45,000	30,000
			Profit on realisation	40,000	20,000
Bank: current assets*	-	5,000	Bank: current assets*	5,000	-
	90,000	50,000		90,000	50,000

£1 Ordinary Shares in CD Ltd

Dr.			Cr.
	£		£
CD Ltd	135,000	Capital accounts:	
		C	90,000
		D	45,000
	135,000		135,000

* The transaction of £5,000 passing through the capital accounts and bank account (in current assets) is a cash adjustment between the partners to compensate for the value of extra shares issued to C above the balance of the capital account. D, whose capital account is above the value of shares issued, receives a cheque for £5,000 from C, via the partnership bank account. By making this adjustment, the capital account balances are brought into line with the number of shares issued to each partner.

BALANCE SHEET OF CD LTD AS AT 1 JANUARY 19-2

	£
Goodwill	20,000
Fixed assets	90,000
Current assets	40,000
	150,000
Less current liabilities	15,000
	135,000
£1 ordinary shares	135,000

The company will deal with goodwill (see Chapter 23.1) by either writing it off to profit and loss account over a number of years, or by writing it off in full to reserves as soon as they become available.

25.3 Purchase of a business

Businesses change hands quite often; examples are:

- a sole trader buys another sole trader's business
- a partnership buys a sole trader's business
- a limited company buys a partnership business

Once the purchase price has been agreed, certain accounting procedures are followed in the seller's books, and in the buyer's books.

Seller's books

The special account used is a *realisation account.*

- Close off the asset accounts except for bank/cash account by transfer to the realisation account
  — *debit* realisation account
  — *credit* asset accounts
- Close off the liability accounts(and provisions accounts) by transfer to the realisation account
  — *debit* liability accounts and provisions accounts
  — *credit* realisation account
- When the purchase consideration is received
  — *debit* bank/cash account
  — *credit* realisation account
- If the purchase moneys received exceed the value of the net assets, a profit on realisation has been made; this is transferred to capital account:
  — *debit* realisation account
  — *credit* capital account
  (If purchase moneys are *less* than the value of the net assets, a loss on realisation has been made, and the transactions are reversed.)
- The balance of capital account is now equal to bank/cash account; this is withdrawn by the owner
  — *debit* capital account
  — *credit* bank/cash accounts

All accounts in the seller's books are now closed and the business has ceased to exist. The owner has withdrawn the balance of capital account.

The layout for the realisation account is:

Dr.		**Realisation Account**	Cr.
	£		£
Assets sold to purchaser		Liabilities transferred to purchaser	
Profit on realisation: to capital account		Purchase moneys received from purchaser	
		Loss on realisation: to capital account	
	———		———
	═══		═══

Buyer's books

The special account used is a *purchase of business account.*

- Assets acquired
  — *debit* asset accounts
  — *credit* purchase of business account
  (Note that assets need not be entered into the buyer's books at the same amount shown in the seller's books: the buyer may choose to revalue them either upwards or downwards.)
- Liabilities taken over
  — *debit* purchase of business account
  — *credit* liability accounts
- Purchase moneys paid to the seller
  — *debit* purchase of business account
  — *credit* bank/cash account
  (If the buyer is a limited company and the seller is to accept shares in full or part payment, the credit will be to ordinary shares account.)

- If a debit balance remains on the purchase of business account, this represents *goodwill,* ie the purchase price was greater than the net assets acquired. This is transferred to goodwill account:
  — *debit* goodwill account
  — *credit* purchase of business account
  Note: if the goodwill is to be written off immediately, it will now be debited to capital account: in the case of a partnership it will be debited to partners' capital accounts in their profit and loss sharing ratio; for a limited company it will be debited to a revenue reserve account.
- If a credit balance remains on purchase of business account, this represents a *capital reserve,* ie the purchase price was less than the net assets acquired. This is transferred to capital reserve account:
  — *debit* purchase of business account
  — *credit* capital reserve
  Note: in the case of sole traders and partnerships, capital reserve will be credited to the capital account(s).

The layout for the purchase of business account is:

Dr.	**Purchase of Business Account**		Cr.
	£		£
Liabilities taken over from seller		Assets acquired from seller	
Purchase moneys paid to seller		Goodwill on purchase of the business	
Capital reserve on purchase of the business			
	___		___
	═══		═══

25.4 A sole trader buys another sole trader's business

In this example, we will look at both the seller's and the buyer's books.

Question
The balance sheets of A and Z, two sole traders, are:

BALANCE SHEETS OF A AND Z, SOLE TRADERS, AS AT 31 DECEMBER 19-1

	A	Z
	£	£
Fixed assets (net book values)	25,000	60,000
Current assets (excluding bank/cash)	10,000	12,000
Bank/cash	5,000	38,000
	40,000	110,000
Less current liabilities	10,000	20,000
	30,000	90,000
Capital	30,000	90,000

- On 1 January 19-2, Z agrees to buy the assets (excluding bank/cash) and liabilities of A at their balance sheet values
- The purchase price is settled at £35,000

Show the transactions in the seller's books and the buyer's books.
Also show Z's balance sheet after the purchase has taken place.

Answer

Seller's books

Realisation Account

Dr.	£	Cr.	£
Fixed assets	25,000	Current liabilities	10,000
Current assets	10,000	Bank/cash: purchase moneys	35,000
Capital account: profit on realisation	10,000		
	45,000		45,000

Fixed Assets

Dr.	£	Cr.	£
Balance b/d	25,000	Realisation account	25,000

Current Assets (excluding bank/cash)

Dr.	£	Cr.	£
Balance b/d	10,000	Realisation account	10,000

Current Liabilities

Dr.	£	Cr.	£
Realisation account	10,000	Balance b/d	10,000

Bank/Cash Account

Dr.	£	Cr.	£
Balance b/d	5,000	Balance c/d	40,000
Realisation account: purchase moneys	35,000		
	40,000		40,000
Balance b/d	40,000		

Capital Account

Dr.	£	Cr.	£
Balance c/d	40,000	Balance b/d	30,000
		Realisation account: profit on realisation	10,000
	40,000		40,000
		Balance b/d	40,000

After these transactions have been recorded, only two accounts remain open: bank/cash, and capital. Both have a balance of £40,000, and the owner, A, can decide whether to draw out all the money, or whether to set up a new business.

Buyer's books

Purchase of Business Account

Dr.	£		Cr. £
Current liabilities	10,000	Fixed assets	25,000
Bank/cash: purchase moneys	35,000	Current assets	10,000
		Goodwill	10,000
	45,000		45,000

Fixed Assets

Dr.	£		Cr. £
Balance b/d	60,000	Balance c/d	85,000
Purchase of business account	25,000		
	85,000		85,000
Balance b/d	85,000		

Current Assets (excluding bank/cash)

Dr.	£		Cr. £
Balance b/d	12,000	Balance c/d	22,000
Purchase of business account	10,000		
	22,000		22,000
Balance b/d	22,000		

Current Liabilities

Dr.	£		Cr. £
Balance c/d	30,000	Balance b/d	20,000
		Purchase of business account	10,000
	30,000		30,000
		Balance b/d	30,000

Bank/Cash Account

Dr.	£		Cr. £
Balance b/d	38,000	Purchase of business account:	
		purchase moneys	35,000
		Balance c/d	3,000
	38,000		38,000
Balance b/d	3,000		

Goodwill Account

Dr.	£		Cr. £
Balance b/d	10,000	Capital account	10,000

Capital Account

Dr.	£		Cr. £
Goodwill account	10,000	Balance b/d	90,000
Balance c/d	80,000		
	90,000		90,000
		Balance b/d	80,000

Note that the balance of goodwill account has been written off in full to capital account.

BALANCE SHEET OF Z AS AT 1 JANUARY 19-2

	£
Fixed assets (net book values)	85,000
Current assets (excluding bank/cash)	22,000
Bank/cash	3,000
	110,000
Less current liabilities	30,000
	80,000
Capital	80,000

25.5 A partnership buys a sole trader's business

In this example, we will look only at the buyer's books.

Question

P and Q are in partnership sharing profits and losses in the ratio 2:1 respectively. On 1 January 19-5, they decide to buy the business of R, a sole trader. The balance sheets are shown on the next page:

BALANCE SHEETS AS AT 31 DECEMBER 19-4

	P and Q	R
	£	£
Fixed assets (net book values)	100,000	40,000
Current assets (excluding bank/cash)	40,000	20,000
Bank/cash	15,000	10,000
	155,000	70,000
Less current liabilities	25,000	15,000
	130,000	55,000
Capital accounts		
R		55,000
P	80,000	
Q	50,000	
	130,000	55,000

- P and Q will take over the business of R at an agreed price of £50,000 (excluding R's bank/cash balance)
- To finance part of the purchase price, P and Q have arranged a bank loan of £30,000, and P will introduce additional capital of £10,000
- In their books, P and Q will revalue R's fixed assets at £42,000 and the current assets at £17,000

Show the transactions in the books of the buyer, P and Q, together with their balance sheet after the purchase has taken place.

Answer

Purchase of Business Account

Dr.			Cr.
	£		£
Current liabilities	15,000	Fixed assets	42,000
Bank/cash: purchase moneys	20,000	Current assets	17,000
Bank loan: purchase moneys	30,000	Goodwill	6,000
	65,000		65,000

Fixed Assets

Dr.			Cr.
	£		£
Balance b/d	100,000	Balance c/d	142,000
Purchase of business account	42,000		
	142,000		142,000
Balance b/d	142,000		

Current Assets (excluding bank/cash)

Dr.	£		Cr. £
Balance b/d	40,000	Balance c/d	57,000
Purchase of business account	17,000		
	57,000		57,000
Balance b/d	57,000		

Current Liabilities

Dr.	£		Cr. £
Balance c/d	40,000	Balance b/d	25,000
		Purchase of business account	15,000
	40,000		40,000
		Balance b/d	40,000

Bank/Cash Account

Dr.	£		Cr. £
Balance b/d	15,000	Purchase of business account	20,000
Capital account: P	10,000	Balance c/d	5,000
	25,000		25,000
Balance b/d	5,000		

Bank Loan Account

Dr.	£		Cr. £
		Purchase of business account	30,000

Goodwill Account

Dr.	£		Cr. £
Purchase of business account	6,000	Capital accounts:	
		P (two-thirds)	4,000
		Q (one-third)	2,000
	6,000		6,000

Partners' Capital Accounts

Dr.	P	Q		P	Q Cr.
	£	£		£	£
Goodwill	4,000	2,000	Balances b/d	80,000	50,000
Balances c/d	86,000	48,000	Bank: additional capital	10,000	-
	90,000	50,000		90,000	50,000
			Balances b/d	86,000	48,000

Note that the balance of goodwill account has been written off to the partners' capital accounts in their profit and loss sharing ratio.

BALANCE SHEET OF P AND Q AS AT 1 JANUARY 19-5

	£
Fixed assets (net book values)	142,000
Current assets (excluding bank/cash)	57,000
Bank/cash	5,000
	204,000
Less current liabilities	40,000
	164,000
Less bank loan	30,000
	134,000
Capital accounts:	
P	86,000
Q	48,000
	134,000

25.6 A limited company buys a partnership business

In this example, we will look at the buyer's books when the buyer is a limited company and shares are issued to the sellers, a partnership.

Question

On 1 January 19-8, A-Z Ltd is to buy the assets (excluding the bank/cash balance), but not the liabilities, of the partnership of S and T. The balance sheets at 31 December 19-7 are:

BALANCE SHEETS AS AT 31 DECEMBER 19-7

	A-Z Ltd	S and T
	£	£
Fixed assets (net book values)	125,000	50,000
Current assets (excluding bank/cash)	55,000	15,000
Bank/cash	20,000	5,000
	200,000	70,000
Less current liabilities	20,000	10,000
	180,000	60,000

(Balance sheet continues on next page)

	A-Z Ltd	S and T
	£	£
Capital		
£1 ordinary shares	150,000	
Revenue reserves	30,000	
Capital accounts:		
S		40,000
T		20,000
	180,000	60,000

- The valuations of the assets of S and T are agreed at:

fixed assets	£70,000
current assets (excluding bank/cash)	£10,000
goodwill	£10,000
purchase consideration	£90,000

- Goodwill is to be written off in full in the books of A-Z Ltd
- The purchase consideration is to be satisfied by:
  - payment of £10,000 in cash
  - the issue to S and T of an appropriate number of £1 ordinary shares at a premium of 25 per cent (see note below)

Show the transactions in the books of the buyer, A-Z Ltd, together with the balance sheet after the purchase has taken place.

Answer

Note: The purchase consideration to be satisfied by the issue of shares is £80,000 (ie total purchase consideration of £90,000, less cash payment of £10,000). As the shares are to be isssued at a premium of 25 per cent, the *number* of £1 ordinary shares to be issued is 64,000 (£80,000 ÷ £1.25); the other £16,000 goes to share premium account. S and T will decide how the shares are to be allocated between them – it will, most probably, be in proportion to their capital accounts.

Purchase of Business Account

Dr.			Cr.
	£		£
Bank/cash: purchase moneys	10,000	Fixed assets	70,000
£1 ordinary shares account: purchase moneys	64,000	Current assets	10,000
Share premium account: purchase moneys	16,000	Goodwill	10,000
	90,000		90,000

Fixed Assets

Dr.			Cr.
	£		£
Balance b/d	125,000	Balance c/d	195,000
Purchase of business account	70,000		
	195,000		195,000
Balance b/d	195,000		

Current Assets (excluding bank/cash)

Dr.	£	Cr.	£
Balance b/d	55,000	Balance c/d	65,000
Purchase of business account	10,000		
	65,000		65,000
Balance b/d	65,000		

Current Liabilities

Dr.	£	Cr.	£
		Balance b/d	20,000

Bank/Cash Account

Dr.	£	Cr.	£
Balance b/d	20,000	Purchase of business account	10,000
		Balance c/d	10,000
	20,000		20,000
Balance b/d	10,000		

Goodwill Account

Dr.	£	Cr.	£
Purchase of business account	10,000	Revenue reserves: written off	10,000

Revenue Reserves

Dr.	£	Cr.	£
Goodwill written off	10,000	Balance b/d	30,000
Balance c/d	20,000		
	30,000		30,000
		Balance b /d	20,000

£1 Ordinary Shares Account

Dr.	£		Cr. £
Balance c/d	214,000	Balance b/d	150,000
		Purchase of business account	64,000
	214,000		214,000
		Balance b /d	214,000

Share Premium Account

Dr.	£		Cr. £
		Purchase of business account	16,000

BALANCE SHEET OF A-Z LTD AS AT 1 JANUARY 19-8

	£
Fixed assets (net book values)	195,000
Current assets (excluding bank/cash)	65,000
Bank/cash	10,000
	270,000
Less current liabilities	20,000
	250,000
Capital:	
£1 ordinary shares	214,000
Capital reserve: share premium account	16,000
Revenue reserves	20,000
	250,000

25.7 Chapter summary

- Conversion of a business into a different form of business unit, eg a sole trader converts to a partnership, requires the use of a *realisation account* in the closing business.
- When one business buys another, a *realisation account* is used in the books of the seller, and a *purchase of business account* in the books of the buyer.
- The broad principles of conversion and outright purchase apply whatever forms of business unit are involved.

In the next chapter we return to year-end accounts to look at the layout used where firms buy in raw materials and manufacture products which are then sold as finished goods.

25.8 Questions

25.1 Green and Harrison are two sole traders who have decided to form a partnership from 1 January 19-2. At the close of business on 31 December 19-1 their separate balance sheets were as follows:

	Green		*Harrison*	
	£	£	£	£
Fixed Assets				
Delivery van		4,500		–
Office equipment		6,000		8,500
		10,500		8,500
Current Assets				
Stock	5,300		7,200	
Debtors	9,500		11,600	
Bank	2,500		3,000	
	17,300		21,800	
Less Current Liabilities				
Creditors	4,700		4,800	
Working Capital		12,600		17,000
NET ASSETS		23,100		25,500
Capital		23,100		25,500

- The new partnership will take over all the assets and liabilities at the balance sheet values, except for the following valuations:

  Green: office equipment £4,000, stock £5,500, bad debts of £500 to be written off

  Harrison: office equipment £8,000, stock £7,000, bad debts of £900 to be written off
- In the new partnership, profits and losses are to be shared equally
- Goodwill is agreed at Green £6,000, Harrison £8,000

Required:
Show the opening balance sheet of the new partnership.

25.2 The balance sheets of Singh and Patel, two sole traders, at 31 December 19-1 are as follows:

	Singh		*Patel*	
	£	£	£	£
Fixed Assets				
Premises		100,000		55,000
Fixtures and fittings		25,000		10,000
		125,000		65,000
Current Assets				
Stock	14,500		6,300	
Debtors	15,800		7,200	
Bank	35,400		2,900	
	65,700		16,400	
Less Current Liabilities				
Creditors	9,700		4,600	
Working Capital		56,000		11,800
NET ASSETS		181,000		76,800
Capital		181,000		76,800

- On 1 January 19-2, Singh agrees to buy the assets (excluding bank) and liabilities of Patel
- The purchase price is agreed at £80,000
- In his books, Singh revalues Patel's premises at £60,000, stock at £5,500, debtors at £6,500, other assets and liabilities at balance sheet values
- To finance part of the purchase price, Singh has arranged a bank loan of £50,000

You are required to show:

(a) the purchase of business account in Singh's books

(b) Singh's balance sheet at 1 January 19-2 after all the above transactions have been completed

25.3* Michael and Norman carried on business in partnership as builders sharing profits and losses, Michael two-thirds and Norman one-third.

They agreed with Oliver, who was in business on his own account, to amalgamate their businesses on 31 May 19-9.

The summarised balance sheets of the two firms at 31 May 19-9 were as follows:

	Michael and Norman	*Oliver*		*Michael and Norman*	*Oliver*
	£	£		£	£
Capital Accounts			**Fixed Assets**		
Michael	140,000		Freehold premises	80,000	–
Norman	90,000		Plant	52,500	35,000
Oliver		60,000			
	230,000	60,000		132,500	35,000
Current Liabilities			**Current Assets**		
Trade creditors	100,000	18,000	Work in progress	170,000	60,000
Bank overdraft	–	33,500	Trade debtors	25,000	16,500
			Cash at bank	2,500	
	330,000	111,500		330,000	111,500

The terms on which the businesses were amalgamated were as follows:

(i) Profits were to be shared Michael one-half, Norman three-tenths and Oliver one-fifth.

(ii) The value of goodwill of the two firms was agreed at Michael and Norman £39,000, Oliver £11,000. (No account for goodwill was to be opened in the books, but adjusting entries for transactions between the partners were to be made in the partners' capital accounts.)

(iii) The new firm was to take over all the assets and discharge all the liabilities of Michael and Norman; for the purpose of the amalgamation fixed assets and work in progress were to be revalued as follows:

	£
Freehold premises	115,000
Plant	45,000
Work in progress	195,000

(iv) Oliver was to collect his own debts and pay off his creditors. The new firm was to take over his plant at book value and his work in progress which was to be written up by £5,000.

(v) The new firm was to raise a new 10% bank loan for £60,000 (secured on the freehold premises); the loan was to be used to repay Oliver's bank overdraft and provide additional working capital.

(vi) The capital of the firm was to be £350,000 contributed by the partners in profit sharing ratio. The balance due to be withdrawn or paid in by each partner was to be entered in a current account.

Requirement:

(a) (i) the partners' capital accounts in columnar form recording the amalgamation adjustments; and

(ii) the opening balance sheet of the new firm.

(b) Where two people join together to manage a business they can either run the business in partnership or under the auspices of a limited company. You are required to explain

(i) TWO main differences in these types of business organisations; and

(ii) the way in which profits may be shared between the partners/managers where they contribute differing amounts of capital and entrepreneurial skills.

[© Northern Ireland Schools Examinations and Assessment Council]

26 Manufacturing Accounts

In previous chapters we have concerned ourselves with the accounts of businesses that trade, ie buy and sell goods without carrying out a manufacturing process. However, many firms buy raw materials and manufacture products which are then sold as finished goods. The final accounts for a manufacturer include a *manufacturing account* which brings together all the elements of cost which make up the production cost. In this chapter we will:

- consider the manufacturing process
- study the elements of cost
- prepare a manufacturing account

26.1 The manufacturing process and elements of cost

Fig. 26.1 shows, in outline, the manufacturing process and the costs incurred at each stage.

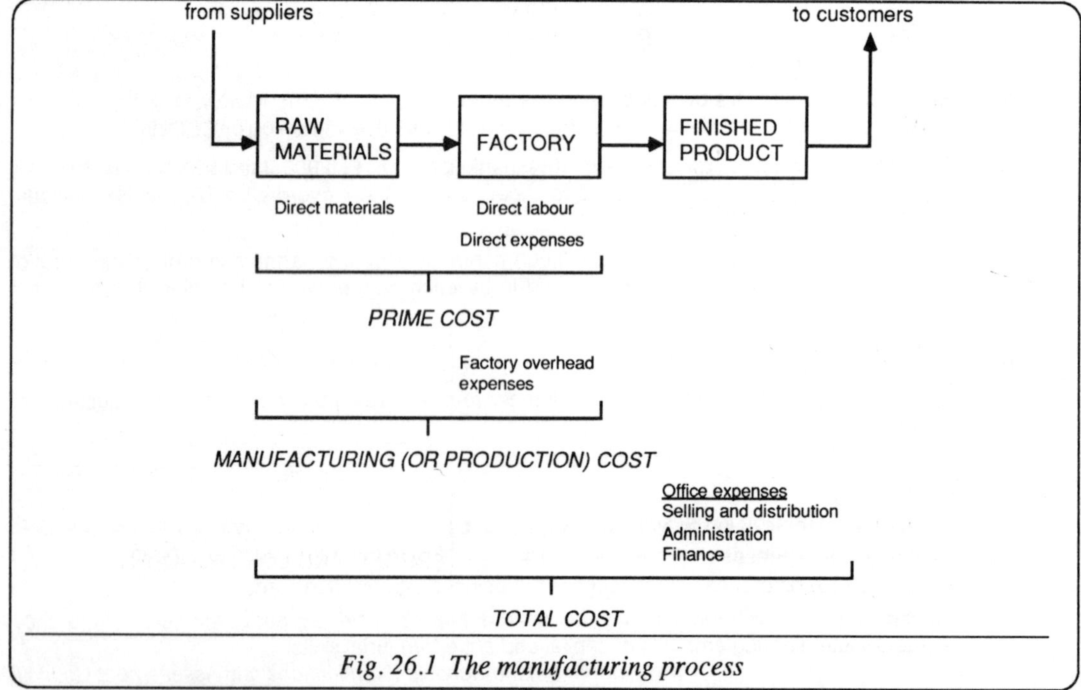

Fig. 26.1 The manufacturing process

There are four main elements of cost which make up the manufacturing (or production) cost for a manufacturer:

- **direct materials** — these are the raw materials that are required in manufacturing the finished product
- **direct labour** — this is the cost of the workforce engaged in production, eg machine operators (note that the wages of supervisors are a factory overhead expense and are usually described as 'indirect labour')
- **direct expenses** — these include any special costs that can be identified with each unit produced, eg a royalty payable to the designer of the product for each unit made, or the hire of specialist machinery to carry out a manufacturing task
- **factory overhead expenses** — all the other costs of manufacture, eg wages of supervisors, rent of factory, depreciation of factory machinery, heating and lighting of factory

Prime cost is the basic cost of manufacturing a product before the addition of factory overhead expenses. It consists of the first three costs, ie

direct materials + direct labour + direct expenses = prime cost

Manufacturing cost is the factory cost of producing the product after the addition of factory overhead expenses, and is:

prime cost + factory overhead expenses = manufacturing (or production) cost

26.2 Manufacturing account

The final accounts of a manufacturer use the following outline:

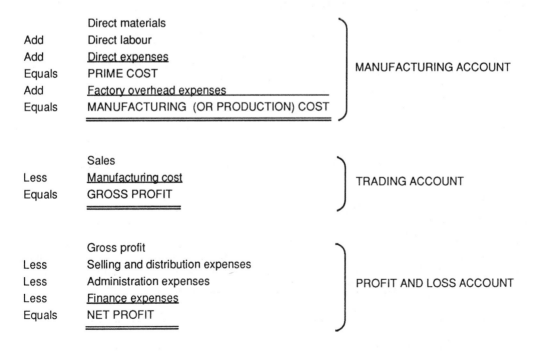

	Direct materials	MANUFACTURING ACCOUNT
Add	Direct labour	
Add	Direct expenses	
Equals	PRIME COST	
Add	Factory overhead expenses	
Equals	MANUFACTURING (OR PRODUCTION) COST	
	Sales	TRADING ACCOUNT
Less	Manufacturing cost	
Equals	GROSS PROFIT	
	Gross profit	PROFIT AND LOSS ACCOUNT
Less	Selling and distribution expenses	
Less	Administration expenses	
Less	Finance expenses	
Equals	NET PROFIT	

The layout of a manufacturing, trading, and profit and loss account (with sample figures) is shown below:

MANUFACTURING, TRADING, AND PROFIT AND LOSS ACCOUNT OF ALPHA MANUFACTURING CO FOR THE YEAR ENDED 31 DECEMBER 19-1

	£	£
Opening stock of raw materials		5,000
Add Purchases of raw materials		50,000
		55,000
Less Closing stock of raw materials		6,000
COST OF RAW MATERIALS USED		49,000
Direct labour		26,000
Direct expenses		2,500
PRIME COST		77,500
Factory overheads		
Indirect materials	2,000	
Indirect labour	16,000	
Rent of factory	5,000	
Depreciation of factory machinery	10,000	
Factory light and heat	4,000	
		37,000
		114,500
Add Opening stock of work-in-progress		4,000
		118,500
Less Closing stock of work-in-progress		3,000
MANUFACTURING (OR PRODUCTION) COST OF GOODS COMPLETED		115,500
Sales		195,500
Opening stock of finished goods	6,500	
Manufacturing (or production) cost of goods completed	115,500	
	122,000	
Less Closing stock of finished goods	7,500	
COST OF GOODS SOLD		114,500
Gross profit		81,000
Office expenses		
Selling and distribution expenses	38,500	
Administration expenses	32,000	
Finance expenses	3,500	
		74,000
Net profit		7,000

Points to note:

- *Manufacturing cost* (or *production cost*) is the final figure of the manufacturing account.
- A manufacturing account forms one part of the year-end accounts for a manufacturing business, and precedes the trading account. The latter is prepared in the usual way except that manufacturing cost takes the place of purchases. However, some businesses both manufacture goods and buy in finished goods, in which case the trading account will show both manufacturing cost *and* purchases of goods for resale.
- In the trading account, the opening and closing stocks are the *finished goods* held by a business.

- Manufacturing businesses usually hold stocks of goods in three different forms:
  - — *raw materials:* commodities and components purchased from suppliers required in manufacturing the finished product
  - — *work-in-progress:* products in course of manufacture at a particular moment in time
  - — *finished goods:* products on which the manufacturing process has been completed and which are ready for sale

  Note that, with raw materials, there may be the cost of *carriage in* to be added, and an amount for *purchases returns* to be deducted.

  The first two stocks appear in the manufacturing account, while finished goods stock is in the trading account. The closing stock valuation of *all three* form the year-end stocks to be shown in the balance sheet.

- Certain expenses might be allocated between the manufacturing account and profit and loss account – for example, business rates might be allocated two-thirds to the factory and one-third to the office.

26.3 Unit cost of goods manufactured

When the manufacturing cost has been ascertained, the unit cost can be calculated as follows:

$$\text{Unit cost} = \frac{\text{Manufacturing cost of goods completed}}{\text{Number of units completed}}$$

For example, if the manufacturing account on page 398 represented production of 200,000 units, the unit cost for the year was:

$$\text{Unit cost} = \frac{£115{,}500}{200{,}000} = \underline{\underline{£0.58 \text{ per unit}}}$$

26.4 Factory profit

Some manufacturing businesses transfer completed goods from the factory to the warehouse at, for example, 'factory cost plus ten per cent'. The objective in doing this is for the factory to make a notional profit which is added into net profit at a later stage. This might enable the unit cost of goods manufactured to be compared with the cost of buying in completed goods from an outside source. In pure accounting terms it might be cheaper to buy in, although there are many other factors to consider. Also, by showing a factory profit, the profit (or loss) from trading activities (as distinct from manufacturing) can be identified separately.

Referring back to the manufacturing account on the previous page and amending the figures to allow for a factory 'profit' of ten per cent, the final part of the manufacturing account, and the trading and profit and loss account appear as follows:

	£	£
MANUFACTURING COSTS		115,500
Factory profit of ten per cent		11,550
MANUFACTURING COST OF GOODS COMPLETED (including profit)		127,050
Sales		195,500
Opening stock of finished goods	6,500	
Manufacturing (or production) cost of goods completed	127,050	
	133,550	
Less Closing stock of finished goods	7,500	
COST OF GOODS SOLD		126,050
Gross profit		69,450
Office expenses		
Selling and distribution expenses	38,500	
Administration expenses	32,000	
Finance expenses	3,500	
		74,000
Loss from Trading		(4,550)
Add Factory profit		11,550
Net profit		7,000

Note that the final net profit is unchanged, but the manufacturing cost is higher, and gross profit is lower. The factory profit is added back in the profit and loss account, after showing separately the profit or loss from trading. As stated earlier, the reason for doing this is to make the factory and the warehouse into separate *profit centres.*

Provision for unrealised profit on finished goods stocks

A business using the 'factory profit' method may choose to value stocks of finished goods at *manufacturing cost plus manufacturing profit.* For example, the business whose manufacturing account is shown above, might value finished goods stocks as:

Opening stock: manufacturing cost (£6,500) + manufacturing profit of 10 per cent (£650) = £7,150

Closing stock: manufacturing cost (£7,500) + manufacturing profit of 10 per cent (£750) = £8,250

The logic behind valuing finished goods stocks in this way is to show more clearly the profit from the separate sections of the business, ie manufacturing and trading. It will apply particularly where goods are both manufactured *and* bought in as finished goods from outside manufacturers. The trading account now compares 'like with like', ie own-manufactured goods are priced in the trading account to include a profit, while the bought-in goods include the supplier's profit. At the end of the financial year the closing stock of own-manufactured goods includes an element of *unrealised profit.*

Statement of Standard Accounting Practice No 9 (Stocks and long-term contracts) – see Chapter 16.4 – requires that stocks should be shown in the balance sheet at cost price if purchased, or cost of production if manufactured. (Note that if realisable value is lower than cost, then this will be used instead.) In order to comply with SSAP 9, it is necessary to account for the element of unrealised profit included in the finished goods stock valuation. This is done through an account called *provision for unrealised profit,* which is used to adjust the closing stock figure in the balance sheet to cost price.

For example, using the adjusted finished goods opening stock figure of £7,150 (above) and the closing stock figure of £8,250, the provision for unrealised profit account appears as:

Provision for Unrealised Profit Account

Dr.		£		Cr.	£
19-1			19-1		
31 Dec.	Balance c/d (adjustment in respect of closing stock)	750	1 Jan.	Balance b/d (adjustment in respect of opening stock)	650
			31 Dec.	Profit and loss account	100
		750			750
19-2			19-2		
			1 Jan.	Balance b/d	750

Note that the *increase* in provision for unrealised profit of £100 is charged as an expense in profit and loss account. It is recorded as a *deduction* from factory profit shown in the profit and loss account, eg

	£	£
Factory profit	11,550	
Less increase in provision for unrealised profit	100	
		11,450

If there is a fall in the value of finished goods stock during the year, then there will be a decrease in the provision for unrealised profit, and this will be *added* to the factory profit shown in the profit and loss account.

Stock account uses the finished goods stock valuations which include the manufacturing profit, as follows:

Stock Account

Dr.		£		Cr.	£
19-1			19-1		
1 Jan.	Balance b/d (opening stock)	7,150	31 Dec.	Trading account	7,150
31 Dec.	Trading account (closing stock)	8,250	31 Dec.	Balance c/d	8,250
19-2			19-2		
1 Jan.	Balance b/d	8,250			

The balance sheet figure at 31 December 19-1 for finished goods stocks shows the net value, ie

	£
Finished goods stocks	8,250
Less Provision for unrealised profits	750
Net value	7,500

As can be seen this reduces the closing stock value of finished goods to cost price, and enables the balance sheet valuation to comply with SSAP 9.

26.5 Fixed and variable costs

Most costs for an organisation can be categorised as *fixed* or *variable*:

- fixed costs, eg factory rent, remain constant despite changes in production levels
- variable costs alter with changed circumstances, such as increases in production

The main variable costs for a manufacturing business are:

- raw materials
- direct labour
- direct expenses, eg a royalty payment

With each of these, as production increases, so the costs will increase in direct proportion to production. In practice, such increases may not be quite so direct, eg the purchase of raw materials in larger quantities may enable a manufacturer to obtain discounts in bulk. Also, direct labour is usually regarded as varying with production: where payment is made on a piecework basis, this will be true; however, piecework is not common nowadays – most production workers are paid a basic wage, plus a production bonus which varies with overall output. Despite this, there is a close relationship between goods produced and the costs of direct labour, because labour can be moved from one production line to another to suit the changing needs of the manufacturing process.

However, these 'rules' are only true within certain restricted limits; for example a rapidly expanding business must eventually reach the point at which more premises are needed, and then rent and other 'fixed' costs will increase. In the short term, though, it is correct to classify costs between those that are fixed and those that are variable.

Accountants can use the relationship between fixed and variable costs in decision-making as a part of management accounting. It is likely that you will study this topic as a part of your other accountancy studies.

26.6 Chapter summary

❑ A manufacturing account brings together all the elements of cost which make up manufacturing (or production) cost.

❑ Prime cost = direct materials + direct labour + direct expenses.

❑ Manufacturing (or production) cost = prime cost + factory overhead expenses.

❑ Trading account deals with the stock of finished goods.

❑ Profit and loss account deals with office expenses.

❑ Most manufacturing costs are either fixed or variable; the management accountant can use the relationship between these two types of costs for decision-making purposes.

In the next chapter we continue the theme of specialised accounting applications by looking at departmental accounts, joint venture accounts and consignment accounts.

26.7 Questions

26.1 Bob Grubb has taken early retirement and has decided to set himself up in business, making and selling children's swings. His turnover for his first year in trading amounted to £250,000.

The following information is also relevant to his first trading year which ended on 30 April 19-0:

	£
Purchases of raw materials	82,000
Factory wages	35,000
Factory expenses	25,000
Office salaries	12,000
Office expenses	4,000
Closing stocks:	
Raw materials	10,000
Finished goods	12,000
Depreciation:	
Factory equipment	6,000
Office fixtures	1,000
Purchases returns	2,000

You are required to:

(a) Prepare a manufacturing account for the year ended 30 April 19-0, showing clearly

(i) the prime cost

(ii) the cost of goods manufactured

(b) Prepare the trading account for the year ended 30 April 19-0

(c) Explain the meaning of *depreciation* and why it appears in the books of a business. Illustrate your answer by reference to *two* depreciation methods.

[Welsh Joint Education Committee]

26.2* From the following information you are required to prepare the manufacturing account of Percival Components Limited for the year ended 31 October 19-9, showing clearly:

(a) Prime cost

(b) Cost of manufactured goods

	£
Purchases of raw materials	383,296
Manufacturing wages	287,136
Factory rent and rates	7,264
Factory insurance	3,184
Factory salaries	11,936
Machinery repairs	4,128
Heating and lighting	14,208
General factory expenses	9,248
Machinery (at cost)	512,000
Stock of raw materials (1 November 19-8)	31,584
Stock of raw materials (31 October 19-9)	32,384
Work-in-progress (1 November 19-8)	36,768
Work-in-progress (31 October 19-9)	39,616

Notes:

- Only one-half of the heating and lighting expenses are to be allocated to the factory
- £496 for the factory insurance was paid in advance
- Depreciate machinery by 7½% per annum on cost

[RSA Examinations Board]

26.3* The balances shown below are from the books of the Protem Manufacturing Company as at 30 September year 9:

	£
Stocks at 1 October year 8:	
Raw materials	39,000
Work-in-progress at prime cost	8,100
Finished goods	51,930
Purchases of raw materials for the year	214,760
Sales	365,752
Returns outwards – raw materials	1,350
Plant and machinery, at cost	93,000
Office equipment	19,800
Factory wages	33,560
Factory – lighting and heating	13,700
– power	7,600
– rates and insurance	3,800

The following details are also available:

1. Stocks at 30 September year 9:

Raw materials	£43,630
Work-in-progress at prime cost	£5,160
Finished goods	£57,400

2. Factory lighting and heating expenses accrued at 30 September year 9 — £760
3. Factory rates and insurance paid in advance at 30 September year 9 — £240
4. Depreciation is to be provided on plant and machinery at the rate of 15% per annum on cost

Required:

Prepare the manufacturing and trading account of Protem Manufacturing Company for the year ended 30 September year 9.

[London Chamber of Commerce]

26.4 Chesterton Plc are manufacturers.

At the end of their accounting year, 30 April 19-0, the following information was available:

	£
Stocks, 1 May 19-9:	
raw materials	17,500
finished goods	24,800
work-in-progress	15,270
Wages and salaries:	
factory direct	138,500
factory indirect	27,200
Purchases of raw materials	95,600
Power and fuel (indirect)	18,260
Sales	410,400
Insurance	3,680
Returns inwards (finished goods)	5,200
Stocks, 30 April 19-0	
raw materials	13,200
finished goods	14,600
work-in-progress	15,700

Notes:

- The company's machinery cost £82,000 and the provision for depreciation on 1 May 19-9 was £27,000. Machinery is to be depreciated by 20% per annum using the reducing balance method.
- Fuel and power £390 is in arrears at 30 April 19-0; at the same date insurance £240 is prepaid.
- Insurance is to be allocated 5/8ths factory; 3/8ths administration

Required:

For Chesterton Plc

(a) A manufacturing account for the year ended 30 April 19-0, showing clearly
 (i) cost of raw materials consumed
 (ii) prime cost
 (iii) total cost of production

(b) A trading account for the year ended 30 April 19-0 showing clearly
 (i) cost of sales of finished goods
 (ii) gross profit

[Southern Examining Group, 1990]

26.5 Makit is in business as a manufacturer and the following balances were extracted from his books on 31 October 19-0:

	£	£
Stocks at 1 November 19-9:		
Raw materials	2,400	
Finished goods	16,750	
Work-in-progress	4,500	
Purchases raw materials	87,900	
Manufacturing wages	94,000	
Factory expenses	22,670	
Rent and property insurance	6,780	
Carriage on raw materials	650	
Plant and machinery at cost	85,000	
Office equipment at cost	9,500	
Motor vehicles at cost	14,500	
Provision for depreciation:		
Plant and machinery		22,000
Office equipment		3,400
Motor vehicles		4,500
Light and heat	6,000	
Office salaries	22,000	
Office expenses	7,800	
Selling and distribution costs	28,000	
Sales		300,000
Drawings	18,000	
Cash in hand	780	
Bank		8,680
Capital		89,280
Debtors	6,400	
Creditors		5,770
	433,630	433,630

You are required to:

Prepare the manufacturing, trading, profit and loss account for the year ended 31 October 19-0 and a balance sheet as at that date, after giving effect to the following adjustments:

(i) The stocks on 31 October 19-0 were:

Raw materials	£2,870
Finished goods	£14,600
Work-in-progress	£4,750

(ii) Light and heat and rent and insurance are to be apportioned three-quarters to manufacturing account and one-quarter to profit and loss account.

(iii) At 31 October 19-0 manufacturing wages of £600 were unpaid and rent had been prepaid by £380

(iv) Depreciation is to be written off fixed assets as follows:

	£
Plant and machinery	8,500
Fixtures and fittings	950
Vehicles	2,500

[RSA Examinations Board]

26.6* The following list of balances as at 30 April 19-0 has been extracted from the books of Fairdeal Manufacturers Limited which commenced business on 1 May 19-9:

	£
Factory plant and machinery at cost 1 May 19-9	120,000
Motor delivery vehicles at cost 1 May 19-9	25,000
Purchases of raw materials	41,000
Factory labour: machine operatives	36,000
supervisory	7,000
Factory plant and machinery repairs	8,710
Heat, light and power	24,750
Rates and insurance	2,550
General administrative expenses	9,400
Administrative salaries	12,090
Trade debtors	12,000
Trade creditors	7,100
Bank overdraft	4,900
Sales	136,500
Ordinary shares of £1 each, fully paid	120,000
Share premium account	30,000

Additional information:

1. Raw material stocks, at cost, at 30 April 19-0 were valued at £3,000.
2. Work-in-progress at 30 April 19-0 was valued at £24,000.
3. Depreciation is to be provided on fixed assets at the following rates on cost:

	per cent per annum
Factory plant and machinery	10
Motor delivery vehicles	25

4. Rates and insurances prepaid at 30 April 19-0 amounted to £600; heat, light and power accrued due at 30 April 19-0 was £2,300.
5. Rates and insurances and heat, light and power charges are to be apportioned three quarters to manufacturing and a quarter to the profit and loss account.
6. Manufactured goods are to be transferred from the manufacturing account to the trading account at wholesale prices; the wholesale price of goods manufactured during the year ended 30 April 19-0 was £100,000.
7. Finished goods stock at 30 April 19-0, at wholesale prices, was valued at £10,000.

Required:

(a) Prepare the manufacturing, trading and profit and loss account for the year ended 30 April 19-0 of Fairdeal Manufacturers Limited

(b) Prepare the balance sheet as at 30 April 19-0 of Fairdeal Manufacturers Limited

[Association of Accounting Technicians]

26.7 Carthorn Manufacturing Limited showed the following balances in its books at 31 December:

	£
Sales	201,200
Quoted investments	35,940
120,000 ordinary shares of £1 fully paid	120,000
(Authorised 150,000 of £1)	
20,000 8% preference shares of £1 fully paid cumulative	20,000
(Authorised 20,000 of £1)	
General reserve	30,000
Purchases	60,920
Freehold property	130,840
Additions to property during year	6,000
Creditors	24,124
Debtors	18,900
Goodwill	30,000
8% Debentures (repayable at par 1 January 19-0)	60,000
Factory wages	76,640
Stock of raw materials (1 January)	16,640
Stock of finished goods (1 January)	4,540
Work-in-progress (1 January)	3,840
Share premium account	4,280
Investment income	3,460
Profit and loss account (credit)	11,180
Plant and equipment (cost £44,000)	22,000
Debenture interest half year to 30 June (paid 1 July)	2,400
Repairs to plant	1,700
Insurances (factory)	1,400
(office)	120
Carriage inwards	2,200
Factory power	8,340
Rent and rates (overheads)	2,120
Salaries	25,260
Directors' fees	720
Office expenses	1,160
Cash at bank and in hand	15,364
Preference share dividend for half year (paid 1 July)	800
Office furniture (cost £10,000)	6,400

You are required to make out a manufacturing, trading and profit and loss account for the period to 31 December and a balance sheet as at that date, taking the following information into account:

(a) Doubtful debts provision of £500

(b) Half-year preference dividend payable 1 January

(c) Accrued charges:

Commissions		£420
Factory power		£620
Repairs to plant		£180
Audit fee		£320
Debenture interest		£2,400

(d) Prepayments:

Rates	£530
Factory insurance	£400

(e) Ordinary share dividend of 5% payable at 28 February

(f) Depreciation: Plant 10% on cost
Office furniture 10% on net book value

(g) Value of stocks at 31 December:

Raw materials	£18,200
Work-in-progress	£3,600
Finished goods	£4,800

(h) The market value of the quoted investments at 31 December was £37,000

[Pitman Examinations Institute]

27 Departmental and other Specialist Accounts

This chapter looks at the following types of accounts:

- *departmental accounts,* which identify the income and expenditure of different departments or divisions within a business, so as to show the separate gross and net profits
- *joint venture accounts,* used to record the transactions of a joint venture, which is an undertaking by which its participants expect to achieve some common purpose or benefit, eg the buying or selling of an agreed quantity of goods
- *consignment accounts,* which cover the shipment of a consignment of goods to an agent (who may well be abroad) for sale

27.1 Departmental accounts

Departmental accounts are used to identify the gross and net profits of different departments or divisions within a business. For example, consider a large store which is divided into several different departments such as furniture, clothes, kitchenware, electrical goods, etc; which of the following statements of profit do you think the management of the business will find more useful?

(a)	Gross profit for store	£150,000	
(b)	Gross profit:		
	furniture	£20,000	profit
	clothes	£80,000	profit
	kitchenware	(£10,000)	loss
	electrical	£60,000	profit
	Total	£150,000	

Clearly the profit analysed between departments enables the management to identify and then investigate the poor performance of a particular department.

With departmental accounting, a department does not usually operate its own book-keeping system. Instead, the book-keeping is kept by a central department, whose accounts distinguish between the purchases and sales made by different departments. This analysis is usually made in analysed day books (see Chapter 6.7) for purchases, sales and returns. In a large store, departmental sales figures are readily obtained from the cash tills, the sales being analysed between the various departments by a coding system at the point of sale.

Although a department usually forms a physical part of the rest of the business, its manager may have considerable autonomy with regard to purchasing goods, staffing levels and selling prices. The manager may well be set targets by the management and then left to decide how to achieve these targets. A departmental accounting system will show if the targets have been achieved.

27.2 Departmental trading accounts

Once an analysis of purchases and sales between departments has been made in the accounting system, it requires a departmental stock-take at the end of the accounting period in order to prepare *departmental trading accounts*.

Worked example

Question

Wyvern Superstore Ltd has the following information about its three departments – carpets, clothes and furniture, for the year ended 31 December 19-1:

		£
Sales:		
Carpets		220,000
Clothes		350,000
Furniture		150,000
Purchases:		
Carpets		130,000
Clothes		180,000
Furniture		100,000
Stock:	1 Jan 19-1	31 Dec 19-1
	£	£
Carpets	50,000	55,000
Clothes	60,000	70,000
Furniture	35,000	30,000

Prepare the departmental trading account for the year.

Answer

WYVERN SUPERSTORE LTD
DEPARTMENTAL TRADING ACCOUNT FOR THE YEAR ENDED 31 DECEMBER 19-1

	Carpet department		Clothes department		Furniture department		Total	
	£	£	£	£	£	£	£	£
Sales		220,000		350,000		150,000		720,000
Opening stock	50,000		60,000		35,000		145,000	
Purchases	130,000		180,000		100,000		410,000	
	180,000		240,000		135,000		555,000	
Less Closing stock	55,000		70,000		30,000		155,000	
Cost of Goods Sold		125,000		170,000		105,000		400,000
Gross profit		95,000		180,000		45,000		320,000
Gross profit percentage (see next page)		43%		51%		30%		44%

The gross profit percentage is calculated as follows:

$$\frac{\text{Gross profit}}{\text{Sales}} \times \frac{100}{1} = \text{Gross profit/sales percentage}$$

The gross profit figures and their relative gross profit percentages (see Chapter 29.2) for each department will lead to an investigation into the reasons for the poor performance of a particular department. For example, the 30 per cent gross profit percentage achieved by Department C is well below that of the other two departments and of the store as a whole; the reasons for this need to be investigated.

27.3 Departmental profit and loss accounts

The departmental analysis can be carried further than the trading account by analysing the profit and loss account items. Each department must be charged with its share of the various expense items, using the following guidelines:

- Expenses directly attributable to a particular department should be charged (or allocated) to that department.
- Selling expenses, for example advertising, should be charged (or apportioned) to departments in the same proportions as their net sales.
- Administration expenses and general expenses are often apportioned on the basis of net sales.
- For other expenses, a suitable basis of apportionment should be used. For example, expenses of running the building, eg heating, lighting, rent, business rates, buildings insurance – might be apportioned on the basis of the floor area occupied by each department. Insurance premiums on the stock might be charged to departments on the basis of the average stock value.
- Interest may be charged to departments based on the estimated amount of capital employed by each department

Worked example

Question

Wyvern Superstore Ltd (see example in Section 27.2) has the following expenses for the year ended 31 December 19-1:

		£
Salaries:	Carpet department	25,000
	Clothes department	40,000
	Furniture department	20,000
Advertising		36,000
Administration		72,000
Rent and business rates		60,000
Heating and lighting		10,000

The expenses are to be apportioned as follows:

- advertising and administration – on the basis of sales
- rent and business rates, and heating and lighting – on the basis of floor area, which is carpets one-quarter, clothes one-quarter, and furniture one-half

Prepare the departmental profit and loss account for the year, commencing with the departmental gross profits from the example in Section 27.2, above.

Answer

WYVERN SUPERSTORE LTD
DEPARTMENTAL PROFIT AND LOSS ACCOUNT FOR THE YEAR ENDED 31 DECEMBER 19-1

	Carpet department		Clothes department		Furniture department		Total	
	£	£	£	£	£	£	£	£
Gross profit		95,000		180,000		45,000		320,000
Salaries	25,000		40,000		20,000		85,000	
Advertising	11,000		17,500		7,500		36,000	
Administration	22,000		35,000		15,000		72,000	
Rent and business rates	15,000		15,000		30,000		60,000	
Heating and lighting	2,500		2,500		5,000		10,000	
		75,500		110,000		77,500		263,000
Net profit/(loss)		19,500		70,000		(32,500)		57,000

Loss-making departments

When a departmental profit and loss account identifies a loss-making department, thoughts will inevitably turn towards closing that department in order to 'save' costs. However, the management needs to remember that, if the department is closed, there is unlikely to be a large reduction in profit and loss account expenses (or 'overheads') – rent and business rates, heating and lighting, and administration costs will continue to be paid and will have to be shared out amongst the remaining departments. Moreover, closing one department may well affect the sales of others: eg closing the furniture department of a store may result in reduced sales in the carpet department.

Faced with a loss-making department, the management should consider one of the following actions:

- keep the department open, identifying the reasons for the loss and correcting them
- close the department and expand other departments into its floor area
- look for a more profitable use of the floor area occupied by the poor-performing department
- lease the floor area to another business

27.4 Departmental balance sheets

While departmental trading and profit and loss accounts are often prepared, it is less common to prepare a departmental balance sheet. Where one is prepared, the assets and liabilities are shown divided between the two (or more) departments, with a total column. The capital section of the balance sheet, however, is not split between departments, but is shown in the total column only.

27.5 Joint ventures

A joint venture is defined as

an undertaking by which its participants expect to achieve some common purpose or benefit.

Those joining in a joint venture agree to contribute capital and/or skills, and to share profits and losses. It is, however, usually limited to one transaction, such as buying and selling an agreed quantity of goods. The main advantage of a joint venture is that it allows the benefits of a partnership, eg combined expertise and capital, for one transaction (or a limited number of transactions agreed at the outset). The main disadvantage of a joint venture is that it carries with it the unlimited liability of a partnership.

The accounting procedure for joint ventures is:

- Each person in the venture opens an account in his/her books entitled *joint venture with ... (name of the other person/persons)*
- This account is debited or credited with the transactions with which he or she is concerned
- Upon completion of the joint venture, each person submits a copy of the account to the one of them who has agreed to prepare a *joint venture memorandum account*
- This account, which is not part of the double-entry system, summarizes all the transactions that have taken place and shows the amount of profit or loss
- Each person transfers his/her share of the profit or loss to their own profit and loss account, respectively debiting or crediting the joint venture account
- Any balance remaining on one person's joint venture account will be settled in cash by the other person or persons, who will have an opposite balance on their accounts: this closes the joint venture accounts

Worked example

Question

Severn and Teme enter into a joint venture: Severn will buy certain goods and Teme will sell them. Profits and losses are to be shared equally. The following transactions take place:

Severn bought and paid for goods costing	£1,740
Severn paid storage costs	£165
Teme paid delivery costs	£135
Teme paid selling expenses	£200
Teme sold goods and received cash	£5,000

Prepare the joint venture accounts in the books of Severn and Teme, and the joint venture memorandum account.

Answer

Both parties will prepare the following accounts in their own records:

Books of Severn

Dr.	Joint Venture with Teme		Cr.
	£		£
Bank: purchases	1,740		
Bank: storage costs	165		

Books of Teme

Dr.	Joint Venture with Severn		Cr.
	£		£
Bank: delivery costs	135	Bank: sales	5,000
Bank: selling expenses	200		

After the goods have been sold and the venture completed, one of the parties in the venture will prepare the joint venture memorandum account as follows:

Joint Venture Memorandum Account: Severn and Teme

Dr.		£		Cr. £
Purchases		1,740	Sales	5,000
Storage costs		165		
Delivery costs		135		
Selling expenses		200		
Net profit:	Severn (one-half)	1,380		
	Teme (one-half)	1,380		
		5,000		5,000

Note: the joint venture memorandum account is *not* part of the double-entry system.

As each person's net profit is now known, it can be entered in their own accounts and the indebtedness between them settled. The joint venture accounts are completed as follows:

Books of Severn

Joint Venture with Teme

Dr.	£		Cr. £
Bank: purchases	1,740	Bank: from Teme in settlement	3,285
Bank: storage costs	165		
Profit and loss account: share of profit	1,380		
	3,285		3,285

Books of Teme

Joint Venture with Severn

Dr.	£		Cr. £
Bank: delivery costs	135	Bank: sales	5,000
Bank: selling expenses	200		
Profit and loss account: share of profit	1,380		
Bank: to Severn in settlement	3,285		
	5,000		5,000

In this example, Teme has paid £3,285 to Severn in settlement of the amount owing.

Note: Sometimes at the end of a joint venture there may be a few items remaining unsold. In these circumstances, it is quite usual for one of the parties to the venture to take the unsold items at an agreed price. The amount is recorded as a credit in the joint venture memorandum account, eg 'stock taken over by . . .' The person taking over the items will, in their own books:

— *debit* purchases account }
— *credit* joint venture account } with the agreed price

27.6 Consignment accounts

Where goods are sent by the owner to an agent to store and sell, a *consignment account* is used to record the accounting transactions. The two persons involved are:

- *consignor* — the owner of the goods
- *consignee* — the agent (who may be abroad) to whom the goods are sent

The goods remain the property of the consignor until they are sold; the consignee earns a commission. Sometimes the consignee agrees to be responsible for any bad debts arising from sales; in this case a higher commission is usually payable, known as *del credere* commission.

The consignor records each consignment in a separate consignment account and, where several agents are used, it is possible to see which agent sells the goods the fastest and has the lowest expenses.

As the goods do not belong to the consignee, they are not entered into his/her accounts, except to keep a record of sales. When the goods have been sold, the consignee sends the consignor an *account of sales* which details the gross sales value received by the agent, expenses in connection with the consignment, and the net amount that is being sent as payment.

Worked example

Question

Exporters Ltd employs an agent, Mrs P Singh in Bombay, India. One hundred cases of goods, which have cost the company £25 per case, are sent to Singh. The freight and insurance charges cost £125 and are paid by Exporters Ltd. Singh sells the goods for £40 per case; her selling costs are £75, and she is entitled to a commission of 10 per cent of the gross proceeds.

Show the account of sales sent by Singh to Exporters Ltd and record the transactions in the books of Exporters Ltd, and of Singh.

Answer

Account of Sales *by Mrs P Singh, Bombay, India*
Consignment of 100 cases of goods sold on behalf of Exporters Ltd

	£	£
Sales of 100 cases of goods at £40 per case		4,000
Less selling costs	75	
commission at 10 per cent	400	
		475
Net proceeds		3,525

Note: Singh pays this amount of money when she sends the account of sales to Exporters Ltd.

Books of Exporters Ltd

Dr.		Goods sent on Consignment	Cr.
	£		£
Trading account**	2,500	Consignment account: Singh*	2,500

Notes:

* Transaction recorded when the goods are sent to the agent

** Transfer to trading account made at the end of Exporters Ltd's financial year; this will appear in the trading account as:

Sales	£x
Goods sent on consignment	£2,500

Consignment Account: Singh

Dr.	£		Cr. £
Goods sent on consignment	2,500	Singh: sales	4,000
Bank: freight and insurance	125		
Singh:			
selling costs	75		
commission	400		
Profit and loss account	900		
	4,000		4,000

Mrs P Singh

Dr.	£		Cr. £
Consignment account: sales	4,000	Consignment account:	
		selling costs	75
		commission	400
		Bank	3,525
	4,000		4,000

The consignment account records the net profit – in this case £900 – and this is transferred direct to the profit and loss account as *profit (or loss) on consignments.*

Books of Singh

Exporters Ltd

Dr.	£		Cr. £
Selling costs	75	Bank receipts from sales (or debtors)	4,000
Commission received	400		
Bank: payment to Exporters Ltd	3,525		
	4,000		4,000

Commission Received

Dr.	£		Cr. £
		Exporters Ltd	400

Notes:

- The agent, Singh, does not record the sales in her own sales account, but in the account of Exporters Ltd.
- Selling costs will, likewise, not be shown in the agent's profit and loss account.
- The commission is the agent's gain, and will be transferred to her profit and loss account at the end of her financial year.
- If Singh is an 'ordinary' agent, any bad debts resulting from sales will be passed on to Exporters Ltd as a reduction in the amount paid. If she is a *del credere agent*, she must send the net amount of £3,525 to Exporters Ltd and stand any bad debts herself (in return for a higher commission), making the usual bad debt entries.

Unsold stock at the financial year-end

At the end of the financial year, some of the goods sent on consignment will probably be unsold. These goods must then be valued, and the profit earned on sales must be taken into the consignor's accounts. Stock on consignment, like the other stock of the business, is valued 'at the lower of cost and net realisable value' (see Chapter 16.4). Cost can include expenditure incurred in bringing the goods to their present location and condition, so freight and insurance charges, and some of the consignee's costs, can be added. To find out costs incurred, it is usual practice for the consignee to be asked to submit an interim account of sales, costs and commission at the end of the consignor's financial year. The valuation of unsold stock is brought down as a debit balance on the consignment account at the start of the next financial year.

Lost or damaged goods

Insured goods

When insured goods on consignment are lost or damaged, the accounting procedure is:

— *debit* insurance company account }
— *credit* consignment account } with the amount of the insurance claim

(When the insurance claim is settled, bank account is debited and the account in the name of the insurance company is credited.)

Uninsured goods

If the goods are not insured, no accounting entries need be made at all – the profit on the consignment will be reduced, or there may be a loss.

27.7 Chapter summary

- ❑ Departmental accounts are used to identify the gross and net profits of different departments or divisions within a business.
- ❑ Separate departmental trading and profit and loss accounts are prepared, although guidelines need to be established for charging expenses to each department.
- ❑ Management needs to make careful decisions about closing loss-making departments – in particular the overheads will have to be shared amongst the remaining departments.
- ❑ A joint venture is an undertaking by which its participants expect to achieve some common purpose or benefit.
- ❑ Joint venture profits are shared in an agreed way.
- ❑ Consignment accounts are used when the owner of goods (consignor) sends goods to an agent (consignee) for sale.
- ❑ The consignee submits an account of sales to the consignor.
- ❑ A consignment account is opened in the books of the consignor to record the transactions, including the profit or loss on the consignment.

In the next chapter we look at the different methods of calculating wages and salaries, including deductions for income tax and National Insurance Contributions.

27.8 Questions

27.1* Martin and Helen Jarvis own and manage a retail store under the trade name of 'Life & Leisure'. It is run as two departments: (G) Games, etc, managed by Martin, and (B) Books, etc, managed by Helen.

The following trial balance was extracted from the books of Life & Leisure at 31 March year 8, the accounting year end:

		£	£
Sales: G			240,000
B			360,000
Stock at cost at 1 April year 7:	G	42,000	
	B	14,000	
Purchases		422,600	
Sales expenses:	G	33,400	
	B	45,700	
Administrative expenses		7,300	
Establishment expenses (rates, insurance, etc)		16,600	
Advertising campaign		8,500	
Debtors		3,200	
Creditors			8,300
Bank and cash balances		14,900	
Ten year lease on business premises, at cost		66,000	
Fixtures and fittings, at cost		18,000	
Motor van at cost		9,000	
Provisions for depreciation at 1 April year 7:			
Amortisation* of lease			13,200
Fixtures and fittings			8,000
Motor van			3,600
Joint capitals at 1 April year 7			68,100
		701,200	701,200

* *Author's note: amortisation is the term used to depreciate a lease.*

The following additional information was available:

1. The analysis of purchases over the year had been inadequate and only an aggregate figure was available.
2. Gross profit as a percentage of sales is earned on average as follows: G 37%; B 24%.
3. Stock-in-hand, valued at cost, 31 March year 8: G £41,400; B £12,400.
4. Establishment expenses, administrative expenses, and cost of the advertising campaign were all to be apportioned in proportion to the sales of each department.
5. Establishment expenses prepaid at 31 March year 8: £400.
6. Sales expenses accrued at 31 March year 8: G £730; B £490.
7. Commission to sales staff was to be allowed in respect of each department, calculated as 4% of each department's gross profit.
8. Depreciation was to be provided as follows, based on the cost of the asset held at the year end:

   Fixtures and fittings — 15% per annum

   Motor van — 20% per annum
9. The fixed asset depreciation was to be apportioned to departments as follows:

	G	*B*
Lease on business premises	$^1/_2$	$^1/_2$
Fixtures and fittings	$^2/_5$	$^3/_5$
Motor van	$^4/_5$	$^1/_5$

Required:

(i) Prepare columnar departmental trading and profit and loss accounts for Life & Leisure for the year ended 31 March year 8.

(ii) (a) Calculate the ratio of aggregate net profit to the amount of capital at 1 April year 7.

(b) No provision has been made in the figures for a payment to either Martin or Helen for the time they have devoted over the year to managing the business. Explain *briefly* whether you consider this to be reasonable.

[London Chamber of Commerce]

27.2 Aire and Dovey entered into a joint venture for the purpose of purchasing and then selling the stock of a company in liquidation. This stock was acquired on 1 March for £105,000, of which Aire contributed £60,000 and Dovey contributed £45,000.

They agreed that profits (or losses) should be shared equally after charging interest at 12% per year on the amounts each venturer had contributed initially (for the period of the joint venture) and a commission of 10% in respect of each venturer's sales. All sales were to be made on a cash basis.

No joint venture bank account was opened.

Relevant transactions were as follows:

1 March	Dovey hired a market stall for £480
5 March	Dovey purchased a delivery van for £6,900
10 March	Aire incurred advertising expenses of £390
16 March	Aire collected £18,000 and Dovey collected £27,000, in respect of sales
7 April	Aire collected £60,000 and Dovey collected £22,500 in respect of sales
10 April	The delivery van broke down and, whilst it was being repaired, Aire agreed to use his own van for the joint venture at an agreed charge of £300
17 April	Dovey paid £1,290 in respect of expenses for the delivery van owned by the joint venture
24 April	Aire collected £7,500 and Dovey collected £12,600 in respect of sales
30 April	Dovey took over the delivery van for his own use at an agreed value of £5,000 and Aire took over the small amount of stock still remaining unsold at an agreed value of £2,620. The debt between the venturers was then settled in cash

Required:

(a) Prepare the memorandum joint venture account

(b) Prepare in Aire's books the joint venture with Dovey account

(c) Prepare in Dovey's books the joint venture with Aire account

(d) Briefly outline the advantages (and disadvantages) of such arrangements as compared with more formal partnership agreements.

[London Chamber of Commerce]

27.3 On 24 February 19-4, D Muir, a London trader, consigned 120 cases of goods to M Batts, an agent in Australia. The cost of the goods was £285 a case. D Muir paid carriage to the port of £2,350 and insurance amounting to £430.

On 31 March 19-4, D Muir received an account sales from M Batts showing that 100 cases had been sold for £35,000 and M Batts had paid freight, at the rate of £7 a case, and port charges amounting to £660. M Batts was entitled to a commission of 5 per cent on sales. A sight draft (cheque) for the net amount due was enclosed with the account sales.

You are required to show the accounts for the above transactions in the ledger of D Muir and to show the transfer to the profit and loss account at 31 March 19-4.

[Pitman Examinations Institute]

28 Wages and Salaries

In the chapter we will look at:

- the methods used to calculate pay
- employer's records of employees' attendance
- the compulsory and voluntary deductions made from pay
- Income tax, National Insurance Contributions and Statutory Sick Pay
- the preparation of a payslip
- payroll, including double-entry book-keeping
- methods of payment of wages and salaries

The income a person receives from being employed is often referred to in terms of 'wages' or 'salary'. Over the years a tradition has been established of describing them as follows:

- Wages: Payment made to manual employees normally working in the areas of production or service. Payment is made weekly and paid in cash or by transfer into the employees' bank or building society accounts.

- Salary: Payment made to non-manual employees normally working in the areas of administration and management. Payment is usually made monthly and paid directly into the employees' bank or building society accounts.

A further distinction is drawn between 'gross pay' and 'net pay'.

- Gross pay: Wages or salary paid by the employer *before* deductions are made.

- Net pay: The wages or salary actually received by the employee *after* compulsory and voluntary deductions.

28.1 Methods used to calculate pay

The methods used to calculate wages and salaries can vary between different employers and between different employees within the same company. The following methods are commonly used for calculating wages and salaries:

- *salary payment* – an agreed annual amount
- *time rate payment* – an hourly rate
- *basic rate plus bonus* – an incentive scheme based on productivity
- *piece rate payment* – based on the number of items produced
- *commission* – payment related to the sales achieved

Salary payment

An annual salary is agreed between employer and employee and an equivalent amount is either paid in weekly or monthly amounts.

Example:
Mr Harris, Production Manager, and Miss White, Receptionist, have just agreed new salaries with their employer. Mr Harris is to receive £24,000 per year, Miss White is to receive £8,320. Their gross pay (before deductions) is as follows:

Mr Harris, monthly paid, will earn £24,000 ÷ 12, ie £2,000 per month gross
Miss White, weekly paid, will earn £8,320 ÷ 52, ie £160 per week gross

Time rate payment

A payment rate for each hour worked is agreed and the employee will be paid according to the number of hours worked. It is common with this system to pay a higher rate of pay when an employee works overtime. Overtime is any time worked beyond what is normal for the working day, or time worked on a day not normally worked. A normal working week usually consists of five days, each of between seven and eight working hours.

Example:
Ron Bourne, a storekeeper, is paid at the rate of £5.00 per hour for an eight hour day, five days a week. Overtime is paid at the rate of time and a quarter (ie 1¼ x £5.00) for weekday work and time and a half (ie 1½ x £5.00) for weekend work. During one week Ron Bourne worked the following hours.

Monday	8 hours
Tuesday	9 hours
Wednesday	8 hours
Thursday	9 hours
Friday	8 hours
Saturday	4 hours

Ron's working hours for the week are therefore as follows:

Basic hourly rate 5 days x 8 hours	=	40 hours
Weekday overtime (Tuesday and Thursday)	=	2 hours
Weekend overtime (Saturday)	=	4 hours

Ron's gross pay for the week is worked out as follows:

Basic hourly rate (40 hours x £5.00)	=	£200.00
Weekday overtime (2 hours x £5.00 x 1¼)	=	£ 12.50
Weekend overtime (4 hours x £5.00 x 1½)	=	£ 30.00
Gross pay for week		£242.50

Basic rate bonus payment

Many businesses operate bonus schemes as an incentive to workers to reach and exceed set targets. An employer will fix the amount of work to be completed in a certain time; if the work target is exceeded, bonus payments will be paid. The bonus payment will be paid either individually to each worker based on his or her performance, or paid as an average bonus to every worker based on the amount by which the target has been exceeded. The bonus, often referred to as a 'productivity bonus', can be paid either as a specific amount of money or as a percentage of the basic pay.

Example:
If we suppose that Ron Bourne, in addition to receiving the gross pay of £242.50 calculated in the previous example, was awarded in that week a productivity bonus of 5% on basic pay. His gross pay will be increased by that bonus.

The bonus is calculated (on basic pay) as follows:

Basic weekly pay £200.00 x 5% = £10.00

His gross pay will therefore be:

Basic pay	£200.00
Weekly overtime	£12.50
Weekend overtime	£30.00
Bonus	£10.00
Gross pay for week	£252.50

Piece rate payments

Piece rate payment is another form of incentive to employees to work more quickly. The employer will agree a rate of pay for each article produced or operation completed and the employees will be paid only for the work that they have completed. Normally, however, there is an agreement between employer and employees that a minimum wage will be paid regardless of the work completed. An agreement of this nature is to provide the employee with a wage when the employer cannot provide work.

Example:
Fred Parry and Helen Morse work at Lowe Electronics which produces electronic alarms. The employer and employees have come to an agreement that piecework rates will be paid as follows:

- 'Red alert' alarm = £3.00 per unit
- 'Klaxon' alarm = £2.50 per unit

The company has also agreed a minimum of £120 per week.

During one week Fred worked hard and produced 80 'Red alert' alarms whereas Helen Morse had a machine breakdown and only managed 40 'Klaxon' alarms. Their gross pay for the week is:

Fred Parry:	80 x £3.00	=	£240
Helen Morse:	40 x £2.50 = £100, *but* because of £120 agreed minimum wage	=	£120

Commission

Commission payment is normally made to employees engaged in selling goods: the commission is usually paid as a percentage of the total sales made. Commission is usually paid in addition to a basic salary.

Example:
Jane Summers, Area Sales Manager of a mail order company, receives a basic £750 per month salary plus commission at the rate of 5% on all the sales in her area. During the past month her area sales were £20,000.

Her monthly pay is calculated as follows:

Basic + (total sales x commission rate) =
£750 + (£20,000 x 5%) =
£750 + £1,000 =
£1,750 per month

Other employee benefits

In addition to the payment of wages and salaries, employees may be offered other benefits, eg

- profit-sharing
- non-contributory pensions
- company car
- loans at favourable interest rates
- luncheon vouchers, or a subsidised canteen
- share ownership schemes

28.2 Records of attendance

In order that an employer can calculate wages, particularly where hourly paid workers are employed, a record of attendance must be kept. Employees' attendance records take a number of different forms which include the following:

- *time book* – a simple 'signing in' book
- *clock cards* – a card used in conjunction with a time 'clock'
- *time sheets* – records used by employees who work away from the premises
- *computerised 'clock cards'* – a card which records the hours on a computer

Time book

A 'time book' is often used in offices and is a simple ruled book in which staff enter against an allocated number:

- their time of arrival
- their signature
- their time of departure

Clock cards

With this method, each employee who works regularly on the business premises has a *clock card* (see fig. 28.1) which is kept in a rack next to a time recorder clock. On arrival at work, the employee removes the card from the 'out section' of the rack and inserts the card into the time recorder clock, which stamps the arrival time on the card in the appropriate place. The card is then removed from the time recorder clock and placed in the 'in section' of the rack indicating that the employee is at work. When the employee leaves work, the card is stamped in the recorder clock and then placed in the 'out section' rack ready for when she or he works the next shift.

The clock cards are used to calculate weekly wages by the wages department of the business which will be able to see the actual hours worked by each employee. Note that the employees' arrival and departure times will vary by a few minutes each day; the employer always allows a margin of lateness – often five minutes – before reducing pay.

MEREFORD CASTINGS LTD

Employee's name: J Hicks

Week ending: 20 January 19-9

Day	In	Out	In	Out	TOTAL HOURS
M	0801	1230	1331	1701	8.00
Tu	0755	1230	1330	1803	9.00
W	0800	1230	1330	1701	8.00
Th	0800	1230	1331	1800	9.00
F	0801	1230	1332	1704	8.00
Total					42.00

Fig. 28.1 An example of a clock card

Time sheets

This method is normally used by employees who work away from the business premises on contract work, or for hourly paid staff who do not 'clock in' with clock cards. The employee completes and signs his or her record of attendance on a specially prepared time sheet, indicating the hour of attendance each day. The foreman or supervisor in charge will normally check and sign the time sheet before it is passed to the wages department. A typical time sheet is shown in fig. 28.2. Note that time is split into three categories:

- time spent working
- time spent travelling
- time spent 'waiting' to do the job in hand, eg if a machine to be serviced is not immediately accessible to the travelling maintenance engineer

WYVERN INSTALLATIONS LTD

TIME SHEET (in hours)

Name .... **Works No** .... **Week ending** ....

Job	Mon	Tues	Wed	Thu	Fri	Sat	Sun
Sub-total							
Travel Waiting time							
Total							

Employee .... **Supervisor** .... **Date** ....

Fig. 28.2 An example of a time sheet

Computer cards

Employers using this method require staff to carry computer cards to and from their place of work and to insert the card in a computersied time clock on arrival or departure. This computerised system automatically records their hours of work.

This method of recording attendance is normally used by organisations who operate a flexitime system. Flexitime is a method that allows staff to arrive at work when they like and leave when they like, provided they are present during a prescribed 'core' time (say, between 10 am and 4 pm). Staff will still need to complete the normal number of hours per week but can arrange their own hours of attendance. With this system, it is also possible to carry forward time worked in excess of the normal time or time owed to the company provided the amount does not exceed a set figure.

Using the computer card system, the daily attendance hours are automatically calculated, totalled for the week and compared with the normal weekly figure. Wages for the week are worked out on the basis of the normal weekly figure.

28.3 Deductions from gross pay

As we saw earlier, *gross pay* is the total wage or salary earned by an employee. It is the basic amount plus any additional payments such as overtime and bonuses. The *net pay* is the amount the employee receives after the employer has made certain deductions.

There are a number of deductions an employer can make from gross pay. Some are compulsory and some are voluntary.

Compulsory deductions

An employer will deduct the following government taxes:

- Income Tax
- National Insurance Contributions

Income tax is collected by the *Inland Revenue*. National Insurance Contributions are collected by the Inland Revenue on behalf of the Department of Social Security.

The compulsory deductions are explained more fully in the following sections.

Voluntary deductions

An employer may make certain voluntary deductions on the authority of the employee. For example:

- pensions/superannuation scheme payments*
- union subscriptions*
- payments to charity* (if the employer operates a voluntary payroll giving scheme)
- payments to savings schemes
- repayment of loans

* payments or contributions to these may be deducted from income before tax is calculated

28.4 Income tax

Income tax is a tax on the income received by an individual. 'Income' for tax purposes includes pay, tips, bonuses, and benefits in kind (eg company car, cheap loans), pensions, most state benefits, and interest and dividends from investments.

For a person in employment, income tax is deducted by the employer from gross pay by means of a scheme known as PAYE (Pay As You Earn). This scheme, as its title suggests, enables taxation to be spread evenly over the year instead of in one amount at the end of the tax year.

Taxable income: the personal allowance

Income which is liable to tax is known as *taxable income*. Taxable income is calculated by deducting the personal allowance from gross income.

Employees do not, fortunately, have to pay tax on all their income. The government gives a *personal allowance*, an amount which can be earned during the tax year (6 April - 5 April), on which no tax is paid at all.

The personal allowance, which is announced by the Chancellor of the Exchequer in his annual budget, is normally increased in line with inflation each year, and is fixed for each tax year. The amount of the personal allowance varies, depending on factors such as whether you are single or married, or over a certain age. The two most common personal allowances, for the tax year from 6 April 1997 to 5 April 1998 are:

- personal allowance £4,045
- married couple's allowance (additional to the personal allowance, and claimed by one partner) £1,830

Income tax calculations

It is the responsibility of the employer to see that the employee pays the right amount of tax through the PAYE system.

There are three rates of income tax applicable to taxable income (for the tax year 1997/98):

- Lower Rate Tax: 20%, charged on the first £4,100 of taxable income
- Basic Rate Tax: 23%, charged on the remaining taxable income up to £26,100
- Higher Rate Tax: 40%, charged on taxable income above £26,100

If a person receives taxable income that exceeds £26,100, that person has to pay income tax at 20% on the first £4,100 of taxable income, 23% on the next £22,000, and 40% *on the excess*.

If we take two employees of the same organisation, an unmarried accounts clerk earning £10,000 gross per year and an unmarried financial controller earning £40,000 per year, it is straightforward to work out how much income tax they pay. Remember that taxable income in each case is gross income less the personal allowance of £4,045.

	Accounts clerk		Financial controller	
		£		£
Gross income		10,000.00		40,000.00
less personal allowance		4,045.00		4,045.00
Taxable income		5,955.00		35,955.00
Income tax @ 20%	£4,100 @ 20% =	820.00	£4,100 @ 20% =	820.00
Income tax @ 23%	£1,855 @ 23% =	426.65	£22,000 @ 23% =	5,060.00
Income tax @ 40%		nil	£9,855 @ 40% =	3,942.00
TOTAL INCOME TAX PAYABLE		1,246.65		9,822.00

These tax calculations cannot, however, be taken in isolation, as the employer will also deduct National Insurance Contributions, and the Inland Revenue may make further adjustments by means of a *tax code*.

28.5 Tax codes and allowances

Additional allowances

The Inland Revenue, as well as granting the personal allowance, gives additional allowances against tax. These could include expenses incurred in employment, professional subscriptions, and clothing and specialist equipment used when working.

The allowance system works so that earnings spent on these items up to the amount of the appropriate allowance will not be subject to income tax.

Allowance restrictions

The Inland Revenue restricts the married couple's allowance (and certain other allowances, but not the personal allowance) so that it is worth the same to all taxpayers. In 1997/98 the married couple's allowance was restricted to 15 per cent, so that it was worth £274.50 (£1,830 at 15%) to all taxpayers, regardless of the rate at which tax is paid. The amount of allowance restrictions (if any) is deducted by the Inland Revenue from the total allowances when calculating the taxpayer's tax code.

Calculation of the tax code

So that the employer knows what allowances have been given to the employee and how much tax to deduct the Inland Revenue gives each employee a *tax code*, a number which is used by the employer to calculate the taxable pay. The tax code incorporates *all* the tax allowances, including the personal allowance less allowance restrictions (if any).

Typical allowances for an unmarried factory worker would be:

Personal allowance	£4,045
Allowance for work clothing	£ 50
Total allowances	£4,095

During the tax year the employee can earn £4,095 which will not be subject to Income Tax. The tax code will be 409, the amount of the total allowances less the last digit. The code will be followed by a letter, the two most common of which are:

L = a Lower code incorporating the basic personal allowance

H = a Higher code incorporating the married couple's allowance

In the case of this factory worker the full code will be 409L.

When the Inland Revenue has allocated the tax code to the employee, the tax is, in principle, easy to calculate. Take, for example, the factory worker with the code referred to above, who earns £12,000 a year.

Gross annual pay	£12,000
Less allowances (code 409L - see above)	£ 4,090
Taxable annual pay	£ 7,910

Tax payable for the year	= £4,100 @ 20%	=	£820.00
	£3,810 @ 23%	=	£ 876.30
			£1,696.30

The employer's task of collecting the tax on a weekly or a monthly basis is less simple. What happens for instance if an unmarried employee starts work, for the first time, halfway through the tax year? No tax will be payable, unless the employee earns over £4,045, ie the personal allowance, in that year. How is the employer to know how much to deduct, and when? The Inland Revenue makes the calculation of tax on a weekly or monthly basis possible for the employer through the PAYE system. The workings of the PAYE system are illustrated in the example in Section 28.7.

28.6 National Insurance Contributions and Statutory Sick Pay

National Insurance Contributions

Both the employer and the employee have to pay Class 1 National Insurance Contributions (NIC) when an employee earns over a certain amount (the 'lower earnings limit'). The employer will have to pay to the Inland Revenue the employee's National Insurance Contributions by deducting it from his or her pay through the PAYE system.

Payment of National Insurance enables the employee in time of need to claim benefits from the State such as retirement pension and sickness benefits.

The amounts payable, for example, for an employee earning between £62.00 and £109.99 per week are: employee 2% on earnings up to £62 and 10% on earnings from £62 to £109.99; employer 3.0% of gross pay. *No* National Insurance is payable by the employee if earnings are less than £62.00 a week and *no* National Insurance Contributions are payable by the employee on any earnings *above* £465 a week. The employer has to pay National Insurance on *all* gross earnings.

The National Insurance 'not contracted-out' rates (which are commonly used) are set out below. Tables for the calculation of the rates are available from the Department of Social Security.

National Insurance Contributions (1997/98)

Total weekly earnings	Employee	Employer
Under £62	Nil	Nil
£62 to £109.99	2% on earnings up to £62, plus 10% on earnings between £62 and £465	3.0%
£110 to £154.99		5.0%
£155 to £209.99		7.0%
£210 to £465		10.0%
over £465	2% on £62 and 10% on £403	10.0%

Statutory Sick Pay

Statutory Sick Pay (SSP) is a payment an employer normally makes to employees when they are ill, for the first twenty-eight weeks of sickness (but *not* for the first three days of illness). SSP is treated like any other earnings for tax and National Insurance Contributions.

Statutory Maternity Pay (SMP) is payable for up to eighteen weeks. An employer is able to recover 92 per cent (for 1997/98) of the amounts paid in SMP by deducting it from the total of National Insurance Contributions and income tax paid over to the Inland Revenue each month. (Small employers can recover 100 per cent of the SMP paid, and also claim 6.5 per cent to compensate for the employer's National Insurance Contributions paid on SMP.)

28.7 Wages calculation: worked example

Question

Bill Baker has just started work as a trainee storekeeper at May's, a mail order company. His terms of employment are a 40 hour week at £4.00 per hour and a rate of time-and-a-half for overtime. His employer uses a clock card system for recording time worked. He is paid on a weekly basis. His tax code is 404L.

Bill started work in April 1997 and worked the following hours in the first fortnight:

week beginning 6 April 40 hours normal rate

week beginning 13 April 40 hours normal rate plus 8 hours at overtime rate

How does May's, work out Bill's take-home ('net') pay for the first two weeks?

Answer

His employer has a number of basic documents to work from. All of these, except for the clock card, are provided by the Inland Revenue:

- **Bill's clock card** showing the hours worked (not illustrated)
- **P11 deduction sheet** on which to work out all the calculations for tax deductions from gross pay (illustrated in fig. 28.3)
- **National Insurance Contributions 'Table A'** (extract not illustrated)
- **Pay Adjustment Tables** showing the employer how much pay, depending on Bill's tax code, is *not* subject to Income Tax (extract illustrated in fig. 28.4)
- **Taxable Pay Tables** showing the employer how much tax is payable on Bill's taxable income (illustrated in fig. 28.5), used in conjunction with the **Subtraction Tables** (extract illustrated in fig. 28.4)

The basis of the calculation is the P11 deduction sheet (fig. 28.3) and we will see how this is completed, first with the Income Tax calculations and, secondly, with the National Insurance calculations.

Income tax calculations: week one

1. Calculate gross pay for week one

Establish how much gross pay Bill has earned:

Hours worked x rate per hour = gross pay

40 x £4.00 = £160.00

Enter £160.00 in column 2 (pay for the week) of the deduction sheet
Enter £160.00 also in column 3 (total pay to date, ie £160.00)

2. Calculate free pay to date

Calculate the free pay, ie untaxed pay, from the Pay Adjustment Table on the page for week 1 (April 6 to April 12)

Locate Bill's tax code of 404 and read off total free pay of £77.87

Enter £77.87 in column 4a of the deduction sheet

3. Calculate taxable pay to date

Deduct total free pay from the gross pay to date (column 3 minus column 4)

In this case, £160.00 – £77.87 = £82.13

Enter £82.13, the taxable pay, in column 5 of the deduction sheet

4. Calculate tax due to date

Select Table B (tax at 23%) of the Taxable Pay tables, and find the tax due on £82 (pence are ignored). This is shown as £18.86

This figure, which shows tax at 23%, now has to be adjusted for the amount of taxable pay taxed at 20%. This is done by deducting from it the figure shown in Table B (Subtraction Tables) under 'Weekly Pay' for week no 1, ie £2.37: the calculation is £18.86 – £2.37 = £16.49

Enter £16.49 in column 6 ('tax due to date') of the deduction sheet

As this is the first week at work for Bill, this 'tax due to date' is also the tax for week one

Enter £16.49 in column 7

Normally at this stage Bill's employer will work out his National Insurance Contribution. We will explain this shortly, but first we will see how the Income Tax is worked out for week two, because the employer will need to base the calculations on the figures for week one.

Income tax calculations: week two

1. Calculate gross pay for week two

As Bill worked eight hours overtime in the second week his gross pay will be as follows:

Normal rate:	40 hours x £4.00	=	£160.00
Overtime rate:	8 hours x £6.00	=	£ 48.00
Total gross pay		=	£208.00

Enter £208.00 in column 2 of the deduction sheet in the line for week 2
Enter £208.00 + £160.00 (last week's pay) = £368.00, in column 3 ('Total pay to date')

2. Calculate free pay to date (week 2)

The figure will be obtained from the Pay Adjustment Table for week 2. In this case, free pay to date against Bill's code of 404 is £155.74. 'Free pay to date' means the amount of money Bill has earned since he started on which he does not have to pay tax.

Enter £155.74 in column 4a of the deduction sheet

3. Calculate taxable pay to date (week 2)

As in week one, deduct free pay to date from total pay to date (column 3 minus column 4a), ie £368 – £155.74 = £212.26

Enter £212.26 in column 5 of the deduction sheet

4. Calculate tax due to date (week 2)

Select Table B (tax at 23%) of the Taxable Pay Tables, and find the tax due on £212 (pence are ignored). As £212 is not shown, the tax is calculated by combining together figures which add up to £212, ie £200 and £12:

	taxable pay	*tax due*
	£200	£46.00
plus	£ 12	£ 2.76
equals	£212	£48.76

This figure of £48.76, which shows tax at 23%, now has to be adjusted for the amount of taxable pay taxed at 20%. This is done by deducting from it the figure shown in Table B (Subtraction Tables) under 'Weekly Pay' for week no 2, ie £4.74: the calculation is £48.76 – £4.74 = £44.02

Enter £44.02 in column 6 ('tax due to date') of the deduction sheet

Note that this tax figure is the 'total due to date'; some of it was paid in week one

5. Calculate the tax due for week two

As £16.49 of the tax 'due to date' was paid in week one, tax for week two is calculated as follows:

Total tax due to date minus tax paid to date, ie £44.02 minus £16.49 = £27.53

Enter £27.53 in column 7 of the deduction sheet

Thus both pay and tax are worked out, paid and deducted, on a week-by-week basis. This is how the Pay As You Earn (PAYE) system gets its name.

As mentioned earlier, the employer will also work out on the same deduction sheet Bill's National Insurance Contributions on a weekly basis. This calculation, explained below, is a completely separate process and is an additional deduction from Bill's gross earnings.

Deductions Working Sheet P11 Year to 5 April 1998

Employer's name: MAYS MAIL ORDER

Tax Office and reference: MEREFORD 777/M339E

National Insurance contributions

For guidance on National Insurance and the completion of columns 1a to 1h see CA27 Quick Reference Cards

For guidance on Statutory Sick Pay figures see leaflet CA30

For guidance on Statutory Maternity Pay figures see leaflet CA29

or contact Social Security Advice Line for Employers - telephone number is in CA27 Quick Reference Cards

At the top of each section in the NI Tables there is a letter, for example *A, B, C, D* or *E*. Copy that letter from the Table you use to the box bottom left overleaf - see ▼ overleaf. If the employee's circumstances change part way through a year the letter may change as well. Record all letters with separate totals for each table letter used. Remember to record under letter *Y* any Class 1a on the last line of the box at ▼.
See the *CA27 Quick Reference Cards* for further information and examples

Earnings recorded in column 1a should not exceed the Upper Earnings Limit

For employer's use	Earnings on which employee's contributions payable *Whole pounds only* 1a £	Total of employee's and employer's contributions payable 1b £	Employee's contributions payable 1c £	Earnings on which employee's contributions at contracted-out rate payable included in col. 1a *Whole pounds only* 1d £	Employee's contributions at contracted-out rate included in column 1c 1e £	Statutory Sick Pay in the week or month included in column 2 1f £	Statutory Maternity Pay in the week or month included in column 2 1g £	Statutory Maternity Pay recovered 1h £	Month no
	160	22 32	11 09						
	208	30 48	15 89						
									1

Employee's surname *in CAPITALS*: BAKER

First two forenames: WILLIAM JOHN

National Insurance no.: AB 60 21 94 A

Date of birth *in figures*: Day 21 Month 08 Year 80

Works no. etc: 1049317

Date of starting *in figures*: Day 02 Month 04 Year 97

Date of leaving *in figures*: Day Month Year

Tax code †: 404L

Amended code †

Wk/Mth in which applied

PAYE Income Tax

For guidance on completing this form see P8 'Employer's Basic Guide to PAYE'

- *Card 6 for general completion*
- *Card 6a specifically for K codes*
- *Card 7 for examples using suffix and K codes*

Week no	Pay in the week or month including Statutory Sick Pay Statutory Maternity Pay 2 £	Total pay to date 3 £	Total free pay to date (Table A) 4a £	K codes only: Total 'additional pay' to date (Table A) 4b £	Total taxable pay to date i.e. column 3 *minus* column 4a or column 3 *plus* column 4b 5 £	Total tax due to date as shown by Taxable Pay Tables 6 £	K codes only: Tax due at end of current period Mark refunds 'R' 6a £	K codes only: Regulatory limit i.e. 50% of column 2 entry 6b £	Tax deducted or refunded in the week or month. Mark refunds 'R' 7 £	K codes only: Tax not deducted owing to the Regulatory limit 8 £	For employer's use
1	160 -	160 -	77 87		82 13	16 49			16 49		
2	208 -	368 -	155 74		212 26	44 02			27 53		
3											
4											

Fig 28.3 P11 Deduction Sheet for Bill Baker (extract)

Note: for ease of illustration this form has been divided in half; in reality the sheet is horizontal in format – Income Tax and National Insurance Contributions would appear on one line for each week. The columns for K codes are used when the Inland Revenue issues the employee with a K code, ie taxable benefits such as a company car exceed allowances and extra taxable pay has to be entered into the calculation.

TABLE A - PAY ADJUSTMENT

WEEK 1
Apr 6 to Apr 12

Code	Total pay adjustment to date	Code	Total pay adjustment to date	Code	Total pay adjustment to date	Code	Total pay adjustment to date	Code	Total pay adjustment to date	Code	Total pay adjustment to date	Code	Total pay adjustment to date	Code	Total pay adjustment to date	Code	Total pay adjustment to date
	£		£		£		£		£		£		£		£		£
0	**NIL**																
1	0.37	**61**	11.91	**121**	23.45	**181**	34.99	**241**	46.52	**301**	58.06	**351**	67.68	**401**	77.29	**451**	86.91
2	0.56	**62**	12.10	**122**	23.64	**182**	35.18	**242**	46.72	**302**	58.25	**352**	67.87	**402**	77.49	**452**	87.10
3	0.75	**63**	12.29	**123**	23.83	**183**	35.37	**243**	46.91	**303**	58.45	**353**	68.06	**403**	77.68	**453**	87.29
4	0.95	**64**	12.49	**124**	24.02	**184**	35.56	**244**	47.10	**304**	58.64	**354**	68.25	**404**	77.87	**454**	87.49
5	1.14	**65**	12.68	**125**	24.22	**185**	35.75	**245**	47.29	**305**	58.83	**355**	68.45	**405**	78.06	**455**	87.68
6	1.33	**66**	12.87	**126**	24.41	**186**	35.95	**246**	47.49	**306**	59.02	**356**	68.64	**406**	78.25	**456**	87.87
7	1.52	**67**	13.06	**127**	24.60	**187**	36.14	**247**	47.68	**307**	59.22	**357**	68.83	**407**	78.45	**457**	88.06
8	1.72	**68**	13.25	**128**	24.79	**188**	36.33	**248**	47.87	**308**	59.41	**358**	69.02	**408**	78.64	**458**	88.25
9	1.91	**69**	13.45	**129**	24.99	**189**	36.52	**249**	48.06	**309**	59.60	**359**	69.22	**409**	78.83	**459**	88.45
10	2.10	**70**	13.64	**130**	25.18	**190**	36.72	**250**	48.25	**310**	59.79	**360**	69.41	**410**	79.02	**460**	88.64

Week 2
Apr 13 to Apr 19

TABLE A - PAY ADJUSTMENT

Code	Total pay adjustment to date	Code	Total pay adjustment to date	Code	Total pay adjustment to date	Code	Total pay adjustment to date	Code	Total pay adjustment to date	Code	Total pay adjustment to date	Code	Total pay adjustment to date	Code	Total pay adjustment to date	Code	Total pay adjustment to date
	£		£		£		£		£		£		£		£		£
0	**NIL**																
1	0.74	**61**	23.82	**121**	46.90	**181**	69.98	**241**	93.04	**301**	116.12	**351**	135.36	**401**	154.58	**451**	173.82
2	1.12	**62**	24.20	**122**	47.28	**182**	70.36	**242**	93.44	**302**	116.50	**352**	135.74	**402**	154.98	**452**	174.20
3	1.50	**63**	24.58	**123**	47.66	**183**	70.74	**243**	93.82	**303**	116.90	**353**	136.12	**403**	155.36	**453**	174.58
4	1.90	**64**	24.98	**124**	48.04	**184**	71.12	**244**	94.20	**304**	117.28	**354**	136.50	**404**	155.74	**454**	174.98
5	2.28	**65**	25.36	**125**	48.44	**185**	71.50	**245**	94.58	**305**	117.66	**355**	136.90	**405**	156.12	**455**	175.36
6	2.66	**66**	25.74	**126**	48.82	**186**	71.90	**246**	94.98	**306**	118.04	**356**	137.28	**406**	156.50	**456**	175.74
7	3.04	**67**	26.12	**127**	49.20	**187**	72.28	**247**	95.36	**307**	118.44	**357**	137.66	**407**	156.90	**457**	176.12
8	3.44	**68**	26.50	**128**	49.58	**188**	72.66	**248**	95.74	**308**	118.82	**358**	138.04	**408**	157.28	**458**	176.50
9	3.82	**69**	26.90	**129**	49.98	**189**	73.04	**249**	96.12	**309**	119.20	**359**	138.44	**409**	157.66	**459**	176.90
10	4.20	**70**	27.28	**130**	50.36	**190**	73.44	**250**	96.50	**310**	119.58	**360**	138.82	**410**	158.04	**460**	177.28

Table B Subtraction Tables

(Lower Rate Relief)

Do not use the subtraction tables for code BR

For all ordinary suffix codes and prefix K codes - When you have used the table on Page 6 to work out the tax at 23% refer to the tables below to give the benefit of the lower rate band. Find the week or month in which the pay day falls (it is the same week or month you have used in Tables A) and **subtract** the amount shown to arrive at the tax due.

There is an example below and further examples on Page 8

Employee paid at Weekly rates

Week No.	Amount to subtract
	£
1	2.37
2	4.74
3	7.10
4	9.47

Employee paid at Monthly rates

Month No.	Amount to subtract
	£
1	10.25
2	20.50
3	30.75
4	41.00

Fig 28.4 Pay Adjustment and Subtraction Tables (extracts)—Crown copyright

Pages 2 and 3 tell you when to use these tables

Table B

(Tax at 23%)

Remember to use the Subtraction Tables on Page 7

Tax Due on Taxable Pay from £1 to £99

Total TAXABLE PAY to date	Total TAX DUE to date	Total TAXABLE PAY to date	Total TAX DUE to date
£	£	£	£
1	0.23	56	12.88
2	0.46	57	13.11
3	0.69	58	13.34
4	0.92	59	13.57
5	1.15	60	13.80
6	1.38	61	14.03
7	1.61	62	14.26
8	1.84	63	14.49
9	2.07	64	14.72
10	2.30	65	14.95
11	2.53	66	15.18
12	2.76	67	15.41
13	2.99	68	15.64
14	3.22	69	15.87
15	3.45	70	16.10
16	3.68	71	16.33
17	3.91	72	16.56
18	4.14	73	16.79
19	4.37	74	17.02
20	4.60	75	17.25
21	4.83	76	17.48
22	5.06	77	17.71
23	5.29	78	17.94
24	5.52	79	18.17
25	5.75	80	18.40
26	5.98	81	18.63
27	6.21	82	18.86
28	6.44	83	19.09
29	6.67	84	19.32
30	6.90	85	19.55
31	7.13	86	19.78
32	7.36	87	20.01
33	7.59	88	20.24
34	7.82	89	20.47
35	8.05	90	20.70
36	8.28	91	20.93
37	8.51	92	21.16
38	8.74	93	21.39
39	8.97	94	21.62
40	9.20	95	21.85
41	9.43	96	22.08
42	9.66	97	22.31
43	9.89	98	22.54
44	10.12	99	22.77
45	10.35		
46	10.58		
47	10.81		
48	11.04		
49	11.27		
50	11.50		
51	11.73		
52	11.96		
53	12.19		
54	12.42		
55	12.65		

Where the exact amount of taxable pay is not shown, add together the figures for two (or more) entries to make up the amount of taxable pay to the nearest £1 below

Tax Due on Taxable Pay from £100 to £26,100

Total TAXABLE PAY to date	Total TAX DUE to date	Total TAXABLE PAY to date	Total TAX DUE to date	Total TAXABLE PAY to date	Total TAX DUE to date	Total TAXABLE PAY to date	Total TAX DUE to date
£	£	£	£	£	£	£	£
100	23.00	6600	1518.00	13100	3013.00	19600	4508.00
200	46.00	6700	1541.00	13200	3036.00	19700	4531.00
300	69.00	6800	1564.00	13300	3059.00	19800	4554.00
400	92.00	6900	1587.00	13400	3082.00	19900	4577.00
500	115.00	7000	1610.00	13500	3105.00	20000	4600.00
600	138.00	7100	1633.00	13600	3128.00	20100	4623.00
700	161.00	7200	1656.00	13700	3151.00	20200	4646.00
800	184.00	7300	1679.00	13800	3174.00	20300	4669.00
900	207.00	7400	1702.00	13900	3197.00	20400	4692.00
1000	230.00	7500	1725.00	14000	3220.00	20500	4715.00
1100	253.00	7600	1748.00	14100	3243.00	20600	4738.00
1200	276.00	7700	1771.00	14200	3266.00	20700	4761.00
1300	299.00	7800	1794.00	14300	3289.00	20800	4784.00
1400	322.00	7900	1817.00	14400	3312.00	20900	4807.00
1500	345.00	8000	1840.00	14500	3335.00	21000	4830.00
1600	368.00	8100	1863.00	14600	3358.00	21100	4853.00
1700	391.00	8200	1886.00	14700	3381.00	21200	4876.00
1800	414.00	8300	1909.00	14800	3404.00	21300	4899.00
1900	437.00	8400	1932.00	14900	3427.00	21400	4922.00
2000	460.00	8500	1955.00	15000	3450.00	21500	4945.00
2100	483.00	8600	1978.00	15100	3473.00	21600	4968.00
2200	506.00	8700	2001.00	15200	3496.00	21700	4991.00
2300	529.00	8800	2024.00	15300	3519.00	21800	5014.00
2400	552.00	8900	2047.00	15400	3542.00	21900	5037.00
2500	575.00	9000	2070.00	15500	3565.00	22000	5060.00
2600	598.00	9100	2093.00	15600	3588.00	22100	5083.00
2700	621.00	9200	2116.00	15700	3611.00	22200	5106.00
2800	644.00	9300	2139.00	15800	3634.00	22300	5129.00
2900	667.00	9400	2162.00	15900	3657.00	22400	5152.00
3000	690.00	9500	2185.00	16000	3680.00	22500	5175.00
3100	713.00	9600	2208.00	16100	3703.00	22600	5198.00
3200	736.00	9700	2231.00	16200	3726.00	22700	5221.00
3300	759.00	9800	2254.00	16300	3749.00	22800	5244.00
3400	782.00	9900	2277.00	16400	3772.00	22900	5267.00
3500	805.00	10000	2300.00	16500	3795.00	23000	5290.00
3600	828.00	10100	2323.00	16600	3818.00	23100	5313.00
3700	851.00	10200	2346.00	16700	3841.00	23200	5336.00
3800	874.00	10300	2369.00	16800	3864.00	23300	5359.00
3900	897.00	10400	2392.00	16900	3887.00	23400	5382.00
4000	920.00	10500	2415.00	17000	3910.00	23500	5405.00
4100	943.00	10600	2438.00	17100	3933.00	23600	5428.00
4200	966.00	10700	2461.00	17200	3956.00	23700	5451.00
4300	989.00	10800	2484.00	17300	3979.00	23800	5474.00
4400	1012.00	10900	2507.00	17400	4002.00	23900	5497.00
4500	1035.00	11000	2530.00	17500	4025.00	24000	5520.00
4600	1058.00	11100	2553.00	17600	4048.00	24100	5543.00
4700	1081.00	11200	2576.00	17700	4071.00	24200	5566.00
4800	1104.00	11300	2599.00	17800	4094.00	24300	5589.00
4900	1127.00	11400	2622.00	17900	4117.00	24400	5612.00
5000	1150.00	11500	2645.00	18000	4140.00	24500	5635.00
5100	1173.00	11600	2668.00	18100	4163.00	24600	5658.00
5200	1196.00	11700	2691.00	18200	4186.00	24700	5681.00
5300	1219.00	11800	2714.00	18300	4209.00	24800	5704.00
5400	1242.00	11900	2737.00	18400	4232.00	24900	5727.00
5500	1265.00	12000	2760.00	18500	4255.00	25000	5750.00
5600	1288.00	12100	2783.00	18600	4278.00	25100	5773.00
5700	1311.00	12200	2806.00	18700	4301.00	25200	5796.00
5800	1334.00	12300	2829.00	18800	4324.00	25300	5819.00
5900	1357.00	12400	2852.00	18900	4347.00	25400	5842.00
6000	1380.00	12500	2875.00	19000	4370.00	25500	5865.00
6100	1403.00	12600	2898.00	19100	4393.00	25600	5888.00
6200	1426.00	12700	2921.00	19200	4416.00	25700	5911.00
6300	1449.00	12800	2944.00	19300	4439.00	25800	5934.00
6400	1472.00	12900	2967.00	19400	4462.00	25900	5957.00
6500	1495.00	13000	2990.00	19500	4485.00	26000	5980.00
						26100	6003.00

Fig 28.5 Taxable Pay Tables (used in conjunction with the Subtraction Tables – see fig 28.4) – Crown copyright

National Insurance Contributions

Both Bill and his employer will pay National Insurance Contributions. In this case, the contributions are 'not contracted-out'. As you will see from the illustration of the P11 deduction sheet (fig. 28.3) there are columns for:

- earnings on which contributions are calculated – column 1a
- total of employer's and employee contributions – column 1b
- employee's contribution - column 1c

The figures for these columns should be copied from columns 1a, 1b, and 1c of the Table A National Insurance Contributions tables (not illustrated) which are available from the Department of Social Security; alternatively they can be calculated on a percentage basis. The figures are as follows:

	column 1a (earnings)	*column 1b (contributions of both employer and employee)*	*column 1c (employee's contribution)*
	£	£	£
week one	160	22.32	11.09
week two	208	30.48	15.89

Note that none of the figures in column 1a of Table A includes pence. If the gross earnings include pence, they are to be ignored.

Bill's net pay calculation

	Week One		Week Two	
	£	£	£	£
Gross Pay		160.00		208.00
Deductions				
Income Tax	16.49		27.53	
National Insurance	11.09		15.89	
Total Deductions		27.58		43.42
Net Pay		132.42		164.58

The table set out above summarises the deductions made from Bill's gross pay and shows his net pay. Bill's employer would set out this information in full each week on a *payslip* (see Section 28.8).

The tax and National Insurance Contributions collected by May's through the PAYE system will be paid to the Inland Revenue, together with the employer's National Insurance Contributions by the 19th of the *next* month.

28.8 Payslip

An employer normally gives each employee details of earnings and deductions when a wage or salary payment is made. This information is presented in the form of a payslip which shows:

- name of employee
- department and/or works number
- current tax code for employee
- basic pay
- overtime and/or bonus payments
- total gross pay (ie basic pay, plus overtime/bonus)
- details of compulsory deductions, ie income tax, national insurance contributions
- details of voluntary deductions, ie pension schemes, union fees, donations to charity
- cumulative totals (since the beginning of the tax year on 6 April) of gross pay, income tax and National Insurance Contributions.

A specimen pay slip for Bill Baker for the week ending 18 April 1997 (see calculations in Section 28.7) is illustrated as follows:

Company:	**Mays Mail Order**		Pay Advice
Payments		**Deductions**	
	£		£
Basic Pay	160.00	Income Tax	27.53
Overtime	48.00	National Insurance	15.89
Bonus	-	TOTAL DEDUCTIONS	43.42
TOTAL GROSS	208.00	NET PAY	164.58
Gross pay to date	368.00	Income Tax to date	44.02
Taxable Pay to date	212.26	National Insurance to date	26.98
Date	**Employee's name**	**Tax Code**	**Tax Period**
18 Apr. 1997	W.J. Baker	404L	week 2

28.9 Payroll

At the end of each week or month, an employer prepares a list of the earnings, deductions and net pay of each employee. This list is known as the *payroll,* and is the master internal record for these items. A typical payroll showing the pay calculations for five employees of Bright Kitchens Ltd is illustrated in fig. 28.5.

Payroll details can be either recorded manually on specially ruled payroll sheets, or can be entered and stored on computer disk (see Chapter 10.9).

Bright Kitchens Ltd		Week ending: 21 July 19-1								Week Number: 16	
Work Number	Name	Earnings				Deductions				Employer's National Insurance Contributions	Net Pay
		Basic £	Overtime £	Bonus £	Total Gross Pay £	PAYE (Income Tax) £	National Insurance £	Pension Contribution £	Total Deductions £	£	£
111	P. Waite	220.00	20.50	15.00	255.50	32.75	19.35	15.33	67.43	26.57	188.07
112	D. Land	220.00	–	15.00	235.00	37.50	17.55	14.10	69.15	24.49	165.85
113	A. Brooks	220.00	40.90	15.00	275.90	47.00	21.15	16.55	84.70	28.65	191.20
114	G. Johnson	220.00	40.90	15.00	275.90	39.50	21.15	16.55	77.20	28.65	198.70
115	S. Barber	220.00	10.25	15.00	245.25	38.25	18.45	14.71	71.41	25.53	173.84
116	T. Lord	220.00	20.50	15.00	255.50	30.50	19.35	15.33	65.18	26.57	190.32
	TOTALS	1,320.00	133.05	90.00	1,543.05	225.50	117.00	92.57	435.07	160.46	1,107.98

Fig. 28.5 Payroll: Employees paid weekly in cash

The payroll, as well as acting as a permanent record, can be used to give:

- total amounts the employer has to pay out in wages and salaries
- totals for income tax and National Insurance Contributions which the employer has to forward to the Inland Revenue on a monthly basis
- a breakdown of the overtime and bonus payments
- total amount of pension contributions which the employer passes to the manager of the pension fund (the employer may also make a pension contribution on behalf of employees)

When employees are paid in cash, an extension to the payroll layout is needed for *cash analysis* (see Section 28.11). A cash analysis is required so that an employer can withdraw from the bank the exact quantities of bank notes and coin required to pay wages due to employees.

Payroll and double-entry book-keeping

It is from the payroll record that the double-entry book-keeping transactions for wages and salaries are made. A *wages and salaries control account*, which is a double-entry book-keeping account, is credited with the total of all the deductions, plus net pay, plus the employer's National Insurance Contributions.

Transactions are as follows (using figures from the payroll shown in fig. 28.5):

- Transfer of totals

  – debit wages and salaries account
  – credit wages and salaries control account
  } with the total from the payroll record, £1,543.05 *plus* the employer's National Insurance, £160.46, equals a total of £1,703.51

- Payment of wages and salaries

  – debit wages and salaries control account
  – credit bank account
  } with the total amount of net pay, £1,107.98

- Transfer to the Inland Revenue account of income tax and NIC

  – debit wages and salaries control account
  – credit Inland Revenue account
  } with the total amount of income tax and NIC, ie £225.50 + £117.00 + £160.46 = £502.96

  Note: Payment to the Inland Revenue (which collects both income tax *and* National Insurance Contributions) is normally made by the 19th of the month after the wages payment.

- Transfer of pension contributions

  – debit wages and salaries control account
  – credit pension contributions account
  } with the total amount of the pension contribution, £92.57

  Note: This amount will be paid (normally on a monthly basis) to the pension fund, which may be managed by the employer or by a specialist organisation on behalf of the employer.

The double-entry accounts appear as follows:

Wages and Salaries Control Account

Dr.		£	Cr.		£
19-1		£	19-1		£
21 Jul.	Bank	1,107.98	21 Jul.	Wages and salaries (payroll for the week)	1,703.51
21 Jul.	Inland Revenue account	502.96			
21 Jul.	Pension contributions	92.57			
		1,703.51			1,703.51

Wages and Salaries Account

Dr.			Cr.		
19-1		£	19-1		£
21 Jul.	Wages and salaries control account (payroll for the week)	1,703.51			

Note: The figure of payroll for the week is the total from the payroll record, £1,543.05, plus the employer's National Insurance, £160.46, equals a total of £1,703.51.

Inland Revenue Account

Dr.			Cr.		
19-1		£	19-1		£
			21 Jul.	Wages and salaries control account	502.96

Note: This account shows the amount due to the Inland Revenue for income tax and National Insurance Contributions. Payment is made on a monthly basis, by the 19th of the month after the wages payment. After payment has been made (debit Inland Revenue account, credit bank account), the account will have a nil balance.

Pension Contributions Account

Dr.			Cr.		
19-1		£	19-1		£
			21 Jul.	Wages and salaries control account	92.57

Note: This account shows the amount due to the pension fund. Payment is normally made on a monthly basis, in the month after the wages payment. After payment has been made (debit pension contributions account, credit bank account), the account will have a nil balance.

28.10 Other pay and tax records: P60 and P45

P60

Each year an employer is required to give a Certificate of Pay and Tax Deductions to every employee from whose pay deductions have been made. This certificate, known as a P60, shows the total amount paid to the employee during the tax year (which ends on 5 April) and the total income tax and National Insurance Contributions deducted by the employer.

P45

When an employee leaves a business, the employer is required to complete form P45. This form gives the following information about the employee:

- tax (PAYE) reference of employee
- National Insurance number of employee
- name and address of employee
- date of leaving
- tax code at date of leaving
- total pay to date during the tax year
- total tax to date during the tax year

Form P45 is in three parts, with parts 2 and 3 being carbon copies of part 1. The employer sends part 1 to the local tax office and parts 2 and 3 are given to the departing employee. When starting a new job, the employee hands these two parts to the new employer, who keeps part 2, completes further information on part 3 and sends it to the local tax office.

28.11 Methods of payment of wages and salaries

The methods of payment of wages and salaries include:

- cash
- cheques
- bank giro credits
- computer (BACS) payments through the banking system

Cash payment

Many manual workers still have their wages paid in bank notes and coin. The cash is placed inside a wage packet marked with the name and pay reference or clock number of the employee. Details showing how the payment is made up and the deductions that have been made are provided to each employee. These details can be shown on a separate pay slip or written on the wage packet itself. Most wage packets are designed so that the employee can check the contents of the packet before it is opened. The employee signs in a record book to confirm receipt of the wage packet.

An employer paying wages in cash can either sub-contract the work to a security firm which will make up the wage packets, or it can be completed by the company's own staff. Preparing wage packets involves collecting sufficient notes and coin from the bank to make up the exact amount for each pay packet. It is normal practice to telephone the bank in advance to tell them the exact denominations of notes and coin needed; these details are taken from a cash analysis (see fig. 28.6).

NAME	£20	£10	£5	£1	50p	20p	10p	5p	2p	1p	TOTAL (£ p)
P. Waite	9		1	3				1	1		188.07
D. Land	8		1		1	1	1	1			165.85
A. Brooks	9	1		1		1					191.20
G. Johnson	9	1	1	3	1	1					198.70
S. Barber	8	1		3	1	1	1		2		173.84
T. Lord	9	1				1	1		1		190.32
Number required	52	4	3	10	3	5	3	2	4		
TOTAL (£ p)	1,040.00	40.00	15.00	10.00	1.50	1.00	0.30	0.10	0.08	0	1,107.98

Fig. 28.6 Cash Analysis Sheet

Cheque payment

This method requires the employer to write out individual cheques made payable to each employee for the net pay earned. Larger employers may well use a computerised wages (or payroll) system which can print out the payment cheques for each employee.

The employer encloses the cheque in each pay packet with the pay advice slip and distributes them to employees who sign in a record book to confirm receipt of their cheque. They can then either cash the cheques at the employer's bank or pay them into a bank or building society account.

Bank giro credits

Almost all salaried staff, and quite a number of manual employees, have their wages and salaries paid directly into their bank or building society account. This reduces the security problem of cash handling by the employer, and the fear of loss or theft of the wage packet by the employee.

Employers can make direct payments by means of bank giro credits. The employer gives each employee a pay slip, stating earnings and deductions, the net pay figure on the pay slip being the amount credited to the employee's bank or building society account.

The procedure for the payment of the giro credits through the banking system is for the employer to list the giro credits on a separate schedule and to take the credits, schedule and a cheque for the total of all the credits to the bank. These are then processed through the banking system. It is quite common for the employer's computer to work out the net pay, and print out the credits and payslips for the employees.

BACS payment of wages

As an alternative to using the bank giro credit system, an employer can make use of BACS (Bankers Automated Clearing Services), which is the banks' computerised payment transfer system. With this system an employer, using his own computer will prepare computer data containing the banking and money amount details relating to each wage payment. This data is then sent to BACS in London, who run it through their computer, crediting the employees' and debiting the employer's bank account on the same day. The data can either be sent in the form of a tape or disk by courier, or alternatively by telephone, using a system known as BACSTEL, which links up the employer's computer directly to the BACS computer by telephone line.

If an employer does not have a suitable computer to prepare the tape or disk for BACS, a computer bureau or a bank may be used to send the payments through the banking system via BACS. All the employer has to do is to provide the bureau or bank with a schedule listing the employees' pay and the date of payment. The bureau or bank will already have been given the employees' banking details which will be held permanently on computer file.

An example of a bank BACS payment system is National Westminster Bank's 'Autopay' system.

28.12 Chapter summary

- ❑ The basis of wage and salary calculations can vary between employees within the same organisation. An employee can be paid a basic wage only or can receive additional income in the form of overtime or a bonus.

- ❑ An employer, in order to be able to calculate wages, must keep records of attendance for all his employees. Different organisations have different methods to suit their own requirements. These include:
  - time books
  - clock cards
  - time sheets
  - computer cards

- ❑ Income Tax and National Insurance Contributions are compulsory deductions from an employee's gross pay.

- ❑ An employee can also make voluntary deductions such as pension payments, savings scheme contributions, or voluntary giving payments.

- ❑ The amount of Income Tax which an employed person will pay depends on their personal allowance, tax coding and total earnings.

- ❑ The PAYE system operated by employers calculates these deductions on a weekly or a monthly basis.

- ❑ When payment is made an employer gives each employee a payslip which gives details of earnings and all deductions.

- ❑ An employer will keep payroll records of all its employees.

- ❑ An employer making payment of wages in cash will need to prepare a cash analysis sheet to ensure that sufficient notes and coin are available to make up each wage packet.

- ❑ An employer can pay wages and salaries by the following methods:
  - cash payment
  - cheques
  - bank giro credit
  - BACS payment

In the next chapter we look at the important area of interpreting, and understanding what accounting statements are telling us about the strengths and weaknesses of a business. To help us in this we shall be calculating ratios, percentages and other performance indicators.

28.13 Questions

28.1* Calculate the following employees' weekly gross wages assuming the following hourly rates of pay apply:

Normal weekday work—	£6.60 per hour
Overtime weekday work—	time-and-a-quarter
Saturday working—	time-and-a-half
Sunday working—	double time

Employee	*Weekday*		*Weekend*	
	Normal hours	*Overtime hours*	*Saturday hours*	*Sunday hours*
F Mariani	37	–	4	–
J Banks	37	4	4	–
R Robson	37	6	5	2
H Wilson	37	–	8	4

28.2 M Marchand works as an electrician with a basic rate of pay of £4.40 per hour for a 40 hour week, overtime is paid at a rate of 1½ times the basic.

During the week ending 28 April 19-0 M Marchand worked 50 hours. He pays National Insurance at 10% of the gross pay, pensions at 8% of the basic pay and income tax at 30% on all earnings after deducting £30 tax free pay. £2 is also paid in union contributions.

You are required to:

(a) calculate M Marchand's gross pay

(b) calculate each of the deductions

(c) show the amount M Marchand will take home

Note: Marks will be awarded if presented in the form of a pay slip

[RSA Examinations Board]

28.3* The following details relate to the earnings of two employees during the week ended 25 May 19-0.

Employee	*J Brown*	*A White*
Piecework rate per unit	120p	130p
Units produced	200	140
Hours worked	40	44
Hourly rate of pay	375p	410p

A 40 hour week is in operation and overtime is paid at time-and-a-quarter.

If an employee's piecework earnings fall below his earnings at the hourly rate then the hourly rate earnings are paid.

Both employees have the following deductions:

Company Pension Scheme	2% of gross earnings
National Insurance	10% of gross earnings
PAYE	25% of all earnings in excess of £75 per week

You are required to calculate:
The gross and net wage of each employee showing clearly the amount of each deduction.

[RSA Examinations Board]

28.4 You have just been appointed wages clerk at Bright's Breweries Ltd. Although most of the wages have been calculated by your predecessor, you have been left to calculate the wages of six new employees for the week beginning 6 April.

The details are:

Employee	*Gross Pay*
J Whitbread	£245.10
R Banks	£220.25
L Foster	£215.50
S Watney	£210.50
F Loveday	£197.75
R Sisson	£201.50

You are to draw up deduction sheets (P11s) for each employee using the example in the chapter as a model, and

(a) calculate their income tax using Pay Adjustment Tables*, Taxable Pay Tables*, and Subtraction Tables* (all of these employees have the personal allowance)

(b) calculate National Insurance Contributions from National Insurance Table 'A' tables*

(c) calculate their net pay

* *Use the latest tables for the calculations: these could be borrowed from your employer or, if you are not in employment, ask if your teacher or lecturer has a set that you can use. (National Insurance Contributions can be calculated by using the percentages shown on page 427.)*

28.5 During the following week in the business referred to in question 28.4, the gross wages earned by the six employees are:

Employee	*Gross Pay*
J Whitbread	£205.75
R Banks	£202.15
L Foster	£198.35
S Watney	£214.97
F Loveday	£202.83
R Sisson	£212.75

You are to calculate the wages of each employee using the deduction sheets drawn up in question 28.4, and calculating:

(a) income tax

(b) National Insurance Contributions

(c) net weekly pay

28.6 C Ponsford manages a small firm employing four workers. During the week ending 31 December 19-9, each worker earned a take home pay as follows:

L Jennett	£160.56
J Smith	£90.75
J Grala	£100.20
G Thomas	£136.40

C Ponsford pays wages at the end of each week in cash using notes and coins of £10, £5, £1, 50p, 20p, 10p, 5p, 2p and 1p. C Ponsford insists that each worker receives at least one £1 coin.

You are required to:

(a) rule up and complete a note and coin analysis in table form using the least number of notes and coins permissible;

(b) reconcile the value of the total notes and coins with the total pay bill

[RSA Examinations Board]

28.7* (a) Rule up and complete a payroll sheet from the following details of weekly pay for the week ending 18 August 19-1:

	A Adams £ p	B Barnes £ p	C Cutts £ p	D Dodds £ p
Basic pay	250.00	250.00	250.00	250.00
Overtime	43.75	–	43.75	29.50
Bonus	10.00	10.00	10.00	10.00
PAYE (Income Tax)	45.25	44.00	46.25	40.75
National Insurance (employees' contribution)	23.67	19.80	23.67	22.41
Pension scheme (employees' contribution)	18.22	15.60	18.22	17.37
National Insurance (employer's contribution)	31.56	27.09	31.56	30.11

(b) Enter the transactions in the double-entry accounts on 18 August 19-1; show payment to the Inland Revenue on 15 September 19-1, and to the pension fund on 20 September 19-1.

28.8* From the information contained in question 28.7, prepare a cash analysis on the basis of the following instruction:

Each employee's pay packet to be made up in the highest value bank notes and coin available with the following exceptions:

- no bank notes in excess of £20 to be paid
- no more than five £20 notes to be paid
- at least four £5 notes to be paid
- at least five £1 coins to be paid

28.9 (a) Rule up and compile a payroll sheet from the following details of weekly pay for the week ending 20 November 19-2:

Name	F Fleming £ p	G Singh £ p	H Hock £ p	L Mehta £ p	M Mann £ p	P Potts £ p
Basic pay	196.00	254.00	284.00	284.00	325.50	226.00
Overtime	–	24.00	20.00	20.00	15.00	10.00
PAYE (Income Tax)	20.75	41.00	54.25	46.50	53.75	31.25
National Insurance (employee's contribution)	14.04	21.42	23.76	23.76	27.00	17.64
Pension scheme (employees' contribution)	11.76	16.68	18.24	18.24	20.43	14.16
National Insurance (employer's contribution)	20.44	28.96	31.67	31.67	35.41	24.60

(b) Enter the transactions in the double-entry accounts on 20 November 19-2; show payment to the Inland Revenue on 10 December 19-2, and to the pension fund on 18 December 19-2.

28.10 From the information contained in question 28.9, prepare a cash analysis using the following instruction:

Each employee's pay packet to be made up in the highest value bank notes and coin available, with the following exceptions:

- no bank notes in excess of £20 to be paid
- no more than five £20 notes to be paid
- at least four £5 notes to be paid
- at least five £1 coins to be paid

Multiple-choice questions: chapters 25-28

- Read each question carefully
- Choose the *one* answer you think is correct (calculators may be needed)
- Answers are on page 486

1. When buying a business, it is usual to pay an extra sum over and above the value of the assets. This is known as the:

   A goodwill
   B premium
   C bonus
   D investment

2. When a business is sold, the transactions in the seller's books pass through a:

   A dissolution account
   B purchase of business account
   C realisation account
   D investment account

3. In manufacturing, direct materials + direct labour + direct expenses equals:

   A factory overhead expenses
   B prime cost
   C manufacturing cost
   D administration costs

4. Which one of the following does *not* appear in a manufacturing account?

   A depreciation of factory machinery
   B supervisors' wages
   C depreciation of office equipment
   D factory heating and lighting

5. In a manufacturing business, royalties are included under the heading of:

   A selling and distributing costs
   B factory overheads
   C raw materials
   D direct expenses

6. For a manufacturing business, which type of stock is recorded in the trading account?

   A raw materials
   B work-in-progress
   C partly manufactured goods
   D finished goods

7. Which one of the following is classified as a variable cost?

A raw materials
B supervisors' wages
C factory rent
D business rates

8. In preparing departmental profit and loss accounts for a large shop, the best method of apportioning rent is on the basis of:

A capital employed
B floor area
C sales
D value of stock held

9. The profit or loss on a joint venture is calculated by means of a:

A joint venture account
B consignment account
C joint venture memorandum account
D departmental account

10. In joint ventures, the consignee sends the consignor:

A a consignment note
B a consignment account
C a del credere commission
D an account of sales

11. Rates of pay and bands of taxable pay are:

- 20% £1 – £4,100
- 23% £4,101 – £26,100
- 40% £26,101 upwards

James Gordon has taxable pay of £28,000 for the year. He will pay tax for the year amounting to:

A £5,600
B £6,440
C £6,640
D £11,200

12. Which one of the following is a compulsory deduction from wages?

A national insurance contributions
B superannuation scheme contributions
C union subscriptions
D payments to savings schemes

29 Interpretation of Accounts

The final accounts – trading and profit and loss account, and balance sheet – of businesses are often interpreted for decision-making purposes. The interpretation will not necessarily be made by an accountant; interested parties include the

- *general management of the business,* who need to make financial decisions affecting the future development of the business
- *bank manager,* who is being asked to lend money to finance the business
- *creditors,* who wish to assess the likelihood of receiving payment
- *customers,* who wish to be assured of continuity of supplies in the future
- *shareholders* of a limited company, who wish to be assured that their investment is sound
- *prospective investors* in a limited company, who wish to compare comparative strengths and weaknesses
- *employees and trade unions,* who wish to check on the financial prospects of the business
- *government departments,* eg Inland Revenue, HM Customs and Excise, that wish to check they are receiving the amount due to them

In all of these cases, the interested party will be able to calculate the main ratios, percentages and performance indicators. By doing this, the strengths and weaknesses of the business will be highlighted and appropriate conclusions can be drawn.

In this chapter we will examine the areas of:

- *profitability,* the relationship of profit to sales turnover, assets and capital employed
- *solvency/liquidity,* which considers the soundness and stability of the business on both a short-term and long-term basis
- *asset utilisation,* the effective and efficient use of assets
- *investment ratios,* specific ratios which examine the returns to shareholders in companies

Note that the general term 'accounting ratios' is usually used to describe the calculations aspect of interpretation of accounts. The term *ratio* is, in fact, partly misleading because the performance indicators include percentages, time periods, as well as ratios in the strict sense of the word.

29.1 Making use of accounting ratios

It is tempting, as an academic exercise, to examine a set of final accounts and calculate a large number of accounting ratios. This might look impressive on paper, but will prove useless in itself because, in order to be relevant, the ratios must be placed in context, and related to some form of reference point or standard. These points of reference might include:

- ratios from past years, to provide a standard of comparison
- comparison with other businesses in the same industry
- comparison with standards assumed to be satisfactory by the interested organisation, eg a bank

Above all, it is important to understand the relationships between ratios: one ratio may give an indication of the state of the business, but this needs to be supported by other ratios.

Another use of ratios is to estimate forward the likely profit or balance sheet of a business. For example, it might be assumed that the same gross profit percentage as last year will also apply next year; thus, given an estimated increase in sales, it is a simple matter to estimate gross profit. In a similar way, by making use of ratios, net profit and the balance sheet can be forecast.

29.2 Profitability

Gross profit percentage

$$\frac{\text{Gross profit for year}}{\text{Sales for year}} \times \frac{100}{1} = \text{Gross profit/sales percentage}$$

This expresses, as a percentage, the gross profit in relation to sales. For example, a gross profit percentage of 20 per cent means that for every £100 of sales made, the gross profit is £20.

The gross profit percentage should be similar from year-to-year for the same business. It will vary between organisations in different areas of business, eg the gross profit percentage on jewellery is considerably higher than that on food. A significant change from one year to the next, particularly a fall in the percentage, needs investigation into buying and selling prices.

Gross profit percentage, and also net profit percentage (below), needs to be considered in context. For example, a supermarket may well have a lower gross profit percentage than a small corner shop but, because of the supermarket's much higher turnover, the *amount* of profit will be much higher. Whatever the type of business, gross profit – both as an amount and a percentage – needs to be sufficient to cover the expenses, and then to give an acceptable return on capital.

Net profit percentage

$$\frac{\text{Net profit* for year}}{\text{Sales for year}} \times \frac{100}{1} = \text{Net profit/sales percentage}$$

* the figure for net profit is taken from the profit and loss account, before the deduction – for limited companies – of taxation and dividends.

As with gross profit percentage, the net profit percentage should be similar from year-to-year for the same business, and should also be comparable with other firms in the same line of business. Net profit percentage should, ideally, increase from year-to-year, which indicates that the profit and loss account costs are being kept under control. Any significant fall should be investigated to see if it has been caused by an increase in one particular expense, eg wages and salaries, advertising, etc.

Expense/sales percentage

A large expense item can be expressed as a percentage of sales:

$$\frac{\text{Specified expense}}{\text{Sales for year}} \times \frac{100}{1} = \text{Expense/sales percentage}$$

For example, the relationship between advertising and sales might be found to be 10 per cent in one year, but 20 per cent the next year. This could indicate that an increase in advertising had failed to produce a proportionate increase in sales.

Note that each expense falls into one of three categories of cost:

- fixed costs, or
- variable costs, or
- semi-variable costs

Fixed costs remain constant despite other changes. Variable costs alter with changed circumstances, such as increased production or sales. Semi-variable costs combine both a fixed and a variable element, eg hire of a car at a basic (fixed) cost, with a variable cost per mile. It is important to appreciate the nature of costs when interpreting accounts: for example, if sales this year are twice last year's figure, not all expenses will have doubled.

Operating profit percentage

Net profit percentage is calculated after loan and bank interest has been charged to profit and loss account. Thus it may be distorted when making comparisons between two different businesses where one is heavily financed by means of loans, and the other is financed by owner's capital. The solution is to calculate the *operating profit percentage* which uses net profit but adds back any loan and bank interest, ie profit before deducting interest.

$$\frac{\text{Net profit for year + loan/bank interest}}{\text{Sales for year}} \times \frac{100}{1} = \text{Operating profit percentage}$$

Return on capital employed (ROCE)

$$\frac{\text{Net profit for year}}{\text{Capital employed at start of year}} \times \frac{100}{1} = \text{Percentage return on capital employed}$$

This expresses the net profit of the business in relation to the owner's capital. For this calculation, the capital at the start of the year should, ideally, be used; if this is not known, the year-end capital figure can be used. The percentage return is best thought of in relation to other investments, eg a building society might offer a return of ten per cent, or a bank might offer eight per cent on a deposit account. A person running a business is investing a sum of money in that business, and the net profit is the return that is achieved on that investment. However, it should be noted that the risks in running a business are considerably greater than depositing the money with a building society or bank, and an additional return to compensate for the extra risk is needed.

While the above calculation is suitable for sole trader and partnership businesses, we need to be more specific for limited companies and to take note of their different methods of financing. It is necessary to distinguish between the ordinary shareholders' investment (known as *equity*) and the capital employed by the company, which includes preference shares and debentures/long-term loans:

	Ordinary share capital
add	Reserves
equals	Equity
add	Preference share capital
add	Debentures/long-term loans
equals	Capital Employed

The reason for including preference shares and debentures/long-term loans in the capital employed is that the company has the use of the money from these contributors for the foreseeable future, or certainly for a fixed time period. These different definitions of capital employed give different calculations.

Return on equity

$$\frac{\text{Net profit for year - preference dividend (if any)}}{\text{Ordinary share capital + reserves}} \times \frac{100}{1} =$$ Percentage return on equity (also known as *Return on Owners' Equity*)

Note that the net profit is *after* deduction of the preference dividend (if any), ie it is the profit available for the ordinary shareholders, *before* deduction of corporation tax.

Return on capital employed

$$\frac{\text{Net profit for year + interest on debentures/long-term loans}}{\text{Ordinary share capital + reserves + preference share capital + debentures/long-term loans}} \times \frac{100}{1} =$$ Percentage return on capital employed

Note that, here, the net profit is *before* deduction of interest on debentures/long-term loans, ie it is the profit available to the providers of capital (shown as the divisor in the calculation), *before* deduction of corporation tax.

The primary ratio

Return on capital employed is perhaps the most effective ratio used in financial analysis. It is often known as the primary ratio, since it can be broken down into the two secondary factors of:

- net profit percentage (see page 448)
- asset turnover ratio (see page 455)

The relationship between the three is:

Net profit percentage		*Asset turnover ratio*		*Return on capital employed*
$\frac{\text{Net profit}}{\text{Sales}}$	x	$\frac{\text{Sales}}{\text{Net assets*}}$	=	$\frac{\text{Net profit}}{\text{Capital employed**}}$

* *Net assets:* defined (for ratio analysis) as fixed assets + current assets – current liabilities

** *Capital employed:* defined as capital/share capital + reserves + long-term liabilities

For example, if a business has a net profit of £50,000, sales of £500,000 and net assets and capital employed of £250,000, the three figures are:

$$\frac{£50{,}000}{£500{,}000} \times \frac{£500{,}000}{£250{,}000} = \frac{£50{,}000}{£250{,}000}$$

10% x 2 times = 20%

The primary ratio is used to help us appreciate that the same return on capital employed can be reached in different ways, depending on the type of business. Thus, one business may have a net profit percentage of 10 per cent, but an asset turnover of 2 times, while for a different business the respective values might be 2 per cent and 10 times: for both the return on capital employed is 20 per cent. These examples illustrate why, for example, an engineering firm and a supermarket can be equally profitable.

Return on net assets employed

$$\frac{\text{Net profit for year}}{\text{Net assets (fixed assets + current assets – current liabilities)}} \times \frac{100}{1} = \text{Percentage return on net assets}$$

This is an important ratio as it relates the profitability of the business to the value of the net assets in use. It is perhaps more easily understood by the non-financial manager who may find difficulty in understanding the concept of capital employed (which, of course, is what this percentage is restating).

29.3 Solvency/liquidity

Working capital

Working capital is needed by all businesses in order to finance day-to-day trading activities. Sufficient working capital enables a business to hold adequate stocks, allow a measure of credit to its customers (debtors), and to pay its suppliers (creditors) as payments fall due. Working capital is calculated as:

Current assets – Current liabilities = Working capital

Working capital can be described as the life-blood of a business because it must keep circulating. For example:

- creditors supply a stock of goods
- stock is sold to debtors (or cash sales, for a retailer)
- debtors make payment (cash/bank)
- payment (cash/bank) made to creditors

Fig. 29.1 (next page) shows the flow of working capital in a business. From this, note that external funds may flow *into* working capital, eg new capital/loans, and the sale of fixed assets will increase the cash/bank balance and, consequently, the amount of working capital. An outflow of funds for the purchase of fixed assets, repayment of capital/loans, dividends/drawings, and payment of expenses and tax will reduce the cash/bank balance and, consequently, the amount of working capital.

The *amount* of working capital required by a business will vary from business to business depending on:

- *the nature of the business* – a shop is likely to need less working capital than an engineering business, because a shop has few, if any, debtors
- *the size of the business* – a small corner shop will need less working capital than a large department store

Because the amount of working capital varies between businesses, it is better to calculate *ratios* which measure the relationship between current assets and current liabilities:

- working capital ratio (or current ratio)
- liquid capital ratio

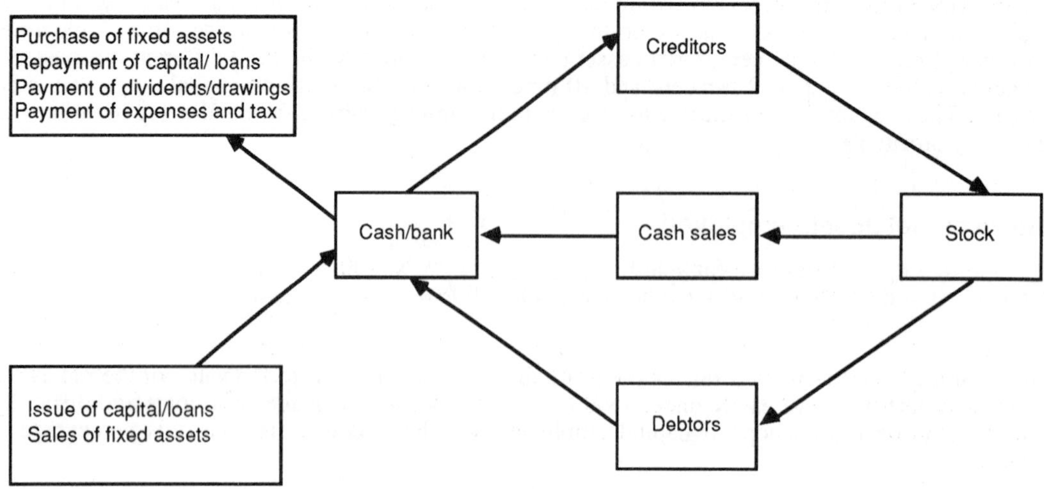

Fig. 29.1 Flow of working capital

Working capital ratio (or current ratio)

Working capital ratio uses figures from the balance sheet and measures the relationship between Current Assets:Current Liabilities

It is usually expressed as:

$$\frac{\text{Current assets}}{\text{Current liabilities}} = \text{Working capital ratio (also known as the } \textit{current ratio}\text{)}$$

Although there is no ideal working capital ratio, an often accepted ratio is about 2:1, ie £2 of current assets to every £1 of current liabilities. However, an organization in the retail trade may be able to work with a lower ratio, eg 1.5:1 or even less, because it deals mainly in sales for cash and so does not have a large figure for debtors. A working capital ratio can be *too* high: if it is above 3:1 an investigation of the make-up of current assets is needed: eg the business may have too much stock, too many debtors, or too much cash at the bank, or even too few creditors.

Liquid capital ratio

Liquid capital ratio is

(Current Assets – Stock):Current Liabilities

It is usually expressed as:

$$\frac{\text{(Current assets – stock)}}{\text{Current liabilities}} = \text{Liquid capital ratio (also known as the } \textit{quick ratio} \text{ or } \textit{acid test}\text{)}$$

This ratio uses the current assets and current liabilities from the balance sheet, but stock is omitted. This is because stock is the most illiquid current asset: it has to be sold, turned into debtors, and then the cash has to be collected from the debtors. Also, some of the stock included in the balance sheet figure may be unsaleable or obsolete.

The balance between liquid assets, that is debtors and cash/bank, and current liabilities should, ideally, be about 1:1, ie £1 of liquid assets to each £1 of current liabilities. At this ratio a business is expected to be able to pay its current liabilities from its liquid assets; a figure below 1:1, eg 0.75:1, indicates that the firm would have difficulty in meeting pressing demands from creditors. However, as with the working capital ratio, certain types of business are able to operate with a lower liquid ratio than others.

Capital gearing

Sole trader and partnerships

$$\frac{\text{Long-term loans}}{\text{Capital}} \times \frac{100}{1} = \text{Gearing percentage}$$

Limited companies

$$\frac{\text{Preference share capital + long-term loans, including debentures}}{\text{Ordinary share capital + reserves}} \times \frac{100}{1} = \text{Gearing percentage}$$

In analysing a set of final accounts it is important to know how much of the business is financed by debt (including, in the case of companies, preference shares). The higher the gearing ratio, the less secure will be the equity capital of the business and, therefore, the future of the business. This is because debt is costly in terms of interest payments (particularly if interest rates are variable); also, some debt can, strictly speaking, be recalled at any time. It is difficult to set a standard for an acceptable gearing ratio: in general terms most investors (or lenders) would not wish to see debt exceeding equity, ie a gearing percentage of greater than 100% is undesirable.

Capital gearing can also be expressed as a ratio, ie *debt:equity*. Thus a gearing percentage of 100% is a ratio of 1:1.

Interest cover

$$\frac{\text{Net profit + interest (ie operating profit)}}{\text{Interest}} = \text{Interest cover}$$

Linked closely to gearing is interest cover. This considers the safety margin (or cover) of profit over the interest payable by a business. For example, if the operating profit of a business was £10,000, and interest payable was £5,000, this would give interest cover of 2 – a low figure. If the interest was £1,000, this would give interest cover of 10 – a much more acceptable figure.

As with most accounting ratios, it is difficult to set a standard – several ratios must be used in conjunction with one another in order to draw appropriate conclusions.

29.4 Asset utilisation

Stock turnover

$$\frac{\text{Average stock}}{\text{Cost of goods sold}} \times 365 = \text{Stock turnover (in days)}$$

This calculation uses information from the trading account: average stock is usually found by taking the simple average of the opening and closing stocks, ie

$$\frac{\text{(opening stock + closing stock)}}{2*}$$

* divide by 2 to calculate the average of the two stock figures

Stock turnover is the number of days' stock held on average. This figure will depend on the type of goods sold by the business. For example, a market trader selling fresh flowers, who finishes each day when sold out, will have a stock turnover of one day. By contrast, a furniture shop – because it may hold large stocks of furniture – will have a much slower stock turnover, perhaps sixty or ninety days. Nevertheless, stock turnover must not be too long, bearing in mind the type of business, and a business which is improving in efficiency will have a quick stock turnover comparing one year with the previous one, or with the stock turnover of similar businesses.

Stock turnover can also be expressed as number of times per year:

$$\frac{\text{Cost of goods sold}}{\text{Average stock}} = \text{Stock turnover (times per year)}$$

A stock turnover of, say, twelve times a year means that about thirty days' stock is held.

Debtors' collection period

$$\frac{\text{Debtors}}{\text{Credit sales for year}} \times 365 \text{ days} = \text{Debtors' collection period (in days)}$$

This calculation shows how long, on average, debtors take to pay for goods sold to them by the business. If the answer is needed in months, or in weeks, then it will, clearly, be necessary to multiply by 12 or 52 respectively. The figure of *credit sales for the year* may not be disclosed in the trading account, in which case the sales figure should be used. Some businesses make the majority of their sales on credit but others, such as shops, will have a considerably lower proportion of credit sales.

The debt collection time can be compared with that for the previous year, or with that of a similar business. In Britain, most debtors should make payment within about 30 days; however, sales made abroad will take longer for the proceeds to be received. A comparison from year-to-year of the collection period is a measure of the firm's efficiency at collecting the money that is due to it.

Creditors' payment period

$$\frac{\text{Creditors}}{\text{Credit purchases for year}} \times 365 \text{ days} = \text{Creditors' payment period (in days)}$$

This calculation is the 'other side of the coin' to that of debtors: here we are measuring the speed it takes to pay creditors. While creditors can be a useful temporary source of finance, delaying payment too long may cause problems.

Note: There is an inconsistency in calculating both debtors' collection and creditors' payment periods: the figures for debtors and creditors *include* VAT, while sales and purchases *exclude* VAT. Strictly, therefore, we are not comparing like with like; however, the comparison should be made with reference to the previous year, or a similar company, calculated on the same basis from year-to-year.

Working capital cycle

A further use of ratios covering the working capital items, ie the turnover of stock, debtors and creditors is to calculate the *working capital cycle* (sometimes known as the cash operating cycle). This calculates the period of time between the payment for goods received into stock and the collection of cash from customers in respect of their sale. The shorter the length of time between the initial outlay and the ultimate collection of cash, the lower the value of working capital to be financed by the business.

The length of the working capital cycle is found by calculating:

1. the time that goods are in stock
2. the time that debtors take to pay
3. deduct from 1 + 2 the period of credit received from suppliers

The cash operating cycle calculations take the following format (with example figures):

WORKING CAPITAL CYCLE	**DAYS**
Time period that goods are in stock Stock turnover: (average stock ÷ cost of goods sold) x 365	37
Time period that debtors take to pay Debtor collection time: (debtors ÷ sales) x 365	40
	77
Less: Period of credit received from suppliers Creditors payment time: (creditors ÷ purchases) x 365	30
WORKING CAPITAL CYCLE	47

Like all accounting ratios, a comparison needs to be made – either with the figure for the previous year, or with a similar firm. The working capital cycle is likely to show either an overall position that is better, ie the cycle has been reduced, or one that is worse, where the total time has been increased. There are three ways in which the cycle can be reduced:

- reducing stocks (which will lower the number of days that stock is held)
- speeding up the rate of debtor collection (ie less time is allowed to debtors to pay)
- slowing down the rate of creditor payment (ie taking longer to pay the creditors)

Any one of these actions will achieve the result of reducing the working capital cycle. However, it may not always be possible to put them into practice, or they may have unexpected consequences for a particular business. For example:

- reducing stocks might mean that a poorer service is offered to customers, who may take their business elsewhere
- giving debtors less time to pay may cause customers to seek alternative suppliers who are offering better terms
- taking extra credit from suppliers may be difficult, and they might decline to supply goods unless immediate payment is forthcoming

Asset turnover ratio

$$\frac{\text{Sales}}{\text{Net assets*}} = \text{Asset turnover ratio}$$

* fixed assets + current assets – current liabilities

This ratio measures the efficiency of the use of net assets in generating sales. An increasing ratio from one year to the next indicates greater efficiency. A fall in the ratio may be caused either by a decrease in sales, or an increase in net assets – perhaps caused by the purchase or revaluation of fixed assets, or increased stockholding, or increased debtors as a result of poor credit control.

Different types of businesses will have very different asset turnover ratios. For example a supermarket, with high sales and relatively few assets, will have a very high figure; by contrast, an engineering business, with lower sales and a substantial investment in fixed and current assets, will have a much lower figure. As we have seen in the primary ratio (page 450), asset turnover and net profit percentage are the two factors which go to making up return on capital employed; therefore, although different types of businesses will have differing asset turnover ratios, they could have the same return on capital employed.

Proprietary ratio

$$\frac{\text{Ordinary shareholders' (or owners') funds}}{\text{Tangible assets*}} = \text{Proprietary ratio}$$

* *Tangible assets:* assets which have material substance

The proprietary ratio, which may also be expressed as a percentage, indicates the proportion of owners' funds to the tangible assets (tangible fixed assets + current assets) of the business. As a guideline a ratio of around 0.5:1, or 50 per cent, should be considered as the minimum desirable figure. This shows that half of the tangible assets are owned by the ordinary shareholders or owners, and half by contributors of other types of share and loan capital and by creditors. Intangible assets, such as goodwill, are excluded from this calculation because they would, most probably, be worthless in the event of the forced sale of the business.

29.5 Investment ratios

Investment ratios are used by business people and investors who intend to buy either a whole business, or holdings of shares in limited companies. The ratios will help to assess the performance of the company in which they wish to invest.

Dividend yield

$$\frac{\text{Ordinary share dividend (in pence)}}{\text{Market price of ordinary share (in pence)}} \times \frac{100}{1} = \text{Dividend yield}$$

Investors in companies which are quoted on the stock market can obtain this information from the share price pages of the financial press. The dividend yield gives the investor the annual percentage return paid on a quoted share. However, dividend yield is an inadequate measure because it ignores the overall profits – or 'earnings' – available for the ordinary shareholders; retained profits (ie that part of profits not paid as dividends) should help to boost the share price, so giving investors capital growth rather than income.

Earnings per share

$$\frac{\text{Net profit, after corporation tax and preference dividends}}{\text{Number of issued ordinary shares}} = \text{Earnings per share}$$

Earnings per share (or EPS) measures the amount of profit *earned* by each share, after corporation tax and preference dividends. Comparisons can be made with previous years to provide a basis for assessing the company's performance.

Earnings yield

$$\frac{\text{Earnings per ordinary share (in pence)}}{\text{Market price of ordinary share (in pence)}} \times \frac{100}{1} = \text{Earnings yield}$$

This compares, in percentage terms, the earnings per ordinary share (after corporation tax and preference dividends) with the market price per share. It is an important calculation for investors because it shows the return earned by the company on each ordinary share. Some part of the earnings will, most likely, have been paid to investors, while the rest will have been retained in the company and should help to increase the capital value of the shares.

Price/earnings ratio

$$\frac{\text{Market price of ordinary share (in pence)}}{\text{Earnings per ordinary share (in pence)}} = \text{Price/earnings ratio}$$

The price/earnings ratio (or P/E ratio, as it is often abbreviated) compares the current market price of a share and the earnings (after corporation tax) of that share. For example, if a particular share has a market price of £3, and the earnings per share in the current year are 30p, then the P/E ratio is 10. This simply means that a person buying the share for £3 is paying ten times the last reported earnings of that share.

Investors make use of the P/E ratio to help them make decisions as to the 'expensiveness' of a share. In general, high P/E ratios (ie a higher number) indicate that the stock market price has been pushed up in anticipation of an expected rapid improvement in earnings: therefore, the share is now expensive. The reason for a low P/E ratio is usually that investors do not expect much (if any) growth in the company's earnings in the foreseeable future.

P/E ratio is simply a reciprocal of the earnings yield (see above). Thus a P/E ratio of 10 is the same as an earnings yield of 10 per cent; a P/E ratio of 20 is the same as an earnings yield of 5 per cent.

Dividend cover

$$\frac{\text{Net profit, after corporation tax and preference dividends}}{\text{Ordinary dividends}} = \text{Dividend cover}$$

This figure shows the margin of safety between the amount of profit a company makes and the amount paid out in dividends. The figure must be greater than 1 if the company is not to use past retained profits to fund the current dividend. A figure of 5 as dividend cover indicates that profit exceeds dividend by five times – a healthy sign. The share price pages in the financial press quote the figure under the column headed 'cover' or 'cvr'.

29.6 Worked example

Earlier in this chapter (Section 29.1) we saw that interpretation of accounts does not require the extraction of a long list of ratios from a set of accounts. Instead, it involves the analysis of the relationships between the figures in the accounts and the presentation of the information gathered in a meaningful way to interested parties.

In the example which follows, we will look at the set of accounts of a limited company. For clarity, one year's accounts are given although, in practice, more than one year's accounts should be used. The comments given should indicate what should be looked for when analysing and interpreting a set of accounts.

Question

The following are the accounts of Wyvern Trading Co Ltd. The business trades in office supplies and sells to the public through its three retail shops in the Wyvern area; it also delivers direct to businesses in the area from its modern warehouse on a local factory estate.

TRADING AND PROFIT AND LOSS ACCOUNTS OF WYVERN TRADING CO LTD FOR THE YEAR ENDED 31 DECEMBER 19-1

	£	£	£
Sales			1,430,000
Opening stock		200,000	
Purchases		1,000,000	
		1,200,000	
Less Closing stock		240,000	
Cost of Goods Sold			960,000
Gross profit			470,000
Less:			
Selling expenses		150,000	
Administration expenses		140,000	
Debenture interest		10,000	
			300,000
Net profit for year before taxation			170,000
Less corporation tax			50,000
Profit for year after taxation			120,000
Less:			
preference dividend paid		25,000	
ordinary dividend proposed		75,000	
			100,000
			20,000
Add balance of retained profits at beginning of year			180,000
Balance of retained profits at end of year			200,000

BALANCE SHEET OF WYVERN TRADING CO LTD AS AT 31 DECEMBER 19-1

Fixed Assets	*Cost*	*Dep'n to date*	*Net*
	£	£	£
Premises	850,000	-	850,000
Fixtures and fittings	300,000	120,000	180,000
Vehicles	350,000	100,000	250,000
	1,500,000	220,000	1,280,000
Current Assets			
Stock		240,000	
Debtors		150,000	
Bank/cash		135,000	
		525,000	
Less Current Liabilities			
Creditors	130,000		
Proposed ordinary dividend	75,000		
Corporation tax	50,000		
		255,000	
Working Capital			270,000
			1,550,000
Less Long-term Liabilities			
10% debentures			100,000
NET ASSETS			1,450,000

(balance sheet continues on next page)

	£	£	£
FINANCED BY			
Authorised and Issued Share Capital			
1,000,000 ordinary shares of £1 each, fully paid			1,000,000
250,000 10% preference shares of £1 each, fully paid			250,000
			1,250,000
Revenue Reserve			
Profit and loss account			200,000
			1,450,000

Note: the current market price of the ordinary shares is £1.25.

We will now analyse the accounts from the point of view of a potential investor.

Answer

PROFITABILITY

Gross profit percentage

$$\frac{£470{,}000}{£1{,}430{,}000} \times \frac{100}{1} = 32.87\%$$

Net profit percentage

$$\frac{£170{,}000}{£1{,}430{,}000} \times \frac{100}{1} = 11.89\%$$

Specified expense: selling expenses

$$\frac{£150{,}000}{£1{,}430{,}000} \times \frac{100}{1} = 10.49\%$$

Operating profit percentage

$$\frac{£170{,}000 + £10{,}000}{£1{,}430{,}000} \times \frac{100}{1} = 12.59\%$$

Return on capital employed

$$\frac{£170{,}000 + £10{,}000}{£1{,}000{,}000 + £250{,}000 + £200{,}000 + £100{,}000} \times \frac{100}{1} = \frac{£180{,}000}{£1{,}550{,}000} = 11.61\%$$

Return on equity

$$\frac{£170{,}000 - £25{,}000}{£1{,}000{,}000 + £200{,}000} \times \frac{100}{1} = \frac{£145{,}000}{£1{,}200{,}000} = 12.08\%$$

Return on net assets employed

$$\frac{£170{,}000}{£1{,}550{,}000} \times \frac{100}{1} = 10.97\%$$

The gross and net profit percentages seem to be acceptable figures for the type of business, although comparisons should be made with those of the previous accounting period. A business should always aim at least to hold its percentages and, ideally, to make a small improvement. A significant fall in the percentages may indicate a poor buying policy, poor pricing (perhaps caused by competition), and the causes should be investigated.

Selling expenses seem to be quite a high percentage of sales. As these are likely to be a relatively fixed cost, it would seem that the business could increase sales turnover without a corresponding increase in sales expenses.

The small difference between net profit percentage and operating profit percentage indicates that finance costs are relatively low.

Return on capital employed is satisfactory, but could be better. At 11.61% it is less than two percentage points above the ten per cent cost of the preference shares and debentures (ignoring the taxation advantages of issuing debentures). Return on equity is better at 12.08%, but needs to be compared with the gross returns available from banks and building societies. This is not to suggest that the directors (who may well own the majority of the shares) should sell up: the business is likely to provide them (and others) with employment – directors' remuneration having been deducted before arriving at the net profit figure used in the calculations. The figure for return on net assets employed confirms the mediocre performance of the company in this area.

SOLVENCY/LIQUIDITY

Working capital ratio

$$\frac{£525{,}000}{£255{,}000} = 2.06:1$$

Liquid capital ratio

$$\frac{(£525{,}000 - £240{,}000)}{£255{,}000} = 1.12:1$$

Capital gearing

$$\frac{£250{,}000 + £100{,}000}{£1{,}000{,}000 + £200{,}000} \times \frac{100}{1} = \frac{£350{,}000}{£1{,}200{,}000} = 29\% \text{ or } 0.29:1$$

Interest cover

$$\frac{£170{,}000 + £10{,}000}{£10{,}000} = 18 \text{ times}$$

The working capital and liquid capital ratios are excellent: they are slightly higher than the expected 'norms' of 2:1 and 1:1 respectively (although many companies operate successfully with lower ratios); however, they are not too high which would be an indication of inefficient use of assets.

The capital gearing percentage is low: anything up to 100% (1:1) is often seen. With a low figure of 29% this indicates that the company could borrow more money if it wished to finance, say, expansion plans (there are plenty of fixed assets for a lender – such as a bank – to take as security for a loan). The interest cover figure of 18 is very high and shows that the company has no problems in paying interest.

All-in-all, the company is very solvent, with no pressures showing at all.

ASSET UTILISATION

Stock turnover

$$\frac{(£200{,}000 + £240{,}000) \div 2}{£960{,}000} = \frac{£220{,}000}{£960{,}000} \times 365 = 83.6 \text{ days (or 4.36 times per year)}$$

Debtors' collection period

$$\frac{£150{,}000}{£1{,}430{,}000} \times 365 = 38.3 \text{ days}$$

Creditors' payment period

$$\frac{£130{,}000}{£1{,}000{,}000} \times 365 = 47.4 \text{ days}$$

Working capital cycle

Stock turnover + debtors' collection period – creditors' payment period =
83.6 days + 38.3 days – 47.4 days = 74.5 days

Asset turnover ratio

$$\frac{£1{,}430{,}000}{£1{,}550{,}000^{*}} \times 365 = 0.92:1$$

* fixed assets + current assets – current liabilities

Proprietory ratio

$$\frac{£1{,}000{,}000 + £200{,}000}{£1{,}280{,}000 + £525{,}000} = \frac{£1{,}200{,}000}{£1{,}805{,}000} = 0.66:1$$

This group of ratios shows the main weakness of the company: not enough business is passing through for the size of the company. Stock turnover is very low for an office supplies business: the stock is turning over only every 83 days – surely it should be faster than this. Debtors' collection period is not too bad on the face of it – 30 days would be better – but quite a volume of the sales will be made through the retail outlets *in cash*. This amount should, if known, be deducted from the sales turnover before calculating the debtors' collection period: thus the collection period is, in reality, longer than that calculated. Creditors' payment period is quite leisurely for this type of business – long delays could cause problems with suppliers in the future. The working capital cycle of over 74 days (approximately 2½ months) is quite leisurely for a retailer of office supplies. The asset turnover ratio says it all: this type of business should be able to obtain a much better figure:

- either, sales need to be increased using the same net assets
- or, sales need to be maintained, but net assets reduced

The proprietory ratio is good: above the suggested minimum figure of 50 per cent, indicating that the ordinary shareholders are financing 66% of the tangible assets.

INVESTMENT RATIOS

*Dividend yield**

$$\frac{£75{,}000}{(1{,}000{,}000 \times £1.25)} = \frac{£75{,}000}{£1{,}250{,}000} = 6\%$$

* like a number of investment ratios, this can be calculated *either* per share, *or* on the total shares in issue (as above).

Earnings per share

$$\frac{(£170{,}000 - £50{,}000 - £25{,}000)}{1{,}000{,}000} = \frac{£95{,}000}{1{,}000{,}000} = 9.5 \text{ pence per share}$$

Earnings yield

$$\frac{9.5\text{p}}{125\text{p}} = 7.6\%$$

Price/earnings ratio

$$\frac{125p}{9.5p} = 13.16 \text{ times}$$

Dividend cover

$$\frac{(£170,000 - £50,000 - £25,000)}{£75,000} = \frac{£95,000}{£75,000} = 1.27 \text{ times}$$

These ratios indicate that the company is not highly profitable for its shareholders (although shares are often bought for potential capital gains rather than income). The dividend yield is only 6 per cent, and the dividend is covered just 1.27 times: if profits were to fall, it is unlikely that the current level of dividend could be sustained. A lower price/earnings ratio would seem appropriate for this company.

CONCLUSION

This appears to be a profitable business, although there may be some scope for cutting down somewhat on the profit and loss account selling expenses (administration expenses could be looked at too). The business offers a reasonable return on capital, although things could be improved.

The company is solvent and has good working capital and liquid capital ratios. Gearing is low – a good sign in times of high interest rates.

The main area of weakness is in asset utilisation. It appears that the company could do much to reduce stock turnover and the debtors' collection period; at the same time creditors could be paid faster. Asset turnover is very low for this type of business and it does seem that there is much scope for expansion within the structure of the existing company. As the benefits of expansion flow through to the final accounts, the investment ratios will show an improvement from their present leisurely performance.

29.7 Limitations in the interpretation of accounts

Although accounting ratios can usefully highlight strengths and weaknesses, they should always be considered as a *part* of the overall assessment of a business, rather than as a whole. We have already referred (in Section 29.1) to the need to place ratios in context and relate them to a reference point or standard. The following limitations of ratio analysis should always be borne in mind:

1. **Retrospective nature of accounting ratios**
   Accounting ratios are usually *retrospective,* based on previous performance and conditions prevailing in the past. They may not necessarily be valid for making forward projections: for example, a large customer may become insolvent, so threatening the business with a bad debt, and also reducing sales in the future.

2. **Differences in accounting policies**
   When the accounts of a business are compared, either with previous years' figures, or with figures from a similar business, there is a danger that the comparative accounts are not drawn up on the same basis as those currently being worked on. Different accounting policies, in respect of depreciation and stock valuation for instance, may well result in distortion and invalid comparisons.

3. **Inflation**

Inflation may prove a problem, as most financial statements are prepared on an historic cost basis, that is, assets and liabilities are recorded at their original cost. As a result, comparison of figures from one year to the next may be difficult. In countries where inflation is running at high levels any form of comparison becomes practically meaningless.

We have already seen (in Chapter 13.7) how revaluation of an asset is used to introduce a higher value for the asset into the accounts – a way of adjusting individual assets, usually property, for the effects of inflation. Over the last two decades there have been several attempts by the accountancy profession to account more generally for the effects of inflation: to date, no widely acceptable solution has been devised.

4. **Reliance on standards**

We have already mentioned guideline standards for some accounting ratios, for instance 2 : 1 for the current ratio. There is a danger of relying too heavily on such *suggested* standards, and ignoring other factors in the balance sheet. An example of this would be to criticise a business for having a low current ratio when the business sells the majority of its goods for cash and consequently has a very low debtors figure: this would in fact be the case with many large and successful retail companies. Large manufacturing businesses are able to operate with lower current ratios because of their good reputation and creditworthiness (and also because many large firms are well-known for the slow payment of their creditors).

5. **Other considerations**

Economic: The general economic climate and the effect this may have on the nature of the business, eg in an economic downturn retailers are usually the first to suffer, whereas manufacturers feel the effects later.

State of the business: The chairman's report for a limited company should be read in conjunction with the final accounts and cashflow statements to ascertain an overall view of the state of the business. Of great importance are the products of the company and their stage in the product life cycle, eg is a car manufacturer relying on old models, or is there an up-to-date product range which appeals to buyers?

Comparing like with like: Before making comparisons between 'similar' businesses (or, indeed, departments or divisions within the same business), we need to ensure that we are comparing 'like with like'. Differences, such as the acquisition of assets – renting premises compared with ownership, leasing vehicles compared with ownership – will affect the profitability of the business and the structure of the balance sheet; likewise, the long-term financing of a business – the balance between share capital/owner's capital and loans – will also have an effect.

29.8 Chapter summary

❑ The following ratios are listed for easy reference for when you are working through interpretation questions:

Profitability

$$\frac{\text{Gross profit for year}}{\text{Sales for year}} \times \frac{100}{1} = \text{Gross profit/sales percentage}$$

$$\frac{\text{Net profit for year}}{\text{Sales for year}} \times \frac{100}{1} = \text{Net profit/sales percentage}$$

$$\frac{\text{Specified expense}}{\text{Sales for year}} \times \frac{100}{1} = \text{Expense/sales percentage}$$

$$\frac{\text{Net profit for year + loan/bank interest}}{\text{Sales for year}} \times \frac{100}{1} = \text{Operating profit percentage}$$

$$\frac{\text{Net profit for year}}{\text{Capital employed}} \times \frac{100}{1} = \text{Percentage return on capital employed}$$

Solvency/liquidity

$$\frac{\text{Current assets}}{\text{Current liabilities}} = \text{Working capital ratio}$$

$$\frac{\text{(Current assets – stock)}}{\text{Current liabilities}} = \text{Liquid capital ratio}$$

$$\frac{\text{Preference share capital + long-term loans, including debentures}}{\text{Ordinary share capital + reserves}} \times \frac{100}{1} = \text{Gearing percentage}$$

$$\frac{\text{Net profit + interest}}{\text{Interest}} = \text{Interest cover}$$

Asset utilisation

$$\frac{\text{Average stock}}{\text{Cost of goods sold}} \times 365 = \text{Stock turnover (days)}$$

$$\frac{\text{Debtors}}{\text{Credit sales for year}} \times 365 = \text{Debtors' collection period (days)}$$

$$\frac{\text{Creditors}}{\text{Purchases for year}} \times 365 = \text{Creditors' payment period (days)}$$

$$\frac{\text{Sales}}{\text{Net assets}} = \text{Asset turnover ratio}$$

$$\frac{\text{Ordinary shareholders' (or owners') funds}}{\text{Tangible assets}} = \text{Proprietary ratio}$$

Investment ratios

$$\frac{\text{Ordinary share dividend (in pence)}}{\text{Market price of ordinary share (in pence)}} \times \frac{100}{1} = \text{Dividend yield}$$

$$\frac{\text{Net profit, after corporation tax and preference dividends}}{\text{Number of issued ordinary shares}} = \text{Earnings per share}$$

$$\frac{\text{Earnings per ordinary share (in pence)}}{\text{Market price of ordinary share (in pence)}} \times \frac{100}{1} = \text{Earnings yield}$$

$$\frac{\text{Market price of ordinary share (in pence)}}{\text{Earnings per ordinary share (in pence)}} = \text{Price/earnings ratio}$$

$$\frac{\text{Net profit, after corporation tax and preference dividends}}{\text{Ordinary dividends}} = \text{Dividend cover}$$

29.9 Questions

29.1* The following information relates to two businesses, A and B:

	BUSINESS A		BUSINESS B	
	£000s	£000s	£000s	£000s
PROFIT AND LOSS ACCOUNT (EXTRACTS)				
Sales		3,057		1,628
Cost of goods sold		2,647		911
Gross Profit		410		717
Expenses		366		648
Net Profit		44		69
SUMMARISED BALANCE SHEETS				
Fixed Assets		344		555
Current Assets				
Stock	242		237	
Debtors	6		269	
Bank	3		1	
	251		507	
Less Current Liabilities	195		212	
Working Capital		56		295
NET ASSETS		400		850
FINANCED BY				
Capital		400		850

One business operates a chain of grocery supermarkets; the other is a heavy engineering company.

You are to:

(i) Calculate the following accounting ratios for both businesses:
   (a) gross profit percentage
   (b) net profit percentage
   (c) stock turnover (use balance sheet figure as *average* stock)
   (d) working capital (current) ratio
   (e) liquid capital ratio
   (f) debtors' collection period
   (g) return on capital employed

(ii) Indicate which company you believe to be the grocery supermarket chain and which the heavy engineering business. Briefly explain the reasons for your choice based on the ratios calculated and the accounting information.

29.2 The following summarised information is available to you:

J.D. ROWLES
TRADING AND PROFIT AND LOSS ACCOUNTS (EXTRACTS)
FOR THE YEAR ENDED 30 APRIL 19-4 AND 30 APRIL 19-5

	19-4	19-5
	£	£
Sales (all on credit)	120,000	200,000
Cost of Goods Sold	80,000	150,000
Gross Profit	40,000	50,000
Expenses	10,000	15,000
Net Profit	30,000	35,000

BALANCE SHEET (EXTRACTS) AS AT 30 APRIL 19-4 AND 30 APRIL 19-5

			19-4			19-5
	£	£	£	£	£	£
Fixed Assets			15,000			12,000
Current Assets						
Stock		7,000			18,000	
Debtors		12,000			36,000	
Bank		1,000			-	
		20,000			54,000	
Less Current Liabilities						
Creditors	6,000			15,000		
Bank overdraft	-			10,000		
		6,000			25,000	
Working Capital			14,000			29,000
NET ASSETS			29,000			41,000
FINANCED BY						
Capital						
Opening capital			22,000			29,000
Add net profit			30,000			35,000
			52,000			64,000
Less drawings			23,000			23,000
			29,000			41,000

Notes:

- there were no purchases or disposals of fixed assets during the year
- during 19-4 and 19-5 Rowles reduced his selling prices in order to stimulate sales
- it may be assumed that price levels were stable

You are to use accounting ratios to analyse and assess the profitability, liquidity and asset utilisation of the business over the two years.

29.3 The following are the summarised balance sheets at 31 December 19-9 and extracts from the trading and profit and loss accounts for 19-9 of Moa Ltd and Dodo Ltd:

SUMMARISED BALANCE SHEETS AT 31 DECEMBER 19-9

	Moa	*Dodo*
	£000	*£000*
Fixed assets at cost	200	640
Less: accumulated depreciation	75	100
	125	540
Stock	92	130
Debtors	76	80
Cash	12	–
	305	750
Ordinary shares of £1 each	100	100
Profit and loss account	125	400
Debenture	–	100
Trade creditors	80	140
Overdraft	–	10
	305	750

EXTRACTS FROM TRADING AND PROFIT AND LOSS ACCOUNTS FOR 19-9

	Moa	*Dodo*
	£000	*£000*
Sales	2,500	7,500
Gross profit	600	900
Net profit	100	300

Required:

(a) State for both Moa and Dodo the values of their current assets, current liabilities and working capital, and calculate the following ratios: working capital; acid test (liquidity); capital gearing; gross profit on sales; and net profit on sales. Your answer should be presented in a table:

	Moa	*Dodo*
Current assets	....	....
Current liabilities	....	....
Working capital	....	....
Working capital ratio	....	....
Acid test (liquidity) ratio	....	....
Capital gearing ratio	....	....
Gross profit on sales	....	....
Net profit on sales	....	....

(b) Comment on the differences between the two companies revealed by the ratios calculated in answer to part (a) of this question.

Notes:

1. You should show how each ratio is calculated
2. Work to two decimal places when calculating the ratios

[The Chartered Institute of Bankers, Spring 1990]

29.4* The summarised balance sheets of Ritt Ltd at the end of two consecutive financial years were as shown below.

SUMMARISED BALANCE SHEETS AS AT 31 MARCH

19-6			*19-7*	
£000	*£000*		*£000*	*£000*
		Fixed Assets (at written down values)		
50		Premises	48	
115		Plant and equipment	196	
42		Vehicles	81	
	207			325
		Current Assets		
86		Stock	177	
49		Debtors and prepayments	62	
53		Bank and cash	30	
188			269	
		Current Liabilities		
72		Creditors and accruals	132	
20		Proposed dividends	30	
92			162	
	96	**Working Capital**		107
	303	**NET ASSETS EMPLOYED**		432

(balance sheet continues on next page)

19-6 £000	19-6 £000		19-7 £000	19-7 £000
		FINANCED BY		
250		Ordinary share capital	250	
53		Reserves	82	
	303	Shareholders' funds		332
	–	Loan capital: 7% debentures		100
	303			432

Turnover was £541,000 and £675,000 for the years ended 31 March 19-6 and 19-7 respectively. Corresponding figures for cost of sales were £369,000 and £481,000, respectively.

At 31 March 19-5, reserves had totalled £21,000. Ordinary share capital was the same at the end of 19-5 as at the end of 19-6.

Required:

(a) Calculate, for each of the two years, the ratios listed below:

gross profit/turnover percentage
net profit/turnover percentage
turnover/net assets employed
net profit/net assets employed percentage
current assets/current liabilities
quick assets/current liabilities

(Calculations should be correct to one decimal place)

(b) Comment on each of the figures you have calculated in (a) above, giving probable reasons for the differences between the two years.

[The Chartered Association of Certified Accountants]

29.5 You are given summarised information about two firms in the same line of business: A and B, as follows:

Balance sheets at 30 June	A £000	A £000	A £000	B £000	B £000	B £000
Land			80			260
Buildings		120			200	
Less: Depreciation		40	80		–	200
Plant		90			150	
Less: Depreciation		70	20		40	110
			180			570
Stocks		80			100	
Debtors		100			90	
Bank		–			10	
		180			200	
Creditors	110			120		
Bank	50	160	20	–	120	80
			200			650
Capital b/forward			100			300
Profit for year			30			100
			130			400
Less: Drawings			30			40
			100			360
Land revaluation			–			160
Loan (10% per annum)			100			130
			200			650
Sales			1,000			3,000
Cost of sales			400			2,000

Required:

(a) Produce a table of eight ratios calculated for both businesses.

(b) Write a report briefly outlining the strengths and weaknesses of the two businesses. Include comment on any major areas where the simple use of the figures could be misleading.

[The Chartered Association of Certified Accountants]

29.6* The summarised trading and profit and loss accounts for the three years ended 30 September 19-8, 19-9 and 19-0 and the balance sheets as at 30 September 19-8, 19-9 and 19-0 of T Carr Limited are as follows:

TRADING AND PROFIT AND LOSS ACCOUNTS

Years ended 30 September		*19-8*		*19-9*		*19-0*
	£000	*£000*	*£000*	*£000*	*£000*	*£000*
Sales		120		180		270
Less: Cost of sales		80		135		216
Gross profit		40		45		54
Less: Overhead expenses						
Variable	18		27		27	
Fixed	10		10		20	
		28		37		47
Net profit		12		8		7

BALANCE SHEETS

As at 30 September		*19-8*		*19-9*		*19-0*
	£000	*£000*	*£000*	*£000*	*£000*	*£000*
Fixed assets		30		60		80
Current assets: Stock	24		25		40	
Debtors	26		40		55	
Balance at bank	20		10		–	
	70		75		95	
Less: Current liabilities						
Creditors	20		35		45	
Bank overdraft	–		–		10	
	20		35		55	
		50		40		40
		80		100		120
Share capital:						
Ordinary shares of £1		50		62		75
Retained earnings		30		38		45
		80		100		120

All the share capital of T Carr Limited is owned by two brothers, James and Henry Carr, who have bought additional shares, at par, in the company in 19-9 and 19-0. The company has not paid any dividends since 19-6.

The major objective of the company in each of the last two financial years has been to increase turnover by 50 per cent on the immediately preceding year.

Required:

(a) Prepare a table of four accounting ratios, each ratio showing a distinctly different aspect of changes in the company during the past three years.
Note: The ratios may be expressed as percentages.

(b) A brief, but reasoned, report addressed to James and Henry Carr concerning the advisability of the company continuing to concentrate on increasing turnover by 50% each year.

[Association of Accounting Technicians]

30 Cash Flow Statements

A balance sheet shows the financial state of a business at a particular date and is usually only prepared once a year. While it is possible to obtain a great deal of information on the progress of the business by comparing one year's balance sheet with that of the next year, it is more difficult to see what has gone on during the period between the two balance sheet dates.

A cash flow statement uses information from the accounting records (including profit and loss account) and balance sheet, and shows an overall view of money flowing in and out of a business during an accounting period.

Such a statement concentrates on the liquidity of a business and explains to the owner or shareholders why, after a year of good profits for example, there is a reduced balance at the bank or a larger bank overdraft, at the year-end than there was at the beginning of the year.

Cash flow statements are especially important because they deal with flows of money. It is invariably a shortage of money that causes most businesses to fail, rather than a poor quality product or service. The importance of the cash flow statement is such that Financial Reporting Standard No 1 (FRS 1) requires all but small companies to include this statement as a part of their accounts which they publish and send to shareholders. For sole traders and partnerships, the information that the statement contains is of considerable interest to the owner(s) and to a lender, such as a bank.

A cash flow statement can look either at what has gone on in a past accounting period, or it can, based on a forecast trading and profit and loss account and balance sheet, demonstrate the effect on cashflow of future alternative courses of action.

30.1 Format of the cash flow statement

Cash flow statements are divided into eight sections:

1. Operating activities
2. Returns on investments and servicing of finance
3. Taxation
4. Capital expenditure and financial investment
5. Acquisition and disposals
6. Equity dividends paid
7. Management of liquid resources
8. Financing

The cash flows for the year affecting each of these main areas of business activity are shown in the statement, although not every business will have cash flows under each of the eight sections.

Fig 30.1 shows the main cash inflows and outflows under each heading, and indicates the format of the cash flow statement. The first section – operating activities – needs further explanation, particularly as it is the main source of cash flow for most businesses.

operating activities

The net cash inflow from operating activities is calculated by using figures from the profit and loss account and balance sheet as follows:

- operating profit (ie net profit, before deduction of interest)
- add depreciation for the year (added to profit because depreciation is a non-cash expense, that is, no money is paid out by the business in respect of depreciation charged to profit and loss account)
- add decrease in debtors, or deduct increase in debtors
- add increase in creditors, or deduct decrease in creditors
- add decrease in stock, or deduct increase in stock

CASH FLOW STATEMENT

Operating activities

- Operating profit (ie net profit, before deduction of interest)
- Depreciation charge for the year (see Section 30.5 for treatment of a profit or a loss on sale of fixed assets)
- Changes in debtors, creditors and stock

Returns on investments and servicing of finance

- *Inflows:* interest received, dividends received
- *Outflows:* interest paid, dividends paid on preference shares (but not ordinary shares – see below)

Taxation

- *Outflow:* corporation tax paid by limited companies during the year

Capital expenditure and financial investment

- *Inflows:* sale proceeds from fixed assets and investments
- *Outflows:* purchase cost of fixed assets and investments

Acquisitions and disposals

- *Inflows:* sale proceeds from investments and interests in
  - subsidiary companies (where more than 50 per cent of the shares in another company is owned)
  - associated companies (where between 20 per cent and 50 per cent of the shares in another company is owned)
  - joint ventures (where a project is undertaken jointly with another company)
- *Outflows:* purchase cost of investments in subsidiary companies, associated companies, and of interests in joint ventures

Equity dividends paid

- *Outflow:* the amount of dividends paid to equity (ordinary) shareholders during the year (where the cash flow statement is for a sole trader or partnership, the amount of drawings will be shown here)

Management of liquid resources

- *Inflows:* sale proceeds from short-term investments that are almost as good as cash – such as treasury bills (a form of government debt), and term deposits of up to a year with a bank
- *Outflows:* purchase of short-term liquid investments

Financing

- *Inflows:* receipts from increase in capital /share capital, raising/increase of loans
- *Outflows:* repayment of capital/share capital/loans

Fig 30.1 Format of the cash flow statement

30.2 Layout of a cash flow statement

A cash flow statement uses a common layout which can be amended to suit the particular needs of the business for which it is being prepared. The following layout – with specimen figures included – is commonly used:

ABC LIMITED
CASH FLOW STATEMENT FOR THE YEAR ENDED 31 DECEMBER 19-1

	£	£
Operating activities:		
Operating profit (note: before tax and interest)	75,000	
Depreciation for year	10,000	
Decrease in stock	2,000	
Increase in debtors	(5,000)	
Increase in creditors	7,000	
Net cash inflow from operating activities		89,000
Returns on investments and servicing of finance:		
Interest received	10,000	
Interest paid	(5,000)	
		5,000
Taxation:		
Corporation tax paid (note: amount *paid* during year)		(6,000)
Capital expenditure and financial investment		
Payments to acquire fixed assets	(125,000)	
Receipts from sales of fixed assets	15,000	
		(110,000)
Acquisitions and disposals		
Purchase of subsidiary undertakings	(–)	
Sale of a business	–	–
Equity dividends paid: (note: amount *paid* during year)		(22,000)
Cash outflow before use of liquid resources and financing		(44,000)
Management of liquid resources:		
Purchase of treasury bills	(250,000)	
Sale of treasury bills	200,000	
		(50,000)
Financing:		
Issue of share capital	275,000	
Repayment of capital/share capital	(–)	
Increase in loans	–	
Repayment of loans	(90,000)	
		185,000
Increase in cash		91,000

Notes:

- The separate amounts shown for each section can, if preferred, be detailed in a note to the cash flow statement.
- Money amounts shown in brackets indicate a deduction or, where the figure is a sub-total, a negative figure.

- The changes in the main working capital items of stock, debtors and creditors have an effect on cash balances. For example, a decrease in stock increases cash, while an increase in debtors reduces cash.
- The cash flow statement concludes with a figure for the *increase or decrease in cash*. This is calculated from the subtotals of each of eight sections of the statement.

30.3 Worked example: a sole trader

Question

Mrs Green runs a children's clothes shop in rented premises in a small market town. Her balance sheets for the last two years are as follows:

BALANCE SHEET AS AT 31 DECEMBER

	19-1			19-2		
	£ Cost	£ Dep'n	£ Net	£ Cost	£ Dep'n	£ Net
Fixed assets						
Shop fittings	1,500	500	1,000	2,000	750	1,250
Current assets						
Stock		3,750			4,850	
Debtors		625			1,040	
Bank		220			–	
		4,595			5,890	
Less Current liabilities						
Creditors	2,020			4,360		
Bank	–			725		
		2,020			5,085	
Working capital			2,575			805
			3,575			2,055
Less Long-term liabilities						
Loan from husband			–			1,000
NET ASSETS			3,575			1,055
FINANCED BY						
Capital						
Opening capital			3,300			3,575
Add net profit for year			5,450			4,080
			8,750			7,655
Less drawings			5,175			6,600
			3,575			1,055

Note: Interest paid on the loan and bank overdraft in 19-2 was £450.

Mrs Green says to you: "I cannot understand why I am overdrawn at the bank by £725 on 31 December 19-2 when I made a profit of £4,080 during the year". She asks for your assistance in seeking an explanation.

Answer

A cash flow statement will give Mrs Green the answer:

CASH FLOW STATEMENT FOR THE YEAR ENDED 31 DECEMBER 19-2

	£	£
Operating activities:		
Operating profit (before interest)	4,530	
Depreciation for year	250	
Increase in stock	(1,100)	
Increase in debtors	(415)	
Increase in creditors	2,340	
Net cash inflow from operating activities		5,605
Returns on investments and servicing of finance:		
Interest paid		(450)
Taxation:		
Corporation tax paid		not applicable
Capital expenditure and financial investment:		
Payments to acquire fixed assets		(500)
Equity dividends paid: (drawings)		(6,600)
Cash outflow before use of liquid resources and financing		(1,945)
Financing:		
Loan from husband		1,000
Decrease in cash		(945)

Points to note:

- Net profit for the year (before interest) is calculated as:

net profit for 19-2	£4,080
interest for 19-2	£ 450
	£4,530

- Depreciation for the year of £250 is the amount of the increase in depreciation to date shown on the balance sheets, that is, £750 minus £500.
- An increase in stock and debtors reduces the cash available to the business (because stock is being bought, debtors are being allowed more time to pay). In contrast, an increase in creditors gives an increase in cash (because creditors are allowing Mrs Green more time to pay).
- In this example there is no tax paid (because Mrs Green is a sole trader who will be taxed as an individual, unlike a company which pays tax on its profits); however, the place where tax would appear is indicated on the cash flow statement.
- As this is a sole trader busines, drawings are shown on the cash flow statement in place of equity dividends.
- The change in the bank balance is summarised as follows: from a balance of £220 in the bank to an overdraft of £725 is a 'swing' in the bank of minus £945, which is the amount of the decrease in cash shown by the cash flow statement.

Explanation to Mrs Green

In this example, the statement highlights the following points for the owner of the business:

- net cash inflow from operating activities is £5,605, whereas owner's drawings are £6,600; this state of affairs cannot continue for long
- fixed assets costing £500 have been purchased
- a long-term loan of £1,000 has been raised from her husband
- over the year there has been a decrease in cash of £945, this trend cannot be continued for long
- by the end of 19-2 the business has an overdraft of £725, caused mainly by the excessive drawings of the owner
- in conclusion, the liquidity position of this business has deteriorated over the two years, and corrective action will be necessary

30.4 Worked example: a limited company

Question

The balance sheets of Newtown Trading Company Limited for 19-6 and 19-7 are as follows:

BALANCE SHEET AS AT 31 DECEMBER

	19-6			19-7		
	£	£	£	£	£	£
	Cost	Dep'n	Net	Cost	Dep'n	Net
Fixed assets	47,200	6,200	41,000	64,000	8,900	55,100
Current assets						
Stock		7,000			11,000	
Debtors		5,000			3,700	
Bank		1,000			500	
		13,000			15,200	
Less Current liabilities						
Creditors	3,500			4,800		
Proposed dividends	2,000			2,500		
Corporation tax	1,000			1,500		
		6,500			8,800	
Working capital			6,500			6,400
			47,500			61,500
Less Long-term liabilities						
Debentures			5,000			3,000
NET ASSETS			42,500			58,500
FINANCED BY						
Ordinary share capital			30,000			40,000
Share premium account			1,500			2,500
Retained profits			11,000			16,000
SHAREHOLDERS' FUNDS			42,500			58,500

Note: Interest paid on the loan in 19-7 was £400.

Prepare a cash flow statement for the year ended 31 December 19-7 and comment on the main points highlighted by the statement.

Answer

NEWTOWN TRADING COMPANY LIMITED
CASH FLOW STATEMENT FOR THE YEAR ENDED 31 DECEMBER 19-7

	£	£
Operating activities:		
Operating profit (before interest)*	9,400	
Depreciation for year§	2,700	
Increase in stock	(4,000)	
Decrease in debtors	1,300	
Increase in creditors	1,300	
Net cash inflow from operating activities		10,700
Returns on investments and servicing of finance:		
Interest paid		(400)
Taxation:		
Corporation tax paid		(1,000)
Capital expenditure and financial investment:		
Payments to acquire fixed assets		(16,800)
Equity dividends paid:		(2,000)
Cash outflow before use of liquid resources and financing		(9,500)
Financing:		
Issue of ordinary shares at a premium ie £10,000 + £1,000 =	11,000	
Repayment of debentures	(2,000)	
		9,000
Decrease in cash		(500)

Notes:

* Calculation of the operating profit for 19-7 before interest, tax and dividends:

	£
increase in retained profits	5,000
interest paid in 19-7	400
proposed dividends, 19-7	2,500
corporation tax, 19-7	1,500
operating profit before interest, tax and dividends	9,400

§ Depreciation charged: £8,900 – £6,200 = £2,700

Both proposed dividends and corporation tax – which are current liabilities at 31 December 19-6 – are paid in 19-7. Likewise, the current liabilities for dividends and tax at 31 December 19-7 will be paid in 19-8 (and will appear on that year's cash flow statement).

How useful is the statement?

The following points are highlighted by the statement:

- net cash inflow from operating activities is £10,700
- a purchase of fixed assets of £16,800 has been made, financed partly by operating activities, and partly by an issue of shares at a premium
- the bank balance during the year has fallen by £500, ie from £1,000 to £500
- in conclusion, the picture shown by the cash flow statement is that of a business which is generating cash from its operating activities and using them to build for the future

30.5 Profit or loss on sale of fixed assets

When a business sells fixed assets it is most unlikely that the resultant sale proceeds will equal the net book value (cost price, less depreciation to date). The accounting solution, as we have already seen in Chapter 13.6, is to transfer any small profit or loss on sale – *non-cash* items – to profit and loss account. However, such a profit or loss on sale must be handled with care when preparing a cash flow statement because, in such a statement we have to adjust for non-cash items when calculating the *net cash inflow from operating activities*; at the same time we must separately identify the amount of the sale proceeds of fixed assets in the *capital expenditure* section.

Example showing profit or loss on sale of fixed assets in a cash flow statement

H & J Wells are electrical contractors. For the year ended 30 June 19-2 their profit and loss account is as follows:

		£	£
Gross profit			37,500
Less expenses:			
General expenses		23,000	
Provision for depreciation:	machinery	2,000	
	vehicles	3,000	
			28,000
Net profit			9,500

Profit on sale

During the course of the year, but not yet recorded in their profit and loss account, they have sold the following fixed asset:

		£
Machine	cost price	1,000
	depreciation to date	750
	net book value	250
	sale proceeds	350

As the machine has been sold for £100 more than book value, this sum is shown in profit and loss account, as follows:

		£	£
Gross profit			37,500
Profit on sale of fixed assets			100
			37,600
Less expenses:			
General expenses		23,000	
Provision for depreciation:	machinery	2,000	
	vehicles	3,000	
			28,000
Net profit			9,600

The cash flow statement, based on the amended profit and loss account, will include the following figures:

CASHFLOW STATEMENT (EXTRACT) OF H & J WELLS
FOR THE YEAR ENDED 30 JUNE 19-2

	£	£
Operating activities:		
Operating profit (before interest)	9,600	
Depreciation	5,000	
Profit on sale of fixed assets	(100)	
(Increase)/decrease in stock	. . .	
(Increase)/decrease in debtors	. . .	
Increase/(decrease) in creditors	. . .	
Net cash inflow from operating activities		14,500
| |		
Capital expenditure and financial investment:		
Payments to acquire fixed assets	(. . .)	
Receipts from sales of fixed assets	350	
		350
| |		

Note that profit on sale of fixed assets is deducted in the operating activities section because it is non-cash income. (Only the sections of the cash flow statement affected by the sale are shown above.)

Loss on sale
If the machine had been sold for £150, this would have given a 'loss on sale' of £100. this amount would be debited to profit and loss account, to give an amended net profit of £9,400.

The effect on the cash flow statement would be twofold:

- In the operating activities section, loss on sale of fixed assets of £100 would be *added*; the net cash inflow from operating activities remains at £14,500 (which proves that both profit and loss on sale of fixed assets are non-cash items)

- In the capital expenditure section, receipts from sales of fixed assets would be £150

Conclusion
The rule for dealing with a profit or a loss on sale of fixed assets in cash flow statements is:

- *add* the amount of the loss on sale, or *deduct* the amount of the profit on sale, to or from the net profit when calculating the net cash flow from operating activities

- show the *total* sale proceeds, ie the amount of the cheque received, as receipts from sales of fixed assets in the capital expenditure section

30.6 Chapter summary

- The objective of a cash flow statement is to show an overall view of money flowing in and out of a business during an accounting period.

- A cashflow statement is divided into eight sections:
  1. operating activities
  2. returns on investments and servicing of finance
  3. taxation
  4. capital expenditure and financial investment
  5. acquisitions and disposals
  6. equity dividends paid
  7. management of liquid resources
  8. financing

- The Financial Reporting Standard No 1 on cash flow statements provides a specimen layout.

- Most limited companies are required to include a cash flow statement as a part of their published accounts. They are also useful statements for sole traders and partnerships.

30.7 Questions

30.1* John Smith has been in business for two years. He is puzzled by his balance sheets because, although they show a profit for each year, his bank balance has fallen and is now an overdraft. He asks for your assistance to explain what has happened. The balance sheets are as follows:

BALANCE SHEET AS AT 31 DECEMBER

		19-1			19-2	
	£	£	£	£	£	£
	Cost	Dep'n	Net	Cost	Dep'n	Net
Fixed Assets						
Fixtures and fittings	3,000	600	2,400	5,000	1,600	3,400
Current Assets						
Stock		5,500			9,000	
Debtors		750			1,550	
Bank		850			-	
		7,100			10,550	
Current Liabilities						
Creditors	2,500			2,750		
Bank overdraft	-			2,200		
		2,500			4,950	
Working Capital			4,600			5,600
NET ASSETS			7,000			9,000
FINANCED BY						
Capital			5,000			7,000
Add Net profit for year			8,750			11,000
			13,750			18,000
Less Drawings			6,750			9,000
			7,000			9,000

Note: Interest paid on the bank overdraft in 19-2 was £250.

You are to prepare a cash flow statement for the year-ended 31 December 19-2.

30.2 Richard Williams runs a stationery supplies shop; his balance sheets for the last two years are:

BALANCE SHEET AS AT 30 SEPTEMBER

	19-5			19-6		
	£ Cost	£ Dep'n	£ Net	£ Cost	£ Dep'n	£ Net
Fixed Assets	60,000	12,000	48,000	70,000	23,600	46,400
Current Assets						
Stock		9,800			13,600	
Debtors		10,800			15,000	
		20,600			28,600	
Less Current Liabilities						
Creditors	7,200			14,600		
Bank overdraft	1,000			4,700		
		8,200			19,300	
Working Capital			12,400			9,300
			60,400			55,700
Less Long-term Liabilities						
Bank loan			10,000			15,000
NET ASSETS			50,400			40,700
FINANCED BY						
Capital			50,000			50,400
Add Net profit/(loss)			10,800			(1,500)
			60,800			48,900
Less Drawings			10,400			8,200
			50,400			40,700

Note: Loan and overdraft interest paid in 19-6 was £2,200.

You are to prepare a cash flow statement for the year-ended 30 September 19-6.

30.3 Using the balance sheets of Richard Williams in question 30.2 (above), prepare revised cash flow statements for the year to 30 September 19-6, to take note of the following:

Situation 1
A fixed asset with a cost price of £5,000 and depreciation to date of £3,000 was sold for £2,500.

Situation 2
A fixed asset with a cost price of £5,000 and depreciation to date of £3,000 was sold for £1,500.

Notes:

- two separate cash flow statements for the year ended 30 September 19-6 are required
- assume that the balance sheet for 19-6 already includes the sale transactions, ie do not adjust the net loss by the amount of the profit or loss on sale, or the bank account by the sale proceeds

30.4 Martin Jackson is a shareholder in Retail News Limited, a company that operates a chain of newsagents throughout the West Midlands. Martin comments that, whilst the company is making reasonable profits, the bank balance has fallen quite considerably. He provides you with the following information for Retail News Limited:

BALANCE SHEET AS AT 31 DECEMBER

	19-4		19-5		19-6	
	£000	£000	£000	£000	£000	£000
Fixed Assets at cost		252		274		298
Add Additions during year		22		24		26
		274		298		324
Less Depreciation to date		74		98		118
		200		200		206
Current Assets						
Stock	50		64		70	
Debtors	80		120		160	
Bank	10		-		-	
	140		184		230	
Less Current Liabilities						
Creditors	56		72		78	
Bank	-		10		46	
Proposed dividends	16		20		16	
Corporation tax	4		5		8	
	76		107		148	
Working Capital		64		77		82
NET ASSETS		264		277		288
FINANCED BY						
Share Capital		200		210		210
Retained profits		64		67		78
		264		277		288

Note: Interest paid on the bank overdraft was: £3,000 in 19-5, and £15,000 in 19-6.

You are to prepare a cash flow statement for the years ended for 19-5 and 19-6.

Multiple-choice questions: chapters 29-30

- Read each question carefully
- Choose the *one* answer you think is correct (calculators may be needed)
- Answers are on page 486

1. The following information is available:

	£
Sales	200,000
Purchases	170,000
Opening stock	40,000
Closing stock	50,000

Gross profit percentage is:

A 10%
B 15%
C 20%
D 25%

2. The following information has been extracted from the accounts of Teme Traders Ltd:

	last year	*this year*
Sales	£300,000	£350,000
Gross profit percentage	30%	31%
Net profit percentage	15%	4%

What conclusion do you draw?

A buying prices have increased, but selling prices have not
B expenses have increased greatly
C closing stock has increased greatly
D the company has paid too large a dividend

3. Which one of the following costs is most likely to be semi-variable?

A purchase of raw materials
B factory rent
C royalties
D telephone charges

4. Operating profit is:

A profit after deducting interest
B profit before deducting interest
C profit before deducting depreciation
D gross profit before deducting expenses

5. The primary ratio is:

A net profit % x asset turnover ratio = return on capital employed
B gross profit % ÷ net profit % = operating profit %
C liquid capital ratio x net profit % = asset turnover ratio
D sales ÷ net assets = gearing ratio

6. Which one of the following would you *not* take into account when calculating working capital?

   A machinery
   B cash
   C debtors
   D accruals

7. Which one of the following would you *not* take into account when calculating the liquid capital ratio?

   A bank overdraft
   B prepayments
   C stock
   D creditors

8. The following information is available:

	£
Sales for the year	450,000
Purchases for the year	230,000
Opening stock	60,000
Closing stock	40,000

   The rate of stock turnover for the year is:

   A 5 times
   B 9 times
   C 4.6 times
   D 4.2 times

9. A cash flow statement shows:

   A net profit for the year
   B change in working capital for the year
   C the cash flowing in and out of the business during the year
   D a reconciliation with the bank statement balance

10. Which one of the following items, in a cash flow statement, would *not* be shown in the *operating activities* section?

   A dividends paid
   B depreciation for year
   C change in debtors
   D change in stock

11. Which one of the following items, in a cash flow statement, would *not* be shown in the *returns on investments and servicing of finance* section?

   A interest paid
   B repayment of long-term loan
   C dividends received
   D interest received

12. In a cash flow statement, which one of the following items would be shown in the *capital expenditure and financial investment* section?

   A interest received
   B sale of fixed assets
   C change in debtors
   D long-term loan raised

Appendix A
Final Accounts – Example Layout

This pro-forma layout for final accounts is for sole trader final accounts, and uses a vertical presentation. For partnerships and limited companies, the layout will need to be adjusted to take into account the different ways in which these businesses are owned and financed (see Chapters Twenty-two and Twenty-four, respectively).

TRADING AND PROFIT AND LOSS ACCOUNT OF ***name***
FOR THE YEAR/PERIOD ENDED ***date***

		£	£	£	
TRADING ACCOUNT	Sales			x	
	Less Sales returns			x	
	Net sales			x	(a)
	Opening stock		x		
	Purchases	x			
	Carriage in	x			
	Less Purchases returns	x			
	Net purchases		x		
			x		
	Less Closing stock		x		
	Cost of Goods Sold			x	(b)
	Gross profit (a) – (b)			x	(c)
PROFIT AND LOSS ACCOUNT	Add other income, eg				
	Discount received			x	(d)
	Reduction in provision for bad debts			x	(d)
	Profit on sale of fixed assets			x	(d)
	Other income			x	(d)
	(c) + (d)			x	(e)
	Less expenses, eg				
	Motor vehicle running expenses		x		
	Rent		x		
	Business rates		x		
	Heating and lighting		x		
	Telephone		x		
	Salaries and wages*		x		
	Discount allowed		x		
	Carriage out		x		
	Other items, eg				
	Provision for depreciation		x		
	Loss on sale of fixed assets		x		
	Bad debts written off		x		
	Increase in provision for bad debts		x		
				x	(f)
	Net profit (e) – (f)			x	(g)

* Wages are sometimes listed as an expense in the trading account section

BALANCE SHEET OF * name *** AS AT *** date *****

		£	£	£	
Fixed Assets		*Cost* (a)	*Dep'n to date* (b)	*Net*	(a) – (b)
Intangible:	Goodwill	x	x	x	
Tangible:	Premises	x	x	x	
	Equipment	x	x	x	
	Vehicles	x	x	x	
	etc	x	x	x	
		x	x	x	(c)
Current Assets					
Stock *(closing)*			x		
Debtors		x			
Less Provision for bad debts		x			
			x		
Prepayments			x		
Bank			x		
Cash			x		
			x		(d)
Less Current Liabilities					
Creditors		x			
Accruals		x			
Bank overdraft		x			
			x		(e)
Working Capital (d)– (e)				x	(f)
(c) + (f)				x	(g)
Less Long-term Liabilities					
Loans				x	(h)
NET ASSETS (g) – (h)				x	(i)
FINANCED BY					
Capital					
Opening capital				x	
Add Net profit (from profit and loss account)				x	
				x	
Less Drawings				x	
				x	(i)

Note: Balance sheet balances at points (i)

Practical point:
When preparing handwritten final accounts it is usual practice to underline all the headings and sub-headings shown in bold print in the example layout.

Appendix B
Answers to Questions

In this appendix answers are given to:
- multiple-choice questions
- questions marked with an asterisk from the chapters

Answers to multiple-choice questions

Question number	*1*	*2*	*3*	*4*	*5*	*6*	*7*	*8*	*9*	*10*	*11*	*12*
Page 48	A	C	D	C	A	A	D	B	A	A	C	D
Page 74	C	A	C	B	C	D	B	B	C	A	D	A
Page 119	B	C	B	D	D	A	D	B	C	A	D	B
Page 192	A	C	A	B	A	C	B	B	B	D	A	C
Page 231	A	B	C	D	C	B	B	C	C	A	C	B
Page 277	D	B	C	A	B	B	B	A	A	B	D	A
Page 324	A	D	A	A	C	D	D	C	B	B	B	A
Page 375	B	C	A	A	D	D	C	B	A	D	B	B
Page 445	A	C	B	C	D	D	A	B	C	D	C	A
Page 482	C	B	D	B	A	A	C	A	C	A	B	D

Answers to selected questions

Answers are given to those questions marked with an asterisk from the chapters. Where answers are given to questions from past examination papers of examining boards, these are the responsibility of the author and not the examining body.

The layout of answers is particularly important in this subject and so full display answers are given so that readers may compare their work with the suggested layout. All final accounts have been set out in vertical format.

CHAPTER 1

1.1
(a) ledger
(b) debtor
(c) creditor
(d) sales day book
(e) cash book
(f) nominal ledger
(g) assets – liabilities = capital
(h) business entity
(i) auditors

1.7

capital	£20,000
capital	£10,000
liabilities	£7,550
assets	£14,100
liabilities	£18,430
assets	£21,160

1.8
(a) Owner started in business with capital of £10,000 in the bank
(b) Bought office equipment for £2,000, paying by cheque
(c) Received a loan of £6,000 by cheque
(d) Bought a van for £10,000, paying by cheque
(e) Owner introduces £2,000 additional capital by cheque
(f) Loan repayment of £3,000 made by cheque

CHAPTER 2

2.2

Dr. **Bank Account** Cr.

19-2		£	19-2		£
1 May	Capital	6,000	4 May	Machinery	3,500
12 May	L Warner: loan	1,000	6 May	Office equipment	2,000
17 May	Commission received	150	10 May	Rent paid	350
			15 May	Wages	250
			20 May	Drawings	85
			25 May	Wages	135

Dr. **Capital Account** Cr.

19-2		£	19-2		£
			1 May	Bank	6,000

Dr. **Machinery Account** Cr.

19-2		£	19-2		£
4 May	Bank	3,500			

Dr. **Office Equipment Account** Cr.

19-2		£	19-2		£
6 May	Bank	2,000			

Dr. **Rent Account** Cr.

19-2		£	19-2		£
10 May	Bank	350			

Dr. **Lucy Warner: Loan Account** Cr.

19-2		£	19-2		£
			12 May	Bank	1,000

Dr. **Wages Account** Cr.

19-2		£	19-2		£
15 May	Bank	250			
25 May	Bank	135			

Dr. **Commission Received Account** Cr.

19-2		£	19-2		£
			17 May	Bank	150

Dr. **Drawings Account** Cr.

19-2		£	19-2		£
20 May	Bank	85			

2.4

Dr. **Bank Account** Cr.

19-2		£	19-2		£
1 Mar.	Capital	6,500	4 Mar.	Office equipment	1,000
5 Mar.	Bank loan	2,500	7 Mar.	Wages	250
8 Mar.	Commission received	150	10 Mar.	Rent paid	200
			12 Mar.	Drawings	175
			15 Mar.	Van	6,000

Dr. **Capital Account** Cr.

19-2		£	19-2		£
			1 Mar.	Bank	6,500

Dr. **Office Equipment Account** Cr.

19-2		£	19-2		£
4 Mar.	Bank	1,000			

Dr. **Bank Loan Account** Cr.

19-2		£	19-2		£
			5 Mar.	Bank	2,500

Dr. **Wages Account** Cr.

19-2		£	19-2		£
7 Mar.	Bank	250			

Dr.	Commission Received Account				Cr.
19-2		£	19-2		£
			8 Mar.	Bank	150

Dr.	Rent Account				Cr.
19-2		£	19-2		£
10 Mar.	Bank	200			

Dr.	Drawings Account				Cr.
19-2		£	19-2		£
12 Mar.	Bank	175			

Dr.	Van Account				Cr.
19-2		£	19-2		£
15 Mar.	Bank	6,000			

2.7 19-4

1 Jan.	Started in business with *capital* of £10,000 in the bank
2 Jan.	Bought *office equipment* for £3,000, paying by cheque
3 Jan.	Paid *business rates* of £1,500, by cheque
4 Jan.	*Commission received* £500, by cheque
5 Jan.	Withdrew £250 *cash* from the bank
6 Jan.	*Drawings* £500, by cheque
7 Jan.	Received a *bank loan* £2,500, by cheque
8 Jan.	Bought a *van* for £7,500, paying by cheque

Note: the name of the other account in the double-entry accounts is shown in italics

CHAPTER 3

3.2

Dr.	Bank Account				Cr.
19-1		£	19-1		£
1 Feb.	Capital	3,000	3 Feb.	Purchases	100
2 Feb.	Sales	250	5 Feb.	Wages	150
7 Feb.	Sales	300	12 Feb.	Purchases	200
15 Feb.	J Walters: loan	1,000	20 Feb.	Computer	1,950
25 Feb.	Sales	150	27 Feb.	Wages	125

Dr.	Capital Account				Cr.
19-1		£	19-1		£
			1 Feb.	Bank	3,000

Dr.	Sales Account				Cr.
19-1		£	19-1		£
			2 Feb.	Bank	250
			7 Feb.	Bank	300
			25 Feb.	Bank	150

Dr.	Purchases Account				Cr.
19-1		£	19-1		£
3 Feb.	Bank	100			
12 Feb.	Bank	200			

Dr.	Wages Account				Cr.
19-1		£	19-1		£
5 Feb.	Bank	150			
27 Feb.	Bank	125			

Dr.	J Walters: Loan Account				Cr.
19-1		£	19-1		£
			15 Feb.	Bank	1,000

Dr.	Computer Account				Cr.
19-1		£	19-1		£
20 Feb.	Bank	1,950			

3.3

Bank Account

19-1		*Debit* £	*Credit* £	*Balance* £
1 Feb.	Capital	3,000		3,000 Dr.
2 Feb.	Sales	250		3,250 Dr.
3 Feb.	Purchases		100	3,150 Dr.
5 Feb.	Wages		150	3,000 Dr.
7 Feb.	Sales	300		3,300 Dr.
12 Feb.	Purchases		200	3,100 Dr.
15 Feb.	J Walters: loan	1,000		4,100 Dr.
20 Feb.	Computer		1,950	2,150 Dr.
25 Feb.	Sales	150		2,300 Dr.
27 Feb.	Wages		125	2,175 Dr.

3.4

Dr.	Purchases Account				Cr.
19-1		£	19-1		£
4 Jan.	AB Supplies Ltd	250			
20 Jan.	Bank	225			

Dr.	AB Supplies Ltd				Cr.
19-1		£	19-1		£
15 Jan.	Bank	250	4 Jan.	Purchases	250

Dr.	Sales Account				Cr.
19-1		£	19-1		£
			5 Jan.	Bank	195
			7 Jan.	Cash	150
			17 Jan.	L Lewis	145

Bank Account

Dr.		£			Cr. £
19-1		£	19-1		£
5 Jan.	Sales	195	15 Jan.	AB Supplies Ltd	250
10 Jan.	J Johnson: loan	1,000	20 Jan.	Purchases	225
29 Jan.	L Lewis	145	31 Jan.	Mercia Office Supplies Ltd	160

Cash Account

Dr.					Cr.
19-1		£	19-1		£
7 Jan.	Sales	150	22 Jan.	Wages	125

J Johnson: Loan Account

Dr.					Cr.
19-1		£	19-1		£
			10 Jan.	Bank	1,000

L Lewis

Dr.					Cr.
19-1		£	19-1		£
17 Jan.	Sales	145	29 Jan.	Bank	145

Wages Account

Dr.					Cr.
19-1		£	19-1		£
22 Jan.	Cash	125			

Office Equipment Account

Dr.					Cr.
19-1		£	19-1		£
26 Jan.	Mercia Office Supplies Ltd	160			

Mercia Office Supplies Ltd

Dr.					Cr.
19-1		£	19-1		£
31 Jan.	Bank	160	26 Jan.	Office equipment	160

CHAPTER 4

4.1

(a) purchase order
(b) invoice
(c) cash discount
(d) trade discount
(e) net
(f) Value Added Tax
(g) credit note
(h) debit note
(i) statement of account

4.2

- Net: £175 + £30.62 VAT = £205.62
- 2½%: £175 + £29.85 VAT (£175 x 97½% x 17½%) = £204.85
- 5%: £175 + £29.09 VAT (£175 x 95% x 17½%) = £204.09

4.6

(a) F Ramsey & Son

(b) 12 Jul: goods sold on credit by F Ramsey & Son to W Hoddle Ltd
14 Jul: payment received by F Ramsey & Son from W Hoddle Ltd, including cash discount allowed to W Hoddle Ltd
20 Jul: goods returned by W Hoddle Ltd to F Ramsey & Son; credit note no 864 issued by F Ramsey & Son

(c) £54

(d) as a creditor

(e)

W Hoddle Ltd

Dr.					Cr.
19-7		£	19-7		£
1 Jul.	Balance b/d	522.80	14 Jul.	Cash/discount allowed	522.80
8 Jul.	Sales	178.00			
12 Jul.	Sales	132.80			

CHAPTER 5

5.2

Bank Account

Dr.					Cr.
19-0		£	19-0		£
1 Feb.	Capital	500	1 Feb.	Purchases	150
10 Feb.	Sales	290	5 Feb.	Rent paid	50
27 Feb.	Sales	240	22 Feb.	Advertising	25
			26 Feb.	Drawings	100
			28 Feb.	Balance c/d	705
		1,030			1,030
1 Mar.	Balance b/d	705	2 Mar.	Purchases	100
14 Mar.	J Lock: loan	450	5 Mar.	Rent paid	50
16 Mar.	Sales	330	23 Mar.	Drawings	75
26 Mar.	Sales	180	29 Mar.	Advertising	30
			31 Mar.	Balance c/d	1,410
		1,665			1,665
1 Apr.	Balance b/d	1,410			

Capital Account

Dr.					Cr.
19-0		£	19-0		£
31 Mar.	Balance c/d	500	1 Feb.	Bank	500
			1 Apr.	Balance b/d	500

Purchases Account

Dr.					Cr.
19-0		£	19-0		£
1 Feb.	Bank	150	31 Mar.	Balance c/d	250
2 Mar.	Bank	100			
		250			250
1 Apr.	Balance b/d	250			

Rent Account

Dr.		£			Cr. £
19-0		£	19-0		£
5 Feb.	Bank	50	31 Mar.	Balance c/d	100
5 Mar.	Bank	50			
		100			100
1 Apr.	Balance b/d	100			

Sales Account

Dr.		£			Cr. £
19-0		£	19-0		£
31 Mar.	Balance c/d	1,040	10 Feb.	Bank	290
			27 Feb.	Bank	240
			16 Mar.	Bank	330
			26 Mar.	Bank	180
		1,040			1,040
			1 Apr.	Balance b/d	1,040

Advertising Account

Dr.		£			Cr. £
19-0		£	19-0		£
22 Feb.	Bank	25	31 Mar.	Balance c/d	55
29 Mar.	Bank	30			
		55			55
1 Apr.	Balance b/d	55			

Drawings Account

Dr.		£			Cr. £
19-0		£	19-0		£
26 Feb.	Bank	100	31 Mar.	Balance c/d	175
23 Mar.	Bank	75			
		175			175
1 Apr.	Balance b/d	175			

J Lock: Loan Account

Dr.		£			Cr. £
19-0		£	19-0		£
31 Mar.	Balance c/d	450	14 Mar.	Bank	450
			1 Apr.	Balance b/d	450

Trial balance of A Thompson as at 31 March 19-0

	Dr. £	*Cr.* £
Bank	1,410	
Capital		500
Purchases	250	
Rent	100	
Sales		1,040
Advertising	55	
Drawings	175	
J Lock: loan		450
	1,990	1,990

5.5 (a) 3 Feb. Celia Donithorn receives a cheque for £190 from Georgina Harrison, and allows her cash discount of £10
6 Feb. Celia Donithorn sells goods £80, on credit to Georgina Harrison
10 Feb. Georgina Harrison returns goods £15 to Celia Donithorn, who issues a credit note

(b) £10 on £200 = 5%

(c) Georgina Harrison owes Celia Donithorn £65

5.6 (a) (i) M Johnston is a debtor of Devenish Interiors: the balance of £150 is brought down from the previous month.
(ii) J Kelly is a creditor of Devenish Interiors: the balance of £220 is brought down from the previous month.

(b) M Johnston.

(c) M Johnston has returned goods £10 to Devenish Interiors, who have issued a credit note.

(d) Devenish Interiors have paid for the purchases made on 6 April from J Kelly: the amount of the cheque was £105, and Devenish Interiors have received £5 discount from J Kelly for quick settlement.

(e) Credit note.

CHAPTER 6

6.2

Sales Day Book

Date	*Details*	*Invoice No*	*Folio*	*Net*	*VAT*	*Gross*
19-6				£	£	£
2 Feb.	Wyvern Fashions			200	35	235
10 Feb.	Zandra Smith			160	28	188
15 Feb.	Just Jean			120	21	141
23 Feb.	Peter Sanders			320	56	376
24 Feb.	H Wilson			80	14	94
26 Feb.	Mercian Models			320	56	376
28 Feb.	Totals for month			1,200	210	1,410

Purchases Day Book

Date	*Details*	*Invoice No*	*Folio*	*Net*	*VAT*	*Gross*
19-6				£	£	£
1 Feb.	Flair Clothing			520	91	611
4 Feb.	Modernwear			240	42	282
18 Feb.	Quality Clothing			800	140	940
28 Feb.	Flair Clothing			200	35	235
28 Feb.	Totals for month			1,760	308	2,068

GENERAL LEDGER

Value Added Tax Account

Dr.		£			Cr. £
19-6		£	19-6		£
28 Feb.	Purchases Day Book	308	28 Feb.	Sales Day Book	210
			28 Feb.	Balance c/d	98
		308			308
1 Mar.	Balance b/d	98			

6.5

Sales Day Book

Date	Details	Invoice No	Folio	Net	VAT	Gross
19-2				£	£	£
5 Jan.	Mereford College	1093	SL 201	3,900.00	682.50	4582.50
7 Jan.	Carpminster College	1094	SL 202	8,500.00	1,487.50	9,987.50
14 Jan.	Carpminster College	1095	SL 202	1,800.50	315.08	2,115.58
14 Jan.	Mereford College	1096	SL 201	2,950.75	516.38	3,467.13
20 Jan.	Carpminster College	1097	SL 202	3,900.75	682.63	4583.38
22 Jan.	Mereford College	1098	SL 201	1,597.85	279.62	1,877.47
31 Jan.	Totals for month			22,649.85	3,963.71	26,613.56

Purchases Day Book

Date	Details	Invoice No	Folio	Net	VAT	Gross
19-2				£	£	£
2 Jan.	Macstrad plc	M1529	PL 101	2,900.00	507.50	3,407.50
3 Jan.	Amtosh plc	A7095	PL 102	7,500.00	1,312.50	8,812.50
18 Jan.	Macstrad plc	M2070	PL 101	1,750.00	306.25	2,056.25
19 Jan.	Amtosh plc	A7519	PL 102	5,500.00	962.50	6,462.50
31 Jan.	Totals for month			17,650.00	3,088.75	20,738.75

Sales Returns Day Book

Date	Details	Credit Note No	Folio	Net	VAT	Gross
19-2				£	£	£
13 Jan.	Mereford College	CN109	SL 201	850.73	148.87	999.60
27 Jan.	Mereford College	CN110	SL 201	593.81	103.91	697.72
31 Jan.	Totals for month			1,444.54	252.78	1,697.32

Purchases Returns Day Book

Date	Details	Credit Note No	Folio	Net	VAT	Gross
19-2				£	£	£
10 Jan.	Macstrad plc	MC105	PL 101	319.75	55.95	375.70
12 Jan.	Amtosh plc	AC 730	PL 102	750.18	131.28	881.46
23 Jan.	Macstrad plc	MC120	PL 101	953.07	166.78	1,119.85
31 Jan.	Totals for month			2,023.00	354.01	2,377.01

SALES LEDGER

Mereford College (account no 201)

Dr.			Cr.		
19-2		£	19-2		£
1 Jan.	Balance b/d	705.35	13 Jan.	Sales Returns	999.60
5 Jan.	Sales	4,582.50	27 Jan.	Sales Returns	697.72
14 Jan.	Sales	3,467.13	31 Jan.	Balance c/d	8,935.13
22 Jan.	Sales	1,877.47			
		10,632.45			10,632.45
1 Feb.	Balance b/d	8,935.13			

Carpminster College (account no 202)

Dr.			Cr.		
19-2		£	19-2		£
1 Jan.	Balance b/d	801.97	31 Jan.	Balance c/d	17,488.43
7 Jan.	Sales	9,987.50			
14 Jan.	Sales	2,115.58			
20 Jan.	Sales	4,583.38			
		17,488.43			17,488.43
1 Feb.	Balance b/d	17,488.43			

PURCHASES LEDGER

Macstrad plc (account no 101)

Dr.			Cr.		
19-2		£	19-2		£
10 Jan.	Purchases Returns	375.70	1 Jan.	Balance b/d	1,050.75
23 Jan.	Purchases Returns	1,119.85	2 Jan.	Purchases	3,407.50
31 Jan.	Balance c/d	5,018.95	18 Jan.	Purchases	2,056.25
		6,514.50			6,514.50
			1 Feb.	Balance b/d	5,018.95

Amtosh plc (account no 102)

Dr.			Cr.		
19-2		£	19-2		£
12 Jan.	Purchases Returns	881.46	1 Jan.	Balance b/d	2,750.83
31 Jan.	Balance c/d	17,144.37	3 Jan.	Purchases	8,812.50
			19 Jan.	Purchases	6,462.50
		18,025.83			18,025.83
			1 Feb.	Balance b/d	17,144.37

GENERAL LEDGER

Sales Account

Dr.			Cr.		
19-2		£	19-2		£
			31 Jan.	Sales Day Book	22,649.85

Purchases Account

Dr.			Cr.		
19-2		£	19-2		£
31 Jan.	Purchases Day Book	17,650.00			

Sales Returns Account

Dr.			Cr.		
19-2		£	19-2		£
31 Jan.	Sales Returns Day Book	1,444.54			

Purchases Returns Account

Dr.			Cr.		
19-2		£	19-2		£
			31 Jan.	Purchases Returns Day Book	2,023.00

Value Added Tax Account

Dr.		£			Cr. £
19-2		£	19-2		£
31 Jan.	Purchases Day Book	3,088.75	31 Jan.	Sales Day Book	3,963.71
31 Jan.	Sales Returns Day Book	252.78	31 Jan.	Purchases Returns Day Book	354.01
31 Jan.	Balance c/d	976.19			
		4,317.72			4,317.72
			1 Feb.	Balance b/d	976.19

6.6

	Source document	Book of prime entry	Account to be debited	Account to be credited
(a)	invoice received	purchases day book	purchases	A Cotton
(b)	invoice issued	sales day book	D Law	sales
(c)	cheque received	cash book	bank	sales
(d)	credit note received	purchases returns day book	A Cotton	purchases returns
(e)	cheque issued	cash book	gas	bank
(f)	credit note issued	sales returns day book	sales returns	D Law

CHAPTER 7

7.1 (a)

Month	Purchases £	VAT £	Sales £	VAT £
April	5,400	945	8,200	1,435
May	4,800	840	9,400	1,645
June	6,800	1,190	10,800	1,890

(b) **Value Added Tax Account**

Dr.		£			Cr. £
19-4		£	19-4		£
30 Apr.	Purchases Day Book	945	30 Apr.	Sales Day Bok	1,435
31 May	Purchases Day Book	840	31 May	Sales Day Book	1,645
30 Jun.	Purchases Day Book	1,190	30 Jun.	Sales Day Book	1,890
30 Jun.	Balance c/d	1,995			
		4,970			4,970
			1 Jul.	Balance b/d	1,995

(c) VAT account has a credit balance of £1,995: this means that Wyvern Computers owes the amount to HM Customs and Excise. The amount is payable not later than 31 July 19-4. The book-keeping entries for payment will be

—*debit* Value Added Tax Account

—*credit* bank account

If Wyvern Computers prepares a balance sheet at 30 June 19-4, the amount owing to HM Customs and Excise will be listed as a creditor.

7.4 (a) **Sales Day Book**

Date	Details	Invoice No	Folio	Net	VAT	Gross
19-1				£	£	£
19 Aug.	E Newman	SI 1547		156.00	27.30	183.30
20 Aug.	Wyvern Traders Ltd	SI 1548		228.00	39.90	267.90
21 Aug.	Teme Supplies	SI 1549		350.00	61.25	411.25
22 Aug.	Lugg Brothers & Co	SI 1550		1,200.00	210.00	1,410.00
23 Aug.	E Newman			400.00	70.00	470.00
23 Aug.	Totals for week			2,334.00	408.45	2,742.45

Sales Returns Day Book

Date	Details	Credit Note No	Folio	Net	VAT	Gross
19-1				£	£	£
22 Aug.	Wyvern Traders Ltd	CN 121		228.00	39.90	267.90
23 Aug.	E Newman	CN 122		78.00	13.65	91.65
23 Aug.	Totals for week			306.00	53.55	359.55

(b) *Sales Day Book:*

- The total of net sales is credited to sales account in the general ledger.
- The total of the VAT column is credited to the VAT account in the general ledger.
- The individual gross amounts for each customer are debited to the debtors' personal accounts in the sales ledger.

Sales Returns Day Book:

- The total of net sales returns is debited to sales returns account in the general ledger.
- The total of the VAT column is debited to the VAT account in the general ledger.
- The individual gross amounts for each customer are credited to the debtors' personal accounts in the sales ledger.

(c) **E Newman**

Dr.		£			Cr. £
19-1		£	19-1		£
1 Aug.	Balance b/d	440.00	7 Aug.	Bank	418.00
19 Aug.	Sales	183.30	7 Aug.	Discount allowed	22.00
23 Aug.	Sales	470.00	23 Aug.	Sales returns	91.65
			31 Aug.	Balance c/d	561.65
		1,093.30			1,093.30
1 Sep.	Balance b/d	561.65			

8.2

Dr. **Cash Book** Cr.

Date	Details	Folio	Discount allowed	Cash	Bank	Date	Details	Folio	Discount received	Cash	Bank
19-2			£	£	£	19-2			£	£	£
1 Jun.	Balance b/d			280		1 Jun.	Balance b/d				2,240
3 Jun.	G Wheaton		5		195	8 Jun.	F Lloyd		10		390
5 Jun.	T Francis		2	53		10 Jun.	Wages			165	
16 Jun.	Bank	C		200		12 Jun.	A Morris		3	97	
18 Jun.	H Watson		30		640	16 Jun.	Cash	C			200
28 Jun.	M Perry		6		234	20 Jun.	R Marks				78
30 Jun.	K Willis			45		24 Jun.	D Farr		2		65
30 Jun.	Balance c/d				1,904	26 Jun.	Telephone			105	
						30 Jun.	Balance c/d			211	
			43	578	2,973				15	578	2,973
1 Jul.	Balance b/d			211		1 Jul.	Balance b/d				1,904

Dr. **Discount Allowed Account** Cr.

		£			£
19-2			19-2		
30 Jun.	Cash Book	43			

Dr. **Discount Received Account** Cr.

		£			£
19-2			19-2		
			30 Jun.	Cash Book	15

8.3

Cash Book (credit side only)

		Discount £	Cash £	Bank £
2 Jan.	Balance b/d			380 (...B...)
4 Jan.	M Hughes	30 (...C...)		570 (...K...)
9 Jan.	Bank		240 (...H...)	
16 Jan.	Motor van			5,850 (...I...)
20 Jan.	Purchases		735 (...A...)	
31 Jan.	Balances c/d		25 (...L...)	260 (...F...)
		30	1,000	7,060

8.5

Dr. **Cash Book** Cr.

Date	Details	Folio	Disc allwd	VAT	Cash	Bank	Date	Details	Folio	Disc recd	VAT	Cash	Bank
19-0			£	£	£	£	19-0			£	£	£	£
1 Oct.	Balance b/d				142		1 Oct.	Balance b/d					177
1 Oct.	Bank	C			250		1 Oct.	HM Customs					
3 Oct.	P Donavon					230		& Excise					535
3 Oct.	G Stevens					690	1 Oct.	Cash	C				250
3 Oct.	Sales			96		736	2 Oct.	Telephone			27		207
4 Oct.	S Turnbull					90	4 Oct.	M Palmer					297
5 Oct.	Sales			57	437		4 Oct.	N Collins					110
5 Oct.	Cash					450	5 Oct.	Bank				450	
							5 Oct.	Balances c/d				379	620
				153	829	2,196					27	829	2,196
6 Oct.	Balances b/d				379	620							

Dr. **Value Added Tax Account** Cr.

		£			£
19-0			19-0		
5 Oct.	Cash Book	27	5 Oct.	Cash Book	153

Dr. **Telephones Account** Cr.

		£			£
19-0			19-0		
2 Oct.	Cash Book	180			

8.8

Petty Cash Book

Receipts	Date	Details	Voucher No.	Total Payment	Travel	Stationery	Postages	Office expenses	Magazines/ newspapers
					Analysis columns				
£	19-7			£	£	£	£	£	£
19.37	1 May	Balance b/d							
60.63	1 May	Cash received							
	1 May	Bus fares		0.41	0.41				
	2 May	Stationery		2.35		2.35			
	4 May	Bus fares		0.30	0.30				
	7 May	Postage stamps		1.70			1.70		
	7 May	Trade journal		0.95					0.95
	8 May	Bus fares		0.64	0.64				
	11 May	Correcting fluid		1.29		1.29			
	12 May	Typewriter ribbons		5.42				5.42	
	14 May	Parcel postage		3.45			3.45		
	15 May	Paper clips		0.42		0.42			
	15 May	Newspapers		2.00					2.00
	16 May	Photocopier repair		16.80				16.80	
	19 May	Postage stamps		1.50			1.50		
	20 May	Drawing pins		0.38		0.38			
	21 May	Train fare		5.40	5.40				
	22 May	Photocopier paper		5.63		5.63			
	23 May	Display decorations		3.07				3.07	
	23 May	Correcting fluid		1.14		1.14			
	25 May	Wrapping paper		0.78		0.78			
	27 May	String		0.61		0.61			
	27 May	Sellotape		0.75		0.75			
	27 May	Biro pens		0.46		0.46			
	28 May	Typewriter repair		13.66				13.66	
	30 May	Bus fares		2.09	2.09				
				71.20	8.84	13.81	6.65	38.95	2.95
	30 May	Balance c/d		8.80					
80.00				80.00					
8.80	1 Jun.	Balance b/d							
71.20	1 Jun.	Cash received							

Other analysis columns and classifications could be used as appropriate

8.9

Petty Cash Book

Receipts	Date	Details	Voucher No.	Total Payment	VAT	Postages	Travel	Meals	Stationery
					Analysis columns				
£	19-1			£	£	£	£	£	£
150.00	1 May	Balance b/d							
	1 May	Postages	455	7.00		7.00			
	1 May	Travel	456	2.85			2.85		
	2 May	Meal allowance	457	6.11				6.11	
	3 May	Taxi	458	4.70	0.70		4.00		
	4 May	Stationery	459	3.76	0.56				3.20
	7 May	Postages	460	5.25		5.25			
	8 May	Travel	461	6.50			6.50		
	9 May	Meal allowance	462	6.11				6.11	
	10 May	Stationery	463	8.46	1.26				7.20
	14 May	Taxi	464	5.17	0.77		4.40		
	17 May	Stationery	465	4.70	0.70				4.00
	21 May	Travel	466	3.50			3.50		
	21 May	Postages	467	4.50		4.50			
	23 May	Bus fares	468	3.80			3.80		
	26 May	Catering	469	10.81	1.61			9.20	
	27 May	Postages	470	3.50		3.50			
	27 May	Stationery	471	7.52	1.12				6.40
	28 May	Travel	472	6.45			6.45		
				100.69	6.72	20.25	31.50	21.42	20.80
100.69	31 May	Cash received							
	31 May	Balance c/d		150.00					
250.69				250.69					
150.00	1 Jun.	Balance b/d							

CHAPTER 9

9.2 (a)

Cash Book (bank columns)

Dr.		£			Cr. £
19-9			19-9		
31 May	Balance b/d*	270	31 May	Mortgage standing order	90
			31 May	Bank charges	14
			31 May	Balance c/d	166
		270			270
1 Jun.	Balance b/d	166			

* Total of debt entries – total of credit entries, ie £716 – £446 = £270

(b)

C COD

Bank Reconciliation Statement as at 31 May 19-9

			£	£
Balance at bank as per cash book				166
Add:	cheque drawn, not yet recorded on the bank statement	N Fish		108
				274
Less:	amounts paid in, not yet recorded on the bank statement	V Perch	90	
		B Tench	48	
				138
Balance at bank as per bank statement				136

9.3 (a)

Cash Book (bank columns)

Dr.		£			Cr. £
19-0			19-0		
31 May	Balance b/d	1,055	31 May	Bank charges	22
31 May	Credit transfer	22	31 May	Direct debit	32
			31 May	Balance c/d	1,023
		1,077			1,077
1 Jun.	Balance b/d	1,023			

(b)

J KEARNS
Bank Reconciliation Statement as at 31 May 19-0

		£	£
Balance at bank as per bank statement			955
Less: cheques drawn, not yet recorded on the bank statement	131	30	
	133	250	
	134	27	
			307
			648
Add: amount paid in, not yet recorded on the bank statement			375
Balance at bank as per cash book			1,023

9.6 (a) The opening cash book balance can be reconciled with the opening bank statement balance as follows:

		£	£
Balance at bank as per cash book (1 March)			4,201
Add: cheques drawn, not yet recorded on the bank statement	543984	1,512	
	543985	68	
	543986	237	
			1,817
			6,018
Less: amount paid in, not yet recorded on the bank statement until 3 March			2,489
Balance at bank as per bank statement			3,529

J C LIMITED
Bank Reconciliation Statement as at 31 March 19-0

		£	£
Balance at bank as per cash book			(12,879)
Less: bank charges		195	
dishonoured cheque (Brown & Co)		234	
standing order (rates)		4,029	
			(4,458)
Adjusted cash book balance			(17,337)
Add: cheques drawn, not yet recorded on the bank statement	543984	1,512	
	543987	279	
	543993	2,305	
	543994	5,242	
			9,338
			(7,999)
Add: errors to be investigated			
• counter credit 14 March, cash book understated by		100	
• counter credit 23 March, cash book understated by £5,332 – £3,246		2,086	
• cheque no 543989, cash book overstated by £11,987 – £1,197		10,790	
• cheque no 543991, cash book overstated by £547 – £57		490	
			13,466
Balance at bank as per bank statement			5,467

(b) Three from:

- verify the cash book balance
- identify unpresented cheques, and amounts paid into the bank, not yet recorded on the bank statement
- identify errors – either in the cash book or on the bank statement
- identify 'stale' unpresented cheques, ie those over six months old

9.8 (a)

	£	£
Balance of statement at 1 October 19-9		1,000
Less: payment credited on statement on 5 October	220	
discount received	4	
		224
Balance of account at 1 October 19-9		776

(b)

	£	£
Balance of account at 31 October 19-9		248
Add: payment made on 30 October	1,235	
discount received	65	
		1,300
Balance of statement at 31 October 19-9		1,548

CHAPTER 11

11.1

MATTHEW LLOYD

TRADING AND PROFIT AND LOSS ACCOUNT FOR THE YEAR ENDED 31 DECEMBER 19-8

	£	£
Sales		125,890
Opening stock	–	
Purchases	94,350	
Less Closing stock	5,950	
Cost of Goods Sold		88,400
Gross profit		37,490
Less expenses:		
Business rates	4,850	
Heating and lighting	2,120	
Wages and salaries	10,350	
		17,320
Net profit		20,170

BALANCE SHEET AS AT 31 DECEMBER 19-8

	£	£
Fixed Assets		
Office equipment		8,500
Motor vehicles		10,750
		19,250
Current Assets		
Stock	5,950	
Debtors	3,950	
Bank	4,225	
Cash	95	
	14,220	
Less Current Liabilities		
Creditors	2,200	
Working Capital		12,020
NET ASSETS		31,270
FINANCED BY		
Capital		
Opening capital		20,000
Add Net profit		20,170
		40,170
Less Drawings		8,900
		31,270

11.3 Business A: gross profit £8,000, net profit £4,000
Business B: gross profit £17,000, expenses £7,000
Business C: sales £36,500, net profit £6,750
Business D: purchases £25,500, expenses £9,800
Business E: opening stock £8,350, net loss £1,700
Business F: closing stock £4,600, expenses £15,000

11.5

JOHN ADAMS

TRADING AND PROFIT AND LOSS ACCOUNT FOR THE YEAR ENDED 31 DECEMBER 19-7

	£	£
Sales		259,688
Opening stock	14,350	
Purchases	114,472	
	128,822	
Less Closing stock	16,280	
Cost of Goods Sold		112,542
Gross profit		147,146
Less expenses:		
Business rates	13,718	
Heating and lighting	12,540	
Wages and salaries	42,614	
Motor vehicle expenses	5,817	
Advertising	6,341	
		81,030
Net profit		66,116

BALANCE SHEET AS AT 31 DECEMBER 19-7

	£	£
Fixed Assets		
Premises		75,000
Office equipment		33,000
Motor vehicles		21,500
		129,500
Current Assets		
Stock	16,280	
Debtors	23,854	
Bank	1,235	
Cash	125	
	41,494	
Less Current Liabilities		
Creditors	19,736	
Working Capital		21,758
		151,258
Less Long-term Liabilities		
Loan from bank		35,000
NET ASSETS		116,258
FINANCED BY		
Capital		
Opening capital		62,500
Add Net profit		66,116
		128,616
Less Drawings		12,358
		116,258

12.3 (a) (i) The balance sheet is a statement of the assets and liabilities of a business *at a particular moment in time.*

(ii) The trading and profit and loss account has been prepared already. Transfers to the ledger accounts have been made, including the recording in stock account of the value of the closing stock at 31 October 19-2.

(b)

BALANCE SHEET OF G WILLIAMS AS AT 31 OCTOBER 19-2

	£	£	£
Fixed Assets			
Premises			27,400
Furniture and fittings			3,075
Vehicles			6,100
Plant and machinery			13,840
			50,415
Current Assets			
Stock		3,073	
Debtors		5,127	
Prepayment		50	
Cash		500	
		8,750	
Less Current Liabilities			
Creditors	2,065		
Accrual	225		
Bank overdraft	1,875		
		4,165	
Working Capital			4,585
			55,000
Less Long-term Liabilities			
Loan from Loamshire Finance Co			7,500
NET ASSETS			47,500
FINANCED BY			
Capital			
Opening capital (missing figure)			45,330
Add Net profit			12,970
			58,300
Less Drawings			10,800
			47,500

(c)

Capital Account

Dr.		£			Cr. £
19-1/-2			19-1/-2		
31 Oct.	Drawings	10,800	1 Nov.	Balance b/d	45,330
31 Oct.	Balance c/d	47,500	31 Oct.	Profit and loss account	12,970
		58,300			58,300
19-2/-3			19-2/-3		
			1 Nov.	Balance b/d	47,500

12.5

PROFIT AND LOSS ACCOUNT OF SANDRA BLACK FOR THE YEAR ENDED 31 MAY 19-0

	£	£
Income from clients		32,500
Commissions from other sources		800
Discount received		150
		33,450
Less expenses:		
Stationery £2,100 – £150	1,950	
Wages	7,600	
Rent and rates £2,350 – £120	2,230	
Vehicle expenses	2,000	
Light and heat £800 + £45	845	
Insurance	850	
Telephone £280 + £52	332	
Sundry expenses	175	
		15,982
Net profit		17,468

BALANCE SHEET OF SANDRA BLACK AS AT 31 MAY 19-0

	£	£	£
Fixed Assets			
Equipment			4,500
Vehicles			6,500
			11,000
Current Assets			
Stock		150	
Debtors		760	
Prepayment		120	
Cash		175	
		1,205	
Less Current Liabilities			
Creditors	670		
Accruals £52 + £45	97		
Bank overdraft	250		
		1,017	
Working Capital			188
NET ASSETS			11,188
FINANCED BY			
Capital			
Opening capital			4,920
Add Net profit			17,468
			22,388
Less Drawings			11,200
			11,188

12.6 (a)

Rates Account

Dr.		£			Cr. £
19-1/-2			19-1/-2		
31 Jan.	Balance b/d	500	31 Jan.	Profit and loss account	400
			31 Jan.	Balance c/d	100
		500			500
19-2/-3			19-2/-3		
1 Feb.	Balance b/d	100			

Rent Receivable Account

Dr.		£			Cr. £
19-1/-2			19-1/-2		
31 Jan.	Profit and loss account	300	31 Jan.	Balance b/d	225
			31 Jan.	Balance c/d	75
		300			300
19-2/-3			19-2/-3		
1 Feb.	Balance b/d	75			

Insurance Account

Dr.		£			Cr. £
19-1/-2			19-1/-2		
31 Jan.	Balance b/d	450	31 Jan.	Drawings	50
			31 Jan.	Profit and loss account	400
		450			450

Wages Account

Dr.		£			Cr. £
19-1/-2			19-1/-2		
31 Jan.	Balance b/d	5,200	31 Jan.	Profit and loss account	5,500
31 Jan.	Balance c/d	300			
		5,500			5,500
19-2/-3			19-2/-3		
			1 Feb.	Balance b/d	300

(b)

PROFIT AND LOSS ACCOUNT OF BILTON POTTERIES FOR THE YEAR ENDED 31 JANUARY 19-2

	£	£
Gross profit		11,507
Add Rent receivable		300
		11,807
Less expenses:		
Insurance	400	
Rates	400	
Wages	5,500	
		6,300
Net profit		5,507

BALANCE SHEET OF BILTON POTTERIES AS AT 31 JANUARY 19-2

	£	£	£
Fixed Assets			
Premises			5,000
Current Assets			
Stock		1,000	
Debtors		434	
Prepayment		100	
Debtor for rent		75	
Bank		3,218	
		4,827	
Less Current Liabilities			
Creditors	870		
Accrual	300		
		1,170	
Working Capital			3,657
NET ASSETS			8,657
FINANCED BY			
Capital			
Opening capital			7,000
Add Net profit			5,507
			12,507
Less Drawings £3,800 + £50			3,850
			8,657

12.8 (a)

Rent Account

Dr.		£			Cr. £
19-1/-2			19-1/-2		
1 Jul.	Bank	480	31 Mar.	Profit and loss account	1,920
30 Sep.	Bank	480			
2 Jan.	Bank	480			
31 Mar.	balance c/d	480			
		1,920			1,920
19-2/-3			19-2/-3		
			1 Apr.	Balance b/d	480

(b)

Rates Account

Dr.		£			Cr. £
19-1/-2			19-1/-2		
1 Apr.	Balance b/d	280	31 Mar.	Profit and loss account	1,180
1 Jul.	Bank	600	31 Mar.	Balance c/d	300
1 Jan.	Bank	600			
		1,480			1,480
19-2/-3			19-2/-3		
1 Apr.	Balance b/d	300			

(c)

Insurance Account

Dr.		£			Cr. £
19-1/-2			19-1/-2		
1 Apr.	Balance b/d	600	31 Mar.	Profit and loss account	600

13.3

HAZEL HARRIS
TRADING AND PROFIT AND LOSS ACCOUNT FOR THE YEAR ENDED 31 DECEMBER19-4

		£	£
Sales			614,000
Opening stock		63,000	
Purchases		465,000	
		528,000	
Less Closing stock		88,000	
Cost of Goods Sold			440,000
Gross profit			174,000
Add Discount received			8,140
			182,140
Less expenses:			
Building repairs		8,480	
Motor expenses		2,680	
Wages and salaries		89,240	
Discount allowed		10,610	
Business rates and insurance		5,620	
General expenses		15,860	
Provision for depreciation:	motor vehicles	2,400	
	furniture and fittings	2,500	
			137,390
Net profit			44,750

BALANCE SHEET AS AT 31 DECEMBER 19-4

	£	£	£
Fixed Assets	*Cost*	*Dep'n to date*	*Net*
Land and buildings	100,000	–	100,000
Motor vehicles	12,000	4,800	7,200
Furniture and fittings	25,000	5,000	20,000
	137,000	9,800	127,200
Current Assets			
Stock		88,000	
Debtors		52,130	
Prepayment		450	
		140,580	
Less Current Liabilities			
Creditors	41,850		
Accrual	3,180		
Bank	2,000		
		47,030	
Working Capital			93,550
			220,750
Less Long-term Liabilities			
Bank loan			75,000
NET ASSETS			145,750
FINANCED BY			
Capital			
Opening capital			125,000
Add Net profit			44,750
			169,750
Less Drawings			24,000
			145,750

13.4 (a)

Provision for Depreciation Account: Car

Dr.		£			Cr. £
19-1			19-1		
31 Dec.	Balance c/d	1,500	31 Dec.	Profit and loss account	1,500
19-2			19-2		
31 Dec.	Balance c/d	2,625	1 Jan.	Balance b/d	1,500
			31 Dec.	Profit and loss account	1,125
		2,625			2,625
19-3			19-3		
31 Dec.	Disposals account	3,469	1 Jan.	Balance b/d	2,625
			31 Dec.	Profit and loss account	844
		3,469			3,469

(b)

BALANCE SHEET (EXTRACT) AS AT 31 DECEMBER 19-1

	£	£	£
Fixed Assets	*Cost*	*Dep'n to date*	*Net*
Car	6,000	1,500	4,500

BALANCE SHEET (EXTRACT) AS AT 31 DECEMBER 19-2

	£	£	£
Fixed Assets	*Cost*	*Dep'n to date*	*Net*
Car	6,000	2,625	3,375

(c)

Disposals Account

Dr.		£			Cr. £
19-3			19-3		
31 Dec.	Car account	6,000	31 Dec.	Provision for dep'n account	3,469
31 Dec.	Profit and loss account (profit on sale)	219	31 Dec.	Bank	2,750
		6,219			6,219

13.8 (a)

Annual depreciation charges

	Straight line	*Diminishing balance*	*Units of output**
Year 1 (19-1)	£7,000	£15,400	£5,600
Year 2 (19-2)	£7,000	£ 6,930	£7,000
Year 3 (19-3)	£7,000	£ 3,119	£7,700
Year 4 (19-4)	£7,000	£ 2,551§	£7,700
	£28,000	£28,000	£28,000

* units of output based on 14p per film processed
§ year 4 depreciation adjusted to leave a nil residual value

(b) (i)

Minilab Account

Dr.		£			Cr. £
19-3			19-3		
1 Jan.	Balance b/d	28,000	1 Jul.	Disposals account	28,000

Provision for Depreciation Account: Minilab

Dr.		£			Cr. £
19-3			19-3		
1 Jul.	Disposals account	17,500	1 Jan.	Balance b/d	14,000
			1 Jul.	Depreciation	3,500
		17,500			17,500

Disposals Account

Dr.		£		Cr.	£
19-3			19-3		
1 Jul.	Minilabs account	28,000	1 Jul.	Prov'n for dep'n account	17,500
			1 Jul.	Bank	10,000
			31 Dec.	Profit and loss account (loss on sale)	500
		28,000			28,000

13.9 A The owner has introduced £30,000 of additional capital, which has been paid into the bank account.

B £4,000 of stock has been purchased on credit.

C Property has been purchased (or improvements made to property) costing £50,000; financed by a bank loan.

D Stock which originally cost £5,000 has been sold on credit for £7,000; profit of £2,000 made.

E £3,000 cash withdrawn from the bank for use in the business.

F Accrued expense of £10,000 paid by cheque.

G A motor van (or vans) which had cost £3,000 has been sold for £4,000 – a cheque received for this amount. The profit on sale of £1,000 has been credited to capital account.

H A creditor for £6,000 has been paid, £5,000 by cheque and £1,000 discount received.

I A loan repayment of £1,000 has been made by cheque.

J A debtor (or debtors) has paid £7,000 by cheque.

CHAPTER 14

14.1 (i) Provision for bad debts:

19-7: £32,350 total debtors – £850 bad debts written off = £31,500 x 5% = £1,575 provision for bad debts.

19-8 £36,500 total debtors x 5% = £1,825 provision for bad debts required. Therefore, *increase* in provision for bad debts is £1,825 – £1,575 = £250.

Provision for Bad and Doubtful Debts Account

Dr.		£		Cr.	£
19-7			19-7		
31 Dec.	Balance c/d	1,575	31 Dec.	Profit and loss account	1,575
19-8			19-8		
31 Dec.	Balance c/d	1,825	1 Jan.	Balance b/d	1,575
			31 Dec.	Profit and loss account (increase in provision)	250
		1,825			1,825
19-9			19-9		
			1 Jan.	Balance b/d	1,825

Bad Debts Account

Dr.		£		Cr.	£
19-7			19-7		
31 Dec.	D Rice	420	31 Dec.	Profit and loss account	850
31 Dec.	T Higgs	310			
31 Dec.	C Clay	120			
		850			850
19-8			19-8		
1 Jul.	H Carr	640	31 Dec.	Profit and loss account	930
1 Oct.	A Moore	290			
		930			930

(ii) **BALANCE SHEET (EXTRACT) AS AT 31 DECEMBER 19-7**

	£	£	£
Current Assets			
Debtors	31,500		
Less provision for bad debts	1,575		
		29,925	

BALANCE SHEET (EXTRACT) AS AT 31 DECEMBER 19-8

	£	£	£
Current Assets			
Debtors	36,500		
Less provision for bad debts	1,825		
		34,675	

14.5

STAMPER
TRADING AND PROFIT AND LOSS ACCOUNT FOR THE YEAR ENDED 31 DECEMBER 19-9

		£	£
Sales			150,750
Opening stock		25,600	
Purchases £112,800 – £450		112,350	
		137,950	
Less Closing stock		27,350	
Cost of Goods Sold			110,600
Gross profit			40,150
Less expenses:			
Wages		12,610	
Rent £2,500 – £500		2,000	
Motor expenses £1,240 + £140		1,380	
Provision for depreciation:	motor vehicle	3,000	
	equipment	3,150	
Bad debt written off		200	
Insurance £1,000 + £450		1,450	
			23,790
Net profit			16,360

15.1

HENRY

	Trial balance as at 31 December 19-9		Adjustments		Trading account		Profit and loss account		Balance Sheet *Assets Liabilities*	
	Dr	Cr	Dr	Cr	Dr	Cr	Dr	Cr	Dr	Cr
	£	£	£	£	£	£	£	£	£	£
Sales		185,500				185,500				
Purchases	97,250				97,250					
Debtors	10,500								10,500	
Creditors		9,000								9,000
Stock at 1 Jan. 19-9	15,250				15,250					
Bad debts	500						500			
Rent	12,750		1,000				13,750			
Wages	33,250			500			32,750			
Provision for bad debts		1,000		50						1,050
Fixed assets (cost)	120,000								120,000	
Provision for depreciation		36,000		12,000						48,000
Bank	11,500								11,500	
Capital		95,000								95,000
Drawings	25,500								25,500	
	326,500	326,500								
Stock at 31 Dec. 19-9:										
• trading account				18,500		18,500				
• balance sheet			18,500						18,500	
Accrued expenses				1,000						1,000
Prepaid expenses			500						500	
Provision for bad debts			50				50			
Provision for depreciation			12,000				12,000			
Gross profit (balancing figure)					91,500			91,500		
Net profit (balancing figure)							32,450			32,450
			32,050	32,050	204,000	204,000	91,500	91,500	186,500	186,500

BALANCE SHEET AS AT 31 DECEMBER 19-9

	£	£	£
Fixed Assets	*Cost*	*Dep'n to date*	*Net*
Motor vehicle	17,000	6,000	11,000
Equipment	15,000	7,650	7,350
	32,000	13,650	18,350
Current Assets			
Stock		27,350	
Debtors		9,750	
Prepayment		500	
Bank		900	
Cash		250	
		38,750	
Less Current Liabilities			
Creditors	8,100		
Accrual	140		
		8,240	
Working Capital			30,510
NET ASSETS			48,860
FINANCED BY			
Capital			
Opening capital			52,500
Add Net profit			16,360
			68,860
Less Drawings			20,000
			48,860

14.7

A Received a cheque for £5,000 from a trade debtor.

B £11,000 of stock has been purchased on credit.

C Stock which originally cost £14,000 has been sold for £20,000 with payment by cheque; profit of £6,000 made.

D Equipment has been purchased for £25,000; financed by a bank loan.

E Owner withdrew stocks costing £10,000 for own use, *or* theft/loss of stock recorded in the accounts.

F £2,000 of expenses, including accrued expenses of £1,000, have been paid in cash.

G Buildings have been revalued to show an increase of £50,000, *or* additional capital of £50,000 has been used to purchase further buildings.

H Bad debts of £3,000 have been written off (or a provision for bad debts of £3,000 has been made).

I A creditor for £6,000 has been paid, £5,000 by cheque and £1,000 discount received.

J A prepaid expense of £2,000 is refunded in cash.

16.3 (a) Consistency concept: he should continue to use reducing balance method (it won't make any difference to bank manager anyway).

(b) Prudence concept: stock valuation should be at lower of cost and net realisable value, ie £10,000 in this case.

(c) Business entity concept: car is an asset of John's firm, not a personal asset (in any case personal assets, for sole traders and partnerships, might well be used to repay debts of firm).

(d) Accruals concept: expenses and revenues must be matched, therefore it must go through the old year's account.

(e) Going concern concept presumes that business will continue to trade in the foreseeable future: alternative is 'gone concern' and assets may have very different values.

16.5 (a) **LIFO**

Date	Receipts		Issues		Balance		
19-9	Quantity	Price	Quantity	Price	Quantity	Price	Total
1 Sep.	Balance b/d				NIL		
3 Sep.	200 @	£1.00			200 x	£1.00 =	£200.00
7 Sep.			180 @	£1.00	20 x	£1.00 =	£20.00
8 Sep.	240 @	£1.50			20 x 240 x 260	£1.00 = £1.50 =	£20.00 £360.00 £380.00
14 Sep.			170 @	£1.50	20 x 70 x 90	£1.00 = £1.50 =	£20.00 £105.00 £125.00
15 Sep.	230 @	£2.00			20 x 70 x 230 x 320	£1.00 = £1.50 = £2.00 =	£20.00 £105.00 £460.00 £585.00
21 Sep.			150 @	£2.00	20 x 70 x 80 x 170	£1.00 = £1.50 = £2.00 =	£20.00 £105.00 £160.00 £285.00

AVCO

Date	Receipts		Issues		Balance		
19-9	Quantity	Price	Quantity	Price	Quantity	Price	Total
1 Sep.	Balance b/d				NIL		
3 Sep.	200 @	£1.00			200 x	£1.00 =	£200.00
7 Sep.			180 @	£1.00	20 x	£1.00 =	£20.00
8 Sep.	240 @	£1.50			20 x 240 x 260 x	£1.00 = £1.50 = £1.46 =	£20.00 £360.00 £380.00
14 Sep.			170 @	£1.46	90 x	£1.46 =	£131.40
15 Sep.	230 @	£2.00			90 x 230 x 320 x	£1.46 = £2.00 = £1.85 =	£131.40 £460.00 £591.40
21 Sep.			150 @	£1.85	170 x	£1.85 =	£314.50

(b) In times of rising prices, LIFO produces lower profits than AVCO. This is because, under LIFO the latest prices are charged to cost of goods sold, whereas under AVCO prices charged to cost of sales are smoothed and are lower than AVCO. In times of falling prices, the reverse will apply.

16.6 **Item DW/04** **STOCK CARD**

Date	*Details*	*Receipts* *Units*	*£*	*Issues* *Units*	*£*	*Balance* *Units*	*£*
1 Sep.	Balance					12	144
6 Sep.	Issue note no A237			8	96	4	48
8 Sep.	Invoice no 784	20	240			24	288
15 Sep.	Invoice no 847	48	576			72	864
17 Sep.	Issue note no D534			18	216	54	648
22 Sep.	Invoice no 984	20	240			74	888
24 Sep.	Issue note no B631			64	768	10	120
30 Sep.	Stock loss			2	24	8	96

Note: A stock loss of two units has occurred during the month. This will have been caused by:
—short delivery, ie incorrect number of units received, two units short, *or*
—over-issue, ie incorrect number of units issued, two units extra, *or*
—theft, if continued stock losses are detected, the matter will need further investigation

16.8 (a)

MARY SMITH
TRADING AND PROFIT AND LOSS ACCOUNT FOR THE QUARTER ENDED 30 NOVEMBER 19-0

	First in, first out £	£	*Last in, first out* £	£
Sales 4 @ £560, 20 @ £680		15,840		15,840
Cost of Goods Sold (see note 1, below)		10,408		11,392
Gross profit		5,432		4,448
Less expenses:				
Overheads	1,520		1,520	
Sales commissions (2½% of gross profit)	136		111	
Provision for depreciation: lawn mower (see note 2)	4		5	
		1,660		1,636
Net profit		3,772		2,812

Note 1
Purchases: 12 @ £384 = £4,608
8 @ £450 = £3,600
16 @ £489 = £7,824
£16,032

FIFO

Date	Receipts			Issues			Balance			
19-0	Quantity		Price	Quantity		Price	Quantity		Price	Total
September	12	@	£384				12	x	£384 =	£4,608
October	8	@	£450	4 1	@ @	£384 £384 (own use)	7 8 15	x x	£384 = £450 =	£2,688 £3,600 £6,288
November	16	@	£489	7 8 5	@ @ @	£384 £450 £489	10 1 11	x x	£489 = £350* =	£4,890 £ 350 £5,240

* net realisable value

Cost of goods sold:
purchases £16,032
less own use £ 384
£15,648
less closing stock £ 5,240
cost of goods sold £10,408

LIFO

Date	Receipts			Issues			Balance			
19-0	Quantity		Price	Quantity		Price	Quantity		Price	Total
September	12	@	£384				12	x	£384 =	£4,608
October	8	@	£450	4 1	@ @	£450 £450 (own use)	12 3 15	x x	£384 = £450 =	£4,608 £1,350 £5,958
November	16	@	£489	16 3 1	@ @ @	£489 £450 £384	10 1 11	x x	£384 = £350* =	£3,840 £ 350 £4,190

* net realisable value

Cost of goods sold:
purchases £16,032
less own use £ 450
£15,582
less closing stock £ 4,190
cost of goods sold £11,392

Note 2
Depreciation: FIFO
(£384 ÷ 8) ÷ 12 (one month's use) = £4

Depreciation: LIFO
(£450 ÷ 8) ÷ 12 (one month's use) = £5 approximately

(b) Quarter ended 31 August 19-0:
salary £3,750
interest on savings at 10% pa £ 175
£3,925

Quarter ended 30 November 19-0:
net profit (FIFO basis) £3,772

(c) *FIFO*

Advantages: realistic; easy to calculate; stock valuation comprises actual prices at which items have been bought; closing stock valuation is close to the most recent prices

Disadvantages: prices at which goods are issued are not necessarily the latest prices; in times of rising prices, profits will be higher than with other methods

LIFO

Advantages: goods are issued at the latest prices; it is easy to calculate

Disadvantages: illogical; closing stock valuation is not usually at most recent prices; when stocks are being run down, issues will dip into old stock at out-of-date prices

CHAPTER 17

17.3 (a)

Vehicle Account

Dr.		£			Cr. £
19-7/-8			19-7/-8		
1 Nov.	Bank	12,000	31 Oct.	Balance c/d	12,000
19-8/-9			19-8/-9		
1 Nov.	Balance b/d	12,000	1 Jan.	Disposals account	12,000
6 Dec.	Bank	18,000	31 Oct.	Balance c/d	18,000
		30,000			30,000
19-9/-0			19-9/-0		
1 Nov.	Balance b/d	18,000	7 Mar.	Disposals account	18,000
7 Mar.	Disposals account (part-exchange allowance)	13,500	31 Oct.	Balance c/d	28,000
7 Mar.	Supatruks Ltd (balance due)	14,500			
		46,000			46,000
19-0/-1			19-0/-1		
1 Nov.	Balance b/d	28,000			

Provision for Depreciation Account - Vehicle

Dr.		£			Cr. £
19-7/-8			19-7/-8		
31 Oct.	Balance c/d	3,000	31 Oct.	Profit and loss account	3,000
19-8/-9			19-8/-9		
1 Jan.	Disposals account	3,000	1 Nov.	Balance b/d	3,000
31 Oct.	Balance c/d	4,500	31 Oct.	Profit and loss account	4,500
		7,500			7,500
19-9/-0			19-9/-0		
7 Mar.	Disposals account	4,500	1 Nov.	Balance b/d	4,500
31 Oct.	Balance c/d	7,000	31 Oct.	Profit and loss account	7,000
		11,500			11,500
19-0/-1			19-0/-1		
			1 Nov.	Balance b/d	7,000

BALANCE SHEET (EXTRACT) OF W E CARRYIT AS AT 31 OCTOBER 19-8

	£ Cost	£ Dep'n to date	£ Net
Fixed Assets			
Vehicle	12,000	3,000	9,000

BALANCE SHEET (EXTRACT) OF W E CARRYIT AS AT 31 OCTOBER 19-9

	£ Cost	£ Dep'n to date	£ Net
Fixed Assets			
Vehicle	18,000	4,500	13,500

BALANCE SHEET (EXTRACT) OF W E CARRYIT AS AT 31 OCTOBER 19-0

	£ Cost	£ Dep'n to date	£ Net
Fixed Assets			
Vehicle	28,000	7,000	21,000

(b)

Date	Details	Folio	Dr £	Cr £
19-9				
1 Jan.	Disposals account		12,000	
	Vehicle			12,000
	Provision for depreciation – vehicle		3,000	
	Disposals account			3,000
	Bank		8,450	
	Disposals account			8,450
	Profit and loss account		550	
	Disposals account			550
			24,000	24,000
	Lorry, registration no .... written off in accident. Insurance proceeds £8,450 received. Loss of £550 transferred to profit and loss account.			
19-0				
7 Mar.	Disposals account		18,000	
	Vehicle			18,000
	Provision for depreciation – vehicle		4,500	
	Disposals account			4,500
	Vehicle		13,500	
	Disposals account			13,500
	Vehicle		14,500	
	Supatruks Ltd			14,500
			50,500	50,500
	Purchase of new lorry, registration no ...., for £28,000. Part-exchange allowance of £13,500 against lorry, registration no ....; balance of £14,500 payable on 7 March 19-1.			

CHAPTER 18

18.2

Suspense Account

Dr.	£		Cr. £
Forest and Co	70	Sales	70
Drystone Brothers	210	Trial balance difference (missing figure)	350
Clair and Sons	140		
	420		420

Notes:

(a) Debit suspense account £70; credit Forest and Co £70. (It is probably better to show this as two debits and two credits of £35 each.)

(b) Debit suspense account £210; credit Drystone Brothers £210. (Instead of recording the difference, it is probably better in practice to take out the wrong amount of £700, and then put through a transaction for the correct amount for £910.)

(c) Debit sales account £70; credit suspense account £70. (As the sales day book has been overcast, the error will have been taken into sales account.)

(d) Debit suspense account £140; credit Clair and Sons £140. (As before, it is better in practice to take out the wrong amount, and then put through a transaction for the correct amount.)

18.4 **Statement of corrected net profit for the year ended 31 December 19-2**

		£	£
Net profit (unadjusted)			3,700
Add:	discount received	100	
	wages overstated	140	
			240
			3,940
Less:	sales overcast	420	
	prepayment of expense overstated (ie expense understated)	18	
	closing stock overstated	30	
			468
Adjusted net profit			3,472

18.7 (a) **JOURNAL**

Details	*Dr*	*Cr*
	£	£
Stock account	33,600	
Trading account		33,600
Profit and loss account	86,000	
Provision for depreciation account:		
property		22,000
equipment		24,000
motor vehicles		40,000
Provision for bad debts account	3,660	
Profit and loss account		3,660
Purchases account*	396	
XJ Supplies*		396
P Next	770	
B Necht		770
Suspense account*	99	
Discount allowed account*		99
Returns outwards (purchases returns) account*	550	
Suspense account*		550

* Alternatively in each case, take out the wrong amount, and then put through a transaction for the correct amount.

(b) **Statement of corrected net profit for the year ended 31 May 19-0**

		£	£
Net profit (unadjusted)			677,220
Add:	closing stock	33,600	
	reduction in provision for bad debts	3,660	
	discount allowed overstated	99	
			37,359
			714,579
Less:	depreciation for the year	86,000	
	purchases understated	396	
	returns outwards overstated	550	
			86,946
Adjusted net profit			627,633

CHAPTER 19

19.2 **Sales Ledger Control Account: Section 1**

Dr.				Cr.			
19..			£	19..			£
1 Jan.	Balances b/d		84,200	1 Jan.	Balances b/d		190
	Sales for year		678,672		Cash received from debtors		697,384
31 Dec.	Balances c/d		281		Sales returns		3,475
					Discount allowed		2,760
					Bad debts written off		3,660
				31 Dec.	Balances c/d		55,684
			763,153				763,153
19..				19..			
1 Jan.	Balances b/d		55,684	1 Jan.	Balances b/d		281

Sales Ledger Control Account: Section 2

Dr.			Cr.		
19..		£	19..		£
1 Jan.	Balances b/d	136,200	1 Jan.	Balances b/d	1,260
	Sales for year	497,285		Cash received from debtors	526,294
31 Dec.	Balances c/d	1,328		Sales returns	1,226
				Discount allowed	887
				Bad debts written off	1,284
			31 Dec.	Balances c/d	103,862
		634,813			634,813
19..			19..		
1 Jan.	Balances b/d	103,862	1 Jan.	Balances b/d	1,328

19.4 **Sales Ledger Control Account**

Dr.			Cr.		
19-0		£	19-0		£
1 Apr.	Balances b/d	95,617	1 Apr.	Balances b/d	613
	Credit sales	759,348		Sales returns	3,549
30 Apr.	Balances c/d	161		Cash received from debtors	703,195
				Discount allowed	25,355
				Bad debts written off	5,123
			30 Apr.	Balances c/d	117,291
		855,126			855,126
1 May	Balances b/d	117,291	1 May	Balances b/d	161

Purchases Ledger Control Account

Dr.			Cr.		
19-0		£	19-0		£
1 Apr.	Balances b/d	782	1 Apr.	Balances b/d	78,298
	Purchases returns	4,581		Credit purchases	621,591
	Cash paid to creditors	612,116	30 Apr.	Balances c/d	329
	Discount received	8,570			
30 Apr.	Balances c/d	74,169			
		700,218			700,218
1 May	Balances b/d	329	1 May	Balances b/d	74,169

Note:

- cash sales and cash purchases do not go through the control accounts
- change in provision for bad debts is not entered in the sales ledger control account

19.6 (a)

Sales Ledger Control Account

Dr.	£		Cr. £
Balances b/d	25,300	Sales returns for year	4,220
Credit sales for year	157,220	Cash and cheques received	133,880
Refunds to customers	440	Discount allowed	5,410
Dishonoured cheques	110	Bad debts written off	750
		Set-offs	690
		Balances c/d	38,120
	183,070		183,070
Balances b/d	38,120		

Purchases Ledger Control Account

Dr.	£		Cr. £
Purchases returns for year	4,040	Balances b/d	19,960
Cash and cheques paid	150,960	Credit purchases for year	161,090
Discount received	3,710		
Set-offs	690		
Balances c/d	21,650		
	181,050		181,050
		Balances b/d	21,650

Note:

- change in provision for bad debts is not entered in the sales ledger control account

(b)
- The sales ledger control account balance agrees with the figure used in the trial balance at 31 May 19-0.
- The purchases ledger control account is £90 more than the figure used in the trial balance at 31 May 19-0. The error occurs in the purchases ledger section of his accounts.

19.7 (a)

Purchases Ledger Control Account

Dr.	£		Cr. £
Purchases returns	4,564	Balances b/d	45,870
Cash/cheques paid to creditors	231,570	Credit purchases	249,560
Discount received	3,608		
Set-off	818		
Balances c/d	54,870		
	295,430		295,430
		Balances b/d	54,870

(b) (i)

	£	£
Balance from control account		54,870
Add: invoice omitted from purchases book		1,850
		56,720
Less: credit note omitted	870	
petty cash payments to suppliers	625	
		1,495
Corrected control account balance		55,225

(ii)

	£	£
Balances of individual creditor's accounts		51,120
Add: invoice not posted to creditor's account	1,125	
invoices omitted from purchases book	1,850	
undercasting error	2,000	
		4,975
		56,095
Less: credit note omitted		870
Revised balances of creditors' accounts		55,225

CHAPTER 20

20.2 (a)

STATEMENT OF ASSETS AND LIABILITIES OF BRIAN WITHERS AS AT 1 MAY 19-9

	£	£
Assets		
Fixed assets		45,000
Stock		6,400
Debtors		6,240
Expenses prepaid		140
Bank		720
		58,500
Less Liabilities		
Creditors	1,330	
Expenses owing	70	
Loan from father	5,000	
		6,400
Capital at 1 May 19-9		52,100

(b)

STATEMENT OF ASSETS AND LIABILITIES OF BRIAN WITHERS AS AT 30 APRIL 19-0

	£	£
Assets		
Fixed assets		46,500
Stock		6,700
Debtors		6,430
Expenses prepaid		180
Bank		790
		60,600
Less Liabilities		
Creditors	1,450	
Expenses owing	50	
Loan from father	4,000	
		5,500
Capital at 30 April 19-0		55,100

(c) net profit or loss for the year = closing capital – opening capital + drawings – capital introduced
£55,100 – £52,100 + £8,400 (£700 x 12) – £2,000 = £9,400

(d)
- greater accuracy – trial balance can be extracted at any time
- receipts and payments correctly recorded
- control of debtors and creditors

(e) expenses matched to the financial year, ie the accruals concept

20.4

GERALD ASH
PROFIT AND LOSS ACCOUNT FOR THE YEAR ENDED 30 NOVEMBER 19-0

	£	£
Work done £52,080 + £2,400		54,480
Less expenses:		
Materials used £15,000 + £3,400 – £560	17,840	
Loan interest	1,500	
Provision for bad debts	180	
Rent	1,200	
Assistant's salary	4,900	
Other expenses £8,640 + £65 – £120	8,585	
Provision for depreciation:		
motor vehicle £14,000 *divide by* 5	2,800	
equipment £11,000 *divide by* 5	2,200	
		39,205
Net profit		15,275

BALANCE SHEET AS AT 30 NOVEMBER 19-0

	£ *Cost*	£ *Dep'n to date*	£ *Net*
Fixed Assets			
Motor vehicle	14,000	2,800	11,200
Equipment	11,000	2,200	8,800
	25,000	5,000	20,000
Current Assets			
Stock		560	
Debtors	2,400		
Less Provision for bad debts	180		
		2,220	
Prepayment of expenses		120	
Bank (missing figure: see below)		11,940	
		14,840	
Less Current Liabilities			
Creditors	3,400		
Accruals £100 rent + £65 expenses	165		
		3,565	
Working Capital			11,275
			31,275
Less Long-term Liabilities			
Loan			8,000
NET ASSETS			23,275
FINANCED BY			
Capital			
Opening capital			20,000
Add Net profit			15,275
			35,275
Less Drawings			12,000
			23,275

Although not required by the question, the bank summary for the year is as follows:

Bank Account

Dr.		£		Cr.	£
19-9/-0			19-9/-0		
1 Dec.	Opening capital	20,000	1 Dec.	Motor vehicle	14,000
	Loan	10,000	1 Dec.	Equipment	11,000
	Debtors	52,080		Loan repayments	3,500
				Creditors	15,000
				Rent	1,100
				Assistant's salary	4,900
				Drawings	12,000
				Other expenses	8,640
			30 Nov.	Balance c/d	11,940
		82,080			82,080
19-0/-1			19-0/-1		
1 Dec.	Balance b/d	11,940			

20.7

JB
TRADING AND PROFIT AND LOSS ACCOUNT FOR EIGHTEEN MONTHS ENDED 30 DECEMBER 19-8

	£	£
Sales £21,250 + £431 + £1,955		23,636
Purchases £2,160 + £7,315 + £749	10,224	
Less Closing stock	1,425	
Cost of Goods Sold		8,799
Gross profit		14,837
Less expenses:		
Rent and rates £1,850 – £300	1,550	
Light and heat £923 + £76	999	
Postage and stationery	474	
Motor expenses	919	
Loan interest	450	
Loss on sale of van £1,500 – £850	650	
Provision for depreciation:		
motor van*	825	
office equipment§	320	
		6,187
Net profit		8,650

* *Motor van depreciation:* (£4,000 – £700) ÷ 3 years = £1,100 pa x 9 months = £825
§ *Office equipment depreciation:* £1,280 ÷ 5 years = £256 pa x 15 months = £320

BALANCE SHEET AS AT 31 DECEMBER 19-8

	£	£	£
Fixed Assets	*Cost*	*Dep'n to date*	*Net*
Motor van	4,000	825	3,175
Office equipment	1,280	320	960
	5,280	1,145	4,135
Current Assets			
Stock		1,425	
Debtors £431 – £189 set-off		242	
Prepayments (rates)		300	
Bank		7,037*	
Cash		697	
		9,701	
Less Current Liabilities			
Creditors £749 – £189 set-off	560		
Accruals (light and heat)	76		
Loan interest owing	450		
		1,086	
Working Capital			8,615
			12,750
Less Long-term Liabilities			
Bank loan			4,500
NET ASSETS			8,250
FINANCED BY			
Capital			
Opening capital			5,000
Add Net profit			8,650
			13,650
Less Drawings			5,400
			8,250

* *Balance at bank:* £6,877 + £160 discrepancy between cash paid into bank of £21,190 and cash book amount of £21,350.

20.9 **Calculation of stock loss on 30 November**

	£	£
Opening stock		94,300
Purchases		187,600
COST OF STOCK AVAILABLE FOR SALE		281,900
Sales	251,200	
Less Normal gross profit percentage (22%)	55,264	
COST OF GOODS SOLD		195,936
ESTIMATED CLOSING STOCK		85,964
Less Value of stock salvaged		6,800
VALUE OF STOCK LOST (ie insurane claim)		79,164

CHAPTER 21

21.1

CARLTON SPORTS CLUB
INCOME AND EXPENDITURE ACCOUNT FOR THE YEAR ENDED 31 DECEMBER 19-9

	£	£
Income		
Members' subscriptions £481 + £23		504
Tuck shop		
Receipts	832	
Less purchases	690	
Profit		142
Competitions		
Entry fees	143	
Less expenses	98	
Surplus		45
		691
Less Expenditure		
Postage and stationery	176	
Rent £120 + £30	150	
Provision for depreciation: equipment £840 x 5%	42	
		368
Surplus of income over expenditure		323

BALANCE SHEET AS AT 31 DECEMBER 19-9

	£	£	£
Fixed Assets	*Cost*	*Dep'n to date*	*Net*
Equipment	840	42	798
Current Assets			
Subscriptions due		23	
Bank		532	
		555	
Less Current Liabilities			
Accrual (rent)		30	
Working Capital			525
NET ASSETS			1,323
REPRESENTED BY			
Accumulated fund			1,000
Add surplus of income over expenditure for year			323
			1,323

21.4 (a) **Calculation of the accumulated fund as at 1 November 19-8**

	£
Assets	
Furniture and equipment	420
Bar stock	120
Bank	380
	920
Less Liabilities	
Accrual (rent)	30
Accumulated fund as at 1 November 19-8	890

(b)

EAST SUTTON SOCIAL CLUB
INCOME AND EXPENDITURE ACCOUNT FOR THE YEAR ENDED 31 OCTOBER 19-9

	£	£	£
Income			
Subscriptions			1,420
Bar			
Sales		2,040	
Opening stock	120		
Purchases	1,485		
	1,605		
Less Closing stock	150		
		1,455	
Profit			585
Dance			
Receipts		750	
Less expenses		580	
Profit			170
			2,175
Less Expenditure			
Rent of premises £840 + £110 – £30		920	
Secretary's expenses		225	
Wages of caretaker		580	
			1,725
Surplus of income over expenditure			450

(c)

BALANCE SHEET AS AT 31 OCTOBER 19-9

	£	£
Fixed Assets		
Furniture and equipment		420
Additions in year		200
		620
Current Assets		
Bar stock	150	
Bank	680	
	830	
Less Current Liabilities		
Accrual (rent)	110	
Working Capital		720
NET ASSETS		1,340
REPRESENTED BY		
Accumulated fund		890
Add surplus of income over expenditure for year		450
		1,340

21.7 (a)

Calculation of the accumulated fund as at 1 June 19-9

	£	£
Assets		
Cash/bank		410
Subscriptions in arrears		200
Stocks of music		6,160
Grants and subsidies receivable		950
		7,720
Less Liabilities		
Subscriptions in advance	50	
Owing to suppliers of music	510	
		560
Accumulated fund as at 1 June 19-9		7,160

(b) **Subscriptions Account**

Dr.		£			Cr. £
19-8/-9			19-8/-9		
1 Jun.	Balance b/d	200	1 Jun.	Balance b/d	50
31 May	Income and expenditure account	1,310		Cash/bank	1,480
31 May	Balance c/d	140	31 May	Balance c/d	120
		1,650			1,650
19-9/-0			19-9/-0		
1 Jun.	Balance b/d	120	1 Jun.	Balance b/d	140

(c) **Purchases of Music Account**

Dr.		£			Cr. £
19-8/-9			19-8/-9		
	Cash/bank	1,300	1 Jun.	Balance b/d	510
31 May	Balance c/d	660		Purchases for year (missing figure)	1,450
		1,960			1,960
19-9/-0			19-9/-0		
			1 Jun.	Balance b/d	660

Depreciation of music:	£
Stocks of music (valuation) at 1 June 19-8	6,160
Purchases for year	1,450
	7,610
Less Stocks of music (valuation) at 31 May 19-9	7,100
Therefore Depreciation of music for the year	510

Grant and Subsidies Account

Dr.		£			Cr. £
19-8/-9			19-8/-9		
1 Jun.	Balance b/d	950		Cash/bank	2,500
31 May	Income and expenditure account	2,950	31 May	Balance c/d	1,400
		3,900			3,900
19-9/-0			19-9/-0		
1 Jun.	Balance b/d	1,400			

(d)

CAPELLA CHOIR
INCOME AND EXPENDITURE ACCOUNT FOR THE YEAR ENDED 31 MAY 19-0

	£	£
Income		
Subscriptions		1,310
Donations		220
Sale of concert tickets		2,680
Grants and subsidies		2,950
		7,160
Less Expenditure		
Secretarial expenses	550	
Rent of rehearsal room	850	
Other rehearsal expenses	350	
Fees and expenses	2,870	
Travelling expenses £490 + £210	700	
Stationery and printing	670	
Depreciation of music	510	
		6,500
Surplus of income over expenditure		660

21.8 (a)

HB TENNIS CLUB
INCOME AND EXPENDITURE ACCOUNT FOR THE YEAR ENDED 30 SEPTEMBER 19-0

	£	£	£
Income			
Subscriptions (£12,600 + £1,500) ÷ 2			7,050
Life membership fees (£4,200 ÷ 10 years) ÷ 2			210
Tournaments			
Fees		465	
Prizes		132	
Surplus			333
Club ties			
Sales		373	
Purchases	450		
Less Closing stock 40 @ £4.50 each	180		
		270	
Profit			103
Interest received			43
			7,739
Less Expenditure			
Groundsman's wages £4,520 + £40		4,560	
Rent and business rates £636 – £68		568	
Heating and lighting £674 + £53		727	
Postage and stationery £41 + £12		53	
Court maintenance		1,000	
Provision for depreciation: equipment (£4,080 – £50) ÷ 10		403	
			7,311
Surplus of income over expenditure			428

(b)

BALANCE SHEET AS AT 31 OCTOBER 19-9

	£	£	£
	Cost	*Dep'n to date*	*Net*
Fixed Assets			
Equipment	4,080	403	3,677
Current Assets			
Subscriptions due £1,500 ÷ 2		750	
Stock of ties		180	
Prepayment (business rates)		68	
Bank		6,148	
		7,146	
Less Current Liabilities			
Subscriptions in advance £12,600 ÷ 2	6,300		
Accruals £40 + £12 + £53	105		
		6,405	
Working Capital			741
NET ASSETS			4,418
REPRESENTED BY			
Accumulated fund			–
Surplus of income over expenditure			428
Reserves			
Life subscriptions account £4,200 – £210			3,990
			4,418

CHAPTER 22

22.2 (a)

Eel: Capital Account

Dr.		£			Cr. £
19-8			19-8		
31 Dec.	Balance c/d	8,000	1 Jan.	Balance b/d	6,000
			30 Jun.	Bank	2,000
		8,000			8,000
19-9			19-9		
			1 Jan.	Balance b/d	8,000

(b)

Eel: Current Account

Dr.		£			Cr. £
19-8			19-8		
1 Jan.	Balance b/d	136	16 Jan.	Bank	136
30 Jun.	Motor vehicle expenses	30	30 Jun.	Salary	800
31 Mar.	Drawings	700	31 Dec.	Interest allowed on capital*	350
30 Jun.	Drawings	900	31 Dec.	Salary	1,000
1 Sep.	Drawings	800	31 Dec.	Share of net profit	1,200
31 Dec.	Balance c/d	920			
		3,486			3,486
19-9			19-9		
			1 Jan.	Balance b/d	920

* (£6,000 x 5%) + (£2,000 x 5% x ½) = £300 + £50 = £350

(c) **BALANCE SHEET (EXTRACT) AS AT 31 DECEMBER 19-8**

	£	£
FINANCED BY		
Capital Accounts		
Eel	8,000	
....	....	
Current Accounts		
Eel	920	
....	....	

Note: For the current accounts, a detailed balance sheet extract could be shown, giving a summary of the transactions that have taken place during the year.

22.5 **WAVE AND TROUGH**

TRADING AND PROFIT AND LOSS ACCOUNT FOR THE YEAR ENDED 30 JUNE 19-0

	£	£	£
Sales			611,300
Opening stock		35,500	
Purchases	426,100		
Less Goods for own use (Wave)	1,500		
		424,600	
		460,100	
Less Closing stock		42,700	
Cost of Goods Sold			417,400
Gross profit			193,900
Discount received			2,700
			196,600
Less Expenses:			
Rates £15,000 – £4,000		11,000	
Wages		36,900	
Motor expenses		6,300	
Bank charges and interest		3,600	
Advertising £21,200 + £4,300		25,500	
Discount allowed		9,800	
Interest on long-term loan		5,000	
Provision for depreciation:			
motor vehicle		3,000	
fixtures and fittings		5,000	
			106,100
Net profit			90,500
Less appropriation of profits:			
Interest allowed on partners' capitals:			
Wave		10,800	
Trough		9,000	
			19,800
Salaries:			
Wave		20,000	
Trough		30,000	
			50,000
			20,700
Share of remaining profits:			
Wave (50%)		10,350	
Trough (50%)		10,350	
			20,700

BALANCE SHEET AS AT 30 JUNE 19-0

	£	£	£
Fixed Assets	*Cost*	*Dep'n to date*	*Net*
Land and buildings	134,000	–	134,000
Motor vehicle	20,000	6,000	14,000
Fixtures and fittings	55,200	15,000	40,200
	209,200	21,000	188,200
Current Assets			
Stock		42,700	
Debtors		101,800	
Prepayments (rates)		4,000	
		148,500	
Less Current Liabilities			
Creditors	35,500		
Bank	15,100		
Accrual (advertising)	4,300		
		54,900	
Working Capital			93,600
			281,800
Less Long-term Liabilities			
Long-term loan			50,000
NET ASSETS			231,800
FINANCED BY			
Capital Accounts			
Wave		90,000	
Trough		75,000	
			165,000
Current Accounts	WAVE	TROUGH	
Opening balance	(1,000)	10,600	
Add: salary	20,000	30,000	
interest on capital	10,800	9,000	
share of profit	10,350	10,350	
	40,150	59,950	
Less: drawings	16,000	15,800	
goods for own use	1,500	–	
	22,650	44,150	66,800
			231,800

22.7 **BRICK AND STONE**

TRADING AND PROFIT AND LOSS ACCOUNT FOR THE YEAR ENDED 30 SEPTEMBER 19-0

	£	£	£
Sales			322,100
Less Sales returns			2,100
			320,000
Opening stock		23,000	
Purchases	208,200		
Carriage in	1,700		
Less Purchases returns	6,100		
Less Goods for own use (Stone)	1,000		
		202,800	
		225,800	
Less Closing stock		32,000	
Cost of Goods Sold			193,800
Gross profit			126,200

(account continues on next page)

	£	£	£
Gross profit			126,200
Discount receivable			370
			126,570
Less expenses:			
Printing, stationery and postages		3,500	
Rent and rates £10,300 – £600		9,700	
Heat and light		8,700	
Staff salaries		36,100	
Telephone charges £2,900 + £400		3,300	
Motor vehicle running costs		5,620	
Discount allowable		950	
Carriage outwards		2,400	
Interest on loan £10,000 x 5% pa x 3 months		250	
Provision for depreciation:			
fixtures and fittings		2,600	
motor vehicles		9,200	
			82,320
Net profit			44,250
Less appropriation of profits:			
Salary: Stone £12,000 x 6 months			6,000
			38,250
Share of remaining profits:			
Brick (60%)		22,950	
Stone (40%)		15,300	
			38,250

BALANCE SHEET AS AT 30 SEPTEMBER 19-0

	£ *Cost*	£ *Dep'n to date*	£ *Net*
Fixed Assets			
Fixtures and fittings	26,000	13,800	12,200
Motor vehicles	46,000	34,200	11,800
	72,000	48,000	24,000
Current Assets			
Stock		32,000	
Debtors	9,300		
Less Provision for bad debts	300		
		9,000	
Prepayment (rent)		600	
Bank		7,700	
		49,300	
Less Current Liabilities			
Creditors	8,400		
Accrual (telephone)	400		
		8,800	
Working Capital			40,500
			64,500
Less Long-term Liabilities			
Loan from Brick			10,000
NET ASSETS			54,500

(balance sheet continues on next page)

	£	£	£
FINANCED BY			
Capital Accounts			
Brick	33,000		
Less transfer to loan account	10,000		
		23,000	
Stone		17,000	
			40,000
Current Accounts	BRICK	STONE	
Opening balance	3,600	2,400	
Add: salary	–	6,000	
loan interest	250	–	
share of profit	22,950	15,300	
	26,800	23,700	
Less: drawings	24,000	11,000	
goods for own use	–	1,000	
	2,800	11,700	14,500
			54,500

CHAPTER 23

23.2

Sundry Creditors Account

Dr.	£		Cr. £
Bank	3,815	Balance b/d	3,815

Stock Account

Dr.	£		Cr. £
Balance b/d	7,945	Realisation account	7,945

Sundry Debtors Account

Dr.	£		Cr. £
Balance b/d	4,417	Realisation account	4,417

Premises Account

Dr.	£		Cr. £
Balance b/d	23,177	Realisation account	23,177

Loan from Crocus

Dr.	£		Cr. £
Bank*	2,450	Balance b/d	2,450

* The partner's loan account is only repaid after the firm's other debts have been paid.

Realisation Account

Dr.	£		Cr. £
Stock	7,945	Bank: stock	7,812
Sundry debtors	4,417	Bank: premises	21,000
Premises	23,177	Bank: debtors	4,305
		Loss on realisation:	
		Rose ($^1/_7$)	346
		Tulip ($^2/_7$)	692
		Crocus ($^4/_7$)	1,384
	35,539		35,539

Partners' Capital Accounts

Dr.	Rose £	Tulip £	Crocus £		Rose £	Tulip £	Crocus £ Cr.
Realisation account: loss	346	692	1,384	Balances b/d	9,170	10,290	12,432
Bank	8,824	9,598	11,048				
	9,170	10,290	12,432		9,170	10,290	12,432

Cash/Bank Account

Dr.	£		Cr. £
Balance b/d	2,618	Creditors	3,815
Stock	7,812	Loan: Crocus	2,450
Premises	21,000	Capital accounts:	
Debtors	4,305	Rose	8,824
		Tulip	9,598
		Crocus	11,048
	35,735		35,735

23.4 (a)

STONE, PEBBLE AND BRICK TRADING AS THE BIGTIME BUILDING SUPPLY COMPANY PROFIT AND LOSS APPROPRIATION ACCOUNT FOR THE YEAR ENDED 31 MARCH 19-0

	9 months to 31 December £	3 months to 31 March £	Total for year £
Net profit from draft accounts	27,225	9,075	36,300
Less interest on loan account (Stone)	–	385	385
Net profit	27,225	8,690	35,915
Less appropriation of profits:			
Salaries: Brick £8,500 ÷ 4	–	2,125	2,125
Interest on partners' capitals:			
Stone	–	250	250
Pebble	–	200	200
Brick	–	125	125
	27,225	5,990	33,215
Share of remaining profits:			
Stone	($^1/_3$) 9,075	($^1/_2$) 2,995	12,070
Pebble	($^1/_3$) 9,075	($^3/_{10}$) 1,797	10,872
Brick	($^1/_3$) 9,075	($^1/_5$) 1,198	10,273
	27,225	5,990	33,215

Notes:

- Interest on Stone's loan account is calculated on a balance of £14,000 (see below) at 11% pa for three months.
- Interest on partners' capitals are calculated on the balances (see below) at 5% pa for three months.

(b)

Partners' Capital Accounts

Dr.	Stone £	Pebble £	Brick £		Stone £	Pebble £	Brick £ Cr.
19-9/-0				19-9/-0			
1 Apr. Goodwill (see below)	–	2,000	6,000	1 Apr. Opening balances	26,000	18,000	16,000
1 Jan. Loan account	14,000	–	–	1 Apr. Goodwill (see below)	8,000	–	–
31 Mar. Balances c/d	20,000	16,000	10,000				
	34,000	18,000	16,000		34,000	18,000	16,000
19-0/-1				19-0/-1			
				1 Apr. Balances b/d	20,000	16,000	10,000

Goodwill calculations at 1 April 19-9

	Goodwill from previous businesses credited to partners' capital accounts £	Elimination of goodwill debited to partners' capital accounts £	Net transaction £
Stone	30,000	22,000	8,000 Cr.
Pebble	20,000	22,000	2,000 Dr.
Brick	16,000	22,000	6,000 Dr.
	66,000	66,000	nil

Partners' Current Accounts

Dr.	Stone £	Pebble £	Brick £		Stone £	Pebble £	Brick £ Cr.
19-9/-0				19-9/-0			
31 Mar. Drawings for year	8,200	9,600	7,200	31 Mar. Salary	–	–	2,125
31 Mar. Balances c/d	4,120	1,472	5,323	31 Mar. Interest on capital	250	200	125
				31 Mar. Share of profits:			
				9 mths to 31 Dec.	9,075	9,075	9,075
				3 mths to 31 Mar.	2,995	1,797	1,198
	12,320	11,072	12,523		12,320	11,072	12,523
19-0/-1				19-0/-1			
				1 Apr. Balances b/d	4,120	1,472	5,323

Note: The interest on Stone's loan account will be credited to his/her current account for the first time on 31 December 19-0. In the meantime it will be credited to a partner's loan interest account, and shown as a current liability on the balance sheet at 31 March 19-0.

CHAPTER 24

24.2

SWIFT TRADERS PLC
APPROPRIATION ACCOUNT FOR THE YEAR ENDED 31 OCTOBER 19-0

	£	£
Net profit for year		52,000
Less dividends proposed:		
preference shares	8,000	
ordinary shares	18,000	
		26,000
		26,000
Less transfer to general reserve		5,000
Retained profit for year		21,000
Add balance of retained profits at beginning of year		12,890
Balance of retained profits at end of year		33,890

BALANCE SHEET (EXTRACT) AS AT 31 OCTOBER 19-0

	£	£
FINANCED BY		
Authorised Share Capital		
100,000 8% preference shares of £1 each		100,000
200,000 ordinary shares of £1 each		200,000
		300,000
Issued Share Capital		
100,000 8% preference shares of £1 each, fully paid		100,000
150,000 ordinary shares of £1 each, fully paid		150,000
		250,000
Capital Reserve		
Share premium account		37,500
Revenue Reserves		
General reserve*	27,760	
Profit and loss account	33,890	
		61,650
SHAREHOLDERS' FUNDS		349,150

* including transfer of £5,000

24.6

SIDBURY TRADING CO LTD
TRADING AND PROFIT AND LOSS ACCOUNT FOR THE YEAR ENDED 31 DECEMBER 19-2

	£	£
Sales		297,462
Opening stock	42,618	
Purchases	189,273	
	231,891	
Less Closing stock	47,288	
Cost of Goods Sold		184,603
Gross profit		112,859
Less expenses:		
Provision for depreciation on motor vans	11,000	
Rent and rates	3,600	
General expenses	9,741	
Wages and salaries	35,043	
Bad debts written off	948	
Increase in provision for bad debts	124	
Directors' salaries	25,000	
		85,456
Net profit for year before taxation		27,403
Less corporation tax		12,000
Profit for year after taxation		15,403
Less ordinary dividend proposed		8,000
Retained profit for year		7,403
Add balance of retained profits at beginning of year		18,397
Balance of retained profits at end of year		25,800

BALANCE SHEET AS AT 31 DECEMBER 19-2

	£ Cost	£ Dep'n to date	£ Net
Fixed Assets			
Land and buildings	142,000	–	142,000
Motor vans	55,000	32,800	22,200
	197,000	32,800	164,200
Current Assets			
Stock		47,288	
Debtors	26,482		
Less Provision for bad debts	1,200		
		25,282	
Prepayment (rates)		400	
Bank		65,958	
		138,928	
Less Current Liabilities			
Creditors	16,974		
Accrual (wages and salaries)	354		
Corporation tax	12,000		
Proposed ordinary dividend	8,000		
		37,328	
Working Capital			101,600
NET ASSETS			265,800
FINANCED BY			
Authorised Share Capital			
300,000 ordinary shares of £1 each			300,000
Issued Share Capital			
240,000 ordinary shares of £1 each, fully paid			240,000
Revenue Reserves			
Profit and loss account			25,800
SHAREHOLDERS' FUNDS			265,800

24.8

MAGINN CO LTD
APPROPRIATION ACCOUNT FOR THE YEAR ENDED 31 DECEMBER 19-9

	£	£
Net profit for year		36,720
Less: interim dividends paid		
preference shares	1,500	
ordinary shares	7,500	
final dividends proposed		
preference shares	1,500	
ordinary shares	11,250	
		21,750
		14,970
Less transfer to reserves		7,500
Retained profit for year		7,470
Add balance of retained profits at beginning of year		17,400
Balance of retained profits at end of year		24,870

BALANCE SHEET AS AT 31 DECEMBER 19-9

	£ Cost	£ Dep'n to date	£ Net
Fixed Assets			
Premises	112,500	–	112,500
Fixtures and fittings	60,000	28,500	31,500
Office equipment	6,750	2,550	4,200
Motor vans	30,000	18,750	11,250
	209,250	49,800	159,450
Current Assets			
Stock		59,730	
Debtors		60,375	
Prepayments		1,800	
Bank		35,005	
		156,910	
Less Current Liabilities			
Creditors	38,400		
Accruals	1,365		
Proposed dividends:			
preference shares	1,500		
ordinary shares	11,250		
		52,515	
Working Capital			104,395
			263,845
Less Long-term Liabilities			
12½% mortgage debentures			13,975
NET ASSETS			249,870
FINANCED BY			
Authorised Share Capital			
175,000 ordinary shares of £1 each			175,000
50,000 8% preference shares of £1 each			50,000
			225,000
Issued Share Capital			
150,000 ordinary shares of £1 each, fully paid			150,000
37,500 8% preference shares of £1 each, fully paid			37,500
			187,500
Capital Reserve			
Share premium account			15,000
Revenue Reserves			
Reserves*		22,500	
Profit and loss account		24,870	
			47,370
SHAREHOLDERS' FUNDS			249,870

* including transfer of £7,500

25.3 (a) (i)

Partners' Capital Accounts

Dr.	Michael £	Norman £	Oliver £	Cr.	Michael £	Norman £	Oliver £
Goodwill deletion	25,000	15,000	10,000	Balances b/d	140,000	90,000	–
Transfer to current accounts	1,000	500	–	Net assets taken over	–	–	66,500
Balances c/d	175,000	105,000	70,000	Goodwill creation	26,000	13,000	11,000
				Revaluation of assets	35,000	17,500	–
				Transfer to current account	–	–	2,500
	201,000	120,500	80,000		201,000	120,500	80,000
				Balances b/d	175,000	105,000	70,000

Notes:

- Net assets of Oliver: plant £35,000, work in progress (at revaluation) £65,000, less bank overdraft £33,500 = £66,500.
- Goodwill £39,000 of Michael and Norman credited £26,000 and £13,000 respectively.
- Deletion of goodwill of £50,000 (£39,000 + £11,000 from Oliver) debited Michael £25,000, Norman £15,000, Oliver £10,000.
- Revaluation of assets of Michael and Norman:

freehold premises	£35,000	increase
plant	£ 7,500	decrease
work in progress	£25,000	increase
net	£52,500	increase

Credited in profit-sharing ratio: Michael £35,000, Norman £17,500.

(ii)

MICHAEL, NORMAN AND OLIVER
BALANCE SHEET AS AT 31 MAY 19-9

	£	£
Fixed Assets		
Freehold premises		115,000
Plant		80,000
		195,000
Current Assets		
Work in progress	260,000	
Trade debtors	25,000	
Bank £26,500 + £2,500	29,000	
	314,000	
Less Current Liabilities		
Trade creditors	100,000	
Working Capital		214,000
		409,000
Less Long-term Liabilities		
Bank loan		60,000
NET ASSETS		349,000

(balance sheet continues on next page)

	£	£
FINANCED BY		
Capital Accounts		
Michael	175,000	
Norman	105,000	
Oliver	70,000	
		350,000
Current Accounts		
Michael	1,000	
Norman	500	
Oliver	(2,500)	
		(1,000)
		349,000

(b) (i)

- legal entity
  - — a limited company is a separate legal entity
  - — a partnership is not a separate legal entity, and thus a person taking legal action proceeds against the partners
- limited liability
  - — the shareholders of a limited company are liable for company debts only to the extent of any money unpaid on their shares
  - — in a partnership every partner is personally liable for the whole debt of the partnership

(ii)

- partnership
  - — profit or loss sharing ratio
  - — partner's salary/commission
  - — interest on capital
- limited company
  - — director's salary/commission
  - — dividends on shares

CHAPTER 26

26.2

PERCIVAL COMPONENTS LTD
MANUFACTURING ACCOUNT FOR THE YEAR ENDED 31 OCTOBER 19-9

	£	£
Opening stock of raw materials		31,584
Purchases of raw materials		383,296
		414,880
Less Closing stock of raw materials		32,384
COST OF RAW MATERIALS USED		382,496
Manufacturing wages		287,136
PRIME COST		669,632
Factory overheads		
Factory rent and rates	7,264	
Factory insurance	2,688	
Factory salaries	11,936	
Machinery repairs	4,128	
Heating and lighting	7,104	
General factory expenses	9,248	
Depreciation of machinery	38,400	
		80,768
		750,400
Add Opening stock of work-in-progress		36,768
		787,168
Less Closing stock of work-in-progress		39,616
MANUFACTURING COST OF GOODS COMPLETED		747,552

26.3

PROTEM MANUFACTURING COMPANY
MANUFACTURING AND TRADING ACCOUNT FOR THE YEAR ENDED 30 SEPTEMBER YEAR 9

	£	£
Opening stock of raw materials		39,000
Purchases of raw materials	214,760	
Less purchases returns	1,350	
		213,410
		252,410
Less Closing stock of raw materials		43,630
COST OF RAW MATERIALS USED		208,780
Factory wages		33,560
PRIME COST		242,340
Factory overheads		
Lighting and heating	14,460	
Power	7,600	
Rates and insurance	3,560	
Depreciation of plant and machinery	13,950	
		39,570
		281,910
Add Opening stock of work-in-progress		8,100
		290,010
Less Closing stock of work-in-progress		5,160
MANUFACTURING COST OF GOODS COMPLETED		284,850
Sales		365,752
Opening stock of finished goods	51,930	
Manufacturing cost of goods completed	284,850	
	336,780	
Less Closing stock of finished goods	57,400	
COST OF GOODS SOLD		279,380
Gross profit		86,372

26.6

FAIRDEAL MANUFACTURERS LIMITED
MANUFACTURING, TRADING AND PROFIT AND LOSS ACCOUNT
FOR THE YEAR ENDED 30 APRIL 19-0

	£	£
Purchases of raw materials		41,000
Less Closing stock of raw materials		3,000
COST OF RAW MATERIALS USED		38,000
Factory labour: machine operatives		36,000
PRIME COST		74,000
Factory overheads		
Factory labour: supervisory	7,000	
Factory plant and machinery repairs	8,710	
Heat, light and power (rounded down to £)	20,287	
Rates and insurance (rounded up to £)	1,463	
Depreciation of factory plant and machinery	12,000	
		49,460
		123,460
Less Closing stock of work-in-progress		24,000
MANUFACTURING COSTS		99,460
Factory profit		540
MANUFACTURING COST OF GOODS COMPLETED (including profit)		100,000

(account continues on next page)

	£	£
Sales		136,500
Manufacturing cost of goods completed	100,000	
Less Closing stock of finished goods	10,000	
COST OF GOODS SOLD		90,000
Gross profit		46,500
Office expenses		
Heat, light and power (rounded up to £)	6,763	
Rates and insurance (rounded down to £)	487	
General administrative expenses	9,400	
Administrative salaries	12,090	
Provision for depreciation: motor delivery vehicles	6,250	
		34,990
Profit from Trading		11,510
Factory profit	540	
Less provision for unrealised profit*	54	
		486
Net profit		11,996

* Provision for unrealised profit:

$$\frac{\text{finished goods stock}}{\text{manufacturing cost (including profit)}} \times \text{factory profit}$$

$$\frac{£10,000}{£100,000} \times £540 = £54$$

BALANCE SHEET AS AT 30 APRIL 19-0

		£	£	£
		Cost	Dep'n to date	Net
Fixed Assets				
Factory plant and machinery		120,000	12,000	108,000
Motor delivery vehicles		25,000	6,250	18,750
		145,000	18,250	126,750
Current Assets				
Stocks: raw materials			3,000	
work-in-progress			24,000	
finished goods		10,000		
less provision for unrealised profits		54		
			9,946	
			36,946	
Debtors			12,000	
Prepayment			600	
			49,546	
Less Current Liabilities				
Creditors		7,100		
Accrual		2,300		
Bank		4,900		
			14,300	
Working Capital				35,246
NET ASSETS				161,996
FINANCED BY				
Issued Share Capital				
120,000 ordinary shares of £1 each, fully paid				120,000
Capital Reserve				
Share premium account				30,000
Revenue Reserve				
Profit and loss account				11,996
SHAREHOLDERS' FUNDS				161,996

CHAPTER 27

27.1 (i)

'LIFE AND LEISURE'
DEPARTMENTAL TRADING AND PROFIT AND LOSS ACCOUNT
FOR THE YEAR ENDED 31 MARCH YEAR 8

	Games Department £	£	*Books Department* £	£	*Total* £	£
Sales		240,000		360,000		600,000
Opening stock	42,000		14,000		56,000	
Purchases (missing figure)	150,600		272,000		422,600	
	192,600		286,000		478,600	
Less Closing stock	41,400		12,400		53,800	
Cost of Goods Sold		151,200		273,600		424,800
Gross profit		88,800		86,400		175,200
(using gross profit percentages)						
Less expenses:						
Sales expenses	34,130		46,190		80,320	
Administrative expenses	2,920		4,380		7,300	
Establishment expenses	6,480		9,720		16,200	
Advertising campaign	3,400		5,100		8,500	
Commission	3,552		3,456		7,008	
Provision for depreciation:						
lease	3,300		3,300		6,600	
fixtures and fittings	1,080		1,620		2,700	
motor van	1,440		360		1,800	
		56,302		74,126		130,428
Net profit		32,498		12,274		44,772

(ii) (a) $\frac{\text{Net profit}}{\text{Capital}} = \frac{£44,772}{£68,100} \times \frac{100}{1} = 65.74\%$*

* the calculation of this percentage is discussed more fully in Chapter 29.2

(b) This is reasonable because, as partners, the net profit belongs to them. They must decide how this should be shared between them. One way would be for each to receive a partnership salary (not to be shown in the profit and loss account, but in the appropriation section), and a share of the remaining profits.

CHAPTER 28

28.1

Name	*Basic (£)*	*Weekday (£)*	*Saturday (£)*	*Sunday (£)*	*Gross (£)*
F Mariani	244.20	–	39.60	–	283.80
J Banks	244.20	33.00	39.60	–	316.80
R Robson	244.20	49.50	49.50	26.40	369.60
H Wilson	244.20	–	79.20	52.80	376.20

28.3

Week ended 25 May 19-0

Name	Earnings				Deductions				
	Basic	*Overtime*	*Bonus*	*Total Gross Pay*	*PAYE*	*National Insurance*	*Pension Scheme*	*Total Deductions*	*Net Pay*
	£	£	£	£	£	£	£	£	£
J Brown	150.00	–	90.00	240.00	41.25	24.00	4.80	70.05	169.95
A White	164.00	20.50	–	184.50	27.37	18.45	3.69	49.51	134.99

28.7 (a)

Week ending: 18 August 19-1											
Work Number	Name	Earnings				Deductions				Employer's National Insurance Contributions	Net Pay
		Basic £	Overtime £	Bonus £	Total Gross Pay £	PAYE (Income Tax) £	National Insurance £	Pension Contribution £	Total Deductions £	£	£
	A. Adams	250.00	43.75	10.00	303.75	45.25	23.67	18.22	87.14	31.56	216.61
	B. Barnes	250.00	—	10.00	260.00	44.00	19.80	15.60	79.40	27.09	180.60
	C. Cutts	250.00	43.75	10.00	303.75	46.25	23.67	18.22	88.14	31.56	215.61
	D. Dodds	250.00	29.50	10.00	289.50	40.75	22.41	17.37	80.53	30.11	208.97
TOTALS		1000.00	117.00	40.00	1157.00	176.25	89.55	69.41	335.21	120.32	821.79

(b)

Wages and Salaries Control Account

Dr.		£	Cr.		£
19-1			19-1		
18 Aug.	Bank	821.79	18 Aug.	Wages and salaries	1,277.32§
18 Aug.	Inland Revenue account	386.12*			
18 Aug.	Pension contributions	69.41			
		1,277.32			1,277.32

* £176.25 (income tax) + £89.55 (National Insurance) + £120.32 (employer's National Insurance)
§ £1,157.00 (gross pay) + £120.32 (employer's National Insurance)

Wages and Salaries Account

Dr.		£	Cr.		£
19-1			19-1		
18 Aug.	Wages and salaries control account	1,277.32			

Inland Revenue Account

Dr.		£	Cr.		£
19-1			19-1		
15 Sep.	Bank	386.12	18 Aug.	Wages and salaries control account	386.12

Pension Contributions Account

Dr.		£	Cr.		£
19-1			19-1		
20 Sep.	Bank	69.41	18 Aug.	Wages and salaries control account	69.41

28.8

NAME	£20	£10	£5	£1	50p	20p	10p	5p	2p	1p	Total (£ p)
A. Adams	5	9	4	6	1		1			1	216.61
B. Barnes	5	5	5	5	1		1				180.60
C. Cutts	5	9	4	5	1		1			1	215.61
D. Dodds	5	8	4	8	1	2		1	1		208.97
No. required	20	31	17	24	4	2	3	1	1	2	
Total (£ p)	400.00	310.00	85.00	24.00	2.00	0.40	0.30	0.05	0.02	0.02	821.79

CHAPTER 29

29.1 (i)

		Business A	*Business B*
(a)	gross profit percentage	13.4%	44.0%
(b)	net profit percentage	1.4%	4.2%
(c)	stock turnover	33 days	95 days
(d)	working capital ratio	1.3:1	2.4:1
(e)	liquid capital ratio	0.05:1	1.3:1
(f)	debtors' collection period	1 day*	60 days
(g)	return on capital employed	11%	8.1%

* sales figure used for this calculation; this is unrealistic because most supermarket sales will be for cash rather than on credit

(ii) Business A is grocery supermarket chain; business B the heavy engineering company. Reasons:

Business A	low net profit percentage; quick stock turnover; short debtors' collection period, with few debtors; low working capital and liquid capital ratios
Business B	higher net profit percentage; slow stock turnover; long debtors' collection period, with a large amount of debtors; 'normal' working capital and liquid capital ratios; quite high fixed assets

29.4 (a) *Note:*

- gross profit is turnover, minus cost of sales
  for 19-6, £541,000 – £369,000 = £172,000
  for 19-7, £675,000 – £481,000 = £194,000

- net profit is increase in reserves, plus dividend
  for 19-6, (£53,000 – £21,000) + £20,000 = £52,000
  for 19-7, (£82,000 – £53,000) + £30,000 = £59,000

	19-6	*19-7*
Gross profit/turnover	31.8%	28.7%
Net profit/turnover	9.6%	8.7%
Turnover/net assets	1.8 times pa	1.6 times pa
Net profit/net assets	17.2%	13.7%
Current assets/current liabilities	2.0:1	1.7:1
Quick assets/current liabilities	1.1:1	0.6:1

(b) *Gross profit/turnover* The fall in the percentage could be caused by an increase in buying prices not passed on in higher selling prices, or by a change in products sold, or by pilfering.

Net profit/turnover The fall in caused partly by the lower gross profit percentage, and/or an increase in selling/administrative costs.

Turnover/net assets During 19-7 there has been a considerable increase in net assets: turnover has not increased by the same proportion. A doubling of year end stocks may indicate that the business is preparing for a major sales campaign; alternatively, some of the stocks could be unsaleable.

Net profit/net assets This percentage has declined for the same reasons as the previous two ratios.

Current assets/current liabilities Despite the doubling of year end stocks and an increase in debtors, this ratio has fallen because of the large increase in creditors, and the higher proposed dividend.

Quick assets/current liabilities This ratio has fallen quite dramatically, mainly because of the large increase in creditors. It would appear that creditors are being used to finance a part of the expansion scheme.

29.6 (a)

	19-8	*19-9*	*19-0*
Gross profit percentage	33.33%	25.0%	20.0%
Net profit percentage	10.0%	4.44%	2.59%
Variable expenses/sales percentage	15.0%	15.0%	10.0%
Fixed expenses/sales percentage	8.33%	5.55%	7.41%
Return on capital employed	15.0%	8.0%	5.83%
Working capital ratio	3.5:1	2.14:1	1.73:1
Liquid capital ratio	2.3:1	1.43:1	1:1
Stock turnover	109 days	66 days	55 days
Debtors' collection period	79 days	81 days	74 days
Creditors' payment period (using cost of sales as purchases)	91 days	95 days	76 days
Asset turnover ratio	1.5 times	1.8 times	2.25 times

Note: The question asks for four ratios/percentages, each showing a different aspect of the company. The four areas could be:

profit/sales, eg gross profit, net profit, expenses

profit/capital, eg return on capital employed

liquidity, eg working capital ratio, liquid capital ratio

asset utilisation, eg stock turnover, debtors' collection period, creditors' payment period, asset turnover

(b) **Report to James and Henry Carr**

The report should include reference to:

- The company has increased turnover by 50% each year in the past two years.
- However, the increase in turnover has resulted in declining profit percentages, eg gross and net profits, and return on capital employed.
- Both working capital and liquid capital ratios have declined during the period, although the 19-0 ratios are perfectly acceptable.
- Control over the working capital items of stock, debtors and creditors has been good: the working capital cycle was 97 days in 19-8, 52 days in 19-9, and 53 days in 19-0.
- As turnover has increased, the overhead expenses have reduced as a percentage of turnover: this shows that overheads are under control.
- The brothers, J and H Carr, have increased their investment in the company, but the return on capital employed has fallen considerably. It might have been better to have invested the funds elsewhere.
- The asset turnover ratio has increased over the three years, a sign that increased turnover has been achieved without a proportionate increase in net assets.
- The urgent task for the company is to return to higher levels of profitability in the trading account. It might be that, in order to increase turnover, the company has had to reduce selling prices. Alternatively, higher buying prices may not have been passed on in the form of higher selling prices. It would probably be better to make fewer sales at a higher profitability: this increased profit would then result in a higher return on capital employed.

CHAPTER 30

30.1 **CASH FLOW STATEMENT OF JOHN SMITH FOR THE YEAR ENDED 31 DECEMBER 19-2**

	£	£
Operating activities:		
Operating profit (before interest)	11,250	
Depreciation	1,000	
Increase in stock	(3,500)	
Increase in debtors	(800)	
Increase in creditors	250	
Net cash inflow from operating activities		8,200
Returns on investments and servicing of finance:		
Interest paid	(250)	
		(250)
Taxation:		
Corporation tax paid		not applicable
Capital expenditure and financial investment:		
Payments to acquire fixed assets		(2,000)
Equity dividends paid: (drawings)		(9,000)
Cash outflow before use of liquid resources and financing		(3,050)
Financing:		–
Decrease in cash		*(3,050)

* Bank balance at start of year	850
Bank balance at end of year	(2,200)
Decrease in cash	(3,050)

Index